Rwanda Before the Genocide

Rwanda Before the Genocide

Catholic Politics and Ethnic Discourse in the Late Colonial Era

J. J. CARNEY

OXFORD
UNIVERSITY PRESS

OXFORD
UNIVERSITY PRESS

Oxford University Press is a department of the University of Oxford.
It furthers the University's objective of excellence in research, scholarship,
and education by publishing worldwide.

Oxford   New York
Auckland   Cape Town   Dar es Salaam   Hong Kong   Karachi
Kuala Lumpur   Madrid   Melbourne   Mexico City   Nairobi
New Delhi   Shanghai   Taipei   Toronto

With offices in
Argentina   Austria   Brazil   Chile   Czech Republic   France   Greece
Guatemala   Hungary   Italy   Japan   Poland   Portugal   Singapore
South Korea   Switzerland   Thailand   Turkey   Ukraine   Vietnam

Oxford is a registered trademark of Oxford University Press
in the UK and certain other countries.

Published in the United States of America by
Oxford University Press
198 Madison Avenue, New York, NY 10016

Library of Congress Cataloging-in-Publication Data
Carney, J. J.
Rwanda before the genocide : Catholic politics and ethnic discourse in
the late colonial era / J.J. Carney.
p. cm.
Includes bibliographical references and index.
ISBN 978-0-19-998227-1 (cloth : alk. paper)
1. Rwanda—History—To 1962.   2. Rwanda—Ethnic relations—History.   3. Hutu
(African people)—Rwanda.   4. Tutsi (African people)—Rwanda.   5. Rwanda—Social
conditions.   6. Church and state—Rwanda—History.   7. Catholic Church—Rwanda—
History.   8. Rwanda—Church history.   I. Title.
DT450.28.C37 2013
967.57103—dc23
2013006147

To Mom, Dad & Becky,
In gratitude for your faith, witness, and support.

Contents

Acknowledgments

THIS BOOK BEGAN over a decade ago in the library of Marquette University in Milwaukee, Wisconsin. Tasked with writing an undergraduate term paper on the intersection of human rights and Christian theology, I located a number of texts on the Rwandan genocide of 1994 and decided to explore one of the great human rights tragedies of the twentieth century. As I delved deeper, I realized the extent to which my own religious tradition, Catholicism, had shaped the entire twentieth-century history of Rwanda. I grappled with seeming church complicity in the massacres of 1994, wondering how such a devout country could fall into the depths of human barbarity. This grappling only grew more intense through later coursework on Rwanda, a trip to Rwanda in 2004, and my own theological reflections on the ecclesiological ramifications of the Rwanda genocide.[1] Although I began my explorations of Rwanda as a student of Christian ethics and theology, I found myself drawn to Rwanda's history in an effort to understand the intersection of colonial politics, Christian ethics, and Rwanda's pernicious Hutu-Tutsi *mythos*. I have come to realize the complexity of this question and the limits to my knowledge—itself an important step on the path to wisdom.

There are many people who have aided me in this journey. This book is a revised version of my dissertation *From Democratization to Ethnic Revolution: Catholic Politics in Rwanda, 1950–1962* (The Catholic University of America, 2011). I owe a major debt of gratitude to my dissertation committee for steering the original project to completion. The late Jacques Gres-Gayer, former director of the Church History program in CUA's School of Theology and Religious Studies, oriented me to the Francophone world that shaped so much of Rwandan church history. Thomas Cohen, Associate Professor of History at CUA, served as an invaluable editor; his detailed comments on every chapter vastly improved the cohesion of the final text. Paul Kollman, Associate Professor of Theology and Director of the Center of Social Concerns at the University of Notre Dame, was an outstanding mentor in modern African church history. I thank Dr. Kollman in particular for giving me the opportunity to speak on my early research at Notre Dame in 2009.

I also thank all of the groups and individuals who helped facilitate my research. CUA's School of Theology and Religious Studies awarded me a Hubbard Dissertation Fellowship in 2010, a scholarship that greatly facilitated my ability to finish the original dissertation. Thanks as well to Lynda Coon and the History Department at the University of Arkansas for inviting me to lecture on my research in 2010. It is largely thanks to Prof. Coon, Tom Kennedy, my other undergraduate history professors at Arkansas, and John Iliffe at the University of Cambridge that I first learned to think historically about the world and Africa. I am greatly indebted to Emmanuel Katongole, Associate Professor of Theology and Peace Studies at the University of Notre Dame. As my mentor during M.Div. studies at Duke Divinity School, Dr. Katongole refined my thinking on Rwanda and gave me my first opportunity to visit the country. Ian Linden, René Lemarchand, Frank Nolan, Paul Rutayisire, and David Newbury offered invaluable insights as I conceived the project in 2007–2008. During the research process, I benefited from the encouragement and insight of scholars like Catherine Newbury, Timothy Longman, Samuel Totten, Scott Straus, Susan Thomson, and the late Allison Des Forges (whose historical work on Rwanda remains a model for me). I owe particular thanks to Profs. Katongole, Rutayisire, Linden and Robert Koerpel for offering detailed feedback on draft versions of the final manuscript. Finally, I thank the Inter-Library Loan Departments at the University of Arkansas and Creighton University for obtaining so many rare texts on my behalf.

I also thank all of the individuals who aided my archival work in Rome and Rwanda in 2009–2010. As director of the General Archives of the Missionaries of Africa in Rome, Fr. Stefaan Minnaert offered me unprecedented access to archival resources for the 1956–1962 period. As a historian and missionary who spent years in Rwanda, Fr. Minnaert also offered me invaluable insights into the complex history of the Catholic Church in Rwanda. I also thank his confrere, Fr. Juan Oses, for generously sharing the General Archives' digital photos with me; several of these are included in this manuscript. Fr. Guy Theunis, M.Afr., the former provincial for the White Fathers in Rwanda, has also provided helpful bibliographic insights for my project. In the midst of their studies at the University of Arkansas, Janvier Kwizera, Thierry Habimana, and Sixbert Uwiringiyimana spent hours teaching me Kinyarwanda prior to my archival work in Rwanda in 2010. The Brothers of Charity hosted me in Kigali, Gatagara, and Butare and facilitated my research in all three places; I am particularly grateful to Eric Ferdinand Twizeyimana and Yves Mugwaneza for their translation assistance. I also thank Fr. Marc François, Jean Marie Vianney Karekezi and the White Fathers' *Centre Missionnaire Lavigerie* in Kigali for opening their archives to me. Thanks also to Bishop Smaragde Mbonyintege, Fr. Jean de Dieu Hodari, and the Diocese of Kabgayi for allowing me broad access to Kabgayi's archival material. Joseph Rurangwa offered tremendous insight and translation assistance during my travels to Ruhengeri, Nyundo, and

Gisenyi. I am also grateful to my former employers at the Diocese of Little Rock and St. Thomas Aquinas University Parish (Fayetteville, Arkansas), who demonstrated remarkable flexibility with me as I conducted this archival research.

I also thank everyone at Oxford University Press for working with me on this project, especially acquisitions editor Theo Calderara. I never would have approached OUP without the encouragement and mentoring of Fr. Bill Harmless, S.J., at Creighton University. Thanks also to OUP's anonymous readers who offered detailed and substantive feedback on the original manuscript.

This book includes material previously published in several academic journals: "Beyond Tribalism: The Hutu-Tutsi Question and Catholic Rhetoric in Colonial Rwanda," *Journal of Religion in Africa* 42.2 (2012): 172–202; "'Far from having unity, we are tending towards total disunity': The Catholic Major Seminary in Rwanda, 1950–1962," *Studies in World Christianity* 18.1 (2012): 82–102; "The Danger of Description: The Ethnic Labeling of the Poor in Colonial Rwanda" *Journal of Religion & Society* Supplement Series 10 (2013), available online at http://www.creighton.edu/jrs. I am grateful to Brill Press, Edinburgh University Press, and the Kripke Center at Creighton University for granting reprinting permissions.

The people to whom I owe the greatest debt of gratitude are my family. My sister Jenny Grimes provided constant encouragement throughout my dissertation and was the first person with whom I celebrated the news of its publication. My children Ruben James, Annabelle Grace, and Samuel Thomas lived with "Daddy's dissertation" for many years. In helping me keep my studies in perspective and reminding me of the joys of human life, they have helped me in ways they will never know.

I have dedicated this book to my parents, Jim and Pinkey Carney, and to my wife Becky. An accomplished author, my Dad taught me and showed me how to write with lucidity. A gifted writer and youth minister, my Mom encouraged me to follow Mother Teresa's maxim to do "small things with great love." Both have embodied a deep but critical Christian faith, and I hope this book reflects echoes of their legacies. Becky has walked with me through every step of graduate studies and the writing of this book, exhorting me to continue through the inevitable doubts and pitfalls of the journey. I am incredibly blessed to share my life with such a remarkable woman, mother, teacher and friend.

J.J. Carney
Omaha, Nebraska
April 2013
A.M.D.G.

Rwanda Before the Genocide

Political Map of Rwanda, 2008 (*Rwanda Map # 3717, Rev. 10, courtesy United Nations*)

Introduction

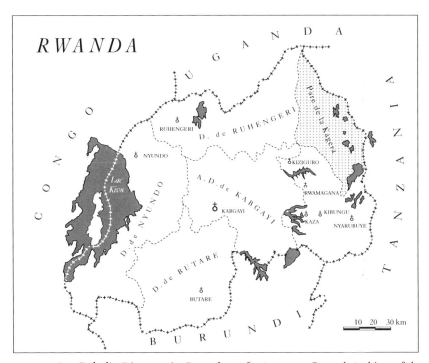

FIGURE I.I Catholic Dioceses in Rwanda, 1962 (*courtesy General Archives of the Missionaries of Africa, Rome*).

ONE OF THE most Catholic countries in Africa suffered the worst genocide of the late twentieth century. Christians slaughtered Christians in Christian schools and parishes, and upward of 800,000 Rwandan Tutsi and moderate Hutu perished over the course of 100 days. In turn, the genocide precipitated a regional war that consumed Central Africa for nearly a decade and took the lives of millions in neighboring Democratic Republic of the Congo. In the years following the genocide, Christian theologians and church leaders have grappled with the seeming failure of Christian mission in a country in which 90 percent of the population claimed the Christian faith and nearly 70 percent identified as Catholics. To echo the words of Catholic papal envoy Roger Cardinal Etchegaray, "the blood of tribalism proved deeper than the waters of baptism."[1]

In explaining how and why the "blood of tribalism" grew so poisonous, two main viewpoints have emerged. In the stereotypical popular view, Rwanda suffered from primordial tribal hatred between Hutu and Tutsi. Manipulated by local political actors, these latent tensions exploded into genocidal violence in 1994. For the majority of scholarly commentators, the root of Rwanda's problems lay less with ancient ethnic grievances and more with the colonial interventions of European actors. Hutu and Tutsi lived peaceably until Belgian colonial officials and Catholic Missionaries of Africa (also known as the White Fathers) taught them to see each other as separate racial groups. Such divisionist rhetoric ultimately gave rise to a zero-sum, "us against them" narrative that culminated with Hutu power advocates calling for the wholesale elimination of Tutsi from Rwandan society.[2]

This latter meta-narrative has led scholars to focus on the early decades of Rwanda's missionary history and the immediate years preceding the genocide of 1994. In church history, the standard story has highlighted early White Fathers' efforts to cultivate close relations with Rwanda's central court, the mass conversions of Tutsi elites in the 1930s (known by the French term *la tornade*), and the establishment of Rwanda as a "Christian kingdom in the heart of Africa" in the 1940s. The story then skips to the 1980s and early 1990s, emphasizing the close ties between Vincent Nsengiyumva, the Hutu Archbishop of Kigali, and President Juvenal Habyarimana. Many critics have noted the church's silence and complicity in the face of the 1994 genocide. If the 1950s and early 1960s are mentioned at all, it is to highlight the Machiavellian role that church leaders played in switching their favor from Tutsi to Hutu elites, thereby ensuring the rise of an ethnicist, Hutu-dominated republic after independence in 1962.

This standard narrative—recently propagated in English through the influential works of Mahmood Mamdani and Timothy Longman—is not without its merits.[3] I will reinforce several of these points, such as church leaders' commitment to church-state partnership, contributions to the hardening of ethnic categories, and obsession with protecting what they perceived to be the Catholic Church's institutional interests. But the simplicity of the standard narrative—and its failure to analyze the crucial political and rhetorical developments of the late 1950s and early 1960s—risks occluding more than it reveals. For example, the focus on top-down evangelization downplays the extent to which early Catholic missions supported a counter-cultural, pan-ethnic community of poor peasants and counter-elites. Not only did the first Banyarwanda converts come from the ranks of Hutu peasants and marginalized *petit* Tutsi, but also the earliest Banyarwanda term for Christian, *inyangarwanda*, literally meant "haters or repudiators of Rwanda."[4] While Longman and others have argued that this populist narrative was lost after the Tutsi *tornade* of the 1930s, I argue that the 1950s represents the resurgence and ultimate triumph of this "church from below." For late colonial Hutu leaders and their missionary allies, the Hutu social revolution was closely connected to the liberation of the poor masses and the establishment of a more egalitarian Rwandan society marked by social justice, democracy, and economic equality.

In addition, late colonial Rwandan history reveals the birth of "Hutu" and "Tutsi" as politically contested labels. This was the moment when Rwandans—and particularly Hutu elites—began to publicly identify themselves first and foremost as "Hutu" and "Tutsi." Clan identities, patron-client relationships, religious affiliations, ideological loyalties, and even national identities were subsumed under the Hutu-Tutsi dynamic. For Hutu elites, the pan-ethnic political reform movements of the early 1950s transformed in the late 1950s into a mission to empower the Hutu masses over and against a perceived Tutsi oligarchy. Tutsi elites responded in kind, refusing to incorporate Hutu elites into Rwanda's local political structures and defining Rwandan nationalism against both Belgian colonialism and the growing movement of Hutu social democracy. Ethno-political mobilization also contributed to one of the primary ideological legacies of the 1950s—the emergence and ultimate dominance of what Catherine Newbury has termed a "corporate view of ethnicity" in which "Hutu" and "Tutsi" are defined in collective, stereotypical terms.[5]

The late colonial period also reveals the extent to which other ideological issues such as democratization, anti-communism, and church-state tensions shaped Catholic leaders' responses to Rwanda's emerging ethnic and political movements. Even as Hutu-Tutsi language came to dominate Rwandan politics in the late 1950s, growing missionary support for Hutu parties had less to do with ethnicism and more to do with perceived institutional self-interest. Namely, missionaries feared for their postcolonial future in light of Tutsi elites' association with the *Union National Rwandaise* (UNAR), an anti-colonial, nationalist party with thinly veiled plans to nationalize Catholic schools and reduce White Father influence in Rwanda.

The 1950s also challenges our understanding of "Catholic Church." Far from the monolithic, missionary-dominated community of the early twentieth century, the Rwandan church of the 1950s included Belgian Africa's first African bishop and a majority of African clergy. Most of these clergy were Tutsi, and their social and political views often differed greatly from the White Fathers or their Hutu confreres. Such analytical divisions extended down into Rwanda's seminaries, revealing deep interracial tensions that are often overshadowed by scholars' exclusive focus on the Hutu-Tutsi dynamic. By the 1950s Catholic seminaries had also formed a generation of Hutu elites denied access to elite colonial schools, creating what Ian Linden has described as a "Hutu counter-elite" notable for their fealty to church authorities and commitment to social democracy.[6]

In addition, two critical—and oft-overlooked—Catholic leaders rose to prominence in the 1950s. After two years working in the Burundian missions, the Swiss White Father André Perraudin became a theology professor at Nyakibanda Major Seminary in 1950. In the wake of a crisis that divided Nyakibanda's Burundian, Rwandan, and Congolese seminarians along nationalist lines, Perraudin was named rector of the seminary in 1952. Three years later, he was the surprise choice to replace Mgr. Laurent Déprimoz as Vicar Apostolic of Kabgayi. At the age of forty-one, Perraudin became the most powerful churchman in the country. His power would soon be matched by controversy.

The second principal church leader of this era was Aloys Bigirumwami. Born in 1904, Bigirumwami was a native of Gisaka in eastern Rwanda. He hailed from one of Rwanda's first Catholic families and became one of Rwanda's first indigenous priests. Bigirumwami served in pastoral ministry for over twenty years before he was named in 1952 as the first indigenous bishop in Belgian Africa. As Vicar Apostolic of Nyundo in northwestern Rwanda, Bigirumwami served as a bridge between Rwanda's increasingly polarized missionaries and its indigenous clergy. As this study will reveal, however, he also adopted an analysis of Rwanda's social and political situation that contrasted with that of Perraudin and his White Father allies, especially as social and ecclesial tensions accelerated in the 1959–1962 period.

A word on terminology. The first half of the book's title, *Rwanda before the Genocide*, alludes to my argument that the late 1950s and early 1960s established the political ideologies, rhetorical dynamics, and patterns of ethnic violence that would ultimately culminate with the 1994 genocide. In turn, if we are to fairly evaluate the Catholic Church's controversial role in Rwandan history, we must consider not just the White Father missions of the early twentieth century but also the late colonial period when Catholic bishops, priests, lay journalists, and politicians dominated Rwanda's social and political discourse. In light of current polemics in Rwanda and elsewhere, however, I should state up front that this book does not "blame" the White Fathers or the colonial Catholic Church for the 1994 genocide, nor do I wish to convey a direct causal link between the events of the 1950s and the much different historical context of the early 1990s. The complexities of history do not allow for such deterministic accounts. Even if the era's revolutionary changes did not make the 1994 genocide inevitable, it is very difficult to understand the deeper roots of the latter without due attention to the former.

The second half of the title reflects my specific focus on the internal and external politics of the Rwandan church between 1952 and 1962. When I say "Catholic politics," I imply three things. First, I investigate how church leaders—primarily bishops, influential clergy, and lay elites working in the Catholic media—interacted with colonial and Rwandan political leaders and envisioned church-state relations. Second, I explore how the Catholic Church itself served as a locus of political contestation, focusing on intraclerical relations between European missionaries and African priests and the nationalist and ethnic tensions that swirled at the Catholic seminary of Nyakibanda. Third, I analyze the theo-political visions of Rwanda's Catholic leaders, particularly their understandings of ecclesiology and the application of Catholic social teaching to Rwanda. I do this for two reasons. First, what Emmanuel Katongole has termed "theological imagination" helps establish what the church deems possible, and the lacunae and silences often reveal as much as the stated visions.[7] Second, the postcolonial tendency to focus solely on the Hutu-Tutsi dynamic has overshadowed other key themes in late colonial Rwandan history, such as the Catholic Church's virulent anti-communism or newfound embracing of democratization and social justice. Late colonial arguments concerned not just Hutu-Tutsi classifications but also how the theoretical ideals of Catholic social teaching should be *applied* to the Hutu-Tutsi dynamic.

Having said this, much of Rwanda's historical controversy revolves around ethnic discourse and especially the contested labels of "Hutu" and "Tutsi." The opening chapter therefore provides a historiographical overview of the complex categories that proved so divisive in Rwanda's late colonial and postcolonial eras. Although "Hutu" and "Tutsi" have at times included racial, ethnic, economic, occupational, and social connotations, I will emphasize the *political* nature of these identities. In particular, I see the late 1950s as the crucial era in which these identities were "triggered" in the midst of accelerating decolonization and democratization movements.

Although my primary focus lies with the late colonial period, this era needs to be placed in proper historical context. The second chapter therefore considers the historical and ecclesial developments of the late nineteenth and early twentieth centuries that established the later contours of Catholic history in Rwanda. I begin by considering the ecclesial and theological vision of White Father founder Charles Lavigerie, placing Lavigerie in the context of a nineteenth-century French Catholic missionary revival that focused in particular on the continent of Africa. Lavigerie emphasized several principles that shaped later White Father missions in Rwanda, including top-down evangelization, missionary adaptation, and the necessity of Christian civilization. I then turn to the White Father missions in Rwanda's neighbor Buganda. Originating in the late 1870s and 1880s, these missions predated Rwanda's own Catholic missions by two decades. In numerical terms, these missions were phenomenally successful. However, the Buganda missions' experience of state persecution and internecine Protestant-Catholic rivalries left an ambivalent legacy for many of Rwanda's earliest missionaries. The heart of the first chapter narrates the first fifty years of Rwanda's Catholic history. This period witnessed the entrenchment of German and later Belgian colonial rule. Despite their support by both colonial powers, the White Fathers were initially rebuffed by Rwanda's Mwami Musinga and nearly all of Rwanda's nobility. Catholic missions were more successful among Rwanda's Hutu and Tutsi peasants, who often viewed the White Fathers as political patrons. In the 1910s and 1920s, the church's evangelical focus shifted back toward Rwanda's predominantly Tutsi elites, leading to the remarkable transformation of Rwanda from a struggling mission outpost to a celebrated "Christian kingdom" in the heart of Africa. In addition to narrating the growth of the church, I consider Catholic contributions to ethnic discourse. In summary, although White Father rhetoric contributed to the hardening of Hutu-Tutsi categories, Catholic political engagement during this period was marked more by institutional self-interest than ethnicism per se.

The third chapter traces Rwandan church history from 1950 to 1955. Here I consider the major political changes that swept through Rwanda after World War II, including Belgium's decision to introduce a ten-year political decentralization plan in 1952. Social and political reforms accelerated inside Rwanda as Mwami Mutara Rudahigwa abolished the traditional institutions of *ubuhake* (patron-client relationships revolving around cattle usage) and *uburetwa* (forced labor imposed on Hutu peasants). After the pastoral triumphs of the 1930s and 1940s, the Rwandan Catholic Church in the early 1950s experienced new tensions between White Father missionaries and Rwanda's rising numbers of indigenous clergy. Unprecedented nationalist tensions flared at the major seminary of Nyakibanda as Rwandan students forced out their Burundian and Congolese colleagues, as well as the seminary's White Father rector. At the same time, pastoral leaders and Catholic journalists were preoccupied with the fate of the *évolués*, the rising generation of Catholic and Belgian-trained elites entrusted with the future leadership of the country. Surprisingly, Hutu-Tutsi terminology appears rarely in Catholic commentaries from the early 1950s. This lacuna reflects a much broader social context than the ethnic dualism that is often read back into the period. Finally, this chapter introduces Perraudin and Bigirumwami, the two prelates who came to dominate Rwandan church politics in the late 1950s and early 1960s. The early 1950s reveal analytical and pastoral tensions between Perraudin and Bigirumwami that became more pronounced in the latter years of the decade.

The fourth chapter begins with Perraudin's consecration to the episcopate in March 1956 and concludes on the eve of the Hutu uprisings of November 1959. This was one of the most volatile three-year periods in Rwandan history, marked by Rwanda's first direct legislative elections in 1956, the emergence of the Hutu-Tutsi question in local newspapers, the 1957 publication of the *Bahutu Manifesto*, Mwami Mutara Rudahigwa's sudden death in July 1959, and the rapid mobilization of ethnic and nationalist political parties in the latter months of 1959. In response, Catholic leaders struggled to gauge and shape the increasingly fractious decolonization movement, releasing important pastoral statements on questions of social justice and church-state relations. In the face of a political dispute framed in increasingly ethnic terms, Bigirumwami and Perraudin published sharply contrasting analyses of Rwanda's ethnic and social challenges in late 1958 and early 1959. After several years of peace, political and ethnic tensions also reemerged at Nyakibanda seminary. I conclude the chapter by considering if and how Catholic leaders—and particularly Mgr. Perraudin—stand responsible for fomenting the revolutionary politics and Hutu-Tutsi divisions that saturated Rwanda at the end of 1959.

The fifth chapter opens with the Hutu *jacquerie* or uprisings of November 1959. Over the course of two weeks, pitched battles broke out between Hutu mobs, militias associated with Mwami Kigeli Ndahindurwa, and Belgium's colonial army, the *Force Publique*. Hundreds died in the violence, and Hutu arsonists forced thousands of Tutsi to flee the country. The events of November 1959 also precipitated vast political changes on the part of Belgium's colonial authorities. Led by Col. Guy Logiest, a devout Catholic and Belgian military resident, colonial officials transformed the *jacquerie* into a veritable political revolution, replacing hundreds of Tutsi chiefs and subchiefs with Hutu elites from Catholic journalist Gregoire Kayibanda's Parmehutu party. Political changes would only accelerate in 1960 when Mwami Kigeli and many of his allies in the Tutsi-dominated UNAR party went into exile, facilitating Parmehutu's establishment of an effective one-party dictatorship. By the time of independence in July 1962, Rwanda had transformed from a Tutsi-dominated monarchy to a Hutu-dominated democratic republic. Multiparty pluralism and ethnic tolerance would prove elusive.

As these momentous events unfolded, Perraudin, Bigirumwami, and other Catholic leaders spoke out on Rwanda's increasing ethnic and political violence while trying to protect Catholic interests in the face of an uncertain political future. Behind the scenes, the two churchmen and their clerical allies engaged in increasingly fractious disputes over how to engage Rwanda's new political leaders and how to resolve the Hutu-Tutsi crisis that threatened to destroy Nyakibanda seminary. The church also lost one of its most promising sons, Mgr. Bernard Manyurane, a Hutu seminary professor who died under suspicious circumstances shortly after his appointment to the episcopate. In addition, this period saw the emergence of a broad pattern of Catholic political discourse that would continue into the postcolonial period. Namely, Catholic leaders took a strong rhetorical stand against political and ethnic violence, but they also betrayed a pro-Hutu analytical partisanship that offered uncritical support for the state and tended to blame Rwanda's increasing violence on Tutsi unwilling to accept Parmehutu rule.

Moving into the postcolonial era, the sixth chapter considers Catholic hierarchical responses to anti-Tutsi violence in 1963–1964, 1973, and 1994. After a failed coup attempt by UNAR exiles in December 1963, Rwanda's Parmehutu government executed a score of prominent Tutsi political opponents and orchestrated the massacre of thousands of Tutsi civilians in the Gikongoro region of southern Rwanda. Led by Perraudin, Catholic leaders denounced the violence but again failed to hold the government responsible for its crimes. After a Tutsi-dominated military regime in neighboring Burundi massacred upward of 200,000 Hutu in 1972, anti-Tutsi violence broke out in Rwandan Catholic schools, universities, and seminaries in early 1973. Again, Catholic leaders condemned the violence but failed to take subsequent steps to distance themselves from the government or address ethnic violence as a distinctly ecclesial problem. I conclude this chapter by narrating key political and ecclesial developments in the years leading up to the 1994 genocide, including Perraudin's own reactions to this epochal event.

While this study is primarily a historical work, it raises important questions for Christian theology and social ethics in Rwanda and beyond. In a brief epilogue, I share six lessons I see emerging from this historical narrative. First and foremost, Rwanda calls the church to embody a politics of repentance. This requires the church to move beyond the institutional defensiveness of Mgr. Perraudin and other church leaders toward a corporate, top-down embracing of confession and reconciliation. Second, this history underlines the necessity of the church leader's prophetic role, especially in terms of maintaining critical distance from state leaders. A third lesson concerns violence. Namely, the church is called to manifest a politics of nonviolence in the midst of a nation-state premised on the love of domination. Fourth, Rwandan history raises the important question of how to pursue Christian ethical prescriptions—namely the love of God, neighbor, and enemy—in the midst of highly contested social contexts and social descriptions. There is not an easy answer to this question, but Rwandan history demonstrates the importance of grappling with what I term the church's "descriptive task." Fifth, Rwandan history challenges the church to preach the social, communal, ethical, and political dimensions of Christian identity in the face of rival nationalist, ethnic, and ideological allegiances. Finally, this history underlines the importance of the purification of memory. Thick, honest, and self-critical historical assessments are therefore crucial to the church's theological task, as Rwanda makes evident.

In his landmark 1977 *Church and Revolution in Rwanda*, Ian Linden shares a revealing anecdote from a 1973 interview with Gregoire Kayibanda, the former Catholic seminarian, founder of Parmehutu, and President of Rwanda during the First Republic (1962–1973). The interview came after the Tutsi schools expulsions of early 1973 and shortly before a military *coup d'état* removed Kayibanda from office in July. Linden writes:

I was impressed during an interview with Gregoire Kayibanda, then President of Rwanda, in June 1973, by the intensity of his feelings against the Tutsi. Interviews with missionaries who had known him intimately during the years 1950–61 convinced me that social Catholicism, rather than any other philosophy, informed his actions and planning.[8]

This book was written in part to uncover the story behind this observation. It is to this intersection—ethnic identity, politics, violence, and Catholic theology—we now turn.

I

Contested Categories

DESPITE THEIR CENTRAL importance in Rwanda's tragic postcolonial history, the categories "Hutu" and "Tutsi" are not easily defined.[1] Variously described as distinctions of race, ethnicity, caste, socioeconomic status, or political power, the terms used to explain Hutu and Tutsi themselves reflect deep ideological presuppositions.[2] The argument over how to define Hutu and Tutsi reflects longstanding divisions on the history of ethnic migration into Rwanda. If there is a narrow consensus, it holds that Bantu-speaking groups later associated with the Hutu arrived in Rwanda beginning around 1100 AD as part of the broader Bantu migrations that shaped so much of Iron Age history in Africa. Although they worked in both agricultural and pastoralist work, Hutu were more associated with the former. Hutu communities maintained a higher degree of political independence in northern and western Rwanda well into the twentieth century; Hutu and Tutsi mixed more frequently in central and southern Rwanda.

The geographic and chronological origins of the Tutsi are more controversial. Colonial theorists tended to trace Tutsi ancestry to Ethiopia or Egypt.[3] Modern scholars locate their origins much closer to Rwanda, perhaps among the Ankole in southwestern Uganda or pastoralists on the plateaus of Tanzania. Tutsi pastoralists were likely to have migrated into Rwanda over the course of several centuries between 1100 and 1650. Colonial commentators and Hutu nationalist historians described these ancient Tutsi migrations in terms of a military conquest.[4] However, contemporary scholars favor a more gradual infiltration and mixing with the local Hutu population, noting that many of the political and religious traditions associated with the Tutsi (e.g., pastoralism, monarchy, military) were likely to have originated among Hutu communities.

Growing out of oral traditions associated with the royal court, two Banyarwanda myths explained the origins of Hutu, Tutsi, and Twa.[5] In the first, Kigwa, the son of the heavenly king Nkuba and first earthly king of Rwanda, had three sons— Gatutsi, Gahutu, and Gatwa. All three of his sons were deprived of a social faculty.

The first son, Gatutsi, suggested that they petition Imana, the high god of traditional Rwandan religion, for new faculties. Imana subsequently bestowed Gatutsi with the quality of anger, Gahutu with the qualities of disobedience and labor, and Gatwa with the quality of gluttony. The second myth relates how Kigwa tested his three sons by entrusting each of them with a calabash of milk. The next morning, Gatwa had drunk his milk, Gahutu had spilled his milk, and Gatutsi had preserved his calabash of milk. For his courage and obedience, Kigwa rewarded Gatutsi with command over the "gluttonous serf" Gatwa and the "clumsy peasant" Gahutu.

While Bernardin Muzungu is correct to note that these traditional myths never posited different geographic or racial origins for Hutu, Tutsi, and Twa, Muzungu fails to note the inherent moral hierarchy implicit in these origin myths. Both stories reinforced traditional ethnic stereotypes while lending an air of divine sanction to Rwanda's traditional social hierarchy, problematizing Muzungu's romanticist claims that "all the millennial history of co-existence between the two groups [Hutu and Tutsi] had been characterized by a flawless harmony."[6] One should note, however, that the Hutu-Tutsi-Twa division was not the sole or even preeminent concern of nineteenth-century royal origin myths; clan alliances, religious power, and warrior narratives appeared even more frequently.[7]

Reacting to the physical, economic, and social differences between the Tutsi royal court and a peasantry that they tended to describe as "Hutu," European missionaries and scholars writing in the first half of the twentieth century viewed the Hutu-Tutsi distinction as racial or biological. Shaped by the early observations of colonial explorers, they tended to distinguish Tutsi from Hutu according to the "Hamitic thesis." Introduced by the nineteenth-century explorer John Hanning Speke and propagated by twentieth-century scholars like C. G. Seligman and Jan Czekanowski, the Hamitic thesis combined the biblical narrative of the "curse of Ham" (Genesis 9:18–29) with the scientific racialism of the late 19th century.[8] Rather than use the curse of Ham to justify slavery as in antebellum America, late nineteenth-century European theorists ranked a so-called "Hamitic race" of North African and Ethiopian pastoralists as superior to what they termed the "Bantu" populations of sub-Saharan Africa. For European theorists in Rwanda, the Tutsi fit the role of Hamitic civilizer; the Hutu were classified as Bantu Africans. In turn, the Tutsi "Caucasians under a black skin" were seen as culturally and racially superior to their Bantu Hutu neighbors. Such theories also implied a foreign origin for the Tutsi.[9] In the words of Louis de Lacger, an early chronicler of Rwandan history, the Tutsi were originally "brothers of the Nubians, the Galla, the Danakil. They have the Caucasian type and have come from Semitic roots in Asia... before being in this way blackened they were bronze."[10] For Léon Classe, the influential Catholic vicar apostolic of Rwanda between 1922 and 1945, the "Tutsi are not Bantu, they are, if one wants, Negroids—they are an African people which possesses the strongest Hamitic indices."[11] As late as the early 1960s, the influential

Belgian anthropologist Marcel d'Hertefelt continued to describe the Tutsi as an "Ethiopian race."[12] It should be noted that colonial theorists developed their Tutsi paradigm from their experiences at the royal court. Although Rwanda's peasantry included thousands of "petit Tutsi" (or poor Tutsi peasants), colonial missionaries tended to describe the poor masses as "Bahutu" and the political and economic elite as "Batutsi."[13]

The Hamitic thesis retained a powerful political mythos throughout the twentieth century and developed an especially vitriolic edge in the years preceding the 1994 genocide.[14] Among scholars, however, understandings began shifting in the 1950s and 1960s. Language of "caste" rather than "race" began to mark studies of the Hutu-Tutsi distinction. Caste underlined the supposedly endogamous and occupational distinctiveness of each group while emphasizing the socially integrated nature of Banyarwanda society. In this sense, the influential Belgian scholar J. J. Maquet described Rwandan society in terms of a caste framework, but Maquet saw this hierarchy as maintaining Rwanda's delicate social harmony. More critical anthropologists like Helen Codere and Luc de Heusch saw the caste system as fraught with social tension, maintained only by Tutsi monopolization of political power and military force. Political studies in the 1960s—particularly the influential work of René Lemarchand—also utilized the terminology of caste to describe Hutu and Tutsi. Critics noted, however, that Hutu and Tutsi contained no connotations of purity and pollution as in south Asia.[15]

The late 1960s and 1970s saw further development toward a "socioeconomic" understanding of the Hutu-Tutsi divide.[16] In this view Tutsi referred to the land-owning aristocracy and Hutu to the landless peasantry. The church historian Ian Linden described this socioeconomic distinction in feudal terms; the anthropologist Claudine Vidal rejected feudal terminology as anachronistic and overly rigid and failing to account for the fluidity of economic status in pre-colonial Rwanda. The language of social class successfully avoided the genetic and biological associations of racial, tribal, or ethnic terminology, and it tended to imply more fluidity between Hutu and Tutsi groups.[17] At the same time, skeptics note that there were many wealthy Hutu who never became Tutsi, and there were thousands of lower-class Tutsi who struggled to eke out a living far from the luxuries of the royal court. Whatever its shortcomings, the socioeconomic school remains influential, especially among Rwanda's RPF government and Westerners writing after the 1994 genocide.[18]

Contemporary reflections tend to break down along two poles. On one side are those who see the Hutu-Tutsi distinction as an ethnic or even racial division that dates from the precolonial period. Composed primarily of Hutu expatriates and Westerners critical of the Rwanda Patriotic Front (RPF) government, this school sees current RPF efforts to subsume Hutu and Tutsi under the national Banyarwanda identity as overtly ideological and historically naïve. While still allowing for a colonial role in exacerbating Hutu-Tutsi tensions, these scholars emphasize the cultural and even biological distinctiveness of Tutsi and Hutu and trace the origins of social discrimination to the precolonial period. For example, while admitting that racist Belgian colonial policies exacerbated Rwandan social tensions, Johann Pottier argues that one should see through the "smokescreen of sameness (same territory, same clans, same political institutions, same language) and must appreciate the divisive institutions and practices which preceded European rule."[19] The French historian Bernard Lugan has gone even further, arguing that Hutu and Tutsi are in fact distinct racial groups.[20]

Other postgenocide scholars emphasize the mutable nature of Hutu and Tutsi identities. This approach highlights the problematic history of racial, tribal, ethnic, or even economic terminology, describing Hutu and Tutsi instead as "social categories."[21] Associated with Tutsi nationalists during the independence period, the current RPF government of Paul Kagame, and the writings of the influential French academic Jean-Pierre Chrétien, this school emphasizes the integrated nature of traditional Rwandan clans and the military, Rwanda's shared linguistic and political heritage, Hutu-Tutsi mixed marriages, and the precolonial fluidity of the Hutu-Tutsi line.[22] More radical voices reject the categories as colonial impositions lacking any foundations in traditional Rwanda, arguing that the nation's only ethnic group is the Banyarwanda. In this sense, Bernardin Muzungu notes that *ubwoko*, the Banyarwanda term for race, referred to a group descending from the same patrilineal ancestor—in other words, clans rather than Hutu, Tutsi, or Twa social groups.[23]

There are elements of truth to both accounts. The first school accurately recognizes that colonial agents did not make up these categories out of whole cloth; the second group reminds us that Hutu and Tutsi categories retained a significant degree of flexibility until the colonial period. In this sense, the precolonial reign of Rwanda's great Mwami Rwabugiri (1860–1895) emerges as an especially important period for consideration.[24] The term *abahutu* came into common usage as a socially derogatory term implying political marginalization; one thinks here of a traditional Kinyarwanda phrase like *Sindi umuhutu wawe*, literally "I am not his servant."[25] Traditional institutions like the cattle-based *ubuhake* became more oppressive; new institutions like *uburetwa corvées* were imposed on Hutu farmers but not Tutsi herders.[26] In addition, Rwabugiri's military conquests extended his authority from central Rwanda to previously independent Hutu regions in the north and west, provoking strong resistance from powerful Hutu lineages in these regions.[27] And while large numbers of *petit* Tutsi continued to live alongside their Hutu peasant neighbors, royal ideology increasingly equated "Tutsi" with political and economic power. In summary, the late nineteenth century saw Hutu-Tutsi labels develop ideological overtones that were missing in earlier periods of Rwandan history.[28]

Having said this, the Hutu-Tutsi line remained comparatively fluid in the years prior to the European encounter, and significant "factors of integration" should not be discounted.[29] Intermarriage continued, wealthy Hutu could still be ennobled as Tutsi, and Hutu and Tutsi coexisted in socially formative institutions like the military. While the Mwami had theoretically unlimited power, three chiefs divided responsibility on each of Rwanda's hills. Each chief had a separate portfolio for agriculture, pastoral herding, or taxes, and one of these chiefs was always Hutu.[30] In addition, the patron-client *ubuhake* system closely connected the welfare of the Hutu client with that of his Tutsi patron; the former provided services to the latter in exchange for protection and advocacy at the Mwami's court. Nor was *ubuhake* limited to a Hutu-Tutsi relationship—it some regions the custom may have been more prevalent between Tutsi.[31] And while precolonial Banyarwanda rulers all came from the Abega and Abanyiginya lineages, the king was viewed as a transcendent, pan-ethnic figure for Hutu, Tutsi, and Twa alike. Finally, a traditional Rwandan was not merely Hutu or Tutsi. Family, clan, and lineage ties were often more determinative, whether on the local hill or in the often-vicious succession struggles at Court.[32] In light of the categories' relative flexibility in the precolonial period, the subsuming of all identities under the supposed dualist struggle of "Tutsi lord" and "Hutu serf" is one of the most regrettable legacies of European colonialism. As Catherine Newbury has argued, European colonial policies "did not create ethnicity; instead they served to mold its social salience."[33]

A century of scholarship has not resolved the seemingly simple question of "who are the Tutsi" and "who are the Hutu," a fact that reminds us to exercise considerable caution when using any label. Notwithstanding the considerable ambiguity of the term, "ethnicity" remains the conventional term for the Hutu-Tutsi distinction and will be used throughout this book.[34] When I use the term "ethnic," however, I do not imply that "Hutu" and "Tutsi" are timeless, unchanging, genetically distinct categories. Nor do I adopt the textbook understanding of ethnicity as a cultural group sharing a common language and religion.[35] Rather, I follow David Newbury's understanding of ethnicity as a largely political identity that shifted through time:

> Ethnic identities were not primordial; they were contextually created, they altered over time, and they evolved differently in different places and contexts. Therefore, ethnic groups cannot be seen as internally homogenous, externally distinct, and constantly in confrontation with other such groups. Like many social categories, ethnicity was not an institution but an identity, and hence ethnic categories were contextually defined... Only with the slow infiltration of state power, and in a complex process of mutual agency, did people come to see themselves as part of a collective Hutu identity that transcended lineage and hill.[36]

And while denying neither the precolonial origins of Hutu and Tutsi nor the shared heritage of Banyarwanda culture, I will focus on how these labels were essentialized, politicized, and institutionalized during the Catholic missionary era. At the same time, I hope to show that many other factors beyond Hutu-Tutsi identities shaped Rwandan politics in the late colonial period. In this sense, I hope to move beyond recent scholars' obsession with "tribalism"—an analysis that assumes that the European transformation of Hutu and Tutsi into racial categories inevitably led to social conflict. While its impact should not be discounted, the Hamitic thesis risks obscuring other key dimensions of Rwanda's political history. In turn, social conflict is not inherently or exclusively racial, nor is racial or ethnic difference inherently conflictual.

In conclusion, while RPF claims concerning the colonial invention of the Hutu-Tutsi distinction are overstated, precolonial Hutu-Tutsi labels were neither static nor wholly determinative for individual or group identity. More important than the origins of these groups are how and why these identities (and not others of clan, family, lineage, or nationality) became politicized and institutionally reproduced in the twentieth century. In the words of Jean-François Bayart, the key issue is to understand why people choose particular "operational acts of identification" that favor one identity over another.[37] In Rwanda, this critical shift happened in the late 1950s in a sociopolitical context dominated by Catholic actors. The roots of this dominance—namely the history of White Father missions in the late nineteenth and early twentieth centuries—is the subject of the next chapter.

2

Building a Catholic Kingdom in Central Africa, 1900–1950

CATHOLIC HISTORY IN Rwanda is a distinctively twentieth-century story. White Father missionaries first arrived at the royal court in 1900; mass conversions began in the 1920s and 1930s; Mwami Charles Rudahigwa Mutara dedicated the country to Christ the King in 1946. That said, the ecclesial visions of Rwanda's first Catholic missionaries were formed in a nineteenth-century European context. The first section of this chapter thus explores the missiological vision of Charles Lavigerie, the French founder of the White Fathers, in the context of a nineteenth-century European missionary revival that led thousands of young men and women to spread a gospel of Christianity and European civilization to the farthest corners of the globe. In the second part of the chapter, I analyze the legacies of early White Father missions in Buganda, Rwanda's northern neighbor. The witness of the "Uganda Martyrs" and subsequent growth of Catholic and Protestant missions served as implicit models for missionaries throughout the region, establishing important legacies concerning state power, Christian rivalry, and mass conversions.

After considering these late nineteenth-century contexts, I delve into a more detailed study of Rwandan Catholic history between 1900 and 1950. Here I highlight how Catholic leaders' concerns for the church's own institutional and evangelical interests shaped their engagement with political and ethnic questions; I focus in particular on the visions of Rwanda's first three vicars apostolic—Jean-Joseph Hirth, Léon Classe, and Laurent Déprimoz. I argue that two lasting—and contrasting—themes emerged in the earliest years of Catholic missions: proclaiming the kingdom of God to the poor and marginalized while simultaneously striving to convert Rwanda's political elites. The early foundations of the church lay with more politically and economically marginalized Hutu and Tutsi populations between 1900 and 1920. Under the leadership of Mgr. Classe, however, the Catholic Church built its pastoral capacity and formed stronger relationships with colonial officials and local Tutsi elites during the transitional decade of the 1920s. This work bore fruit in the 1930s as Tutsi elites converted en masse, helping Rwanda to become one of the most Catholic countries in Africa. I conclude by considering the 1940s, a decade in which Rwanda publicly embraced Catholicism as a national creed. Even in the midst of this golden era, however, new intra-ecclesial divisions emerged, foreshadowing deeper tensions that would come to dominate ecclesial and political life in the 1950s.

Charles Lavigerie's Vision for the White Fathers

As the Archbishop of Algiers and Carthage, founder of two missionary congregations, international crusader against slavery, and confidant of Pope Leo XIII, Charles Lavigerie remains one of the seminal figures in nineteenth-century Catholic history. In turn, his Missionaries of Africa—better known as the White Fathers— were arguably the most significant missionary congregation in twentieth-century Africa.[1] Nicknamed "kings without crowns" by the early German colonial official Richard Kandt, the White Fathers were the most influential Europeans to arrive in Rwanda during the early twentieth century.[2]

Charles Martial Allemand Lavigerie was born in 1825 in a Europe still recovering from the calamities of the French Revolution and the Napoleonic period. The France of his early years remained bitterly divided over the legacy of the Revolution and the role of Catholicism in French society. Lavigerie's family embodied the emergent tensions in French society; Lavigerie pursued his priestly vocation over the opposition of his anticlerical family. The extent to which a French Catholic could engage the French Republic would remain a central issue throughout Lavigerie's life; Lavigerie himself would play no small role in resolving this controversy in his final years.[3]

For all of the challenges, though, Lavigerie joined a European Catholic Church experiencing a major renewal at home and abroad. This nineteenth-century Catholic revival shared its early modern predecessor's close association of internal renewal with overseas mission; 82 missionary congregations were founded in France alone during the 1800s.[4] Recovering from the dechristianization of the revolutionary period, most nineteenth-century European missions correlated Christianity with Western civilization and envisioned mission territories as a birthplace for a modern Christian renewal. The Vatican played a central role in this nineteenth-century missionary revival, beginning with the pontificate of Pope Gregory XVI (1831–1846). Former prefect of *Propaganda Fide*, the Vatican's congregation for evangelization, Gregory supported multiple missionary congregations focusing exclusively on the African continent such as Francis Libermann's Spiritans and Daniel Comboni's Verona Fathers. In spearheading Catholic outreach in nineteenth-century Africa, these new groups supplanted traditional Catholic missionary orders such as the Franciscans, Dominicans, and Jesuits.

Daniel Comboni's 1864 plan for the evangelization of Africa—particularly its concern for medical missions and vision of "saving Africa through Africa"—had particular influence on Lavigerie as he began envisioning his own missionary societies of men and women religious.[5]

Lavigerie's early biography is noteworthy in three ways. First, he pursued doctoral work in church history, developing a particular interest in the ancient catechumenate. His later introduction of a four-year catechumenate in the White Fathers' Buganda missions placed a distinct emphasis on Christian formation, rejecting past missionary practices of mass baptisms. Second, he spent a crucial period in the early 1860s coordinating Catholic relief work for Lebanese orphans. This experience taught him the importance of the humanitarian dimensions of mission. Finally, Lavigerie in the early 1860s served in the Roman Rota, the Holy See's highest appellate tribunal. This allowed Lavigerie to gain *entrée* into the Vatican circles that would facilitate the work of his missionary congregations in the 1870s and 1880s.

Lavigerie traced his missionary vocation to a revelation in November 1866. On the feast of St. Martin of Tours, Lavigerie dreamed of "dark-skinned people" asking him to restore the African Church.[6] Already the Bishop of Nancy and groomed for probable succession to the important French archdiocese of Lyons, Lavigerie abruptly changed course. In 1867 he petitioned the Vatican to appoint him to lead the long-dormant diocese of Algiers. Lavigerie supported French colonies in Algeria and Tunisia and saw French influence as critical to reversing Muslim dominance in North Africa. In going to Algeria, Lavigerie envisioned the revival of the ancient North African church, the inauguration of an apostolate to North African Muslims, and the establishment of a missionary gateway to the African continent.[7]

After his appointment to the see of Algiers, Lavigerie launched two new missionary congregations for men and women that he named the "Missionaries of Africa." Adopting the white gandourah dress common in Arab North Africa, the Missionaries of Africa become locally known as the "White Fathers" and "White Sisters." In the words of their initial charter, the White Fathers were intended to be a "society of secular priests, dedicated to the Missions of Africa, living in community, practicing the same rule, and bound to each other and to the common work by an oath to consecrate themselves to the Missions of Africa, either within the Delegation or beyond its boundaries, according to the rules of the Society and in obedience to its Superiors."[8] Stymied by an unsupportive colonial government, a hostile settler population, and a committed Muslim populace, White Father missions in North Africa struggled throughout the late 1860s and early 1870s. The missions attracted Arab orphans eager for shelter, food, and education, but few others demonstrated much interest. Frustrated with his failures in North Africa, Lavigerie in the 1870s turned his proselytizing zeal to the emerging mission fields south of the Sahara desert. Working through his new missionary congregations, the Missionaries of Africa and the Sisters of Africa, Lavigerie established Catholic outposts stretching from present-day Mali to Malawi.

Lavigerie's influence in the late nineteenth century stretched beyond his missionary communities. He became a leading advocate for the abolition of the international slave trade, thereby lending humanitarian sanction to the growing European "Scramble for Africa." After a century of French ecclesial intransigence toward the postrevolutionary order, Pope Leo XIII asked Lavigerie to begin building bridges between the French church and French leaders of the Third Republic. This "First Ralliement" was symbolized by Lavigerie's famous 1890 "toast of Algiers" in which Lavigerie, surrounded by French naval officers, raised a glass to the French Republic. Shaped by his own experiences in Lebanon, Lavigerie also worked throughout the 1880s to improve relations with Eastern Rite Catholics. In the meantime, Lavigerie's White Father missions continued to grow, especially in Central Africa. He died in November 1892, surrounded by confreres from as far away as Jerusalem and Buganda and praised in Paris and Rome alike. On hearing of his death, Pope Leo XIII is said to have remarked, "I loved him as a brother, as Peter loved Andrew."[9]

If Charles Lavigerie's missiological vision could be summarized in one scriptural verse, it would be St. Paul's exhortation to adaptation in 1 Corinthians 9:22: "To the weak I became weak, to win over the weak. I have become all things to all, to save at least some." As early as 1868, Lavigerie exhorted his missionaries to "adopt the diet, language, dress, [and] sleeping habits of the Arabs."[10] Lavigerie repeated these instructions at the White Fathers' first general chapter meeting in 1874, calling on his missionaries to adopt the exterior habits—clothing, language, diet—of the people they were trying to convert.[11] He mandated that White Fathers speak the local vernacular exclusively within six months of arrival. In part due to such expectations, the White Fathers became some of the preeminent linguists of modern Africa.

Lavigerie began his missionary congregations at the advent of the colonial era in Africa. His reflections on nationality and mission reflect the tensions of this era. On one hand, Lavigerie emerges in retrospect as a staunch French patriot. In the early years of his missions, he recruited missionaries almost exclusively from France and Belgium.[12] As noted earlier, Lavigerie was especially praised for initiating reconciliation between church and state in France and successfully enlisting the French government in the anti-slavery efforts of the 1880s and 1890s.[13] At the same time, Lavigerie would also remind his missionaries that their primary identity should be one of "Christian" and "apostle" rather than "Frenchman" or "European."[14] He also argued that it would be "absurd" to educate African students in the same way as French students. "These are Negroes of the African interior, which one must elevate in a way which offers them the greatest possible utility to their compatriots, and not as children destined to live in France."[15] Like Libermann and Comboni, Lavigerie also shared a strong commitment to developing local clergy, going so far as to initiate a new congregation of lay doctor-catechists.[16] His openness to cultural adaptation thus reflected both a spirit of colonial paternalism and a relatively optimistic anthropology. For Lavigerie, the death-knell of the missions would not be polygamy or idolatry, but rather Jansenist expectations for a pure church.[17]

After witnessing the withering of his early Algerian missions among impoverished orphans, Lavigerie would never again underestimate the importance of social norms and elite opinion, and he quickly became a committed devotee of top-down evangelization. For Lavigerie, converting rulers and chiefs would facilitate the rapid growth of Christianity and allow the faith to develop deep roots within a local culture. As he instructed his first caravan of missionaries traveling to central Africa, "Once the chiefs convert, all the rest will follow after them."[18] For this reason Lavigerie also insisted on a four-year catechumenate, leaving ample time for the formation necessary for the long-term implanting of Christianity in African soil. Yet while emphasizing rigorous formation, Lavigerie also conveyed surprising flexibility on key ethical questions like polygamy—probably as much out of a spirit of *realpolitik* as adaptation.[19] His emphasis on communal rather than individual conversion helps explains why he became so deeply involved in eradicating social sins such as slavery. This is also why the White Fathers became such devoted purveyors of education, medical care, social services, and indigenous culture.

For all of his rhetorical commitment to cultural adaptation, however, Lavigerie shared his generation's commitment to civilizing and transforming Africans through the introduction of European art, trade, and religion. While he favored working through local leaders whenever possible, he saw colonial protection as critical to suppressing the slave trade and protecting missionaries from local persecution. Like many of his Catholic contemporaries, Lavigerie also traced any "civil" quality in European civilization to Europe's embrace of Christianity, a commitment that appeared increasingly tenuous in the late nineteenth century. The Rwanda missions did not begin until seven years after Lavigerie's death, but Lavigerie's emphases on top-down conversion, Christian formation, cultural adaptation, and the mission's civilizing role would become hallmarks of Rwanda's Catholic experience.

The Legacy of the Buganda Missions

Charles Lavigerie was not the only major influence on early Catholic missionaries in Rwanda. In the late nineteenth and early twentieth centuries, the Buganda missions in southern Uganda served as the shining success story and implicit model for other White Father communities in Africa. Buganda bordered Rwanda and shared Rwanda's strong monarchical tradition and political centralization. If Lavigerie took his inspiration from the ancient catechumenate and early medieval monasteries, Buganda inspired early White Fathers' dreams of mass conversions in Rwanda.

By the time Catholic and Protestant missionaries arrived in Buganda in 1878–1879, the region had undergone a mild Islamization and economic modernization stemming from Buganda's contacts with Zanzibari traders from the East African coast. Mutesa, Buganda's *kabaka* or king, viewed the competing Catholic and Anglican missionaries as French and British emissaries, and he expertly played off their rivalries in hopes of discerning the intentions of the encroaching European powers.[20] As with the Rwandan court's reaction to European leaders after 1900, Mutesa saw European missionaries as potential allies in his own struggle to withstand colonial power and suppress local rivalries. The missionaries proved impotent in this regard, failing to cultivate economic relations between Buganda and their home countries. This reflected a crucial difference between Ugandan and Rwandan mass evangelization movements. Introduced before the advent of British colonialism, Christianity and especially Catholicism were never as intricately connected with the colonial project in Uganda as in Rwanda, where Catholic missionaries arrived in the company of German soldiers.[21]

Even as Mutesa distanced himself from Christian missionaries, young elites at his court flocked to the missions. Fr. Simon Lourdel and his fellow White Fathers were so impressed with the quality of the young Catholic postulants that they proceeded to baptize several lay leaders after only one year of formation, breaking with Lavigerie's instructions concerning the requisite four-year catechumenate. This confidence would be vindicated when Mutesa expelled foreign missionaries from Buganda in 1882, leaving the nascent Catholic communities in the hands of local lay leaders. Far from disintegrating, Catholic and Protestant communities alike grew rapidly under the leadership of local elites, laying the roots for the more extensive expansion of Christianity in Buganda in the 1890s.

By the mid-1880s there were strong Anglican and Catholic parties at the court of Mwanga, the new *kabaka*. In late 1885 Mwanga turned resolutely against the Christians, suspecting their connections with European powers and frustrated with their refusals to indulge his sexual advances. In October, Mwanga ordered the execution of the Anglican Bishop James Hannington as his caravan approached the eastern border of his Buganda kingdom. When this failed to stem the Christian tide, he unleashed more widespread attacks on Christian nobles in May–June 1886. Far from crushing the missions, however, Mwanga's persecution and the later stories of the steadfast and joyful witness of court page Charles Lwanga and his companions became renowned in African mission circles. In 1920, the "Uganda Martyrs" developed a global cult when Pope Benedict XV beatified twenty of the martyrs as the first sub-Saharan African saints.

While Anglican and Catholic missionaries showed little tolerance for each other, their converts did not immediately inherit the age-old denominational and national rivalries between Britain and France. After the persecutions subsided, the Christian parties even joined forces during the late 1880s political struggle with Muslims and adherents of traditional religion. Relations quickly soured, however, culminating with the 1892 Battle of Mengo in which British soldiers helped the Anglican party defeat the more numerous Catholics. The British subsequently divided territory according to a *cuius regio, eius religio* principle: the local chief's religious preference would become the established religious tradition in each region. In part due to these political divisions, Uganda's intra-Christian struggle became one of the fiercest in Africa in the 1890s and early 1900s.

Despite or perhaps because of this competition, Anglican and Catholic communities grew rapidly in Uganda. By 1910 a majority of local chiefs and thousands of their people had received Christian baptism. Ganda catechists spread into surrounding territories, sharing the gospel of Christianity and Ganda culture in an imperialistic mix not unlike their European counterparts. Anglican and White Father missionaries marveled at the maturity and growth of the young churches even as they lamented the political and religious divisions in Uganda.

In summary, the Buganda model was one of mass conversion led by youthful Christian elites. Missionaries initially targeted the king but learned to work around royal intransigence by recruiting young elites open to Christianity's modernizing project. Martyrdom, persecution, and denominational competition helped foster the early growth of Christianity. For all of the numerical successes, however, Anglican and Catholic missionaries lamented the extent of religious and political divisions. In turn, Catholic missionaries who moved from Uganda to Rwanda in the early 1900s obsessed over potential religious rivals. Their commitment to elite conversion was also tempered by a certain ambivalence concerning the role of state politics in Christian mission. For some, the marginalized masses appeared as a more suitable audience for a gospel message that had proclaimed "blessed are you who are poor, for the kingdom of God is yours" (Luke 6:20). The question of whether to follow Lavigerie's vision of top-down conversion or to build a more egalitarian church of the poor would remain one of the central issues facing the first generation of Rwandan missionaries.

The First Catholic Missions in Rwanda

Christian missions had a relatively late start in Rwanda; the first White Father missions began almost a generation after their Ugandan counterparts. Like Christianity in Uganda, however, Rwandan Christianity would grow tremendously during the first half of the twentieth century. Having considered the missiological and historical contexts that preceded the White Father missions in Rwanda, the rest of this chapter takes up the story of Rwandan Catholicism between 1900 and 1950, focusing on Catholic evangelization practices, church-state relations, and missionary views of Hutu-Tutsi identities and relations.

After a mixed record in the late nineteenth century, Christian missions began to lay much deeper roots across Africa during the first decades of the twentieth century. This growth was particularly marked on the Catholic side. By 1910, the overall Catholic missionary population in Africa reached 6,000, surpassing the Protestant missionary population for the first time.[22] The White Fathers stood at the heart of this expansion, nearly doubling in the decade following the death of Lavigerie.[23] Local conversions were also growing. Although there were only seven million baptized African Catholics in 1914, the upward trajectory was notable. This was especially evident in areas of strong colonial influence like Uganda, South Africa, and Nigeria.[24]

Unlike its neighbors in Buganda and Tanganyika, Rwanda withstood colonial encroachment until the end of the nineteenth century. The kingdom had never entered into the regional East African trading system, avoiding entanglement with the Zanzibari slave trade that ravaged the region in the latter decades of the 1800s. Rwanda had become a feared regional power in its own right under Mwami Rwabugiri, an Abanyiginya king who massively expanded Rwanda's territory during his three-decade rule. His unexpected death in 1895 left a power vacuum at the Rwandan court. His chosen successor, Rutarindwa, lost favor after a Congolese-Belgian force inflicted a humiliating defeat on the Rwandan army at Shangi in 1896. Leaders of the Abanyiginya's rival clan, the Abega, staged a successful and violent *coup d'état*, executing Rutarindwa and hundreds of his allies and placing fifteen-year-old Musinga on the throne in February 1897. The young Musinga ruled under the close tutelage of his mother, Kanjogera, and his uncles Kabare and Ruhinankiko. In the long term, Musinga's uncertain succession claims would make him highly suspicious of rivals inside and outside of the court.[25] Several weeks after his elevation to the throne, a small German military force marched into Musinga's court, presenting the young king with a new rival.

Germany's arrival in the country came at the peak of the thirty-year "Scramble for Africa" inaugurated by Otto von Bismarck's Congress of Berlin in 1884–1885. Bismarck had called the European conference to defend Germany's commercial interests and establish clearer guidelines for European colonial protectorates in Africa. The Berlin conference recognized King Leopold's claims to the Congo Independent State and acknowledged existing French and British protectorates in southern and western Africa. Although initially more skeptical than Britain or France concerning the financial burdens of colonization, Germany in the 1890s established colonies in southwestern Africa (today's Namibia) and eastern Africa (modern-day Tanzania and Burundi). Rwanda's military reputation preceded itself, and German officials were anxious to outflank their Belgian and British rivals in forming an alliance with one of the most powerful kingdoms in the region.[26]

More puzzling is why the historically isolationist and militaristic Rwandans did not resist German overtures. Several explanations emerge for Musinga's openness to the German offer of a protectorate. First, in light of the Rwandan army's 1896 defeat at Shangi, Musinga and his advisors recognized the superior firepower of the Europeans and determined that a German alliance would be preferable to Belgian conquest. Second, Musinga's own uncertain claims to the throne made the offer of German military protection particularly attractive. And it should be noted that while he agreed to let German colonial officials into his kingdom, Musinga did not lose all of his authority. Rwandan elites retained more political autonomy than many of their counterparts in other African colonies.

The German partnership proved beneficial to Musinga in other ways. Namely, Germany helped Musinga extend and strengthen central court authority in recalcitrant territories on Rwanda's northern, western, eastern, and southern borders. At the time of the German arrival, the heart of the Rwandan kingdom lay on a central plateau near Nyanza, the home of the Mwami's royal court. The court also administered nearby areas beyond central Rwanda, working through local Tutsi notables who served on behalf of the court. Finally, there were outlying frontier zones of weaker government influence. Particularly contested regions included the Congo-Nile border area of northwestern Rwanda, the Bushiru province in the northeast, and Bukunzi and Busozo in the southeast. Significantly, local Hutu lineage chiefs controlled all of these territories. Musinga's court also faced opposition from local Tutsi leaders in eastern Gisaka and the western territory of Kinyaga. As discussed later in the chapter, German and then Belgian military support enabled Rwanda's central court to achieve sovereignty over these contested regions in the 1910s and 1920s.[27]

If German colonial officials were eyeing Rwanda in the late 1890s, so were Catholic missionaries. With mission stations in Buganda, eastern Congo, Tanganyika, and Burundi, the White Fathers surrounded Rwanda geographically. After the Germans established their 1897 alliance with the Rwandan court, the White Fathers sought permission from Germany to establish a mission outpost in Rwanda. German colonial officials initially resisted these entreaties but ultimately saw the merit of utilizing Catholic missionaries to educate and pacify the Rwandan people, especially considering colonial budgetary and staffing limits.[28] Opening to the White Fathers would entail German Lutheran officials working with predominantly French Catholic missionaries. However, the Germans viewed the latter as less threatening than religious emissaries from Great Britain, the dominant geopolitical power of the day who had already colonized Rwanda's northern neighbor Uganda. After the Germans gave their approval in 1899, the White Fathers organized a missionary caravan under the leadership of Jean-Joseph

FIGURE 2.1 Mwami Musinga with Fr. Charles Lecoindre, M.Afr., Fr. Paulin Loupias, M.Afr., and Br. Anselme (Nicolas Illerich), M.Afr., early 1900s (*courtesy General Archives of the Missionaries of Africa, Rome*).

Hirth, a French-speaking Alsatian of German descent. Accompanied by German soldiers, Hirth's caravan arrived at Rwanda's royal court in Nyanza in February 1900. Fearing a possible religious curse, Mwami Musinga sent out another noble to pose as the king. Skeptical about missionary entreaties yet aware of Germany's support, Musinga agreed to a compromise option: the Catholics could establish mission stations in outlying territories but not in the immediate vicinity of Nyanza.

The White Fathers set up five mission stations over the next three years: Save and Mibirizi in the south, Zaza in the east, Nyundo in the northwest, and Rwaza in the northeast. All were strategically positioned beyond the royal capital yet within the court's sphere of influence. Musinga aimed to keep the missionaries at a distance while using them to extend his own influence over restive local populations. After their mixed experience at the royal courts of Buganda's Mutesa and Mwanga, the White Fathers in Rwanda were also open to a plan in which they would maintain some distance from Rwanda's central court. Like the Germans before them, the White Fathers were greeted as political liberators in some areas, but their religious message met with a cool reception. Unlike Buganda, the White Fathers attracted not elites but rather the socially marginalized, especially women, children, and poor Hutu and Tutsi men looking for economic patronage and political protection. They found particular favor in the eastern territory of Gisaka, where local elites had launched a rebellion against Rwanda's central court in the mid-1890s.[29]

This emphasis on the poor and marginalized also reflected the missiological cal vision of Mgr. Jean-Joseph Hirth, the leader of the first missionary caravan who would serve as the regional Vicar Apostolic until 1920.[30] Hirth had joined the Missionaries of Africa during Lavigerie's first recruiting efforts in the early 1870s and later served in Uganda in the 1880s and 1890s. These experiences in the thriving but politically unsettled Ganda missions profoundly shaped Hirth's ministry in Rwanda. After seeing Anglicans and Catholics fight a civil war in Uganda, he looked to ensure a Catholic monopoly of Christian missions and never lost his deep suspicion of Protestant missionaries.[31] Although Hirth hoped for royal conversions, his experience in Buganda also revealed the dangers of a politicized church and the importance of both religious freedom and what he termed "protect(ing) the poor and feeble from the abuses of the powerful."[32] Unlike his successor Léon Classe, Hirth conveyed little ambivalence about establishing the church among the "poor suffering peasants" who showed openness to the Christian gospel. Significantly, Hirth generally described such poor peasants as "Hutu" and associated the Tutsi with the royal court.[33] While Hirth opposed forced conversion or political revolution, he saw social development as necessary for both evangelizing poor Hutu and Christianizing Rwandan society. This commitment to development also reflected Hirth's intertwining of Christianity and civilization and his strong degree of colonial paternalism. "We should make the blacks in the manner of being human before bringing about their Christianization."[34] For all of the later emphasis on top-down conversion of Tutsi elites, we see in these earliest days a strong focus on evangelizing from below. These two competing approaches—one following Lavigerie's emphasis on top-down conversion, the other building a more egalitarian church of the poor—would remain important contrasting legacies for the twentieth-century Rwandan church.

The latter tendency seemed dominant during the first five years of the White Father missions in Rwanda. While Hirth shared his colleagues' tendency to juxtapose class and ethnicity, the mission stations themselves embodied a certain pan-ethnic egalitarianism. For noted Rwandan historian Gamaliel Mbonimana, this "phenomenon of [pan-ethnic] friendship between baptized people" existed across multiple Rwandan mission posts.[35] These early converts also viewed the White Fathers as political patrons. The White Father Alphonse Brard and several other missionaries obliged them, advocating for Hutu peasants and petit Tutsi over and against the exactions of local Tutsi notables known as abaatware.

Brard's legacy was not just one of cultivating a pan-ethnic church of the poor, however. He also developed a reputation for using force to keep Rwandan children in school and their parents in mission stations.[36] His heavy-handed instincts were only reinforced by the proselytizing tactics of zealous Baganda catechists who assisted the White Fathers at many Rwandan mission stations. In turn, the missions' expropriation of land and increasing usage of forced labor further alienated local populations. Nor was such force limited to Brard's southern Rwandan mission of Save. In 1904, several White Fathers—including Léon Classe, who will be discussed in depth later—organized a military campaign to help pacify hostile clans surrounding the White Fathers' northern mission stations at Rwaza and Nyundo.[37]

Although he took no punitive action against the northern White Fathers, Hirth acted to assuage both German authorities and the Nyanza court by reprimanding Brard.[38] After Brard publicly challenged Hirth at a White Father chapter meeting in 1906, Hirth expelled him from the country. He also replaced the Ganda catechists with indigenous Rwandans, reiterated the mission's official opposition to forced conversion, and restated Catholic support for Musinga. Despite Hirth's actions, these would be tense years for the embryonic Catholic mission in Rwanda. Powerful voices in Nyanza called for their ouster, and the Germans sided with the royal court in several legal and land disputes with the missionaries. Fearful of political retribution against the *inyangarwanda*—the Kinyarwanda name given to early Christian converts which meant "haters or repudiators of Rwanda"—the Hutu and *petit* Tutsi who had frequented the missions now kept their distance.[39] The contrast with Buganda is telling. After five years, the Buganda missions were thriving without missionary tutelage. In 1905 the Rwandan missionaries were struggling to find any converts at all.[40]

A Poor Church Seeks Power

The year 1905 to 1906 marked a turning point in the early history of the Catholic Church in Rwanda.[41] Mwami Musinga relented and allowed the White Fathers to establish a mission station at Kabgayi in central Rwanda, only 50 kilometers from the royal capital at Nyanza. Kabgayi would quickly become the center of Catholic life in Rwanda. In 1906, Léon Classe—an upper-class French missionary who had arrived in Rwanda in 1901—replaced Alphonse Brard as superior of the Save mission station in southern Rwanda. As noted earlier, Classe spent his first five years in Rwanda ministering at the Rwaza and Nyundo stations in the Hutu-dominated north. Classe enthusiastically supported Musinga's territorial claims in a politically contentious region, urging local Christians at Rwaza mission to show their "obedience to the chiefs." He also had a reputation for maintaining high standards for baptism.[42]

In 1907 Classe became vicar general of the Rwandan missions, serving under the titular leadership of Bishop Hirth. He also moved from the Save mission to the new Kabgayi mission station near the royal court at Nyanza. Although Classe and Hirth stood by each other in the years to come, Hirth remained warier of the risks of church-state cohabitation, focusing more on lobbying for religious freedom and ensuring missionary independence. In contrast, Classe unequivocally embraced Lavigerie's goal of spreading Christianity through elite conversion, fearing that Tutsi elites were dismissing Christianity because of "our ideas of justice, our defense of the rights of the poor... Our dear mission can look forward to some dark days if we take no interest in the apostolate to the ruling class, if, by our acts, we give ground for the opinion that the Catholic faith is that of the poor."[43] Classe's arrival and the weakening of anti-Catholic forces at court marked the first tentative rapprochement between Nyanza and the Catholic missions, symbolized by a 1907 meeting in which Musinga's pagan uncle Kabare shared sorghum beer with a newly-baptized Christian.

The following two years saw both the strengthening of German colonial rule and the arrival of the Catholics' first religious rivals. Richard Kandt, a medical doctor and one of the first European settlers in Rwanda, began serving as German colonial resident in 1908. Kandt raised the German profile in Rwanda in the years preceding World War I. He also lent German military support to the royal court's efforts to pacify restive Tutsi notables in the east and Hutu chiefs in the north and west. On the religious front, the colonial office invited German Lutherans to establish new missions in 1907 and 1908. Facing a new religious rival, the White Fathers accelerated their efforts to reach out to Rwandan elites. For his part, Musinga lost no time in playing off the Europeans' religious antagonisms even as he remained far more concerned with their political ambitions.

Musinga's fears were not without merit. While Hirth encouraged missionaries to disengage from local political conflicts, this proved difficult in practice, especially in the unsettled northwest region of Rwanda. Here Kandt praised the White Father missions for "contributing in large part to the pacification of the district."[44] Such political engagement reached a nadir with the shooting death of the White Father Paulin Loupias in 1910. Loupias was killed while attempting to mediate tense negotiations between Musinga's representatives and Lukara, a northern Hutu chief rebelling against Musinga's rule. Loupias allegedly precipitated his own shooting by losing his temper and threatening to shoot Lukara.[45] The death of the White Father missionary led to a brutal German scorched earth policy in the north. When another Hutu of mixed descent, Ndungutse, revolted in 1912, the White Fathers defended Musinga's territorial claims and actively discouraged Christians from joining in the uprising.

In the meantime, the Catholic Church in Rwanda was growing at a slow but steady rate, counting 10,000 baptized members in 1914. This outnumbered the 3,000 Christians in Burundi, where Catholic missions had faced more vociferous opposition from the state. However, it fell far short of Uganda's population of 100,000 Christians.[46] As a sign of the Holy See's commitment to the region, Propaganda Fide in 1911 created a new Vicariate of Kivu that included Rwanda,

Burundi, and eastern provinces of Belgian Congo. The White Fathers' rhetorical commitment to adaptation was becoming a reality under the leadership of Hirth, the "father of the East African seminaries," who made the indigenization of the Catholic priesthood one of his top pastoral priorities.[47] Hirth established major and minor seminaries in Rwanda during the first decade of the 1900s, enrolling both Hutu and Tutsi youth. Founded in 1913, the indigenous Benebikira sisters grew rapidly and spread to Uganda and elsewhere in the surrounding region.[48]

On the eve of World War I, the tenuous early years of the Rwandan missions were giving rise to something more permanent. Uncertainties remained, however. Bishop Hirth focused on the ordination of native clergy yet failed to develop Catholic schools, the training grounds for a future generation of Catholic elites. At the same time, Classe's outreach to the Rwandan nobility led royal pages to approach the Kabgayi mission station for secret instruction; such gestures echoed the White Fathers' Buganda model of reaching out to young royal pages.[49] Despite Classe's efforts to nurture better relations with the royal court, Musinga and his allies remained wary of the White Fathers and moved closer to their German Lutheran rivals. For his part, Musinga was in his strongest position since taking power in 1897, controlling more territory than even his legendary father Rwabugiri. Yet Musinga continued to fear the encroachment of German rule and potential challengers to his own ambiguous claims to the throne. The Germans themselves were divided over whether to work through Musinga or implement more direct colonial rule in Rwanda. In the midst of these competing local agendas, global history intervened.

World War I and the Belgian Takeover

The African Great Lakes region experienced some of the worst effects of the First World War on the continent.[50] This was in large part because the German territories of Rwanda, Burundi, and Tanganyika bordered Belgian Congo and the British territories of Kenya and Uganda. The burden of war was keenly felt by Rwanda's civilian population. Porterage and food requisitions rose, and Rwanda in 1915 suffered through its worst famine in nearly twenty years. Some Catholic mission stations experienced 50 percent mortality rates during this famine. Despite Bishop Hirth's commitment to missionary neutrality, the Germans suspected the loyalties of French White Fathers and ordered non-German missionaries to stay 70 kilometers from the Congolese border. Many priests were called up to serve in their respective national armies, and mission activity disappeared within several months of the outbreak of war. In contrast to the European theater, however, World War I ended relatively quickly in Rwanda. Germany retreated from Rwanda in early 1916, and the Belgians marched across the Congolese border and captured Nyanza in March. A new epoch had begun.

Far from welcoming the Belgians into Rwanda, Mwami Musinga feared the implications of this shift in the European balance of colonial power. After all, he had entered into the original German protectorate in 1897 in part to fend off Belgian influence. After the First World War commenced in 1914, Musinga had gone so far as to mobilize his army on behalf of the Germans. Stories from Belgian Congo convinced him that Belgium would exercise more onerous rule than Germany, and he feared—rightly as it turned out—that the Belgians would depose him in favor of a more pliable monarch.[51]

Although the Belgians flirted with direct military rule in 1916–1917, they concluded that it would make more financial and political sense to follow the German model of indirect rule.[52] For the next decade, the Belgians proved to be as supportive of Musinga as their German predecessors. The inherent contradictions of indirect colonial rule—such as reifying perceived "tradition" in the context of unprecedented modernization and social change—became ever more apparent. In this regard, a revealing commentary emerges from the pen of Belgian colonial official Louis Franck. While claiming that Belgium should respect indigenous institutions, Franck also insisted that Belgium should modify these institutions to enhance economic productivity. And although he reiterated the Belgian commitment to protecting the Hutu from arbitrary injustice, he also argued that Belgium should resist an "egalitarian temptation" which might disturb the "ancient" political institutions established by the Tutsi. Achieving what Filip Reyntjens has termed a "double consensus" of both the rulers and the ruled would prove elusive for the Belgians.[53]

Relieved by the end of the war and the prospect of restarting their missions, the White Fathers were also grateful for what the later commentator Louis de Lacger termed a "Catholic and Latin" victory.[54] Facing Lutheran encroachment and German intransigence in the immediate pre-war years, Catholics welcomed the far more accommodating Belgian power. While Belgium's twentieth-century domestic politics were marked by a degree of church-state tensions, this metropolitan struggle did not influence the mission field in the early 1900s.[55] Whether or not they supported Catholic influence at home, Belgian politicians agreed that Catholic missions offered the best means of civilizing and pacifying the African, ensuring the economic productivity of the colony and the humanitarian uplift of a benighted people. The Belgians would offer unflagging financial and infrastructural support for Catholic missions until independence.

Belgian pressure also began to shift Rwanda's local political calculus in favor of the Catholic missions. Under orders from Belgian military officials, Musinga in 1917 issued a decree on religious freedom that officially legalized Christian missions in Rwanda. Musinga also relinquished the right to impose the death penalty, ceding significant judicial authority to the Belgian courts. The Mwami's loss of the right over life and death should not be underestimated, as this had been crucial to his legitimacy as a semidivine religious figure. Combined with later Belgian proscriptions of traditional court rituals, what Reyntjens terms the "secularization of Rwandan society" helped pave the way for the growth of the Catholic Church in Rwanda.[56] The first elite Tutsi postulants, including several of Musinga's relatives, arrived at the Catholic missions at the end of 1917, the same year that three Hutu were ordained as Rwanda's first indigenous priests.

Yet for all of these positive developments, the missions were also experiencing great strains in the immediate postwar period. Missionaries based in Burundi accused Hirth and Classe of focusing all of their energies and resources on Rwanda. For their part, missionaries in Rwanda criticized Hirth as a remote administrator obsessed with indigenous ordinations. Classe's critics saw him as a heavy-handed micromanager. Hirth stood by Classe and defended his own seminary policies, blaming his declining health for his inattention to details. Despite these protestations, the White Fathers in 1920 recalled Classe to Europe for consultations, and Hirth resigned the vicariate two months later. It remained to be seen who would lead the Rwandan church into its next decade.

Léon Classe, Ethnic Discourse, and the Christian Coup d'état

The thirty-year "Scramble for Africa" that followed the 1885 Berlin Congress slowed under the weight of colonial overextension and nationalistic rivalries that culminated in the global conflagration of World War I.[57] The postwar League of Nations acknowledged the principle of national self-determination, especially for former German and Ottoman Empire colonies. Such principles did not yet apply to Central Africa, however. Rather, the League classified Rwanda as a Mandate B territory and formally entrusted the territory to Belgian supervision. In return, Belgium was expected to guarantee freedom of religion and commercial access, maintain public order and good morals, and administer the territory "to the benefit of the population."[58]

This colonial mission faced its first major test in 1922. As part of the Versailles peace treaty, which ended World War I, Great Britain gained economic access to Rwanda's eastern province of Gisaka that bordered the British colony of Tanganyika. Gisaka had a long history of political tensions with the Nyanza court, and most local elites welcomed the potential economic opportunities and political autonomy offered by the prospect of British rule. Musinga, on the other hand, saw this as the first step in the dismemberment of his kingdom and implored the Belgians to preserve the territorial integrity of his country. After blustering on both sides—and thanks in part to a crucial intervention from Léon Classe in favor of Musinga—the British withdrew in 1923.[59]

Classe's intervention marked his return to prominence after a brief exile in the political and ecclesial wilderness.[60] After his 1920 recall to Europe, Classe spent two years consulting with his superiors, writing about Rwanda, and dialoguing with Belgian colonial officials. He managed to restore his reputation and was consecrated to the episcopate in 1922, returning in triumph to head the newly established Rwanda vicariate. Classe moved quickly to entrench a Catholic religious monopoly in Rwanda by expanding Catholic missions, increasing the local church's financial assets, and recruiting Tutsi elites. He also focused on indigenizing Catholic clergy and women religious. Between 1922 and Classe's death in 1945, Rwandan clergy grew twelve-fold from five to sixty. The number of Benebikira sisters surpassed 120 during the same period. In addition, Classe proved to be a strong supporter of both lay catechists and *Bakura b'inama,* the local branch of the international lay movement known as Catholic Action.[61]

Classe also shifted the church's relations with Rwanda's indigenous leaders. If Hirth discouraged the White Fathers from disrupting Rwanda's predominantly Tutsi hierarchy, Classe went a step further and established the church as a close ally of Musinga's court. As noted earlier, Classe adopted this view not long after arriving in Rwanda. Positing that "in this country, as in Uganda, the King is the soul of the country," Classe argued in 1911 that failing to recruit chiefs would "give Catholicism a situation of inferiority and slavery, condemning it to be forever taken with the difficulties of oppression."[62] As already noted, Classe in the 1920s supported the "rights of Musinga and the Batutsi" in the contested region of Gisaka. Classe also supported the Belgian and Tutsi pacification campaigns across the northern and western regions of Rwanda—campaigns that often entailed replacing local Hutu lineage heads with imported Tutsi notables.[63]

In this vein, Classe helped ensure that political and class issues were analyzed through the lens of the Hutu-Tutsi distinction. First, he made a broad association between "Tutsi" and "nobility," writing in 1911 that "it is a grave error to say that the people will be Catholic without the chiefs as the chiefs and the people are not of the same race."[64] Classe echoed this language in 1922, writing that "when we speak of the Batutsi, we think very uniquely of the great Tutsi chiefs, who constitute a very restrained aristocracy."[65] Second, Classe argued that colonial policy should favor Tutsi chiefs as much as possible. As early as 1906 he exhorted the German administration to "augment their [Tutsi chiefs'] existing authority," positing that "the more the authority of the Europeans is established in the country, the more they [the Hutu] believe in the power of the Tutsi."[66] As noted previously, Classe supported Musinga's claims in Gisaka and northwestern Rwanda in the 1910s and 1920s. And when Belgian officials wavered in their commitment to an all-Tutsi ruling class in 1927–1928, it was Classe who insisted that reinstituting Hutu chiefs would lead the country to "anti-European communism and anarchy."[67] Even as he turned against Musinga

FIGURE 2.2 Mgr. Léon Classe, Vicar Apostolic of Rwanda, 1922–1945 (*courtesy General Archives of the Missionaries of Africa, Rome*)

after 1927, Classe favored a Tutsi monopoly of the *chefferies* and *sous-chefferies*, the chiefdoms and sub-chiefdoms that Belgian colonial authorities established in the 1920s. "Generally speaking, we have no chiefs who are better qualified, more intelligent, more active, more capable of appreciating progress and more fully accepted by the people than the Tutsi."[68] To be clear, Classe favored not the older court nobles but young Tutsi elites who had been trained in Catholic schools. Openness to European modernization and Christianization were as important as ethnic identity or hierarchical rank.[69]

Under Classe's watch, ethnic stratification grew inside the Catholic Church as well. This was most evident in the area of schooling, a pastoral priority that Classe saw as essential to determining whether "the leadership elite will be for us or against us."[70] Although Hutu and Tutsi students had been educated together before 1920, Classe introduced a two-tiered Catholic educational system in the 1920s. Students were segregated by ethnic group, and Tutsi received a far more rigorous course than their Hutu colleagues. This helped ensure that only Tutsi qualified for the most influential positions in the colonial administration. For Classe, Hutu children should receive an education, but it should be an education suited to those who "would have places to take in mines and farming."[71] In 1913,

Classe started an indigenous congregation of Josephite brothers. This religious congregation would become increasingly dominated by Tutsi elites.

However, Classe did not categorically oppose Hutu advancement in the church. For example, Classe ordained multiple Hutu to the priesthood, appointed Hutu priests and catechists to lead mission stations, and named the Hutu Gallican Bushishi to teach at the major seminary in Kabgayi. In fact, the Catholic seminary remained one of the only avenues for Hutu advancement in colonial Rwanda. Furthermore, writing in the Belgian magazine *Congo* in 1922, Classe rejected the notion of inherent Tutsi intellectual superiority and hinted at the complexity of the Hutu-Tutsi distinction. "I would say that the Tutsi are not, in general, more intelligent than the Hutu...Tutsi refers not to origin but social condition, a state of fortune...whoever is a chief, or is rich, will often be called Tutsi."[72]

If anything, Classe's shifting rhetoric shows how difficult it was to classify "Hutu" and "Tutsi" during the 1920s–1930s period when Belgium was undertaking just such a task. In the same 1922 article, Classe wrote that "the Tutsi and the Hutu speak the same language, they have the same religion and the same customs."[73] In 1935 Classe propagated a more racialist vision, writing in the White Fathers' journal *Grands Lacs* that "the Tutsi are not Bantu, they are, if you will, Negroids—they are the African people which displays the strongest Hamitic indications."[74] Here Classe posited differing geographic origins for the Tutsi and Hutu, arguing that the former emigrated from Asia Minor through Ethiopia while the latter traced their ancestry to western and central Africa. Even in the mid-1930s, however, Classe admitted that many Hutu "have a certain proportion of Tutsi blood" and that Rwanda's 80,000 Tutsi "are not a pure race, and for those which fortune does not favor, alliances with female Hutu are not rare."[75] Classe also continued to emphasize the political horizon that underlay the Hutu-Tutsi distinction, noting that when he used the term "Tutsi" he was speaking of "the great Tutsi chiefs" rather than the broader Tutsi population. And yet even here he recognized that the ranks of the great chiefs included Hutu and Twa alike.[76] Louis de Lacger—the historian that Classe commissioned to write the first official history of the Rwandan church—also emphasized Rwandan national unity over ethnic disunity, writing in 1939 that "there are few peoples in Europe in which one finds together the three factors of national cohesion: the same language, the same religion, and the same customs."[77]

More than a racist ideologue convinced of the biological superiority of Tutsi over Hutu, Classe was a pragmatic churchman protecting what he perceived to be the political interests of the Catholic Church. As discussed earlier, his early push to evangelize the Tutsi nobility stemmed more from political interests than Hamitic anthropology. "We should absolutely work to destroy the opinion of the governing authorities that we are men of the Bahutu, of a party opposed to the chiefs...Whether the chiefs are Batutsi or Bahutu matters little, we have only to recognize those to whom God has given authority."[78] His much-quoted 1930 essay supporting Musinga's removal from power called for an exclusively Tutsi ruling caste. Often overlooked, however, were his subsequent statements proscribing any sort of permanent ban on Hutu leadership and rejecting any Tutsi favoritism in employment or high school enrollment.[79] In other words, Classe's insistence on a temporary Tutsi monopolization of chiefdoms was a tactical move to ensure that the Catholic Church (and not its Protestant rivals) shaped the next generation of Tutsi political leaders. As he said in 1927, "the question is whether the ruling elite will be for us or against us, whether the important places in native society will be in Catholic or in non-Catholic hands; whether the Church will have through education and its formation of youth the preponderant influence in Rwanda."[80] This does not lessen Classe's responsibility for his divisive rhetoric, nor does it deny that Catholic institutions exacerbated ethnic tensions in Rwanda. But as will be evident in the 1950s, Classe and other Catholic leaders acted more out of perceived institutional self-interest than explicit racialist bias.[81]

In the meantime, Hutu-Tutsi divisions were hardening in the 1920s and 1930s. This stemmed from colonial innovations that linked political power to Hutu and Tutsi categories, creating what Filip Reyntjens has termed a "more and more pronounced ethnic consciousness."[82] Notable here was Belgium's 1926–1932 reorganization of Rwanda's hill-based chiefdoms into unitary *chefferies* and *sous-chefferies*. This made for more efficient tax collection but destroyed the delicate balance of power that had existed between precolonial Hutu and Tutsi hill chiefs. As already noted, all of the Belgian appointees were Tutsi, most of them young elites trained at the official government school in Nyanza (later moved to the Group Scolaire d'Astrida).[83] Derisively nicknamed *abakaraani* ("clerks") by local residents, the new chiefs' inexperience and lack of local legitimacy only encouraged the chiefs to further emphasize Tutsi privilege. Drawing from cattle ownership data along with church records and physical measurements, the Belgians conducted an ethnic census in 1933–1934 and issued identity cards that legally classified Rwandans as Tutsi, Hutu, and Twa.[84] And even as they reduced Hutu *corvée* requirements within the traditional *uburetwa* system, the Belgians increased colonial labor and tax obligations for the Hutu people. This contributed to mass Hutu emigrations to Uganda and Tanganyika in the late 1920s and to the Rwakayihura famine of 1928–1929 in which upward of 35,000 Rwandans died.

In the face of these social upheavals, Classe and Belgian colonial officials pondered whether to force political change on Rwanda. Classe had defended Musinga against a reform-minded Belgian official looking to depose the Rwandan king in 1925–1926, arguing that the Mwami had improved Rwandans' material living conditions and consistently sided with Belgian interests. But as Musinga continued to vacillate in his posture toward the Catholic missions and their Protestant rivals, Classe gave up on the notion that Musinga would ever become the Rwandan

Clovis.[85] Committed to traditional religion and Rwandan sovereignty, Musinga had no place in the emerging Belgian-Catholic order.[86]

By 1930 Classe and the Belgians were secretly grooming Rudahigwa, one of Musinga's sons, to assume his father's position as *mwami*. While not initially associated with the modernizing Tutsi party, Rudahigwa had begun administering the province of Nduga-Marangara in January 1929. This chiefdom included Kabgayi, Classe's see and the traditional center of Rwandan Catholic life. Later that year he became a secret catechumen, even as he maintained close relations with his father until the final months of Musinga's rule.

The Belgians made their move in November 1931. Calling Rwanda's chiefs to Nyanza for an economic briefing, colonial officials whisked Musinga off to exile on Lake Kivu and installed Rudahigwa as *mwami*. Even as Musinga retained a popular following among the people, Rwandan elite opinion seemed resigned to this outcome, muting any public dissent. Not surprising, Mwami Mutara Rudahigwa's first royal trip was a visit to the Catholic mission at Kabgayi. Within a year, 4,000 Rwandans received baptism, and 10,000 catechumens had enrolled at Kabgayi.[87] After thirty years of frustration, Catholic missionaries had found their Clovis, and Rwanda's Tutsi elites would soon transform Rwanda into the first daughter of the African church.

The Tutsi Tornade *of the 1930s*

Although Rwanda's mass elite conversions emerged in the years following Mutara Rudahigwa's accession to the throne, the process had already begun in the 1920s.[88] Between 1922 and 1927, the number of catechumens grew four-fold from 5,000 to 20,000. This figure quintupled to 100,000 at the time of Mutara's installation in 1931. At this point Rwanda counted 70,000 baptized Catholics, 17 indigenous priests, 43 mission stations, and over 1,100 lay catechists. The number of Catholics then trebled to over 200,000 in the first four years of Mutara's reign and grew to 300,000 by 1939.[89] Although less than 20 percent of the total Rwandan population had converted to Christianity, elites were disproportionately represented; 80 percent of chiefs and subchiefs identified as Catholic in 1936.[90]

In contrast, Protestant numbers remained comparatively low. In 1936 Adventist, Anglican, and Belgian Protestant missions included a combined 13,800 adherents and 6,800 baptized Christians. Although small in number, these churches left important legacies for the future. For example, Rwanda played a central role in the regional East African Revival, leading to sizeable increases in the Anglican population that continued growing after World War II.[91] As Catholicism grew into a veritable state religion in the 1940s, Anglicanism drew the theologically disenchanted and politically marginalized. It would remain a small but vigorous alternative to established Catholicism into the postcolonial period.

If Protestantism remained on the margins, what explains the phenomenal growth of the Catholic Church in the 1930s? A frequently overlooked factor is Classe's expansion of the Catholic Church's institutional capacity during the 1920s. Long before *la tornade*,[92] Classe embarked on an ambitious program to build new mission stations, increase the ranks of clergy and catechists, and encourage local Catholic Action groups. And even when fellow missionaries questioned the authenticity of some of the 1930s elite conversions, Classe argued that the key to developing these new Christians was not to make baptism more difficult but to improve the church's pastoral capability to form new Christians.

Another crucial factor was the close association of Christian mission and Western modernization. Far from their European perception as bastions of conservative traditionalism, Catholic churches in Rwanda were notable for their cosmopolitan association with Belgian francs, literacy, health, and emancipation from traditional hierarchies.[93] For the young Tutsi elite, traditional religion had become not so much idolatrous as anachronistic and ineffective; the 1928–1929 famine had disillusioned many Rwandans concerning the efficacy of traditional religion. This association of religious conversion with Western civilization was not lost on contemporary observers. Classe's determination to build the church's pastoral capacity in the 1920s reflected his belief that spiritual conversion and material progress could not be separated. "We must try hard to give these good populations true civilization which is founded on Christian morals and which alone can assure the future."[94] He later credited Belgian government, road construction, famine relief, and the demystification of traditional religion for the mass conversions of the 1930s. Louis de Lacger echoed these comments in his 1939 history of Rwanda, praising the *tornade* as "a second birth of the Rwandan people in a baptism of Christianity and civilization."[95] In this sense Justin Kalibwami accurately describes the goal of the 1930s missions as creating a new man, the "Catholic Rwandan," who would transform Rwanda into a distinctly modern, European, and Christian society.[96]

The Catholic monopolization of schooling also facilitated elite *entrée* into the church. Always valued for teaching the technical and literacy skills necessary for colonial service, Catholic schools received a virtual monopoly on primary schooling after 1925. In 1930, Classe convinced the colonial administration to allow Catholic educators to run the colonial government's secondary schools. This included the new *Group Scolaire d'Astrida*, the training ground for future Tutsi elites that was entrusted to the Brothers of Charity, a Catholic religious community based in Belgium. Catholic theology and ethics became key components for the education of a new cadre of Tutsi leaders. Significantly, Hutu enrollment in the *Groupe Scolaire* never rose above 5 percent until the 1950s.[97]

In addition, Mutara's and the Rwandan nobility's public attachment to Catholicism clearly aided *la tornade*. Classe noted in 1935 that "the catechumen king and the Christian chiefs are great forces for the mission."[98] Three years of further conversions only strengthened this conviction. As Classe said, "giving confidence to our Christian chiefs is the first duty of all of us" for achieving Lavigerie's dream of establishing a Christian kingdom in central Africa.[99] Elite opinion was especially important in the case of Rwanda, a hierarchical society in which patrons brought clients with them into the church. Regardless of its veracity, the early 1930s rumor that Mutara had ordered his Rwandan subjects to become Catholic captured the broad sense of Christian conversion as an act of social and political obedience.[100]

At the same time, it would be inaccurate to reduce all of Rwanda's conversions to a strictly socio-political logic. The 1935 issue of the White Fathers periodical *Grands Lacs* highlighted the number of converts. Commentators also marveled at the fervor of the new Christians. This was reflected in the distances that Christians walked for church, the frequency with which laity received communion, the catechists' proselytizing zeal, and the six to seven-hour Saturday confessional lines that one missionary described as "apostolic *corvées*."[101] Although Classe reduced what he termed "special [baptismal] rules of exaggerated severity" to facilitate the *entrée* of young Tutsi into the church, White Father missions still required a three-year catechumenate prior to baptism.[102] Even Mwami Mutara did not receive preferential treatment; the king was not baptized until 1943. There were more mundane factors at work in the 1930s *tornade* than the blowing of the Holy Spirit, but political and spiritual motivations were not necessarily mutually exclusive.

It should be noted that a minority of White Father missionaries raised objections to the mass conversions happening in their midst. Critics protested looser baptismal requirements, the reduction of the catechumenate from four to three years, the heavy-handed proselytizing attributed to Catholic chiefs and Catholic Action cadres, and the rising numbers of apostasies to Protestantism and traditional religion. Led by Mgr. Classe, the majority of missionaries retained a more gradualist understanding of conversion, trusting that over time God would deepen the faith of the political convert. In Classe's words, "the motive is perhaps not the most disinterested, but with the help of God's grace they will be turned into good Christians."[103] Classe and his allies also accused their opponents of rigorism and racism and accused them of trying to stifle the growth of a burgeoning African church.

This section has been entitled "the Tutsi *tornade*," for the unique aspect of Rwanda's 1930s Catholic growth was the conversion of large numbers of formerly recalcitrant Tutsi elites. Although the vast majority of Rwandan peasants continued traditional religious practices, elites embraced Western Christianity and then made it their own.[104] Roman Catholicism offered a new spiritual legitimacy for Mwami Mutara and served as a religious glue for an emergent stream of Rwandan nationalism propagated by Fr. Alexis Kagame and other Tutsi elites.

In the words of Gérard Prunier, "Catholicism after Mutara III Rudahigwa became not only linked with the highest echelons of the state but completely enmeshed in Rwandan society from top to bottom. It was a legitimizing factor, a banner, a source of profit, a way of becoming educated, a club, a matrimonial agency and even at times a religion."[105] The next section traces Rwanda's Catholic story into the 1940s, a decade that saw the public triumph of Catholicism amid signs of a growing pastoral crisis.

Triumphs and Tensions in Africa's Catholic Kingdom

If the seeds of church growth were planted in the 1920s and flowered in the 1930s, Catholicism became Rwanda's national religion in the 1940s. In addition to the church's qualitative and quantitative growth, three events signified what Bernard Lugan has described as the "complete alliance between throne and altar"[106]: the 1943 baptism of Mwami Mutara Rudahigwa, Mutara's 1946 dedication of Rwanda to Christ the King, and the 1950 golden anniversary of Rwanda's first Catholic mission at Save. At the same time, the Rwandan church experienced new strains during World War II and the immediate postwar period. Baptismal numbers and ecclesial participation flattened near the end of the war, raising concerns about the church's pastoral strategy. In turn, the first significant strains between European and Rwandan clergy arose, foreshadowing a 1950s period in which intraclerical cracks would become full-scale fissures.[107]

To an outside observer, the Rwandan church seemed healthy in the 1940s. The number of Rwandan clergy more than doubled between 1937 and 1948 from 30 to 81. By the end of the war, 155 Rwandan women were serving as Benebikira sisters. Nor were these indigenous priests and sisters toiling in obscurity; by 1948 the White Fathers had turned over nearly half of Rwanda's 40 mission stations to indigenous clergy.[108] In 1950 Rwanda counted over 230,000 Catholic catechumens and nearly 400,000 baptized Catholics, and Easter communion rates—measuring the number of Catholics who fulfilled their "Easter duty" to receive the sacraments of reconciliation and Eucharist—approached 80 percent. Together with Burundi and Belgian Congo, Rwanda formed the largest block of Catholics in Africa; this Catholic population exceeded much larger and more populated territories such as South Africa, Nigeria, Tanganyika, Uganda, and Angola.[109] In the words of Adrian Hastings, Rwanda in 1950 "might have appeared to the observer the nearest approach to a Catholic country in black Africa."[110]

As discussed earlier, Rwanda's Catholic identity was even more visible in the echelons of power. The symbolic culmination of the 1930s *tornade* came in October 1943 when the Catholic Church baptized Mwami Mutara after a twelve-year catechumenate. Mutara had divorced his pagan wife in 1941, ostensibly on the grounds of infertility.[111] His subsequent marriage to Rosalie Gicanda, a Christian, paved the way for his public baptism. Standing at Mutara's side for the baptismal ceremony were Léon Classe, his spiritual mentor, and Pierre Ryckmans, his godfather and Belgium's colonial governor-general. Mutara took the Christian name Charles Léon Pierre to signify his admiration of Classe and Ryckmans and his commitment to following Charlemagne's model of Christian kingship.

In 1946 Rwanda's Christian king followed through on his pledge by dedicating Rwanda to Christ the King. Instituted by Pope Pius XI in 1922 to combat rising European tides of secularism, fascism, and communism, the feast of Christ the King had become a symbol of Catholicism's continuing claims to the public sphere. Although Classe did not live to see the moment, Mutara's October 1946 dedication also symbolized the fulfillment of Classe's dream for his adopted country—the creation of a "Christian kingdom" in the heart of Africa. In Mutara's words,

> Lord Jesus, it is you who have formed our country. You have given us a long line of kings to govern in your place, even though we did not know you. When the time fixed by your Providence had arrived, You have been made known. You have sent us your apostles; they have opened to us the light...Now that we know you, we recognize publicly that you are our Lord and our King.[112]

While sacrificing any lingering claims to divine right, Mutara's dedication placed him in the good graces of the Vatican. In 1947, the Apostolic Nuncio, Mgr. Dellepiane, duly rewarded Mutara by enrolling him in the prestigious order of St. Gregory the Great. The Holy See would retain positive ties with Mutara and his allies long after the White Fathers began to distance themselves from Rwanda's king in the mid-1950s.

Finally, the August 1950 jubilee of the founding of Save Mission represented an apogee for a young church celebrating the advent of Catholic civilization in Rwanda. Thousands of Rwandan Catholics gathered for three days of festive celebrations, including Pierre Sigismondi, the Vatican's apostolic delegate to Congo, Rwanda, and Burundi, and representatives from all 40 Catholic missions. Demonstrating the sociopolitical salience of the Catholic missions, the highest-ranking political leaders in the region also attended this ostensibly ecclesial gathering.[113] Although scholars like Catherine Newbury and Ian Linden have retrospectively highlighted the Save gathering's importance for conscientizing Hutu political elites, the major theme of the meeting itself was celebrating "Christian civilization and Belgian material assistance" to Rwanda.[114] Church leaders noted the extent to which Christianity had shaped Rwandan political and social organizations, contributed to social justice, and given people a sense of duty before the law.[115] As we will see in chapter 3, concerns with maintaining Christian civilization shaped early 1950s Catholic literature far more than the Hutu-Tutsi question.

FIGURE 2.3 Mwami Mutara Rudahigwa dedicating Rwanda to Christ the King, 1946 (*courtesy Centre Missionnaire Lavigerie, Kigali, Rwanda*).

For all of the public spectacle, however, the 1940s also saw emerging challenges for Rwanda's Christian kingdom. After experiencing exponential growth throughout the 1930s, the Rwandan Catholic population declined slightly in the first half of the 1940s from 330,000 to 312,000. Part of this fall stemmed from the effects of World War II, especially the Ruzagayura famine of 1943–1944 that killed upward of 300,000 people.[116] Colonial forced labor, crop failures, and higher export requirements also took their toll on the local Hutu population, leading to more widespread protests and higher Hutu emigration rates to neighboring Congo, Uganda, and Tanganyika. Protestant churches were also making inroads during the postwar period. By 1958, nearly 100,000 Rwandans and Burundians professed the Anglican faith, and the Seventh Day Adventists counted 120,000 adherents.

As Catholic growth stalled, tensions rose between European and Rwandan clergy. Many of the strains revolved around the perceived paternalism of the White Fathers. In a 1946 petition to the superior general of the White Fathers, three indigenous priests wrote of a "difficulty of comprehension between blacks and whites," arguing that "indigenous priests are not destined to be auxiliaries of the whites, but it is the whites who should be the auxiliaries of the indigenous."[117] The Hutu-Tutsi question is not wholly absent from this document. Tutsi are described as "more intelligent than Bahutu," and Catholic mission history is divided into phases of "the first conquests of the Bahutu" and "the second hour of the Batutsi." However, the black-white question emerges as the dominant theme.[118] As we will see in chapter 3, European-Rwandan tensions emerged in the early 1950s as a prominent strain in the local church, especially at the major seminary of Nyakibanda.

In the midst of the turmoil, the Rwandan Catholic Church underwent its first leadership transition in two decades. Léon Classe suffered a stroke in 1940, and three years later Rome named Laurent Déprimoz as coadjutor of the Vicariate of Rwanda. Déprimoz officially succeeded Classe upon the latter's death in January 1945. Like Classe, Déprimoz came from an upper-class French background. After joining the Missionaries of Africa in 1901 at the age of seventeen, Déprimoz served for several years in the Burundian missions before joining the faculty of the minor seminary in Kabgayi in 1913. Over the next thirty years, he served as Catholic schools inspector, vicar general, and rector of the major seminary at Nyakibanda.[119]

After Classe's death, Déprimoz laid out a new catechetical strategy that prioritized qualitative formation over quantitative growth. This shift reflected Déprimoz's sense that in their efforts to attract Rwandan elites during the 1930s *tornade*, missionaries had allowed initiation standards to slide. For Déprimoz, the "conversions of opportunity" of the 1930s helped explain the flattening of Catholic growth in the early 1940s.[120] Déprimoz subsequently restored the four-year catechumenate, expanded oversight in the seminaries, undertook more pastoral visits to mission stations, and attempted to strengthen clerical unity by organizing national synods in 1945 and 1950. These efforts bore visible fruit. Easter communion rates rose from 50 percent in 1945 to 90 percent by the early 1950s.[121]

Whatever his ambiguities about the legacy of the *tornade*, Déprimoz did not give up Classe's commitments to elite conversion and church-state cohabitation. On the contrary, he actively recruited chiefs to join Catholic Action. In the early 1950s, he expanded Catholic Action by introducing apostolic movements such as the League of the Sacred Heart, the Legion of Mary, and the Eucharistic Crusade. A former editor of *Kinyamateka*, the Kinyarwanda-language Catholic newspaper, Déprimoz also recognized the importance of the press for forming Rwanda's rising generation of middle-class elites. Toward this end, he started the academic journal *Theologie et Pastorale* for local priests and the monthly review *L'Ami* for former seminarians and other Catholic elites.[122] And although Déprimoz was by no means a theological or political radical, he encouraged *Kinyamateka's* editors to more explicitly engage with contemporary social and political questions. Perhaps most importantly, in 1953 he appointed a young Hutu teacher and former seminarian named Gregoire Kayibanda as co-editor of *L'Ami*. Kayibanda subsequently became one of the most influential voices shaping the Rwandan social and political conversation in the 1950s.

Finally, Déprimoz continued and even expanded upon Classe's commitment to the indigenization of the local church. Having served as rector in both the minor and major seminary, Déprimoz had helped train nearly all indigenous

Rwandan clergy by the mid-1940s. Alexis Kagame, the Tutsi priest and chronicler of Rwanda's royal histories, served as his personal secretary.[123] In 1947 Déprimoz appointed one of his former students, Aloys Bigirumwami, as the first Rwandan priest on the priest-advisory committee known as the Council of the Vicariate. He also named indigenous priests to serve as vicar general and inspector general of Catholic schools. Deogratias Mbandiwimfura became the first Rwandan priest to pursue higher studies abroad, traveling to Rome in 1947 to pursue a doctorate in canon law. By the time Déprimoz retired in 1955, there were over 100 indigenous priests in Rwanda, and Bigirumwami had become the first indigenous bishop in Belgian Africa.[124]

As Rwanda celebrated a half century of Catholic evangelization in 1950, Lavigerie's, Hirth's, and Classe's dream to create a Christian kingdom in the heart of Africa had become a visible reality. From its nondescript beginnings in the early 1900s, the Rwandan church had become a model of rapid growth and indigenization. The Catholic Church crossed ethnic and political lines, including both Hutu and Tutsi in its ranks. After early trepidations, Rwandan elites had embraced the Catholic faith as colonial politics shifted in the 1920s and 1930s. Journalists at *Kinyamateka*, missionary anthropologists, and indigenous scholars like Fr. Alexis Kagame shaped Rwanda's social milieu, historical understanding, and modern vision of itself. And yet even as the church's power grew, deep internal cleavages also emerged in the 1940s. These reflected lingering tensions over the church's dual commitments to popular uplift and elite conversion, as well as church leaders' meddling in ethnic discourse and colonial politics. These political, racial and clerical tensions would only rise in the early 1950s, as we will see in the next chapter.

3

Success Breeds Restlessness,
1950–1955

SUBTLE BUT IMPORTANT shifts in Rwandan politics occurred during the early 1950s. Belgium announced a ten-year economic and political plan in 1952 that promised regional and national councils, democratic elections, and increasing local autonomy. In the midst of these reforms, local Rwandan politics were becoming more complex and variegated. New divisions arose between conservative traditionalists associated with Mwami Mutara, pro-Belgian Tutsi reformists, and a rising class of Hutu intellectuals who had received much of their academic formation in Catholic seminaries.

On the surface, the Rwandan Catholic Church appeared to be flourishing in the early 1950s. The church celebrated record numbers of baptisms, a growing catechumenate, higher rates of lay sacramental practice, and the 1952 consecration of Mgr. Aloys Bigirumwami, the first African bishop in the Belgian colonies. Although Mgr. Laurent Déprimoz, the Vicar Apostolic of Kabgayi, never enjoyed the same rapport with Mwami Mutara that Mutara had shared with Léon Classe, public relations remained amicable among Catholic missionaries, Belgian colonial officials, and local Rwandan authorities. Beneath this seeming tranquility, however, new fissures were bubbling to the surface. These included divisions between the White Fathers and Belgian colonial officials, rising tensions among the Rwandans, Burundians, and Congolese studying in Rwanda's major seminary, and a burgeoning power struggle between European missionaries and Rwanda's indigenous clergy.

In addressing the interrelated ecclesial, social, and political dimensions of Catholic history in the early 1950s, I divide this chapter info five sections. First, I offer a brief overview of economic, social, and political developments in Rwanda during the late 1940s and early 1950s, highlighting the abolition of Rwanda's traditional *ubuhake* and *uburetwa* practices and growing tensions within Rwanda's ruling elites. Second, I consider how Catholic Church leaders continued their mission to build Christian civilization by embracing democratization and virulently opposing international communism, establishing an ideological paradigm that would last through the final years of colonial rule. Third, I analyze how Catholic leaders sought to keep Rwanda's *évolués*—Western-educated social and political elites—within the church's sphere of influence. Perhaps surprising, in light of later historical developments, Catholic literature was far more preoccupied with the future of the "*évolués*" than with any social tensions between Hutu and Tutsi. The lacuna of Hutu-Tutsi references challenges the common historiographical assumption that these categories dominated colonial and Catholic discourse throughout the post-World War II period.

In the final half of the chapter, I turn to the Catholic Church's internal politics, focusing on the two men who would emerge as the dominant Catholic leaders of the late 1950s and early 1960s. First, I consider the appointment of Aloys Bigirumwami as the third indigenous Catholic bishop in sub-Saharan Africa and first in the Belgian colonies. Overlooked in most histories of Rwandan Christianity, Bigirumwami will emerge in this narrative as one of the most important churchmen in the late colonial period. Second, I consider the meteoric rise of the Swiss White Father André Perraudin. In 1950 Perraudin arrived at Nyakibanda as a thirty-six-year-old seminary professor with only two years of missionary experience. He would quickly be immersed in the nationalist and interracial tensions that broke out at Nyakibanda Seminary in 1952. Praised for his handling of the aftermath of this near-schism, Perraudin would be named three years later to succeed Déprimoz as Vicar Apostolic of Kabgayi.

This chapter offers three primary contributions concerning the nature of Catholic politics in the early 1950s. First, the advent of democratization and decolonization did not fundamentally alter Catholic missionaries' vision of the state as an indispensable partner in maintaining Rwanda's status as a Christian kingdom in central Africa. Rather, these political developments merely altered the means that missionaries used. Rather than convert the king and his court, the Christian *polis* of the 1950s required the adherence of a new class of rising lay elites (*évolués*) who would determine the course of postcolonial Rwandan politics.

Second, Catholic politics in Rwanda in the early 1950s concerned a far wider array of themes than the Hutu-Tutsi question, challenging the scholarly tendency to read Rwandan history exclusively through this lens. In turn, Catholic ideological concerns with communism, democracy, and anti-clericalism help contextualize the positions that church leaders later adopted toward the Hutu-Tutsi question. This chapter also shows how divisions of race, nationality, and social class divided Catholic clergy and seminarians. Whatever their public protests of undivided unity, internal correspondence reveals a deep-seated mistrust between the White Fathers and Rwanda's Tutsi-dominated clergy long before the public irruption of the Hutu-Tutsi question in 1956 and 1957.

Third, this narrative provides crucial insight into the backgrounds and personalities of Mgr. Perraudin and Mgr. Bigirumwami. Perraudin emerges here
as a popular professor of missiology, advocating for social justice but steering
clear of controversial ethnic questions. We also see Perraudin as a consummate
church politician, laboring to publicly reconcile opposed factions even as he
worked behind the scenes to achieve his own agenda. Bigirumwami, on the other
hand, found himself encountering resistance from both Perraudin and the White
Fathers in Rome as he strove to move the Vicariate of Nyundo beyond missionary
tutelage. Bigirumwami's advocacy earned him few missionary allies but marked
him as an independent voice—a voice that would ultimately challenge some of the
stereotypical shibboleths of Rwandan politics in the late colonial period.

Postwar Developments in Rwandan Society

The early 1950s was an era of anticipation across sub-Saharan Africa. Horizons
broadened by the Second World War, nationalist movements gained ground
across the continent. These took various forms, including Kwame Nkrumah's
pan-Africanism in Ghana, the Senegalese Leopold Senghor's *négritude* movement, Mau-Mau uprisings against the British in Kenya, and the African National
Congress's anti-apartheid protests in South Africa.[1] Exhausted and overstretched
after World War II, European colonial powers increasingly spoke of devolution and local autonomy if not yet independence. By the mid-1950s, even officials in paternalistic Belgian Congo had begun using language of "partnership,"
"non-racialism," and the "Belgian-Congolese community," although these officials
were still envisioning decolonization in terms of decades rather than years.[2]

As in the rest of Africa, political change in Rwanda accelerated with the end
of World War II and the advent of the United Nations. The U.N. placed Rwanda
under an international *tutelle* (guardianship) in 1946. Consisting of members of
the Belgian colonial administration, the five permanent members of the U.N.
Security Council, and three rotating nations, this *tutelle* replaced the permanent
commission of the League of Nations that had exercised official oversight of the
Rwanda-Burundi trust territory since 1922. The *tutelle's* responsibilities included
examining colonial reports, evaluating petitions from Rwanda and Burundi, and
conducting triennial visits to assess Belgium's oversight of the two colonies.
Conducted in 1948, 1951, 1954, 1957, and 1960, these visits precipitated flurries of
political lobbying. Each visit also sparked a degree of political reform.[3]

Following the 1948 U.N. Charter's calls for national self-determination, the U.N.
tutelle instructed Belgium during its 1948 and 1951 visits to accelerate Rwanda's
and Burundi's paths toward political autonomy.[4] In response, Belgium announced
on July 14, 1952 the inauguration of a ten-year political devolution plan for both territories. This plan called for the institution of representative structures in 1953 and

democratic *sous-chefferie* (sub-chiefdom) elections in 1956. The new *sous-chefferies* would consist of one sub-chief and five to nine counselors; each counselor represented 500 inhabitants. In turn, each of the higher *chefferie* (chiefdom) councils would include five to nine appointed members from the lower *sous-chefferies*. The *chefferie* councils then sent representatives to the territorial councils. The highest consultative body, the *Conseil Supérieur du Pays* (CSP), included the presidents of the nine territorial councils, six additional chiefs, nine notables, and four royal appointees. Although these systems offered a measure of representative democracy, local chiefs had to endorse candidates for higher councils. This requirement tended to reinforce Rwanda's existing oligarchies rather than infuse new blood into the system. In particular, Tutsi nobility from the royal Abega and Abanyiginya clans continued to predominate in Rwanda's higher offices. As we will see, while two-thirds of the sub-chiefs elected in 1956 legislative elections were Hutu, 31 of the 32 CSP members remained Tutsi.[5]

The most significant socioeconomic changes of the postwar period were Mwami Mutara's 1949 decision to abolish *uburetwa* and the 1954 elimination of *ubuhake*. As discussed earlier, *uburetwa* required Hutu workers to spend two days per week cultivating a local Tutsi patron's land. The Mwami's decision to abolish the practice appeared to confirm his prewar reputation as a reformist and modernizer. However, Mutara's subsequent failure to address the issues of pasturages and land redistribution exacerbated social tensions as Rwanda's population grew rapidly due to improved medical care and higher agricultural yields.[6]

The abolition of *ubuhake* in the mid-1950s had even greater symbolic value. As discussed in chapter 1, *ubuhake* was a patron-client relationship in which a patron lent land and cattle to a client in exchange for the client's services. Although *ubuhake* relationships had originally predominated among Tutsi elites, it increasingly stratified Tutsi from Hutu during the colonial era. When he announced the abolition of *ubuhake* in 1952, Mwami Mutara justified this in the context of the advent of modern capitalism. For Mutara, *ubuhake* had helped to "peacefully regulate relations between Tutsi and Hutu" in past eras and underlay the social, political, and economic stability of Rwanda's *ancien régime*. However, the emergence of a wage-based and property-based capitalist system during the colonial era had made *ubuhake* anachronistic.[7]

The abolition of *ubuhake* happened as a new class of Hutu elites emerged in Rwanda. Many of these Hutu were prosperous emigrants returned from Uganda. If there ever was an "ethnic gap" in Banyarwanda socioeconomic status, it disappeared in the 1950s. In fact, a survey of family incomes in the mid-1950s revealed an average annual Hutu family income of 4,249 Belgian francs, just below the Tutsi figure of 4,439 francs. In 1959, a Belgian working group for Rwanda and Burundi concluded that only 6,000 to 10,000 of Rwanda's 150,000 Tutsi should be classified as upper class elites. If Tutsi status retained a certain social prestige, it connoted little to no financial advantage. In the words of the Belgian Working Group's final report, "the advantages [of being Tutsi] are situated more in the plan of social organization and of prestige; they do not necessarily imply elevated revenues, out of proportion with the level of the life of the masses."[8]

In fact, the primary political division in the early 1950s did not divide Hutu from Tutsi. Rather, a split emerged between traditionalist Tutsi chiefs and the "Astridiens," younger Tutsi chiefs trained at the *Groupe Scolaire d'Astrida* in Butare in southern Rwanda. This school was led by Br. Secundien, a politically savvy Brother of Charity noted for his patronage of several young, ambitious Tutsi students and his alleged involvement in a 1940s plot to topple Mwami Mutara.[9] Seeing themselves as a reforming, nonhereditary meritocracy, the Astridiens embraced Western democracy and the continuing liberalization of Rwanda's economy. Their leader was Prosper Bwanakweri, a prominent Tutsi chief based in Nyanza who hailed from the Abega, the rival clan to Mwami Mutara's Abanyiginya clan. Bwanakweri took the lead in initiating land reform in his own chiefdom and briefly became a lionized figure for pro-European Tutsi and Hutu alike.[10] Bwanakweri was not without his critics, however, who accused him of cozying up to the Belgian *tutelle* and undermining Mwami Mutara's own efforts to achieve more political autonomy from Belgium. Mutara ultimately convinced the Belgians to relocate Bwanakweri from his chiefdom in the Kigali region to Gisenyi in northwestern Rwanda. Yet by publicly challenging a Mwami who had cultivated a supra-political image, Bwanakweri legitimized political debate in Rwanda for Tutsi and Hutu alike.[11]

Bwanakweri also symbolized an early 1950s period before Hutu and Tutsi labels emerged as dominant Rwandan political identities. Bwanakweri was one of the founders of *L'Association des Amitiés Belge-Rwandaises* and the *Mouvement Politique Progressiste* (MPP). Launched in 1951 to support the "moral, intellectual and material progress of Rwanda," *L'Association des Amitiés* had a diverse membership. Key figures included Fr. Arthur Dejemeppe, a progressive White Father missionary who briefly served as vicar general of Kabgayi; Gregoire Kayibanda, Hutu journalist and emerging leader of a rising group of former seminarians; Fr. Alexis Kagame, the Tutsi intellectual godfather of the Banyarwanda nationalist revival of the 1940s; and Lazare Ndazaro, a moderate Tutsi chief and political ally of Bwanakweri.[12]

Initiated in 1955, the *Mouvement Politique Progressiste* (MPP) was the successor of *L'Association des Amitiés Belge-Rwandaises*. Like its predecessor, the MPP charted a moderate course between nationalism and ethnicism, striving to improve relations between Rwandans and Europeans while avoiding both "anti-European nationalism" and what it termed "social discrimination based on race."[13] The MPP's roster included Bwanakweri, Kayibanda, the Hutu journalist Aloys Munyangaju, the Burundian prince and nationalist leader Pierre Baranyanika, and 39 other Tutsi chiefs. For a moment in the mid-1950s, pan-ethnic social reform appeared to be the harbinger of Rwanda's postcolonial future. As we will see, this moment proved ephemeral as Hutu-Tutsi tensions increased in the latter years of the decade.

For all of their spirit of collaboration, however, Tutsi and Hutu elites in the early 1950s faced different professional ceilings. If ambitious Tutsi elites could anticipate rising through the colonial administration or serving on a *chefferie* or territorial council, Hutu opportunities were more circumscribed—teaching in a village school, serving on a local sub-council, providing medical care in a rural dispensary, or writing for a Catholic newspaper. At the same time, such opportunities proved valuable in light of the growing democratic turn in 1950s Rwandan politics. While Tutsi elites sought influence through traditional hierarchical offices and tended to emphasize the necessity of elite rule, Hutu leaders like Kayibanda were mobilizing the people through the mass media and Catholic Action groups, building relationships between the new "elites of the country" and the rural masses.[14] The top-down Tutsi approach had worked for decades, but the grassroots work of Kayibanda and his allies established a better base for electoral democracy. In turn, Kayibanda and his supporters would quickly realize the electoral potential of mobilizing voters on the basis of their Hutu identity.

A New Civilizing Mission: Anti-communism and Democratization

As Rwanda's political changes accelerated in the early 1950s, Catholic leaders recalibrated their traditional vision of Christian civilization. Rather than emphasize the top-down, hierarchical models of the pre-World War II period, a new generation of postwar missionaries embraced democratization, anti-communism, and a managed devolution from colonial rule. Even as they began distancing themselves from the Belgian administration, the White Fathers worried whether they would retain the social and religious influence to which they had grown accustomed in Belgian Rwanda.

This ambiguity was reflected in missionary commentaries on anti-colonial movements. In particular, Catholic commentators feared that decolonization would open Africa's doors to international communism, godless atheism and religious indifference. The division of Berlin in 1948, communist triumph in China, Cold War stalemate in Korea, and ongoing struggle in French Indochina (Vietnam) appeared to confirm this pessimism and colored Catholic views of African nationalism, especially the movement's most vociferous pan-Africanist and anti-colonial streams. At a magisterial level, Pope Pius XII's 1951 and 1957 encyclicals on Christian mission, *Evangelii Praecones* and *Fidei Donum*, neither condemned nor endorsed Africa's anti-colonial movements. However, the pope warned of the "proponents of atheistic materialism...stirring up the emotions of the natives by encouraging mutual envy among them and distorting their unhappy material condition in an attempt to deceive them…or to incite them to seditious acts."[15] Such suspicions were echoed in the White Fathers' publications in Rwanda, especially the journal *L'Ami* that was aimed at Rwandan Catholic elites. Here the White Fathers critiqued the political philosophy of Karl Marx and described Maoist China's persecution of Catholics. One article even related a supposed Soviet plot to have communist agitators impersonate black Catholic priests![16] Even the White Fathers' growing emphasis on social justice and land reform stemmed in part from the fear of peasant resentment opening Rwanda to "the subversive ideas of communism."[17] As André Perraudin expressed in 1955, after "swallowing" Indochina and India "the red monster will turn its eyes toward Africa…the future [of communism] is not perhaps that far off."[18]

To fight communism, Rwandan Catholic elites advocated the Catholic social teaching tradition first initiated by Pope Leo XIII's 1891 encyclical *Rerum Novarum*.[19] Namely, they called for a robust defense of private property rights while simultaneously encouraging workers' associations that could improve conditions for the laboring poor. In rural Rwanda, this took the form of mutualities and cooperatives, joint associations of farmers, workers and artisans who sold products collectively and distributed the profits equitably among members. Just as Belgian and Swiss cooperatives had organized Christian workers while rejecting Marxist visions of class warfare, Rwandan Catholic commentators saw local cooperatives as an "effective anecdote against the opposition of classes and races" which would "build mutual confidence between the great and the small, between the races, between the evolved and the less evolved."[20] For the White Fathers, cooperatives tempered the excesses of capitalism, encouraging profit while avoiding the individualism and business abuses that had left capitalism with such a mixed legacy in stratified European societies.[21] Cooperatives had the potential to address the direct material suffering of the poor, provide social security for workers, and counter the secular humanism that had come to dominate Europe's working classes.[22]

It was this very "secularization" that loomed as another perceived ideological threat for Catholic missionaries in early 1950s Rwanda. This challenge emerged most prominently in the lay schools debate of 1954-55. Supported by Augustin Buisseret, Belgium's minister for colonies, Mwami Mutara and many nationalist Tutsi elites advocated for Belgium to curtail missionary influence in Rwandan schools and develop an independent state school system. A similar debate was underway in Belgium and Burundi at the same time.[23] Part of the objection to Catholic schools was ideological; some critics also raised concerns over the academic rigor of Catholic education.[24] The argument also reflected a broader debate on the extent to which the Rwandan state should chart an independent course from the Catholic Church, particularly as instantiated in the White Fathers and other missionary clergy. Tensions had also grown between Mutara and the

White Fathers after two incidents in the early 1950s. First, a missionary denied Mutara communion in 1951. Second, the Belgian government in 1952 moved a Jesuit humanities college from its planned location in Nyanza to Burundi.[25] While Mutara bristled at what he saw as deliberate missionary snubs, the White Fathers saw the opposition of Mutara and his allies as part of a larger "masonic" conspiracy to eliminate Catholic influence from society.[26]

In response, Rwanda's Catholic bishops launched a vociferous attack against the laicization of schools.[27] In an October 1954 joint pastoral letter on "the danger which menaces teaching in Rwanda," Déprimoz and Bigirumwami reiterated the centrality of religion for Rwanda's moral formation and argued that the Catholic Church had a "sacred right" to educate children. "IN A CATHOLIC COUNTRY as is Rwanda, THE ONLY OFFICIAL TEACHING SHOULD BE CATHOLIC TEACHING. We must protect the most sacred rights of the church, those of the education of children."[28] For Déprimoz, Catholic schooling was critical to preventing a nation like Rwanda with its "pagan shadows" and "barbarous superstitions" from sinking into "total moral anarchy," thereby exposing the population to the temptations of communism. In contrast, lay schools would "prepare children for materialist and liberal ideas which are in opposition to Christian religion."[29] The formula was simple. Morality undergirded civilization, and Catholic education underwrote morality. Therefore, the decline of Catholic education would open Rwanda to tides of neo-paganism and communism.[30] Whatever its merits, such rhetoric proved convincing. Two-thirds of the Superior Council voted against Buisseret's and Mutara's plan in 1955, and the Catholic Church maintained a near monopoly on primary and secondary schooling for another decade.[31]

As evidenced by the rhetoric of the lay schools debate, Catholic leaders continued to see the upbuilding of Christian civilization as a key plank in their evangelical mission. Europeans like Déprimoz or the Belgian primate Cardinal Van Roey praised missionaries for being "messengers of Christian civilization" in black Africa.[32] Tutsi elites like the Catholic priest and royal *biru* (advisor) Alexis Kagame thanked the White Fathers for developing the written Kinyarwanda language that facilitated the cultural renaissance of the 1930s and 1940s, noting that "religious formation is an irreplaceable element in the initiation of Black Africa to Western civilization."[33] Meanwhile, young Hutu elites like Gregoire Kayibanda, editor of *L'Ami* after 1953, associated this civilizing mission with the Catholic duty to protect the common good and defend Rwanda's status as a bulwark of African Christianity.[34] Even as European colonization entered its twilight years, prominent European, Tutsi and Hutu commentators agreed on the priority of the Christian civilizing mission.

Developing Christian civilization in turn required an ongoing alliance between church and state. As discussed in chapter 2, missionaries and colonial officials assumed a close working relationship between church and state through much

of the first fifty years of Rwandan Catholic history. However, the election of a
Socialist government in Belgium in the early 1950s offered a robust challenge
to this colonial status quo.[35] In response, church leaders attempted to walk a
tightrope, recognizing the autonomy of the state while reiterating the church's
right to exercise its voice in public life. While at least one missionary spoke of
his duty to "remain in the sacristy and leave the Mwami to his politics,"[36] most
Catholic commentators stressed how the holistic and material dimensions of the
gospel required Christians to evangelize both state and society. In the 1955 words
of André Perraudin, "the Catholics are strong and do not fear to speak up...We
do not have any desire to create here a religion of the sacristy."[37] From his editorial perch at *L'Ami*, Kayibanda exhorted Rwandans to "baptize the structures and
institutions" of their emerging postcolonial society. While this would not require a
theocracy, only an *entente* between church and state could provide a healthy basis
for the continued evolution of Rwandan society.[38]

If such a church-state entente had propagated a neo-traditional, hierarchical vision of Rwandan society during the first half of the twentieth century, new
winds were blowing in the early 1950s. In the face of Belgium's proposed political decentralization and Mutara's abolition of *uburetwa* and *ubuhake*, 1950s missionaries and indigenous Catholic elites exhorted Catholics to join and shape
Rwanda's evolving "march for progress."[39] In practical terms this meant replacing Rwanda's ancestral customs with Western economic, political and human
rights standards, closely associating the building of the Christian kingdom with
democratization and calling for a new focus on Rwanda's "social problem."[40] In
this vein, missionaries rejected *ubuhake* as "non-Christian" and "the Middle Ages
in miniature," advocating instead for private property, mutualities and cooperatives.[41] Mwami Mutara himself described the 1953 decree establishing the *Conseil
supérieur du pays* (CSP) as "introducing democratic principles in the functioning
of our institutions...posing the foundations for the transformation of a feudal
Rwanda into a modern state."[42] For his part, Kayibanda saw the Christian task
as "challenging barbarous mentalities which cloaked themselves in the language
of the sacred custom of the country."[43] In turn, the Hutu journalist and former
Catholic seminarian Aloys Munyangaju called his readers to the "ballot boxes"
and celebrated the suppression of *ubuhake* as the "the beginning of democracy."[44]
Even the White Fathers began rewriting the history of Belgian occupation through
the lens of elevating the masses out of feudal oppression, filling the pages of *L'Ami*
with sympathetic analyses of democratic theory.[45] *Kinyamateka* also supported the
abolition of *ubuhake* and *uburetwa* in the early and mid-1950s.[46]

To summarize, Catholic leaders in the early 1950s positioned the church
to oppose communism and secularism while supporting democracy and economic modernization. Christianity emerged here as an ethical faith that encouraged fraternity between all, respected the rights of each human person, and

supported justice for the "proletariat."[47] If Léon Classe had spent three decades establishing the Catholic missions as firm supporters of the Mwami and the Tutsi nobility, the egalitarian ghosts of the earliest Catholic missions appeared to be stirring.

Elites, Évolués, *and the Ethnic Lacuna*

To withstand the threats of communism and secularism and further a more egalitarian vision of Christian civilization, the Catholic Church needed to win over a new generation of political and social elites who would lead Rwandan society toward political autonomy and democracy. Conversant in French and filling the lower echelons of the Belgian colonial administration, these elites were known as *évolués*. Comprised of both educated young Tutsi and former Hutu seminarians, the *évolués* owed their social status to European commerce and Catholic schools like the *Groupe Scolaire d'Astrida* rather than Rwanda's ancestral institutions.[48] As Mutara's generation aged, these younger elites emerged as Rwanda's rising leadership class. Tempted by communism, secularism, and anti-colonial nationalism, the *évolués* were also seen as a volatile group whose long-term Catholic sympathies could not be assumed. In the words of Louis Gasore, the Tutsi vicar general of Nyundo, "one day they [the missionaries] will be surprised to find pagan, the country which they believed entirely converted because ... certain *évolués*, working in the manner of Renan, Voltaire and Diderot, will in a century render void the land of missions."[49]

On paper, Rwanda in the early 1950s had become one of the most Catholic countries in Africa.[50] In 1950 Rwanda's population numbered just over 1.8 million. Of these, 370,000 had received Catholic baptism, and an additional 200,000 were enrolled in the Catholic catechumenate. This Catholic population represented a 900 percent increase since the church's silver jubilee in 1925. In 1951 a record 20 indigenous priests were ordained to the priesthood. Qualitative zeal matched this quantitative growth. In 1955 over 90 percent of Rwanda's Catholics made their Easter duty, up from 65–70 percent in the mid-1940s. And as in the 1930s and 1940s, Catholicism dominated Rwanda's elite class even more than its peasantry. By 1950, 647 of Rwanda's 674 Tutsi chiefs had converted to Catholicism, while nearly all educated Hutu had been trained in Catholic schools and seminaries. In contrast to Catholicism's dominance among elites, only one-third of the Rwandan population had received baptism or entered the Catholic catechumenate.[51] Recognizing that Catholics outnumbered Protestants by fifteen to one and Muslims by one hundred to one, longtime White Father missionary R.P. Endriatis wrote that "it is not exaggerated to say that all the elite of this country are Catholic."[52] The 1953-54 annual report from Kabgayi boldly claimed that "Rwanda has made its choice—it wants to be a Catholic country."[53]

And yet for all of the church's evangelical successes, missionary doubts remained.[54] In addition to the ideological risks discussed earlier, Anglicanism, Seventh-Day Adventism and the Belgian Protestant Missionary Society continued to make inroads in Rwanda's northern, northwestern, and eastern territories.[55] And while Rwandan elites may have accepted Christian baptism, this did not mean that they had embraced Christian morality. Here missionaries criticized what they described as Rwanda's "elastic" view of justice, "hateful" political intrigues, and lingering "pagan attitudes." Many wondered more openly if elite conversions reflected the Holy Spirit or a spirit of political expediency. Others questioned whether Banyarwanda Christians would continue to support Rwanda's missionary clergy or seek a more independent course. The nineteenth- and twentieth-century history of Europe—namely the alienation of intellectual elites and the urban working class from the church—played no small role in raising the anxieties of the White Fathers. In the face of all these challenges and ambiguities, one can better understand the prominent Tutsi priest Stanislas Bushayija's worries that religious indifference, anti-clericalism, and "neo-paganism" were threatening to subsume the Tutsi *tornade*. For André Perraudin, the primary pastoral challenge of the 1950s was to "strengthen the converts of yesterday and form Christian elites capable of training the masses."[56]

To achieve this goal, the Catholic Church undertook three primary pastoral strategies. First, they enlisted the *évolués* in Catholic Action leadership. Launched in the 1920s by Pope Pius XI, Catholic Action aimed to re-Christianize European society through forming committed cadres of young Catholics, enlisting them in a social movement that would counter communism on the left and fascism on the right.[57] In Rwanda Catholic Action focused on empowering lay leaders to further evangelize the pagan peasantry and to reform social structures to better reflect gospel values. Catholic Action leaders applied the movement's "see, judge, act" methodology to topics ranging from instructing children and influencing political institutions to serving as Christian professionals in agriculture, commerce or administration.[58]

Second, the Catholic Church commissioned groups of indigenous clergy, advanced seminarians, and lay elites to study Rwanda's social problems. These included the *Cercle Lavigerie* at the royal capital of Nyanza, the *Cercle Sant Paul* at Kabgayi, and the national *L'association d'anciens* for former seminarians.[59] While missionaries preferred to describe these circles as "social" rather than "political," these groups represented a concerted Catholic effort to influence political conversation in Rwanda on topics like democracy, economic development, and education. Mwami Mutara participated in the *Cercle Lavigerie* gatherings in Nyanza, and members of these groups also served on *chefferies*, territorial councils and even the CSP. So while claiming that "in these meetings we have never spoken of politics...but have discussed social problems," the influential White Father Arthur

Dejemeppe also celebrated the inclusion of two former members of the *Cercle Léon Classe* on Rwanda's first Superior Council.[60]

Third, the Catholic hierarchy initiated an "apostolate of the press."[61] Started in the 1930s, the Kinyarwanda-language Catholic weekly *Kinyamateka* was intended to be read orally to Rwanda's masses of illiterate peasants. Under the 1940s editorship of Alexis Kagame, the journal emphasized the synthesis between Roman Catholicism and Rwanda's monarchy and traditional institutions. The White Fathers' 1953 decision to send Kagame to Rome to pursue doctoral studies in theology facilitated a major change in *Kinyamateka's* editorial policy.[62] With the socially progressive missionary Arthur Dejemeppe at the helm, *Kinyamateka's* editorial vision shifted from a top-down focus on the monarchy to more grassroots emphases on social justice, the Hutu peasantry, and democracy. Over the next two years, the newspaper's circulation more than doubled from 10,000 to 22,000. As we will see, the newspaper also provoked more controversies as the decade progressed.[63]

In the early 1950s, *L'Ami* was the primary Catholic journal directed at lay elites. The White Fathers started *L'Ami* in 1950 to offer a Christian perspective on the complex questions of Rwandan social and political life. They also looked to fight what they termed the "materialist tides" which threatened to swamp Rwanda's Christian elites.[64] Seminarians filled the pages of *L'Ami* with articles on various dimensions of Catholic social teaching. For example, members of the *Cercle Sant Paul* penned over 60 articles for the Catholic press between January 1953 and June 1954.[65] *L'Ami* tended to adopt a pro-Belgian editorial policy, chastising unnamed Rwandan elites for their "unnecessary" and "destructive" criticisms of Belgian authorities.[66] In 1953 the White Fathers appointed Gregoire Kayibanda as the first lay editor of *L'Ami*, giving the emerging Hutu spokesman a key platform from which to develop and propagate his political thought.

Considering his later notoriety as coauthor of the 1957 Bahutu Manifesto, founder of the *Mouvement Social Muhutu*, and president of the Hutu-dominated First Republic, what is perhaps most striking in Kayibanda's early 1950s writings is his failure to frame social questions in Hutu-Tutsi terms. For example, while Kayibanda laments the "feudal mentality" infecting the wealthier classes, he never labels this mentality "Tutsi."[67] Even his famous 1954 manifesto, "Marching toward Progress," reads like a paean for interracial and intraclass collaboration on the pressing social issues of the day.[68] Significantly, Kayibanda does not name the Hutu-Tutsi question as one of these pressing social issues. And even after taking over the editorship at *Kinyamateka* in 1955, Kayibanda's social critiques did not include Hutu-Tutsi language until early 1957.[69] As we will see in subsequent chapters, his language would change markedly with the release of the Bahutu Manifesto in March 1957.

The early 1950s absence of Hutu-Tutsi language was not limited to Kayibanda's writings. While themes of anti-communism, secularization, democratization,

land reform, and elite conversion emerged prominently in White Father literature in the early 1950s, Hutu-Tutsi ethnic discourse was almost completely
absent. Brief anthropological studies in Catholic newspapers focused instead
on the categories of clan and family.[70] The interracial question emerged as the
decade progressed, but these commentaries concerned black-white relations in
Belgian Congo and apartheid South Africa, not Hutu-Tutsi relations in Rwanda.[71]
Nor did the Hutu-Tutsi distinction dominate the White Fathers' political analysis.
For example, an anonymous October 1952 study of Rwandan politics described
the Rwandan mentality as "characterized by duplicity, xenophobia, and a lack
of scruples in choosing means to an end."[72] While colonial writers would later
associate such language with Tutsi, the labels in 1952 were national rather than
ethnic.

In concluding this section, then, I would argue that the dominant socio-political
category of the early 1950s was "évolué" rather than "Hutu" or "Tutsi." Integrating
the best of European and Rwandan tradition, évolués were distinguished from
both Rwanda's traditional nobility and the common masses. "The évolués are the
elites of Africa: a category of men who by their intellectual, moral and religious
formation, and often through their social situation and material assistance, find
themselves in the forefront of progress."[73] For both Kayibanda the Hutu journalist
and Gasore the Tutsi priest, the "evolved men" of Rwanda had emerged from the
Banyarwandan masses. They were now entrusted with leading the lower classes to
a higher level of civilization.[74] Likewise, for the Tutsi priest Innocent Gasabwoya,
the key social division was not Hutu-Tutsi but the cleavage between "the class of
évolués at the head of the country which have in their hands [the nation's] destiny, and the class of the peasants."[75] As will be seen in chapter 4, this pan-ethnic
évolué identity would not last. In the face of democratizing currents, elitist identities proved no match for ethnicity and nationalism in mobilizing the Rwandan
masses.

Aloys Bigirumwami, the Banyarwanda Bishop

By the early 1950s, Catholic Rwanda was no longer the exclusive province of
the White Fathers. Many new priests belonged to other missionary orders. The
Jesuits arrived in 1949, while the Salesians started a secondary school in Kigali in
1954. Others came from diocesan backgrounds, like the *Fidei Donum* priests who
responded to Pius XII's 1957 exhortation for more African missionaries. Many
of these younger missionaries came from working class backgrounds and harbored suspicions of the traditional Rwandan ruling class.[76] In addition, the White
Fathers were handing over a majority of mission stations and pastoral leadership
positions to Rwanda's growing indigenous clergy.[77] Several indigenous clergy traveled abroad for the first time, exposing them to a broader milieu of intellectual

and ideological streams. Lay leaders were also asserting themselves in apostolic movements like the Sacred Heart of Jesus and the Legion of Mary.

It was the elevation of Aloys Bigirumwami, however, that symbolized the most decisive shift in ecclesial leadership in Rwanda's colonial history.[78] Since the 1939 appointment of Uganda's Joseph Kiwanuka as the first black Catholic bishop in modern Africa, the Vatican's Propaganda Fide and the White Fathers had pondered the idea of restructuring the Rwandan church and appointing an indigenous bishop to lead one of Rwanda's new vicariates.[79] Many expected an indigenous episcopal appointment during the jubilee year of 1950, but the reticence of leaders like Louis Durrieu, the Superior General of the White Fathers, delayed the appointment by another two years. Even then colonial and White Father officials helped ensure that the new vicariate of Nyundo would be far smaller than the vicariate of Kabgayi. Allegedly described by the Belgian minister of colonies as a "token indigenous vicariate" to satisfy black nationalists, Nyundo received only nine of Rwanda's forty-five mission stations and included one-eighth of Rwanda's Catholic population. In 1952 there were 54,000 baptized Catholics and 27,000 catechumens in Nyundo and 350,000 baptized and 150,000 catechumens in Kabgayi.[80] Nyundo also contained Rwanda's largest Adventist and Anglican populations—populations suspected of being "agents of British propaganda and zealots of pan-Africanist xenophobia."[81] Due to this religious competition as well as emigration to Congo and Uganda, Nyundo's Catholic population growth remained stagnant throughout the 1950s.[82] Like Kiwanuka's diocese of Masaka in southwestern Uganda, however, Nyundo would serve as a test-run for the broader indigenization of the church. In this vein, Nyundo's ratio of indigenous to European clergy was three to one—a near reversal of the ratio in Kabgayi.

Bigirumwami came from a noble family with mixed Hutu-Tutsi ancestry in the eastern Rwandan province of Gisaka.[83] He was a direct descendant of the Gisaka royal line through the king's Hutu son, although Bigirumwami would be publicly classified as a Tutsi. (Bigirumwami's mixed ethnic heritage exerted no small influence on his later political views, as we will see in chapters 4 and 5.) The Gisaka royal line represented a regional rival to the Mwami's central court in Nyanza. As discussed earlier, this region had served as a political hotbed from the first German encounter in the 1890s through the brief British takeover of Gisaka in 1923-24. The British had even considered installing Bigirumwami's father, the devout Catholic and former seminarian Joseph Rukambwa, as an autonomous regional chief. Considering this context, Bigirumwami was fortunate to receive a name that meant "all things belong to the *mwami*."

Bigirumwami's Catholic *bona fides* were no less impressive than his noble pedigree. His family converted to Christianity in the early 1900s; his 1904 baptism was one of the first at Zaza mission station. At the tender age of nine, Bigirumwami became one of the first Rwandans to enter Kabgayi's minor seminary, the first

Catholic school for boys considering the priesthood. Significantly, Laurent Déprimoz, the seminary's rector and future Vicar Apostolic of Kabgayi, became his spiritual mentor. It was Déprimoz who shepherded Bigirumwami through the seminary system, witnessed his ordination in 1929, appointed him as superior of Muramba mission, and named him as one of the first indigenous members of the church's presbyteral (priest) council.

The day of Bigirumwami's ordination, June 1, 1952, rivaled the 1950 Save jubilee as a day of national celebration.[84] 25,000 Rwandans gathered for Bigirumwami's consecration at Kabgayi, including 350 European representatives, all of Rwanda's fifty-two chiefs, representatives from Rwanda's forty-five Catholic missions, official delegations from Burundi and Belgian Congo, and two of the first three African Catholic bishops in modern history (Uganda's Joseph Kiwanuka and Tanzania's Laurean Rugambwa). Déprimoz formally consecrated Bigirumwami as a bishop and spoke of how this event fulfilled Lavigerie's nineteenth-century dream of "evangelizing Africa through Africa." Days of celebration preceded and followed the event as tens of thousands of people lined the roads leading to and from Kabgayi. In his own public remarks, Bigirumwami professed his fidelity to Rwanda and to the missionaries who had brought the gospel to his native land, stating that "they were and remain our Fathers in the faith."[85] If the Mwami's 1946 dedication of Rwanda to Christ the King marked the apogee of Rwandan Christendom, the 1952 ordination of Aloys Bigirumwami to the Catholic episcopate symbolized the pinnacle of European-Rwandan cooperation in building one of the most robust Catholic churches in Africa. As Durrieu wrote in a congratulatory letter to Bigirumwami, "whether secular African clergy or foreign missionary clergy, our providential destiny is to work together in this divine work...in perfect fraternal unity."[86]

As so often in Rwandan history, however, the public façade of unity masked deeper internal divisions. First among these were rising intraclerical tensions between indigenous clergy and European priests. Whatever his collegial words to Bigirumwami, Durrieu was already on record in 1949 positing "the profound differences which psychologically separate us [Europeans] from the blacks." In turn, the 1950–51 Kabgayi annual report described black-white relations in the vicariate as "very delicate."[87] Missionaries in 1952 lamented the "xenophobic nationalism, lack of candor, schismatic spirit, and Machiavellian conduct" of African priests. At the same time, the Belgian minister for colonies distinguished between indigenous priests "tinged with white" and "integrally black priests" who betrayed an African materialism more concerned with secular influence than spiritual gain.[88] For his part, Bigirumwami grew increasingly frustrated with European missionaries' refusal to serve under secular Rwandan clergy, a pattern that he saw contributing to a "lack of understanding and fraternal charity" on the side of the Rwandan priests or *abbés*.[89]

FIGURE 3.1 Aloys Bigirumwami speaking at his installation as Vicar Apostolic of Nyundo, June 1952 (*courtesy General Archives of the Missionaries of Africa, Rome*).

Nor did European observers spare Bigirumwami from critique. Shortly after his consecration, the aforementioned Belgian colonial official W.V. Hove offered a comprehensive summary of the critiques directed at Nyundo's new vicar apostolic.

"[Bigirumwami] is too pledged to the politics of the White Fathers for the nationalist priests, too indifferent to indigenous public life for the chiefs and the sub-chiefs, too rigid from a disciplinary point of view and too heretical for the Hutu priests, too foreign for the chauvinist Tutsi, a little old for the priests of the new school."[90]

Nor was Bigirumwami a close confidant of Mutara or his Nyanza circle. He even refused the Mwami's 1954 invitation to serve on Rwanda's first Superior Council despite the presence of two other priests.[91] At the same time, Bigirumwami challenged the White Fathers when he deemed it necessary, defending the boundaries of his vicariate and protesting the treatment of Nyundo seminarians.[92] As we will see in subsequent chapters, Bigirumwami's independent streak would leave him in an awkward if often-prophetic political position as Rwandan ecclesial and political life became more polarized in the late 1950s and early 1960s.

The Nyakibanda Seminary Crisis and the Rise of André Perraudin

The major seminary of Nyakibanda replaced the former major seminary at Kabgayi in 1936. Intended as a regional seminary for African students from Rwanda, Burundi, and the Kivu districts of eastern Congo, Nyakibanda graduated 143 African priests in the 1930s and 1940s—over 25 percent of all African Catholic priests ordained during those two decades.[93] Since the Catholic seminary remained one of the few avenues for higher education in Rwanda, the seminary served an important social role, as many former seminarians moved into politics, business, journalism, and education. In light of this, the church faced considerable pressure to ensure that the seminary contributed to both religious and social unity. As André Perraudin wrote in a 1954 letter to his brother, "we know well that the religious and even human future of these regions is at play in the Major Seminary."[94] By the early 1950s, however, morale was sinking as unprecedented numbers of seminarians left Nyakibanda. While 47 percent of major seminarians persevered to ordination between 1909 and 1946, 66 percent of the major seminarian population turned over between 1949 and 1953.[95] In light of the seminary's continuing importance for forming Rwanda's future social and political elites, the divisions that wracked Nyakibanda in the early 1950s had the potential to subvert Rwandan society.

Nyakibanda's turnover resulted from divisions between faculty and students and tensions between the seminarians themselves. Durrieu attributed much of the blame to the seminary's White Father professors. Rather than form "men of the church," Nyakibanda professors were alienating the seminarians and driving them into the hands of anti-Belgian nationalists and other "propagators of subversive doctrine."[96] Notable here was the degree to which missionary commentators analyzed these tensions in nationalist rather than ethnicist language, writing for example that "the mentality of the Banyarwanda is very different than that of surrounding peoples, and it seems that we cannot employ the same means with them as with the others."[97] While Tutsi comprised a sizeable majority of Rwandan Catholic seminarians at the time, the language of "Bahutu" and "Batutsi" does not appear here. Nyakibanda's divisions are described in international rather than intra-ethnic terms.

This stemmed in part from the fact that national rather than ethnic identities were driving the seminarian community apart in the early 1950s.[98] In 1951, the seminary's Banyarwanda majority demanded the establishment of a separate

FIGURE 3.2 Nyakibanda Major Seminary (*Author Photo, 2010*)

seminary for Burundian and Congolese students. Rather than acquiesce to these demands, Nyakibanda's rector, the White Father Xavier Seumois, dismissed four of the Rwandan seminarians. Following this, a small coterie of the remaining Rwandans took the unusual step of sending an official letter to Rome requesting Seumois's dismissal, highlighting his Belgian identity, previous missionary service in Burundi, and alleged bias in favor of the Burundian students. During the first three months of 1952, twenty-three seminarians departed Nyakibanda, including over half of the Burundian student population.

The White Fathers themselves disagreed on the proper response. On one side was Déprimoz, the champion of the indigenous clergy who had stated as early as 1949 that Seumois should resign and sided with the Rwandan seminarians in the latest dispute. On the other side was Durrieu, the White Father superior general who had resisted the appointment of an indigenous bishop and feared the consequences of acquiescing to seminarian pressure. Whatever his frustrations with Nyakibanda's White Father professors, Durrieu had no love for Rwanda's indigenous clergy. He accused the Rwandan clergy of corrupting the seminarians and even chastised Déprimoz for tolerating insubordination in the seminary and undermining Seumois's authority. As the situation continued to deteriorate throughout 1952, however, Déprimoz's position grew stronger. In September, the White Fathers agreed to limit Nyakibanda to Rwandans and reassigned the seminary's Burundian and Congolese students to Burundi's new major seminary at

Burasira, reducing Nyakibanda's population from eighty-three to fifty. The White Fathers also decided to appoint a new Swiss rector to replace the Belgian Seumois. The man they chose, Fr. André Perraudin, was one of the few Nyakibanda professors whose reputation had improved between 1950 and 1952.

Born in 1914 in the mountainous region of Valée de Bagnes in French-speaking Switzerland, André Perraudin was one of nine children of a devout Catholic schoolmaster.[99] Two aspiring White Fathers in his rural parish encouraged André and his brother Jean to join the Missionaries of Africa. His parents enthusiastically supported their sons' vocations. As early as 1925, they wrote glowingly of their "future missionaries." A decade later, they expressed their hopes that "God will bless you and grant you all that you need to become good missionaries after the heart of Jesus."[100] After attending a White Father minor seminary in Valais, Perraudin pursued his philosophy studies in France before completing his novitiate in Algeria and his scholasticate in Tunisia. After ordination in 1939, he initially dreamed of undertaking an apostolate to Muslims in North Africa or the Middle East like his cousin Hubert Bruchez.[101]

As the shadows of the Second World War spread across Europe, such dreams were placed on hold. The White Fathers sent Perraudin back to Switzerland where he spent the war years directing a minor seminary in his hometown of Valais and overseeing a new White Father scholasticate in Fribourg. These years saw the French-speaking Perraudin develop a deep antipathy for Nazism and its sympathizers in German-speaking Switzerland. As we will see later, he would read political developments in late 1950s Rwanda in part through the Nazi prism.[102]

By the end of the war, Perraudin's evangelical interests had shifted from the Middle East to the White Fathers' most successful missions in Africa's Great Lakes region. His missionary opportunity finally came in 1947. Dispatched to replace his brother Jean in Burundi, Perraudin ministered for two and a half years in the rural mission station of Kibumbu. This mission included 20,000 Christians, representing over 25 percent of the local population. It was also dominated by Tutsi pastoralists. For all of its potential, Kibumbu struggled to sustain a regular worshiping community.[103] Despite these challenges, Perraudin's early comments reflected the enthusiasm of a new missionary. "Our brave people are certainly far from perfection, but their Christian behavior can well serve as a lesson to Europe where religion too often tends to become a religion of Sunday...Missionary life seems magnificent to me in Burundi."[104]

Perraudin did note Hutu-Tutsi distinctions in his early letters. He described a Hutu man in one letter as "one of the subjects of an inferior caste" and elsewhere mentioned his own experience instructing a "semi-circle of Batutsi of the purest kind." Overall, though, this early correspondence does not dwell on ethnic distinctions or tensions. Rather, Perraudin celebrated the cultural and spiritual transformation wrought by Christianity in Burundi—a nation Perraudin described as existing in a "miserable state" prior to the arrival of the first Catholic mission-aries.[105] He also noted the challenge of translating Burundians' frequent confessional practice into behavioral change, lamenting that "the old pagan blood still circulates very vividly in our neophytes."[106]

For all of his pastoral zeal, Perraudin was an intellectual with years of experience forming young seminarians back in Switzerland. Because of this, he was not left toiling in rural mission stations for very long. In June 1950, the White Fathers appointed him as a professor at Nyakibanda major seminary.[107] Perraudin arrived in Rwanda during the August 1950 golden jubilee of Save mission. Not surprisingly, his first impression of Rwanda was that of a flourishing church. In a reflection written shortly after Save's three-day celebration, Perraudin highlighted "white and black ministers fraternally united in service of the same Master." He also praised the White Fathers and Belgium for placing Rwanda on a path to "true progress," describing the Eucharistic host as a "sun for destroying the pagan night and its miseries."[108]

Perraudin himself flourished in his new role as seminary professor. Echoing Lavigerie, he wrote early in his tenure that the faculty's goal was "not to make them Europeans but good priests of the country from which they come."[109] Perraudin taught a wide range of courses including sociology, morality, pedagogy, canon law, and a two-month diaconal course on justice. His most popular class was missiology.[110] Engaging questions of ethnology, local culture, and church growth, missiology was a perennial favorite among the Rwandan seminarians. Perraudin gained even more adherents by expanding the curricular focus to include broader questions of European-African race relations, the tensions between Western and customary law, and "the problem of evolution," namely Rwanda's development from a feudal monarchy to a modern capitalist democracy. Perraudin also deemphasized the traditional ethnological component of Catholic missiology. "This course should be conceived differently than in Europe: treating systematically ethnology seems to me extremely delicate considering the reactions which would be produced in the audience."[111] His superiors seemed less hesitant, however, recommending that Perraudin address the "delicate questions" through a full presentation of Catholic social doctrine. Unmentioned, however, is the content of these "delicate questions," whether the Hutu-Tutsi distinction or something else.[112]

As Perraudin developed a devoted following at Nyakibanda, he became the logical choice to succeed Seumois as seminary rector after the crisis of 1951–52. His nomination documents praise his intellectual gifts, linguistic skills, pastoral judgment, personal holiness, and political moderation. As a Swiss native, he also stood outside of the Belgian paradigm; Perraudin's nationality would serve him well as he advanced up the church ladder in the early 1950s. He also appeared to be one of the few European professors who retained a "great and profound influence" on the seminarians.[113] Perraudin himself attributed his positive relations with the Rwandan seminarians to his lack of "caste" prejudice, a seeming reference to Hutu-Tutsi distinctions which Perraudin at this point never described in racial terms. "I do not believe... that I have a very bad press among the Banyarwanda. I have not come here like others with the ideas of caste."[114] Perraudin's only short-coming was his initial posting in the Burundian missions; Rwandan seminarians tended to oppose missionaries seen as having Burundian sympathies. But this issue was fading with the transfer of the Burundian seminarians in 1952, and the White Fathers subsequently appointed Perraudin as the new rector of Nyakibanda in September.

After being appointed rector, Perraudin cleaned the slate. He worked with his superiors to replace or reassign all six of Nyakibanda's faculty members. Four were transferred from the seminary, and the other two were assigned new subjects.[115] He also decided not to inform newly hired professors about Nyakibanda's recent problems. "It is perhaps better moreover for the orientation of new personnel that they not know the former atmosphere."[116] As we will see in subsequent chapters, this would not be the last time that Perraudin would attempt to "clean the slate" after a particularly controversial period.

In his years as rector, Perraudin also developed an uneven relationship with Bigirumwami.[117] In light of the seminary's recent struggles, the White Fathers asked Perraudin in 1952 to coordinate a curricular overhaul at Nyakibanda. Perraudin consented to his superiors' plans to exclude Bigirumwami from this process, preferring to keep the new curriculum firmly under White Father control. In early 1953, he antagonized Bigirumwami when he refused to allow several Nyundo minor seminarians to commence studies at Nyakibanda. Tensions increased further when Perraudin expelled several Nyundo major seminarians during 1954. In addition, Perraudin vigorously opposed Bigirumwami's 1952–1953 requests to send Nyundo seminarians to Rome in part because Perraudin saw Pontifical Urbaniana, the Roman college dedicated to the missions, as "anti-white." He went so far as to describe Bigirumwami's plans as "premature innovations on the part of a young Vicar Apostolic," language that he later came to regret.[118] Although Déprimoz supported Bigirumwami's plans to send his seminarians abroad, Perraudin temporarily convinced Bigirumwami to follow the strictures of a recent episcopal conference that counseled against sending Africa seminarians to Rome.[119] But after Bigirumwami sent several seminarians to Louvain, Belgium in 1954, Perraudin lamented Bigirumwami's seeming lack of confidence in Nyakibanda seminary.[120]

Like Durrieu, Perraudin also worried that indigenous clergy were corrupting Rwanda's seminarians.[121] Calling for a reduction in seminarian vacation time, Perraudin lamented the "critical spirit" in the mission stations. Significantly, he attributed this spirit in part to the "psychosis of independence" which had grown "especially since the consecration of His Excellency Mgr. Bigirumwami."[122]

Although Perraudin lauded improvements in seminarian formation during the course of 1953 and 1954, he continued to view the sanctification of the clergy and clerical unity as the most pressing problems facing the Rwandan church. He feared that social changes in Rwanda would spark further intraclerical divisions and worried especially about inter-racial clerical tensions in the parishes. While admitting the reality of racist European attitudes toward Africans, Perraudin also worried about black racism toward whites, insisting that the church's catholicity provided the only long-term solution to the problem. In an effort to address the problem directly, Perraudin in 1955 instituted recollection days for local clergy at Nyakibanda.

Like many of his confreres, Perraudin saw Catholic social teaching as the antidote to many of the nationalist and inter-racial tensions that threatened to divide Rwanda's clergy.[123] Shaped especially by the French theologian Jacques Leclerq—a writer who shared Jacques Maritain's commitment to a "new Christendom" which would embody Christian values in an increasingly pluralistic European context—Perraudin saw the clergy as teachers who would guide laity in living out their Christian vocations in the world.[124] In his 1952 annual report from Nyakibanda, Perraudin wrote of the need to "form their [seminarians'] consciences on questions of justice." A year later, he agreed that the key to Rwanda's healthy political evolution was the influence of Catholic social doctrine on Banyarwandan morals and institutions. In turn, Perraudin's lectures frequently addressed contemporary political events, and his missiology curriculum engaged problems of public security, the judiciary, and the distribution of public offices.

But while Professor Perraudin showed a definite concern for issues of social justice, one must be careful about transforming him into some kind of proto-liberation theologian.[125] Although his views would shift during Rwanda's revolutionary years of 1959–1962, the early Perraudin comes across as a man of Catholic Action, more concerned with forming strong Catholic elites (e.g., chiefs, teachers, *évolués*) than in demanding any kind of preferential option for the poor (Hutu or otherwise). And contrary to the anti-statist critique of much liberation theology, Perraudin continued to support a broad alliance between church and state, writing as early as 1947 that missionary works had resulted from the "fruit of the sincere collaboration of the Church and the government of the colony."[126] If anything, the real proto-liberationist churchman of the mid-1950s was Arthur Dejemeppe, the aforementioned vicar general of Kabgayi. In his two years at the helm of the Catholic newspaper *Kinyamateka*, Dejemeppe shifted the newspaper's editorial line from Kagame's focus on Rwanda's cultural past toward a strong and at times strident emphasis on social justice.[127]

With the exception of the "caste" language mentioned earlier, Perraudin rarely referenced a Hutu-Tutsi problem in the early 1950s.[128] To be sure, Perraudin wrote in the 1952 Nyakibanda annual report of wanting to foster "a more forthright fusion between subjects of the different races and vicariates" and attributed seminary tensions to "the human tendency of people of the same ethnic group to come together." Yet in this same report he noted that the White Fathers' decision to relocate the Burundian and Congolese seminarians stemmed from a desire to "suppress at its root certain difficulties stemming from ethnic differences"—a comment which reflected how easily ethnic and national language could meld and overlap. Later in 1953, Perraudin traced intra-ecclesial divisions to political agitation, the promise of independence, and "fights between blacks and whites," but he never mentioned Hutu-Tutsi tensions. Likewise, White Father superiors praised Perraudin for "maintaining perfect union between the two clerical factions in Rwanda." The language of "two" rather than "three" should be noted—the division here was black-white, not Hutu-Tutsi-European. Even in his 2003 autobiography, Perraudin wrote that "there were no visible ethnic problems during my sojourn at the major seminary of Nyakibanda," claiming that he only realized the extent of Tutsi clerical domination after being named Vicar Apostolic of Kabgayi in 1956. Namely, of the 100 priests that Perraudin ordained between 1951 and 1962, 75 were classified as Tutsi.[129]

Whatever their origins, the divisions that rent the Nyakibanda community in the late 1940s and early 1950s healed considerably by the 1954–1955 academic year.[130] The seminarian population rebounded from its 1953 low of fifty to a 1955 high of sixty-seven. White Fathers in Rome described the students as "serious" and "submissive to authority," the professorial staff as "homogenous," and Perraudin as "supernatural." In particular, Perraudin's superiors attributed the improvement to Perraudin's calm but resolute leadership as well as the decision to turn Nyakibanda into an exclusively Banyarwanda seminary (thus eliminating the Burundian-Rwandan-Congolese tensions of previous years). European-African clerical tensions remained problematic but now stood alongside more perennial challenges like a new clerical petition to remove the obligation of priestly celibacy. As 1955 began, the major seminary of Nyakibanda seemed restored to its former stability, the infighting of the early 1950s a distant memory. And as Nyakibanda's atmosphere improved, the reputation of its rector rose to the point that a priest who had only worked in the country for five years became the leading candidate to assume the most important ecclesial post in Rwanda.

The sudden vacancy at the head of the Kabgayi vicariate came about through unfortunate circumstances. Although the seventy-year-old Déprimoz had struggled with medical problems for years, he continued serving as Vicar Apostolic until he broke his leg in an overnight accident on January 17, 1955.[131] The injury required him to seek treatment in Belgium. In March Déprimoz decided that Kabgayi's demands were too much for him to bear. As Déprimoz tendered his resignation to the Vatican, the search began for a suitable replacement.[132]

An obvious contender was Fr. Arthur Dejemeppe, the man appointed as interim administrator of Kabgayi vicariate after Déprimoz's January injury.[133] Dejemeppe had replaced Déprimoz's close confidant R. P. Endriatis as vicar general in 1954, perhaps in response to Endriatis's and Déprimoz's perceived biases toward the indigenous clergy and traditionalists at court.[134] Close to Prosper Bwanakweri and the other Astridiens, Dejemeppe had also accompanied Gregoire Kayibanda to the international *Jeunesse Ouvrière Chrétienne* (JOC) conference in Belgium in 1950. He later proved instrumental in Kayibanda's appointments as editor of *L'Ami* in 1953 and editor of *Kinyamateka* in 1955. Dejemeppe also attended the February 1954 opening of Rwanda's new Superior Council, an event that he celebrated as "a commencement of the democratization of [Rwandan] institutions."[135] By 1955, however, Dejemeppe's activism had become as much of a liability as Déprimoz's perceived passivity. He was criticized for needlessly alienating the Mwami, Rwanda's traditional leadership, the majority of *évolués*, and even the Belgian colonial resident. Even as a few indigenous priests spoke up in his defense, Dejemeppe was never seriously considered for the final appointment as Vicar Apostolic.[136]

Rather than Dejemeppe, the White Fathers proposed three candidates to Propaganda Fide in May 1955—Johannes Hartmann, Alphonse Van Hoof, and André Perraudin.[137] In nominating three Europeans, the White Fathers demonstrated that they were not quite ready to concede full leadership of Rwanda's church to indigenous clergy. Born in the Flemish-speaking area of Belgium in 1921, Hartmann served as superior of the minor seminary of Kabgayi. Praised for improving discipline and morale in the seminary, the thirty-four-year-old Hartmann was also criticized for his youth and deemed too "timid" for the job.[138] Van Hoof, himself a Flemish native of Antwerp in Belgium, offered a stronger portfolio. In fact, the White Fathers had just appointed Van Hoof to serve as their regional superior for the Rwandan and Burundian vicariates. While praised for his intelligence, piety, zeal, and lack of racial bias, Van Hoof was also known for his brusque manner, a particular liability for a bishop in Rwanda. Even more significantly, he was a Flemish Belgian at a moment when Belgian-Rwandan relations were becoming increasingly tenuous.

Perraudin thus emerged as the leading candidate for the job.[139] A Swiss national whose country had no colonial designs in the region, Perraudin was also an intellectual whose passion for social justice did not trump his overriding commitment to ecclesial and national unity. Unlike the more traditionalist Déprimoz or the social democrat Dejemeppe, Perraudin was not strongly associated with the growing ideological and ethnic factions within the church.[140] His nominating documents highlight his success in restoring harmony to Nyakibanda and his positive relationships with white and black clergy. His superiors also praised Perraudin's spiritual depth and diplomatic skills while underlining his willingness to stand up to indigenous authorities, Rwandan priests, and Mgr. Bigirumwami. Most importantly, Perraudin was not French or Belgian. In the words of Antoine Grauls, the Vicar Apostolic of Gitega in Burundi, "there is an anti-Belgian movement which has developed for a long time and in particular in recent times, and I believe that a foreigner would be more easily accepted."[141] Even Perraudin's relative novelty on the Rwandan stage could be viewed as a strength—he appeared as an attractive new face for a new moment in the history of the Rwandan church. In Durrieu's concluding recommendation, "I know little personally about Fr. Perraudin, but what I know makes me think that he is the man of the situation in Rwanda." In a nonbinding survey of White Fathers in Rwanda, Perraudin outpolled Van Hoof by twenty-five votes to thirteen.[142]

Despite the approbations, however, the Holy See's decision did not come for months.[143] By October, missionaries openly worried about the delay, noting that the issue of episcopal succession in Kabgayi had become a point of political gossip. The Nyanza superior described the royal capital as reaching a "boiling point," while the Italian superior of Save depicted Rwanda as "akin to a stormy sea." Even Durrieu sent an impassioned letter to Propaganda Fide demanding an immediate decision. Local clergy wondered if the delay portended the appointment of another indigenous bishop.

Christmas finally brought the long-awaited news. Privately notified on December 19, 1955, Perraudin was publicly announced as the new Vicar Apostolic of Kabgayi on December 30.[144] The initial reaction was enthusiastic. Missionaries lauded Perraudin as "the man of the moment," noting the positive reaction of the indigenous clergy to the selection of a non-Belgian known for assuaging white-black tensions at Nyakibanda. "Mgr. Perraudin...is universally known and liked in Rwanda for his supernatural spirit, his clear views, his good will and his simplicity. We are all of one heart with him."[145] The extent to which "the most chic brother in the Vicariate" retained this initial popularity will be considered in the next chapter.[146]

In describing Catholic politics in early 1950s Rwanda, I have underlined three important points for the overarching study. First, the Catholic Church continued to support a top-down approach to mission. The new element in the 1950s was the church's focus on the *évolués*, the rising generation of Rwandan elites who had been trained in Catholic and colonial schools. In this sense, church leaders recalibrated rather than rejected Lavigerie's and Classe's focus on elite conversion.

Second, Rwandan politics in the early 1950s concerned a far wider array of themes than the Hutu-Tutsi question. These issues of secularization, democratization, anti-communism, and Christian civilization in turn provide important ideological contexts for understanding the polarizing nature of later Hutu-Tutsi disputes in the late 1950s. In turn, nationalist and racial tensions predated the emergence of the Hutu-Tutsi question inside the Rwandan church. Rwandan, Congolese and Burundian seminarians were already separating in 1951 and 1952, reflecting the salience of national identity in a political era marked by accelerating calls for decolonization and African nationalism. These nationalist and anti-colonial tensions also divided European missionaries from African priests inside Rwanda.

We have also been introduced to Perraudin and Bigirumwami, the two church-men who would come to symbolize the contrasting poles of Catholic politics in Rwanda. Bigirumwami has emerged here as an independent figure, close to White Father mentors like Déprimoz while retaining a critical distance from Mwami Mutara and younger White Father missionaries. For his part, Perraudin cultivated a largely apolitical image in the early 1950s. However, his correspondence and seminary work revealed his commitments to social justice, church-state partner-ship, and the importance of maintaining an influential Catholic voice in the public sphere. In contrast, Perraudin largely steered clear of ethnic issues in the early years of the decade, rarely framing his political and social views in Hutu-Tutsi terms. This would change as the decade progressed.

4

The Irruption of Hutu-Tutsi Tensions, 1956–1959

IF NARRATIVES OF democratization and anti-communism dominated Rwandan politics in the early 1950s, the Hutu-Tutsi question emerged in the latter years of the decade as the polarizing division in Rwandan political life. The surfacing of the ethnic question stemmed in part from Tutsi elites' failure to share political power and in part from Hutu elites' growing recognition of the electoral salience of ethnic labels. Belgian colonial officials played their part as well, moving away from Mwami Mutara and his court and toward a rising group of Hutu elites who promised fealty to Belgium, the Catholic Church, and majoritarian democracy. The 1957 Bahutu Manifesto and an increasingly independent Catholic media broke previous taboos in publicly criticizing Mwami Mutara and many of Rwanda's customary chiefs. For their part, the Mwami and his allies adopted a more adversarial position toward both Belgium and Hutu counter-elites, claiming the anti-colonial mantle and demanding immediate independence. At the same time, political debates from the period reveal the continuing fluidity of Hutu-Tutsi categories; even in the late 1950s these categories are presented in alternatively economic, social, and racial terms. Finally, the unexpected death of Mwami Mutara in July 1959 and the anticipation of "winner take all" elections in early 1960 unleashed a three-month political mobilization which left Rwanda deeply polarized between Hutu ethnicist and Tutsi nationalist parties.

Appointed Vicar Apostolic of Kabgayi for his perceived political moderation, lack of Belgian colonial ties, and newness on the Rwandan stage, Mgr. André Perraudin publicly avoided political and ethnic issues during the first three years of his episcopate. While Catholic lay elites like Gregoire Kayibanda, Joseph Gitera and Aloys Munyangaju led an increasingly strident grassroots campaign for Hutu rights, Perraudin, Aloys Bigirumwami, the White Father Guy Mosmans and other ecclesial leaders did not speak out publicly on the Hutu-Tutsi question until late 1958. When these churchmen finally entered the debate, however, they revealed a fundamental analytical divergence over the nature of the political and social problems facing Rwanda. In an influential European newspaper article in September 1958, Bigirumwami cast doubt on the nature of the Hutu-Tutsi distinction and called for Rwanda to embrace national unity and pan-ethnic social justice. In February 1959, Perraudin released his famous Lenten pastoral "*Super omnia caritas.*" Even as he shared Bigirumwami's broad Catholic emphases on charity, justice, and unity, Perraudin framed Rwanda's political and social problems in explicitly Hutu-Tutsi terms. This divergence on the ethnic question placed Rwanda's two Catholic leaders on opposite sides of a growing analytical divide between Hutu and Tutsi elites and undermined both leaders' cherished goal of clerical unity. In turn, Perraudin's perceived efforts to push the Catholic Church away from its traditional cohabitation with the Tutsi monarchy to a new egalitarian emphasis in favor of the Hutu masses led to charges of ethnic divisionism and revolutionary incitement, charges we will consider in the conclusion of this chapter.

Perraudin's Consecration and the Emergence of the Hutu-Tutsi Question

1956 began with great promise for Rwanda. Following the introduction of a degree of representative government in 1953, U.N.-mandated triennial elections were scheduled for September 1956. For the first time, all Rwandan men (if not yet women) would be able to vote to elect representatives for Rwanda's *sous-chefferie* councils. In turn, the *Mouvement Politique Progressiste* (MPP) offered a potential pan-ethnic nationalist movement for pursuing democratic political reform. Mwami Mutara's reputation as a Western modernizer and recent suppression of *uburetwa* and *ubuhake* reflected an openness to political change. And within the Catholic Church, the elevations of Aloys Bigirumwami and André Perraudin represented a generational shift in Catholic missionary leadership, portending a new era in the life of the Rwandan Catholic Church.

   The iconic image of this new era came on March 25, 1956, the day of Perraudin's installation as vicar apostolic. To emphasize the indigenization of the church, Perraudin requested that Bigirumwami serve as the official episcopal consecrator rather than the Apostolic Nuncio to Belgian Africa.[1] This would become the first known instance in modern history of a black bishop consecrating a white priest to the Catholic episcopate. In the midst of South Africa's anti-apartheid struggle, growing racial tensions in the southern United States, and rising nationalist currents across Africa, the image of Bigirumwami laying his hands on Perraudin splashed across international newspapers, symbolizing the seeming interracial harmony of the global Catholic communion. Perraudin recognized the symbolic moment in his homily. "This is the first time perhaps in the annals of the world (that) a black bishop has conferred the plenitude of the priesthood on a white priest…the Church is in all the races, in the heart of all the races, unifying them from the inside."² Inside Rwanda, Bigirumwami's consecration of Perraudin offered much-needed political capital for the beleaguered White Fathers. In the words of Leo Volker, soon to be named Superior General of the White Fathers, "the event should be exploited to the maximum."³

Whatever the visual audacity of his consecration, Perraudin's early statements represented more a spirit of continuity than radical change. A February 1956 letter to Catholic clergy in the vicariate of Kabgayi spoke of the need to continue the "march of Christian progress" in Rwanda. His first pastoral letter focused on the importance of hierarchical authority in the church while warning of the continuing danger of communism.⁴ In his homily on the day of his consecration to the episcopate, Perraudin reiterated the importance of a close alliance between church and state for protecting the common good. "When the spiritual power and the temporal power get on well, the world is well-governed...you will find always in the Vicar Apostolic of Kabgayi a servant fully devoted to the dear country of Rwanda."⁵ Perraudin's first annual report stressed his obligation to Christianize Rwanda "in its institutions, in its cultural, social, and familial life, so that the word of Christ will be the uncontested King."⁶

FIGURE 4.1 Mgr. Perraudin greets wellwishers after his installation as Vicar Apostolic of Kabgayi, March 1956 (*courtesy General Archives of the Missionaries of Africa, Rome*)

FIGURE 4.2 The Catholic Cathedral at Kabgayi (*Author Photo, May 2010*)

If Perraudin retained Classe's and Déprimoz's emphases on Christian civilization, anti-communism, and church-state cohabitation, the new Vicar Apostolic showed a particular interest in questions of social justice. Even before his consecration, he organized a February 1956 gathering on Catholic social teaching that addressed themes like worker pensions and universal suffrage. Weeks after becoming Vicar Apostolic, Perraudin announced that the summer retreat for priests would consist of four study days concerning social questions in Rwanda. These July seminars reinforced what Perraudin termed the "very grave obligations of social justice" for preaching and confessional practice alike. While reminding priests that they were "men of God and the Church" and should not partake in "partisan political fights," Perraudin also instructed his priests to take responsibility for the social education of their parishioners. This included encouraging laity to take part in syndicates, mutualities, and cooperatives and reminding lay Catholics of their duty to participate in political life.[7]

As he took the bishop's miter, Perraudin encountered an increasingly recalcitrant Mwami Mutara. As discussed in chapter three, relations between the Mwami and the White Fathers had begun declining with the 1945 death of Léon

Classe. The Astridien and lay schools controversies only furthered these growing tensions. At the same time, Mutara continued to enjoy a reputation in Rome
and Brussels as a devout African Catholic king and trusted friend of Belgium.[8]
As Mutara prepared to celebrate his 25th anniversary as Mwami in 1956-57, the
Vatican proposed elevating Rwanda's king to the honorary rank of papal nobility. Although missionaries had celebrated when the Holy See enrolled Mutara in
the papal order of Gregory the Great in 1947, many White Fathers now saw the
Mwami as an obstacle to the future growth of the church. When asked his opinion
on the proposed papal honor, Perraudin refused to endorse Mutara while revealing his typical diplomatic caution. "I find the decision very delicate for reasons
which are difficult to write."[9] Ultimately, Rome granted Mutara the honor. As we
will see in subsequent chapters, this was not the last time that the Vatican and the
White Fathers differed over Rwandan politics.

Even as Perraudin struggled to develop a rapport with Mwami Mutara,
Kabgayi's new Vicar Apostolic looked with anticipation to Rwanda's September
1956 legislative elections.[10] In offering a universal male franchise for the first time,
these elections raised popular expectations for continued reform and sparked
deeper interest in a political process that had been heretofore an elite domain.
Anticipating a popular mandate, the national *Conseil Supérieur du Pays* (CSP) proposed a new executive office of CSP president. While suspicious of this potential
rival to his authority, Mutara embraced universal suffrage in hopes of establishing his government's democratic *bona fides*. For his part, Perraudin welcomed the
democratic turn in Rwandan politics, publishing a pastoral letter in September
1956 in which he embraced the principle of universal suffrage, reminded Catholic
laity of their civic obligation to vote for virtuous candidates, and encouraged
Rwandan politicians to avoid undue partisanship.[11]

Over 75 percent of Rwandan men voted in the 1956 legislative elections. Most
supported Hutu candidates at the local level—the percentage of Hutu sub-chiefs
rose from 50 percent in 1953 to 66 percent after the 1956 elections. At the higher
appointed levels of Rwanda's government, Rwanda's customary authorities remained
entrenched. After the elections Tutsi elites controlled 81 percent of Rwanda's territorial
council seats, 57 percent of colonial administrative positions, and 31 of the 32 seats on
Rwanda's superior council. Members of Rwanda's traditionally dominant Abanyiginya
and Abega clans led over 50 percent of the colony's *sous-chefferies* and 80 percent of its
chefferies after the elections.[12] While the elections appeared to reinforce Rwanda's traditional rulers, they also contained signs of coming change. Although Mwami Mutara
had denied the existence of a Hutu-Tutsi problem as recently as February 1956, the
major discrepancy between Hutu and Tutsi representatives at the local versus national
levels of government did not bode well for the future.[13]

Even before the September elections, the ethnic question was emerging more
prominently in Catholic newspapers. In July 1956, the Bukavu, Congo-based

La Presse Africaine published *"Un Abbé ruandaise: nous parle."*[14] Purportedly reflecting the views of an anonymous Rwandan priest, the article was dismissed by some as a colonial effort to sully the local clergy.[15] It detailed the rivalry between Prosper Bwanakweri and Mwami Mutara, positing that the former's progressive vision offered hope for a Hutu people "abused by centuries of servitude and famine." The interview sparked a series of replies and ripostes in *La Presse Africaine*, Leopoldville's *Le Courrier d'Afrique*, and the White Fathers' Bujumbura-based *Temps Nouveaux d'Afrique.*[16] These articles raised taboo subjects such as the machinations surrounding Mwami Mutara's 1931 accession to the throne, the history of Hutu-Tutsi relations, the nature of the Hutu-Tutsi distinction, and even the Mwami's own ethnic identity. In contrast to the traditional vision of Rwanda as a harmonious society of integrated social groups, this new literature painted a highly conflictual picture of deep social and ethnic stratification. In the words of one anonymous polemicist, "the reign of Tutsi terror has existed since before the arrival of the whites."[17] Regardless of its veracity, this media controversy made what colonial governor Jean-Paul Harroy later termed "an enormous impact" on Rwandan social discourse.[18]

The controversy reached the point that Mwami Mutara intervened. Writing in a September 1956 issue of *Temps Nouveaux d'Afrique*, Mutara reemphasized the traditional image of precolonial Rwanda as a place of social mobility, ethnic intermingling, and cultural unity. "Rwanda is a habitat of one homogenous people where rights should be the same for all and not a field of quarrels between racial and social factions."[19] A month later a group of Tutsi chiefs echoed these sentiments, writing that after centuries of intermixing, "Rwanda has become a land of one homogenous people" where "all ethnic distinction is impossible."[20]

After years of focusing on the *évolué* question, Catholic missionary leaders in 1956 also began framing political questions in more explicitly Hutu-Tutsi terms. Guy Mosmans, the Belgian provincial of the White Fathers, reacted with cynicism to Mutara's decision to embrace universal suffrage. "One thinks that he has adopted this attitude in hopes that the result of the votes would favor the Batutsi and that this would demonstrate that the Council which is composed of a majority of Batutsi represents all the country."[21] Perraudin admitted privately that many Rwandans traced the emergence of the ethnic question to the Kabgayi vicariate and the Catholic *Kinyamateka* newspaper. He also noted that the mission posts of Nyagahanga and Rwaza had experienced Hutu-Tutsi strains ahead of the September elections.[22] In these early comments, Perraudin framed the Hutu-Tutsi question in terms of political access and abuse, placing the blame on the shoulders of local authorities and defending the church's right to speak on moral issues.

> One notes rising tension between Bahutu and Batutsi; the Bahutu want more and more the lead and do not want to trail behind…I have permitted

myself to say to the Governor and the Mwami that one of the immediate remedies is to fight more and more seriously against certain exactions of those who are in power, and that the Church can only be for justice and truth.[23]

Whatever Perraudin said to the Mwami in private, he did not yet share his views more publicly, and both Perraudin and Mutara maintained public decorum throughout 1956. Mutara congratulated Perraudin on his appointment as Vicar Apostolic in March, and Perraudin's limited 1956 correspondence with Mwami Mutara offered little in the way of political advocacy.[24]

The Hutu-Tutsi question also circulated in other Catholic missionary quarters in 1956. In his influential study of Rwanda and Burundi, the Nyakibanda seminary professor Jan Adriaenssens noted growing Hutu peasant resentment of Tutsi authorities. Writing in August, another missionary serving at the minor seminary of Kabgayi excoriated the "racist spirit of the Tutsi," critiqued the Tutsi-dominated Josephite brothers for their "anti-white racism," and traced all seminary problems to the Tutsi students who comprised 80 percent of the seminary population. By the end of the year, the superior of Save mission in southern Rwanda joined the chorus, criticizing his fellow missionaries for first promoting the Tutsi and then switching their favor to the Hutu.[25]

Whatever the White Fathers' growing frustrations with Rwanda's Tutsi-dominated social order, they did not undertake any kind of Hutu affirmative action plan inside the Catholic Church. While Perraudin retained Gregoire Kayibanda as lay editor of *Kinyamateka*, he also appointed the Tutsi priest Innocent Gasabwoya as overall director of the controversial Catholic weekly. The Tutsi priest Jean-Marie-Vianney Rusingizandekwe also served on Kinyamateka's editorial staff in 1957-58; Hutu priests in fact remained conspicuously absent from *Kinyamateka's* editorial board throughout the rest of the 1950s.[26] And although Perraudin's April 1956 shakeup of mission staffing was described in some quarters as an "audacious coup," the controversy stemmed more from his promotion of indigenous clergy than any fomenting of Hutu-Tutsi tensions. For example, Perraudin named Gasabwoya to replace Dejemeppe as vicar general of the Kabgayi vicariate and appointed the Tutsi priest Gerard Mwerekande to lead the Kabgayi mission station.[27]

It would also be a mistake to reduce all of Catholic life in 1956 to the Hutu-Tutsi question. The biggest ecclesial event of the year was Kabgayi's 50th anniversary, and missionaries were preoccupied with pastoral issues such as expanding infrastructure, developing Catholic Action, and recruiting foreign missionaries.[28] In 1955-56 alone, Perraudin approved seven new mission stations for Kabgayi's burgeoning Catholic population. Some commentators even wondered if Rwanda's population was growing too quickly. For example, the 1956-57 Kabgayi annual report highlighted Rwanda's population growth rate of 5 percent per annum, noted that the Rwandan population had doubled in 40 years, and expressed concerns over the employment prospects for Catholic school graduates.[29] In his own study, Adriaenssens named population growth, not Hutu-Tutsi relations, as Rwanda's greatest social problem. Such sentiments were echoed by the U.N. Trusteeship Council.[30] In a December 1956 letter to Perraudin, Fidele Nkundabagenzi—the Hutu seminarian who later served in Rwanda's first postcolonial government—wrote of Rwanda's struggles with ideologies of liberty, religious freedom, democracy, authority, and church-state relations. Notably missing was any mention of the Hutu-Tutsi question.[31]

In addition, a key tension from the early 1950s—interracial tensions between Europeans and Rwandans—remained salient in 1956. In February, Mosmans critiqued two Nyundo priests looking to study in Belgium as "politicians whose anti-white attitudes are well-known" and expressed fears that Belgian Communist agents would target them upon arrival. He later argued that in light of ongoing interracial tensions, the *évolué* question remained the most important social issue in Rwanda. Leo Volker, Durrieu's assistant at the White Fathers' headquarters in Rome, claimed that professors in Rome and Europe did not understand the African mentality. "It is nearly impossible for professors and directors from there to know and understand well the mentality of our blacks." Nor was the importance of the interracial question limited to the conservative wing of the church. For example, left-wing commentators like Adriacnssens mentioned the emergence of the Hutu-Tutsi strains but saw black-white and Asian-African tensions as more pressing. Significantly, Adriaenssens lay most of the blame on what he termed a "white superiority complex" and denied that proto-nationalist movements had direct communist inspirations. Such sentiments were echoed by Louis Gasore, a Tutsi priest and vicar general of Nyundo.[32]

In turn, these debates reflected the Catholic hierarchy's continuing struggle to offer an authoritative ethical voice as Africa inched closer to independence. Globally, the Bandung, Indonesia conference of April 1955 marked a symbolic escalation of the anti-colonial movement as representatives from 30 African and Asian countries condemned racial segregation and colonialism.[33] Perhaps because Belgian Africa chose not to send any representatives to Bandung, Catholic bishops from Belgian Congo, Rwanda and Burundi took the initiative to discuss similar issues at Leopoldville, Congo in June 1956. Looking back decades later, Perraudin described this Leopoldville meeting as "the [African Catholic] Church disassociating itself from the colonial state."[34] While Perraudin may exaggerate, the language of the Leopoldville pastoral letter does reveal a measure of openness to decolonization. Noting that a legitimate state could take diverse forms ranging from clans and tribes to modern kingdoms and republics, the bishops posited that "all the inhabitants of a country have a duty to actively collaborate in the common good...The autochthonous have the obligation to become conscious of the complexity of their responsibilities and to make themselves capable of assuming them."[35] In this statement the regional bishops defined the church as a "supernatural society founded by Jesus Christ for conducting people to eternal life" and limited its primary jurisdiction to "purely spiritual matters," entrusting the state with responsibility for the common good. Church and state in turn shared authority over key "social" issues like education and youth associations. As we will see later, the bishops' decision to entrust the common good to the state while defining the church in exclusively spiritual terms left the Catholic hierarchy incapable of challenging the Rwandan state when the state itself became an enemy of the common good.[36] Regardless, this 1956 statement showed the Catholic hierarchy distancing itself from Belgium while beginning to envision the church's postcolonial future.[37] Not insignificantly, the bishops passed over the Hutu-Tutsi question—or other ethnic issues—in silence.

The Leopoldville conference sparked several important Catholic initiatives in the Great Lakes region.[38] First, Catholic bishops established a regional bureau of Catholic works encompassing Catholic Action, Catholic schools, social and medical apostolates, and the press. In September 1956, Perraudin agreed to allow Fr. Louis Pien to start the agricultural cooperative "Trafipro" (taken from *Travail, Fidélité, Progrès*, or "work, fidelity, progress"). By organizing producers of sorghum, rice, corn, peanuts, manioc, soap, sugar, and coffee, the cooperative aimed to promote the social and economic interests of its members by improving price stability, working conditions, and infrastructure. This initiative grew out of Perraudin's own familiarity with cooperative movements in Switzerland; Swiss development workers would provide no small contribution to Trafipro's success in the late 1950s and early 1960s. Led from its earliest days by Gregoire Kayibanda, Trafipro helped the Rwandan church develop stronger grassroots networks in the countryside. It would also serve as a highly effective means for mobilizing peasants after Kayibanda entered politics.

As 1956 drew to a close, Rwanda's traditional rulers seemed to be successfully managing Rwanda's transition from oligarchy to representative democracy. On the surface, the September council elections gave Mutara and Rwanda's CSP a new popular mandate. But by not including more Hutu leaders in the top echelons of the government, the Mwami and his allies were undermining their own claims to stand above ethnic politics and sowing deep discontent among Hutu counter-elites.[39] As for the Catholic Church, its national scope, ethnically mixed clergy, and European missionary presence made it the most diverse social institution in Rwanda. In 1956 Catholic leaders could still speak in broad platitudes of social justice, charity, and the common good, publicly avoiding the more contested Hutu-Tutsi question. Likewise, Perraudin could maintain cordial relations with Mwami Mutara and his fellow chiefs while also starting a Hutu-dominated cooperative like Trafipro. The hardening of ethnic language in 1957 would make this balancing act substantially more difficult.

The Year of Manifestoes

If 1956 saw the emergence of the Hutu-Tutsi question in Rwandan political and ecclesial discourse, this issue still competed with older narratives of interracial tensions, anti-communism, church-state relations, and the local implications of Catholic social teaching. Many of these themes would continue through 1957.[40] However, the release of rival Tutsi and Hutu manifestoes in early 1957 elevated the Hutu-Tutsi question to the top of Rwandan politics. And even as the Catholic hierarchy resisted entering this debate, ethnic tensions emerged more prominently inside the Catholic Church, particularly at Nyakibanda major seminary.

Scheduled for September 18 through October 8, 1957, the U.N. *tutelle's* fourth triennial visit to Rwanda and Burundi loomed over the Rwandan political scene in early 1957.[41] As discussed in chapter 3, the United Nations established the *tutelle* in 1946 to exercise oversight over the Belgian colonies of Rwanda and Burundi. Each of its subsequent visits sparked a flurry of political activity and reform. The U.N. *tutelle's* 1948 visit praised the "constructive work" of the Belgians while also encouraging further political reforms, leading Mutara and the Belgian colonial government to establish local advisory councils. The 1951 visit criticized Belgium for not incorporating more indigenous representatives into territorial administration, spurring Belgium to announce a ten-year development plan and the initiation of local elections. On the eve of the 1954 U.N. mission, Mwami Mutara announced the abolition of *ubuhake*. Expectations were high as U.N. officials prepared to travel to Rwanda in September 1957, and rival groups began mobilizing to influence the views of the visiting commission.

Rwanda's Superior Council initiated the year's political debate. Released in February 1957, the Tutsi-dominated CSP's *Mise au point* described black-white racial tensions as the dominant social cleavage in Rwanda and criticized the extent to which Belgians continued to dominate Rwanda's local government.[42] Favoring the rule of an experienced elite as Rwanda moved toward democracy, the authors demanded a rapid timeline for national independence. They also noted Rwanda's internal "social" and "economic" inequalities but argued that these could be resolved through expanding secondary school and university enrollment. Perhaps most telling, the *Mise au point* wholly ignored the question of ethnic inequality and never addressed the Hutu-Tutsi relationship or the concerns of the rural poor. Rather, the CSP focused on the political grievances of the nation's dispossessed (and Tutsi-dominated) elites. "It is an error to believe that one must refuse the recognition of political rights to an elite which possesses political maturity." In summary, the *Mise au point* outlined the emerging principles of Tutsi nationalism in the late 1950s: anti-colonial nationalism, political elitism, calls for rapid indepen-dence, and a resistance to framing social and economic challenges in ethnic terms.

In response to the *Mise au point*, nine Hutu intellectuals released the Bahutu Manifesto in March 1957. Controversy continues to swirl over who actually wrote this document; several historians have implicated the White Fathers.[43] Decades later, Perraudin rejected such insinuations, claiming that Kayibanda kept his own political counsel and never shared this document with him.[44] Justin Kalibwami, a Tutsi journalist, historian, and former priest who served as general editor of *Kinyamateka* between 1958 and 1960, posited that "the manifesto of the Bahutu is without the least doubt the work of those who have signed it."[45] Without doubt, the authors of the Bahutu Manifesto were Catholic-trained *évolués* who had cultivated amicable relations with the White Fathers. Three were former seminarians, two served as editors at *Kinyamateka*, one worked as Perraudin's personal secretary, and two were employed in Kabgayi by a Catholic school and Catholic press, respec-tively.[46] At the same time, it should be recalled that the church represented one of the only avenues of Hutu social advancement.[47] And while the Bahutu Manifesto reflected key principles of Catholic social teaching, it also went beyond the public and private positions of Perraudin and other key White Fathers in 1957. We may never know the extent to which Hutu intellectuals consulted with European mis-sionaries in drafting the Bahutu Manifesto, but I follow Perraudin and Kalibwami in seeing the nine Hutu signers as the principal authors of the document rather than missionary puppets.

The Bahutu Manifesto's social analysis contrasted sharply with that of the CSP's *Mise au point*.[48] For the authors of the Manifesto, the primary political cleav-age in Rwanda was not black-white colonial tension but rather the "indigenous racial problem" between "Hamitic" Tutsi and the Hutu peasantry. This racial prob-lem had social, cultural, economic and political dimensions; the division had been exacerbated by the Tutsi monopolization of all influential political offices under Belgian colonial rule. Therefore, ethnic democratization of Rwandan society had to precede national independence. In turn, the Bahutu Manifesto expressed ample skepticism about anti-colonial nationalism and praised European colonial-ism for protecting the Hutu masses. "Without the European we would have been subjected to a more inhumane exploitation...to total destruction."[49] The authors advocated for what could be termed a Hutu affirmative action plan, calling for an "integral and collective promotion of the Muhutu" which would include nam-ing Hutu as chiefs, sub-chiefs, and judges, expanding rural development to ben-efit Hutu cultivators, and raising the percentage of Hutu in secondary schools.[50] The authors opposed eliminating ethnic identity cards for fear that Tutsi rulers would continue to occlude the ethnic biases in Rwanda's educational and politi-cal systems. The petitionaries concluded by distancing themselves from any revo-lutionary labels, arguing that they were simply "collaborators conscious of their social rights" struggling against a "racist monopoly in Rwanda."[51] Like the *Mise au point* for Tutsi nationalists, the Bahutu Manifesto encompassed the key principles of Hutu nationalism in the late 1950s—the primacy of the ethnic question, the positive view of Europeans, the increasingly strident critiques of Tutsi rulers, and the demands for socio-ethnic democratization and redistribution prior to independence.

Whether the Manifesto accurately represented the beliefs of the "Hutu people" is another matter altogether. In the telling 1957 words of Jean-Paul Harroy, the colonial governor, "the manifesto expressed the views of a still-limited group of Bahutu but reflected a tendency which in a confused form was already part of the consciousness of a great many members of that social group."[52] Harroy himself doubted the Bahutu Manifesto's racial analysis, writing in July 1957 that "I am personally convinced that the distinction at stake between Hutu and Tutsi concerns nowadays two social groups identified less and less with two racial groups recognized by physical anthropology."[53]

Sharing Harroy's own ambiguities, the U.N. Visiting Mission expressed mixed views on the Hutu-Tutsi question after visiting Rwanda in September and October 1957.[54] The subsequent U.N. report warned of the dangers of a continued Tutsi monopolization of power and admitted the existence of an internal Hutu-Tutsi problem, even if *tutelle* members still disputed the exact nature of the Hutu-Tutsi distinction. For example, a preliminary U.N. study in March 1957 borrowed Hamitic language in describing Hutu as "Negroes of Bantu origin and average height" and Tutsi as "[of] Hamitic or Nilotic origin...remarkable for their size and statures."[55] Likewise, the December 1957 U.N. report described how Rwanda's "different racial groups" had lived in a "symbiotic relationship" in the precolonial period. Yet the Commission also warned against "placing undue stress upon the opposition between Bahutu and Batutsi" and even claimed that Belgian economic and social reforms had helped "break down and change the nature of the distinction between the Batutsi and the Bahutu, so that the terms have come to denote social rather than racial or political groups."[56] And in the words of a Belgian representative on the U.N. Visiting Commission, "these classes are not castes...the terms Batutsi and Bahutu should be understood as names of common usage and not as exclusive predicates of closed castes."[57]

If the U.N. Visiting Commission's analysis of the Hutu-Tutsi distinction betrayed a degree of ambiguity, the Commission showed no reticence about pushing Rwanda toward full-fledged democracy. After forty years of Belgian political reforms and Western modernization, the U.N. *tutelle* concluded that Rwanda was ready to take its place in the pantheon of modern democracies. While "not anticipating spectacular and revolutionary changes overnight," the Commission envisioned the transformation of a "regime still characterized by vestiges of feudalism to institutions that are more in keeping with democratic principles."[58] Betraying a naïve optimism that would be betrayed by later events, the Commission wrote that "we have every reason to hope that the transition will take place with a minimum of tension, friction, and difficulties." What is striking in this narrative is the extent to which the U.N. *tutelle* continued to echo Louis Franck in the 1920s or Pierre Ryckmans in the 1930s—namely that Belgium and the international community should, in Ryckmans's memorable words, "dominate to serve." In the words of the December 1957 report, "[Rwanda-Burundi] has confronted the Administering Authority with a well-established political and social structure that may have been suited to conditions in bygone centuries but is basically incompatible with the democratic principles which it was Belgium's mission to gradually implant in the country."

This excursus reveals two important points for our broader study. First, the colonial project contained obvious authoritarian impulses, but these were often framed in terms of an uncritical embracing of democratization. The *tutelle* never questioned Belgium's "mission" to democratize Rwanda. Second, colonial officials seemed incapable of considering how democratic institutions—particularly those imposed from the top down—could undermine social and national unity. The failure to critique the darker side of democratization remained a major analytical problem for church and state alike into the 1960s.[59]

In the midst of rising ethnic and political ferment in 1957, the Catholic hierarchy tried to steer a middle course.[60] After several missionaries critiqued the Tutsi-dominated Josephite brothers for their allegedly anti-European nationalism, their superiors cautioned against taking sides in Rwanda's growing ethnic disputes. To this end, Louis Durrieu reminded one missionary of the necessity of "prudence for not compromising the mission in questions of a political order...we are not men of one or another fraction of the population; we must be all for all (*omnibus omnia factus sum*)." Perraudin echoed similar sentiments in a September-October exchange of letters with Fr. Noti, a mission superior at Nyabahanga. Noti had rankled local Tutsi authorities when he publicly preached against the exactions of local chiefs. Even as he reiterated the importance of social justice, Perraudin reminded Noti that souls were won to the truth through "persuasion" and "interior conversion," not prophetic denunciation. He also advised Noti to take up such questions in Catholic Action study groups rather than in Sunday sermons. This cautious effort to keep the church above ethnic politics extended to seminary teaching. For example, Leo Volker, the new Superior General of the White Fathers, demanded in December 1957 that Nyakibanda professors cease lecturing on the Hutu-Tutsi question and exercise great prudence in all matters related to the seminarians' "diverse tribes of origin."

While attempting to steer clear of public conflict, the missionary hierarchy also betrayed a racialist understanding of Hutu-Tutsi categories in their private correspondence. In February 1957, Perraudin utilized a combination of racial and social language to describe the Hutu-Tutsi distinction. "The inhabitants [of Rwanda] all have the same language but they are of a different race: there are the Batutsi—the privileged class—around 10 percent—and the Bahutu—cultivators—which form the mass, near 90 percent—and some Batwa, pygmies, of very few numbers."[61] And even as he cautioned against taking sides in ethno-political quarrels, the superior general of the White Fathers, Louis Durrieu, spoke of the "Tutsi tribe's real qualities for governing" and attributed much of the political tension in Rwanda to the "inferior class" challenging the Tutsi monopoly.[62]

Even as they discussed ethnic issues in private, Catholic leaders offered public guidance for the Catholic lay faithful as Rwanda and Burundi moved toward democracy and self-determination. Following the regional Leopoldville statement of June 1956, the Catholic bishops of Rwanda and Burundi released a pastoral letter on justice in March 1957.[63] As in 1956, the bishops attempted to offer an apolitical commentary on politics, "shedding light on the moral laws that should reign" in society rather than "offering directives of an economic or political order" that would "substitute for the people in their temporal relations." After these opening caveats, the bishops described justice in distributive terms as "that virtue which disposes man to render to each his due." For the bishops, a just society ensures economic progress, civil peace, familial love, and the common good. Injustice, on the other hand, "renders human relations unsupportable, summoning tyranny and provoking revolt. It will foment and keep alive hatreds." The church in turn had a duty to expose social abuses and to state the moral principles that should guide the laity in resolving social injustices.

The 1957 pastoral letter on justice was significant for three reasons. First, it demonstrated that the church hierarchy would continue to follow the course set by the 1956 Leopoldville conference in speaking to issues of social injustice. Whereas previous episcopal statements had concerned issues directly related to the church's institutional interests like the 1954–1955 debate over Catholic schools, the 1956–1957 pastoral letters focused more explicitly on Rwanda's broader social context. In this way these latter statements stood squarely within the post-*Rerum Novarum* tradition of Catholic social teaching. Second, while not directly addressing the Hutu-Tutsi question, the 1957 statement on justice offered much stronger critiques of indigenous authorities than the 1956 Leopoldville document. The church appeared here as the moral soul of society, the prophet drawing attention to great evils in hopes of inspiring the powerful to change their ways. Finally, the statement marked the last time for three years that the bishops of Rwanda and Burundi spoke together on social and political issues. As we will see, Perraudin and Bigirumwami diverged on the Hutu-Tutsi question in 1958–1959. In addition, Rwanda and Burundi charted increasingly independent political courses after 1957.[64]

The 1957 statement on justice was also significant for what it did not accomplish or even attempt—namely, resolving the fundamental analytical dispute on how to interpret the ethno-political divisions in Rwandan society. In this sense the bishops' efforts to stand above politics and "avoid technical solutions" ensured that each side could interpret Catholic principles in whatever way it saw fit. Thus Tutsi nationalists emphasized Catholic teachings on unity, dismissing the writers of the Bahutu Manifesto as treasonous insurrectionaries dividing Rwandan society into illusory ethnic groups. Hutu leaders emphasized the Catholic principle of justice and its corresponding demands for an equitable distribution of political and economic power, rejecting Tutsi calls for unity as smokescreens for perpetuating a fundamentally unjust system. Catholic Hutu and Tutsi elites agreed with their bishops that Rwandan society should be unified, charitable, and just, but episcopal pronouncements on these matters had little transformative effect since lay leaders interpreted the church's teachings in whatever way suited their own group's interests.

In addition, Rwanda's growing fissiparous tendencies were reflected in the rise of new ethnic political movements in 1957. While the *Mouvement Progressiste Politique* (MPP) united progressive Hutu and Tutsi elites for a brief moment in 1954–1955, the party lost momentum by early 1956, and the 1956 press disputes and 1957 manifestoes finished it off.[65] Three months after the release of the Bahutu Manifesto, Gregoire Kayibanda founded the *Mouvement Social Muhutu* (MSM) in Kabgayi in June 1957. This movement advocated for the political, social, cultural and economic uplift of a distinctively "Hutu" peasantry. After founding the MSM, Kayibanda traveled to Belgium in late 1957 to begin an internship with *Vers l'avenir*, a liberal Catholic publication based in Namur. Kayibanda used this experience to cultivate important political and financial relationships with center-left Christian political parties and trade unions like the *Parti Social Chrétien* (PSC) and the *Confédération des Syndicats Chrétiens* (CSC).[66] Far from defusing the political situation, however, Kayibanda's departure left a political vacuum filled by the devoutly Catholic and passionately anti-Tutsi Joseph Gitera. Gitera launched *L'association pour le promotion des masses bahutu* (Aprosoma) in southern Rwanda in November 1957. During this same month, a group of conservative nationalist Tutsi started *L'association des éleveurs du Ruanda-Urundi*, a movement that would grow into the *Union Nationale Rwandaise* (UNAR) in 1959. While not yet official political parties, the rival movements demonstrated the growing salience of ethnicity for political mobilization.[67]

Rising ethnic tensions in Rwandan politics also began to spill over into the Catholic seminary if not yet Catholic mission stations.[68] If the four years between 1953 and 1956 had been calm ones at Nyakibanda seminary, 1957 began a four-year period which saw the entire faculty turn over and two-thirds of the student body depart. The celebration of Mwami Mutara's twenty-fifth jubilee from June 29 to July 1, 1957 brought some of the latent ethnic tensions into the open. The jubilee days turned into a boisterous celebration of the monarchy and traditional

Rwandan culture, including a laudatory sermon from Bigirumwami and lavish tributes from Belgian colonial officials and Rwandan chiefs alike.[69] Some seminarians embraced the jubilee. Others lamented how the Mwami overlooked both the Hutu-Tutsi question and the need for further social democratization. In the words of Nyakibanda's rector, Pierre Boutry, "the Mwami's jubilee days have revealed the Hutu-Tutsi antagonism, and the seminarians are avoiding each other."[70] And in an illuminating commentary on the extent to which ethnic identity stemmed from political imagination, the Nyakibanda annual report admitted frictions between Hutu and Tutsi students after "certain seminarians became conscious of a problem of which they were [previously] ignorant."[71] Having said this, however, one should not retrospectively exaggerate the impact of the twenty-fifth jubilee—even the Mwami's media foil, *Kinyamateka*, included positive accolades for Rwanda's king.[72]

Nine seminarians—seven Tutsi and two Hutu—left Nyakibanda at the beginning of the 1957–1958 academic year, marking the largest student withdrawal since 1952. The controversy was precipitated by Fr. Corneille Slenders, a seminary professor who taught on social issues and provided much of the spiritual direction in the seminary. Slenders had only joined the faculty in 1956 and initially cultivated positive relations with the seminarians.[73] By 1957, however, his public engagement of the Hutu-Tutsi question and criticisms of some Tutsi seminarians had proven

FIGURE 4.3 Mwami Mutara and the White Fathers in happier times (*courtesy Centre Missionnaire Lavigerie, Kigali, Rwanda*)

more controversial, and his superiors directed him to cease speaking publicly on ethnic issues.[74] Both Slenders and an ally, Fr. Cogniaux, were removed from the seminary at the end of the 1957–1958 academic year. Since both were known for their strident critiques of Tutsi seminarians, their dismissals point more to a hierarchy trying to avoid political entanglements rather than to a church switching over to the Hutu side.[75]

If Nyakibanda was sliding back into a familiar pattern, the seminary's former rector was also sparking new controversies. But as in 1956, the critique of Perraudin in 1957 concerned not his social justice views or pro-Hutu leanings but rather the rapid pace at which this relative newcomer to the Rwandan scene was indigenizing the local church. A fellow White Father described him in late 1956 as "a spiritual man, but a little political. He came to the seminary without missionary background. He wants, they say, at all costs to get on well with the king and the *abbés* [indigenous priests]."[76] A year later Jan Hartmann—the same Hartmann who had been a finalist to replace Déprimoz in 1955—lamented the low morale of the White Fathers. He traced this to Perraudin's favoring "all which is indigenous," including the construction of a new minor seminary for the Josephites.[77] Behind the scenes, Perraudin lobbied for the establishment of a new vicariate in Kigali headed by an indigenous bishop, a doubling of indigenous clergy, and a 50 percent reduction in European missionary priests.[78] Since in 1957 the vast majority of indigenous Catholic priests were Tutsi, this can hardly be seen as the first step in an anti-Tutsi conspiracy.

In addition to clerical indigenization, Perraudin also continued to advocate on social justice issues. For example, he wrote in the 1956–1957 Kabgayi annual report of the importance of exposing the Rwandan population to the social teachings of the popes and the local bishops "which is absolutely necessary in these difficult times where democracy tends to replace the former feudalism."[79] A November speech to the alumni of the *Groupe Scolaire d'Astrida* offered a synopsis of Perraudin's social vision at the end of 1957:

> The Church is not a Society of the sacristy, but the community of the children of God, who pray always and sanctify themselves individually and together, but who try also to work with all their strength for the construction of a truly just, truly free, truly fraternal world on the basis of Christian principles...If she [the church] does not destroy social inequalities, she works to reduce them to just and healthy proportions.[80]

If Perraudin had not lost his social commitment, he spent four months outside of the country in early 1957 and was not even in Rwanda when the regional bishops released their letter on justice. He continued to maintain amicable relations with the ruling regime, focused on indigenizing the local clergy and building pastoral capacity, and worked to improve "fraternal charity" between European and African clergy through a series of reflection days.[81] In retrospect, it is difficult to imagine that a man criticized in 1957 for being too close to the Mwami and the church's Tutsi clergy would find himself facing accusations of regicide and inciting ethnic revolution just two years later.

The Hutu-Tutsi Study Commission

By 1958 the Hutu-Tutsi question had risen to the top of the Rwandan political agenda. Rival political movements had mobilized to contest anticipated 1959 elections, and the U.N. and the Belgian government were struggling to balance their mandate's dual commitments to devolution and democratization. In the words of the U.N. Visiting Commission Report of December 1957, "the Belgian authorities must do everything within their power to hasten the Bahutu's emancipation so as to be able to accelerate still further the current transfer of power to the constituted indigenous authorities without endangering democratic principles"[82] At the same time, rhetoric surrounding the Hutu-Tutsi distinction showed a striking degree of variability, reflecting the extent to which "Hutu" and "Tutsi" remained shifting political labels. In particular, the April-June 1958 debates of the Mwami's special Hutu-Tutsi Study Commission revealed the complexities of ethnic discourse. These debates also demonstrated that Rwanda did in fact have alternatives to the "tribal construction of politics" that Philip Gourevitch and others have claimed dominated Rwanda in the final years of Belgian rule.[83]

After publicly ignoring the Bahutu Manifesto for nearly a year, Mwami Mutara in March 1958 agreed to establish a special commission to study the Hutu-Tutsi question.[84] The ten-man commission included the conservative Tutsi chief Justin Gashugi, the former Astridien Prosper Bwanakweri, and the Hutu advocates Joseph Gitera and Calliope Mulindahabi. The ethnic and ideological diversity of the commission offered hope for resolving Rwanda's increasingly intractable political situation. One could argue that the Hutu-Tutsi Study Commission's ultimate failure to achieve consensus—and the Mwami's rejection of their other conclusions—placed Rwanda on a road to revolution.[85]

The study commission gathered three times in April 1958 and a fourth time in June.[86] The initial meeting did not start well. When fifteen Hutu petitioners requested an early audience with the Mwami on March 30, Mutara initially refused to see them. The Mwami then engaged in a heated exchange with the Hutu leaders, allegedly grabbing Gitera by the throat. Shortly thereafter, Mutara issued a statement dismissing the petitioners as separatists and enemies of Rwanda.[87] This train of events further politicized the Mwami in the eyes of Hutu elites. In subsequent committee dialogues on the Mwami, Gitera agreed to call Mutara the "common father of us all" yet also posited that "the Mwami belongs to the Tutsi group." This contradicted the traditional view that the Mwami stood above ethnic categories, that in the words of one Tutsi commission member he was "neither Muhutu nor Mututsi nor Mutwa."[88]

Despite this rocky beginning, a broad, pan-ethnic majority concurred on several key issues. First, the commission admitted the existence of an ethnic problem in secondary and higher education, recognizing that Tutsi comprised over 60 percent of secondary students and over two-thirds of the student populations at elite schools like the *Groupe Scolaire d'Astrida*.[89] Second, the commission agreed that Hutu were vastly underrepresented in administrative and judicial positions and that Hutu had suffered disproportionately under traditional institutions like *uburetwa* and *ubuhake*. Third, a majority of commission members envisioned an independent Rwanda with a constitutional monarchy, representative democracy, and universal male suffrage. Reflecting the Mwami's increasingly precarious political future, Tutsi chiefs like Bwanakweri and Gashugi enthusiastically endorsed circumscribing the Mwami's powers in a new Rwandan parliamentary democracy.[90]

If commission members agreed on the necessity of political reform and the reality of Hutu-Tutsi inequality, they differed on the underlying reasons. Tutsi members blamed the Belgian colonial administration for favoring Tutsi chiefs and limiting secondary education to Tutsi in the 1920s and 1930s.[91] Other Tutsi members went further. Chief Gashugi highlighted the past failures of Hutu chiefs and the unwillingness of Hutu peasants to live under the rule of fellow Hutu. Gitera and his Hutu colleagues placed more responsibility at the feet of the Mwami and the precolonial Rwandan political system, highlighting the exclusion of Hutu from the royal court and the social inculcation of a Hutu inferiority complex.[92]

Commission members also differed over how to resolve the ethnic gap in political representation. Dismissing the current Belgian and Tutsi-dominated system as a "feudal system of courtesan culture and favoritism,"[93] Mulindahabi and his Hutu colleagues advocated for "Hutu representatives" on the Superior Council. Despite Tutsi protestations, the Hutu advocates could claim some precedent for their demand. After admitting the existence of racial discrimination against the Twa, the CSP agreed to admit a Twa representative in June 1955.[94] And in light of the continuing Tutsi dominance of the CSP, some Belgian officials had proposed Hutu representatives as early as 1956.[95] But embracing Hutu delegates who could claim to represent 85 percent of the population posed a more direct political challenge than a token Twa minister representing one percent of the Rwandan population. Making ethnicity the basis of political representation also challenged the Superior Council's trans-ethnic, nationalist ideal.[96]

The Tutsi members of the Hutu-Tutsi study commission therefore stood united against the idea of Hutu representatives on the CSP. Rather, they argued that existing educational and political discrepancies would resolve themselves as Rwandan schools improved, the Belgians withdrew, and Rwanda embraced a more meritocratic political system. In the words of the commission chair Chief Bagirishya, the state should "give equality of opportunity to all three ethnic groups to access public office" but avoid a "representation by racial group that could only engender harmful rivalries based on race."[97] Even a reformist chief like Bwanakweri disputed Gitera's proposal for a Hutu representative. "We would not base this choice on either intelligence or capacity…it's an unjust method which can only be separatist and anti-democratic."[98] Although he showed some openness to the idea of a special Hutu advisor to the Mwami, Bwanakweri took issue with Gitera's tendency to speak in collective ethnic terms, reminding him that the majority of Tutsi were poor and that the Tutsi class did not conspire to discriminate against Hutu. For his part, Gashugi claimed that Kayibanda had rejected the Mwami's earlier offers of a chieftaincy, demonstrating that Kayibanda was merely looking to gain electoral leverage with the Hutu masses.[99]

These arguments over Hutu representatives on the CSP symbolized a broader debate over which side bore most responsibility for Rwanda's growing political divisions. While the Tutsi chiefs blamed Hutu polemicists for dividing the country into contrived ethnic groupings, Gitera, Mulindahabi, and their Hutu allies pointed to recalcitrant Tutsi elites who refused to share political power. In this view, Hutu elites were not undermining national unity but making people aware of a nation that had already been rent asunder. Given the current political impasse, some even argued that national division was inevitable. In the words of Gitera, "the division that we want is equalizing, that which you want is division by monopoly."[100]

Even as the political debate became increasingly contentious, the rhetoric concerning the nature of the Hutu-Tutsi distinction was remarkably ambiguous. For example, the Hutu Balthazar Bicamumpaka offered a socioeconomic understanding of these categories. "Our sense of Bahutu encompasses all the poor people, so that a poor Mututsi is at the same time Muhutu, that is Hutu in a social sense."[101] Another Hutu representative, Bendantuguka, provided a more biological definition, positing that "I understand a Muhutu in the genealogical sense, a Muhutu by race." Gitera appeared to retain both understandings yet emphasized the solidarity of all poor Rwandans.

> A Muhutu in our sense then is the poor and simple man, excluding at the same time the racial Hutu who becomes socially Hamitic. The Mututsi for us is the super-human…who socially is higher and mistrusts the Hutu, so that the Tutsi who sympathizes [with us]…is not a Tutsi in our sense.[102]

Even after the hardening of ethnic discourse in 1957 and early 1958, three prominent Hutu could still publicly disagree on how to understand the term "Tutsi."[103] This does not mean that the distinction was invented out of whole cloth by

Europeans bent on dividing Rwanda. But as with the language of "black" in apartheid South Africa, "Hutu" and "Tutsi" reflected a far more complex reality than later polemicists would make it appear.

In early June, the Hutu-Tutsi Study Commission gathered a third time to consider the ethnic divergence in schools enrollment. The commission proposed four reasons to explain this discrepancy. First, the Belgians had given Tutsi elites a monopoly over Rwanda's political and economic life, and Hutu had not been promoted in the colonial school system. Second, Rwandan society had inculcated Tutsi superiority and Hutu inferiority complexes. Third, local authorities had not encouraged Hutu parents to send their children for more advanced education. Fourth, the onerous demands of *uburetwa* work *corvées* had interfered with Hutu schooling.

Recognizing the empirical reality of Tutsi dominance of secondary education, the commission offered several tangible suggestions.[104] First, they urged the CSP and the Belgian government to launch a propaganda campaign to recruit and retain Hutu students. Second, the commission demanded that the *Group Scolaire d'Astrida* eradicate any Tutsi favoritism in their admissions and promotions policies. Third, the commission urged the government to rapidly expand schools construction. Fourth, committee members suggested the creation of a permanent commission to monitor the government's progress in strengthening educational equality. Finally, the committee unanimously agreed that secondary schools should adopt an ethnic-blind admissions policy.[105] A key testimonial here came from none other than Mgr. André Perraudin. Perraudin wrote in a May 1958 letter to the Study Commission that "an individual has never been dismissed [from Catholic schools] because of his race" and claimed that Catholic schools based promotion on exit exams rather than ethnic identity.[106]

In the midst of the Hutu-Tutsi Study Commission debates, a group of conservative Tutsi chiefs threw in a bombshell in the form of two May 1958 letters from the "Twelve Great Servants of the Court" (in Kinyarwanda *"Bagaragu b'ibwami bakuru"*).[107] These writers accused Hutu advocates of treasonous rebellion and reaffirmed their support for Mwami Mutara and Rwanda's monarchical system. In more inflammatory language, the Great Servants denied any fraternity between Tutsi and Hutu and argued that the superior Tutsi had conquered and enslaved the weaker Hutu. "Those which claim the sharing of common patrimony are those who share bonds of fraternity. Now the relations between us Tutsi and those Hutu has from all time been based on slavery; between us and them there is no foundation of brotherhood." The document seemed to confirm the worst fears of Hutu reformers, and the text would be cited for years as evidence of Tutsi malfeasance.[108]

Called by Mutara in a special night session on June 12, 1958, Rwanda's Superior Council gathered to consider the recommendations of the Hutu-Tutsi Study Commission. On the Mwami's recommendation, the CSP rejected all of the committee's conclusions. Seemingly contradicting the commission's *raison d'être*, Mutara issued a statement denying the existence of a Hutu-Tutsi problem in Rwanda, claiming that such polemics had originated from "the foreign influence of some whites on blacks, from communist ideas whose intention is to divide the country."[109] Over stringent Hutu protests, the CSP went so far that night as to ban any further usage of the terms Hutu, Tutsi and Twa in official documents.[110] Even as he avoided the polemical language of the Great Servants document, Mwami Mutara adopted its one-sided political analysis rather than the more nuanced critique of the Hutu-Tutsi Study Commission.

In response, Hutu elites took their argument to the hills.[111] Gitera's aprosoma released "*La voix de petit peuple*" ("The Voice of the Peasants") in late June 1958.[112] This publication turned the CSP's "enemies of the people" discourse on its head, positing that the only enemies of Rwanda were those who "sucked the blood of their brothers," hated foreigners, opposed the reign of Christ and Europeans, and suppressed all voices of progress. For Aprosoma, the spirit of Hutu brotherhood stood in sharp contrast to the "Hamitic spirit of exploitation and extermination." Aprosoma's concluding exhortation could have been mistaken for a Jacobin rally in 1793 Paris: "Young men and young women of the Hutu movement: Liberty! Let's liberate ourselves from Tutsi slavery. We have had enough. Justice!" Political rhetoric had undergone a radical shift in three years. The pan-ethnic moderation of the *Mouvement Politique Progressiste* had given way to a much more radical spirit.

Catholic Divisions on the Hutu-Tutsi Question

Where did missionary leaders stand in the midst of these momentous debates? As usual, the White Fathers did not speak with one voice. Fr. Louis Gilles, one of the more politically active White Fathers, called the Tutsi-dominated CSP a "distortion" in a majority-Hutu country, anticipating major political changes in the next round of elections.[113] Another White Father continued to worry about the old problem of the *évolués*, noting that it was "harder to manage 20 of them than 10,000 peasants."[114] The rector of Nyakibanda, Pierre Boutry, lamented the "aggressive" tone of the Bahutu Manifesto as well as the Mwami's failure to make a conciliatory gesture at his 1957 jubilee.[115] But as was the case in 1956–1957, most missionaries did not mention political or ethnic problems in reports to their superiors back in Rome.[116] Even the hierarchy seemed to be playing a cautious waiting game. Although Perraudin later called Mutara's rejection of the recommendations of the Hutu-Tutsi Study Commission the turning point in a "volcanic" year for Rwandan politics, he made no mention of such issues in his limited correspondence with his White Father superiors in 1958.[117] For his part, Leo Volker, the new superior general of the White Fathers, instructed Boutry "not to enter into problems of a political order."[118]

If missionary superiors were instructing the White Fathers to avoid "problems of a political order," indigenous Catholics sensed no such strictures. As discussed earlier, Hutu lay activists like Joseph Gitera and Aloys Munyangaju led the movement for political change, utilizing sympathetic European journals like *La Libre Belgique, Témoignage Chrétien, La Cité, La Revue Nouvelle,* and *Les Dossiers de l'Action Sociale Catholique* to present their case to the French and Belgian public.[119] On the other side of the divide, Louis Gasore, the Tutsi vicar general of Nyundo, continued to focus on the black-white colonial problem. In a 1958 article in the White Fathers' monthly *Vivante Afrique,* Gasore noted the rising tensions between Tutsi and Hutu. Here he described these categories as "the traditional nobility and minority" and "the large peasant masses"; he also expressed his fears that ethnic parties would "compromise the unity of the country." After this brief paragraph on the Hutu-Tutsi question, he then devoted the next thirteen paragraphs to discussing what he saw as the more pressing issue of white-black racism in the Great Lakes region.[120] Reflecting the presence of both Tutsi and Hutu elites, the White Fathers' weekly *Temps Nouveaux d'Afrique* possessed the most conflicted editorial policy in 1958. Cover stories alternated between the traditional European preoccupation with communism, pro-Hutu articles that openly questioned Rwanda's traditional institutions, and ongoing Tutsi critiques of Belgian colonialism.[121]

Perhaps the most complex Catholic voice came from Bigirumwami. Unlike the "Great Servants of the Court" or many of the Superior Council chiefs, Bigirumwami could not be stereotyped as a Tutsi royalist unconcerned with the conditions of poor Hutu peasants. He had joined the other bishops of Rwanda and Burundi in drafting the 1957 pastoral letter on justice and issued several other stinging rebukes of customary abuses during the spring of 1958.[122] In contrast to Perraudin, however, Bigirumwami was less convinced of the need or potential efficacy of major political change. For the Vicar Apostolic of Nyundo, advocating for social justice should never entail undermining traditional authorities or supporting revolutionary political change. Rather, Catholic social teaching should serve as a conscience for Rwanda's political authorities, reminding them that Rwanda's long-term stability and prosperity rested on the nation's treatment of the poor masses. "Well-treated, they [the peasants] are grateful; poorly treated, they revolt."[123]

Bigirumwami expanded on this commentary while traveling in Europe during the fall of 1958. Here he penned an article entitled "The Problem of Hutu, Tutsi and Twa" in the Belgian Catholic weekly *Témoignage chrétien.*[124] In this article, Bigirumwami rejected any historical theories concerning a violent Tutsi conquest of the Hutu, arguing that the Tutsi established a political dynasty in Rwanda because local Hutu wanted access to Tutsi cattle and valued patron-client relations. Even as he admitted a growing crisis between the "'social' or 'racial' groups of Batutsi, Bahutu and Batwa," Bigirumwami also questioned the categories of Hutu,

Tutsi, and Twa themselves. Pointing to the discrepancy between his so-called Tutsi appearance and mixed ethnic background, Bigirumwami lambasted the "inanity of physical criteria" in determining Hutu and Tutsi identities. He also downplayed ethnic discrepancies in secondary schools, claiming that Hutu and Tutsi elites comprised a privileged class over and against the impoverished masses of Hutu cultivators and *petit* Tutsi. Democratizing education meant expanding educational opportunities for both Hutu and Tutsi peasants. Bigirumwami also criticized the writers of the Bahutu Manifesto for addressing their petition to an imagined "Tutsi collectivity" rather than the actual leaders of the country—namely the Belgian government and Rwanda's Superior Council. He concluded by issuing a pan-ethnic call for social justice along with a plea for Rwandans to avoid discord, tension and hate. Here again Bigirumwami described Rwanda's problems as fundamentally "social" and "economic" rather than "ethnic" or "racial." "The very rapid evolution that passes through our country should not and cannot blind us to the point of misunderstanding realities, such as social and economic differences."[125]

Just as Perraudin's February 1959 "Letter on Charity" symbolized Perraudin's public adoption of Hutu social analysis, so Bigirumwami's September 1958 *Témoignage chrétien* article appeared to place him in the ideological camp of moderate Tutsi nationalists. The article also signaled a shift in Bigirumwami's attitude toward Rwanda's traditional authorities. Although he had critiqued Tutsi chiefs on social justice grounds throughout 1957 and 1958, he began to worry in late 1958 that growing Catholic media critiques of Rwanda's leadership risked undermining Rwanda's social fabric. After returning to Rwanda in December, Bigirumwami began pressuring Fr. Sebastian Grosjean and Abbé Justin Kalibwami, the editors of *Temps Nouveaux d'Afrique*, to moderate their critiques of the Mwami, chiefs, and sub-chiefs.[126]

Within weeks of the publication of Bigirumwami's article in *Témoignage Chrétien*, two influential White Fathers penned their own political analyses of the Rwandan situation. First came Dominique Nothomb.[127] An influential spiritual director and respected intellectual from an upper-class French family, Nothomb maintained close ties with both Bigirumwami and Perraudin into the 1960s, earning a reputation as a political moderate. It is noteworthy, then, that Nothomb claimed in his September 1958 political analysis that the Hutu-Tutsi debate reflected not merely a social conflict but a "racial problem" with "hereditary, physiological, innate factors (e.g., height, form of head, blood) and a fixed discrimination of rights and of duties." According to Nothomb, the Catholic Church was neither "racist" nor blind to racial difference. So even if "the Tutsi seem to possess certain qualities for command, the Hutu certain qualities for work," the Catholic Church also "rejects absolutely all definitive and fixed superiority of one race over another race."[128] Since all humans were created in the image of God and redeemed from original sin through Christ's sacrifice on the Cross, all were destined for the same eternal home and deserved the same rights and responsibilities. Nothomb expressed his hopes for an egalitarian, multiracial society yet also argued that Rwanda should attribute "social and political functions to those who have the competencies and the requisite qualities to exercise them in view of the common good." Far from encouraging demagoguery, Nothomb's church condemned the fomenting of conflict and hatred even as she promised not to stand idly by while a regime abused its citizens. "The church's will for peace and justice does not mean that she preaches the passive acceptance of all regimes so as to avoid conflicts."[129]

The second important missionary statement came from the pen of Guy Mosmans, the Belgian provincial of the White Fathers. In a September 21, 1958 letter to the Belgian foreign ministry, Mosmans exhorted Belgium to help establish a new Hutu republic.[130] Claiming that Tutsi elites preferred retaining a political monopoly to instituting a genuine democracy, Mosmans encouraged Belgium to break with Mwami Mutara and to strengthen the colonial administration's own authority over the Rwandan people. This would set the stage for the indigenization of the colonial administration by promoting Hutu elites, suppressing the Tutsi-dominated CSP, and offering the "genuine LIBERATION" of the people.[131] Mosmans admitted that his plan risked national division, but he saw the alternatives as even worse. Namely, Belgium's continued support for Tutsi indirect rule would foment anti-Belgian nationalism among Tutsi elites and anti-Western communism among the Hutu masses. Faced with such a stark choice, the Belgians had only one option: "suppress the privileges of the castes and make justice reign." Here Mosmans reminded his Belgian interlocutors of Belgium's colonial mission to deliver social justice to the masses. As it completed its "magnificent work in Rwanda-Burundi," Belgium would have to once again impose its benevolent will on the Rwandan people. "The only acceptable method is to act with authority and impose indispensable measures for the general good and evolution of the country."

Mosmans's ecclesial advice echoed his political vision. Facing the inevitable rise of the Hutu people, the local church should distance itself from Tutsi elites. Clergy should also maintain a united front across ethnic lines. In this area, Mosmans offered special praise for Bigirumwami for defending Hutu peasants against Tutsi nobles. "Mgr. Bigirumwami has many times taken the defense of unjustly condemned Hutu. This has strongly annoyed the Tutsi. The rumor has spread that Mgr. was the bishop of the Hutu but not the bishop of the Tutsi."[132] He also warned his fellow priests to be on guard against Mwami Mutara, noting Mutara's recent criticisms of missionaries and indigenous priests for fomenting the "false problem" of Hutu-Tutsi tension. If the Catholic clergy could resist the Mwami's entreaties and maintain a united front in favor of social justice, Mosmans envisioned the Rwandan feudal system collapsing like a house of cards. If they caved in to nationalist temptations, however, it was the church that stood at greatest risk.[133]

Maintaining a unified clerical front was proving difficult in the cauldron of 1958 Rwanda, however. First were the perennial tensions between white and black clergy and especially between Kabgayi and Nyundo priests. European missionaries issued frustrated critiques of their Rwandan colleagues, highlighting the spiritual poverty of the indigenous *abbé* as well as his alleged materialism, politicization, and anti-White Father bias.[134] Another tension concerned the shortage of priests in the vicariate of Nyundo, especially in comparison with the much larger Kabgayi vicariate. In his 1957–1958 annual report, Bigirumwami lamented that forty priests, thirty sisters, and sixty-four lay auxiliaries could not possibly shepherd 60,000 Catholics, especially in light of the vigorous pastoral challenge arising from growing Anglican and Seventh Day Adventist communities.[135]

The priest shortage only exacerbated the longstanding tensions over seminary admissions and dismissals.[136] In June 1958, Bigirumwami could barely contain his rage with Boutry when the latter rejected three Nyundo candidates for Nyakibanda major seminary. Far from his 1952 rhetoric about sharing "absolutely the same apostolic ministry" as the White Fathers, Bigirumwami wrote here that Nyundo seminarians "had without a doubt a mentality other than that inculcated by the White Fathers." While admitting that many seminarians would not ultimately persevere to priestly ordination, Bigirumwami argued that the seminary formed not just priests but many of the nation's future political elites, and it was important not to alienate these future leaders by dismissing them without just cause. This controversy over seminarian admissions and dismissals lingered throughout 1958 and foreshadowed even greater tensions between Bigirumwami and the White Father leadership during the revolutionary upheavals of 1959 to 1962.

The seminarian dispute also reflected a broader crisis of leadership at Nyakibanda.[137] After losing nine seminarians at the beginning of the 1957-58 academic year, Nyakibanda saw sixteen more seminarians depart by the fall of 1958. Growing mistrust marked relationships between seminarians and professors, and the professors themselves divided along ideological and generational lines. The rector, Pierre Boutry, found himself under increasing scrutiny, criticized by old opponents like Corneille Slenders and former supporters like André Perraudin. While Boutry himself blamed the "critical spirit of the Banyarwanda" for Nyakibanda's problems, his colleagues pointed to Boutry's dearth of leadership skills. Perraudin recommended Boutry's replacement in March 1958. The Vatican acquiesced in June. Boutry was replaced for the 1958–1959 term by Paul Baers, a White Father who had been teaching in a Catholic seminary in Belgian Congo.

Perraudin attempted to address these intraclerical problems by holding a series of clerical study days at Nyakibanda Seminary in July 1958.[138] In addition to local European and Rwandan priests, the gathering included Perraudin, Mosmans, several Jesuit leaders, and the African representative for the *Jeunesse Ouvrier Chretienne* (JOC). Bigirumwami was notably absent. The gathered leaders reiterated their vision of the church as a "purely spiritual" community lacking specific expertise in economic, social and political matters. At the same time, speakers emphasized the importance of church leaders for guiding the political formation of elites and the masses, avoiding partisanship and passivity alike. Perraudin encouraged priests to study socio-political problems like the Hutu-Tutsi question and to develop engaged "social apostolates" that moved beyond the more religious orientation of Catholic Action groups. Significantly, he also appointed a four-member commission to study the Hutu-Tutsi question.[139]

To summarize, the increasingly polarized Rwandan political environment of 1958 took its toll on intraclerical relations. This polarization was especially evident in the major seminary of Nyakibanda. Ideological divisions were also becoming more public, as expressed in the writings of prominent churchmen like Guy Mosmans, Dominique Nothomb, Louis Gasore, and Aloys Bigirumwami. Following the 1956 Leopoldville statement and 1957 letter on justice, André Perraudin encouraged his clergy to engage social questions. Overall, though, one does not see the Catholic hierarchy mobilizing a political or ethnic movement in 1958. Hutu-Tutsi divisions remained an intra-elite dispute with little noticeable impact in the mission stations themselves. Perraudin's late 1958 circulars concerned broader Catholic issues like the death of Pope Pius XII and subsequent election of Pope John XXIII.[140] Even when Perraudin engaged political issues, he avoided taking controversial stands. For example, Perraudin refused Joseph Gitera's impassioned October 1958 request for an official Catholic condemnation of the Kalinga drums, the chief symbol of Rwanda's monarchy.[141] If Perraudin maintained a semblance of public neutrality throughout 1958, his February 1959 pastoral letter on charity would bring him off the ideological fence.

Perraudin's Super Omnia Caritas

When he was named Vicar Apostolic in 1956, Mgr. André Perraudin had developed two reputations. On one hand, he was seen as a social justice advocate who had revamped Nyakibanda's seminary courses to offer a more explicit engagement with Catholic social teaching. On the other hand, he had developed a reputation as a diplomatic seminary rector, praised for his mediation skills, commitment to strengthening clerical unity, and success in avoiding political controversy. Between his consecration in March 1956 and the end of 1958, Perraudin seemed to track more closely to the rector's path of ecclesial neutrality. Even as colleagues like Bigirumwami and Mosmans waded into the political fray, Perraudin retained his characteristic public caution, careful not to take sides in the rising disputes between Hutu and Tutsi elites. Rather, he focused on pastoral care for his burgeoning vicariate—building new parishes and substations, constructing schools and seminaries, initiating work on vernacular translations of the liturgy, and blessing the first Benedictine monastery in Rwanda.[142] Even as he described Africa as "boiling over" from anti-colonial tensions and Rwanda as an "unsettled country searching for equilibrium," Perraudin as late as January 1959 expounded far more on Rwanda's pastoral needs than its political problems. So the same month that Mosmans wrote hopefully of the Belgians' newfound commitment to a "real democratization" of Rwandan political structures, Perraudin lamented priest shortages and requested funds for a new medical center.[143] If a poll had been taken at the beginning of 1959 concerning the most politicized leader of the White Fathers, Mosmans would surely have beaten Perraudin.

These perceptions changed on February 11, 1959 when Perraudin issued his Lenten pastoral *Super omnia caritas* ("above all things charity").[144] This letter established Perraudin's public reputation as a Hutu partisan, marking the definitive break in the missionary-monarchy alliance forged in the 1930s by Mgr. Classe and Mwami Mutara. If Hutu elites celebrated Perraudin's message, Tutsi nationalists came to view Perraudin as the embodiment of negative European influence in Rwanda. Despite the controversy, Perraudin at the end of his life still described *Super omnia caritas* as "the charter of my episcopate," arguing that his letter did not represent an inappropriate episcopal intervention into political life but an appropriate application of Catholic social teaching to a "regime of servitude and humiliation for the large proportion of the population."[145]

Whatever the later polemics, Perraudin's Lenten pastoral began on an uncontroversial note by underlining the essential connection between charity and Christianity. "Without charity one is not truly Christian, even if one is baptized."[146] More than a sign of harmonious interpersonal relationships, however, charity undergirded the social order and provided the foundation for social tranquility, justice, and peace. Citing the call of John 15:13 to "lay down his life for his friends" and the command to serve the "least of these" from Matthew 25:34–46, Perraudin argued that charity was embodied in one's sacrifice for the common good and commitment to serving the needs of the marginalized. By aiding his nation's enemy, St. Luke's Good Samaritan (Luke 10:29–37) emerged as a biblical model of charity in Perraudin's letter.[147]

Controversy arose not from Perraudin's biblical analysis but rather from his subsequent application of these Christian principles to the Rwandan social context. For Perraudin, Rwanda's social divisions broke down along a Hutu-Tutsi axis. In perhaps the most important line in the document, Perraudin claimed that "in our Rwanda social differences and inequalities are for a large part linked to racial differences." Whatever this empirical reality, Perraudin exhorted Rwandan Christians to love everyone in light of God's equal love and care for all races. Therefore, the racial differences between Hutu and Tutsi should not divide Christians who "find themselves in the higher unity of the Communion of Saints."[148] Perraudin did not elaborate on either his grounds for describing Hutu and Tutsi as separate races or the practical implications of what it would mean for Christians to coexist in the communion of saints.

Perraudin concluded his pastoral letter by listing key principles that should guide the "city of man."[149] Here he called on the state to facilitate universal access to public office, respect the right to political association, serve the common good, and oppose class struggle and factionalism. Here Perraudin seemed closer to post-war Catholic social teaching than post-Vatican II liberation theology, writing that "the common good cannot consist finally in an ongoing [class] struggle but only in a real and fraternal collaboration." Perraudin also reminded his readers not to separate means from ends. "Hate, mistrust, a spirit of division and disunity, lies and calumnies are means of dishonest struggle and are severely condemned by God. Do not listen, dear Christians, to those who, under pretext of love for one group, preach hate and mistrust to another group."

In an effort to ensure that Catholic clergy modeled such fraternal collaboration, Perraudin issued an accompanying circular to guide priests in their interpretation and presentation of *Super omnia caritas*. Here he instructed priests to avoid partisanship on one side and social indifference on the other, charting a middle course that recognized the need for structural reform, the centrality of Catholic social doctrine, and the importance of the priest's witness of fraternal charity.[150] Mindful that many priests would ignore the letter or manipulate it for their own political purposes, Perraudin directed his clergy to read the letter without commentary. He also requested that catechumens and lay Catholic Action groups study the document as they strove to "impregnate a Christian spirit in the social milieu, the laws and the institutions of the country."[151] Finally, Perraudin reaffirmed the church's support for the right to association, offering a tacit endorsement for Hutu political gatherings viewed with great suspicion by Rwanda's customary authorities.

Looking back over fifty years later, how should we judge Perraudin's momentous letter? First, the document was consistent with Perraudin's vision. Following his missionary predecessors and much (if not all) of the Rwandan intelligentsia, Perraudin described Hutu and Tutsi as racial groups.[152] Likewise, he echoed previous bishops' statements in calling for pan-ethnic and trans-racial unity, the right to association, the importance of Catholic social teaching, and the necessity of political nonpartisanship. Even the title of the letter reflected "charity above all," the episcopal motto that Perraudin had chosen at his consecration in 1956. In some ways, then, Perraudin's statement was only radical for those who did not know the man or his writings.

What explains, then, the controversial historical legacy of *Super omnia caritas*? First was Perraudin's timing. The document was released in early 1959 after the 1957 *Mise au point* and Bahutu Manifesto, the 1957 U.N. Report, and the 1958 Hutu-Tutsi Study Commission debates. Despite growing ambiguity about Hutu and Tutsi categories, Perraudin's letter contained no calls for further study of Rwanda's contested social and ethnic categories. Perraudin's letter did not even reflect the complexity of this debate but simply adopted Hutu social analysis. Published only months after Bigirumwami's *Témoignage Chrétien* article, Perraudin's letter also represented a radical departure from Bigirumwami's own analysis, reinforcing a perception of clerical division (ironic in light of Perraudin's obsession with presenting a united ecclesial front). Its release in early 1959 also came in the midst of Rwanda's escalating political mobilizations. Perraudin's statement was thus used—and abused—by partisans on both sides to galvanize supporters and influence public opinion. In this sense the document's contextual effect was greater than its language might retrospectively convey.

In addition, the document's analytical lacunae contributed to *Super omnia caritas's* reputation as a pro-Hutu diatribe. Whereas Bigirumwami's article nuanced ethnic and political stereotypes, Perraudin argued without qualification that (1) Hutu and Tutsi were racial groups, (2) Rwandan social, economic, and political inequalities fell along a Hutu-Tutsi axis, and (3) Christian charity entailed a duty to oppose this structural sin. Notably missing were any comments on the historical roles that European colonists and Catholic missionaries had played in establishing an exclusively Tutsi aristocracy. The document did not delve further into what lay behind the racial description of the Hutu-Tutsi distinction, nor were there any caveats concerning the shared cultural heritage of the Banyarwanda. Perraudin never mentioned the masses of poor Tutsi peasants. So if *Super omnia caritas* was not a call to arms or a blueprint for Hutu power ideology,[153] it betrayed what could be termed an "analytical partisanship." Its social imagination was wholly that of the Hutu counter-elite. In Weberian terms, one could argue that Perraudin's pastoral letter legitimized Hutu ideology inside the church and for a broader international public.

What were the reactions to Perraudin's document? Whatever Perraudin's later description of this document as a "declaration of war on feudalism" or recent critics' claims that the letter "unleashed" years of ethnic hostility, there was no immediate political backlash in February 1959.[154] Rwandans did not gather to burn the document, and clergy did not organize public boycotts or protests of the letter. The colonial governor, Jean-Paul Harroy, expressed his "very great satisfaction" at how "the action of the representatives of the Church, whose role is supernatural, has developed in fertile harmony with the efforts of the secular authority in favor of the well-being of the laboring population of Rwanda."[155] While he continued to build contacts with the Anglican missions, Mwami Mutara issued no objections to Perraudin's letter. In fact, Perraudin recalled the Mwami commenting only that the document "came too late."[156] The international Catholic press celebrated Perraudin's statement.[157] Inside Rwanda, Joseph Gitera's February 15 announcement of the formal establishment of a new political party, *"Mouvement actuel de la Promotion Sociale de la Masse Paysanne"* (Aprosoma), garnered more local attention.

Despite their evident analytical divergence on the nature of the Hutu-Tutsi distinction, Bigirumwami did not publicly challenge Perraudin's vision. In fact, Bigirumwami's circular letter of March 10, 1959 exhorted local clergy to read Perraudin's pastoral letter and study Rwanda's political and social problems in their local contexts. In this vein, Bigirumwami touted the Nyundo vicariate's commitment to all the poor (whether Hutu, Tutsi or Twa) and celebrated Nyundo's model of intra-ethnic harmony. Bigirumwami publicly defended Catholic periodicals like *Kinyamateka* and *Temps Nouveaux d'Afrique* for their "impartial" defense of the poor and marginalized, noting that the church had never shied away from critiquing the "feudal regime of the Mwami, the chiefs, the sub-chiefs, and the judges."[158] And even as he condemned late-night political meetings and implicitly linked Nyundo's social stability to the region's slower political mobilization, Bigirumwami attached to his circular a political manifesto from none other than Joseph Gitera. Here Bigirumwami praised Gitera's "dynamism," voicing his hope that Aprosoma would continue evolving into a pan-ethnic movement defending the collective interests of the Rwandan peasantry.

Even in his private correspondence, Bigirumwami directed his harshest criticism not at Perraudin but at the editorial staffs of *Temps Nouveaux d'Afrique* and *Kinyamateka*. For Bigirumwami, Catholic journalists were "helping to create cold relations between Hutu and Tutsi" and "being more destructive than constructive."[159] If anything, Bigirumwami worried less about Perraudin and more about how other White Fathers might utilize *Super omnia caritas* to further their own agendas. In this vein, Bigirumwami expressed his hopes that Perraudin would remind missionaries in Nyundo to "be on guard against those who want to trouble public order under the pretext of defending the weak."[160] In his own diocesan newspaper, Bigirumwami publicly castigated the "unfair critiques" of European missionaries circulating in some Rwandan circles.[161] Whatever their differences, Bigirumwami stood by Perraudin in the early months of 1959.

The Dawn before the Storm

Bigirumwami's relative optimism also reflected the extent to which Rwanda's early 1959 political atmosphere was improving after the acrimonies of 1958. Strident voices remained, as evidenced by the Hutu polemicist Gaspard Cyimana's description of Rwanda as a "tripartite society" whose social troubles could be traced to the historic Tutsi enslavement of the Hutu.[162] And yet most Hutu elites in early 1959 emphasized the pan-ethnic nature of their political visions. This was symbolized by Joseph Gitera's February 1959 decision to strike the word "Bahutu" from the end of Aprosoma's name (the party was formerly known as *L'association pour le promotion des masses Bahutu*). For Gitera, the new party name demonstrated that "it is in its essential interests to promote indistinctly the Rwandan mass, to know those Twa, Hutu and Tutsi which in their social condition are reduced to being poor people."[163]

Recently returned from Belgium, Aloys Munyangaju shared Gitera's rhetorical commitment to pan-ethnic social justice. Even as he argued that Rwanda's key political challenge in the late 1950s was moving from "the execrable feudal absolutism of the old regime" to popular democracy, Munyangaju targeted his critiques at Rwanda's customary authorities rather than the Tutsi as a race or collectivity.[164] He also claimed that Hutu demands would benefit poor Tutsi who were "practically assimilated to the Hutu in all domains of life." And even as he argued that the "Hamitic Tutsi" had always looked down upon the Hutu as a "congenitally inferior race," he also admitted that these groups were not closed castes. "The Hutu-Tutsi duality results from two distinct races but permeable to the infiltration one by the other...all generalization without nuance constitutes an error in this domain."[165]

Gregoire Kayibanda also struck a conciliatory tone in the early months of 1959. Writing in *Kinyamateka*, Kayibanda claimed that Hutu petitioners did not aim to establish their own ethnic monopoly. "I have never appreciated a regime based on slavery...their [the Hutu] manifesto stipulates well that a mono-ethnic regime should not cede to another of the same genre."[166] Extending an olive branch to any Tutsi who shared the Hutu vision of egalitarian democracy, Kayibanda presented a populist vision of pan-ethnic solidarity among Rwanda's poor masses. "I can assure you that the Hutu and the simple Tutsi who are with me support you in fighting for their development."[167] And countering accusations that Hutu agitators were closet communists determined to overthrow the monarchy, Kayibanda concluded that "those who love Rwanda want to destroy all who could separate the Banyarwanda."[168]

On the other side of Rwanda's ideological divide, the *Conseil Superieur du Pays* also sounded mollifying notes during the early months of 1959. In their first public statement on the ethnic question since their June 1958 rejection of the findings of the Hutu-Tutsi Study Commission, the CSP admitted that "the problem of relations between different ethnic groups in the country is certainly of first importance. The commission estimates that the problem is more social, but that it has a tendency to become racial."[169] At the same time, the CSP continued to condemn those propagating "racial hate" and "division." Reflecting its growing independence from Mwami Mutara, the CSP also recommended the establishment of a constitutional monarchy and the CSP's transformation from a consultative to a deliberative legislative body.[170]

For their part, Belgian colonial officials seemed more receptive to Hutu critiques by the beginning of 1959. After steering clear of the "delicate" issues of ethnicity in 1956 and 1957, Governor Harroy changed tack in early December 1958. Claiming that it would be worse to remain silent on Rwanda's social question than to engage in a "frank and direct exposé" of the subject, Harroy posited that "there is a problem, not precisely a problem of Tutsi and Hutu, but of rich and poor, of capitalists and workers, of governors and governed."[71] At the same time, Harroy argued that members of the "anthropological group of the Tutsi" comprised the vast majority of those in authority while Hutu made up the vast majority of disenfranchised peasants. Therefore, it was licit to incorporate "Hutu" and "Tutsi" terms in describing this social problem.[72] Recognizing the extent to which Rwanda's political "misunderstandings were often the fruit of a discordance of vocabulary," Harroy tried to overcome the Hutu-Tutsi question by positing that "a Hutu is one who says he is Hutu, a Twa one who says he is Twa, a Tutsi one who declares that he is Tutsi." Lest he be construed as unabashedly pro-Hutu, however, Harroy noted his sympathy with the Superior Council's resistance to incorporating ethnic discourse into official legislation or political representation. From a juridical point of view, "there are only Banyarwanda in Rwanda. In Burundi, there are only Barundi."[73]

Responding to Harroy's admission of a Rwandan social problem, the Belgian government announced in January 1959 that it would send a *Groupe du Travail* (Belgian Working Group) to tour Rwanda and Burundi, interview local leaders, and recommend a framework for resolving the colony's social and political problems as devolution progressed.[74] The commission included prominent colonial officials like M. A. De Schrijver and Augustin Buisseret as well as J. J. Maquet, the anthropologist whose *Premises of Inequality in Rwanda* would become one of the most influential texts in postcolonial Rwandan studies.[75] Arriving in April 1959, the *Groupe du Travail* received over 500 written testimonies and conducted over 700 interviews over the course of three weeks.[76]

In its final report released in September 1959, the Belgian Working Group saw the political trend in Rwanda pointing toward democratization. For all of their differences over ethnic discourse and Belgian colonialism, Rwanda's political leaders accepted basic democratic principles of universal suffrage, constitutional monarchy, and separation of powers.[77] The Belgian Working Group also recommended the institution of a land reform commission, the establishment of a loose political federation between Rwanda and Burundi, and the granting of equal political rights to "non-autochthonous" Africans living in Rwanda or Burundi.[78] Crucially, however, the Belgian Working Group sided with Hutu elites in favoring a longer-term political devolution rather than immediate independence, claiming that the latter would only benefit an "oligarchic minority."

Even as they described the Hutu-Tutsi question as the "grave socio-racial problem" of the territories, the Belgian Working Group's ethnic analysis retained a degree of nuance.[79] Their concluding document described Rwanda and Burundi as "peopled by three ethnic groups that represent…three distinct cultures," yet they also wrote that European colonists found populations "at once homogenous and strongly stratified." If Tutsi occupied 99 percent of Rwanda's *chefferies*, 94 percent of Rwanda's Superior Council positions, 81 percent of Rwanda's territorial council seats, 67 percent of Rwanda's colonial administrators, and 61 percent of Rwanda's secondary school placements, the vast majority of these elites came from only two royal clans, the *Abanyiginya* and the *Abega*.[180] The Working Group admitted that only 6,000 to 10,000 Rwandan Tutsi benefitted from the spoils of public office; the other 140,000 Tutsi were no wealthier than their fellow Hutu peasants.[181] If anything, the ethnic distinctions in neighboring Burundi were even less evident.[182] If Harroy had correctly noted that Tutsi comprised the vast majority of Rwanda's political authorities, the corollary that the vast majority of Tutsi possessed economic or political leadership had no basis in reality.

If most Tutsi were poor, what explained the rise of a uniquely Hutu social movement in Rwanda? For the Belgian Working Group, responsibility lay largely with the Catholic Church. First, the commission argued that "it is among the Rwandan priests that the working group has found the most convinced democrats," a revealing claim in light of the Tutsi dominance of the Catholic priesthood in the late 1950s. In addition, the church had trained most Hutu elites in seminaries, giving them the education necessary to participate in public affairs. Most critically, "the [Christian] doctrine of the functional equality of all men" raised Hutu consciousness of their own relative deprivation. But rather than blame the missions for inciting ethnic discord, the Belgian Working Group praised them for "making people conscious of a social state founded on oligarchy and privilege." In turn, missionaries and colonial officials did not create the Hutu-Tutsi problem but rather changed attitudes toward it. "Little by little, the spirit of courtesan culture was replaced by the consciousness of human rights equal for all."[183] Regardless of whether one accepts this positive analysis of the church's role, it again underlines the extent to which the Hutu social movement grew out of a distinctly Catholic political imagination.

As the Belgian Working Group finished its research in Rwanda in May 1959, the U.N. *tutelle* for Rwanda-Burundi released its long-awaited summary of its 1957–1958 deliberations. Reflecting a growing analytical divergence between Belgium and the United Nations, the U.N. report downplayed the Hutu-Tutsi dynamic, criticized Catholic schools, and emphasized the problem of over-population. The report briefly mentioned the "so-called 'problem' of the two kingdoms, or the Batutsi-Bahutu relationship," noting presciently the "danger that a racial discrimination complex might represent for the territory."[184] For the U.N., however, Rwanda and Burundi's most serious problem was not the Hutu-Tutsi question but the postwar demographic explosion that had exacerbated land tension and sparked a flood of emigrants to neighboring Congo and Uganda.[185] In addition, multiple *tutelle* members critiqued the Catholic dominance of the Rwandan school system and favored the cultivation of secular state schools as a viable educational alternative. For all of these divergences, however, the U.N. *tutelle's* final recommendations echoed the emerging consensus of Belgian colonial officials, Hutu elites, and even Rwanda's customary Tutsi authorities: (1) expand local elections according to the principle of universal suffrage, (2) devolve political authority to the local level, (3) integrate European and indigenous administrations, and (4) develop explicit benchmarks for the path toward self-government and independence.[186] In summary, gradual democratization appeared far more likely than ethnic revolution in the middle of 1959. These prospects would change rapidly in the final months of the year.

As in Rwandan society, the first months of 1959 saw a relative amelioration of sociopolitical tensions within the Catholic Church. To be sure, interracial relations between European missionaries and Rwanda's predominantly Tutsi clergy remained fraught with tension.[187] At the historic Save mission in southern Rwanda, two missionaries quit over interracial disputes with local clergy. At Cyanika mission on the Burundian border, a Belgian missionary critiqued the church's embrace of inculturation for opening the door to African materialism and the politicization of the clergy. Fr. Watteuw, the Flemish superior of Kinyaga mission, expressed his reluctance to live in a racially mixed community, especially since his Tutsi superior, Gerard Mwerekande, belonged to a local family of chiefs. One wonders if Watteuw's oblique reference to the Hutu-Tutsi question masked his deeper fears about the loss of missionary privileges in Rwanda. "The simple people are becoming conscious of their state and desire to catch up culturally to their compatriots...The Hutu here have started to wake up and are opposed to the majority of subchiefs."[188]

Notwithstanding these concerns, the overall ethnic situation within the Rwandan church appeared stable during the spring of 1959. Kabgayi missionary reports from the first six months of 1959 do not mention Hutu-Tutsi tensions at all.[189] In addition, calm had returned to Nyakibanda seminary. Reporting on his 16-day visit to Nyakibanda in April 1959, the regional superior of White Father seminaries admitted that he arrived with apprehensions but left hopeful about the seminary's future. Even as he expressed concerns over the spiritual depth of the seminarians, white-black tensions, and the seminary's "anti-hierarchical, critical atmosphere," the regional superior never mentioned the Hutu-Tutsi question.[190] Nor did lingering seminary tensions necessarily reflect a zero-sum Hutu-Tutsi struggle. For example, André Makarakiza, a Burundian White Father appointed to the Nyakibanda faculty in 1958, wrote in June 1959 of his difficult relations with Hutu and Tutsi seminarians alike. "For the Hutu I have the shortcoming of being Tutsi, for the Tutsi the shortcoming of not wanting to mix myself in their particularism, and for all the shortcoming of being Murundi."[191] Yet even in the face of his own personal challenges, Makarakiza expressed relief that the atmosphere at Nyakibanda had improved since the fall of 1958.

Whatever the lingering interracial tensions, the White Fathers did not express particular concerns about the prospects of further indigenizing Nyakibanda seminary.[192] After appointing Makarakiza to serve on the Nyakibanda faculty for the 1958–1959 academic year, Volker in May 1959 requested the services of Fr. Louis Gasore, Bigirumwami's Tutsi vicar general, as a spiritual director at Nyakibanda. In May 1959, the White Fathers announced that the Hutu priest Bernard Manyurane would serve as a moral theologian on the Nyakibanda faculty for the 1959–1960 academic year. Rumors circulated of the imminent appointment of an indigenous rector. With the notable exception of Manyurane, all of the possible candidates were Tutsi.[193] Ethnic identity would become a major factor in seminary appointments in the early 1960s, but this was not yet the case in 1959.

Compared to the travails of 1950–1952 or 1957–1958, the Rwandan Catholic Church appeared to be on the upswing in mid-1959. Nyakibanda seminary's atmosphere had substantially improved, the mission stations were not wracked by political or ethnic tensions, and the church was conducting a gradual but steady shift from missionary to indigenous leadership. Whatever their differences, Perraudin and Bigirumwami maintained public unity as they spoke out in favor of social justice, national unity, and reconciliation. Even the Catholic king turned missionary *bête noire*, Mwami Mutara, was regularly confessing to a local Tutsi priest and future bishop, Jean-Baptiste Gahamanyi, who in turn received effusive missionary praise for improving relations between the church and the royal court.[194] It is no wonder that the Holy See made the critical decision at this time to reclassify Rwanda from a mission territory to a local church. Before the announcement of this decree in November 1959, however, Rwanda would undergo seismic political changes.

Mutara's Death and Its Aftermath

In comparison to its neighbor Belgian Congo, Rwanda seemed to be undertaking a much more orderly decolonization process in mid-1959. While Congo faced January 1959 popular riots in Leopoldville, Rwanda experienced no public protests.[195] In turn, the specter of communism that so worried European observers in Congo had not gained traction in Rwanda.[196] With Rwanda's January 1960 elections looming in the distance, a growing consensus in Kigali and Brussels favored the establishment of a constitutional monarchy, further devolution of power to indigenous authorities, and the expansion of a meritocratic system of secondary schools and universities. Most importantly, political and ethnic rhetoric inside Rwanda had moderated during the first six months of the year. For all of its unresolved challenges, then, Rwanda appeared to be in the early stages of a relatively smooth political transition in July 1959.

This all changed on Saturday, July 25. While seeing his personal physician in Bujumbura, Burundi, Mwami Charles Mutara Rudahigwa fell gravely ill. Rushed to a local hospital, he died later that afternoon, likely felled by an overdose of penicillin.[197] Although Mutara's health had declined in the late 1950s, his sudden death came as a shock to the Rwandan people, local Rwandan elites, and Belgian colonial officials. His passing was even more destabilizing since Mutara died without a male heir or publicly named successor. In addition, his death in the care of Belgian doctors stoked widespread rumors of another colonial-missionary plot to replace an obdurate Rwandan king with a more compliant pro-Western figure.[198] For their part, colonial officials speculated that Mutara may have killed himself to protect his family's honor and boost popular support for independence.[199]

Condolences poured in from throughout the Catholic world, including a telegram from Pope John XXIII. The White Fathers issued a glowing tribute to Mutara in their August 2, 1959 edition of *Temps Nouveaux d'Afrique*. Here they praised the late Mwami's "true progressive spirit" and highlighted Mutara's suppression of *ubuhake* and central role in Christianizing the Rwandan people.[200] In private, White Father leaders in Rome were less mournful, hoping that Mutara's death would present an opportunity for the "Belgian government to make known its new politics."[201] Implicated in many of the conspiracy theories that circulated in the days following the Mwami's death, Perraudin neither left Kabgayi nor travelled at night until mid-August.[202] His only public comments came during his eloquent eulogy at Mutara's funeral on July 28. Here he praised the late king for championing the Christianization of Rwanda and steadfastly supporting the Catholic Church, highlighting his 1943 baptism, 1946 dedication of the country to Christ the King, and membership in the papal order of Gregory the Great. Perraudin also underlined how Mutara supported "the great and fruitful principle of loyal collaboration between the temporal and spiritual powers."[203]

As mourning continued for Rwanda's late king, European and Rwandan leaders jockeyed to determine who would succeed Mutara. Hutu agitators like Aloys Munyangaju lobbied for Belgium to use this opportunity to establish a republican regime with universal suffrage; Tutsi nationalists sought a constitutional monarch who would maintain Rwanda's traditional institutions. Fr. Alexis Kagame, who served as one of Rwanda's *biru* or "keepers of the traditions," informed Perraudin and other officials that Mutara had named his half-brother Jean-Baptiste Ndahindurwa as his successor in March 1959 and entrusted the young chief to Kagame's tutelage.[204] Unlike in 1931, the Belgians did not have a well-groomed candidate ready to step into office, which may offer the strongest argument against the theory of a Belgian conspiracy in the Mwami's death. Instead, colonial officials favored a slower transition, allowing for an interregnum of several weeks while a Belgian-Rwandan regency council determined a new constitutional monarch.

In contrast to the 1930s, however, the Belgians in 1959 could not simply impose their will on Rwanda's local authorities. During Mutara's funeral, Tutsi notables associated with the royal court staged what a critical Belgian observer termed the "*coup d'état* of Nyanza."[205] Claiming that Rwandan custom required the public installation of a new *mwami* before the burial of his predecessor, the royal *biru* proclaimed Ndahindurwa as Rwanda's new king. Belgian colonial officials did not protest, cowed into silence by the heavily armed Twa guards that surrounded them. The crowd acclaimed Ndahindurwa, a slight, bespectacled twenty-four-year-old who had entered the Catholic Church as a teenager, studied at the *Groupe Scolaire d'Astrida*, and recently finished his second month as a territorial administrator in southern Rwanda. The new Mwami took the name Kigeli V.[206]

Considering the polemics that had swirled in Rwanda since 1956, Mwami Kigeli garnered surprisingly widespread support in his early weeks. This stemmed in part from Ndahindurwa's reputation as a Tutsi modernizer who had cultivated good relations with Hutu elites in his district. Court traditionalists in turn saw Kigeli as a man who would maintain Rwanda's monarchical tradition. Even Catholic missionaries were enthused by his selection. In a letter to Rome, Alphonse Van Hoof remarked on the "extraordinary enthusiasm" which greeted the announcement of Kigeli's elevation. Here Van Hoof highlighted the new mwami's positive relations with the Astrida mission and the fervent Catholic faith of Ndahindurwa's mother.[207] Even a Hutu nationalist like Aloys Munyangaju struck an optimistic note. In an August 1959 postscript to his January 1959 essay *L'actualité politique au Ruanda*, Munyangaju pointed to Ndahindurwa's reputation as a "popular, modest, and simple" man and praised him as one of the few prominent Tutsi who had not publicly opposed the Hutu emancipation movement.[208] Kigeli's early gestures appeared to support Catholic optimism. On July 31, he undertook his first official trip to Kabgayi to ask for Perraudin's blessing. Although this precedent had been established by Mutara in 1931, Kigeli's last-minute decision seemed designed to quell the swirling rumors of church involvement in his half-brother's death. He visited Aloys Bigirumwami three weeks later, greeted by 100 cyclists, lines of cars, and festive shouts of "long live the king."[209]

As Kigeli would discover over the next three months, however, Mutara's death had ushered in a new era in Rwandan politics, an era in which the Mwami no longer set the political agenda. By mid-August Kigeli's natural allies—conservative nationalists based at the Nyanza court, northwestern Tutsi chiefs, and Muslim traders—had formed a new political party, the *Union Nationale Rwandaise* (UNAR). Growing out of the *Association des Eleveurs Ruandais* (Association of Rwandan Cattle Breeders) founded in 1958, UNAR proclaimed a political program first outlined in the 1957 *Mise au Point*. Namely, they supported a rapid timeline for independence from Belgium, celebrated Rwanda's precolonial traditions, denied the empirical reality of a Hutu-Tutsi problem, and emphasized national unity above all else. The UNAR charter also included a more visceral current of anti-colonialism, comparing the Belgian persecution of Rwanda to racial and colonial oppression in the southern United States, South Africa, and Vietnam. In the words of UNAR's first charter, "the West wants always to enslave Africa, to exploit her without pity or respite, and to deny to the black man the fundamental rights of man."[210] Retaining the hierarchical vision of traditional Rwandan society, the writers of the UNAR charter criticized Hutu elites' egalitarian discourse for "according the same valor to the vulgar thought of ordinary man as to the perspicacious judgment of the capable man." UNAR also promised to transform independent Rwanda into a constitutional monarchy and establish a representative parliamentary system in which Hutu and Tutsi would receive the same rights and responsibilities. To symbolize their supposed pan-ethnic vision, UNAR named François Rukeba, a half-Congolese Hutu, as their party spokesman.[211]

On September 13, 1959, UNAR gathered 3,000 members in downtown Kigali for its first party conference. Here UNAR leaders launched fierce diatribes against the Catholic Church and Belgium. As cars circled the streets of Kigali, partisans chanted, "Long live Rwanda! Long live the Mwami! Long live independence! Down with the whites, the missionaries, the dividers of the people!"[212] UNAR's new manifesto called for the secularization of Rwandan schools and an "urgent revision of the agreement with the teaching missions," reviving the lay schools debate of 1954–1955.[213] In a more sinister tone, UNAR equated national patriotism with party loyalty. "Those who do not enter this party will be considered as enemies of the people."[214] In turn, the manifesto described the Hutu-Tutsi problem as "the creation of the missionaries." For UNAR, Europeans were using the ethnic question to divide the country and delay Rwanda's rightful claims to independence. Michel Kayihura, the influential Tutsi chief and brother of the future bishop Jean-Baptiste Gahamanyi, concluded the meeting with a rousing call to arms:

> We share with all the same will of fighting for the unity of the country, for its autonomy first and for its independence following, against those who look to divide all that you know, combating the white monopoly and that of the missions in the schools, fighting against other Banyarwanda who are not of this party, since they are against unity, against Rwanda, against the Mwami, against the customs of the country.[215]

Perhaps doubting the young Mwami Kigeli's ability to mobilize the masses, UNAR looked to establish itself as the anti-colonial nationalist party in Rwanda.

In response to UNAR's manifestoes, Joseph Gitera's Aprosoma party lost whatever pan-ethnic elements it had briefly embraced in early 1959. Following a September 20 Twa assault on Gitera thought to be ordered by UNAR leaders,[216] Aprosoma titled its September 27 press communiqué as the "date of Hutu liberation from the secular slavery of the Batutsi." This document described the Tutsi people as "exploiters by nature, xenophobic by instinct, and communist by need, as manifested by the UNAR party."[217] Claiming the mantle of the church, Aprosoma falsely posited that Catholic authorities had condemned the Kalinga drums, the symbol of the monarchy. They also invoked Christian rhetoric in predicting the coming "resurrection" of Hutu society.[218] If anything, Aprosoma's call to arms was even more extreme than UNAR's earlier proclamations. "Long live the liberation of the Hutu! Down with Tutsi slavery! The cohabitation of Tutsi with Hutu is a gnawing wound, a leech in the body, and a cancer in the stomach. Hutu, from now on believe and hope in God and in each other, never in the Tutsi!"[219]

Aprosoma soon had an official political rival on the Hutu side. Since its inception in 1957, Gregoire Kayibanda's *Mouvement Social Muhutu* (MSM) had built a grassroots network across Rwanda, taking advantage of Kayibanda's and Calliope Mulindahabi's extensive connections within TRAFIPRO, the *Association of Moniteurs*, and the Legion of Mary.[220] In October 1959, Kayibanda announced that the MSM was becoming a formal political party, the *Parti du Mouvement de l'Emancipation Hutu* (Parmehutu). Like UNAR, Parmehutu attempted to present itself as a national party that could unify the Rwandan people. But if UNAR saw national unity threatened by the Hutu social movement, Parmehutu's manifesto described Rwanda as an ethnically stratified country that would unite only with "the end of 'Tutsi colonialism' and the feudal regime instituted by the Tutsi."[221] Unlike Aprosoma, Parmehutu shied away from extremist ethnic rhetoric. In its October manifesto, Parmehutu invited Tutsi sympathizers into its ranks, differentiated between the feudal system and "our Tutsi brothers," and admitted that injustices had been suffered "not only by the Bahutu, but also by the poor Tutsi."[222] Favoring gradual democratization over immediate independence, Parmehutu's manifesto otherwise echoed themes shared by the other major parties—a constitutional monarchy, separation of administrative and judicial powers, support for private property rights, and a "refusal of tribal fights." At the same time, Parmehutu offered a far more sanguine vision of the European and Catholic roles in Rwandan society than UNAR. Parmehutu explicitly rejected anti-European xenophobia and "thanked the missions for their work of educating the masses of the country."[223]

The fourth of the major parties to emerge in 1959 was perhaps closest to the Catholic hierarchy's and Belgian government's own political views. Encouraged by the Belgian Resident, André Preud'homme, and led by the pro-Western Tutsi chiefs Prosper Bwanakweri and Lazare Ndazaro, the *Rassemblement Démocratique Rwandais* (Rader) issued its own manifesto on October 1, 1959. Here Rader proclaimed its support for universal suffrage, the democratization of Rwandan institutions, private property, economic cooperatives, and foreign investment. Rader also distanced itself from the ethnic rhetoric of Aprosoma and Parmehutu, proclaiming that "it is profoundly erroneous to think that the good of one [ethnic group] depends on the crushing of the others."[224] Embracing both UNAR's emphasis on national unity and Parmehutu's commitment to democratization, Rader surpassed both parties in its praise for Belgian and Catholic influence. In its opening manifesto, Rader noted "the civilizing work accomplished by the Belgians in the political, social, economic and cultural domains" and claimed that "it is impossible to give a true education to people without the foundation and animation of true religion."[225] It may be that Rader's awkward melding of pro-Western rhetoric and pan-ethnic nationalism foiled the party from the start; the party of reforming Tutsi elites never developed a popular following. Rader's efforts to reach out to Hutu elites were also rebuffed. Shortly after the release of Rader's manifesto, Bwanakweri approached Kayibanda to discuss the possibility of merging their parties into a pan-ethnic movement that could challenge UNAR. Ever the opportunist, Kayibanda demurred, sacrificing a golden opportunity to form a truly pan-ethnic political movement.[226]

The Bishops Respond

As political mobilization accelerated in the months following Mwami Mutara's death, the Catholic hierarchy attempted to reassert its magisterial authority. Over the course of sixty days between mid-August and mid-October, Perraudin and Bigirumwami brought the nation's priests together for a major synod at Nyakibanda, argued over the role of the Catholic media in Rwanda's disputes, and issued warnings against two of Rwanda's new political parties. The Catholic bishops of Rwanda, Burundi, and Belgian Congo also published two important statements on the relationship between Christianity and politics.

The first statement, *"Le chrétien et la politique,"* was released on August 15 and signed by all of the bishops of Belgian Congo, Rwanda, and Burundi. On August 25, Perraudin, Bigirumwami, and their Burundian colleagues released *"Consignes et directives des Vicaires Apostoliques du Ruanda-Urundi."*[227] Collectively, the bishops argued for a stricter separation of church and state, exhorted their clergy to avoid politics, and vowed to defend church institutions from state interference. At the same time, Catholic leaders looked to expand the church's social engagement beyond the "purely religious questions in the sanctuary or sacristy" to include areas of education, youth formation, social work, medical institutions, property rights, and government subsidies for the missions. Significantly, the bishops also viewed political engagement as a central aspect of lay Catholic identity. "A Christian who, in his place, following his age and social condition, is not preoccupied with the political, economic and social problems of his country, would not be a true Christian."[228] And if lay Catholics should generally follow Romans 13 in accepting duly constituted authority, they "cannot accommodate a Constitution of aggressive laicization which eliminates all reference to God, the principle of legitimate authority."[229] Such language appeared to offer tacit justification for rebellion against a Marxist or Communist government that "opposes the fundamental theses of Christian dogma and applies methods contrary to Christian morality, notably the respect due to the human person...God will not continue to mandate an authority which does not fulfill its mission and does not serve the good of all on whose behalf she serves."[230] Without delving deeply into the ethnic question, the Burundian and Rwandan bishops' statement also followed Perraudin's "Letter on Charity" in describing Rwanda and Burundi's social problem as "particularly delicate since it doubles as a racial problem."[231] For its part, the broader episcopal statement *Le chrétien et la politique* avoided the Hutu-Tutsi question all together.

In the aftermath of the publication of *Le chrétien et la politique* and *Consignes et directives*, Perraudin and Bigirumwami gathered Rwanda's priests for a national synod at Nyakibanda Seminary between August 24 and August 29.[232] Topics ranged from improving training for lay catechists and inculturating the liturgy to strengthening clerical unity and reevaluating the relationship between the priesthood and politics.[233] Sixty priests from Kabgayi and eighteen from Nyundo participated; most were superiors of mission stations. Publicly, the synod members expressed their commitment to clerical unity, their filial obedience to the bishops, and their regret at the "injuries and calumnies" suffered by their bishops.[234] In their concluding statement, Bigirumwami and Perraudin agreed that the church should avoid political entanglements except in matters of faith and morals. They also instructed priests to form lay faithful who could make responsible political decisions in light of their Catholic faith. Perraudin and Bigirumwami also reiterated the importance of Christian unity and demanded that Christians avoid political parties that contradicted the "core truths" of Catholic teaching.[235] For better or worse, these "core truths" remained unnamed.

If the two bishops publicly concurred on the importance of clerical and national unity, they differed on how to achieve this goal. For Bigirumwami, the primary culprit remained the artificial Hutu-Tutsi problem; downplaying this distinction would restore unity within church and state alike. In contrast, Perraudin saw the solution to clerical disunity as keeping the clergy out of politics. But if Perraudin instructed his priests to leave political action to the laity, he also believed that clerics retained the right and responsibility to teach boldly on the nation's pressing social issues. "We cannot be a partisan clergy; but the priest is a man of all the world, and we do not have the right to close our eyes before the problems which are posed to us; we must form our faithful, to each group to which they belong, to take all their temporal responsibilities as convinced Christians."[236]

Even as Perraudin and Bigirumwami worked hard to maintain a united public front, they clashed behind the scenes. In particular, the two bishops disagreed over whether Catholic newspapers bore some responsibility for Rwanda's increasingly volatile political atmosphere. As noted above, Bigirumwami had already expressed his frustration with the Catholic media in late 1958 and early 1959. In a private letter in March 1959, he argued that Catholic journals should speak more of tradition, civility, and ethnic *entente* than democracy, revolution and Hutu emancipation.

Our journals TN [*Temps Nouveaux*] and KM [*Kinyamateka*], Catholic journals in Rwanda-Burundi...should smell more of a 'good sanctified odor'
and in their expressions should stir hearts to sentiments of justice, love
and obedience...Our journals have made much evil, and already we are
undergoing the consequences which will become more pronounced if we
do not stop our democratic propaganda which tends to destroy what has
been constructed.[237]

In August 1959 Bigirumwami took his critiques of *Kinyamateka* and *Temps
Nouveaux d'Afrique* to the leaders of the White Fathers. Here he accused these
newspapers of inciting ethnic divisionism and undermining his own authority
as bishop.[238] Even as he admitted that the Catholic press had the right to criticize
abuses of power and anti-Christian customs, Bigirumwami worried that Catholic
editors had forgotten the fundamental principle that "all authority comes from
God."[239] In a moment of rhetorical hyperbole, Bigirumwami went so far as to claim
that the missionary journals had attacked the Mwami and Rwanda's traditional
authorities for "10 to 15 years."[240] Bigirumwami feared that these newspapers were
now turning against the indigenous church, thereby giving more ammunition to
the church's true enemies. "I believe that in attacking local civil and ecclesiastical
authority, legitimately established, the missionary journals can create an immense
and irreparable evil in our country and in our Church and at the same time attract
hatreds and maledictions on the missionaries."[241] For Bigirumwami, the missionary press had contributed to Rwanda's growing internal divisions by "accentuating
incomprehension and malaise" between Hutu and Tutsi.[242]

   Bigirumwami's critiques had an effect. Even as the White Fathers' Superior
General, Leo Volker, described Bigirumwami's diatribes as "very exaggerated,"
Volker also instructed the editors of *Temps Nouveaux* to exercise more prudence
when writing on ethnic and political questions.[243] For his part, Perraudin agreed
to ban all political writing in *Kinyamateka* and to expand the newspaper's editorial
voices. In October, Perraudin removed Kayibanda from *Kinyamateka's* editorial
staff, ostensibly because Kayibanda had started a political party.[244] At the same
time, Perraudin's appointments helped ensure that *Kinyamateka* maintained a
broadly pro-Hutu outlook. As the newspaper's general editor, Justin Kalibwami
was one of the few Tutsi priests known for his overt sympathies for the Hutu
emancipation movement. And after the November 1959 Hutu uprising, Perraudin
added the Hutu priest Alphonse Ntezimana to the editorial staff.[245]

   Even as they privately grappled over the political culpability of Catholic newspapers, Rwanda's bishops united in the face of Rwanda's new political parties. On
September 24, Bigirumwami and Perraudin issued a confidential circular to their
priests expressing grave concerns over UNAR's nationalistic rhetoric. Perraudin's
wartime experiences in Switzerland reemerged in the bishops' critiques of

UNAR. "This [UNAR] tendency resembles strongly the 'national socialism' that other countries have known and which have caused them so much grief."[246] Perraudin and Bigirumwami especially criticized UNAR's anti-missionary language and opposition to Catholic schools, sentiments that they attributed to possible Communist and Muslim influences. As with the lay schools debate of the mid-1950s, perceived anti-clericalism served to unite Catholic leaders across ideological lines. As Bigirumwami stated in a circular letter released just days after the anti-UNAR statement, "the bishops will not oppose any [political] party unless it is manifestly anti-Catholic."[247]

Rumors have persisted that the White Fathers leaned on Bigirumwami to sign a document that essentially reflected Perraudin's personal views. Guy Mosmans's September 21 visit to Nyundo lends a measure of credence to such theories. However, Bigirumwami never hinted at such pressure, and his individual September 26 pastoral letter echoed the September 24 joint circular.[248] Here Bigirumwami asked his flock to "understand the role of the good Pastor who must look over his sheep" and to judge a political party "by its fruits." If anything, Bigirumwami does not come across in this letter as a man obsessed with Rwandan politics. Rather, his focus lay with maintaining Catholic fidelity and charity in the midst of an overheating political cauldron. Reminding his priests that one "cannot oppose the Church of missionaries with the autochthonous or national Church," he banned clergy from attending political meetings and exhorted lay Catholics to "make a politics of silence, calm, prayer, peace, prudence, and confidence in your Bishops." Bigirumwami exhorted his people to "love all Banyarwanda whether small or great, rich or poor, good or malicious, just or unjust." He also instructed them to surround themselves with Christian teachers and catechists "without neglecting good relations with the chiefs, sub-chiefs, and *évolués* and without forgetting to defend the poor for love and justice and truth."[249] To his credit, Bigirumwami recognized the risks that political mobilization—or partisanship of any type—posed to the universal demands of Christian charity.

After criticizing UNAR, the bishops also released a sharp critique of Aprosoma, UNAR's ideological opposite. Despite or perhaps because of Aprosoma's proclaimed fealty to Catholic teaching, Perraudin and Bigirumwami did not welcome the party's late September manifesto. On October 11, Perraudin and Bigirumwami issued another circular to the Rwandan clergy condemning Aprosoma's "spirit of non-Christian racial hatred [which is] incompatible with the teachings and the exhortations of Our Lord and of the Holy Church."[250] Here the bishops demanded that Gitera retract his statement claiming that the Catholic bishops had condemned the Kalinga drums.[251] Gitera proved to be a loyal son of the church. Two days after the release of Perraudin and Bigirumwami's letter, Gitera resigned his leadership of Aprosoma and apologized for any statements that could be misconstrued as inciting racial hatred. In parting, however, he reiterated his belief that the Bahutu Manifesto embodied "the social doctrine of the Church in a Christian spirit."[252]

As October progressed, Bigirumwami and Perraudin withheld any further political critiques, offering tacit approval to both Rader and Parmehutu and reiterating the church's officially nonpartisan stance. On October 31, Perraudin penned an angry protest letter to the Belgian newspaper *La Libre Belgique* for recently claiming that Perraudin had "taken up the cause, by word and by action, for the emancipation of the Hutu." While admitting that his February 1959 letter on charity had "publicly affirmed the existence of a grave moral problem and took to heart the interests of the poor people," Perraudin denied that he had any racialist motives and expressed his desire to be a bishop for all Rwandans. Unlike in February, this letter carefully avoided juxtaposing "poor" with "Hutu."[253]

Clearly, then, church leaders did not stand idly by while political tensions increased in Rwanda in late 1959. However, their statements and critiques seemed to have little on-the-ground impact. If anything, the political atmosphere in September and October 1959 only worsened as Rwanda's politicians accused each other of communism, atheism, and inciting national division and racial hatred.[254] UNAR protested its opponents' charges of anti-Catholicism, xenophobia, feudalism and communism.[255] At the same time, the party circulated anonymous tracts calling for the elimination of ten "enemies of Rwanda" including Perraudin and Rader's Tutsi leadership.[256] Despite his initial promise, Kigeli V was proving to be a weak monarch, overshadowed by UNAR partisans at his own court. In particular, his failure to condemn some of UNAR's more excessive claims cost him the Mwami's most important traditional attribute—namely the king's reputation as an impartial figure standing above political disputes.[257] Belgian colonial authorities were also losing legitimacy, especially after their decision in mid-October to exile three prominent Tutsi chiefs for inciting political violence. This led to the first public split between Kigeli and the Belgians, mass protests in Kigali, and the Belgian shooting of a Rwandan protester on October 17.[258]

After weeks of escalating political tension, Rwanda stood on a knife's edge as Christians celebrated the Feast of All Saints on the morning of November 1, 1959. The combustible political environment needed only a spark, and it was not long in coming.

Did the Catholic Hierarchy Incite an Ethnic Revolution?

In light of the narrative we have just shared, a key question remains. Through their actions and statements in the late 1950s, did Catholic leaders lay the groundwork for the November 1959 Hutu political uprising that precipitated the revolutionary transformations of 1959–1962? This is after all a widespread view in the post1994 academy and on the Rwandan street alike.[259] In particular, Mgr. Perraudin has been accused of political divisionism, regicide, and offering tacit approval for ethnic massacres. Gourevitch, Mamdani and other critics have repeatedly underlined the connections between the institutional church and emerging Hutu political movements, implying that the church served as a revolutionary vanguard in Rwandan society. Mamdani has gone so far as to describe the church as "the womb that nurtured the leadership of the insurgent Hutu movement."[260] Recent RPF government officials have made even stronger claims, implicating Perraudin as "the author of the 1994 genocide."[261] Perraudin in turn has defended himself and his record to the United Nations, the Vatican, and ultimately to a broader reading public in a 2003 memoir published shortly before his death.

Examining the historical record, it seems easy to parry the charge that Perraudin was a radical liberation theologian advocating for Hutu revolution. He never called on the Hutu masses to rise up and throw off their Tutsi rulers. If there is one theme repeated in all of the bishops' pastoral writings, it is not the demand for liberation but the importance of unity. On the eve of the revolution, Perraudin condemned extremists on both sides of the Rwandan political debate, from UNAR radicals threatening to extirpate their political opponents to Aprosoma militants calling for the violent overthrow of Tutsi authorities.

In addition, Perraudin's and Bigirumwami's writings in 1958–1959 belie any stereotypical division between Perraudin as the "progressive advocate of Hutu rights" and Bigirumwami as the "conservative defender of Tutsi privilege." For sure, there were important ideological differences between the two churchmen. For example, if Perraudin emphasized social justice and Christian unity and utilized racial categories to describe Hutu and Tutsi, Bigirumwami highlighted national unity, defended customary authorities, and downplayed the Hutu-Tutsi distinction. Yet in terms of their overarching politics, both come across as moderate progressives committed to the gradual democratization of Rwanda's political institutions and opposed to anti-clerical nationalism, anti-Tutsi racialism, and the political exploitation of the peasantry.

Inside the church, Perraudin showed a judicious balance in his ecclesial appointments, increasing Hutu enrollment in the seminaries and naming Tutsi to prominent positions in his vicariate.[262] Perraudin made Kayibanda work under Tutsi priests at *Kinyamateka* and removed him from the newspaper's editorial board after Parmehutu formally organized as a political party in October 1959. And as we will see in chapter 5, when violence broke out in November 1959, Perraudin and Bigirumwami issued an immediate condemnation and opened up mission stations and churches to thousands of Tutsi refugees. Unlike in 1994, these missions were not later compromised. So while Perraudin had a passion for social justice and tended to view social distinctions in ethnic terms, he was far from the violent revolutionary of UNAR mythology.[263]

If Perraudin was not a revolutionary, was he simply reincarnating Leon Classe's Constantinian vision in liberal democratic clothing?[264] Like his predecessor, Perraudin believed that the church had a central role to play within Rwandan civil society, and he continually defended the church's right to address pressing moral and social questions. He celebrated the extent to which Mwami Mutara had institutionalized Catholicism as a national religion. Like many of his postwar missionary colleagues, Perraudin saw political independence as a gift only in so far as Rwanda retained its Catholic heritage (especially as embodied in Catholic schools and laws respecting Christian marriage). Perraudin therefore stood in a long line of African missionaries looking to strengthen the church by cultivating close relations with the state. This inclination would only deepen in the postcolonial period, as we will see in subsequent chapters.

It would be inaccurate, however, to dismiss Perraudin as a court prophet. He moved sharply away from Rwanda's traditional authorities in the late 1950s. Along with Bigirumwami, he joined his fellow bishops in condemning colonial and customary abuses in 1956 and 1957 pastoral statements. His 1959 letter *Super omnia caritas* spoke even more definitively of structural evil in Rwandan society. He helped start the TRAFIPRO cooperative and encouraged Catholic Action to consider social justice questions. And unlike Guy Mosmans, Perraudin never wrote of the virtues of colonialism or Belgium's "magnificent work" in Africa.[265] Perraudin in this sense was a distinctively postwar missionary, preoccupied with balancing the church's traditional commitment to church-state cohabitation with growing concerns for decolonization, democratization and social justice. And although some recent scholars see his pro-Hutu leanings as a cynical effort to maintain the church's traditional social privileges,[266] the ultimate political success of the Hutu social movement was by no means evident prior to the November 1959 revolution. Unlike his White Father confreres Arthur Dejemeppe, Mosmans or even Alphonse van Hoof, André Perraudin does not come across as a politically obsessed man in his private correspondence. On the contrary, he emerges as a cautious Catholic churchman, concerned with developing the Catholic Church's pastoral capacity, maintaining internal unity, and resisting secularization.

Another complicating factor is the extent to which ethnic discourse developed in two directions. As we have seen in the "Great Servants of the Court" letter, the early discourse of UNAR, and the general attitudes of the Tutsi-dominated Superior Council, ethnicist attitudes were not limited to Hutu elites. If postgenocide writers look to the 1950s for the roots of "Hutu power," earlier commentators like Ian Linden, Catherine Newbury and René Lemarchand saw the Tutsi as the first Rwandan social group to develop ethnic consciousness.[267] There is truth in both accounts. For example, Mwami Mutara's failure to countenance any of the proposed Hutu-Tutsi Study Commission reforms further alienated Hutu leaders and emboldened radicals on both sides. On the other hand, Hutu leaders' melding of egalitarian and ethnic discourse undermined the hierarchical social institutions of traditional Rwandan society and further essentialized Hutu and Tutsi categories. Regardless, it was likely impossible for Perraudin and Bigirumwami to wholly extricate themselves from ethnic politics in the late 1950s. To say nothing would have maintained Léon Classe's concordat between the missionary church and Rwanda's customary authorities.[268] As it is, Perraudin's attempts to speak out on Rwandan social injustice were invariably construed by his opponents as pro-Hutu propaganda.

In turn, this study reveals the complexity of "the church" or Catholic politics in the late 1950s. Kayibanda, Munyangaju, and Bicamumpaka had their clerical supporters, but so did Mwami Mutara, Michel Kayihura, and Prosper Bwanakweri. Furthermore, all of these individuals were part of "the church," and we should be careful about turning them into lay puppets for missionary puppeteers. As Paul Rutayisire has said, the violence of 1959 arose as much through the agency of Rwandan *évolués* as through their supposed missionary masters. "Two very small groups of candidates for power opposed themselves through third-party popular masses."[269]

And yet it is more difficult to defend Perraudin against the charges that he further hardened ethnic discourse and helped lay the rhetorical groundwork for the Rwandan revolution. His invoking of Hutu-Tutsi language in the post-1956 period seems incongruous after he barely mentioned the distinction in his years at Nyakibanda. Most of all, Perraudin's *Super omnia caritas* exacerbated the zero-sum nature of ethnic discourse by describing Hutu and Tutsi as racial groups and associating this distinction with Rwanda's social and economic divisions. Perraudin's dualistic ethnic vision remained in his memoirs. "Similarly if the Hutu population had enough to eat and was protected by the Tutsi patron, [the Hutu] was considered as inferior, a workhorse to do his master's bidding...living in very humiliating dependence on his patron, ultimately neither free nor independent."[270] Strangely missing from Perraudin's analysis is the postwar rise of a Hutu-dominated middle class. If it ever held true, the stereotypical notions of the wealthy Tutsi cattleholder and poor Hutu subsistence farmer no longer applied in the late 1950s. In this sense, Perraudin erred grievously in framing social justice questions in exclusively ethnic terms and failing to nuance the complex categories of "Hutu" and "Tutsi." He would have done better to borrow the analysis of an anonymous Hutu contributor to a 1958 issue of *Temps Nouveaux d'Afrique*.

> The majority of high dignitaries respond to certain bodily characteristics that immediately classify them among the Tutsi...yet we know well that the problem is more social than racial. It is not because they

have other characteristics that Bahutu and Batutsi are posing a problem: it is because one has in practice...the power and that the others
do not have it. If one says "Batutsi-Bahutu," the problem takes a racial
cast, and it is too easy then to remark that there are many are poor and
miserable Tutsi and rich and fat Bahutu who are very successful in
their affairs.[271]

More than anything, this narrative reminds us that the Rwandan revolution—
like all revolutions—arose first from a revolution of ideas. Postwar support for free
markets, democracy, and social egalitarianism shifted missionary attitudes toward
Rwandan society. The organic social hierarchy celebrated by the White Fathers in
the 1920s and 1930s became anachronistic feudalism by the 1950s. Missionary
commentators from Dominic Nothomb to André Perraudin claimed that the
church did not create the Hutu-Tutsi problem but merely made people aware of
it. Awareness, however, is the crucial issue. In other words, Hutu-Tutsi social divisions existed before the 1950s, but it was Christian egalitarianism that made these
divisions seem problematic. In a sense, then, one could argue that Catholic human
rights discourse did in fact divide Rwanda by raising the peasant's consciousness of
his own relative deprivation. Jan Adriaenssens argued as much in a 1960 political
analysis of Rwanda, noting that the development of Catholic education and evangelization opened Hutu eyes to the injustices they were suffering.[272] As we will
see in the next chapter, "raised Hutu consciousness" was repeatedly named as a
precipitating cause of Rwanda's November 1959 violence.[273] Even Perraudin con-
ceded this point, writing in 1962 that "the revolution has not been only political; it
is above all psychological and social. The masses have become conscious of their
rights as human persons and will no longer accept...the return to a regime which
suppressed them."[274] Nor can it be denied that Catholic media played a central role
in this conscientizing process. For example, whereas *Temps Nouveaux's* articles in
1956 and 1957 generally steered clear of the ethnic question and avoided directly
critiquing Rwanda's Tutsi authorities, the newspaper's tone changed markedly in
1958 under the influence of the Hutu journalist Aloys Munyangaju. Soon *Temps
Nouveaux* was publishing cover stories that openly questioned Rwanda's traditional
institutions.[275]

Rwandan Catholic leaders suffered from other shortcomings in the late
1950s. First, the church could not reach consensus on the primary social division of the day—the nature of the Hutu-Tutsi distinction. No matter Perraudin's
or Bigirumwami's exhortations to unity and consensus, church leaders diverged
on how to *describe* emerging political tensions in the late 1950s. For Perraudin,
Rwanda's social problems stemmed from the economic and political marginalization of the Hutu majority in a Tutsi-dominated state. For Bigirumwami, the blame
lay with Hutu propagandists sewing discord across Rwandan society. Because of

this fundamental analytical division, church leaders failed to present a unified voice in the face of rising political polemics.

Second, the church's triumphal ecclesiology prevented leaders from taking responsibility for their own shortcomings. As noted previously, Perraudin's *"Super omnia caritas"* included no apologies for past missionary meddling, whether through their anthropological analyses or favoring of Tutsi in administrative positions and colonial schools. No one in the late 1950s (or even in Perraudin's memoirs) apologized for Léon Classe's role in the illegal *coup d'état* against Mwami Musinga in 1931. If anything, Perraudin in the late 1950s was trying to leave the past behind rather than grapple with its incontrovertible legacies.

Third, Catholic leaders failed to consider how the church could embody a distinct alternative to electoral party politics. The Catholic Church had remarkable political and social capital in the late 1950s, and it was the only social institution that encompassed both Hutu and Tutsi elites. But rather than envision how Catholic sacramental practices like the Eucharist could themselves challenge the imaginative world of ethnicity or nation-state, Catholic leaders rarely considered what a truly "Christian politics" could look like.[276] In this vein, Perraudin vacillated between defending the church's right to offer moral guidance on social or racial questions and insisting that the church had no explicitly political mission. But to echo Ian Linden, "what politics are not about social or racial issues?"[277] Reducing themselves to moral and social lobbyists, Catholic leaders were both overly ambitious and not ambitious enough—overly ambitious in thinking they could Christianize the democratization process in Rwanda; not ambitious enough in failing to envision the nature of Catholic politics beyond the nation-state. In this sense, one regrets the failure of Catholic leaders to initiate alternative social movements like Martin Luther King's civil rights movement or Desmond Tutu's nonviolent resistance to apartheid.[278] In turn, Perraudin's conflicted rhetoric on the church's political role—trying to influence politics while still claiming a spiritual mission "above" politics—left the church looking simultaneously hypocritical and impotent. In the meantime, Rwandan elites identified first and foremost as Hutu or Tutsi, anti-colonial or pro-Belgian, monarchist or republican.[279] Christian identity was socially and politically irrelevant. Writing in early 1959, Bigirumwami sensed the church's failure to establish its own distinctive political voice.

> As for me, I have apprehensions for the direction given to our country. [Media] propaganda wants to destroy all which is Tutsi but does not say what the Hutu party should become. I myself imagine that we are indisposing thousands of our sheep by our *not neutral* politics. We should be making a Catholic and apostolic and peaceful politics.[280]

Dismissed as a traditionalist by many missionaries and ignored by more radical Tutsi clergy, Bigirumwami's voice remained a lonely one. By the early 1960s, he would be writing for the archives rather than for contemporary public opinion. In hindsight, his words seem prophetic, reminding us that while the church cannot avoid politics, Christian politics should look very different than the politics of Parmehutu, UNAR, or the partisan politics of any day and age.

As we will discover in chapter 5, these three shortcomings—analytical divergence, triumphalist ecclesiology, and the failure to explore an alternative political imagination—would leave the Rwandan Catholic Church deeply divided, dangerously unrepentant, and ultimately impotent in the face of the violence which swept Rwandan society between 1959 and 1962.

5

The Catholic Church and Political Revolution in Rwanda, 1959–1962

THE YEARS 1959 to 1962 marked a profound rupture in Rwanda's long history as a unified state. Already weakened by decades of Belgian colonial rule, the monarchy gave way to a democratic republic. Aided by Belgian military and political officials, a Hutu-dominated one-party state replaced the former Tutsi oligarchy. The bloodshed, ethnic cleansing, and mass refugee movements profoundly destabilized Rwandan society and established the zero-sum ethnic logic that reaped such a terrible harvest in the postcolonial period, culminating with civil war and genocide in the early 1990s. Reflecting the lasting legacy of the 1959 events, Hutu Power advocates in the run-up to the 1994 genocide described Rwanda's enemies as "Tutsi inside or outside the country, who are extremist and nostalgic for power and who have never recognized and still do not recognize the realities of the 1959 Social Revolution."[1]

Recent commentators such as Mahmood Mamdani and Philip Gourevitch have highlighted the ideological significance of the revolutionary period for shaping postcolonial consciousness in Rwanda.[2] Older studies by Filip Reyntjens, Donat Murego, and René Lemarchand offer detailed historical studies of the 1959–1962 period.[3] In addition, Ian Linden, Justin Kalibwami, Tharcisse Gatwa and most recently Timothy Longman have mentioned the Hutu social revolution in their surveys of Christian history in Rwanda.[4] Largely missing in the historical literature, however, is sustained attention to the Catholic hierarchy's public and private reactions to Rwanda's political upheavals of 1959–1962. In addition, few scholars have explored the impact of Rwanda's Hutu revolution on the Catholic Church's internal life, particularly in the areas of intraclerical relations and seminary life.[5]

Continuing the chronological approach of previous chapters, the chapter begins with the November 1959 Hutu uprisings.[6] Here I analyze the complex and contested history of the first two weeks of November 1959, highlighting the political dimensions of the violence and noting the complicity of both Tutsi and Hutu partisans. I also argue that it was the subsequent Belgian reaction—specifically the military resident Col. Guy Logiest's decision to install hundreds of Hutu as interim chiefs—that ensured the long-term political ramifications of the Hutu *jacquerie*. I then consider Mwami Kigeli's fallout with Belgian authorities over the Belgian response to the November uprisings, the growing polarization of Rwanda's political parties in early 1960, and the reasons why Gregoire Kayibanda's Parmehutu party came to dominate Rwandan politics by 1961. I also analyze how and why ethnic and political violence became entrenched in Rwandan society during 1961 and 1962.

While grounding this narrative in Rwanda's political history, my goal in this chapter is to explain the Catholic Church's complex history during a period of rising political polemics. On one hand, Catholic parishes served as places of refuge during the 1959 violence (in contrast to later ethnic violence in both 1973 and 1994).[7] At the same time, Catholic missionary leaders increasingly demonized the leaders of the Tutsi exile community and acquiesced in the rise of Parmehutu's one-party rule. And although Catholic leaders continued to speak of the virtues of ecclesial unity, their own institutions were increasingly marked by ethnic, ideological, and racial divisions, particularly after the White Fathers embarked on an unprecedented Hutu affirmative action program in both the seminary and the episcopacy. In addition, relations between the White Fathers and the Vatican grew more strained. Although the documentary record is far from complete, our limited archival evidence shows the Holy See sympathizing more with Bigirumwami and Rwanda's indigenous clergy than Perraudin and the White Fathers.

At the same time, the Rwandan church underwent extraordinary pastoral changes during this three-year period. The Vatican reclassified Rwanda from a "mission territory" to a "local church" in November 1959 and added two new dioceses in 1961 and 1962. Several new indigenous church leaders emerged on the scene. These included Bernard Manyurane, Rwanda's first Hutu bishop who died suddenly and suspiciously in May 1961; his successor Joseph Sibomana, a Hutu priest known for his political moderation; and Jean-Baptiste Gahamanyi, the first bishop of Butare in southern Rwanda, close confidant of André Perraudin, and Tutsi brother of the UNAR political leader Michel Kayihura.

The two most important Catholic leaders remained the same two churchmen who led the Rwandan Catholic Church in the late 1950s—Archbishop André Perraudin of Kabgayi and Bishop Aloys Bigirumwami of Nyundo. Surprisingly, Perraudin and especially Bigirumwami have been largely ignored in the secondary literature on Rwanda. In many ways scholars have been too enamored with the legacy of Mgr. Léon Classe, ignoring the extent to which Perraudin's contrasting political emphases on social justice, democracy, and Hutu rights shaped the contours of postcolonial Rwandan politics.[8] In turn, Bigirumwami reminds us of the complexity of Catholic politics at the time of independence, recovering an important contrary voice in light of Rwanda's later history.

In my presentation of Bigirumwami, Perraudin, and Catholic politics during the Rwandan revolution, I make three primary arguments. First, the caricatures of Bigirumwami as a conservative traditionalist and Perraudin as a Machiavellian revolutionary do not do justice to their ecclesial visions.[9] Both supported the political ends of democracy and social justice, rejected violence, opposed clerical involvement in secular politics, and shared a Pauline vision of the church as a unified Body of Christ. Having said this, the two bishops continued to disagree over the nature of the Hutu-Tutsi distinction and the extent to which social justice and democracy could be mapped on a Hutu-Tutsi axis. Since the Hutu-Tutsi question came to dominate every aspect of Rwandan life during 1959-62, this analytical divergence undermined their cherished goal of clerical unity. Finally, in his efforts to defend himself and what he perceived to be the Catholic Church's institutional interests, Perraudin and his missionary colleagues established the framework of church politics in the postcolonial period: (1) a pro-Hutu analytical partisanship that underplayed the risks of conflating democracy, social justice, and ethnicity, (2) an ideological paranoia about the Tutsi exile community which led to a "blame the victim" attitude toward local Tutsi, and (3) a close collaboration with the state which protected the church's institutional interests but undermined the church's ability to challenge state-sanctioned ethnic violence.

As a Tutsi bishop who witnessed tremendous suffering in northwestern Rwanda, Bigirumwami offers what in hindsight appears as a lonely prophetic voice. While never renouncing social justice and democratization, Bigirumwami recognized the darker side of these movements—namely, the Hutu majority's violent persecution of the minority Tutsi on the grounds of their alleged social intransigence, authoritarian elitism, communist ties, and opposition to the Catholic Church. More than Perraudin and the White Fathers, Bigirumwami highlighted the mortal danger of ethnicism and argued that the church's ultimate political enemy was not a political *end* like feudalism, communism, or monarchy but rather the political *means* of violence. Bigirumwami also offered a more self-critical ecclesial voice, questioning the depth of Rwanda's Christian identity and wondering why so many Christians had abandoned what he termed the "politics of Jesus" for the politics of Parmehutu and UNAR. In summary, Bigirumwami reveals the ecclesiological promise of the persecuted church—a church that can speak truth to power, identify with the victims, and strive toward an alternative Christian political imagination that challenges the idols of ethnic and national identity.

The November 1959 Hutu Uprisings

The violence that erupted during the first week of November 1959 had been anticipated for weeks.[10] Political tensions had risen precipitously in preparation for Belgium's November 1959 response to the Belgian Working Group document as well as communal elections anticipated for January 1960. As discussed in chapter 4, precipitating incidents included the fiery UNAR and Aprosoma speeches and manifestoes of August-September 1959 and UNAR's attack on Aprosoma leader Joseph Gitera on September 20. Anticipating further disturbances, the Belgian governor, Jean-Paul Harroy, banned political meetings in October and reassigned three chiefs who served in UNAR leadership. Despite this, the three deposed chiefs—Michel Kayihura of Bugoyi, Pierre Mungalurire of Kigali, and Christian Rwangombwa of Byumba—rallied thousands of mostly Hutu supporters and refused to leave their territories.[11] During one mass protest in Kigali on October 17, Belgian soldiers shot and killed three protestors, further exacerbating local tensions. On October 25, anonymous pamphlets calling for the death of "all traitors of Rwanda and their chief, Mgr. Perraudin" appeared on trees across southern and central Rwanda.[12] Rumors circulated that Belgium was about to announce its withdrawal from the country, transforming January 1960 communal elections into a possible gateway to independence. The political stakes in Rwanda had never been higher.[13]

Despite the anticipation, however, the scale and style of the November disturbances came as a surprise. First, the uprisings took on an explicitly ethnic caste as Hutu militias attacked thousands of local Tutsi. The pillaging, arson, and forced displacement of thousands of Tutsi families and hundreds of Tutsi chiefs broke from any precedents in Rwanda's history; this was the first time in Rwandan history that Hutu attacked Tutsi *qua* Tutsi. In addition, the early days of November saw a concerted effort at counter-revolution instigated by Mwami Kigeli and other high authorities in Nyanza, resulting in the targeted assassination of nearly twenty Hutu political leaders and an aborted military campaign against Save hill, the home of Joseph Gitera's Aprosoma movement. In part due to rapid Belgian intervention, these incidents in central and southern Rwanda never evolved into full-scale civil war. But because of the one-sided nature of its intervention, Belgium lost whatever reputation it retained as a neutral arbiter, precipitating a final break between the colonial power and Rwanda's customary authorities.

The spark that lit the early November revolution was the November 1 beating of Dominique Mbonyumutwa by nine partisans associated with UNAR's youth wing. One of only ten Hutu sub-chiefs in Rwanda, Mbonyumutwa also served in the leadership of Gregoire Kayibanda's Parmehutu party in the Gitarama region near Kabgayi. While grudgingly admired by the late Mwami Mutara, Mbonyumutwa had earned recent UNAR wrath through his refusal to sign a protest letter over the October transfer of the three chiefs.[14] Accosted as he left Sunday Mass on All Saints Day, Mbonyumutwa fought off his attackers and made it back to his home in Byimana. Perhaps at his own instigation, rumors of his death quickly spread. By Monday evening, November 2, a large group of Hutu had gathered outside the local Tutsi chief Athanase Gashagaza's house in nearby Ndiza. While the crowd dispersed peacefully that night, an even larger group of 1,000 men returned the next day. A confrontation ensued, and by nightfall a Hutu mob proclaiming themselves for "God, the Church, and Rwanda" had killed two local Tutsi officials and driven Gashagaza into the home of a sympathetic Hutu member of the Legion of Mary. The mob thus accomplished by force what Mbonyumutwa had intended to do at the ballot box—namely, replace Gashagaza as chief in the forthcoming communal elections.[15]

Fires erupted across Ndiza district on November 3 and spread quickly to north-central and northwestern Rwanda.[16] Bands of Hutu arsonists roamed the countryside, pillaging and burning Tutsi homes and driving thousands of Tutsi onto the grounds of local Catholic missions and Belgian colonial posts. Thousands more fled across Rwanda's borders into neighboring Uganda and Congo. The destruction spread to central and eventually southern Rwanda by the end of the week, affecting eight of Rwanda's ten territories.[17] While Belgian troops intervened to arrest some arsonists, colonial officials claimed they lacked sufficient manpower to stop a popular insurrection that was literally spreading like wildfire. After the tensions of September and October, however, one wonders why the Belgians had a token force of 300 soldiers on the ground on November 1—a military presence that the White Father Alphone van Hoof described as "a few jeeps speeding along the road."[18] As Belgium called in reinforcements from Congo on November 5, Mwami Kigeli appealed to Harroy and the local resident André Preud'homme to allow him to mobilize local militia to restore order in the country. Preud'homme refused, fearing the outbreak of a wider civil war and allegedly claiming that he "didn't give a damn" about the violence sweeping the country.[19] If accurate, such sentiments must have been undermined by the subsequent mob that surrounded Harroy and Preud'homme as they tried to leave the Mwami's residence on November 5. Kigeli had to personally rescue the Belgian governor and the colonial resident and drive them to Kigali in his own vehicle.[20] The Belgian refusal to support the Mwami's counter-attack was the first of a series of critical colonial decisions that would help determine the direction of Rwanda's rapid political transformation.

Despite Belgian recalcitrance, Kigeli and other customary chiefs initiated a more targeted counter-revolution on November 7. This aimed to decapitate the Hutu political movements. Comprised of Twa, Tutsi and sympathetic Hutu, these parties assassinated 20 suspected Aprosoma and Parmehutu political leaders, including Joseph Gitera's brother who served as secretary-general of Aprosoma. Hundreds of other Hutu leaders were arrested, and many were tortured. This counter-revolution culminated with the November 9-10 mobilization of thousands of militia to attack Save hill, Gitera's home and the locus of anti-UNAR feeling in southern Rwanda. In response, Gitera began mobilizing thousands of his own supporters to defend Save. The royalist militia's lack of coordination as well as the rapid intervention of Belgian soldiers prevented a bloodbath; it also marked the effective end of Kigeli's counter-revolution.[21]

On November 8 Harroy placed Rwanda under Belgian military authority and imposed an overnight curfew. The next day Kigeli and Harroy issued a joint call for peace and civil obedience and agreed to airdrop 200,000 leaflets with this message. Kigeli simultaneously released a second statement defending himself against accusations of partisanship and reiterating that "the Mwami is the Mwami of all. He cannot join one party and cannot favor one over the others."[22] On November 11 Harroy declared a state of emergency in Rwanda and appointed Colonel B.E.M. "Guy" Logiest, a Belgian *Force Publique* officer serving in Congo, as military resident. Logiest was given wide latitude to restore order, including the imposition of curfews, the establishment of roadblocks, and the arrests of suspected instigators of violence. Such heavy-handed techniques helped end the violence. After two weeks of arson, looting, forced displacement, and political assassinations, an uneasy calm descended on Rwanda on November 14–15.

How should one describe the November violence? While some commentators have tagged these events as the first genocide in Rwanda's history, such descriptions seem overly polemical.[23] Although a conclusive number remains elusive, the November death toll likely remained in the hundreds. The White Father Jan Adriaenssens estimated a death toll of 150. The U.N. Visiting Mission noted the official death toll of 200 but argued that the actual figure was much higher due to rapid burials.[24] In addition, most of these casualties stemmed not from civilian massacres but from violent clashes between Hutu arsonists and ethnically mixed local defense units.[25] The November events were notable more for displacement and property damage than loss of life. Tens of thousands of Tutsi fled the country, over 8,000 homes were destroyed, and 7,000 Tutsi were internally displaced inside Rwanda.[26] In the words of the Hutu priest and future bishop Bernard Manyurane, most Hutu "did not want to kill the Tutsi but only oblige them to leave."[27]

Underlying this ethnic cleansing was an intensely political logic. I have already commented on the electoral campaign that shaped the violent incidents against both Dominique Mbonyumutwa and Athanase Gashagaza on November 1 and 2. One should also highlight here the November 16 commentary of an anonymous Belgian official who described the past fortnight of violence as a dispute between rival political elites.

> [Elites] learned that far-reaching reforms were soon to be carried out and that those reforms would mean another step toward self-determination. As of that moment, the parties and movements had begun to prepare for their future roles as interpreters of the people's wishes in the more authoritative

representative institutions, and they had come into a conflict. It was not simply a tribal conflict between the Tutsi and Hutu but a political and social struggle.[28]

The uprising also showed the complexity of political allegiance in late 1959. Many of the Hutu arsonists claimed to be acting at the behest of the Mwami who was rumored to be imprisoned by a cabal of Tutsi chiefs. When Mwami Kigeli toured Rwanda in late 1959 and early 1960, numerous Hutu peasants requested salaries for the services they had performed on his behalf.[29]

It was not the riots themselves but the subsequent Belgian reaction that ensured the November events would go down in history as the "Hutu Social Revolution." This reaction was largely determined by Col. Logiest, the military resident. A devout Catholic and committed social democrat, Logiest interpreted the November violence as a justified rebellion of oppressed Hutu peasants against oppressive Tutsi overlords. In response, Logiest unilaterally replaced the hundreds of exiled Tutsi chiefs with Hutu teachers, businessmen, merchants, and catechists. By late December 1959, 158 of Rwanda's 489 *sous-chefferies* and 23 of Rwanda's 45 *chefferies* had changed hands. In fairness to Logiest, the top tiers of Rwanda's pre-revolutionary political structures were heavily tilted toward the Tutsi. For example, in mid-1959 43 of Rwanda's 45 chiefs were Tutsi, as were 549 of its 559 sub-chiefs. There was also some precedent for Logiest's action. The Belgian Administration removed 152 sub-chiefs from office between 1955 and 1957, although the Mwami had always retained the sole right to appoint new sub-chiefs and chiefs.[30]

Logiest also continued the Belgian colonial pattern of making ethnicity the seemingly sole criterion for leadership. He justified this on security grounds, arguing that placing Tutsi chiefs over restive Hutu populations would only lead to further violence and instability. Logiest also pointed to the "intermediary" nature of the new chiefs' mandates; Hutu chiefs could be voted out of office if they failed to satisfy popular expectations.[31] Whatever the authenticity of these protestations, the power of incumbency—and the fact that a vast majority of the new chiefs and sub-chiefs were Parmehutu members—went a long way toward turning Rwanda into a Parmehutu-dominated, one-party "democracy." Logiest admitted as much in retrospect, writing in his memoirs that "it was evident that this decision to eviscerate the Tutsi authorities had political consequences, but was this not the only means of ensuring that truly democratic elections could take place?"[32]

The colonial government's judicial proceedings furthered this pro-Hutu trend. The military administration targeted prominent UNAR chiefs and supporters; nearly all of those sentenced to death or long prison terms were UNAR members.[33] At the same time, Parmehutu and Aprosoma leaders remained unmolested despite suspicions that they had incited much of the anti-Tutsi violence. For example,

Fr. De Renesse, one of the White Father leaders of Catholic Action, thought that Parmehutu leaders were utilizing their Legion of Mary networks to initiate the November disturbances. "It is the legionary chiefs of Kabgayi (Gregoire Kayibanda and Calliope Mulindahabi, respectively president and secretary of the Committee of Kabgayi) who have triggered this entire revolt of the Bahutu which is bathing Rwanda in blood at the moment."[34] De Renesse noted that after he confronted Kayibanda and Mulindahabi with these charges, they reacted in an "unpredictable and uncontrollable" manner, implying the likelihood of "implacable racial fights for the future."[35] Despite these suspicions, Kayibanda, Mulindahabi and other Hutu leaders were neither questioned nor disciplined, although the Belgian administration arrested hundreds of lower-level Hutu cadres. To be sure, many of Rwanda's Tutsi chiefs were responsible for targeted assassinations, torture, and other heinous crimes. But Belgium's decision to hold UNAR accountable while giving Parmehutu a free pass not only decapitated the internal UNAR movement but greatly strengthened the hand of its political rivals.

Adding to the atmosphere of political instability was the Belgian government's November 10 announcement of a new long-term political framework for Rwanda and Burundi. In Belgium's transitional plan, Rwanda's traditional *chefferies* were reclassified as administrative bureaucracies, turning Rwanda's customary chiefs into "functionaries without a political mandate"—in other words, bureaucrats without any political authority.[36] In shifting the locus of political power from the *chefferie* to the local commune, Belgium boosted the importance of local burgomasters and communal councils. This in turn strengthened Parmehutu's hand since its political strength lay in Rwanda's hills rather than the corridors of power in Nyanza.[37] Finally, Mwami Mwambutsa of Burundi and Mwami Kigeli of Rwanda were reclassified as constitutional monarchs, further circumscribing their authority and opening a future path to elected executives.

Four other significant political decisions followed in December 1959. First, Harroy sent Preud'homme, the long-time colonial resident of Rwanda, into early retirement on December 5. Harroy replaced Preud'homme with Logiest who assumed the new title of "special civil resident."[38] Harroy and Preud'homme had a longstanding rivalry, in part due to the latter's more cautious approach to political reform and more favorable attitude toward the Catholic missions.[39] In addition to eliminating a potential counter-weight to Logiest, Preud'homme's ouster precipitated the first tensions between the Belgian government and Preud'homme's Tutsi allies in the Rader party, furthering the perception that Belgium was reducing Rwandan politics to a binary Hutu-Tutsi conflict.[40] Second, the Belgian government announced that a new eight-member Special Provisional Council would replace the Superior Council as Rwanda's highest legislative body. Comprised of two members of each of Rwanda's four major political parties, the committee was supposed to embody a government of national unity. But since six of the eight members were hostile to Mwami Kigeli and Rwanda's customary authorities, it also represented a seismic shift in national leadership.[41] Third, Belgium on Christmas Day issued an interim decree that gave Logiest and Harroy the legal right to depose the Mwami and veto any of his decisions.[42] Finally, Belgium announced in December that it was delaying the January 1960 elections until June 1960. This gave Parmehutu time to consolidate its recent gains and expand its already considerable network of supporters across Rwanda's hills. The results of this would become clear in 1960.

Catholic Reactions to the November Violence

If November 1959 marked a turning point in Rwandan political history, it also marked a historic month for the Catholic Church in Rwanda. On November 10, the Holy See issued the apostolic constitution *Cum parvulum sinapsi*. This document announced that the Rwandan vicariates of Kabgayi and Nyundo would now be classified as local dioceses. Perraudin was named Archbishop of Kigali, and Bigirumwami was named Bishop of Nyundo. Significantly, Nyundo was classified as a "suffragen diocese" of Kabgayi, making Perraudin and not Bigirumwami the unofficial primate of the Rwandan church.[43]

The ethnic violence that erupted during the first week of November overshadowed this momentous ecclesial event, however. Meeting together in Nyakibanda for their annual seminary review, Bigirumwami and Perraudin issued their first statement on the violence on November 6. Addressing themselves to "dear Christians of Rwanda" with "much pain in our hearts," they condemned the atmosphere of "mutual fear, hate and vengeance" existing "between Banyarwanda" (never utilizing the terms "Hutu" and "Tutsi").[44] Calling for Christians to live into a Pauline vision of the church as a single united body, Perraudin and Bigirumwami appealed to civil authorities and political leaders to hold a "frank and fraternal" conversation on the social and political problems which sparked the violence. The statement was notable for its categorical denunciation of violence. "In the name of our Lord Jesus Christ of whom we are representatives on earth, we say to you that all of this is not Christian and we deplore it and condemn it absolutely."

Even in his private correspondence, Perraudin seemed genuinely shaken by the violence that swept Rwanda in early November. In a November 8 letter to the White Fathers' General House in Rome, he described Rwanda's "civil war" as "tragic," writing of an atmosphere "heavy with hate and vengeance" and noting the concentration of violence in northern and central Rwanda.[45] Four days later, he distanced the church from both customary and colonial authorities, recalling Abbé Stanislas Bushayija from his role as a spiritual counselor to Mwami Kigeli on Rwanda's Superior Council (CSP). Perraudin explained that "in the current circumstances the place of a priest is not on a Council operating under a military government."[46] In a subsequent November 21 circular letter on the crisis, Perraudin struck some unusually critical notes. Here he bemoaned the "superficiality" of Rwandan Christianity, called for a day of reparation for "the very grave sins" committed against justice and charity, and reminded his readers that authentic politics must be "submitted to the law of God and consequently excludes methods of deception, calumnies, hate, menace, violence and dictatorship."[47] In turn, Perraudin's pastoral actions in late November 1959 reveal a man preoccupied with a Tutsi refugee crisis that he described as "the urgent problem of the day."[48]

For all of Perraudin's critiques of Rwanda's escalating political violence, opponents continued to perceive him as a pro-Hutu partisan. Already named by UNAR as one of the leading enemies of the Mwami in October 1959, Perraudin faced resurgent critiques from UNAR exiles in the early weeks of November 1959. The exiles alleged that Perraudin encouraged Joseph Gitera to start Aprosoma, harbored Hutu extremists, and conspired in the death of Mwami Mutara.[49] Nor were these menaces merely rhetorical. During the first days of the November crisis, UNAR supporters threatened Perraudin's Kabgayi see, viewing it as a bastion for the Hutu emancipation movement. Reputedly aided by two indigenous priests, a local Tutsi chief led a large crowd in burning 1,000 homes in Byimana, Mbonyumutwa's village near Kabgayi. Belgian soldiers intervened after hearing that the crowd was planning to torch Perraudin's residence and Kabgayi cathedral. Perraudin stayed under close *Force Publique* guard until the violence subsided in mid-November.[50]

It was not just Perraudin's opponents, however, who viewed Perraudin as a closet Hutu partisan. Pointing to his February 1959 "*Super omnia caritas*," the White Fathers' newspaper *Temps Nouveaux d'Afrique* praised Perraudin on November 8 for "taking up the cause of Hutu emancipation by word and deed."[51] And even after hearing Perraudin's impassioned claims to political neutrality, the U.N. Visiting Commission concluded in mid-1960 that "a large part of the population felt that the situation was not quite so simple. Many thought that the Archbishop of Kabgayi was the central figure in the support given to the Hutu parties." For the U.N. Commission, this explained the vehemence of the attacks against Perraudin and his public efforts to move toward the political middle.[52] Similarly, the White Father Jan Adriaenssens described Parmehutu leaders like Gregoire Kayibanda, Calliope Mulindahabi, and Maximilien Niyonzima as Perraudin's "collaborators," claiming that Perraudin "has looked after the Hutu leaders at Kabgayi for a long time" since he "favors Hutu emancipation as well as the installation of more humane political and social structures."[53] For his part, Guy Logiest claimed later that Perraudin had informed him that political changes were necessary in light of the "injustices of which the Hutu had constantly been the victims." In this sense, Logiest credited Perraudin for "restoring the Hutu people to its dignity as children of God. In a profoundly Christian country, [the bishop's] perspicacious action took on capital importance."[54]

Nor did Perraudin's writings in November 1959 wholly embody the political and ideological neutrality that he retrospectively claimed. For example, his November 21 circular letter danced around the issue of refugee reintegration, and Perraudin never mentioned the risk of ethnicism in Rwandan politics. Rather, Perraudin criticized the "defeatism" and "useless lamentations" stemming from some clerical quarters, arguing that "individual reparation will be difficult if not impossible."[55] He also continued to present Rwanda's crisis as symptomatic of a broader struggle between Christianity and communism, privately blaming UNAR for starting the troubles and claiming that their incitements "pushed the Hutu over the edge."[56] Despite ample evidence of lay Catholic leadership in the November riots, Perraudin wrote in January 1960, "I believe that all in all the Christian reactions were good."[57] And demonstrating his own awareness of the political impact of the November events for the Catholic Church, Perraudin closed his aforementioned November 8 letter by demanding the immediate appointment of the Hutu seminary professor Bernard Manyurane as bishop.[58] The White Fathers viewed Manyurane—a Ruhengeri native and recent recipient of a canon law doctorate from Rome—as the most suitable Hutu candidate for the episcopate in the anticipated see of Kigali. As we will see, his candidacy took on increasing urgency for Perraudin as Rwandan politics accelerated in a pro-Hutu direction in 1960.

If André Perraudin was trying to position the church to benefit from the Hutu uprisings, Aloys Bigirumwami was becoming more publicly critical. Bigirumwami had also faced threats of violence in early November, stopped by angry crowds at two separate roadblocks before finally reaching his Nyundo church on November 12.[59] Perhaps reflecting these encounters, his November 15 circular letter forcefully condemned arsonists and pillagers. "Those who have chosen to participate in attacks, massacres and fires are rendered gravely culpable, they are enemies of Rwanda, they have sinned against God and against their neighbor."[60] In this letter Bigirumwami exhorted Christians to resist the temptation to retaliation but also called on perpetrators to offer reparations and assist in reconstruction. While he joined Perraudin in crediting mission stations for welcoming so many refugees, Bigirumwami was also far more critical of Christian behavior than the Archbishop of Kabgayi. Worrying that other nations would think that "Christianity is impossible in Rwanda," Bigirumwami called on Christian catechists and local leaders to "show others how to live in harmony" and reminded perpetrators that "the Lord present in the Eucharist that you receive guards you against the sacrilege of hate, rancor, mistrustful words, and reprehensible attitudes." He also exhorted Nyundo Catholics to oppose any efforts to "depose the chiefs and the subalterns named by the King, the Resident, and the Governor," a message that may have been directed primarily at Col. Logiest.[61]

In addition to issuing his own statements, Bigirumwami ensured that his diocesan newspaper took a strong stand against the violence. While the Diocese of Kabgayi's *Trait d'Union* remained silent and the White Fathers' *Temps Nouveaux d'Afrique* continued to offer broad ideological support for the Hutu revolution,[62] Nyundo's *Civitas Mariae* condemned the "massive destitution of chiefs and sub-chiefs" as well as the forced exile of thousands of refugees into foreign lands. Bigirumwami's newspaper rejected the thesis that the Banyarwanda consisted of "three races opposed to each other" and reminded Christians that "racial hate is incompatible with the religion of Christ."[63] Over the next six months, *Civitas Mariae* castigated the evils of ethnic and racial hatred and described Rwanda's ongoing revolutionary violence in far more detail than Kabgayi's *Trait d'Union*.

While Rwanda's bishops spoke out on the violence, Rwanda's Catholic parishes experienced it firsthand. Writing from Muyunzwe on November 8, the Hutu priest Damien Nyrinkindi described three deaths at his mission and credited the local Tutsi sub-chief for preventing further bloodshed by guarding the church's doors.[64] Likewise, mid-November reports from Janja and Runaba missions in northern Rwanda offered day-by-day accounts of the violence in the region. The Janja superior, Fr. Pierre Cattin, recounted the burning of all Tutsi homes in his parish "without exception, those of the old and the young."[65] In southern Rwanda the Save superior and future Hutu bishop, Joseph Sibomana, noted that many brigands with machetes stopped in to pray before heading back out to the hills, foreshadowing similar practices during the 1994 genocide.[66]

In turn, mission reports reveal the social power that priests retained even in the midst of armed conflicts. For example, the Runaba superior brokered a peace accord between Hutu incendiaries and Tutsi refugees, stopping the violence in his region.[67] Fr. Cattin planted the Vatican's flag to mark Janja mission as a place of asylum, encouraging over 1,400 Tutsi to take up temporary residence at the mission. Cattin nearly lost his job due to this bold gesture and the subsequent accusations that Janja mission was harboring a pro-UNAR priest.[68] Even Perraudin drew rare cheers from Tutsi refugees when he paid an unexpected visit to Janja on November 23, handing out gifts and promising that "he was going to do all he could to find a rapid solution to the plight of the refugees."[69]

Catholic parishes also served as welcome refuges from the violence. In addition to the Runaba and Janja examples cited earlier, Ruhengeri priests harbored 1,600 displaced Tutsi, and two Hutu priests faced strong local opposition after they took in 90 Tutsi refugees in their isolated rural sub-station.[70] 800 Tutsi sought refuge at the Rwankuba mission in northern Rwanda, and the Nemba mission took in over 900 refugees who had been expelled from their homes.[71] Even reputedly anti-clerical groups such as the UNAR militias attacking Save hill did not target Catholic missions or religious clergy.[72] To be fair, several pro-UNAR priests fled the country, and multiple Hutu priests refused to take in Tutsi refugees.[73]

However, the vast majority of clerics responded on a humanitarian rather than ethnicist level.

After the initial violence subsided, the refugee issue emerged as an increasingly intractable social problem. Although many Tutsi were reintegrated into villages in southern and central Rwanda, the Hutu population proved more hostile in northern Rwanda. Catholic mission stations were bursting at the seams, and the government decided to set up a permanent refugee camp at Nyamata south of Kigali. Convinced that they would lose their lands if they left the region, most of the displaced Tutsi in northern Rwanda refused to relocate. These Tutsi also feared reports of malaria and tsetse fly epidemics in the Nyamata camps.

These displaced Tutsi received an endorsement when Bigirumwami paid an unexpected visit to Janja mission on November 27. Speaking in unusually blunt terms, Bigirumwami described the Nyamata relocations as "deportations" and demanded that Logiest and Harroy restore Tutsi lands and property. The Belgian leaders demurred, threatening to expel the refugees from Janja mission. Despite these threats and the menacing of a local Hutu crowd, only 40 of the 1,400 displaced Tutsi agreed to relocate.[74] After days of rising tensions, Logiest backed down in early December, describing Nyamata as a "voluntary" and "temporary" solution and encouraging Tutsi to return to their hills of origin if they wished. Belgium provided scant support for reintegration, however, and many Tutsi ultimately chose Nyamata over the uncertainty of living with hostile Hutu neighbors. Nyamata's refugee population bulged to 2,500 by the end of 1959 and over 5,000 by January 1960.[75]

In response to the refugee crisis, Bigirumwami grew more critical of Belgian colonial authorities. Reflecting on why "all the Tutsi" of Nyundo had seen their homes burned to the ground, Bigirumwami in a November 28 letter to Leo Volker accused the Belgian government of using "fire and blood and the massive destitution of all officials even to deportation" to achieve its political goals.[76] His attitude toward Parmehutu was no less scathing. He associated Kayibanda's party with "communist agents" who were trying to hand Rwanda over to the "the representatives of a single party destined to place the whole country under the tyranny of a popular dictatorship." Bigirumwami also critiqued Catholic factionalism for contributing to Rwanda's political deadlock. Catholic conservatives falsely claimed that "we cannot preach on justice and charity without leading the population into hate and vengeance"; more progressive voices sanctioned anti-Tutsi violence on the grounds of social justice.

Bigirumwami's anger reflected the extent to which the refugee crisis disproportionately affected him and other Tutsi clergy. A majority of indigenous clergy and religious saw family members forced into internal or external exile, including relatives of Bigirumwami, Alexis Kagame, the future bishop Jean-Baptiste Gahamanyi, the journalist Justin Kalibwami, Kabgayi's vicar general Innocent

Gasabwoya, and the leading intellectuals of Nyundo diocese, Janvier Mulenzi and Louis Gasore.[77] All of these priests were Tutsi, and many were associated with the more nationalist, pro-UNAR wing of the clergy. Their political sympathies may also explain the mixed attitudes that some White Fathers adopted toward the Tutsi refugees. Rather than condemn ethnic cleansing or call for the reintegration of refugees, the White Father Louis Gilles recommended prudent silence. "In the north we must not speak of the Tutsi, they [the Hutu] no longer want them."[78]

Gilles's words reflect the analytical framework that many Catholic missionaries and Hutu priests later adopted in the early 1960s. First, they pinned all responsibility for the revolution on UNAR. Alphonse Van Hoof's shifting rhetoric provides a good example of this. After violence erupted in early November, Van Hoof initially blamed both sides, cautioning his White Father confreres in mid-November that "it would be unjust to endorse the political leaders responsible for the bloody troubles in which we have come to live."[79] By early December he had changed his tone, praising the new Hutu interim chiefs as "very good Christians" and describing Kayibanda as "very reliable from the doctrinal point of view."[80] Manyurane offers another telling example. While admitting that the "reaction of the other parties was terrible, above all the two parties Aprosoma and Parmehutu," Manyurane still argued that it was UNAR's campaign of intimidation, terrorism and nationalism which incited Rwanda's "fratricidal fight."[81] And as noted previously, Perraudin himself blamed UNAR for provoking the crisis.[82]

If UNAR was becoming the missionary scapegoat for all that ailed Rwanda, missionary opposition to UNAR stemmed more from ideological preoccupations than ethnicism *per se*. In other words, missionaries opposed UNAR more for its perceived communist sympathies and anticlericalism than because of some deep-seated bias against Tutsi. For example, even as he defended Tutsi refugees in northern Rwanda, Mgr. Cattin lambasted UNAR as "full of communism" and declared UNAR to be an existential threat to the church.[83] For his part, the more left-wing Fr. Adriaenssens described the revolution as the "logical (and tragic) outcome of a political and social situation which was deteriorating for a long time. The revolution of November was 'inscribed' in the history of the feudal regime."[84]

If the roots of missionary opposition were primarily ideological, the close association of "UNAR" with "Tutsi" made these two terms increasingly synonymous in public discourse. This led missionaries into a worrying pattern of distinguishing "deserving" and "undeserving" Tutsi victims. Van Hoof wrote in December 1959 that the Hutu arsonists indiscriminately burned down Tutsi homes, "making no distinction between the good and the bad. The bad ones were those who had declared openly for UNAR."[85] He later associated these "bad ones" with indigenous clergy in Nyundo diocese who were allegedly distributing the UNAR publication *Rwanda Nziza*.[86]

The year 1959 began with the promise of Belgian reforms and Catholic optimism about continued church growth. It ended with social upheaval, ethnic violence, and political revolution. But if Rwanda's national politics remained in flux, the Catholic Church had survived the November troubles with its reputation largely intact. Catholic bishops and mission superiors had responded well to the crisis, rapidly denouncing the violence and opening Catholic mission stations to Tutsi refugees. Perraudin and Bigirumwami's rhetoric differed according to their temperaments, but both proclaimed their commitment to maintaining official church neutrality while working to resolve the refugee crisis. A worrying trend, however, was the linking of ethnic labels with moral attributes as well as growing critiques of UNAR without any corresponding cautions about Aprosoma or Parmehutu.[87] As we will see, this analytical partisanship only grew deeper in 1960 and 1961, eliminating the church's ability to serve as a fair arbiter in Rwanda's accelerating political conflicts.

Parmehutu's Rise to Power

The year 1960 began with an uneasy calm in Rwanda.[88] In response to the November troubles, Belgium delayed communal elections from January to June. Hutu political movements were clearly on the rise, led by Aprosoma in southern Rwanda and Parmehutu in central and northern Rwanda. But no single national leader had emerged. Rather, a coterie of Hutu leaders dominated in their home regions—Balthazar Bicamumpaka in northern Rwanda, Dominique Mbonyumutwa and Gregoire Kayibanda in central Rwanda, and Aloys Munyangaju and Joseph Gitera in southern Rwanda. Although many of his strongest allies in the UNAR party were now in exile, Mwami Kigeli retained the symbolic power of Rwanda's monarchy. On a *de facto* level, however, Col. Guy Logiest was the single most powerful political figure inside Rwanda as he continued his mission to empower the Hutu majority and protect Belgian interests. In response to the efforts of Logiest and others, UNAR's internal presence diminished while its exile community built what would become one of Africa's most influential expatriate movements.

As the United Nations Visiting Mission prepared for its triennial visit in March 1960, Rwanda's political parties maneuvered for position. Having broken with the Belgian administration, UNAR shifted its advocacy to the United Nations, hoping that the U.N. would adopt UNAR's political and social analysis, facilitate the return of refugees, declare a general amnesty, and agree to supervise the upcoming communal elections. UNAR continued to believe that it could contest and even win a free and fair election. There is some merit to this claim. Far more than the "Tutsi party" caricatured by its opponents, UNAR had a majority Hutu membership in January 1960. While by no means a mass political movement,

UNAR's 7,000 card-carrying members represented Rwanda's largest committed political bloc. This number continued to grow after the November revolution, tripling to 25,000 by June 1960.[89] In contrast, Parmehutu remained nervous about its electoral prospects despite its boastful claims to represent Rwanda's 85 percent Hutu population. Even after Logiest appointed hundreds of Hutu political leaders in late 1959, Parmehutu implored Belgium to delay the scheduled January 1960 elections until after "the Hutu people were sufficiently emancipated to be able to defend their rights effectively."[90] Fearful of UNAR's electoral power, Parmehutu tried to convince the U.N. to dissolve UNAR before the summer elections. In the meantime, Rader staked out a middle ground, opposing Logiest's appointments for "favoring the antagonism of the two races" while continuing to decry UNAR as a group of "fanatics."[91]

The arrival of the U.N. Visiting Mission in March 1960 initiated an intense electoral campaign. Even as they scheduled official meetings with the U.N. commission, Rwanda's political leaders mobilized thousands of supporters to rally along the U.N. caravan's travel route. Even as all four parties issued a joint March 14 statement appealing for political calm, street politicking spiraled into violence in the provinces of Gitarama, Gisenyi, Shangugu and Byumba.[92] Shangugu and Byumba had not seen violence during the November troubles, making these new outbreaks all the more worrying.[93] Bishop Bigirumwami's see in Nyundo became the site of particular disruptions. As the U.N. convoy passed, pro-UNAR clergy led their predominantly Hutu schoolchildren in shouts of "independence"; the students' Hutu parents responded with cries of "democracy." In the meantime, UNAR literature speculated that the U.N. was going to restore Rwanda's exiled chiefs.[94] This politicking soon turned into something much more sinister. Between March 18 and March 22, Hutu mobs destroyed nearly every Tutsi home in the district and forced over 1,000 Tutsi to flee to the grounds of Nyundo parish. After four days of rioting, Belgian soldiers arrived to quell the disturbances, possibly saving Bigirumwami's life and his cathedral on Nyundo hill.[95] As violence continued into April and May, the number of internally displaced Tutsi rose to over 10,000.[96]

These events had a sobering effect on the U.N. Visiting Commission. The Commission subsequently broke with Belgian policy in April 1960. Rather than proceed with the Belgian plan for June elections, the U.N. Commission called for the establishment of a "round table" conference that would gather Belgian officials and representatives from Rwanda's four major political parties. UNAR celebrated the news; Rader met it with indifference. Parmehutu and Aprosoma appealed to Belgium to maintain its electoral timeline and commitment to the Hutu goal of "democracy before independence."

In the meantime, the relationship between Mwami Kigeli and Rwanda's emerging political parties became increasingly strained. On March 23 the Special Provisional Council submitted a series of seven reforms to the Mwami, including a multi-party cabinet, the suppression of the customary *biru*, and the symbolic replacement of the *Karinga* drums with a national flag. When the Mwami rejected all of these stipulations on April 23, Parmehutu, Aprosoma, and Rader broke with Kigeli, formed a "Common Front," and called for Kigeli's replacement with a more amenable constitutional monarch.[97] By June Parmehutu had gone further, changing its name to *Mouvement Démocratique Républicaine-Parmehutu* (MDR-Parmehutu) and demanding that Belgium end Rwanda's monarchy. Debates over the future of the monarchy split an already weakened Rader—Lazare Ndazaro called for Kigeli's deposition while Prosper Bwanakweri stood by the Mwami.[98] Under heavy Belgian pressure, Kigeli went into exile in late June 1960, taking refuge first in Tanzania and then with Patrice Lumumba's new government in Congo.

In the meantime, Parmehutu's political rhetoric became increasingly ethnocentric. Reformulating Rwandan nationalism in an ethnicist key, Parmehutu wrote in June 1960 that "Rwanda is the country of Hutu and of all those, whites or blacks, Tutsi, Europeans, or other neighbors, who will rid themselves from feudal-imperialist designs."[99] More than an oppressive oligarchy, the Tutsi were now described as foreigners in their own country. In the words of a Parmehutu manifesto, "when they [the Tutsi] claim to represent Rwanda, it is as if the French were representing their colony before independence."[100] If Mamdani's indigeneity thesis lacks credence in the 1950s, it accurately describes the development of Rwandan political rhetoric after 1960.[101]

In the meantime, Belgium attempted to placate both the U.N. and Hutu leaders by scheduling an early June colloquy in Brussels and retaining its midsummer timetable for communal elections. Parmehutu, Aprosoma and Rader attended the Brussels colloquy. UNAR boycotted, however, undermining any potential for political reconciliation. Even more momentously, UNAR announced on May 20 that it was pulling out of the Special Provisional Council and boycotting the June communal elections. This proved to be a disastrous political move. While the boycott was successful in UNAR strongholds such as Nyanza, Astrida, Shangugu, and Kibungo, it failed everywhere else in Rwanda. Overall turnout approached 80 percent, and 70 percent of voters supported Parmehutu. Thanks to its strength in southern Rwanda, Aprosoma polled second with 17 percent. Despite protests from UNAR, Rader, and Mwami Kigeli, the United Nations refused to invalidate the results or schedule new elections. Controlling a vast majority of Rwanda's 230 new burgomasters and 2,900 new communal councilors, Parmehutu had achieved a near political monopoly as Rwanda moved closer to independence.[102] Accusing Parmehutu of becoming a "totalitarian republican party causing terrorism and intimidation across Rwanda," Rader pulled out of the Common Front in July 1960, eliminating the chance for any serious Tutsi participation in the transitional government.[103]

Meanwhile Congo officially declared its independence from Belgium on June 30. Led by Patrice Lumumba, Congo's first postcolonial government took a strong nationalist line against Belgium and welcomed financial support from the Soviet Union. Lumumba also hosted Mwami Kigeli and several UNAR leaders in Leopoldville during the summer of 1960, furthering suspicions that UNAR was building links with African nationalists and communists alike. In mid-July, Belgium forcibly disarmed the Congolese *Force Publique* soldiers guarding the Nyamata refugee camp, fearing that Congolese soldiers might arm the Tutsi refugees inside the camp.[104]

In October 1960 Belgium approved a provisional government based on the results of the summer elections and announced another round of legislative elections in January 1961. The Provisional Council of Rwanda was installed on October 26 with Joseph Gitera as president and Gregoire Kayibanda as prime minister. Logiest continued to control the military as Belgium's special resident. Parmehutu's commanding majority raised hopes for political stability, and a confident Kayibanda even reached out to his Tutsi rivals in an early November statement. "The inhabitants of the country should arrive at a sincere entente, regardless of ethnicity, and live happily."[105] At the same time, Parmehutu's political dominance alienated even its ideological allies. Joining UNAR and Rader in a new "Common Front" in December 1960, Aprosoma accused Parmehutu of fomenting a "dictatorial and terrorist period marked by racial hate" and exhorted Rwandans "not to justify Tutsi feudalism, nor Parmehutu dictatorship, but [rather] a multi-ethnic and multi-party country."[106]

In the meantime, UNAR continued to look to the United Nations as its last political hope. It called on the U.N. to facilitate the reintegration of Rwanda's foreign exiles and the return of Mwami Kigeli, suppress the internal refugee camp at Nyamata, replace Belgium's Force Publique with an international peacekeeping force, and supervise new elections. In response to these demands, the United Nations released Resolution 1579 on December 20, 1960. The statement supported many of UNAR's aims, including general political amnesty, the return of Mwami Kigeli and other UNAR leaders, the reintegration of refugees, and the postponing of elections until after a national reconciliation process. Even as it lost ground inside Rwanda, then, UNAR appeared to be winning the battle for international opinion.

This in turn had an effect on Belgian policy. Reversing course, Belgium announced in December that it would host a reconciliation conference in early January 1961 that would include representatives from UNAR's external wing. At what became known as the "Colloquy of Ostende," Belgium announced the postponement of the anticipated national elections of January 15 until the summer of 1961 (despite the opposition of three-quarters of the Rwandan delegates). Belgium also expressed openness to a political amnesty for prisoners who had not committed murder or torture.[107] The colonial administration agreed to hold a separate referendum on the Mwami that would determine whether Rwanda remained a constitutional monarchy or became a democratic republic. Mwami Kigeli was so optimistic that he prepared to return to Rwanda in February 1961. Before he could do so, however, Harroy signed a decree on January 15 granting Rwanda much broader internal autonomy.[108] The effects of this decision would become evident by the end of the month.

Catholic Political Reactions in 1960

In contrast to their proactive roles in late 1958 and early 1959, Bigirumwami, Perraudin and their fellow church leaders did not shape political discourse after the November revolution. Rather, they assumed a more reactive role as they tried to keep their priests out of politics, defend their political neutrality, respond to sporadic outbursts of ethnic violence, and grapple with Rwanda's ongoing refugee crisis. In analyzing Catholic politics in 1960, I address three areas. First, the bishops' views evolved on the proper relationship between clergy, laity, and secular politics, especially as church leaders struggled to maintain both political neutrality and social influence and argued over whether communism or ethnicism posed the greatest political threat to Rwanda. Second, UNAR's anti-Perraudin diatribes only exacerbated the White Father tendency to blame UNAR for all that ailed Rwanda. Finally, even as the bishops continued to condemn political and ethnic violence in Rwanda, Bigirumwami distanced himself further from Rwanda's increasingly poisonous political atmosphere.

Officially, Catholic leaders' understanding of the relationship between religion and politics did not undergo a marked change after the November 1959 uprisings. Politics remained the proper domain of the laity; clergy were responsible for forming Catholic lay consciences to make political decisions in light of the church's social and ethical teachings. But where episcopal teachings in the late 1950s stressed the duty of lay participation, the emphasis in 1960 fell more on clerical abstention. Thus Leo Volker instructed Perraudin in January 1960 that "priests and religious should be men of God, and politics is not their domain," adding in a letter to Pierre Cattin that "it does not suffice to avoid being political in the proper sense of the word, but it seems necessary that our priests abstain absolutely from referencing politics in their conversations."[109] Writing in June 1960, Cardinal Agagianian, the head of the Vatican congregation Propaganda Fide, ordered that Rwandan clergy "abstain from immersing themselves in purely political quarrels and fights."[110] Perraudin echoed this guidance, reminding clergy that "political meetings are not your affair, but that of the laity" and informing Agagianian that Rwanda must "avoid all confusion between the civil and the ecclesiastic."[111] Perraudin also intervened to remove an indigenous priest from his posting at a Belgian academic center due to suspicions that he was organizing meetings with UNAR agents.[112]

Nor were such sentiments limited to Rwanda's missionary leaders. Bigirumwami echoed the White Fathers' cautions, arguing that the priest's mission to be "*omnia omnibus*" precluded political involvement. However, Bigirumwami struggled with how to keep priests out of politics while still ensuring that politics mirrored a Catholic vision of society. He therefore instructed his clergy to avoid partisanship yet encouraged them to teach Catholic social doctrine to lay Christians. Such teachings included the preeminence of the natural law, the fundamental dignity due to the human person, and the rights of parents to educate their children in Catholic schools. Volker agreed with Bigirumwami's commitment to maintaining the church's cultural influence, writing in a circular to White Father missionaries that "the enemies of Christ are trying to eliminate the influence of the Church in society."[113]

In this sense, Rwanda's Catholic leaders generally concurred that the church hierarchy should maintain cordial relations with state leaders, reflecting the continued salience of the Christendom vision of church-state partnership. In Perraudin's words, the church should oppose either a "confusion" or "separation" between church and state, seeing the "Christian solution in collaboration."[114] Perraudin himself maintained public decorum with Mwami Kigeli, sending him New Year's Day 1960 greetings. The Mwami in turn congratulated Perraudin on his elevation as archbishop and visited Bigirumwami in Nyundo on at least two separate occasions.[115] In addition, Perraudin maintained friendly relations with several of Rwanda's major political leaders, exchanging correspondence with Rader's Lazare Ndazaro and receiving an honorary membership card from Aprosoma's Joseph Gitera.[116]

The seeming unanimity of this vision of church-state relations, however, masked underlying tensions. For example, the bishops' tidy lay-clerical distinction was complicated by the sizeable subset of laity who served the Catholic Church as catechists, teachers, and Catholic Action leaders. In this area, Alphonse Van Hoof counseled that such lay workers should "abstain from politics in their function of serving the Church" while maintaining their political obligations outside of the parish. Such a teaching essentially bifurcated the Christian lay leader, assuming for example that the Rwandan people could distinguish Kayibanda the Legion of Mary leader from Kayibanda the Parmehutu chief. Nor did Van Hoof and other Catholic leaders resolve the issue of whether Catholic lay leaders should resign their ecclesial positions if elected to public office. This was not just a theoretical issue, as evidenced by the election of three Legion of Mary leaders as burgomasters in Kanyanza mission.[117] This underlined perhaps the greatest tension in the Catholic approach to national politics in revolutionary Rwanda. On one hand, church leaders reiterated their rhetorical commitment to political neutrality. At the same time, they also reaffirmed the Catholic Church's traditional role as arbiter of Rwanda's moral and cultural order. One wonders if it is possible to be both neutral and influential, especially if a nation's political parties no longer concur on the proper relationship between church, state, and society.

Since Rwanda's Catholic leaders agreed that the church retained an important voice in the public square, arguments inevitably arose over the extent to which silence itself contained an implicit political message. For example, Bigirumwami complained privately in August 1960 about the church's failure to establish a clerical colloquy on Rwanda's political developments, thereby allowing secular politicians to determine Rwanda's political discourse.[118] Publicly Bigirumwami voiced his frustration with clergy and laity who urged the Catholic hierarchy to exercise prudent silence, arguing that church leaders could not stand silent in the face of withering internal and external attacks.[119] Reflecting this ambiguity, critics interpreted Perraudin's public silence toward Parmehutu as a tacit endorsement; supporters viewed this as Perraudin's effort to stay out of politics.

Catholic leaders also differed on whether ethnicism or communism posed the greatest ideological threat to Rwanda—and whether Parmehutu or UNAR should be tagged with the dreaded "anti-Catholic" label. White Father leaders generally saw communists—and by implication UNAR—as greater threats to Catholic interests in Rwanda. For missionary leaders like Leo Volker, the church's primary enemies were "communists," "masons," and "free thinkers" who were trying to divide Christians of diverse races and social classes.[120] At an episcopal conference in Bujumbura in February 1960, Perraudin spoke passionately about the risks of communism to Africa and Rwanda alike. Privately, he remonstrated with Bigirumwami in an effort to convince him of UNAR's communist influences. Six months later, Perraudin reiterated to his priests the urgent necessity of fighting communism in Africa.[121] On the other hand, while critical of UNAR's tactics, Bigirumwami remained unconvinced of the party's supposed communist leanings. Rather, Bigirumwami saw the greatest ideological threat facing Rwanda as ethnicism. In January he warned the Nyundo faithful to avoid political parties based on ethnic identity. "The political party that advocates for the interests of the Bahutu exclusively, refuse it; the one which advocates for the Tutsi exclusively, keep equal distance."[122] In the run-up to the summer elections, he continued to exhort the Rwandan people to "cease to divide ourselves in parties based on Hutu and Tutsi ethnicity."[123] If Bigirumwami's comments offered a thinly veiled rejection of Parmehutu, Perraudin remained conspicuously silent on the risk of ethnicism.[124] Van Hoof was even less circumspect, writing in late 1960 that "all the members of the [Parmehutu-dominated] provisional government are good Catholics and good family fathers...[they are] not contrary to the doctrine of Jesus Christ."[125]

Both competing visions merged in *"Vérité, Justice, Charité,"* the pastoral letter on politics issued by the Catholic bishops of Rwanda and Burundi in October

1960.[126] This was the only such letter jointly issued by the Rwandan and Burundian bishops during the revolutionary period of 1959–1962; it also represented one of the few statements signed by both Perraudin and Bigirumwami. The document was released after Rwanda's communal elections of June and July 1960 but before anticipated legislative elections in January 1961. It included the voices of Burundi's Archbishop Grauls, Bishop Martin, and Bishop Ntuyahaga, churchmen more associated with Bigirumwami's moderate social conservativism than Perraudin's pro-Hutu social democracy.[127] In many ways, then, *Vérité, Justice, Charité* offers this period's most comprehensive and authoritative Catholic statement on politics. If the document broke new ground in distancing the church from the state and critiquing ethnicism, it fell short in not exploring political alternatives to those offered by the region's political parties.

Perhaps recognizing the extent to which the concept of justice had been manipulated by all sides in Rwanda's political disputes, the bishops dedicated the longest section of *Vérité, Justice, Charité* to describing a Christian vision of justice. Here the bishops demanded the restitution of goods and property to refugees, condemned social vengeance and popular tribunals, and proclaimed their support for liberty of conscience. Following Perraudin's anti-UNAR spirit, the bishops prohibited Christians from voting for any candidate whose party program "is not inspired by a Christian spirit," such as parties who favored state schools over Catholic schools, supported irregular marriages, or opposed Catholic institutions. On the other hand, trademark Bigirumwami emphases emerged as well, such as the document's insistent calls for reparations for refugees and excoriation of popular tribunals whose leaders were "gravely culpable" and "do not merit the name of Christians."

The document also dealt with the justice an individual owed to society as a whole. Here the bishops highlighted the Christian duty to respect the divine law in areas of family life, marriage, Christian schools, and Catholic associations. They also supported multi-party democracy, arguing that the parties' complementary emphases would together build up the common good. Finally, they condemned parties that claimed a political monopoly or utilized propaganda to incite political violence. Christians of good faith could differ in their political preferences, but all must oppose the dissemination of "lies and calumnies in propaganda and electoral campaigns," unfounded critiques of Catholic bishops, and the elevation of group interests over the common good. Despite their cautions against political abuses of all types, the bishops never offered Christians the option to opt out. In strong language, the bishops reminded local Christians that "to refuse to vote—to refuse to acquit oneself of the obligations of justice toward society—would be to sin by omitting an important duty."

The bishops then addressed the "justice" society should ensure for its citizenry. Again Bigirumwami's voice emerged in the bishops' questioning of the state's commitment to social order and peace. Highlighting the fires, ethnic cleansing, and deaths that marked recent Rwandan history, the bishops asked "how the campaign of peace can succeed if the constituted authorities continue to show such deficiencies in their exercise of power?" The bishops also called for the state to exercise neutrality toward political parties except in the case of subversive activity, noting the state's obligation to guard against racism that "constitutes a very great danger to the Christian spirit." In addition, the state had a particular obligation to care for the "hundreds of families brutally chased from their homes who had their goods expropriated from them."

The bishops of Rwanda and Burundi concluded *Vérité, Justice, Charité* by addressing the idea of "charity." Perhaps reflecting Perraudin's own longstanding embrace of charity as an episcopal motto, this section bore the imprint of the Archbishop of Kabgayi. Calling on Twa, Hutu, Tutsi, and Europeans to live "side by side in the country, respecting each other and loving each other," the document lambasted "Communist" and "Masonic" agents that were allegedly dividing Catholic clergy, religious, and laity. While resisting the temptation to "identify communism or the danger of communism with existing political parties, as has happened too often," the bishops noted the propensity for communism to transform nationalism into xenophobia. They concluded by recalling the Virgin Mary's promise of "victory over the forces of atheism and notably of communism" in the 1917 apparitions at Lourdes, France.[128]

"Vérité, Justice, Charité" represented the most comprehensive political statement from the Catholic hierarchy of Rwanda-Burundi since the regional bishops' August 1959 statement *"Le chrétien et la politique."* The bishops' tone in this October 1960 document was much more critical of Belgium and the emerging postcolonial state, reflecting the episcopal majority's pessimism toward recent political developments in Rwanda. In addition, the broad platitudes of 1959 gave way to precise injunctions in 1960, including details on refugee suffering and specific criteria for voting. Above all, *"Vérité, Justice, Charité"* revealed the advantages of having Perraudin and Bigirumwami in the same episcopal conference. For example, the document's alternating emphases on anti-communism and anti-ethnicism come across here as more complementary than conflictual. Similarly, Bigirumwami's critiques of state power balance Perraudin's typical calls for political obedience.[129] Yet the bishops' vision of Christian politics still seems limited by the conventions of modern democracy. Although the bishops' condemnations of local political behavior would seem to open the possibility of voter abstention or even the necessity of a Catholic voter boycott, *Vérité, Justice, Charité* continued to describe nonvoting as a "sin of omission." In doing so, the bishops lost an opportunity to chart a "third way" between the excesses of Parmehutu and UNAR alike.

Whatever the omissions of their formal documents, alleged sins of clerical commission were garnering the most public attention in 1960. This was especially the case for Perraudin, the churchman most closely associated with the Hutu emancipation movement and most virulently opposed by UNAR. The allegations against Perraudin and the Kabgayi church were wide-ranging. According to its critics, the Catholic press had incited the Hutu rebellion by propagating irresponsible, racist and revolutionary propaganda. The White Fathers had supported this campaign in the spirit of colonial divide-and-rule, recognizing that they needed to win over the Hutu masses to ensure their future as a popular church. For their critics, Catholic leaders had acquiesced in Kayibanda's vision of dividing Rwanda into ethnic zones.[130] Other allegations targeted Perraudin more personally: the Archbishop of Kabgayi conspired in the death of Mwami Mutara in July 1959 and opposed the Rwandan monarchy; Perraudin served as a patron for Hutu leaders like Kayibanda, Bicamumpaka, and Gitera and provided material support to Hutu parties; Perraudin falsely connected UNAR with communism and Islam in his clerical directives of September 1959.[131]

At first, Perraudin tried to ignore these diatribes and refused to comment publicly. Soon, however, Perraudin's fellow White Fathers were pressuring him to defend himself, fearing that the negative publicity could jeopardize the future of the Catholic Church in Rwanda. Thus Leo Volker urged Perraudin to submit a formal defense to the United Nations General Assembly.[132] Perraudin acquiesced, testifying to the U.N. Visiting Commission when the commission visited him in Kabgayi on March 13. In late April Perraudin sent a copy of this defense to the United Nations General Assembly in New York.[133]

Even as he expressed his discomfort with defending himself in a political forum, Perraudin began his defense to the U.N. Visiting Commission by stating the Catholic Church's obligation to "redress errors and proclaim the truth" so as to protect its credibility in Rwanda and the wider world. After outlining the accusations, Perraudin quoted *Super omnia caritas*, noting that this document critiqued Rwanda's social structures but rejected class warfare and omitted technical political prescriptions best left to Catholic laity. Perraudin also argued that Catholic newspapers like *Kinyamateka* and *Temps Nouveaux d'Afrique* "denounced a unity based on multiple injustices" but denied that they incited ethnic division or political upheaval. On the issue of his alleged involvement in Mwami Mutara's July 1959 death, Perraudin noted that he was closing a clerical synod in Nyakibanda when Mutara died 200 kilometers away in Bujumbura. Concerning his alleged support for Hutu political leaders, Perraudin admitted that Gregoire Kayibanda resided near Kabgayi yet noted that Rwanda's Queen Mother and her UNAR supporters lived in the area as well. And although he admitted that Kayibanda once served as *Kinyamateka* editor, Perraudin noted that he forced Kayibanda to resign as soon as the MSM (*Mouvement Social Muhutu*) undertook political activity. In turn, Perraudin claimed that he always opposed the ethnic zoning of Rwanda and stated that "the Catholic White Fathers and Bishop Perraudin remain open to all political leaders, Hutu and Tutsi."[134] As arbiters of the moral order, however, the bishops retained the right to issue moral judgments on problematic political doctrines and behavior.

Perraudin also requested that the Hutu seminary professor Bernard Manyurane speak to the U.N. Visiting Commission. In his March 10 testimony, Manyurane noted that the Catholic media employed both Hutu and Tutsi and claimed that Catholic journalists were attempting to find a disinterested solution to the problem of customary authority. Rwanda's bishops had not attacked an ethnic group but simply "preached justice without equivocation, defending the rights of the poor and the oppressed." In an unguarded moment, however, Manyurane spoke of the Hutu need to "liberate themselves from despotism and Tutsi monopoly."[135] In betraying his Hutu nationalist sympathies, Manyurane made it necessary for Perraudin to enlist the support of other indigenous clergy.

Here Perraudin turned to Jean-Baptiste Gahamanyi, the superior of Nyanza parish. Gahamanyi was the ideal Rwandan priest to defend Perraudin against UNAR's charges. A Tutsi member of Rwanda's elite Abanyiginya clan and brother of the UNAR leader Michel Kayihura, Gahamanyi had cultivated a strong relationship with Mwami Mutara in the final months of Mutara's life. In his April 1960 letter to the U.N. Trusteeship Council in New York, Gahamanyi argued that there was no documentary evidence that Perraudin ever opposed the Mwami or other Rwandan authorities; the archbishop simply spoke out on the imperatives of justice and the rights of man. Gahamanyi defended Perraudin against the accusation that he helped assassinate Mwami Mutara, reiterating that Perraudin was closing a priest retreat in Nyakibanda when the Mwami died in Bujumbura. Gahamanyi also claimed that Perraudin condemned problematic political positions in all parties, from UNAR's xenophobic nationalism to Aprosoma's anti-Tutsi racism. Finally, Gahamanyi admitted that the missionary press took a strong position on social justice questions but argued that their writings did not sanction revolution.[136]

How convincing are these testimonies? Clearly some of UNAR's most extreme accusations are easier to parry. For example, there is little to no evidence that Perraudin ever advocated for the ethnic zoning of the country; the White Fathers almost universally opposed such a plan. Likewise, UNAR documents themselves do not concur on the alleged conspiracy surrounding the Mwami's death; only one actually implicates Perraudin himself. However, Perraudin's claims to have fired Kayibanda from Kinyamateka "as soon as the MSM undertook political activity" seem disingenuous, as the MSM was already organizing party meetings, building up local councils, and issuing manifestoes in 1957 and 1958. Despite this overtly political activity, Perraudin did not ask Kayibanda to step down until October 1959 when MSM reinvented itself as the Parmehutu party.[137] Finally, it is perhaps unsurprising that Gahamanyi never addressed the accusation that Perraudin provided protection for Hutu political leaders. As already noted, even Adriaenssens and *Temps Nouveaux d'Afrique* thought as much.

While Perraudin defended himself before the UN, he and other White Father leaders escalated their rhetorical attacks on UNAR, furthering the perception that UNAR stood at the root of all of Rwanda's political problems. This tone was set by Leo Volker, the superior general of the White Fathers. After saying relatively little in his late 1959 correspondence with Bigirumwami, Perraudin, and Van Hoof, Volker revealed his own views in a blistering January letter to Mgr. Pierre Sigismondi, former apostolic nuncio to Belgian Congo and secretary of the Vatican congregation Propaganda Fide.[138] Here Volker accused UNAR of imagining that a few great families in Rwanda had a "divine right" to rule the country and that "racial superiority is inscribed by nature by the Creator." Volker warned Sigismondi that UNAR would fight all who threatened its agenda, including the popular masses who had "become conscious of the abnormal state of inferiority in which they were maintained," the Church whose social justice doctrines preached the "functional equality of all men," and the Belgian Administration in whom the Hutu placed their hope. For Volker, UNAR's lies, calumnies, and premeditated assassinations recalled the Nazi program condemned by Pius XI in his 1937 encyclical *Mit Brennender Sorge*.

What should we make of Volker's accusations? Clearly UNAR deserved criticism. Party cadres launched premeditated assassinations of Hutu political leaders in November, and UNAR's political rhetoric could rival Aprosoma in its unsubstantiated extremism. As we will see, UNAR's armed incursions into Rwanda triggered most of the worst ethnic violence in Rwanda in the early 1960s. But again, what stands out here is the one-sided nature of Volker's interpretation of Rwandan politics. For example, he did not criticize the Hutu rioters; rather he credited them with preventing a Nazi-style takeover by UNAR. "The riots, which have their origins in the provocations and cruelties exercised by this party in regard to the popular masses, have not given UNAR the time to realize its plan." Even more dangerously, Volker's hatred for UNAR led him to denigrate Rwanda's broader Tutsi refugee population. "These Batutsi, as we have seen in different camps of refugees organized by the Missions during the civil war, are devoid of all sensibilities or marks of Christian charity." And while commending Perraudin for his bravery, commitment to social justice, and unwavering defense of the church's "spiritual" mission, Volker painted Bigirumwami as an ideological sympathizer of UNAR. "The anti-Christian racism of UNAR (born of communism and benefitting from the sympathies of French freemasonry in the person of the high agents of the Administration) is assured of the sympathy and favor of Mgr. Bigirumwami who, blinded by the interests of his race, does not see the deeper tendencies of this party."[139] Volker's accusations here went far beyond the March 1960 commentary of the local Belgian colonial administrator in Nyundo who who said "he was certain that [Bigirumwami] was not for anything."[140] Van Hoof himself told Volker later in 1960 that he retained "full confidence in Mgr. Bigirumwami, who is certainly a 'true Catholic man,' although he doesn't seem to understand anything about politics."[141]

Volker's anti-UNAR sentiments likely reflected the convictions of Van Hoof and Perraudin, the two White Fathers who communicated most regularly with Rome. Van Hoof wrote in January 1960 that UNAR adherents were staying away from church and claimed that "the facts that prove that UNAR is a subversive party multiply every day."[142] As discussed earlier, Perraudin in February banned priests from supporting UNAR due to its allegedly *laïcist* program, communist sympathies, and attacks on the Catholic hierarchy.[143] The Diocese of Kabgayi's annual report of June 1960 attributed the onset of violence in November to UNAR's determination to "suppress the political leaders of the opposition."[144] Perraudin went further in October, arguing that UNAR's two founding principles were communist-inspired "noncollaboration" and "a sort of Nazi racism" based on the alleged superiority of the Tutsi race over Hutu and Twa alike.[145] *Temps Nouveaux d'Afrique* shared this critique, highlighting UNAR's alleged anti-clericalism and fascist methods.[146]

In contrast to their repeated diatribes against UNAR, the White Father leadership offered few critiques of Parmehutu. If anything, the scale of Parmehutu's electoral victory in the summer of 1960 took the missionaries by surprise. Van Hoof claimed to be "stupefied" at Parmehutu's rapid rise to political dominance, claiming that the church would be in deep pastoral trouble "if she had the evil of having the Hutu against her."[147] While expressing some concerns over Rwanda's transformation into a one-party state, Van Hoof never implicated Parmehutu in the mass ethnic cleansing happening in Rwanda during the middle of 1960.[148] For his part, Perraudin expressed no reservations as the Parmehutu-dominated provisional government took office in October 1960. Even as he predicted that UNAR would form a government in exile, Perraudin confidently stated that "the movement of democratization should be irreversible, and the return to the political and social situation of another time should be unthinkable."[149] By the end of the year, an increasingly optimistic Van Hoof wrote that the Parmehutu regime's commitment to social justice pointed to the "blossoming of a more authentic Christianity than that which we have ever known here in Rwanda."[150]

Again, Bigirumwami offers an important contrary voice. While the White Fathers attacked UNAR and acquiesced to one-party Parmehutu rule as the manifest will of the people, Bigirumwami publicly distanced himself from all parties. As early as March 1960, Bigirumwami castigated Rwanda's political parties for dividing the country into partisan factions and inciting racial hate. "One searches in vain for a political party who, for love of their country, takes a categorical and true position for the pacification of its country."[151] Unlike many of the White Fathers and many indigenous clergy, Bigirumwami recognized the inherent risks that political affiliation posed to Catholic identity, as reflected in his comments in a June 1960 pastoral letter to the Catholic faithful in Nyundo Diocese.

> The height of calamities is that parties are introduced into our communities. We should not be for one or the other. The political parties have intruded in our words, in our walking, in our visits, in our agitations, and even in our sermons in which we name the gospel....In this we give the impression of having joined the parties of Hutu and Tutsi, abandoning that which is of Jesus.[152]

Bigirumwami never fully developed this inchoate vision of alternative Christian politics. This should not surprise us. As noted earlier, European commentators lampooned him for "not knowing anything about politics." But Bigirumwami at least recognized the risks that political and ethnic identities could pose to Christian solidarity; one looks in vain for similar warnings in the writings of Perraudin and other White Fathers.

Bigirumwami's skepticism about national politics also stemmed from the growing violence which surrounded Rwanda's purportedly democratic elections. Rwanda continued to suffer paroxysms of anti-Tutsi violence throughout 1960. These included the mass ethnic cleansings at Byumba and Nyundo during the U.N. Visiting Commission mission of March 1960, riots near Astrida in April 1960, and the reciprocal political violence of the electoral season of summer 1960.[153] The violence was increasingly dividing Catholic parishes along ethnic lines. During the March unrest in Byumba, for example, the parish's Hutu superiors refused to take in Tutsi refugees.[154]

To their credit, Bigirumwami, Perraudin and even Van Hoof all spoke out against the pillaging, arson, and murder that afflicted Rwanda in 1960. Perraudin went further in March 1960 than he had in November 1959, calling for more refugee aid and stating that the guilty faced a "grave duty" to "make reparation for the injustices that they have committed."[155] His actions supported the rhetoric. Perraudin paid multiple visits to refugee populations in Janja, Nemba, Runaba, Rwambuba and Nyamata, and he also established a new bureau of assistance for refugees.[156] For a period, he even appeared to recognize the risk of conflating "UNAR" with "Tutsi" in the popular mind. In the words of Perraudin's White Father ally Jean Massion, "he [Perraudin] has more than one time insisted that his warning against UNAR was not a warning against the Tutsi but that it was since he loved the Tutsi that he issued the warning against the party, who pretended to be their guardians."[157] For his part, Van Hoof described the violence of March 1960 as "nasty Hutu riots against the Tutsi," expressing empathy for the "poor Batutsi" who comprised the vast majority of the victims. And yet even here Van Hoof cast more blame on Tutsi intransigence rather than the Hutu perpetrators themselves. "These poor Batutsi, betrayed by blind leaders who cannot accept the new situation created by the revolt of the Bahutu, are in the end going to be expelled from all the corners of Rwanda"[158]

But while all of Rwanda's church leaders expressed regret at Rwanda's ethnic violence, Bigirumwami probed further in exploring the deeper reasons for the violence. Rather than just isolate one factor like UNAR provocation or communist propaganda, Bigirumwami cast a wide net, citing the abuses of Tutsi chiefs, Hutu provocateurs "looking to oppose Hutu and Tutsi and to separate them," years of destructive media propaganda, and ignorant arsonists claiming to act on the Mwami's orders.[159] Bigirumwami also turned the critique on himself and the church, questioning the seeming failure of Christian discipleship in Rwanda. While the writings of Perraudin and other White Father leaders offered little in the way of self-critical introspection, Bigirumwami saw Rwanda's violence as a direct contradiction of the nation's supposed consecration to Christ the King. Thus Bigirumwami wrote in January 1960 that the "worst calamity" in Rwanda's recent history was that "the propagators of evils of which I have spoken, were not pagans, nor notorious apostates who had abandoned Christianity, but rather Christians who were known as good models among others."[160] In particular, Bigirumwami rejected the commonplace notion—often repeated by the White Fathers—that the "irresistible will" of the "unchained masses" produced at worst a "necessary evil" and at best a "just social vengeance" against Tutsi.[161]

If Perraudin tended to focus on clerical behavior, Bigirumwami saw Rwanda's violence as a deeper challenge to the very mission and identity of the church. Perraudin could be quite eloquent in his calls on clergy to live into their vocations. "Open your eyes, do not make concession to error or lies, fight against false rumors and calumnies, practice and preach justice and charity. We are the Church, that is to say ministers of God who are all for all, marking only our predilection for the poorest and most suffering. *Beati pacifici!*"[162] Yet his writings rarely held lay Christians accountable for their sins, particularly in political life. In contrast, for Bigirumwami "the church" consisted not just of clerical elites but the whole community of the baptized. "You are children of Rwanda and children of the Church…you have always been brothers…you are more than brothers since you have received baptism which has made you children of God and of the Church."[163] In this sense, Bigirumwami the supposed Tutsi paternalist was in fact the least paternalistic of all of Rwanda's Catholic leaders. Bigirumwami would not excuse his fellow Rwandans as illiterate peasants when they asked priests in the confessional "if killing or wounding a Tutsi is a sin." Rather, he questioned how they had learned to think that way—and why church leaders had not already corrected such misperceptions. In summary, Bigirumwami's ecclesiology envisioned the church as "perfect people faithful to the commandments of God and the Church" rather than "one who calls himself Tutsi" or "one who calls himself Hutu."[164]

Unfortunately for Bigirumwami, the Rwandan Catholic Church itself was breaking up over these very terms. The Hutu-Tutsi cleavage that had divided Rwandan politics and society also threatened those entrusted to lead the postcolonial church—namely Rwanda's missionaries, indigenous priests, and seminarians. It is to this story that we now turn.

An Epicenter Radiating Tensions

If the hierarchy maintained a unified public voice and the institutions of the church held together through 1959, ethnic and political pressures exerted a more visible toll on Catholic unity during 1960. This was particularly evident in the areas of seminary life and episcopal appointments. If not wholly accurate in the late 1950s, Mahmood Mamdani's description of the Rwandan Catholic Church as not just a "passive mirror reflecting tensions…[but] more of an epicenter radiating tensions" aptly described the Catholic Church of 1960.[165]

Looking at the surface of church life in 1960, one could have concluded that the Catholic Church was moving from strength to strength. The Catholic population of Kabgayi diocese grew from 560,000 to over 600,000 between 1959 and 1960. Rwanda had a record 600 minor seminarians and over 100 major seminarians, including 38 new Nyakibanda students for the 1959-1960 academic year. Easter communion rates continued to surpass 80 percent. As Perraudin wrote in January 1960, Rwanda was witnessing a "magnificent hour" in its religious history.[166]

This "magnificent hour" had its shadows, however. First, priestly vocations were not keeping up with the growing Catholic population. Only two priests were ordained in 1960; an additional sixteen either left Rwanda or left the priesthood during the same year.[167] Second, many Tutsi seminarians were struggling with the impact of the revolution, having seen family members and teachers exiled because of their Tutsi identity. Third, sacramental practice was declining due to political tensions, particularly among the Tutsi. In the words of the Kabgayi annual report, "many believe that their political options stop them from communing, and they do not dare to confess…Many of our Tutsi Christians have not practiced since the events of November, [reflecting] a mistrust for religion, the Church, priests, and a penchant towards Protestantism which supports UNAR."[168] While Perraudin would embrace ecumenical outreach after Vatican II, the colonial association between Protestantism and political dissent remained strong in the early 1960s, especially as the Anglican Church embraced UNAR's social analysis.

As Tutsi Catholics pulled back, Hutu Catholic numbers were growing in Rwanda's parishes. In order to keep these Hutu Catholics coming to church, the White Fathers saw the appointment of a Hutu bishop as a pastoral imperative. As the nation's political and business capital, Kigali remained the likeliest center for a Hutu-led diocese, and the White Fathers had been working with the Holy See toward this end since 1957. Several potential roadblocks had emerged, however. First, since Tutsi elites had dominated the priesthood since the 1930s, Rwanda lacked credible Hutu candidates for the episcopate. Second, Kigali was home to a large concentration of Tutsi economic and political leaders and displaced Tutsi from other parts of Rwanda, making the imposition of a Hutu bishop politically difficult. Perhaps reflecting these concerns, the Vatican took the Kigali diocesan plan off the table in February 1960. Three months later, Rome released revised plans to establish two new dioceses in Rwanda—one based at Ruhengeri in the northern mountains, the other in Astrida (later Butare), the nation's intellectual center in southern Rwanda. Perraudin admitted that these plans developed in light of "recent events" and "factors of religious sociology," including the new-found importance of "confiding an ecclesiastical jurisdiction to a bishop of the Hutu race."[169]

For his part, Perraudin advocated strongly for the appointment of a Hutu bishop. Before departing for his 1960 *ad limina* visit to Rome, Perraudin sent a letter to Propaganda Fide nominating two Hutu priests to fill the new positions. Perraudin expected the nominations to provoke some discontent among the Tutsi-dominated clergy but argued that Hutu appointments were imperative in light of rising Hutu political power in Rwanda.

> One must not forget…that there is already a Tutsi Bishop in the person of His Excellency Mgr. Bigirumwami, that the population of Rwanda is 85 percent Hutu, and that the Hutu parties are practically in power. I fear strongly that a Tutsi Bishop would be poorly accepted, and he could find himself in an extremely pitiful situation…I think, on the contrary, that the Hutu Bishops could have much influence in the years to come.[170]

Neither the racist ideologue of UNAR mythology nor the disinterested church-man committed solely to "charity above all things," Perraudin emerges here as a consummate ecclesial politician, positioning the church for future growth by ensuring that its leadership reflected Rwanda's shifting political and ethnic tides. In this regard Perraudin proved himself a worthy successor to León Classe, what-ever their other differences.

As Perraudin pushed for the appointment of a Hutu bishop, relations between Bigirumwami and the White Fathers reached a nadir.[171] These tensions erupted in public with the release of a Bigirumwami pastoral letter in July 1960. Calling the missionaries our "fathers in the faith," Bigirumwami reminded missionaries that priests should never justify nefarious political means in hopes of achieving a desired political end. Namely, democracy and social justice should not arrive via "hate, division, fire, deaths, or pillaging." Nor should missionaries speak poorly of local priests or favor one ethnic group over another. Rather, missionaries should serve as "our [Rwandans'] advocates, our arbiters, our judges, and our liberators" while fighting against ethnicism, communism, materialism, paganism, and anarchy. Bigirumwami's letter served as an unusually public rebuke to the White Fathers in Rwanda. Perraudin took note, reminding his priests in an early September circular that they "do not have the right to demolish the reputation of a neighbor especially when that neighbor is a brother in the priesthood." In a cautionary note, Perraudin added that a priest can fall into mortal sin through unholy conversation marked by lies, mistrust, and criticism.[172] Even the Holy See stepped into the fray, reminding both indigenous and foreign clergy of their duties to maintain fraternal unity and direct their mission toward the "glory of God and the salvation of souls."[173]

Bigirumwami followed this public critique with a stinging private censure of the White Fathers in August 1960. After recounting Rwanda's months of fire, expulsions, massacres, and surveillance, Bigirumwami wondered how so many missionaries could support such things in the name of "normal evolution," "justice," or "social vengeance." "I am suffering cruelly when I think that many Europeans and missionaries find this normal, indifferent, or perfectly good. I am more and more convinced that certain European and African conceptions are not the same, and I do not admit that evil means justify the end."[174] When the White Fathers failed to respond to Bigirumwami's letter, he requested a neutral Vatican arbiter to combat what he termed a "conspiracy of inaction."[175] This dialogue reminds us that while most White Fathers did not explicitly sanction anti-Tutsi violence, many did not speak out against it, particularly since Hutu elites were notable for their opposition to communism, support for Catholic privileges, and commitment to democracy and social justice. Even Alphonse Van Hoof admitted that some White Fathers had "not always been sufficiently understanding...in regards to those who have suffered from the revolution."[176]

If the analytical divisions between Bigirumwami and the White Fathers became increasingly apparent in 1960, this is in part because Rwanda's ethnic tensions were undermining Nyakibanda major seminary. If Nyakibanda remained tense if relatively calm during the November 1959 troubles,[177] student relations at the seminary quickly deteriorated in 1960, and this took a toll on seminary enrollment. Eighty-five students—fifty-five Tutsi and thirty Hutu—started the 1959–1960 academic year. Over the next twelve months, twenty-nine seminarians departed Nyakibanda. An additional sixteen seminarians quit during the first three months of the 1960–1961 year. The majority of these leavers were Tutsi who accused their White Father professors of favoring Nyakibanda's Hutu students. Other leavers came from the seminary's Hutu minority, claiming they had no place in a seminary dominated by Tutsi ideology.[178]

In light of this crisis of both vocations and perceptions, Fr. Paul Baers, Nyakibanda's rector, prepared a special report on "the state of the spirit of the seminary." In drafting his report, Baers solicited input from professors and seminarians alike. A deluge of complaints, diatribes, and testimonies followed, centering on the Hutu-Tutsi cleavage at Nyakibanda. Three major themes emerge in this literature: (1) the rise of a virulent form of Hutu nationalism marked by zero-sum ethnic stereotyping; (2) missionary concerns for preserving Hutu vocations in light of Rwanda's shifting political terrain; and (3) a major divergence between Bishop Bigirumwami and Fr. Baers on how to resolve the seminary's ethnic tensions.

First, this correspondence is marked by an especially strong strand of ethnic nationalism. On one level, this reflected a continuation of the longtime Nyakibanda current of Banyarwandan nationalism; one recalls here the successful purge of Burundian and Congolese seminarians in the early 1950s. The new current in 1960 was provided by a growing population of Hutu seminarians from northern Rwanda. Reflecting the historic independence of their region, these northern Hutu were much less inclined to adapt to what they called the "fully Tutsified" culture of Nyakibanda. In the words of one seminarian, "it is impossible to change what to us is essential; it would seem to us a betrayal…there is a logical impossibility of sincere entente between Tutsi and *true Hutu.*"[179] This rhetoric of "true Hutu" helped the northern seminarians explain why all Hutu seminarians did not yet share their views—namely they were not sufficiently aware of the reality of their oppression. In this spirit, these Hutu advocates rejected missionary calls for fraternal unity, arguing that this would only lead to the "depersonalization" of the Hutu seminarian as he acquiesced to Tutsi cultural norms. Rather than fraternal unity, these Hutu seminarians called on the church to encourage peaceful coexistence between Hutu and Tutsi based on mutual respect. In the words of one Hutu seminarian, the Tutsi needed to recognize that "the Hutu are men, that they have personalities."[180] The more measured words of Hutu professor Bernard Manyurane captured the same sentiment. "The Hutu wants also to be himself; he no longer wants to be dominated, nor to be influenced by his Tutsi brother; he wants to be his equal."[181] This process entailed recognizing what one White Father professor termed the "instinctual differences" between Hutu and Tutsi, rejecting the stereotypical Tutsi predilection toward flattery, egoism and insincerity.[182]

As ethnic nationalism became a dominant ideological presence in the seminary, Rector Baers and his allies grew increasingly concerned about the potential loss of Hutu vocations.[183] This reflected a growing pastoral concern that the Tutsi-dominated Rwandan church would be disadvantaged and even persecuted in a Hutu-dominated state. In the face of this prospect, one anonymous writer went so far as to encourage Tutsi seminarians to "present themselves in the manner of Hutu so that they will be received by the population of that race."[184] So while

Baers explained the departure of Tutsi seminarians as a necessary evil to forestall the ordination of "political priests," he described the departure of one-third of the Hutu seminarians as a "pastoral crisis." Baers also worried about the "danger of a future violent anti-clericalism" if Tutsi priests did not adapt to the new social and political reality facing them in Rwanda. "Without Hutu priests, what is the future of the Church in Rwanda?"[185]

If Catholic leaders concurred that there was an ethnic crisis at Nyakibanda, they differed on how to resolve it. Possible solutions included dividing the students into separate classes according to ethnicity, establishing a new seminary for each diocese, separating philosophy and theology students, or closing the seminary for an interim period. Led by Fr. Baers, a slim majority of Nyakibanda professors supported closing the seminary "to bring about important purifications in the ranks of Tutsi seminarians." The White Fathers would then reopen the seminary later in 1961 with a more equitable ethnic balance.[186]

This debate in turn reflected Catholic leaders' contrasting analyses of Rwandan society. For Paul Baers, the Hutu seminarians had finally realized that Rwanda's traditional society offered a "fallacious regime of unity and concord which required the Hutu to sacrifice his rights." Thanks to the "social doctrine of the Church based on the rights of the human person," the Hutu were now rightfully demanding that Tutsi respect Hutu "valor and respectability."[187] Bernard Manyurane agreed, claiming that Catholic social teaching had helped the Muhutu to "become conscious of his human personality" and "right to full participation in public life"; the Hutu would no longer be content simply "serving others."[188] In contrast, Bigirumwami saw the crisis as stemming from the "virus" of ethnicism introduced by scheming politicians and their missionary allies. Closing the seminary would only sacrifice the church to the "demons" which had already divided the Rwandan polity, obliterating a church that had been the "the pearl of Africa" and the "joy and the glory of the White Fathers."[189] The Nyundo priest and Nyakibanda professor Deogratias Mbandiwimfura agreed, claiming that "the spirit of paternalism on the part of Tutsi seminarians toward the Hutu seminarians for me does not exist here in the major seminary."[190] He attributed the controversy to the intrusion of national politics into the seminary. Unable to agree on a future course in November 1960, Catholic leaders postponed a final decision on Nyakibanda's future until January 1961.

In essence, the divisions at Nyakibanda reflected a deeper crisis of trust inside the Rwandan church. Tutsi seminarians spoke out about the "incompetent" and "inopportune" nature of Perraudin's 1959 "*Super omnia caritas*," suspecting that missionaries had "created a problem that did not exist" to curry favor with the new government.[191] For their part, Hutu students claimed that their seminary professors looked down on them and ignored their presence. One Nyakibanda professor traced the crisis to the age-old problems of disobedience and "incomprehension" between black and white priests.[192] Bigirumwami himself no longer trusted the seminary's White Father leadership, calling in November 1960 for Baers's resignation.[193] As Baers himself recognized, most Tutsi clergy and seminarians no longer believed that the White Fathers "could comprehend what is truly good and opportune for the Banyarwanda."[194] Reflecting the deep mistrust that pervaded Rwandan society at the end of 1960, the crisis of Nyakibanda seminary would continue through 1961 and beyond.

If at first glance 1959 appears to be the chronological turning point in Rwandan church politics, the year 1960 established the long-term pattern of Catholic engagement with Rwandan political and ethnic questions. 1959 garnered more headlines, beginning with Perraudin's February pastoral letter and ending with the mass ethnic cleansing of November. But Catholic leaders maintained broad unity throughout all of these events, gathering in synod at Nyakibanda in August 1959, issuing joint condemnations of UNAR and Aprosoma in September and October, and quickly denouncing the violence of November 1959. Mission stations served as places of sanctuary during the November revolution, and Nyakibanda seminary did not yet show signs of serious ethnic strife.

The real cleavages emerged, then, in 1960. It was in this year that Bigirumwami broke privately and publicly with the White Fathers. By 1960 Perraudin and other White Fathers were attributing nearly all responsibility for Rwanda's political ills to UNAR. In turn, Bigirumwami's more prophetic stance against the Rwandan state emerged in contrast to Perraudin's renewed emphasis on church-state collaboration. 1960 marked a decisive transition in Rwanda's secular politics—a year that began with Perraudin's New Year's greetings to Mwami Kigeli ended with Kigeli in exile and Gregoire Kayibanda leading a Parmehutu-dominated government. The transformation was no less radical for Catholic politics in Rwanda. The patterns established in 1960 would continue through independence in 1962.

The Bloody Road to Independence

As discussed previously, the United Nations and Belgium agreed to a political compromise at the beginning of January 1961. Belgium offered to delay legislative elections until June, hold separate referendums on the monarchy and Rwandan independence, and institute a more inclusive transitional government in Rwanda. A power-sharing government including UNAR exiles seemed possible. Mwami Kigeli even began preparations to return to Rwanda in February.[195]

On January 28, however, Hutu elites took matters into their own hands. Kayibanda, Gitera and Bicamumpaka gathered over 2,800 of Rwanda's 3,125 burgomasters for an impromptu national assembly at Gitarama.[196] Twenty-five thousand Rwandans rallied outside the convention hall in support. Inspired by Gitera's rousing oratory, the assembly abolished the monarchy, replaced the Kalinga drums with a new national flag, and declared Rwanda to be a democratic republic. After the assembly split regionally on whether to elect Kayibanda, Gitera, or Bicamumpaka as president, the delegates settled on Dominique Mbonyumutwa, the symbolic victim of the November 1959 violence. Meanwhile, Belgian para-commandos stood guard outside the assembly. Although he initially denied Belgian knowledge of the coup, Logiest later admitted that Kayibanda approached him on January 25 to gain his prior approval.[197] The declaration of Rwanda as a republic sparked celebrations across the country, especially in Parmehutu strongholds like Ruhengeri where the massive crowds included a substantial number of missionaries and religious sisters.[198]

What came to be known as the *"coup d'état of Gitarama"* ratified the Parmehutu-dominated political order that Col. Logiest had initiated after the November 1959 violence. It took Brussels only four days to offer official recognition to Rwanda's *de facto* authorities, and in early February Mbonyumutwa embarked on a three-week goodwill tour of Rwanda in an effort to take the symbolic place of the Mwami. Notwithstanding a March U.N. declaration that "one racist dictatorship had been replaced by another" and an overwhelming U.N. General Assembly condemnation of the Gitarama coup in April,[199] the U.N. agreed to move forward with expected referendums on the republic and the monarchy in September 1961. Further marginalized by the Gitarama events, UNAR suffered from internal divisions, split between a Kigali wing that agreed to contest the forthcoming elections and an exile community that rejected Rwanda's new political institutions.

After a brief period of relative stability in late 1960 and early 1961, the electoral season of 1961 saw Rwanda's worst violence since November 1959.[200] Facilitated in part by a Belgian decision in July to release over 3,000 political prisoners, clashes between Parmehutu, Aprosoma and UNAR partisans in southern Rwanda killed hundreds, destroyed over 3,000 homes and produced over 22,000 refugees. Parmehutu and UNAR factions clashed in four separate incidents in July 1961, culminating with a major battle east of Kigali that left 130 dead and nearly 10,000 displaced. Whereas much of the 1959-1960 violence had been concentrated in northern Rwanda, anti-Tutsi violence shifted in 1961 to southern Rwanda. The territory of Astrida alone produced 15,000 refugees by mid-August, including nearly 5,000 who took refuge at Nyakibanda Seminary. Political overtones marked the seemingly ethnic violence, from UNAR voter intimidation in the east to Parmehutu clashes with Aprosoma supporters in the south. In the meantime, increasing numbers of Rwandan Tutsi fled the country all together. By the end of 1961, 18,000 had taken refuge in Burundi and 20,000 in Uganda. Even *Temps Nouveaux d'Afrique* published an article on the refugee crisis, its first on the topic in two years.[201]

After three months of violence and instability, the September 25 legislative elections ratified Parmehutu's political mandate. In fact, Parmehutu's share of the vote rose from 70 percent in the July 1960 elections to nearly 80 percent in September 1961. Rejecting the advice of its external wing, the internal UNAR party contested the elections and came second with 17 percent of the vote. In turn, the elections eliminated Aprosoma and Rader as significant political movements. In a concurrent referendum on the Mwami, the Rwandan people rejected the institution of the monarchy by a four to one ratio. This demonstrated the remarkable political shift in Rwanda since the November 1959 days when Hutu incendiaries claimed to be acting at the behest of Mwami Kigeli. In late October the Parmehutu-dominated national assembly named Kayibanda to replace Mbonyumutwa as president. Belgium approved Rwanda's new political institutions in December 1961. In February 1962, the internal wing of UNAR agreed to recognize the new government in exchange for two cabinet positions. Shortly thereafter, the U.N. recognized Rwanda's new government and called for greater political reconciliation and reintegration of refugees.

While Rwanda was achieving a measure of institutional stability in early 1962, it was also developing the trappings of a police state. Belgian and Rwandan troops patrolled nearly every road and park in the country, imposing a night curfew on travel. Prominent personalities like Fr. Alexis Kagame and Joseph Gitera remained under house arrest— Kagame for his alleged association with UNAR, Gitera for his December 1961 decision to join a common front against Parmehutu.[202] Despite these security efforts, UNAR commando raids in early 1962 led to the deaths of several Belgian tourists and local government officials in the northern town of Byumba. In response, Byumba Hutu unleashed a genocidal massacre at the end of March 1962. Over the course of three nights, local Hutu militias killed between 1,000 and 3,000 (predominantly male) Tutsi in Byumba and the surrounding hills. Belgian paratroopers and Rwandan soldiers restored order after several days, but Rwanda's political violence had taken a foreboding turn. Forced displacement had given way to ethnic massacre.[203]

Despite the terror of Byumba, preparations for independence continued apace. Republican Rwanda and monarchical Burundi agreed to part ways in the months preceding independence, breaking the European amalgamation of "Ruanda-Urundi" which the Germans had first initiated at the beginning of the century. On July 1, 1962, Rwanda formally declared its independence from Belgium. Flanked by Archbishop Perraudin and Belgium's first ambassador, Guy Logiest, Kayibanda offered an inaugural address in which he thanked the Catholic missions for their "civilizing influence," praised Belgium's four decades of political stewardship, and trumpeted Rwanda's new credo of "liberty, cooperation, and progress." In his remarks, Perraudin thanked God for the "gift of independence" and proclaimed that "on this memorable day, the Church rejoices with the entire country."[204] Whatever its outward display of rhetorical unity, however, Rwanda's Catholic leadership no longer shared a unified voice on how to engage Rwanda's emerging Parmehutu-dominated state.

FIGURE 5.1 Flanked by President Kayibanda and members of the Rwandan military, Mgr. Perraudin preaches at Independence Day ceremonies, July 1962 (*courtesy Centre Missionnaire Lavigerie, Kigali, Rwanda*)

As Parmehutu expanded its political monopoly in 1961 and 1962, several important trends developed in Catholic circles. First, Perraudin and other White Father leaders increasingly emphasized UNAR's supposed communist connections. In contrast, they did not critique Parmehutu's ethnicist foundations and in fact encouraged closer collaboration between church and state. Second, although Bigirumwami ceased his public critiques of the government, he continued to lobby the White Fathers behind the scenes to adopt a more critical stance toward Parmehutu and its Belgian supporters. Bigirumwami's perceived intransigence along with the more open opposition of many of Rwanda's Tutsi clergy led Rwanda's Hutu authorities to condemn what they described as a "Tutsified" church. Not surprising, Catholic parishes themselves became sites of ethnic and political violence, foreshadowing even worse developments in the postcolonial period. To their credit, Bigirumwami, Perraudin and other Catholic leaders united in forcefully condemning the violence. Behind the scenes, however, Perraudin and his allies continued to ascribe almost exclusive responsibility to UNAR insurgents rather than the Hutu militias who were actually conducting the massacres.

Throughout 1961, Perraudin continued to describe communism as the preeminent threat to Rwanda's political future. In February, Perraudin placed Catholic Action leaders on guard "before the Communist danger" while warning his diocese that "there was no compromise possible" with atheistic and immoral communism.[205] In his first national radio address in April 1961, Perraudin informed Rwandans that international communism was the greatest enemy of the church and "authentic human values."[206] In an April letter to donors, Perraudin expanded his political critique to include other ideologies, noting that "our masses are strongly worked up by news of disastrous ideologies: communism, neo-paganism, a return to ancient customs, *laïcite*."[207] Notably missing here was the ideology of racism or ethnicism. At the same time, Perraudin encouraged political participation, instructing clergy to "give an example" by going to the polls and voting according to their consciences.[208] Since UNAR was the only party associated with international communism, *laïcite* or a "return to ancient customs," the underlying political message was clear: clergy and lay Catholics should vote, so long as they did not vote for UNAR. Even after the September elections, Perraudin remained silent on the risk of ethnicism, writing in a circular to priests that Africa was "menaced and already strongly attacked by materialistic communism and atheism; Islam remains here also very active as well as the forces of laicizing French freemasonry."[209] For Perraudin, UNAR communism loomed as a much larger ideological threat than Parmehutu ethnicism.

Publicly, Bigirumwami pulled back from national politics in 1961. He issued few circular letters, and *Civitas Mariae* focused on strictly pastoral concerns. Privately, however, he continued to emphasize the divisive role that ethnic discourse had played in Rwanda's recent history. In a passionate January 1961 letter to Volker that Bigirumwami claimed to write "for the archives," he defended himself against missionary accusations while offering his own interpretation of Rwanda's recent history.[210] According to Bigirumwami, White Fathers in Rwanda had accused him of being a "communist, schismatic and nationalist." In response, Bigirumwami claimed that he had always "stood with the masses" and spoken out against political abuses. At the same time, he had staunchly opposed the ethnic ideology and violence that marked the November 1959 revolution. For Bigirumwami, the November 1959 revolutions stemmed from the formation of ethnically based parties aided and abetted by sympathetic Catholic missionaries and a strident Catholic media that "incited hatred and division" in the pages of *Temps Nouveaux d'Afrique* and *Kinyamateka*. "In effect, shortly after Parmehutu and Aprosoma were started, we knew that the origin of these parties was in the clergy." While rejecting the theory that Catholic missionaries helped kill Mwami Rudahigwa, Bigirumwami accused the White Fathers of acquiescing to social vengeance in the name of social justice, lamenting that the laudable goal of democracy had degenerated into anarchy and violence. He also raised uncomfortable historical parallels, arguing that missionaries had sided with the Hutu so as not to repeat the nineteenth-century European church's loss of the working classes.

While Bigirumwami lamented missionary collaboration with Hutu politics, Perraudin emphasized the necessity of church-state cooperation to promote the common good. After the *coup d'état* of Gitarama, he promised President Mbonyumutwa in February 1961 that "the true Christians will always be the best citizens."[211] As independence approached in 1962, Perraudin instructed Kabgayi Catholics that "the only reasonable and Christian attitude in the face of the Government is loyalty and collaboration."[212] The collaboration of church and state also emerged as a predominant theme in the bishops' pastoral letter on independence and Perraudin's inauguration sermon in June and July 1962. Echoing Romans 13:1–7, the bishops' statement reiterated the citizenry's obligation to obey state authorities. "All power emanates from God: family power, political power, social power, spiritual power...the authorities of the Republic, from the most elevated to the most humble, must be considered always as the providential instruments of the supreme Authority of God."[213] In his inauguration sermon, Perraudin expressed his "great hope for a sincere and generous collaboration, respectful of the sovereign rights of each of the two societies." Here he challenged the new government to resist the temptation to hide behind a false screen of neutrality in its attitudes toward the Catholic Church.[214]

In celebrating the prospects for church-state collaboration in postcolonial Rwanda, Perraudin found common cause with his fellow White Fathers as well as Hutu politicians. Advocating for continued state support for Catholic schools, Kabgayi parish's pastor Jean Permentier wrote to the Belgian Ministry of African Affairs of the "long tradition of sincere collaboration between State and Church."[215] For his part, Van Hoof continued to see the new Rwandan political leaders as "excellent Christians" and "good fathers of Christian families," calling on reluctant clergy to "convert sincerely to the new regime."[216] Such sentiments were repeated by Rwanda's new political leaders. Gregoire Kayibanda promised to follow the dictates of John XXIII's encyclical *Mater et Magistra*; Rwanda's burgomasters knelt before Jean-Baptiste Gahamanyi at his episcopal consecration in January 1962.[217]

Bigirumwami, on the other hand, worried about the enthusiasm with which church leaders were embracing Rwanda's new state. While he acknowledged that missionaries thought they were acting in the church's interests, Bigirumwami warned his confreres against becoming too close to the emerging Rwandan government. "I believe that the missions should no longer follow the trail of the Government; this could cost them dearly. Priests should remain on guard against involving themselves in political parties."[218] In public, though, Bigirumwami's posture did not consist of Oscar Romero-like condemnations of the regime. More like Thomas More, he fell silent, refusing to either endorse or condemn the new government.[219] While Perraudin gave the official independence-day sermon, Bigirumwami sat on a side *dais* and made no public comments. Bigirumwami did not issue a circular letter between August 1960 and July 1962, and even his limited 1962 correspondence with the White Fathers avoided political issues.[220]

As with Thomas More in sixteenth-century England, Bigirumwami's silence was interpreted as malfeasance by his nation's ruling authorities. This reflected the growing sense among Hutu politicians that the Catholic Church's Tutsi-dominated clergy included a large number of UNAR sympathizers. Several Tutsi clergy had been involved in the production of *Rwanda Nziza*, UNAR's monthly magazine, and the government viewed Nyundo's Young Christian Worker (*Jeunesse Ouvrier Chrétien* or JOC) movement as both a UNAR front and a rival to Parmehutu's own youth wing. In October 1962, the Rwandan government took their case to the highest echelons of the Vatican. Armand Vandeplas, the Belgian magistrate who served as Rwanda's state prosecutor in Kayibanda's first government, presented the Kayibanda government's charges to Cardinal Sigismondi, the former apostolic nuncio in Central Africa and secretary for Propaganda Fide. In a private audience with this Vatican official, Vandeplas accused the Diocese of Nyundo of playing a "very important role in this [external UNAR] terrorist activity" and issued a not-so-subtle threat of violence against Bigirumwami and his associates. "The government fears that it cannot keep the situation in hand, if the Diocese of Nyundo continues to systematically oppose legal power." Sigismondi reacted with indignation, threatening to break the Vatican's diplomatic relations with Rwanda's government if it harmed a Catholic bishop. The Holy See's robust support for Bigirumwami appeared to make a difference, as Bigirumwami remained unmolested during his final decade as Bishop of Nyundo.[221]

Catholic parishes also became centers of political and ethnic conflict in 1961 and 1962.[222] In late April 1961 Hutu and Tutsi fought each other at a Nyundo school preparing future Catholic school teachers. Several weeks later UNAR commandos attacked the White Father editor of the Diocese of Kabgayi press as he left his office. In July Hutu militia stormed the mission of Mururu in southwestern Rwanda, binding the hands of the mission's two Tutsi priests and locking them in a room. In August Perraudin had to reassign a Tutsi priest to Nyakibanda in the face of mounting threats from the Hutu population around his parish. In September a Hutu mob lynched four Tutsi who had taken refuge in a religious school run by the Benebikira sisters. In December UNAR commandos raided the residence of Joseph Sibomana, the newly appointed Hutu bishop of Ruhengeri, and murdered the lay director of the local mission school. During the Byumba massacre in March 1962, Hutu militia entered the house of the Tutsi president of the Legion of Mary. He in turn pulled out a Bible, read the story of Judas's betrayal of Jesus, and ordered his sons to line up since they were "certainly in a state of grace." The militia then killed the father and his sons.

The violence reached the point that Perraudin and Bigirumwami stepped into the breach, issuing their first joint circular since November 1959.[223] Their August 1961 "anguished appeal" came closest to a whole-scale denunciation of the political process itself. Recognizing that "many of the disorders stem from the divergences of the political parties," the bishops condemned any partisans who would force Rwandans to vote for a certain candidate or party. What stands out in this letter is the force of the bishops' language: "death and fire" reign in Rwanda; political

violence is "evil and criminal and plunges the country into misery and disaster";
the destruction of property, pillaging of goods, and occupation of land can never
be justified. The bishops also adopted a nonpartisan approach. Rather than couch
their recommendations in anti-communist or anti-ethnicist language that would
signal UNAR or Parmehutu as the primary culprit, Perraudin and Bigirumwami
wrote that "the political parties oppose each other by violence in lieu of working together to construct the Country." Even the Belgians came under critique.
Rwanda's bishops exhorted the colonial administration to guard the "public
order without compromise or partisanship" and to robustly prosecute arsonists.
Following this statement, Bigirumwami commissioned Dominic Nothomb to
offer a theological and canonical analysis of homicide, theft, restitution and reconciliation in the pages of *Civitas Mariae*.[224] Perraudin also continued this critique in
the subsequent issue of *Trait d'Union*, condemning as "not Christian" acts of steal-
ing, burning, killing, discrediting the Church, denying people the sacraments,
and "exciting hate and vengeance between groups, parties or races." Perraudin
also reminded his readers that they did not have the right to hurt others even if
they belonged to a "bad party."[225] For once in Perraudin's writings, the reality of
ethnic violence overshadowed the ideological specter of communism. At the same
time, Perraudin continued to have misgivings about the Tutsi refugee community.
He had even tried to force these refugees out of Kabgayi mission in June 1961 due
to his worries about potential refugee alliances with nationalist clergy.[226]

The March-April 1962 massacre at Byumba discussed earlier led the Catholic
bishops to issue both a radio address and a pastoral letter. Since the violence happened in the newly established Diocese of Ruhengeri, the new diocesan bishop,
Mgr. Joseph Sibomana, gave the radio address. Reflecting Rwanda's long intertwining of Christianity and the civilizing mission, Sibomana's condemnation of
the "terrible and inhumane reactions" emphasized the incompatibility of popular
violence with modern civilization. "In a civilized country, the simple citizens cannot arrogate to themselves the right to make justice and to avenge themselves as
they will . . . What civilized people can pardon the massacring of men, women and
children without judgment?"[227] The bishops' subsequent episcopal letter traced
the violence to the destabilizing raids of the "criminal bands of terrorists" while
also "condemning with the same severity the bloody reactions of those who kill
their fellow man without being in a state of legitimate defense."[228] To their credit,
the bishops also condemned any recourse to collective ethnic retribution. "Bloodily
massacring the people of a race or a social group, because some among them are
responsible for terrorist assassinations, is not permitted . . . It is never permitted to
kill innocents." As will be discussed in the conclusion, notably missing in these
discourses was any sustained appeal to Christian nonviolence. If anything, the
bishops' tolerance of violence in the name of state security or self-defense left room
for perpetrators to justify their actions under the broad rubric of civil defense. The

bishops' analysis also acknowledged the missionary right to self-defense, a prospect that seemed more imminent in light of the January 1962 massacre of White Father missionaries in the Katanga province of Congo.[229]

If these public statements retain an admirable analytical balance, behind the scenes missionaries still traced all of Rwanda's violence to UNAR. Perraudin blamed the Byumba tragedy on political reactionaries "who could not accept the new order" and wished to restore the former regime.[230] Pierre Boutry, the former rector of Nyakibanda, claimed that the Byumba violence was "terrible, but the former leaders do not want to admit the new state of affairs."[231] Van Hoof posited that he had anticipated the Byumba massacre in light of the ongoing raids by the "irregular and despicable Unarists," hoping that these "extremists would understand this terrible lesson"—namely that their raids were precipitating massacres of the local Tutsi population. In a worrying rhetorical turn, Van Hoof conflated ethnic and political language, describing the UNAR raid on Sibomana's residence as the work of a "band of Tutsi scum" and noting that the Byumba victims included many "guilty" Tutsi. "The guilty by complicity or calculated silence were many, but others, God only knows the number, were certainly innocent."[232] Missionaries also failed to apportion moral responsibility to the Hutu killers themselves, again attributing the violence to "irresistible" popular passions. Thus while recounting the summer 1961 electoral violence in Kigali and its environs, Van Hoof described the Hutu reactions in terms of "anger" and "liberation from social inhibitions."[233] Perraudin used similar language in retrospectively describing the April 1961 violence at Byumba, arguing that UNAR assassinations of two local burgomasters "unleashed the anger of the population."[234]

The 1961–1962 refugee flows also sparked further tensions between Kabgayi and Nyundo dioceses. In response to the ongoing refugee crisis, Bigirumwami ordered Louis Gasore, Nyundo's vicar general, to undertake a European fundraising tour on behalf of displaced Tutsi in Congo, Uganda, and Tanzania. In correspondence sent to the Dutch and Swiss press, Gasore claimed that upwards of 500,000 Rwandans fled the country between November 1959 and April 1962, including over 100,000 refugees under the age of two. White Fathers like Alphonse Van Hoof had long suspected Gasore and his fellow Nyundo clergy of funneling money to UNAR,[235] and the publicity surrounding Gasore's trip pushed Perraudin to issue an internal protest letter in May 1962.[236] While reiterating his commitment to helping Rwanda's refugees, Perraudin contested Gasore's social analysis and his statistics. First, Perraudin claimed that social injustice in precolonial and colonial Rwanda fell along an explicitly Hutu-Tutsi axis. Second, he questioned how 500,000 Rwandans could have fled the country if the total 1959 Tutsi population numbered only 350,000. Finally, Perraudin repeated his fears that refugee donations were benefiting terrorists, implying a link between Nyundo's vicar general and UNAR exiles. The private war of words continued through the rest of

1962. In October, Gasore accused Kabgayi officials of "defamation" in a terse letter to Pierre Boutry.[237]

Overall, the 1961–1962 period saw the institution of several important Catholic political narratives that would continue into the postcolonial period. First, missionary leaders publicly lamented ethnic violence. In private, however, they placed the lion's share of blame on UNAR insurgents rather than the Hutu militias who were actually conducting the massacres. Second, the Parmehutu government increasingly saw the local Catholic Church as a Tutsi-dominated institution that needed to be ethnically cleansed. Not surprisingly, Catholic parishes themselves became sites of ethnic and political violence. Third, after criticizing state authorities in late 1959 and early 1960, Bigirumwami ceased his public critiques as Rwanda neared independence under Hutu nationalist leadership. His silence still contrasted with Perraudin's and the White Fathers' vociferous support for the new political regime. Finally, Perraudin and his allies increasingly spoke of the state as a close partner in the construction of Christian civilization, failing to consider how the state itself could become the enemy of the common good.

The Death of a Bishop and a Seminary in Turmoil

As Rwanda moved toward independence in 1961 and 1962, the Catholic hierarchy struggled to manage its own transition from mission territory to local church. This included internal struggles over new episcopal appointments, a process complicated by the suspicious May 1961 death of Mgr. Bernard Manyurane, the first bishop of Ruhengeri and the most widely respected Hutu churchman of his generation. In the meantime, ethnic tensions and seminarian withdrawals continued at Nyakibanda major seminary, precipitating unprecedented changes in the seminary's leadership.

As already discussed, in May 1960 the Holy See jettisoned the original 1957 arrangement to create a diocese of Kigali, drafting alternative plans to establish new dioceses in northern Rwanda (Ruhengeri) and southern Rwanda (Butare/ Astrida). Despite pleadings from Perraudin, Volker and Van Hoof, the Vatican did not follow up on these plans during the rest of 1960. Finally, at the end of January 1961, the Holy See named Bernard Manyurane as the first bishop of Ruhengeri.[238] The appointment made sense on many levels. The recipient of a doctorate in canon law from the College of St. Peter in Rome, Manyurane possessed an impressive academic record. He also possessed over a decade of pastoral experience as the superior of Nemba and Rulindo missions stations.[239] His Hutu family hailed from Rwaza in northern Rwanda, giving him immediate credibility in a region that had purged over 90 percent of the local Tutsi population. While far more sympathetic to the emerging Parmehutu government than Bigirumwami, Manyurane had cultivated a public reputation of spiritual depth and political moderation. He had also developed a close friendship with Perraudin and positive relations with the White Fathers.[240] Ruhengeri would give him a safe see in which to develop his leadership skills, preparing him to step into the anticipated future metropolitan see of Kigali.

Before Manyurane could even take up his new post at Ruhengeri, he fell gravely ill.[241] After resting in Nyakibanda for nearly a week, Manyurane moved to Kabgayi on February 11. Here he was diagnosed with arterial hypertension and possible kidney failure. Manyurane convalesced in Kabgayi through the end of February. On March 3, Perraudin arranged for Manyurane to fly to Belgium for more specialized care. His condition initially improved in mid-March before regressing in April. Even then, Manyurane expressed hopes that he could return to Rwanda for his scheduled May 21 consecration to the episcopate, and he moved to Rome in late April to prepare for his return journey to Rwanda. His health declined rapidly in early May, and Manyurane died in Rome on May 8, 1961 in the company of a retinue of White Fathers and African seminarians, "offering his life for the peace of Rwanda." One week later, he was buried in Ruhengeri in the presence of Perraudin, Bigirumwami, and President Mbonyumutwa.

The cause of Manyurane's death was never officially announced. It seems likely that he was poisoned. While he had suffered from periodic insomnia, angina, and fatigue during his years as a canon law student in Rome, nothing in Manyurane's health profile suggested a natural cause for the precipitous decline he experienced between February and May 1961. In addition, toxicology reports showed the presence of antinomies associated with arsenic poisoning. The list of potential assassins would be even more speculative. However, the expectation that this Hutu churchman would become the future leader of the Rwandan church suggests a plot among UNAR sympathizers either inside or outside the church. A few contemporary Rwandan historians have implicated Perraudin and his White Father allies, although this seems highly unlikely in light of the White Fathers' vociferous support for Manyurane between 1958 and 1961.[242]

A "dear friend" whose death represented a great personal loss to Perraudin, Manyurane was the linchpin in Perraudin's plan for the postcolonial indigenization of the Catholic Church.[243] Given Perraudin's commitment to promoting Hutu clergy and the dearth of qualified Hutu candidates for the episcopate, Manyurane's death left no obvious successors for the see of Ruhengeri. Rwanda's political instability and the suspicious manner of Manyurane's death also made the Vatican even more cautious about naming a new bishop. Despite Perraudin's increasingly strident pleas for a "more representative episcopal body,"[244] the Holy See did not announce Manyurane's successor until October 1961. And rather than follow Perraudin's suggestion of appointing two Hutu bishops, Rome named the Hutu priest Joseph Sibomana to replace Manyurane and the Tutsi priest Jean-Baptiste Gahamanyi as the first bishop of Astrida.

At first glance, Sibomana and Gahamanyi came from different worlds.[245] A member of the elite Abanyiginya clan, Gahamanyi joined the church as a twelve-year-old during the height of the Tutsi *tornade* in the early 1930s. Sibomana, in contrast, hailed from Save mission in southern Rwanda, representing a minority Hutu clergy that traced its roots to the earliest days of Rwandan Catholicism. In other ways, though, the two churchmen had similar profiles. Both studied at Kabgayi minor seminary and Nyakibanda major seminary and later served as professors at the minor seminary. Both were also familiar with Rwandan church-state relations from their time serving at Nyanza mission. Perhaps most importantly for the White Fathers, both were seen as allies of Perraudin rather than Bigirumwami. Gahamanyi had famously defended Perraudin before the U.N. Commission in April 1960; Sibomana was working in Perraudin's shadow at Kabgayi minor seminary when he received the call to the episcopate. On hearing news of their episcopal appointments, Gahamanyi and Sibomana expressed their commitment to working cordially with the White Fathers as "their true brothers in Christ."[246] Both quickly acted on these words by enlisting White Father missionaries to serve in prominent positions in their chanceries.[247]

The need for European-Rwandan cooperation was evident in light of the ongoing crisis at Nyakibanda seminary. Following the seminary council debates of November 1960 in which Bigirumwami requested a leadership change at Nyakibanda, Perraudin and Baers visited Rome and Brussels in late 1960 to explore possible solutions to the stalemate. They convinced Leo Volker, the White Fathers' superior general, to return with them to Rwanda in January 1961 to help determine a final resolution. In the meantime Bigirumwami remained in Rwanda, pleased with the Sulpician priest leading the seminary in Baers's absence yet still suspicious of White Father intentions.

Gathering at Nyakibanda a day after the *coup d'état* at Gitarama, Volker, Bigirumwami, Manyurane, Van Hoof and Perraudin attempted to reach a compromise over two days of intense meetings on January 29–30, 1961. As the superior general of the White Fathers, Volker had the most influential voice in the gathering. In some ways his analysis echoed previous critiques of Nyakibanda in the 1950s: the seminarians lacked a "supernatural spirit," they resisted authority, and their worldviews were marked by "rationalism." But while Volker attributed much of the blame here to external political causes, he also cited the presence of troublemakers inside the seminary as well as Bigirumwami's lack of confidence in the professorial staff. In contrast, Bigirumwami thought the crisis could be resolved by replacing Nyakibanda's White Father leadership with Sulpicians or indigenous Rwandan clergy. In particular, Bigirumwami lobbied for Baers's dismissal, arguing that Baers had lost the confidence of a majority of the seminarians. The other prelates pushed back, positing that further leadership changes would only further destabilize the seminary.[248]

Although they differed on the key question of seminary leadership, Perraudin, Volker, Baers, Manyurane and Bigirumwami agreed to a range of other actions designed to improve Nyakibanda's atmosphere. First, major seminarians would all undertake a mandatory 30-day retreat between their philosophy and theology studies; retention had proven most difficult during this transition. Second, the admission of minor seminary candidates to the major seminary would depend on the approval of the local bishop rather than the seminary faculty. Third, Nyakibanda's Seminary Council—composed of seminary professors – would secretly vote on whether to retain or dismiss any current seminarian. Fourth, seminarians departing Nyakibanda would be polled on their reasons for leaving. Finally, the bishops would separate philosophy and theology students into different seminaries beginning in September 1961. The White Fathers would run the philosophy school, and diocesan priests would take over Nyakibanda.[249]

Oddly missing in these plans were the Sulpicians. One of the leading French Catholic religious congregations for teaching, the Sulpicians were known for their work in diocesan seminaries. In 1959 the White Fathers had invited the Sulpicians to send several representatives to Rwanda to facilitate Nyakibanda's transition from missionary to indigenous leadership. After acclimatizing to their new country during a year in Rwanda's mission stations, the two Sulpicians, Fr. Cavolleau and Fr. Forissier, joined the Nyakibanda faculty for the 1960–1961 academic year. After only a semester, however, major tensions emerged between Nyakibanda's White Father professors and the two Sulpicians. While agreeing that Nyakibanda faced a major internal crisis, the Sulpician professors adopted a position of neutrality in the ongoing Hutu-Tutsi disputes. They also refused to compile lists of suspect Tutsi seminarians for the Nyakibanda Seminary Council. The White Father professors were furious, complaining to their superiors that the Sulpicians had come under "Tutsi influence" and were giving the seminarians the opportunity to play their European professors off each other. For their part, Tutsi seminarians described the Sulpicians as the "liberators of the Seminary," especially after Cavolleau took over as interim rector in Baers's absence in December 1960.[250]

Despite these tensions, the Sulpicians later claimed that Perraudin reiterated his support for them in November 1960, alleging that Perraudin "could not have been more explicit" in stating that "Cavolleau will take direction of the seminary next October." But in a rapid *volte-face* that left the Sulpicians "surprised, humiliated, and sadly deceived," Perraudin and Volker announced at the January 29 gathering that Cavolleau would not be named rector for the 1961-1962 academic year.[251] Volker also requested that the Sulpicians withdraw their members from Rwanda. Volker justified this decision by arguing that the White Fathers and the Sulpicians had "two different conceptions of the seminary," thereby giving seminarians

the opportunity to "serve St. Sulpice by opposing the White Fathers." A subsequent White Father report to Propaganda Fide accused the Sulpician professors
of "moral deficiency, psychological problems, character incompatibility, and doctrinal incompetence." However, it appears that the Holy See largely accepted the
Sulpician version of the story, attributing the White Fathers' diatribes to Rwanda's
escalating political tensions.[252]

The Sulpician episode is important in that it inserts a new outsider's voice
into the longstanding debates between White Fathers, Hutu seminarians, and
Tutsi clergy. The Sulpicians arrived in Rwanda before the November revolution
and departed after the *coup d'état* of Gitarama; they therefore witnessed the revolutionary changes that swept Rwandan society between 1959 and 1961. Yet while
recognizing the gravity of what they described as Rwanda's "tribal revolution," the
Sulpicians did not follow the White Fathers in ascribing sole blame to UNAR and
its ideological allies within the Tutsi nationalist clergy. Most of all, they refused
to reduce Nyakibanda's many problems to a binary ethnic logic. The dismissal
of the Sulpicians in turn reflected the increasingly zero-sum nature of the power
struggle between Tutsi indigenous clergy and the White Father missionaries. This
debate also shows that the White Fathers were only willing to cede ecclesial power
if they could assure the ideological sympathy of their successors.

As the Sulpicians departed Rwanda in February 1961, Bigirumwami backed
away from the consensus reached at the January 29 Nyakibanda gathering. His
intransigence may have stemmed from perceived marginalization. According to
the Sulpicians, Perraudin, Volker and Manyurane met early on January 29 to compile a list of suspect Tutsi seminarians hours before Bigirumwami arrived; they
then demanded that he acquiesce to this *fait accompli*.[253] Bigirumwami's opposition also arose from his continuing mistrust of Baers and suspicions that the
Nyakibanda rector was using the seminary council to eliminate all of the rector's
ideological opponents. The case of Eustache Rutabingwa emerged as a particular
flash point. Although Rutabingwa had never broken seminary rules, the seminary council voted in early February to remove him because of his "cast of mind"
and "deviating restlessness."[254] Bigirumwami sent official protests to Perraudin,
Volker, and Propaganda Fide, arguing that the bishops had agreed to dismiss politicized troublemakers, not "undesirable" seminarians who had never transgressed
the rules. For Bigirumwami, it was not the Tutsi seminarians but Baers and his
fellow White Fathers who threatened to undermine the very mission of the seminary. "You [Baers] and your [White Father] brothers make much evil in mistreating
the young men that God has confided to you...Why should your Hutu and Tutsi
seminarians regard themselves as dogs before a bone? Why have you not built
unity between Hutu and Tutsi? Why do you not have peace in your seminary?"[255]

Ignoring Bigirumwami's appeals for his support, Perraudin sided with Baers
and wrote two scathing replies to Propaganda Fide and Bigirumwami. Attributing

the "deplorable spirit" at the seminary to Bigirumwami's opposition to Baers, Perraudin called on the Holy See to intervene to "stop this situation from becoming catastrophic not only for the seminary, but also for the exterior." In his letter to Bigirumwami, Perraudin chastised the Bishop of Nyundo for "gravely troubling ecclesiastical discipline," accusing Bigirumwami of making seminary education impossible through his attitude of "open mistrust and near systematic opposition to the Seminary directors." Unfortunately, Perraudin never addressed Bigirumwami's *reasons* for mistrusting Baers and his colleagues. Instead, Perraudin appealed to authority (in this case his status as Rwanda's metropolitan archbishop) and demanded that Bigirumwami change his mind for the sake of public perception. Even as Perraudin professed continued respect for Bigirumwami's "holy person," Perraudin came close to pinning all of Nyakibanda's problems on him, promising to "save my own seminarians against the spirit that your attitude provokes in this house." Volker also stood by Baers and issued a stinging rebuke of Bigirumwami.[256]

Despite the White Fathers' accusations, the Holy See sided with Bigirumwami, reflecting the Vatican's general tilt toward Bigirumwami and Rwanda's indigenous clergy in the early 1960s.[257] Propaganda Fide announced in April that Nyundo's Matthieu Ndahoruburiye would be named the first indigenous rector of Nyakibanda major seminary. In turn, the White Fathers recalled Paul Baers to Belgium for a "well-merited rest." Nyakibanda's new rector arrived in triumph on May 1, accompanied by Bigirumwami and twelve Nyundo clergy. Maintaining public decorum, Perraudin welcomed Ndahoruburiye at the doors of the seminary.[258]

While Catholic leaders battled over the seminary's future direction, Nyakibanda itself continued to decline.[259] Far from defusing the situation, the dismissal of the Sulpicians was decried by the majority Tutsi seminarian population. In an effort to mitigate the damage, Volker gave a series of lectures to the seminarians in early February. However, his emphasis on fraternal unity annoyed the Hutu students, and his insistence on hierarchical obedience alienated most Tutsi seminarians. Led by a White Father noted for his sympathies for the Burundian monarchy, the subsequent mandatory retreat for theology students precipitated further departures in the ranks of the advanced seminarians.[260] The losses were especially high among the minority of Hutu seminarians. Eighteen of these students left the seminary between February and May 1961, including nearly all of the Hutu seminarians from the Diocese of Ruhengeri. Altogether, twenty-nine of Nyakibanda's one hundred and eight seminarians quit between October 1960 and May 1961. An additional twenty-two seminarians were placed on probation or sent to study in Europe, leaving only fifty-seven seminarians in residence. As in 1960, the Hutu departures worried the White Fathers the most. Van Hoof described them as "very sad" and "humanly speaking a catastrophe," noting that Hutu students were now pulling out *en masse* from the minor seminaries as well.[261] Just as Rwanda's national politics were turning in their favor, the White Fathers appeared to be losing their standing among the Hutu masses, particularly in a northern Rwanda region that already had the lowest percentage of baptized Catholics.[262]

The rest of 1961 played out as a sort of stalemate at Nyakibanda.[263] With Mbandiwimfura and Ndahoruburiye installed as spiritual director and rector, respectively, Bigirumwami temporarily had the upper hand in his ongoing confrontation with Perraudin over the direction of the seminary. In the meantime, Hutu seminarians continued to depart in large numbers after Ndahoruburiye's appointment as rector. At one point in 1961 only two Hutu students remained in the entire seminary. In Perraudin's words, the dearth of Hutu seminarians posed a "very grave problem for the [church's] future" in a majority Hutu country. Nor were Nyakibanda's problems limited to Hutu-Tutsi tensions. In July 1961 three White Father professors resigned from the Seminary Council and from their respective roles in spiritual direction and admissions decisions, reflecting ongoing tensions between the White Fathers and Nyakibanda's new Tutsi leadership.

These tensions eased a bit during late 1961 and early 1962.[264] Gahamanyi announced in February 1962 that Astrida would build a new minor seminary based at Save. In turn, minor seminarians from other dioceses would now be required to attend their local seminaries in Kabgayi, Ruhengeri, or Nyundo. While not yet reconciled to the idea of two major seminaries, Bigirumwami himself was attempting to rebuild fences with the White Fathers. In early 1962, he met regularly with Rwanda's other bishops, distanced himself from some of Nyundo's nationalist clergy, and in Van Hoof's words showed "great confidence in regard to members of the Society." Ndahoruburiye called together Nyakibanda's African and European clergy for a special February 1962 council in which both sides aired their grievances. In addition, Rwanda celebrated twelve new ordinations in 1962, far surpassing its annual totals since the late 1950s.

The continuing crisis of Hutu vocations, however, pushed Perraudin to attempt a backroom coup in June 1962. The September 1961 total of seventy-nine major seminarians had fallen to forty-six by June 1962. Only twenty-eight of these students actually resided at Nyakibanda, and over half came from Nyundo diocese. Writing to Propaganda Fide in June 1962, Perraudin and Gahamanyi described Nyakibanda as a "sort of scarecrow," noting that the vast majority of Hutu minor seminarians from northern Rwanda refused to enter the major seminary. The two bishops proposed replacing Rector Ndahoruburiye with Michel Ntamakero, the Hutu vicar general of Ruhengeri. They also requested the removal of Ndahoruburiye and Mbandiwimfura from the seminary faculty. Perraudin's and Gahamanyi's claims to have "unanimously arrived at this conclusion" were undermined by the fact that the document failed to include the signatures of either Bigirumwami or Sibomana. Bigirumwami learned of the plan belatedly and protested accordingly. This may explain in part why the Vatican rejected Perraudin's request.

Ultimately Rwanda's bishops resolved the stalemate by agreeing to the construction of separate diocesan seminaries. Nyakibanda remained the major seminary for the Archdiocese of Kabgayi. In the meantime, St. Joseph's Seminary in Nyundo opened its doors in October 1963. For their part, Fr. Deogratias Mbandiwimfura remained on the Nyakibanda faculty throughout 1962–1963. Fr. Matthieu Ndahoruburiye became rector of the new St. Joseph seminary in 1963, serving in this role until the 1973 uprisings discussed in chapter 6.[265] Whatever the marginalization of Tutsi in broader Rwandan society, Tutsi seminary professors retained prominent roles in the Catholic seminary system in postcolonial Rwanda. As late as 1991, a Hutu critic alleged that Tutsi professors at Nyakibanda "inculcate(d) toward their little Tutsi brothers a visceral hatred toward the Hutu" and hoped that the recent appointment of four Hutu professors would remedy the situation.[266]

Ecclesial politics in 1961–1962 reveal a Catholic Church increasingly divided by ethnic and political factors. The death of Manyurane eliminated the most promising Hutu churchman of his generation. If the subsequent appointments of Sibomana and Gahamanyi strengthened Perraudin's position in Rwanda, developments at Nyakibanda seminary seemed to favor Bigirumwami while revealing the extent to which the church's major seminary had become a political and ethnic battleground. As even apologists for the Catholic Church have noted, the "virus of ethnicism" dominated the Catholic seminary, reflecting "an evil conception of power in the church."[267] And if Bigirumwami and Perraudin remained cordial on a personal level, their vastly different visions of ethnic politics made it increasingly difficult for them to retain the fraternal unity that both cherished.

The Limitations of Catholic Politics between 1959 and 1962

This chapter on Catholic politics during Rwanda's revolutionary changes of 1959–1962 points to five major conclusions. First, Catholic leaders across the ideological spectrum supported the political objective of majority-rule democracy and opposed violence and clerical involvement in politics. If Perraudin and the White Fathers offered more robust rhetorical support, Bigirumwami never fundamentally questioned the goal of political democracy, whatever his hesitations about the means of the Belgian-engineered Hutu revolution. In turn, Perraudin and Bigirumwami repeatedly denounced political and ethnic violence between November 1959 and April 1962 and offered extensive pastoral support for refugee communities both inside and outside Rwanda. Both exhorted their clergy to abstain from politics.

Second, Perraudin and his allies focused on defending Catholic institutional interests, reestablishing the traditional Catholic vision of church-state cohabitation in service of the common good.[268] One can understand their reasons. Namely,

the White Fathers feared for the institutional future of the Catholic Church if
UNAR should take power or if Parmehutu should turn against them. In contrast
to its alleged communist ties, UNAR's anti-clericalism was real—at least to the
extent of rejecting missionary influence in Rwanda and pushing toward a more
national church. What surprised missionaries in 1961 and 1962, however, was the
extent to which their former Hutu acolytes could turn against them if Catholic
clergy did not embrace Rwanda's new political reality. To quote Van Hoof, "the
Hutu have said that they do not see how [the Church] can purify herself of these
elements opposed to the new regime and that perhaps they have a duty to follow
their path without any longer including the Church in Rwanda."[269] But if one can
understand the political reasons for the White Fathers' tacit pact with Parmehutu,
this alliance cost the church its independence and its prophetic voice, leaving it
impotent in the face of the growing violence committed by its state partner. In this
sense, Catholic leaders confused the "common good" with the church's institutional prerogatives and the interests of the Hutu majority. One sees this in subtle
ways, such as Van Hoof's statement in late 1960 that the Rwandan political situation was "not bad for us"—"us" clearly referencing the White Fathers and not
the thousands of Tutsi exiles forced out of their parishes.[270] Most of the White
Fathers supported Parmehutu because their leaders worshiped regularly at church
and offered rhetorical commitment to Catholic doctrine, Catholic schools, and
Catholic social teaching. Missionary affection for this apparent "Catholic party of
the people" contributed to their silence in the face of Parmehutu's ethnicist foundations and abetting of political violence.[271]

Third, this narrative points to the importance of social analysis. Bigirumwami,
Perraudin and others supported broad ideals of social justice and democratization. However, Bigirumwami and Perraudin fundamentally differed on their
understanding of the Hutu-Tutsi distinction and the extent to which social justice
and democracy could be mapped onto an ethnic axis.[272] There is a common narrative in Rwandan historiography that local actors were imprisoned by the Hamitic
thesis, locked into the binary categories of Hutu and Tutsi. In the words of Philip
Gourevitch, "nobody in Rwanda in the late 1950s had offered an alternative to a
tribal construction of politics. The colonial state and the colonial church had made
that almost inconceivable."[273] But as the preceding narrative has demonstrated,
the racial description of the Hutu-Tutsi distinction was a highly contested point
in the late 1950s and early 1960s, along with the "tribal construction of politics"
offered by Parmehutu. To be sure, Perraudin continued to present Hutu and Tutsi
as distinct racial categories, writing in 1962 that Rwanda's "traditional political
organization had its origin in the distinction of races."[274] But Perraudin was not
the only voice in the conversation. Outside observers like the Sulpicians described
Hutu and Tutsi as "two social classes" and described the Hutu as "proletariat if not
slaves."[275] Bigirumwami questioned the very demarcations between "those who

look like Hutu" and "those who look like Tutsi," arguing that "we cannot consider in the Church Hutu or Tutsi races or clans, but see only souls all equal before God."[276] If anything, the political arguments in revolutionary Rwanda grew out of this fundamental analytical division over the nature of the Hutu-Tutsi description.

This reminds us that social description can be far more divisive than ethical prescription. Shared rhetorical support for democracy, social justice, and national defense do not guarantee a united ecclesial voice in political ethics or church-state relations, particularly if church leaders disagree on how to apply these ideals in a contested social context. It is not so much that the White Fathers were out to destroy the local church, as Bigirumwami claimed in several heated exchanges during the Nyakibanda crisis of 1960–1961. Rather, they applied modern Catholic ideals—defending the poor, propagating social justice, supporting democratization—without properly analyzing the context in which they worked. Bigirumwami noted as much in his January 1961 manifesto to Leo Volker, writing that clerical disunity had resulted from the missionary tendency to uncritically apply the church's social encyclicals in a non-European socio-cultural context.

Fourth, missionary sympathies for Parmehutu's politics contributed to what I have termed an "analytical partisanship" on the part of Perraudin and his allies and a concomitant failure to name the link between ethnicism and political violence. Most White Fathers in turn demonized UNAR as anti-clerical communists and terrorists and attributed to them all responsibility for Rwanda's growing culture of political violence. The rhetorical linking of "Tutsi" and "UNAR" further politicized ethnicity and contributed to two dangerous tendencies in postcolonial Rwandan politics—the tendency to blame the victim's perceived intransigence for his or her suffering and the notion of collective ethnic retribution.[277]

Fifth, Perraudin's analytical shortcomings stemmed in part from his failure to explore how Catholic politics could transcend the alternatives offered by democratization and the modern nation-state. On one hand, Perraudin attempted to place the church above politics. One thinks here of his assertions of ecclesial neutrality before the March 1960 U.N. Visiting Commission. On the other hand, Perraudin also pushed the church toward what he perceived to be the "right" side of late colonial politics, favoring decolonization, social democracy and Hutu emancipation while opposing Tutsi nationalism, feudalism and communism. Notably missing in Perraudin's thought, though, was any consideration of how what Bigirumwami termed the "politics of Jesus" challenged the politics of UNAR and Parmehutu alike. In fairness to Perraudin, this was not his mistake alone. If the Catholic Church had struggled to retain an independent voice during Europe's interwar period of fascism and totalitarianism, the challenge became all the more daunting during the 1950s and 1960s when the politics of democracy, decolonization and social justice offered a new generation of missionaries a chance to break with their checkered past. Rare indeed was the postwar churchman who could see the potential shadows in Catholic social teaching's vociferous commitments to social justice and racial equality, shadows that Mahmood Mamdani has aptly described as "when victims become killers." Rare as well was the church leader who recognized the necessity of nonviolence to forestall abuses committed in the names of social justice and collective security. And in light of the violent schisms subsuming Catholic parishes and the Catholic seminary between 1959 and 1962, the Catholic Church would have offered a more transformative witness to Rwandan society by placing its own house in order.

To borrow Enrique Dussel's phrase, it is perhaps only those on the "underside of history" who can see both the shadows of secular politics and the necessity of a distinctively Christian alternative.[278] In this sense Aloys Bigirumwami emerges as an unlikely prophet. It is not so much that Bigirumwami was a model of moral perfection. For all of his deserved rehabilitation in contemporary Rwanda,[279] Bigirumwami's writings reflect a man who could be alternatively obsequious, paranoid, and judgmental. Rather, Bigirumwami's prophetic voice can be traced to his painful pilgrimage from a celebrated indigenous bishop to a suspected Tutsi churchman. While Perraudin *responded* to ethnic violence and subsequent refugee needs, Bigirumwami *experienced* these issues from the side of the victim. In November 1959 he was threatened at multiple roadblocks. In March 1960 Hutu militia attacked his church at Nyundo. And unlike the threats against Perraudin that subsided quickly after the November 1959 disturbances, Bigirumwami continued to face a hostile political climate until the end of his episcopate in the early 1970s. It is not surprising, then, that Bigirumwami saw Rwanda's revolutionary violence as not just a regrettable but inevitable political evil but as a deeper sign of the failure of Christian mission itself.

> The true fires are not those of the thousands and thousands of burned huts and homes, but the true fires are those in the souls killed and scandalized by those who should console and love them. The true expulsions of Tutsi are not those who are confined to the interior of Rwanda and outside but those who are expelled from the chancel and nave of our churches.[280]

The next chapter examines how these "true fires" and "true expulsions" developed in the postcolonial period, focusing on the anti-Tutsi massacres in Gikongoro in 1963–1964, the expulsions of Tutsi students from Catholic schools in 1973, and most infamously the 1994 genocide.

6

The Catholic Church and Postcolonial Ethnic Violence

THE ETHNIC AND political violence that marked the revolutionary period of 1959–1962 did not end with Rwanda's independence in July 1962. If the frequency of the violence declined, the intensity only increased as Tutsi civilians suffered collective retribution at the hands of state and local militias. In the first decade following independence, the largest paroxysms of anti-Tutsi violence occurred in 1963–1964 and 1973. The most infamous example of postcolonial ethnic violence is the 1994 genocide, an event that will be discussed briefly at the end of this chapter.

First, however, I consider the Catholic hierarchy's responses to both the UNAR invasions of December 1963 and the subsequent government massacres of Tutsi that unfolded over the next several weeks. Church leaders largely maintained the political paradigm outlined in chapter 5. Rwanda's bishops offered early and strong condemnations of the 1963–1964 violence and provided extensive support for the resulting Tutsi refugees. At the same time, their pastoral statements continued to reflect a mix of institutional defensiveness, analytical partisanship, and paternalism that failed to hold accountable the Hutu perpetrators of the massacres. Rather, church authorities blamed the violence on the provocations of external UNAR "terrorists" as well as Tutsi civilians' intransigence toward Rwanda's new government. In turn, Catholic leaders appeared far more concerned with defending the international reputations of the Catholic Church and the Rwandan state than with ensuring that Hutu never again massacred Tutsi on account of their ethnic identity and political views.[1]

The narrative then moves to the anti-Tutsi purges that erupted in Catholic schools and seminaries in early 1973. This violence erupted in several key contexts within both church and state—contexts of *de facto* Parmehutu dictatorship, muted church-state strains over political corruption and education, ongoing intraclerical tensions, a burgeoning Catholic population, and a growing crisis of priestly vocations. As they had in 1959, 1962, and 1964, the Catholic hierarchy responded quickly to the anti-Tutsi violence of February and March 1973. While the bishops offered an admirable (and controversial) bluntness on the explicitly ethnic nature of the violence, they did not critique the government of Gregoire Kayibanda or take concrete pastoral steps to hold Hutu Christians responsible for their crimes. Still enamored with the pro-clerical, democratic and social justice vision of Rwanda's First Republic, Mgr. Perraudin and his fellow bishops failed to assume critical distance from their former acolytes in the Parmehutu government. Such patterns continued after Kayibanda's forced resignation and the advent of Rwanda's second republic under the leadership of General Juvenal Habyarimana, the minister of defense and Hutu native of northern Rwanda. A new generation of Catholic leaders, especially Mgr. Vincent Nsengiyumva, the Hutu Archbishop of Kigali, developed close relations with Habyarimana's government during the 1970s and 1980s.

The final part of the chapter considers the developments of the early 1990s that brought Rwanda into global consciousness. These events include the government's 1990–1993 war with the Tutsi-dominated Rwanda Patriotic Front's (RPF), the return of multiparty politics, and escalating ethnic violence that culminated with the genocide of April–July 1994. In the midst of this political upheaval, elements of the Catholic hierarchy and media began to speak out against government corruption and the war. When the genocide actually began, however, the official Catholic response was more pussilanimous than prophetic, even as parishes themselves became the sites of some of the worst massacres. For his part, Mgr. Perraudin condemned the genocide from his home in Switzerland. At the same time, he continued to betray the pro-government and pro-Hutu analytical partisanship that had become the dominant ideology of much of Rwanda's Catholic hierarchy.[2]

The UNAR Invasions and Gikongoro Massacres of 1963–1964

Rwanda's declaration of independence on July 1, 1962 did not stop its opponents from challenging the legitimacy of the new Parmehutu-dominated state.[3] Even after the internal UNAR party made its peace with the government by accepting two cabinet positions in February 1962, UNAR exiles increased their raids into Rwandan territory. On one level, UNAR had never given up its ambitions to rule Rwanda. In turn, UNAR exiles saw the Parmehutu government as a Belgian-imposed ethnic dictatorship lacking democratic legitimacy. UNAR's determination to topple the government only grew in 1963, especially after Parmehutu's February decision to suspend the government's only two Tutsi cabinet officials. When Parmehutu claimed a 98 percent majority in August 1963 parliamentary elections, any remaining internal opposition crumbled.[4] In late 1963, UNAR exiles conceived plans for a major invasion and toppling of the Parmehutu government.

UNAR's first plan mobilized 1,500 exiles to cross Rwanda's southern border with Burundi on November 25, 1963. However, the Tutsi-dominated Burundian government stopped this militia before it could reach the border, and UNAR abandoned the plan. In subsequent weeks relations further soured between Rwanda and Burundi, and Burundi broke off economic and diplomatic relations with Rwanda in mid-December 1963. Despite Mwami Kigeli's opposition, UNAR hardliners developed an elaborate plan for a coordinated attack across the Tanzanian, Ugandan, Congolese, and Burundian borders.[5]

This complex plan spun into motion on Saturday, December 21. Several hundred UNAR exiles crossed the Burundian border with Rwanda. These exiles quickly overwhelmed a military outpost and arms depot at Gako in southern Rwanda. The exiles then moved through the internal refugee camps at Nyamata south of Kigali, recruiting hundreds of sympathetic Tutsi who had been displaced during the violence of 1959 to 1962. The expanded UNAR militia continued its northern march and reached the outskirts of Kigali. Ably assisted by several Belgian military officers, the Rwandan army finally halted the UNAR force 20 kilometers from Rwanda's capital. Most of the exiles were killed, arrested, or chased back across the border. Expected UNAR reinforcements from Congo, Uganda, and Tanzania never materialized. Unlike Burundi, governments in all three countries refused to allow the exile militias to cross their borders into Rwanda.

As they battled the exile militias on December 21–22, the Rwandan government rounded up suspected UNAR sympathizers across the country. Claiming to have discovered plans for a new presidential cabinet on the body of a dead Congolese soldier, the government arrested all of those named in this document. These arrests decimated the leadership of UNAR's and Rader's internal wings and included such Catholic stalwarts as UNAR's Jean-Baptiste Rutsindintwarane and Etienne Rwagasana and Rader's Prosper Bwanakweri and Lazare Ndazaro.[6] The government then transported these leaders to Ruhengeri in northern Rwanda on December 21. Over twenty were convicted of treason in a secret overnight trial, and they were executed on December 22 under the alleged orders of a Belgian military attaché. Most lower-level UNAR sympathizers were incarcerated but not executed; the Vatican's Apostolic Nuncio in Rwanda even intervened to stop the planned execution of several Bugesera Tutsi who had collaborated with the UNAR exiles. Significantly, the government also arrested four Tutsi priests for their alleged cooperation with the exiles.

Controversy remains over whether the Rwandan government planted the cabinet document on the dead Congolese soldier or whether the document reflected the actual plans of the UNAR exiles. It seems more likely that Parmehutu fabricated the document and used it as a pretext to eliminate any remaining political rivals. As Reyntjens notes, there was no love lost between UNAR exiles and internal UNAR leaders. The former tended to view the latter as traitors and collaborators, especially after the internal UNAR party disavowed violence and broke off relations with the exiles in 1962–1963. In addition, Rwanda's National Guard arrested hundreds of Tutsi leaders on the initial day of the invasion, reflecting the premeditated nature of government action. Finally, Rader leaders like Bwanakweri and Ndazaro had never developed close relations with their rivals in UNAR.[7]

The day after the government executed the political opposition, anti-Tutsi massacres broke out across Rwanda. On December 23, Hutu militia killed 98 Tutsi in Cyangugu in southwestern Rwanda and 100 in Kibungo in eastern Rwanda.[8] The worst violence occurred in the prefecture of Gikongoro in southern Rwanda. This region had a high concentration of internally displaced Tutsi and bordered the vast Nyungwe forest on the Rwanda-Burundi border, raising Hutu fears that the region might contain a "fifth column" of UNAR sympathizers. In the weeks preceding the invasion, local Tutsi had also raised tensions by boasting of the impending restoration of the monarchy. Finally, the area around Gikongoro had elected one of the nation's few UNAR-affiliated burgomasters in the August 1963 elections, reflecting the continuing salience of electoral politics beneath the veneer of ethnic violence.[9]

Beginning on Christmas Day, a veritable reign of terror consumed the Gikongoro region. Local self-defense units mobilized under the leadership of André Nkeramugaba, the local Parmehutu burgomaster in Gikongoro town. Hutu militia killed between 8,000 and 14,000 Tutsi over the course of five days. Thousands of other Tutsi took refuge at local Catholic missions in Kaduha and Cyanika.[10] Despite missionary appeals that began on Christmas Day, government authorities did not halt the massacres until December 29. More sporadic killings continued through the first two weeks of January 1964. In the words of René Lemarchand, "the impression from various eyewitness reports is one of unspeakable brutality. Popular participation in violence created a kind of collective catharsis through which years of pent-up hatred suddenly seemed to find an outlet."[11]

The Catholic hierarchy did not delay in addressing the violence. Archbishop Perraudin condemned the invasions and initial counter-reactions in his Christmas 1963 sermon.[12] Speaking from the pulpit at Kabgayi Cathedral, Perraudin "implored God for peace in our dear country" and proclaimed that the "sad events that have happened over the past week...afflict us profoundly [and] sadden much more the Good God who is a God of Peace and not of war." In a veiled critique of the government's executions of the political opposition, Perraudin also argued that "the measures of justice and legitimate defense which should be taken by those who retain power can only be approved by God if we make a generous effort of perfect fidelity to his holy laws." Perraudin also addressed the growing risk of popular retribution. "Certain people can be tempted, in the midst of the current difficulties, to want to harm others and even kill innocents. My dear Brothers, these thoughts are not Christian and can only draw divine condemnation on our Country." Writing in the heat of the moment, Perraudin issued one of his most forceful statements, committing the church to peace, opposing government repression, and condemning popular retribution.

After a week of brutal violence in Gikongoro, Rwanda's four Catholic bishops released a more formal and authoritative statement on January 1, 1964.[13] During the previous week, Perraudin and Sibomana had traveled to Nyundo to consult directly with Bigirumwami and ensure that the subsequent statement reflected the views of all four bishops.[14] Unlike Perraudin's impassioned Christmas sermon, however, the bishops' New Year's Day address seemed more one-sided. Emphasis fell more heavily on the "armed incursions of terrorists" and on the UNAR exiles. The exiles were described as "criminals, above all those knowing very well the incalculable evils resulting from their machinations." While admitting the intractable problem of the Tutsi refugee crisis, the bishops posited that "when the country has pronounced itself more than 80 percent for the regime, and that under the watchful eyes of the U.N., it is not through means of terrorist attacks of a minority that the situation will improve." Addressing the refugee crisis, the bishops exhorted the international community to resolve the problem but said nothing about the Rwandan government's own responsibility to reincorporate refugees. As it is, the refugee crisis grew exponentially after the 1963–1964 events; the external Tutsi refugee population nearly tripled from 120,000 in 1962 to 336,000 in 1964.[15]

Addressing Rwanda's government, the bishops critiqued what they termed the "repression" of December 21–22. Even in the face of an "extremely difficult situation" with "limited means of police," the government "who in the exercise of their powers are representatives of God should scrupulously respect His holy Law." Namely, the government had an obligation to ensure that arrested persons were not tortured or killed prior to legal judgment. The bishops admitted, however, that they did "not know the dossiers of those who were victims of the condemnations." Turning to the popular violence in Gikongoro, the bishops condemned the "rage [*colère*] of violent reactions which have not always spared the innocent," describing these as "undignified for Christians but also as simply disgraceful and degrading." They attributed much of the violence to popular passions, noting that even if such passions could "attenuate guilt," they made the violence "no less condemnable."[16]

Reviewing this statement, several important themes emerge. Continuing the pattern of "analytical partisanship" that we noted in the 1959–1962 period, Perraudin and his associates saw the UNAR terrorists as primarily responsible for Rwanda's violence. This overlooked the fact that the vast majority of killers were Hutu militia members executing innocent Tutsi civilians. As in 1962, massacres organized by local Parmehutu cadres were described in terms of "popular rage" and "violent reactions of the population." In other words, the bishops condemned the violence but did not hold anyone responsible for it; even the guilty masses were partially excused by their irrational passions. Likewise, condemning a "rage of reactions which have not always spared the innocent" tacitly implied the moral legitimacy of killing the guilty.[17] A more consistent nonviolent ethic would recognize that retribution furthers a cycle of self-destructive violence, no matter the alleged guilt of the accused party. (The Apostolic Nuncio to Rwanda seemed to recognize this when he convinced the government to commute the death sentences of the Bugesera Tutsi who had joined in the UNAR invasion.) In turn, the bishops' language reflected a deeper ambiguity in their attitudes toward state-sanctioned violence. In fairness, the bishops did critique government detentions of the political opposition, claiming that they "cannot remain silent any longer on their repression." But when one considers the Catholic reputations of leaders like Bwanakweri and Ndazaro, the bishops' subsequent caveats that "they do not know the dossiers of the victims" and "do not want to judge" undermined the force of their argument and seemed to give the benefit of the doubt to the government.

In turn, Perraudin's accompanying commentary in his diocesan newspaper Trait d'Union reinforced the Rwandan hierarchy's tendency to blame Tutsi victims for their own sufferings. Even as he reminded the Catholic faithful of their "sacred duty to respect the life, honor and goods of the neighbor and the duty of making reparations for injustices committed," Perraudin also implied that the root of the problem lay with recalcitrant Tutsi's failure to embrace the new Parmehutu government.

> If there is not in all the inhabitants of the country a loyalty and good respect in regard to the institutions put in place by the referendum of 1961—which does not stop the existence of a healthy and constructive opposition—there will never be serious peace. Without mixing ourselves in one or another partisan politics, we should be realistic about the choices facing us. We do not have the right, by an equivocal attitude, of exposing the country to much greater evils than those we have known.[18]

For a political realist, Perraudin made a valid point: people living under a dictatorship may need to mute their opposition to preserve social peace. But for a bishop who would later claim that "peace is not just the absence of war but a work of justice," such a statement looks in retrospect like a capitulation.[19] And even if the average peasant did not have the freedom to voice his or her views, a missionary Catholic bishop should surely serve as a voice for the voiceless. Perraudin's Christmas 1963 sermon came close, as did his Lent 1964 pastoral in which he wrote that "some however, profiting from the trouble caused by perfidious terrorist attacks, are sadly allowing themselves to commit abominable crimes."[20] Yet one never really senses that Perraudin perceives Rwanda's ongoing ethnic violence as a pastoral crisis requiring the church to reassess the nature of its mission. If anything, subsequent statements only reinforced his tendency to blame UNAR for all of Rwanda's ills and to focus more on alleged Tutsi complicity with UNAR than on Hutu complicity with ethnic massacres. As Perraudin wrote in a March 1964 issue of *Trait d'Union*, "all collaboration with terrorists in the interior or the exterior of the country is a gravely guilty disorder...It is, in effect, the terrorist actions which are at the origin of the miseries that we deplore."[21] So rather than cause the church to pause and reconsider its mission, Gikongoro appeared as a regrettable interruption of the church's inexorable evangelical march. As Perraudin commented in a February 1964 letter to a Spanish missionary organization, Rwanda had been at peace for four weeks, and "missionary work has resumed as before."[22] In response to such language, one can understand the frustrations of White Fathers like Henri Bazot, the superior at Cyangugu who witnessed so much violence in the environs of his parish. "Where is the cry of indignation, of horror on the part of our pastors?"[23]

Yet even as they tried to move on from Gikongoro, Perraudin and his fellow missionaries found themselves facing an increasingly hostile media. While the local Catholic paper *Kinyamateka* took a strong pro-government line in December 1963 and January 1964,[24] a series of more critical articles appeared in February 1964 in the European press. On February 4, *Le Monde* wrote of the ongoing massacres of "tens of thousands of Tutsi" and alleged a *"véritable génocide"* at Gikongoro. The French newspaper also claimed that while certain priests had "taken with courage the party of the victims, the high authorities seem to desire above all to not deny the reputation of a government attached to church institutions."[25] Soon the Catholic press joined in. The February 6 issue of *Témoignage Chrétien* lamented that a majority of the killers were Christians, and the February 15 edition of *Informations Catholiques Internationales* cited 15,000 deaths and 135,000 exiles produced by a "Christmas Day plan of repression" hatched by the Rwandan government.[26] One Rwandan exile attributed the violence to the "triumph of a Perraudinesque Catholicism"—namely Perraudin's efforts to ally the church with the Hutu emancipation movements.[27] Most seriously, Vatican Radio's February 10 broadcast described the Gikongoro massacres as "the most terrible, systematic genocide since the genocide of the Jews by Hitler."[28]

Perraudin and the White Fathers immediately launched a vociferous defense of themselves and Kayibanda's government. Perraudin sent a protest telegram to the Holy See disputing Vatican Radio's usage of the term "genocide," noting that the massacre was limited to Gikongoro and did not represent a systematic government plot to eliminate the Tutsi. "To speak of genocide without having proof in hand is a gravely reckless judgment...The comparison with Hitler is monstrous and gravely offensive for the head of a Catholic state."[29] In response, Pope Paul VI sent a conciliatory personal message to the Rwandan bishops on February 14 expressing how "profoundly saddened" he was by the violence and addressing a "fervent appeal for appeasement of spirits, respect of persons, and peaceful cohabitation in fraternal charity."[30] In the meantime, the White Fathers ensured that their own international periodical, *Vivante Afrique*, offered a more sympathetic analysis. Shortly after the violence, *Vivante Afrique* described Rwanda as an "oasis of peace, work and efforts for all the people," expressed relief at the limited nature of the 1963–64 massacres, and praised Kayibanda for his "politics of austerity" and success in "remain[ing] integrally faithful to the Christian ideal of his youth."[31] A less glowing account came from Dominic Nothomb. The long-time White Father missionary admitted that "manifest injustices were perpetrated by official persons exercising recognized authority" even as he resisted implicating the entire Kayibanda government in the Gikongoro violence.[32]

Other White Fathers were not as nuanced as Nothomb. In a March 1964 statement sent to the Vatican, anonymous White Fathers looked to restore the reputation of the local Catholic Church against "gross calumnies that have been launched against the Church in Rwanda."[33] The authors began by dismissing the Vatican Radio allegations as "most incredible" and "gravely injurious for Rwanda and the government of the country whose leaders have consistently given unequivocal signs of their profound and respectful adherence to the Church."[34] The authors attributed the Vatican Radio critiques to the machinations of Michel Kayihura and Fr. Jean Bosco Kayonga. As discussed before, Kayihura was a leader of the UNAR exiles and a brother of Bishop Jean-Baptiste Gahamanyi of Butare. Fr. Kayonga had served as a Josephite priest and then as a Benedictine monk before fleeing Rwanda in 1959. The two Tutsi exiles had traveled to Rome in early 1964 to present the Vatican with a detailed list of accusations against Perraudin and the White Fathers. Many of these accusations concerned missionaries' alleged efforts in the 1950s to "sow discord between Rwandans" in a craven political ploy to help ensure the Catholic Church's postcolonial future.[35] However, Kayihura and Kayonga also alleged that the Catholic hierarchy remained silent in January 1963 so as not to jeopardize their privileged relationship with the Kayibanda government.

Rather than combat this charge, the missionary authors of the "*Bréve rèponse*" argued that the political assassinations of December 1963 "do not concern the Church" and claimed that "we do not want to pass judgment on the motives for arresting certain Rwandan priests."[36] The missionaries also tried to undermine the credibility of Kayihura and Kayonga by challenging their statistics. Here they took issue with Kayihura's and Kayonga's estimates of 25,000 to 50,000 deaths in Gikongoro, claiming that this far surpassed the Red Cross and U.N. estimates of 5,000 to 8,000 dead. They accused their Tutsi critics of "desiring to overthrow the postrevolutionary order by blaming all troubles on the Hutu leaders."[37] They also reminded them of Perraudin's public denunciations of revolutionary violence between 1959 and 1962. Finally, the missionaries noted how the Archbishop of Kabgayi had recently founded *Secours Catholique Rwandaise*, a diocesan ministry for refugee relief, and enlisted the services of Catholic Relief Services and Caritas-Belgium in assisting displaced Tutsi.[38]

In summarizing the UNAR critique of Perraudin and the defense offered by his missionary allies, "*Brève réponse*" offers a synopsis of a polemic that began in 1959 and has continued to rage for over fifty years. Several consistent themes emerge. One, "polemic" is the right word to describe this argument. Whatever the sufferings of Rwanda's Tutsi in the early 1960s, UNAR activists consistently exaggerated their case, thereby undermining the credibility of their argument. Examples here included an alleged government massacre of 7,000 in Nyamata refugee camp, government killings of 25,000 Tutsi during January 1964, and the claim that the White Fathers since the 1950s had "oriented and supported the politics of extermination of an ethnic group."[39] For their part, the White Fathers continued to give Kayibanda's government the benefit of the doubt, blamed Tutsi exiles for nearly all of Rwanda's internal problems, and focused on defending their own international reputation. In the words of the "*Brève réponse*," rather than reflect a calculated political move by a local Parmehutu prefect, the 1963–1964 violence stemmed from "racial opposition [that grew] out of a violent explosion, a social struggle provoked by the prospect of returning to the former regime." For the missionaries, Rwanda's bloodshed reflected the inevitable violence of "all revolutions, civil wars, and movements of liberation and resistance."[40] If this was the case, however, one wonders why revolutionary violence did not engulf the entire country, especially since the authors elsewhere emphasize the weakness of government police. In addition, the authors seem more concerned with European press descriptions of the massacres than with the massacres themselves. "Speaking of a systematic genocide of thousands of men killed each day in Rwanda is a monstrous and undignified calumny. There had been, in reality, an explosion of rage of a peaceful people perfidiously attacked from the exterior. Since the second week of January, the country has been at peace."[41] Somewhat flippantly, the White Fathers concluded by arguing that the only "veritable genocide" would occur if the international community suspended development assistance for the Rwandan people.[42] Perraudin himself echoed this argument in a June 1964 press conference in Switzerland in which he claimed that his opponents' criticisms were designed to convince the Swiss to suspend critical economic aid.[43]

In summary, the 1963–1964 Gikongoro massacres and subsequent church reactions carried forward several of the patterns that we noted in chapter 5. First, the Catholic hierarchy offered early opposition to ethnic violence, condemning the massacres in their first days. Perraudin's Christmas 1963 sermon and the bishops' January 1 pastoral letter preceded Kayibanda's own halting denunciations on January 10. Second, while Perraudin later claimed to have remonstrated with Kayibanda behind the scenes, he and his fellow bishops failed to hold the Parmehutu government accountable in their official statements on the violence. Rather they described the violence as an uncontrollable and popular rage triggered by UNAR exiles.[44] Third, while church leaders should be credited with reaching out to refugees, there was little reflection on the lessons of Gikongoro for the church's mission. The focus lay rather on defending the hierarchy and disputing international press accounts that jeopardized Rwanda's pipeline of international funds and foreign missionaries.[45] Even Dominic Nothomb's more balanced analysis stopped short of any categorical reassessment of Christian mission in Rwanda.

> If in 1964 the fervent Christians go astray, we should suffer on this account and experience, as we do for our personal failings, an extreme sadness. All the more so since racial hatred is in absolute opposition to Christian charity. But we do not have the right to prejudge divine action by concluding that what happened represents the defeat of a great missionary hope.[46]

So if UNAR (and later RPF) accusations that the White Fathers plotted a Tutsi extermination seem far-fetched—especially when one recalls how White Fathers at Cyanika and Kaduha parishes protected thousands of Tutsi from the violence— Perraudin and his allies should have used the Gikongoro tragedy to distance themselves from a corrupt government and apply a more self-critical eye to their own pastoral work. After all, even outsiders could recognize that "Christian life in Rwanda has often been influenced by its attitude toward political power" and could express concerns over the extent to which devoutly religious believers were transfixed by "political passions."[47] As we will see, the events of 1973 demonstrated continuing Catholic struggles to heed these lessons.

The 1973 Tutsi Schools Expulsions

The final paroxysm of ethnic violence during Rwanda's First Republic occurred in early 1973. Unlike previous episodes of ethnic violence, church institutions served not as refuges but as epicenters of the conflict. Anti-Tutsi purges began in Catholic secondary schools and minor seminaries in Kabgayi, the Dominican-run National University of Rwanda in Butare, and the Catholic major and minor seminaries in Nyundo. As in the early 1960s, the Catholic hierarchy mitigated their rhetorical denunciations of popular violence through their uncritical loyalty to the Rwandan state. Ironically, the Rwandan military would break with the Kayibanda regime before the Catholic Church, toppling Rwanda's "father of the nation" in a bloodless coup on July 5, 1973.

Political disenchantment with Kayibanda began long before the 1973 events.[48] Although a full study of Rwanda's political history under the First Republic lies outside the scope of this project, a few important themes should be noted. First, the repulsion of the 1963 UNAR exile invasion and subsequent elimination of

Parmehutu's internal political rivals represented the apex of Parmehutu rule. The 1965 legislative elections were the first in Rwanda in which only one party—Parmehutu—proposed candidates for office.[49] Even former Aprosoma stalwarts like Aloys Munyangaju and Joseph Gitera acquired Parmehutu cards. At the same time, UNAR exiles' December 1963 incursion proved to be their Waterloo. While conducting sporadic raids until 1967, the party's organization withered. UNAR unofficially gave up its stated goal of toppling the Parmehutu regime even as it kept the door open to potential internal coups.[50]

Even as Parmehutu eliminated its external rivals, however, internal tensions simmered. If anything, these only worsened in the absence of the rallying points of national security and contested elections. When a 1968 government commission on corruption returned with a damning indictment of what it described as Kayibanda's "Gitarama clique," Kayibanda and his allies suppressed the report and sacked Parmehutu members suspected of conspiring against the president. Several of the luminaries of the 1959 revolution—including Dominique Mbonyumutwa, Bathazar Bicamumpaka, and Aloys Munyangaju—were cast out of government office and into political exile. Even the Catholic media, the great allies of the Hutu emancipation movement in the late 1950s, found themselves under attack. After publishing a thinly veiled political fable about government corruption, the Rwandan editor of *Kinyamateka*, Félicien Semusambi, was imprisoned, and the government subsequently deported the newspaper's general editor back to Italy. In an ironic turn, Kayibanda then temporarily banned production of the Catholic newspaper that he had used to facilitate Parmehutu's political rise in the late 1950s.[51]

Even as *Kinyamateka* rediscovered its anti-government edge in the late 1960s, broader relations between church and state remained amicable.[52] In a sign that the Gikongoro events had not overly strained these relations, Kayibanda and his entire cabinet attended the 25th jubilee of Perraudin's priestly ordination in July 1964.[53] And in a remarkable *volte-face* from the hierarchy's attitudes during the lay schools debates of 1954–1955, Perraudin agreed in 1966 to a new statute that transferred authority over primary schooling from the church to the state. While defenders justified this decision as a further step in the indigenization of Christianity in Rwanda, experienced observers questioned whether the church was sacrificing its independent voice in the name of political expediency. In the words of Perraudin's erstwhile ally Jan Adriaenssens, "I have the impression ... that we are in a 'conspiracy of silence' that suppresses personal reflection and personal judgment. I am certain, for example, that I could not write a true article today on the situation in the schools or on the future of the schools in Rwanda."[54]

It may be that Perraudin no longer saw the need to protect Catholic schools from state influence. After all, the 1962 constitution had adhered closely to church teaching in its near-prohibition of divorce, emphasis on the family as the cornerstone of society, banning of communist parties, and generous subsidies for Catholic schools.[55] As Perraudin wrote in a 1966 pastoral letter on Christian education, "the church trusts that state schools will educate children in a Christian manner conforming to the convictions of their parents" and hire "good Christians" to serve as teachers in public schools.[56] He even convinced state officials to include Catholic social teaching in the official primary school curriculum. In turn, Perraudin may have trusted the government's Hutu leaders as much or more than the Tutsi priests running the majority of Catholic schools. In a 1968 interview, he attributed Rwanda's social and political development to the fact that Rwanda's political leaders were "truly convinced Christians" whose only lingering vice was a tendency to "separate Christianity and politics."[57] Finally, the rapid growth of the Rwandan population and concomitant crisis of religious vocations made it nearly impossible for the church to maintain its traditional dominance of education.[58]

Beyond the schools debate, three other pastoral issues marked Rwandan Catholic life in the 1960s. Demographically, the Catholic population was exploding.[59] Even during the difficult years of 1961–1963, the Catholic population grew from 744,000 to over 809,000. More tellingly, catechumen numbers grew by nearly one-third during the same period after years of stagnant growth in the 1950s. The number of adult baptisms doubled between 1955 and 1963 from 16,000 per annum to over 33,000 per year. These numbers continued to grow throughout the 1960s. By 1971, over 56 percent of Kabgayi's population had become Catholic. The Rwandan church founded 36 new missions between 1961 and 1970, matching its total in the entire 1900–1945 period. The growth was especially notable in the Diocese of Ruhengeri, the heart of the Hutu uprising in November 1959. In the course of the 1960s, Ruhengeri rose from the least populous to the most populous Catholic diocese in Rwanda, counting 900,000 Catholics and catechumens in 1969. As in the Tutsi *tornade* of the 1930s, it appears that the Catholic Church's "opportunistic politics" facilitated a remarkable growth in its own numbers.[60] By 1970 one in eight African Catholics lived in Rwanda and Burundi, two of the continent's smallest countries. Not coincidentally, both hierarchies had embraced their nations' contrasting postcolonial politics; the Burundian Catholic hierarchy consistently supported the Tutsi-dominated military government of Michel Micombero in the late 1960s and early 1970s.[61]

At the same time, Rwanda's population of seminarians, priests and religious continued to atrophy. Despite efforts to establish separate major seminaries in each Rwandan diocese, the church struggled to foster new vocations. As discussed in chapter 5, the major seminary at Nyakibanda counted only 18 theology students and 27 philosophy students in 1962. After Bigirumwami opened St. Joseph's major seminary in Nyundo in November 1963, the discrepancy between Nyundo and Rwanda's other three dioceses became even more pronounced. Bigirumwami's diocese had 25 seminarians in 1963; Butare, Kabgayi and Ruhengeri counted 24 combined. And while Nyundo's priest population rose to 56 in 1970, Butare counted only 35 priests while Kabgayi and Ruhengeri each included only 20 indigenous clergy. Priest-faithful ratios were approaching 10,000-to-1 in parts of Rwanda. Nor were the numbers any better for male and female religious. During the course of the 1960s, the number of religious brothers declined from 170 to 149, and the number of religious sisters fell from 425 to 420. If there was one consistent theme in Perraudin's missionary appeals in the late 1960s, it was the urgent necessity of priests to meet the burgeoning needs of Rwanda's growing Catholic population.[62]

Even as the number of Rwandan priests continued to decline throughout the 1960s, the smaller clerical population struggled to achieve the oft-touted ideal of clerical unity. After the fiftieth anniversary jubilee of the indigenous priesthood in December 1967, local priests founded the *Union Fraternelle Clergé Rwandaise* (UFCR). For its supporters, the UFCR strengthened clerical unity while embodying the post-Vatican II spirit of building collegiality between bishops and priests. For its detractors, the organization represented a clique of Tutsi priests who undermined the authority of Archbishop Perraudin and divided black and white priests. Perraudin banned his diocesan clergy from participating in UFCR gatherings, launching a rival clerical network in February 1968. In contrast, Bigirumwami, Sibomana, and Mgr. Wenceslas Kalibushi, the new bishop of the Diocese of Kibungo, not only gave their blessing to UFCR but joined the organization themselves. Bishop Sibomana noted the bishops' "quasi-unanimous approval" for UFCR; Bigirumwami described UFCR as a sign of the "coming of age" of the Rwandan clergy. Some Kabgayi clergy—including Perraudin's longtime vicar general Innocent Gasabwoya—were so frustrated at their exclusion from UFCR that they published a protest letter in *Cum Paraclito*, a journal published out of Nyundo diocese. UFCR continued to meet periodically over the next three years until Perraudin convinced his colleagues to disband the organization in November 1970.[63]

The tensions over the UFCR also reflected Hutu frustrations that, despite years of enforced Hutu quotas, Tutsi elites continued to dominate the Catholic clergy, business circles and higher education.[64] Clerical life remained a sanctuary for Tutsi locked out of Parmehutu's postcolonial politics, just as the church had served as a path of advancement for Hutu excluded from the colonial Belgian administration. In the words of Ian Linden, "[the church] had come to epitomize for young Rwandans the wily retention of power by their former [Tutsi] overlords, now disguised in *soutanes*."[65] Perhaps due in part to these Hutu-Tutsi tensions, the Vatican bucked the continental trend toward the Africanization of the episcopate. When the Archdiocese of Kigali was finally created in 1968 after over a decade of discussion, Perraudin was named archbishop. At the same time, Perraudin retained his titular see in Kabgayi. In the meantime, Sibomana was transferred to the new eastern diocese of Kibungu. He was replaced in Ruhengeri by Phocas Nikwigize, a Hutu churchman whose theories of "double genocide" would further taint the church in the 1990s.[66]

Before turning to the 1973 events, one other crucial background event must be mentioned—the Burundian genocide of 1972.[67] As noted earlier, Burundi's initial postcolonial politics offered an inverse mirror image of the Rwandan case. However, the nation's initial postcolonial stability did not last. Resentment grew in the late 1960s following the 1966 death of Burundi's Mwami Mwambutsa and the contemporaneous rise of Colonel Michel Micombero's Tutsi-dominated military dictatorship. In late April 1972, a group of low-ranking Hutu military officers and bureaucrats launched an attempted *coup d'état*. During the intial uprising Hutu militias killed several thousand Tutsi, but the attempted coup collapsed during the first week of May. After suppressing the coup, Micombero and his military allies unleashed one of the largest genocides since World War II, executing more than 200,000 Burundians—nearly all educated Hutu elites—between May and August 1972. Seventeen Hutu priests were killed during the violence, and two bishops were placed under house arrest. Tens of thousands of Hutu fled across Burundi's border with Rwanda, further adding to the Hutu resentment and Tutsi fear that marked Rwandan society at the beginning of 1973. It should be noted that the Burundian bishops largely exonerated the Micombero government for the massacres. In a formal statement, the Burundian bishops claimed that "it would be wrong to see the problem as a classical instance of internal politics, a conflict between Hutu and Tutsi. It is rather a diabolical plot to deceive the people in order to foster racial hatred... there are those who, under the pretext of protecting the little people, are grossly biased in favor of one tribe."[68] Two of Burundi's bishops—including Mgr. André Makarakiza, the former seminary professor at Nyakibanda—wholly misrepresented the causes of the violence, describing the massacres as "resulting from the attack of a foreign power."[69] These examples demonstrate that Rwandan bishops did not have a monopoly on slanted, pro-government political analysis.

In contrast to his more circumspect language after Gikongoro as well as the halting statements of the Burundian hierarchy, Perraudin did not hesitate to name the Burundian massacres as "genocide." After publicly critiquing the Burundian authorities for their "perversion" and "lies" in November 1972, Perraudin wrote an impassioned December 1972 letter to his donor base.[70] Here he utilized the uncompromising language missing in his commentaries on Rwanda in 1959, 1962, 1964, or even 1994. "This perversion of a government which should protect its citizens instead exterminates them." For Perraudin, the 1972 events in Burundi demonstrated the difference between revolutionary and genocidal violence. "A revolution is a revolution. There are deaths for sure and many injustices, but in

Burundi they have committed an extermination—genocide by the Government."
In addition to the unprecedented scale of the Burundian massacres, two other
dimensions may explain the force of Perraudin's language. First, Perraudin could
critique the state without facing its wrath. Second, Burundi's Tutsi-dominated military dictatorship was the antithesis of Perraudin's pro-Hutu democratic leanings.
After 1967 Perraudin never traveled to Burundi for regional bishops' meetings
due to the antipathy of both the Burundian government and Rwandan Tutsi exiles
living in Burundi.[71]

Even as Perraudin described the Burundian massacres as "genocide,"
anti-Tutsi purges were breaking out in Catholic schools in and around Perraudin's
see of Kabgayi. The forced removal of Tutsi students began in Catholic schools
in Byimana, Save and Nyamasheke in late 1972. The purges spread to Rwanda's
National University (UNR) in Butare in January and February 1973 and eventually to Nyundo's Catholic schools and seminaries in northwestern Rwanda. 190
students were forced out of UNR on the evening of February 15-16, 1973.[72] After
students divided along ethnic lines at Nyundo's St. Pius X minor seminary on
February 25, over twenty seminarians and Tutsi professors fled Nyundo's St.
Joseph's major seminary for the Congolese border. Meanwhile, the violence
spread to banks, commercial centers, and other Rwandan civil institutions seen
as havens of Tutsi influence. While the bloodshed never approached the level of
Gikongoro in 1963–1964, several hundred Tutsi died between February and April,
including two Josephite religious brothers dragged out of their home by a Hutu
mob. Northern Hutu also chased southern and central Hutu from their homes in
Kibuye and Gisenyi provinces, reflecting ongoing regional and political tensions
among Parmehutu's disparate factions. After maintaining a conspicuous silence
until late March, the Kayibanda government gradually restored order across the
country. The government appointed Gen. Alexis Kanyarengwe, the military's
second-ranking officer, to take over St. Joseph's seminary on March 26. On April
4, the government finally condemned the violence and the "judgment of people by
reason of their racial origin." Sporadic outbursts of violence continued, however,
such as a student attack on the parish of Nyamasheke on April 12 that left three
priests wounded.[73]

In May 1973, Kayibanda used the pretext of Rwanda's national crisis to convince
the National Assembly to end presidential term limits. In light of Parmehutu's
consolidation of power over the preceding decade, even Kayibanda's ideological supporters began to fear that Rwanda's republican dream was turning into
a dictatorial nightmare. After hearing word of a threat to his own life, Juvenal
Habyarimana—the head of national defense, former Kayibanda ally, and native
of Gisenyi in northwestern Rwanda—turned on the president and removed
him from office on the night of July 4–5, 1973. Rwanda's new leader then put
Rwanda under an officially nonpartisan military government, placed Kayibanda

under house arrest, and promised to work toward the reconciliation of Rwanda across ethnic and regional lines. Whatever his stirring rhetoric, Habyarimana continued some of Kayibanda's unsavory political practices. Thirty imprisoned Parmehutu leaders died under suspicious circumstances between 1973 and 1976, and Kayibanda himself died under house arrest in December 1976.[74]

How did the Catholic hierarchy react to the 1973 violence? According to one retrospective account, Perraudin stood between a Hutu mob and Tutsi students at Kabgayi minor seminary, shouting "I am in charge" until the Hutu dispersed.[75] Church leaders also did not hesitate to speak out on the situation. On February 23—more than a month before any official government commentary—the bishops issued a joint statement on the violence. In this statement, the bishops condemned the schools disturbances that "looked to eliminate the students of an ethnicity" and lamented that "the men of one race want to dominate those of another race, to humiliate them and make them disappear." Such crimes contradicted the "law of God," the 1948 U.N. Human Rights Declaration, and the 1962 Rwandan constitution, dividing neighbors and contravening Christ's evangelical command to love one's enemies. "Because of this not only does [Christ] ask that we not do evil to others, but he orders you to love your neighbor, even if he is an enemy." The bishops also instructed Rwandan laity to resist "temptations of hate and racial fights" so as not to jeopardize Rwanda's estimable international reputation. "Thanks to the wisdom and moderation of your governing authorities, the country has known ten years of peace during which it has developed and has acquired the esteem and friendship of other nations. Do not dishonor it in the face of the world."[76]

This statement reflected patterns noted in previous hierarchical commentaries on ethnic violence in Rwanda. First, church leaders were the first local authorities to condemn the violence, speaking weeks before their government counterparts. This raised the ire of some Hutu students studying in Belgium. In an April 1973 protest letter, these students accused Perraudin and the bishops of shifting their favor back to the Tutsi.[77] Second, the bishops condemned the explicitly ethnic nature of the violence. Their strong condemnations may have reflected the fact that the 1973 violence did not arise from an external security threat as in 1962 or 1964. At the same time, their analysis continued to betray a fundamentally divisive vision of Rwandan society. One appreciates the bishops' call for Christians to embody perhaps the hardest message of the Sermon on the Mount—namely to "love your enemies and pray for those who persecute you" (Matthew 5:44). At the same time, asking Rwandans to love their neighbor "even if he is an enemy" did little to promote a vision of pan-ethnic national harmony, particularly in the absence of any subsequent reflections on the shared aspects of Banyarwanda culture. And perhaps most tellingly, the bishops' praise for the Kayibanda government's "wisdom and moderation" reflected the bishops' continuing struggles to distance themselves from the state. Missing here was the type of categorical denunciation we saw in Perraudin's late 1972 statements on the Burundian genocide.

The bishops' subsequent March 23, 1973 pastoral letter further nuanced several of these emphases. For example, the bishops continued to condemn the exclusion of students on ethnic grounds, rejecting "scornful attitudes" and "violence" as "contrary to the Gospel." At the same time, they dedicated far more text to expressing their empathy for the social demands of the Hutu students. In this regard, the bishops claimed to share Hutu students' frustrations with Rwanda's problem of "socio-ethnic equilibrium." But if the "solution does not lie in disorder and violence," the "sudden explosion of demands is not only negative" in that it reflects the "profound aspirations of the young." Conveniently overlooking the Kayibanda regime's weeks of inaction, the bishops also praised "the Authorities of the County and the army for rapidly stopping this outrage." And although the bishops demanded accountability for perpetrators—calling for "penitence, reparation and Charity" and requesting that "those who have killed, burnt or pillaged should repent"—they did not offer concrete specifics here. If anything, the bishops rejected public actions such as suspending sacraments in a particular region. Such decisions might have signaled a broader commitment to addressing ethnic violence as a serious pastoral problem for the church.[78]

Not all observers shared the bishops' ambiguity. In a passionate March 4 letter to Perraudin, Fr. Francesco Cerri, an Italian missionary recently arrived in Rwanda, described the scene at his Mushishiro parish as a "spectacle of blood, fighting, pillaging, and fires above all."[79] Cerri claimed that while some Hutu "risked their lives for their brothers, 98 percent of the catechists and laity have done nothing to avoid what has happened." According to Cerri, many Christian leaders even participated in the violence. In this context, Cerri wondered whether typical Catholic sacramental practice could and should continue.

> Above all I have been concerned by the fact that Christians pillage and sack their brothers, only because they are Tutsi....How can I celebrate Mass in a community divided by hate? How can I give the sacraments to a community in which the majority has been complicit in these events, led by politicians with a diabolical plan to eliminate the Tutsi?[80]

Accusing Perraudin of a "fear of clearly speaking the truth," Cerri requested that the bishops publicly withhold the sacraments from all responsible parties, beginning with Kayibanda and the other politicians responsible for the massacres. He also called on the bishops to work harder on refugee reintegration, seeing this as the key to long-term peace in Rwanda. Perhaps anticipating that his appeal would fall on deaf ears, Cerri concluded by announcing his impending departure from Rwanda, claiming he could no longer exercise his priestly ministry in good conscience. In leaving, he hoped that Rwandan Christians would see that "we [missionaries] are not here for the Hutu only, we are here for all."[81] Like the Sulpicians at Nyakibanda in 1960–1961, an outsider like Cerri offered a far stronger critique of ethnicism than many of the veteran White Fathers around him.

Cerri's departure may have had short-term ramifications. Just weeks after the Italian missionary left Rwanda for what was officially termed a "holiday," Kabgayi's presbyteral council took up such previously taboo subjects as sacramental practice after periods of communal violence, the nature of the church's "prophetic role" toward civil institutions, and the relationship between Catholic schools and the government. At the same time, the council also included a provision concerning an improved "initiation" of new missionaries into Rwanda's political and social context.[82]

Judging from Perraudin's subsequent 1973 statements, it does not seem that the Catholic hierarchy actually altered its long-term pastoral or political vision in light of the schools expulsions. Even as Perraudin's Easter 1973 homily challenged Christians to embody their baptismal promises, it included no specific vision for ethnic reconciliation.[83] Rather Perraudin continued to present Rwanda's ethnic problem as an extra-ecclesial challenge best addressed by Rwanda's governing authorities. Not only did Perraudin ignore the extent of state complicity in Rwanda's 1973 violence, but he missed an opportunity to consider these events as a distinct challenge for the church itself. Individual Christians were called to repent, but Catholic institutions themselves were not critiqued. Likewise, later 1973 statements showed no hint of critical distance from the state. Perraudin never spoke publicly against the government takeover of St. Joseph's Seminary in Nyundo despite the fact that this action clearly transgressed canonical norms concerning seminary jurisdiction.[84] And far from critiquing the *coup d'état* which ushered in the Second Republic, Perraudin commended Habyarimana in late July as a "Christian and an apostle, a disciple of the Prince of Peace." In his Christmas 1973 sermon, Perraudin called on Christians to listen to the "appeals of religious and civil authorities" to reconcile across ethnic lines, and he apparently never spoke out on Gregoire Kayibanda's detention, torture or death in 1976.[85] It seems that even the ethno-political traumas of 1973 could not shake Perraudin's commitment to the partnership of church and state in service to the common good.[86]

In the years following the 1973 events, the Catholic Church continued to flourish on an institutional level. The percentage of the Rwandan population claiming the Catholic faith rose from 46 percent to 63 percent between 1973 and 1991. In 1987 the church signed a convention with the state reiterating the state's commitment to ensuring a Catholic orientation for primary and secondary education. In addition,

Rwanda became internationally famous in Catholic circles in the early 1980s after news emerged of alleged Marian apparitions to three young mystics in Kibeho.[87]

After 1973, major changes also occurred within Rwanda's Catholic leadership. In January 1974, Aloys Bigirumwami stepped down as Bishop of Nyundo. Since he had not yet reached the mandatory retirement age of seventy, some have attributed his early retirement to political pressure following the 1973 events.[88] After his retirement, Bigirumwami immersed himself in studying Rwanda's traditional culture and religions. He wrote frequently in the White Fathers' journal *Dialogue* as well as *Foi et Culture*, the Catholic theological journal which he started in the late 1960s. He also continued to serve in pastoral ministry in a parish near Nyundo until his death in 1986. His passing ushered Bigirumwami into the pantheon of national Rwandan heroes, saluted by fellow churchmen, President Juvenal Habyarimana, and ideological allies and opponents alike.[89]

Bigirumwami's successor as Bishop of Nyundo was Vincent Nsengiyumva, a Hutu native of northern Rwanda. Two years after his appointment to Nyundo, the Vatican named Nsengiyumva to replace Perraudin as Archbishop of Kigali. Only forty at the time of his appointment to the Kigali see, Nsengiyumva cultivated close relations with Habyarimana, Habyarimana's wife Agathe, and a coterie of Hutu political leaders from Gisenyi known as the *akazu* (or "little house"). Nsengiyumva even served on the central committee of Habyarimana's *Mouvement Révolutionnaire Nationale Développement* (MRND) until stepping down in 1990 on the eve of Pope John Paul II's visit to Rwanda.[90] Even after the pope's visit, Nsengiyumva retained a direct phone line to the president's office and served as a personal confessor to Habyarimana's wife Agathé. Other bishops shared Nsengiyumva's high esteem for Habyarimana. On his appointment as Bishop of Cyangugu in 1982, Mgr. Thadee Ntihinyurwa exclaimed, "Excellent President, I dedicate to you the diocese of Cyangugu. It is yours. Direct it yourself!"[91]

After handing over the Kigali see to Nsengiyumva in 1974, Perraudin continued to lead the Diocese of Kabgayi for another fifteen years before retiring in 1989 at the age of 75. In his final decade as bishop, Perraudin received two major national honors, including a Commander of the Revolution award in 1981.[92] Looking back over his thirty-three-year episcopate, Perraudin in 1989 expressed satisfaction at the depth of Christian evangelization in Rwanda. "Despite its many problems, Rwanda is, with Burundi, a country profoundly marked by the Gospel."[93] Even after his retirement, Perraudin remained an active member of Rwanda's episcopal commission, collaborating in the bishops' early 1990s pastoral statements on justice and peace. When Pope John Paul II visited Rwanda in 1990, he celebrated mass at Kabgayi Cathedral and saluted Perraudin as the "model missionary bishop." Perraudin left Rwanda in December 1993 for a medical visit to Switzerland, anticipating that he would return in 1994. He would never see his adopted country again.[94]

The Catholic Church and the 1994 Genocide

The events that prevented Perraudin's return were Rwanda's genocidal massacres of April-June 1994. A wealth of detailed literature exists on the political and religious dimensions of the genocide,[95] and this book has intentionally focused on the late colonial and early postcolonial periods rather than the 1990s. Having said that, no study of Rwandan history can overlook the genocide—and the controversial Catholic politics that surrounded it. As we will see, many of the patterns of Catholic discourse noted in the late colonial period emerged again in the run-up to the genocide.

As many scholars have described, the 1994 genocide grew out of a particular economic, political and military context. Praised as a development darling during the early years of the Second Republic, Rwanda began to decline economically during Africa's "lost decade" of the 1980s. This culminated with the collapse of the coffee market in 1989. Adding to the economic malaise, the Rwanda Patriotic Front (RPF)—comprised of descendants of the UNAR leaders and Tutsi refugees who had settled in Uganda in the 1960s—invaded northern Rwanda in October 1990.[96] The Rwandan government quickly repulsed the RPF, but the exiles regrouped and settled into a long-term insurgency campaign that profoundly destabilized northern Rwanda.[97] In addition, the democratization movement that swept Eastern Europe and other parts of Africa in the early 1990s also had an effect in Rwanda as political opponents rallied for an end to the MRND's monopoly on power. After initial resistance, Habyarimana's government agreed in 1991 to the introduction of multiparty politics. This offered hope for a new political dawn after decades of one-party rule. Unfortunately, hardliners in the emerging parties would manipulate the political process—and especially the parties' youth wings—to persecute their opponents and exacerbate Hutu-Tutsi tensions between 1991 and 1993. Such tensions only grew worse in October 1993 when Burundi's Tutsi-dominated military assassinated Melchior Ndadaye, a Hutu political leader who had been recently installed as Burundi's first democratically elected president.

Even as Rwanda's government conducted public negotiations with the RPF, the MRND was trying to rally Hutu political support by scapegoating the Tutsi. As the military tide turned in favor of the RPF in 1992 and 1993, the government agreed to U.N.-brokered peace negotiations. This led to the Arusha Accords of August 1993 that called for the reincorporation of thousands of Tutsi exiles, the integration of the RPF into the Rwandan military (the *Forces Armées Rwandaises*, known by its acronym FAR), and a government of national unity.[98] Led by Canadian General Romeo Dallaire, a U.N. peacekeeping force arrived in Rwanda in late 1993 to help secure the peace. Behind the scenes, however, hard-line Habyarimana supporters had been arming MRND youth militias (who would be known during the genocide as *"interahamwe"* or "those who work together"). These militias carried out six major massacres of Tutsi between October 1990 and January 1993; Hutu hardliners noted the international community's muted reaction.[99] In late 1993 the government compiled death lists of prominent Tutsi, Hutu political opponents, and other intellectuals. By February 1994 large shipments of machetes, machine guns, and artillery were arriving in Rwanda, causing Dallaire to send alarmed cables to New York that were effectively ignored by his U.N. superiors.

The assassination of Rwanda's president triggered the genocide itself. In early April Habyarimana and Cyprian Ntaryamira, Ndadaye's successor as president of Burundi, traveled to Arusha, Tanzania for another round of peace talks and power-sharing negotiations with the RPF. As the presidential plane returned to Kigali's airport on the evening of Thursday, April 6, 1994, a surface-to-air missile destroyed the plane.[100] Within an hour, the Rwandan military and Hutu militias established roadblocks across Kigali and began executing leaders of the political opposition and other members of the Rwandan intelligentsia. This political repression grew into ethnocide as Hutu militias executed thousands of Tutsi (or those who appeared to be Tutsi) in and around Kigali. In subsequent days, government-ordered massacres spread across Rwanda, consuming northwestern Rwanda and reaching the last holdout of Butare in southern Rwanda in late April. By the time the RPF captured Kigali in July and stopped the genocide, between 500,000 and 800,000 Tutsi and tens of thousands of Hutu had been killed. The RPF also killed thousands of Hutu as they advanced across Rwanda between April and July 1994.[101] In front of the RPF advance, nearly two million Hutu fled to Tanzania and Zaire. After 1996, the Congolese refugee crisis and ongoing cross-border violence precipitated two major wars that drew eight African nations into what scholars have described as "Africa's World War." Upward of four to five million died from war-related causes over the next decade, most of them Congolese civilians.[102]

What role(s) did the Catholic Church play in the years leading up to the Rwandan genocide? The answer is of course multifaceted, and one should avoid either exonerating the church from all corporate responsibility or "blaming the church" for the genocide. Nor can one adequately address all of the dimensions of this question in the few pages that follow. Having said this, several patterns carry forward themes that emerged in our more detailed study of the late colonial period. First, as in the late 1950s, the Catholic Church did not speak with one unified voice. Even as bishops like Phocas Nikwigize of Ruhengeri and Vincent Nsengiyumva of Kigali remained close to the government, the attitude of Perraudin's successor Thadée Nsengiyumva seemed to echo Bigirumwami's prophetic distance. In collaboration with several Kabgayi priests, Thadée Nsengiyumva issued a December 1991 pastoral letter entitled *"Convertissons-nous pour vivre ensemble dans la paix."*

FIGURE 6.1 Local Genocide Memorial Site, Ndera, Rwanda (*Author Photo, 2010*)

This statement offered a strong internal critique of the Catholic Church's role in society. For Bishop Thadée, the Catholic Church had lost credibility due to its ethnic segregation and failure to examine the deeper social causes of corruption, injustice, war and AIDS. The letter reserved particular opprobrium for the hierarchy's failure to speak prophetic truth to state power, especially Catholic bishops' silence in the face of recent Tutsi massacres in Kibilira, Bigogwe, Murambi and Bugesera.[103] Such letters remind us that "the bishops" included a plurality of voices, some of whom strongly opposed the violence and ethnic extremism that saturated Rwandan society in the early 1990s.

Second, the Catholic press continued to serve as an important gadfly. As it had in the late 1950s and late 1960s, *Kinyamateka* in the late 1980s published articles critical of Rwanda's government. Not coincidentally, *Kinyamateka's* editor, Sylvio Sindambiwe, died in a suspicious car accident in November 1989. Fr. André Sibomana, a Hutu priest and human rights advocate, took over *Kinyamateka* and continued to push the case against government authoritarianism. Sibomana received little overt support from most of the Catholic hierarchy with the significant exception of Thadée Nsengiyumva.[104] At the same time, *Kinyamateka* and the White Father journal *Dialogue* remained avenues for the free exchange of ideas—ideas that were increasingly critical of the Habyarimana regime. Church-affiliated human rights organizations also became more active in the early 1990s.

Third, the Catholic hierarchy encouraged democratization and political reconciliation in the midst of the civil war and Rwanda's uneven transition to multiparty politics. In many ways, church leaders played a far more active mediating
role in the early 1990s than in the early 1960s. As early as 1990, the bishops
offered public support for multiparty democracy, and in 1992 the bishops agreed
to participate in national peace talks (even before the MRND government had
officially committed itself). Led by a group of clergy known as "le comité du
contacts," church leaders continued to mediate between the MRND government and the RPF until the signing of the Arusha Peace Accords in August
1993.[105] Mgr. Giuseppe Bertello, the Vatican's apostolic nuncio or ambassador
in Rwanda, was especially notable for his efforts to reach out to the RPF in
northern Rwanda in late 1992.[106] And after 1990, Catholic leaders became more
publicly outspoken on the need to peacefully reintegrate the thousands of Tutsi
refugees living outside the country.[107]

As they had in the early 1960s, however, Rwanda's bishops continued to offer
broad support for the government in the name of national security. After the initial
RPF invasion of October 1990, Vincent Nsengiyumva reminded Catholics that
love of country was a "duty incumbent on each of us" and praised Rwanda's social
progress under the Second Republic. Even as he cautioned Rwandans against the
"temptation of bloody hate which has above all an ethnic basis," Nsengiyumva
reminded Catholics that "we have the duty of protecting the country against all
peril and against all menace, from wherever it comes—from the interior or the
exterior."[108] Similar appeals to national unity against the "foreign" RPF army and
a supposed "fifth column" of internal Tutsi collaborators would be one of the primary justifications for the killings of 1994.[109] In turn, while episcopal statements
preached love of enemies and deplored political intolerance, the bishops failed
to name or condemn the Tutsi massacres unfolding across Rwanda between late
1990 and 1993. When killings were mentioned, blame was apportioned equally to
"Tutsi" and "Hutu" (not the "MRND government" and the "RPF"). A good example
comes from the bishops' Lent 1992 statement, issued shortly after the Bugesera
massacre of March 1992. "Trust is missing in people's homes, to the point that
certain communities have known massacres: Hutu and Tutsi are fighting each
other and the regions are set one against the other."[110] As Timothy Longman has
argued, the Catholic bishops did not exhort people to kill, but they contributed to
the creation of a "moral climate" of silence and pro-government complicity where
genocide could become ethically permissable.[111]

When the genocide began in April 1994, Catholic institutions became the
scenes of unprecedented violence. This happened in part because thousands
of Tutsi initially took refuge at Catholic parishes. But while Catholic parishes
served as asylums during the anti-Tutsi violence of 1959 to 1964, they became
mortuaries in 1994. In fact, more Tutsi died in churches than anywhere else,

including an estimated 65,000 to 75,000 on the grounds of Kabgayi parish. In addition to the hundreds of thousands of lay Catholics who lost their lives, nearly 200 priests and religious were killed, most of them Tutsi.[112] Clerical victims included Jesuit human rights activists at the Centre Christus in Kigali; Fr. Innocent Gasabwoya, Perraudin's long-serving vicar general in Kabgayi; and Fr. Felicien Muvara, the Tutsi priest and scholar whose 1988 promotion to the episcopate had been scuttled by Vincent Nsengiyumva.[113] Bigirumwami's episcopal successor in Nyundo diocese, the Tutsi bishop Wenceslas Kalibushi, survived a machete attack on May 4.[114]

Despite the deaths of clergy and Kalibushi's grave injury, the Catholic hierarchy did not speak with a strong voice in the early weeks of the genocide.[115] Even as Pope John Paul II denounced the massacres as "genocide" at the First African Synod on April 10, Rwanda's bishops remained conspicuously silent.[116] Vincent Nsengiyumva issued a vague statement on April 27 denouncing "grave troubles" that had cost the lives of "many innocent people" but did not link this to the interim government.[117] Collectively, the bishops did not address the violence until May 13, and even here the bishops attributed responsibility to both the RPF and the government, describing the massacres as "tragic events" rather than "genocide."[118] In the meantime, the bishops accompanied the interim government when it moved from Kigali to Gitarama.[119]

It may be that Nsengyiumva and his colleagues had a change of heart in Gitarama. When government leaders fled Gitarama for the western city of Gisenyi on June 2, Vincent Nsengiyumva, Thadée Nsengiyumva, and Joseph Ruzindana, the Bishop of Byumba, chose to stay behind.[120] They would pay dearly for this decision to remain with their people. The next day, RPF soldiers assigned to guard the Catholic bishops assassinated them and nine other clergymen. More than any other single event, these assassinations poisoned postgenocide relations between the RPF and the Catholic hierarchy. On June 20, Catholic bishops and Protestant leaders issued a joint statement blaming both sides for the violence and attributing "this dramatic situation" to the October 1990 war launched by the RPF with the assistance of Uganda.[121] This document again failed to hold the interim government directly responsible for the genocide, arguing instead that "this [Habyarimana's] assassination has been the occasion of a chain of ethnic reactions which have inspired massive massacres known by all in the country."[122]

The RPF marched into Kigali on July 4 and effectively ended the genocide. In fear of retaliation, two million Hutu refugees (including many Hutu priests and Mgr. Phocas Nikwigize, the bishop of Ruhengeri) migrated into eastern Congo. Supported by Nikwigize, a group of Hutu priests in a Goma refugee camp wrote an August 1994 letter to John Paul II alleging a "double genocide" of both Tutsi and Hutu and pleading for international intervention to prevent the Hutu majority from falling back into the "pre-1959 slavery."[123] In the Arusha trials that followed the genocide, 34 Catholic clergy and religious were charged with abetting genocide during the 1990s, including Augustin Misago, the Bishop of Gikongoro. Many of these charges were politically motivated, but a minority of clergy, religious, and lay leaders were either actively or tacitly involved in the killings.[124] One thinks here of a devout lay Catholic like Euprasie Kamatanu, a local MRND party leader who helped organize *Interahamwe* killers while praying the Divine Mercy Chaplet daily in hopes that "the Virgin Mary will help me discover hidden enemies."[125] At the same time, many clergy and lay leaders also protected Tutsi fleeing the *interahamwe*, often sacrificing their own lives in the process. In Rokoma parish in the eastern province of Kibungo, Fr. Evode Mwanangu gathered Christians together in his church for prayer, protecting hundreds of Tutsi before *interahamwe* assassinated him and massacred the refugees.[126]

From Switzerland, Perraudin watched in dismay as the genocide unfolded. In mid-April, he decided to speak out on the violence, granting a rare interview to a local Swiss newspaper.[127] Here we see that Perraudin's basic conceptual paradigms from the early 1960s remained three decades later—namely his condemnation of violence, his dualistic and racialist vision of Rwandan society, and his tendency to blame Tutsi exiles for the abuses that Hutu militias were inflicting on Tutsi peasants. For example, Perraudin exhorted Rwandans to "stop, stop this escalation of horror! No more war between you, nor ever more. Reconcile yourselves, love one another!" At the same time, he also expressed his empathy for the Hutu killers. "I condemn them but I try to understand. They act out of anger and fear. By anger against the death of their president, Juvenal Habyarimana . . . and by fear of returning to slavery." For Perraudin, international media had misrepresented the Rwanda story since journalists did not understand the country. Here Perraudin highlighted the Tutsi's sense of his own "natural right to command and dominate" and Rwandan society's precolonial history as a "system of slavery, an institution of pride and of domination by one race over the other." Betraying lingering pseudo-Hamitic biases, Perraudin also claimed that the Tutsi were "smarter, shrewder and have a European appearance," comparing Rwanda's Hutu-Tutsi relationship to that between the peasants of his home region of Bagnes and the urbane city-dwellers of the Swiss city of Sion. And as in the 1960s, Perraudin still saw Tutsi exiles rather than Hutu militias as primarily responsible for the massacres of the Tutsi. In invading Rwanda in 1990 and (allegedly) shooting down Habyarimana's plane in April 1994, the RPF had committed a "suicidal act" that inexorably led Rwanda down the path to genocide.[128] Nor did Perraudin express any ambiguity about the wisdom of his own pastoral decisions in the late 1950s or early 1960s. Positing that he stood "in favor of justice, liberation and human dignity for all the children of God," Perraudin claimed that "I am ulcered by all the sufferings, but I do not regret having spoken."[129]

This air of self-righteousness remains in Perraudin's 2003 memoir. Even after the 1994 genocide, Perraudin never publicly questioned his own pastoral decisions. Nor could he accept that Rwanda's unparalleled ethnic violence offered a stinging indictment of a century of Catholic evangelization. Perraudin spilt much ink describing the false "calumnies" to which he had been subjected, and many of his criticisms were merited. However, it is regrettable that Perraudin could never admit any fault, either on a personal level or on behalf of the church he led for so many years.

Epilogue

LESSONS FROM RWANDA

I CONCLUDE THIS book by venturing into the dangerous territory of "lessons." This is dangerous ground in that the historian's primary task is to seek a more honest and comprehensive understanding of the past. Whatever Lord Acton's famous dictum that "those who do not learn from the mistakes of the past are destined to repeat them," history does not inevitably run in circles. One can detect patterns, but there are also discontinuities. Historical circumstances differ. And we always read history through our own contemporary lenses and cultural locations. In this sense, our histories say as much about us and our own values as they do about the "past in its pastness."

Caveats to the side, I am always asked what we can learn from Rwanda. As a Catholic scholar who teaches theology, the "we" with whom I am most concerned is "Christians." In concluding this book, therefore, I will venture five ecclesial and theological lessons that emerge from this historical narrative. Here I highlight the necessity of ecclesial repentance, reiterate the need for the church to maintain prophetic distance from the state, and argue for the centrality of nonviolence for Christian politics. In addition, while ethical and political debates often center around the question of "what should we do," the Rwandan case reminds us of the importance of social description and theological imagination—namely the question of "who are we." Following from this, one of the church's most important tasks after Rwanda is to highlight the social and communal dimensions of Christian identity in the face of rival nationalist, ethnic, and ideological allegiances. Finally, the complexities of Rwandan history underline the importance of the "purification of memory" for the theological project. My "theopolitical" reflections here emerge from the Rwandan context, but I believe they have salience for Christian leaders in many other parts of the world.[1] What I offer here is the briefest of theological sketches; I hope to develop these themes further in a future work exploring historical and contemporary case studies in the Christian politics of reconciliation.

I concluded my historical analysis by admitting my own frustrations with Perraudin's air of self-righteousness. Whether one sees him as a progressive champion of social justice or a manipulative schemer of Machiavellian proportions, few would classify Perraudin as a symbol of repentance. If there is one consistent theme in nearly all of Perraudin's writings, it is his defensiveness toward the "calumnies" of his detractors. This highlights perhaps the greatest challenge facing the Catholic Church in Rwanda: the importance of repentance. To be sure, church leaders have encouraged individual Christians to repent for their sins during and after the genocide, and Catholics have been involved in parish reconciliation initiatives, prison ministries, and the state-led *gacaca* process.[2] However, with the notable exception of Mgr. Smaragde Mbonyitege, the current bishop of Kabgayi, the hierarchy has resisted offering a confession of corporate sin similar to the 1997 statement issued by the Protestant Council of Rwanda.[3] Part of this reluctance has stemmed from tensions between the contemporary Catholic Church and the Rwandan government, as well as the church's fears concerning the political manipulation of any institutional confession. The church is also not a monolithic institution, and there were heroic martyrs and resistors in every period of violence since 1959.[4] However, the admission of sin, necessity of repentance, and promise of redemption stand at the heart of the Christian gospel. In the words of St. Paul, "all have sinned and are deprived of the glory of God" (Romans 3:23). To limit repentance to individuals is to lose sight of the communal, social, and institutional nature of the Catholic Church. It is also to ignore the structural nature of sin. As Timothy Longman has demonstrated in his detailed study of Christian politics in the years leading up to the 1994 genocide, the churches embodied the worst tendencies in ethnic chauvinism, power politics, and silent complicity.[5] Even Bishop Mbonyintege named the greatest problem in Rwandan Catholic history as an "evil conception of power in the church."[6]

Embodying what Mary Grey has termed the "*via purgativa*" entails modifying the almost univocal defensiveness that marked so many Catholic episcopal statements in the 1950s, 1960s, and 1990s.[7] There will surely be "gross calumnies" against the church, and church leaders have the right to offer their side of the story. But the apologetic impulse should not overshadow the call to repentance, a far more central component of the gospel of Jesus Christ. Church leaders should therefore be their own toughest critics, recognizing in the words of Vatican II's *Lumen Gentium* that the church stands "always in need of purification, following constantly the path of penance and renewal."[8] Far from a *societas perfecta* marching unscathed through history, the church is deeply immersed in both the shadows and lights of human history. Pope John Paul II recognized this when he called for an "ecclesial examination of conscience" ahead of the jubilee year of 2000.[9] And as Pope Benedict XVI has said in the context of the recent clerical sex abuse scandal, "we see in a truly terrifying way that the greatest persecution of the Church does not come from outside enemies but is born of sin within the Church."[10]

One of the Rwandan church's greatest sins has been the general failure of church leaders to maintain prophetic distance from state leaders. Between 1930 and 1994, every major Rwandan political leader had his perceived ecclesial champion—Mutara Rudahigwa and Léon Classe; Gregoire Kayibanda and André Perraudin; Juvenal Habyarimana and Vincent Nsengiyumva. In embodying a prophetic alternative, then, the church recognizes that its primary political task is not to run the state, partner with the state, or use state power to pursue its own institutional interests. This does not mean that the church withdraws into a ghetto; this would be impossible anyway given the nature of the church as a global communion immersed in local communities. But like the Old Testament prophets Samuel and Amos or past witnesses of conscience like Thomas More or Oscar Romero, the church's posture vis à vis the state should offer what the former White Father provincial Guy Theunis has termed a "prophetic charism in service to the gospel of peace."[11] The church is called to be a prophetic herald of the common good, calling the state away from its tendencies toward self-love and national pride and toward a politics of self-sacrificing service on behalf of the marginalized. Building the common good entails speaking out on the core social issues of the day, whether war, abortion, labor relations, immigration, the environment, ethnic bias, or political corruption. What the prophetic mission does not entail is campaigning for the political party that appears to favor the church's institutional interests—what Antoine Mugesera has termed offering a partisan rather than prophetic message.[12]

One should also distinguish the church's prophetic role from the oft-repeated claims to political neutrality that limit church leaders to a strictly "mediating" role. Although Catholic communities like the Roman lay congregation Sant'Egidio should be praised for their mediating work in countries like Mozambique, the "politics of neutrality" can also reduce the church to an essentially passive, value-neutral community.[13] In their efforts to be "neutral"—such as persistent claims in church circles concerning a "double genocide" in 1994—church leaders can be dishonest and complicit to great evil.[14] In the words of the Rwandan bishops themselves, "if we do not clearly denounce lies, corruption, theft, oppression, arbitrary imprisonment, and assassinations *with their authors*, whether this be an individual, a group or the power, we cannot avoid a sense of culpability, which may appear to be complicity."[15]

In turn, the church's prophetic mission entails embodying an alternative Christian politics within its own common life. This means admitting that the church does in fact have a politics, a claim that Perraudin and his allies liked to deny in the late 1950s.[16] The key issue here is not *whether* Christianity has a politics but rather *what type of politics* is faithful to the Christian gospel. In particular, the church is called to embrace the self-sacrificing politics of the cross, forming beatudinal communities of mercy, justice, righteousness, and peace who may be "persecuted for the sake of righteousness" (Matthew 5:10). Such Christian communities are likely to exist in tension with the mainstream secular political parties of the day. To echo Augustine of Hippo, politics based on the self-sacrificing love of Christ is not easily reconcilable with the national pride and love of glory that so often marks the "city of man."[17] One thinks here of transformative ministries like Paride Taban's Kuron Holy Spirit Village in Sudan or Maggy Barankitse's Maison Shalom in Burundi.[18] In advocating for an alternative Christian politics, I am not claiming that Christian communities will be somehow immune from the sins that plague the nation-state. Whatever its claims to a divine mission or Spirit-led guidance, the church comprises fallen human beings. This is of course where the principle of repentance is so important, reminding the church of its constant need for confession, renewal, and reconciliation (traits not often associated with nation-state leaders for whom apologies are tantamount to admitting defeat).[19] Such a politics does not envision a wholescale Christian withdrawal from electoral politics, but it does entail an Augustinian sense of the fallenness of state politics.[20]

Third, Rwanda's history reveals the savage nature of ethnic and political violence, challenging the church to speak more forcefully and openly about the ethical challenge and scandal of violence. The violence of Rwandan history demonstrates the inadequacy of all slogans, be they for social justice, democracy, national unity, or liberation of the poor. Whether in the form of Parmehutu mobs expropriating Tutsi land in the name of social justice or UNAR assassins killing Parmehutu leaders in the name of national unity, Catholic social teaching was twisted to serve a political agenda counter to the gospel. For all of the laudable and necessary focus on the manipulation of ethnicity in colonial and postcolonial Rwanda, one should not lose sight of the issue of political violence. From Rwabugiri's territorial expansions in the late 1800s to German and Belgian "pacification" campaigns in the early 1900s, modern Rwanda was molded in a crucible of bloodshed.[21] This book has focused in particular on the revolutionary violence of 1959–1962, the UNAR incursions and Gikongoro massacres of the early 1960s, the ethnic purgings of 1973, and the genocide of 1994. One should not forget the wars in Eastern Congo that emerged out of the Rwandan genocide and refugee exodus of 1994–1995. Beginning in 1996, these wars have taken the lives of over six million and continue to fester over fifteen years later.

An alternative Catholic politics thus recognizes the necessity of a Christian nonviolent witness, recognizing in the words of Desmond Tutu that "true security will never be won through the barrel of a gun."[22] While they often lamented violence, Perraudin and even Bigirumwami rarely preached on the *priority* of Christian nonviolence, preferring instead to focus on themes of justice, truth, charity, or national unity. As we have seen, such ideals could be easily manipulated by political and military actors, whether in the name of national defense or in the name of social justice. One should not forget that in the years leading up to the

1994 genocide, the Rwandan government justified its massive military buildup and its mobilization of youth militias in the name of national defense against the RPF. Not surprising, Hutu *génocidaires* later claimed "self-defense" as one of their primary motivations for participating in the 1994 massacres.[23]

Addressing violence as an ethical challenge for the church raises difficult questions. For example, the ecumenical march for peace on New Year's Day 1994 gathered over 30,000 in eight towns and cities across Rwanda. On this world day of peace, Rwandans proclaimed a message very much in keeping with my argument here.

> Life is sacred and inviolable...[We say] No to Violence, no to the destruction of our country, no to the killings, no to the lies, no to hypocrisy and manipulation.... We want peace and we are committing ourselves to being instruments of this peace. We now want to live a life centered in love, a nonviolent life. We demand that truth, justice and tolerance become the foundation of our society.[24]

Whatever these noble sentiments, the genocide still followed three months later. In turn, a convincing argument can be made that rapid international military intervention in April 1994 could have stopped the genocide.[25] So a strict pacifist position may not be the right lesson to draw from Rwanda's history. Regardless, I would still argue that Christians have become too enamored with state violence. To even raise questions in this area jeopardizes one's patriotism, the unforgiveable sin in the civil religion(s) that dominate modern nation-states. In turn, Rwanda's history reminds Christian leaders of the dangers of condemning generic violence while failing to hold state leaders accountable for their own abuses.

Christian leaders should therefore preach the Christocentric nature of nonviolence, draw public attention to questions of military ethics, and offer healing ministries for soldiers and militia members alike. From Rwanda to Burundi to DRC, state militaries and local militias have been responsible for nearly all of the worst human rights abuses in the region. In the recent wars in Congo, civilian mortality rates were perhaps 100 times higher than military casualties.[26] Military culture in Africa's Great Lakes region thus stands in need of an intentional and public politics of repentance. In particular, the church's sacramental practice of reconciliation could aid in this process of repentance and reconciliation. One thinks here of the medieval demand that churches ritually cleanse crusading soldiers returning to their home communities. One thinks also of Mozambican *cuarandeiro* healers who helped to ritually reincorporate child soldiers after the horrors of that country's civil war.[27]

Fourth, Rwandan history reminds us of the importance of social description in any ethical or political conflict. The church is called to embody Christ's calls to "love your neighbor as yourself" (Luke 10:27) and to "love your enemies and pray for those who persecute you" (Matthew 5:44). Yet such prescriptive commands must be embodied in particular social contexts. Jesus himself refused to let "the neighbor" remain an abstract concept in the parable of the Good Samaritan (cf. Luke 10:29:37). In the Rwandan context, the church did not split over the efficacy of ideals like social justice, democracy, or the Christian obligation to aid the poor. Rather, the church divided over how to *apply* and *describe* these principles in Rwanda's social, cultural, and ethnic contexts. I am not naïve enough to think that all parties could have completely agreed on the nature of the Hutu-Tutsi distinction or the extent to which Rwanda's social problems could be mapped on a Hutu-Tutsi axis. But what often seemed missing was a concerted effort to openly discuss, debate, and seek a modicum of consensus on the social descriptions that should underlie Catholic social teaching.[28] Perraudin and Bigirumwami spoke often of the necessity of social unity, but they offered vastly different descriptions of Rwanda's social reality. Unity was lost in the very terms they used to describe the problem.

I admit that this may be the most difficult principle to embody. I write in the aftermath of the 2012 U.S. electoral campaigns, a $6 billion exercise in negative politics that revealed the deep ideological chasms that exist in America and the Catholic Church alike. But I do not see a way to avoid the challenge. Catholic social teaching calls for the upbuilding of the common good, but the common good does not explain itself. Quoting Pope Paul VI's counsel that "if you want peace work for justice" neither explains the nature of justice nor how to build justice in a particular society. Nor do such mottos sufficiently grapple with the often close intertwining of violence and justice in the modern world. One thinks here of the controversies swirling around the legacy of André Perraudin, the "Valasian rock who spoke openly of justice."[29] In turn, social analysis should transcend simplistic sloganeering that pose as "explanations." For example, one can recognize that the Belgians inappropriately racialized Tutsi and Hutu categories, but this does not singlehandedly explain the violence that dominated Rwandan society after 1959. In fact, overemphasizing this point can itself reveal a problematic analytical argument—namely, the idea that racial groups are more prone to conflict than social groups.

Fifth, Rwanda's history challenges Christians to reflect concretely on the risks posed by identity politics, whether of a national, ethnic, racial, social, class, or even religious hue. All such allegiances threaten Christians' fundamental identity as brothers or sisters in the Body of Christ called to love their neighbors as themselves. In their Lenten pastoral of 1993, Rwanda's Catholic bishops posited that "for those who belong to Christ there are no more Jews, Greeks, Hutu, Tutsi, Twa, Mukiga, Munyanduga. All are one in Christ Jesus."[30] And yet it was the political instrumentalization of ethnic identities that helped lead tens of thousands of

Christians to kill hundreds of thousands of their fellow Christians during the genocide of 1994. Recognizing this discrepancy, Cardinal Roger Etchegaray famously asked Rwandan church leaders "if the blood of tribalism ran deeper than the waters of baptism."[31] The rhetorical answer seems to be yes. As Gerard Prunier has shown, only Rwanda's minority Muslim community corporately resisted the violence of the genocide, placing its shared Muslim identity ahead of the Hutu-Tutsi dynamic.[32] Likewise, one of the problems with the Rwandan government's current focus on Banyarwanda identity is that this rhetoric fails to name the oppression propagated in the name of the nation-state and national identity. One thinks here of Banyarwandan seminarians forcing out their Burundian and Congolese confreres from Nyakibanda seminary in 1952. More seriously, one recalls the massive Rwandan atrocities in the 1990s in Eastern Congo in the name of national defense.[33] Nor does an exclusive focus on ethnicity explain the nationalist currents embedded in Rwanda's late colonial political conflicts, including Belgium's efforts to safeguard its colonial influence, UNAR's accusing its political opponents of treason, and Parmehutu's demands that Belgium "give the country to its true inhabitants, the Hutu."[34] To embody an alternative Catholic politics is thus to relativize identities that threaten to become idolatrous (including at times religious ones), recognizing that identity politics always poses a risk to the Christian's two-fold command to love God and to love one's neighbor. It is to remember with Aloys Bigirumwami that each Christian is called ultimately to embody the "politics of Jesus," not the politics of Parmehutu, UNAR, Rwanda, Belgium, or the United States. It is to recall that when the scribes asked Jesus who *qualified* as a neighbor, Jesus responded by describing what it meant to *act* like a neighbor, offering Israel's political enemy, the Samaritans, as a model (cf. Luke 10:29–37).

In this sense, Christian leaders would do well to reflect more publicly on the social implications of sacramental practices. In sharing the Eucharist, Christians encounter Christ in communion with each other. To share in the Eucharist while committing violence against one's brothers or sisters thus profanes the very essence of the sacrament. In the words of Pope Benedict XVI,

> The most effective means for building a reconciled, just and peaceful society is a life of profound communion with God and with others. The table of the Lord gathers together men and women of different origins, cultures, races, languages, and ethnic groups. Thanks to the Body and Blood of Christ, they become truly one. In the Eucharistic Christ, they become blood relations and thus true brothers and sisters, thanks to the word and to the Body and Blood of the same Jesus Christ. This bond of fraternity is stronger than that of human families, than that of our tribes.[35]

To this extent, one must credit the Rwandan Jesuit Octave Ugirashebuja's cat-echetical initiative to reteach the Mass through emphasizing the complementar-ity of loving God and neighbor.[36] One thinks also of the witness of Sr. Félicitas Niyitegeka, a Hutu Catholic sister serving in Gisenyi in April 1994. Sr. Félicitas's brother worked as a military officer with the Rwandan government and offered her the opportunity to flee the growing violence around her. Despite her brother's entreaties, Sr. Félicitas refused to abandon her fellow Tutsi sisters or the forty-three Tutsi who had taken refuge in her community. She was killed along with her Tutsi sisters on April 21, 1994.[37] To echo the German Lutheran theologian Dietrich Bonhoeffer, Sr. Félicitas's martyrdom reminds us of the "cost of disciple-ship."[38] It also offers hope that a deeply Eucharistic Christian identity can tran-scend the divisions of nation, ethnicity, and race that have wreaked such havoc in the modern world.

This is primarily a historical work, and the theological lessons I raise in this brief epilogue can and should be further developed. That is the task of another project. What I hope this work has achieved, however, is to demonstrate the theo-logical importance of grappling with what René Lemarchand has described as the "labor of memory."[39] Theological reflection on Rwanda is full of unexamined mythologies, trite assumptions, and simplistic analysis. For example, a genuine liberation theology could serve a constructive purpose in postgenocide Rwanda, but proponents would do well to consider the risks as well—namely, how liber-ationist rhetoric precipitated some of the worst violence in Rwanda's postcolo-nial history. I am reminded here of the epitaph on Gregoire Kayibanda's tomb in Gitarama describing him as "the liberator of the children of God."[40] And arguing that poisonous Hutu-Tutsi relations can be attributed solely to European colonial anthropology fails to recognize the importance of local agency and the complex-ity of late colonial views of ethnicity.[41] It may be, in fact, that Rwanda's historical complexity itself contains implicit theological lessons—namely, the importance of humility, the risks of polemic, and the necessity of perspectival pluralism.[42] As on the annual April commemoration of the beginning of the genocide, one is reminded of the inadequacy of words, the necessity of lament, and the importance of silence.

Timeline

1880s

1884–1885: The Congress of Berlin divides Africa between European powers; Rwanda, Burundi, and Tanganyika will become German colonies; Uganda will become a British colony; Congo is a trust territory for King Leopold before becoming a Belgian colony.

1885–1886: Anti-Christian persecution in Buganda leads to deaths and resulting cult of Uganda Martyrs.

1885–1895: Protestant and Catholic missions flourish in Buganda and become model Christian missions in late nineteenth-century East Africa.

1890s

1891: Anglicans favored in Uganda after winning sectarian war with Catholic elites.

1892: Charles Cardinal Lavigerie dies in Algiers; his Missionaries of Africa symbolized the resurgence of Catholic mission in nineteenth-century Europe.

1895: Mwami Rwabugiri dies in battle; his 34-year reign was notable for hardening of Hutu-Tutsi identities and regional military expansion.

1896: Belgian/Congolese force defeats Rwandan army at Shangi, demonstrating importance of European firepower.

1895–1897: Brief reign of Mwami Rutarindwa ends with *coup d'état* that brings Mwami Musinga to throne.

1897: Germans arrive at Musinga's court and establish protectorate over Rwanda.

1900s

1900: Led by Jean-Joseph Hirth, the first White Father caravan arrives at Rwandan court; Catholics establish Save mission in southern Rwanda.

1902–1904: White Fathers establish missions at Zaza (east), Nyundo (northwest), Rwaza (north), and Mibirizi (southwest); Musinga does not allow missionaries to establish posts near royal capital at Nyanza, preferring that they help pacify outlying territories and work among more marginalized poor Hutu and *petit* Tutsi populations.

1904: Violence erupts around mission stations due in part to missionary exactions on local populations; Aloys Bigirumwami born in Gisaka.

1906: Musinga allows missionaries to establish Kabgayi mission near Nyanza; White Fathers send Save superior Alphonse Brard back to Europe.

1907: Léon Classe becomes vicar general under Hirth; first signs of rapprochement between royal elites and Rwandan Christians.

1908: Richard Kandt named German resident; Kandt strengthens colonial presence and invites Lutherans to enter Rwanda.

1910s

1910–1911: Paulin Loupias, M.Afr., is killed in dispute with Hutu chief in northern Rwanda, leading to fierce German pacification campaign against Hutu communities in northern Rwanda.

1911: Creation of Vicariate of Kivu including Burundi, Rwanda, and eastern Congo; Hirth continues to serve as Vicar Apostolic.

1913: Hirth starts Kabgayi seminary, Josephite order, and Benebikira sisters.

1914: 10,000 baptized Catholics in Rwanda; André Perraudin born in Valais, Switzerland.

1914–1916: World War I affects Great Lakes region as Belgians, British and Germans struggle for control; major famine ensues; Germans withdraw from Rwanda; Belgians establish new colonial protectorate.

1917: Musinga issues decree on religious freedom, sparking further growth in Christian missions; first Rwandans are ordained to Catholic priesthood.

1920s

1920: Classe recalled to Europe for consultations; Hirth resigns as Vicar Apostolic.

1922: Classe returns from Europe and is named Vicar Apostolic of new Vicariate of Rwanda.

1922–1924: British briefly take over province of Gisaka in eastern Rwanda.

1924: League of Nations gives Belgium official trusteeship of Rwanda and Burundi.

1925: 40,000 baptized Catholics in Rwanda.

1926–1929: Belgium centralizes Rwandan chiefdoms and reserves leadership and higher education to Tutsi.

1928–1929: *Rwakayihura* famine kills upwards of 35,000.

1929: Aloys Bigirumwami ordained priest.

1930s

1931: Classe and Belgians conspire to depose Musinga, replacing him with one of his sons, the Christian catechumen Rudahigwa; 70,000 baptized Catholics in Rwanda.

1932–1933: Belgians introduce ethnic identity cards legally classifying Rwandans as Hutu, Tutsi, and Twa.

1932–1939: Tutsi *tornade* brings thousands of Tutsi elites and their Hutu clients into church.

1933: *Kinyamateka* Catholic newspaper launched.

1935: The Catholic Brothers of Charity take over the *Groupe Scolaire d'Astrida*, a new school for Tutsi elites training for colonial service.

1936: Nyakibanda Major Seminary opens, providing final formation for Rwandan men training to become Catholic priests.

1939: World War II begins; 300,000 baptized Catholics in Rwanda; Perraudin ordained as White Father priest in Carthage.

1940s

1941: Classe suffers stroke; Laurent Déprimoz becomes co-adjudicator of Vicariate of Rwanda.

1943: Mwami Mutara Rudahigwa receives Catholic baptism in national celebration.

1943–1944: Famine again wracks Rwanda, leading to 300,000 deaths.

1945: Classe dies; Déprimoz named Vicar Apostolic of Rwanda.

1946: Mutara dedicates Rwanda to Christ the King; U.N. *tutelle* established to oversee Belgian rule in Rwanda and Burundi.

1947: Mutara enrolled in papal order of St. Gregory the Great.

1948: Catholic population growth flattens, leading to renewed focus on Christian formation.

1948–1949: Tensions emerge between Mutara and graduates of *Groupe Scolaire d'Astrida.*

1949: Mutara officially abolishes *uburetwa.*

1950–1952

1950: Rwanda counts 400,000 baptized Catholics; Save mission celebrates 50th anniversary; André Perraudin arrives in Rwanda as professor at Nyakibanda Seminary.

1951: Founding of *L'Association des Amitiés Belge-Rwandaises*; new organization looks to strengthen relationships between Europeans and Rwandan elites.

1951–1952: Nationalist rivalries at Nyakibanda lead to expulsion of Congolese and Burundian students.

1952: Déprimoz expands Catholic Action by introducing League of Sacred Heart, Legion of Mary, and Eucharistic Crusade; Vatican establishes new Vicariate of Nyundo in northwestern Rwanda; Aloys Bigirumwami named as Vicar Apostolic of Nyundo, becoming first indigenous bishop in Belgian Africa; Belgians introduce ten-year development plan and announce intentions to hold local elections in 1953 and 1956; Perraudin appointed as rector of Nyakibanda seminary; Mutara abolishes *ubuhake.*

1953–1955

1953: Elections for *chefferies* and *sous-chefferies* leave most Tutsi notables in place; Alexis Kagame sent to Rome; Gregoire Kayibanda named editor of *L'Ami*; Arthur Dejemeppe named editor of *Kinyamateka.*

1954: Bwanakweri publicly challenges Mutara, leading to his political exile; *Conseil Superieur du Pays* (CSP) meets for first time.

1954–1955: Lay schools debate leads to major rift between Mutara and the White Fathers and other Catholic chiefs.

1955: Déprimoz breaks leg in accident and resigns as Vicar Apostolic; Dejemeppe serves as temporary administrator; Perraudin later named as permanent successor; Kayibanda named editor of *Kinyamateka*; founding of *Mouvement Politique Progressiste* (MPP) by Tutsi chiefs and Hutu elites.

1956

February: Perraudin organizes priestly retreat on the social question.

February-September: Hutu-Tutsi question emerges in political and media discourse.

March: Bigirumwami consecrates Perraudin to episcopate.

June: Regional bishops release pastoral letter on social question.

September: Expanded elections bring new cadre of Hutu sub-chiefs into government, but Tutsi continue to dominate upper tiers; Perraudin approves new TRAFIPRO cooperative.

1957

February: Tutsi-dominated Superior Council releases *Mise au point*, demanding independence and downplaying Hutu-Tutsi question.

March: Hutu elites release *Bahutu Manifesto*, emphasizing indigenous ethnic problem and Tutsi monopoly of political power.

April: Bishops of Rwanda-Burundi publish pastoral letter on justice.

June: Kayibanda starts *Mouvement Social Muhutu* (MSM) in Kabgayi.

September: U.N. Visiting Commission publicly names Hutu-Tutsi relationship as social problem and calls for democratization and decolonization.

November: White Fathers send Kayibanda and Hutu journalist Aloys Munyangaju to intern for Belgian Catholic newspaper; Joseph Gitera starts *Aprosoma* political movement.

1958

April–June: Mwami creates special commission to study Hutu-Tutsi question; commission agrees on ethnic discrepancies but deadlocks on how to resolve them.

May: Tutsi "Great Servants of the Court" publish letter denying shared brotherhood with Hutu.

June: Mutara and Superior Council reject recommendations of Hutu-Tutsi Study Commission and vote to ban ethnic identity cards; Hutu elites radicalize argument in media.

July: Perraudin leads two clerical study days to enhance clerical unity and study socioeconomic questions.

September: Bigirumwami downplays Hutu-Tutsi distinction in widely-read article in *Témoignage Chrétien*.

October: Gitera unsuccessfully lobbies Perraudin to condemn *Karinga* drums, the symbol of the monarchy.

November: Mutara visits Belgium; perceived snub furthers tensions with Belgian administration.

December: Jean-Paul Harroy, colonial governor, publicly declares Hutu-Tutsi problem.

1959

February: Perraudin's *Super Omnia Caritas* directly links Rwanda's socioeconomic problems to Hutu-Tutsi racial categories; Gitera establishes Aprosoma as formal political party.

April: Belgian Working Group visits Rwanda to draft plan for future political development.

July: Mutara dies unexpectedly in Bujumbura; rumors circulate claiming that Perraudin and Belgian colonial officials were complicit in his death; Rwandan *biru* name Mutara's half-brother, Kigeli V Ndahindurwa, as new Mwami without consulting Belgians; Kigeli pays first official visit to Perraudin.

August: Catholic synod at Nyakibanda studies political questions and clerical unity; bishops release two statements on Christian politics.

August–October: Rwandan political parties mobilize to contest anticipated January elections; new parties include UNAR, a Tutsi-dominated nationalist party, and Rader, a more pro-Belgian, pro-church party also led by Tutsi elites; Kayibanda transforms MSM into Parmehutu party; Perraudin and Bigirumwami condemn UNAR and Aprosoma for extremist rhetoric.

November: Hutu *jacquerie* erupts on November 1, precipitating limited counter-revolution from Mwami against local Hutu leaders; thousands of Tutsi are exiled and hundreds of Hutu and Tutsi are killed; Col. Guy Logiest pacifies country and appoints hundreds of new Hutu chiefs to replace exiled Tutsi; Perraudin and Bigirumwami condemn violence but differ on causes; Holy See establishes local hierarchy in Rwanda.

December: Belgium's "Christmas decree" establishes new intermediary government hostile to Mwami Kigeli.

1960

January: 650,000 baptized Catholics in Rwanda.

March: U.N. Visiting Commission visits Rwanda to investigate November violence and determine future electoral course, sparking renewal of ethnic and political violence; Perraudin defends himself before U.N. commission.

April: Rader, Parmehutu and Aprosoma form common front against Kigeli and UNAR.

May: UNAR decides to boycott communal elections.

June: Mwami Kigeli forced into exile, taking up residence in Tanzania and then Congo.

June–July: Parmehutu wins 70 percent majority in legislative elections; other political parties form common front against Parmehutu.

October: Regional bishops issue *Vérité, Justice, Charité* on sociopolitical developments in region.

October–November: Growing tensions and student withdrawals at Nyakibanda Seminary; Perraudin lobbies Rome to appoint Hutu bishop in Rwanda.

December: U.N. condemns political developments in Rwanda.

1961

January: Belgium delays anticipated legislative elections until June; Hutu elites organize *coup d'état* of Gitarama, abolishing monarchy and unilaterally declaring Rwanda as a Hutu republic.

February: Hutu Bernard Manyurane named first bishop of Ruhengeri before falling sick and dying of apparent poisoning in May.

March: U.N. warns of political dictatorship in Rwanda; Perraudin and Bigirumwami argue over future of Nyakibanda Seminary.

April–May: Vatican appoints first indigenous rector at Nyakibanda in effort to quell ongoing tensions and seminarian withdrawals.

July–August: Electoral season sparks new violence between political parties, leading to joint Bigirumwami-Perraudin condemnation.

September–October: Legislative elections give Parmehutu 80 percent majority; popular referendum overwhelmingly rejects institution of monarchy; Kayibanda named president.

December: Aprosoma joins common front with Rader and Unar against Parmehutu.

1962

January: Joseph Sibomana and Jean-Baptiste Gahamanyi consecrated as Catholic bishops of Ruhengeri and Astrida, respectively.

February: U.N. recognizes Rwandan government after Parmehutu agrees to include two UNAR members in cabinet.

March–April: Increasing UNAR exile raids into Rwanda; Hutu militias massacre 3,000–5,000 Tutsi at Byumba in retaliation.

July: Rwanda celebrates independence and beginning of First Republic; Perraudin delivers sermon at independence day celebrations.

October: Second Vatican Council opens; Perraudin, Bigirumwami, Sibomana and Gahamanyi will attend all four sessions between 1962 and 1965.

1963–1969

1963: Over 800,000 baptized Catholics in Rwanda; Parmehutu sacks Tutsi cabinet members and establishes political monopoly after August 1963 elections.

1963–1964: UNAR exiles launch major invasion in December and nearly reach Kigali, leading to government executions of political opposition and massacres of 8,000–10,000 Tutsi in Gikongoro; Catholic hierarchy condemns violence in January but downplays government role.

1964: Vatican Radio describes Gikongoro violence as "genocide" in February, sparking angry protests from Perraudin and White Fathers.

1964–1969: UNAR raids decline and ultimately cease; Tutsi exile community continues to oppose both Perraudin and Rwanda's Hutu-dominated government; Parmehutu rules as one-party dictatorship but faces more internal and intra-regional tensions as decade progresses.

1967: Founding of *Union Fraternelle Clergé Rwandaise* (UFCR) sparks further tensions between Perraudin and indigenous clergy.

1968: *Kinyamateka* editors sacked and exiled for critiquing government.

1970s

1970: Rwandan Catholic population tops 2 million; UFCR disbanded under pressure from Perraudin.

1972: Burundian genocide begins after failed *coup d'état* by Hutu military officers, leading to deaths of over 200,000 Hutu at hands of Tutsi-dominated military dictatorship; thousands of Burundian Hutu exiles stream into Rwanda.

1973: Government-instigated Hutu student groups force Tutsi students and professors out of Rwandan seminaries, universities, and secondary schools; hundreds killed in violence; bishops condemn violence but fail to critique

Kayibanda regime; Gen. Juvenal Habyarimana leads bloodless *coup d'état* against Kayibanda, establishing Rwanda's Second Republic.

1974: Vincent Nsengiyumva, a Hutu from Habyarimana's home region, replaces Aloys Bigirumwami as Bishop of Nyundo.

1976: Nsengiyumva is named Archbishop of Kigali, replacing Perraudin who continues to serve as Archbishop of Kabgayi; Nsengiyumva joins central committee of Habyarimana's *Mouvement Révolutionnaire Nationale Défense* (MRND).

1980s

1982: Rwandan Tutsi refugees in Uganda unsuccessfully petition Habyarimana government to allow them to return to Rwanda.

1986: Bigirumwami dies in Nyundo and is celebrated as national hero.

1988: Tutsi priest Felicien Muvara resigns episcopal appointment under pressure on eve of consecration; allegations swirl concerning Vincent Nsengiyumva's involvement.

1989: *Kinyamateka* editorials take stronger line against Habyarimana regime, leading to mysterious death of editor and arrests of Catholic journalists; Perraudin retires and is replaced by Thadée Nsengiyumva, a Hutu who will take a stronger line against church and government corruption and ethnicism.

1990–1993

1990: Vatican pressure leads Vincent Nsengiyumva to resign his position on MRND central committee on eve of Pope John Paul II's visit to Rwanda; JPII praises Perraudin as "model missionary"; "October war" begins as Rwanda Patriotic Front (RPF) invades northern Rwanda with stated aim of repatriating Tutsi exiles and toppling Habyarimana regime.

1990–1993: RPF war continues in north; government-organized local militias carry out targeted massacres of Tutsi.

1991: Habyarimana announces that Rwanda will introduce multiparty elections.

1991–1993: Rwandan bishops come out in favor of multiparty democracy and attempt to mediate between RPF and government.

1993: Arusha peace accords establish power-sharing agreement between RPF and Rwandan government; U.N. peacekeeping force arrives in Rwanda.

1994

January: Churches organize New Year's Day "March for Peace" that draws tens of thousands.

February–March: massive shipments of machetes and other weapons raise fears of impending massacres.

April: Habyarimana's plane is shot out of sky on April 6 as he returns from peace talks in Arusha; government militias begin rounding up and executing both Hutu and Tutsi political opponents; Perraudin offers newspaper interview in which he condemns violence but blames RPF for instigating Hutu counter-attacks.

April–July: Genocide spreads across Rwanda, killing an estimated 800,000 Tutsi, Hutu political opponents, and Hutu who appeared to be Tutsi; 75% of Rwanda's Tutsi population is killed before RPF captures Kigali and ends genocide; victims include 200 priests and religious.

July–August: 2 million Hutu flee across Congolese border; RPF establishes power-sharing government; Paul Kagame will be most important leader in new government.

1995–1999

1995: RPF engages in counter-reprisals in Rwanda and Zaire (Congo); thousands of Hutu massacred at Kibeho; Hutu militias continue to raid northwestern Rwanda; International Criminal Tribunal for Rwanda (ICTR) established at Arusha, Tanzania to try genocide suspects.

1995–1999: 100,000 Rwandans arrested on suspicion of genocide involvement, including Bishop Augustin Misago and several Catholic priests and sisters.

1996–1997: Rwandan military invades Zaire, claiming self-defense against Hutu militias; Rwandan army and allied Congolese militias pursue Hutu militants and other refugees across Zaire, toppling Mobutu regime and installing Laurent Kabila as president of Democratic Republic of Congo; estimated 4 million die in Congo from war-related causes between 1996 and 2002.

1997: Rwanda's Protestant Council issues apology for Christian complicity in genocide; Catholic Church confesses sins of individual members but continues to deny corporate or institutional responsibility.

1999: Jean-Baptiste Gahamanyi and Joseph Sibomana die in Rwanda.

2000s

2000: Bishop Misago acquitted on genocide charges, symbolizing the controversy over Catholic hierarchical role in the Rwandan genocide and its aftermath; Catholic Church celebrates hundredth anniversary of Save mission.

2002–2005: Community *gacaca* courts established to help resolve thousands of lower-level genocide cases languishing in Rwandan prison system; churches work extensively in prison ministry and local reconciliation efforts.

2003: RPF wins landslide election; Paul Kagame elected president; Perraudin publishes autobiography and dies in Switzerland.

2005: White Father Guy Theunis arrested on genocide-denial charges, symbolizing the continuing controversies over history, rhetoric, and the church in Rwanda.

2010: Kagame reelected for second seven-year term, reflecting RPF's monopoly of political life; ongoing controversy over Rwanda's meddling in Eastern Congo; four White Fathers remain in active ministry in Rwanda.

Glossary

Key Terms

Abakaraani: the Kinyarwanda nickname given to European-trained Tutsi chiefs in the 1920s and 1930s, reflecting the perception that they served as "clerks" for the Europeans; reflected growing tensions between Tutsi chiefs and predominantly Hutu peasantry under Belgian colonial rule.

Abanyiginya: elite clan that traditionally supplied Rwanda's kings; ongoing rivalry with Abega clan; Tutsi elites from Abanyiginya and Abega clans controlled the vast majority of Rwandan chiefdoms until 1959.

Abbé: French term for diocesan priest.

Abega: rival clan to the *Abanyiginya*; implicated in coup to overthrow Mwami Rwabugiri's chosen successor in 1897; Queen Mother often came from this clan; along with *Abanyiginya* controlled half of sub-chiefdoms and four-fifths of chiefdoms in late 1950s.

Aprosoma (Association pour le promotion des masses bahutu): Hutu populist movement founded by Joseph Gitera in 1957; became a political party in February 1959; rotated between virulent pro-Hutu ethnicism and populist pan-ethnic rhetoric; ultimately marginalized and incorporated into Parmehutu in the 1960s.

Bahutu-Batutsi-Batwa: conventional terms for describing Rwanda's three major social/ethnic groups; reflect a highly complex political, social, economic, ethnic and linguistic history; most post-colonial violence in Rwanda and Burundi centered around the political manipulation of the Hutu-Tutsi distinction.

Bakura b'inama: the local branch of Catholic Action in Rwanda, started by Léon Classe; particularly influential among local chiefs.

Banyarwanda: Kinyarwanda name for the Rwandan people, reflecting Rwanda's historic sense of nationhood and shared religious, cultural and linguistic traditions.

Benebikira: indigenous congregation for women religious founded in Rwanda in 1913; similar congregations started in Uganda and other areas of east and central Africa.

Biru: keepers of Rwandan custom and royal advisors who played an especially important role in consecrating the Mwami's successor; Fr. Alexis Kagame served as a *biru* and advisor to Mwami Mutara during the 1950s; *Biru* appointed Kigeli V Ndahindurwa as Mwami in July 1959.

Burgomasters: local government officials who served at Rwanda's commune/district level after 1959; replaced sub-chiefs as primary local political leaders.

Chefferies and *Sous-Chefferies*: "chiefdoms" and "sub-chiefdoms" established by Belgians in 1920s; Belgians limited these positions almost exclusively to Tutsi between 1920s and 1950s; represented a marked centralization of power in comparison to pre-colonial Rwandan traditions.

Conseil Supérieur du Pays (CSP): Rwanda's highest national advisory council in the late 1950s; Tutsi filled 31 of the CSP's 32 seats after 1956 elections, precipitating tensions with Hutu elites who demanded more representation; CSP released *Mise au point* in February 1957 which established core principles of Tutsi nationalism in late colonial period.

Évolué: French term describing the European-trained African elites of the 1940s and 1950s; many began advocating for more autonomy from colonial rule in the 1950s; early 1950s Catholic media reflected major concerns with future loyalties of this group.

Groupe du Travail: Belgian working group which conducted official visit to Rwanda and Burundi in April-May 1959; subsequent report favored land reform, democratization, and Hutu empowerment and shaped the Belgian government's own devolution plan announced in November 1959.

Hamitic Thesis: propagated by John Hanning Speke and other nineteenth century explorers and scholars, the Hamitic thesis posited that a North African/Ethiopian mixed race (traditionally descended from Noah's son Ham (cf. Genesis 9:18–29)) had migrated, conquered, and civilized the Bantu African peoples of central and eastern Africa, thereby explaining the physical differences between African peoples and the signs of Western civilization present in these cultures; colonial officials and Catholic missionaries applied this theory to Tutsi and Hutu in Rwanda, transforming them into racial categories.

Inyangarwanda: early Kinyarwanda name given to Christian converts in the first years of the twentieth century; literally meant "haters or repudiators of Rwanda."

Irivuze umwami: Kinyarwanda term meaning "the word pronounced by the king" or "what the king has said you must follow"; used in the 1930s to symbolize the nature of elite Christian conversion as an act of social and political obedience.

Jacquerie: "uprising"; originally applied to peasant revolts in 1350s France; used to describe Hutu revolts and anti-Tutsi violence of November 1959.

Karinga Drums: traditional symbol and repository of power for Abanyiginya monarchy; in late 1950s Hutu leaders increasingly criticized this as a pagan symbol reinforcing traditional Tutsi dominance in Rwanda; in 1959 Catholic bishops condemned Karinga "superstitions" but reaffirmed its status as national symbol; replaced by new national flag in January 1961.

Mouvement Politique Progressiste: broad, pan-ethnic political reform movement that briefly gained traction in Rwanda and Burundi during the mid-1950s; early leaders included Kayibanda, Bwanakweri, and the Burundian prince Louis Rwagasore; movement eventually splintered into rival Tutsi and Hutu-dominated political factions.

Mwami: Kinyarwanda name meaning "king"; *mwami* had semi-divine claims to authority, but *de facto* power was mitigated by intra-court and intra-clan rivalries.

Nyakibanda Major Seminary: founded in 1936 in southern Rwanda just west of Butare; offered final years of formation for Rwandan seminarians training for Catholic priesthood; became contested site for nationalist and then ethnicist tensions in 1951–52 and 1960–62; tensions led to establishment of new diocesan major seminaries in 1963.

Parmehutu (*Parti du Mouvement de l'Emancipation Hutu*): Hutu nationalist party launched in October 1959 which grew out of Kayibanda's *Mouvement Social Muhutu* (MSM); built extensive grassroots networks across Rwanda's hills through church organizations and cooperatives; developed increasingly ethnicist vision after 1959; won large majorities in legislative elections in 1960 and 1961 and established political monopoly after independence; lost favor during Second Republic before brief revival under MDR (*Mouvement Démocratique Républicaine*) label in early 1990s.

Propaganda Fide: Vatican congregation responsible for Catholic missions between 1622 and 1965; appointed Vicars Apostolic in Rwanda until 1959; leaders often adopted contrasting social and political analyses of Rwanda than White Father missionaries inside the country.

Rader (*Rassemblement Démocratique Rwandais*): pro-Belgian, pro-Catholic, Tutsi-led party launched with Belgian encouragement in October 1959; leaders included Bwanakweri and Ndazaro; opposed both UNAR authoritarianism and Parmehutu ethnicism; never succeeded in mobilizing popular support.

Rwanda Patriotic Front (RPF): predominantly Tutsi army which invaded northern Rwanda in October 1990 with the stated aim of repatriating Tutsi exiles and toppling Habyarimana government; 1990–1993 war led to deaths of thousands and destabilized Rwandan politics; ended Tutsi genocide in July 1994 after marching on Kigali; RPF political party continues to rule Rwanda under leadership of President Paul Kagame.

"Sindi umuhutu wawe": Kinyarwanda phrase meaning "I am not his servant"; reflected the increasingly political overtones of Hutu and Tutsi categories in the late nineteenth century prior to the colonial encounter.

Sulpicians: French congregation which directed many of France's seminaries in the nineteenth and twentieth centuries; recruited in 1959 to take over interim leadership of Nyakibanda seminary and help prepare seminary for indigenous leadership; White Fathers expelled Sulpicians after two Sulpician professors sided with Tutsi seminarians in 1960–1961.

"Super omnia caritas": Latin phrase meaning "charity above all"; Perraudin adopted this as his episcopal motto; title of Perraudin's famous 1959 pastoral letter which interpreted Rwandan social and political divisions through a Hutu-Tutsi lens.

Tornade: used in a 1935 issue of the White Father journal *Grands Lacs* to describe the mass conversions happening in Rwanda; symbolized the adherence of the Tutsi elite class to Catholicism after the catechumen Mutara Rudahigwa's 1931 accession to the throne.

TRAFIPRO: acronym for *"travail, fidélité, progrès"* ("work, faith, progress"); Rwanda's most important worker cooperative in late 1950s and early 1960s; launched in 1956 by Fr. Louis Pien with Perraudin's approval; Kayibanda served as first director and utilized TRAFIPRO networks to build his own political movement in 1958–1959.

Tutelle: trusteeship; refers to U.N. council entrusted with overall supervision of Rwanda-Burundi after World War II; Belgium served on council with a rotating group of three to five nations; U.N. tutelle visits in 1948, 1951, 1954, 1957, and 1960 precipitated major political reforms and power struggles inside Rwanda.

Ubuhake: patron-client system in traditional Rwandan society; clients (*garagu*) offered their services (fieldwork, nightwatch, etc.) to patrons (*shebuja*) in exchange for the patron's protection and usage of patron's land and cattle; patron provided for the client's family after death, and the patron could choose to extend the *ubuhake* relationship to a deceased client's heirs; *Ubuhake* existed between Tutsi and between Tutsi patrons and Hutu clients; it was rare for a Tutsi *garagu* to enter into such a relationship with a Hutu *shebuja*.

Uburetwa: labor system that required Hutu clients to devote two of every five days to working Tutsi patron's land; Belgians later reduced this rate to two days per week and made further exceptions for government and mission workers; the work itself became more onerous as Belgians enlisted peasants for colonial projects; imposed exclusively on Hutu.

Ubwoko: Kinyarwanda term loosely translated as "race" or "classification" (literally a "specific nature that can reproduce itself"); in precolonial Rwanda this term was never used to describe Hutu and Tutsi but rather those descended from a particular patrilineal clan (clans included both Hutu and Tutsi).

Union Fraternelle Clergé Rwandaise (UFCR): association of mostly Tutsi priests which organized after Vatican II; Bigirumwami and Sibomana allowed their priests to participate in UFCR; Perraudin established a rival network and banned his clergy from UFCR participation; dispute revealed ongoing ethnic and racial tensions in Rwandan church.

Union Nationale Rwandaise (UNAR): predominantly Tutsi nationalist party which formed in August 1959 to contest upcoming legislative elections in Rwanda; noted for its anti-colonial and anti-missionary rhetoric and demands for immediate independence; staunchly opposed Hutu emancipation movements as divisionist and ethnicist; marginalized after November 1959 uprising; split into internal and external wings after 1962; external wing led raids into Rwanda between 1962 and 1964.

Key Historical Figures

Adriaenssens, Jan: Belgian White Father missionary, seminary professor, and political commentator during 1950s to 1960s; Perraudin credited Adriaenssens with influencing his early social and political views; known for his center-left views and sympathy for emerging Hutu social movements; became more critical of Parmehutu in 1960s.

Baers, Paul: White Father who served as seminary rector at Nyakibanda between 1958 and 1961; his tenure was marked by unprecedented seminarian withdrawals and rising Hutu-Tutsi tensions after 1959; lost trust of Bigirumwami during bitter 1960–1961 disputes over how to resolve seminary crisis; replaced by indigenous rector in the spring of 1961 and later served as diocesan chancellor under Bishop Joseph Sibomana in Ruhengeri.

Bicamumpaka, Balthazar: key Hutu leader in northern Rwanda during the late 1950s and early 1960s; served on Hutu-Tutsi Study Commission and assumed prominent positions in Kayibanda's postcolonial government before falling out with Kayibanda at end of 1960s.

Bigirumwami, Aloys: indigenous priest, Vicar Apostolic and then Bishop of Nyundo between 1952 and 1973; first African bishop in Belgian Africa; notable for his opposition to ethnicist discourse in Rwandan politics and fears of ethnic division within the church; dedicated later years to exploring Rwanda's traditional culture and religion.

Boutry, Pierre: White Father who served as rector of Nyakibanda Seminary between 1956 and 1958; later served as advisor to Perraudin in Kabgayi; dismissed as rector in part for his failure to resolve growing intra-ethnic disputes and seminarian withdrawals at Nyakibanda.

Bwanakweri, Prosper: Tutsi chief and Abega clan member who broke with Mwami Mutara in the early 1950s; favored Catholic influence in Rwandan society but castigated Hutu movements as divisionist; helped found Rader in 1959; executed by Rwandan government in December 1963.

Bushayija, Stanislas: Tutsi priest, scholar and Superior Council member in the 1950s; known for his sympathies for White Fathers and opposition to Mwami Mutara.

Cerri, Francesco: Italian missionary who arrived in Rwanda in early 1970s; left country in protest over anti-Tutsi violence in his parish during 1973 schools expulsions.

Classe, Léon: French Vicar Apostolic of Rwanda between 1922 and 1945; notable for his efforts to cultivate close ties with Rwanda's monarchy; contributed to hardening of Hutu-Tutsi distinctions and led Rwandan Catholic Church during its period of fastest growth.

Dejemeppe, Arthur: served as editor of *Kinyamateka*, vicar general and administrator of Kabgayi vicariate in early 1950s; notable for his political advocacy for Mutara's rivals like Kayibanda and Bwanakweri; White Fathers decided in 1955 to appoint Perraudin rather than Dejemeppe as Vicar Apostolic in part due to the latter's reputation as a political partisan.

Déprimoz, Laurent: French Vicar Apostolic of Kabgayi between 1945 and 1955; focused on strengthening pastoral formation after the mass conversions of the 1930s; political moderate who lacked Classe's close relations with Mwami Mutara but did not advocate strongly on social justice questions; strong supporter of indigenous clergy.

Durrieu, Louis: Superior General of the White Fathers in the late 1940s and early 1950s; notable for his paternalist attitudes toward Africans and relatively conservative politics.

Gahamanyi, Jean-Baptiste: Tutsi priest and later bishop of Astrida/Butare between 1962 and 1999; defended Perraudin before U.N. Commission in 1960; notable for his staunch support for post-colonial Hutu governments and strong opposition to UNAR exiles (which included his brother Michel Kayihura).

Gasabwoya, Innocent: Tutsi vicar general of Kabgayi under Perraudin in late 1950s and 1960s; maintained good working relationships with both Perraudin and Bigirumwami; killed during 1994 genocide.

Gashugi, Justin: conservative Tutsi chief who served on Hutu-Tutsi Study Commission in the spring of 1958; opposed idea of appointing Hutu representatives to the Superior Council and dismissed Hutu representatives as divisionists.

Gasore, Louis: Tutsi vicar general of Nyundo under Bigirumwami throughout 1950s and 1960s; prominent writer who propagated Tutsi nationalist vision; later accused by some missionaries of funneling money to UNAR exiles; killed during 1994 genocide.

Gitera, Joseph: devout Catholic leader of Aprosoma; his incendiary political and ethnicist rhetoric helped lay the ideological groundwork for the Hutu uprisings which broke out in November 1959; split with Kayibanda and Parmehutu in the 1960s and retired from politics.

Habyarimana, Juvenal: Hutu native of Gisenyi in northwestern Rwanda who served as head of military defense under Kayibanda; overthrew Kayibanda in bloodless *coup d'état* in July 1973, becoming president of Rwanda's Second Republic; initially adopted pan-ethnic rhetoric before scapegoating Tutsi in early 1990s to rally flagging political support; the shooting down of his plane on April 6, 1994 triggered 1994 genocide.

Harroy, Jean-Paul: Belgian colonial governor of Rwanda-Burundi between 1955 and 1962; initially suspected by many missionaries for his leftist political leanings; possessed complex views of Hutu-Tutsi question but came out in favor of Hutu social movement in late 1958; retired from Rwanda after independence in 1962 but remained a hero for post-colonial Hutu leaders.

Hirth, Jean-Joseph: White Father who led first missionary caravan to Rwanda in 1899–1900 and served as region's Vicar Apostolic until 1920; notable for his concern with avoiding political entanglements of all kinds, respecting Rwanda's traditional leaders, and encouraging evangelization among the peasant masses.

Kagame, Alexis: Tutsi priest, scholar, and close advisor to Mwami Mutara Rudahigwa; one of the great twentieth century African intellectuals notable for his contributions to African philosophy & theology; served as editor of *Kinyamateka* during 1940s and early 1950s; historical works propagated Tutsi nationalism and reinforced Abanyiginya clan's claims to royal authority.

Kayibanda, Gregoire: Gitarama native, Hutu seminarian, *évolué*, journalist, and later leader of the *Mouvement Social Muhutu*, a political party dedicated to the empowerment of Hutu in Rwandan society and government; served as president of Rwanda between independence in 1962 and his toppling in a 1973 *coup d'état*; died suspiciously under house arrest in 1976.

Kayihura, Michel: Tutsi chief and vice-president of the Superior Council during late 1950s; exile leader of UNAR during 1960s; brother of Gahamanyi; lobbied Vatican against Perraudin and White Fathers in early 1960s.

Kigeli V (Jean-Baptiste) Ndahindurwa: half-brother of Mutara appointed Mwami by royal *biru* after Mutara's death in July 1959; arrived in office with reputation as youthful, devout Catholic and reforming Tutsi chief; closely associated with UNAR by end of 1959; accused of acquiescing in torture and targeted assassinations of Hutu leaders during November 1959 uprisings; forced out of Rwanda in June 1960 after Parmehutu electoral victories; deposed in popular referendum in September 1961.

Lavigerie, Charles: French archbishop of Algiers/Carthage in North Africa and nineteenth-century founder of the Missionaries of Africa or White Fathers; his commitments to top-down evangelization, cultural indigenization, and Christian civilization left lasting marks on White Father pastoral strategy.

Logiest, Guy: military and then civil resident of Rwanda between 1959 and 1962; helped quell November 1959 uprisings; his decision to replace exiled Tutsi chiefs with hundreds of Hutu chiefs and sub-chiefs was one of the most important political decisions of the period; strong partisan for Catholic civilization and Hutu democracy; gave tacit approval to *coup d'état* of Gitarama in January 1961.

Makarakiza, André: Burundian priest appointed as first African professor at Nyakibanda Major Seminary in 1958; resented at various times by both Rwandan Hutu and Rwandan Tutsi; appointed bishop of Gitega in Burundi in 1961; failed to critique Burundian government during 1972 genocide of Hutu.

Manyurane, Bernard: first Hutu priest to study abroad in Rome; appointed as first Rwandan seminary professor at Nyakibanda in 1959; named first bishop of Ruhengeri in January 1961; fell ill in February 1961 after apparent poisoning; died in Rome in May 1961.

Mbandiwimfura, Deogratias: first Tutsi priest to study in Europe in late 1940s and early 1950s; later named professor and spiritual director at Nyakibanda; independent figure, but generally seen as ideological ally of Tutsi nationalists and UNAR.

Mbonyumutwa, Dominique: rare Hutu sub-chief during the 1950s; served in leadership of Kayibanda's Parmehutu party; his beating by UNAR youths on November 1, 1959 helped precipitate Hutu uprisings; served as Rwanda's first president during 1961 and in Parmehutu government until his expulsion from party in 1968.

Misago, Augustin: Bishop of Gikongoro in late 1980s and 1990s; accused of failing to protect Tutsi in his diocese during 1994 genocide; his 2000 trial became a symbol of church-state tensions in postgenocide Rwanda.

Mosmans, Guy: Belgian provincial for the White Fathers in the late 1950s; exercised significant political influence on Belgian colonial policy in Rwanda and Burundi; favored establishment of Hutu democracy after 1958.

Mulindahabi, Calliope: Gitarama native who played major role in Hutu social movement of late 1950s; former Catholic seminarian who also served as Perraudin's personal secretary in the late 1950s; served on Hutu-Tutsi Study Commission in 1958; key political advisor to Gregoire Kayibanda in 1960s.

Munyangaju, Aloys: Hutu journalist and later minister in post-colonial government; major propagandist for Hutu social movement in late 1950s as editorial writer for the White Fathers' newspaper *Temps Nouveaux d'Afrique*; early leader of Aprosoma party; remained close ally of Kayibanda until fallout over government corruption in 1968–1969.

Musinga: Rwanda's mwami between 1897 and 1931; came to power after violent intra-clan feud following Rwabugiri's death; skilled politician who utilized German soldiers and Catholic missionaries to pacify outlying regions; never showed serious interest in the Christian faith, leading to growing opposition from Classe; increasingly marginalized in 1920s before Belgians exiled him in 1931.

Mutara Rudahigwa: son of Musinga who was appointed Mwami after 1931 Belgian *coup d'état*; a Catholic convert, he dedicated his country to Christ the King in 1946 before falling out with Belgian and missionary leaders in the 1950s; ended traditional practices of *ubuhake* and *uburetwa*; died in Burundi under suspicious circumstances in July 1959.

Ndazaro, Lazare: ally of Bwanakweri who supported missionary influence in Rwandan society and helped start Rader in 1959; executed by Rwandan government in December 1963.

Ndahoruburiye, Matthieu: Tutsi priest named as first indigenous rector of Nyakibanda major seminary in April 1961; later served as rector of St. Joseph Major Seminary in Nyundo between 1963 and 1973; forced out of Rwanda during Tutsi seminary and schools expulsions of 1973.

Nikwigize, Phocas: Hutu priest named Bishop of Ruhengeri in 1968; known for his strong anti-Tutsi views and theories of a "double genocide" in 1994; exiled in Congo between 1994 and 1996 before disappearing near the Rwandan border in November 1996.

Nothomb, Dominic: influential White Father writer and spiritual director who served as a liaison between Perraudin and Bigirumwami; penned influential political analysis in 1958 claiming that Hutu and Tutsi were distinct racial categories.

Nsengiyumva, Thadée: Hutu priest named in 1989 to succeed Perraudin as Bishop of Kabgayi; strong critic of ethnicism and corruption within Catholic Church and Rwandan government; assassinated in June 1994 by RPF soldiers.

Nsengiyumva, Vincent: Hutu priest from northern Rwanda who replaced Bigirumwami as Bishop of Nyundo in 1974; succeeded Perraudin as Archbishop of Kigali in 1976; notable for his close relations with President Habyarimana; served as personal confessor to Habyarimana's wife Agathe; served on the central committee for the MRND ruling party until 1990; killed along with T. Nsengiyumva in June 1994.

Perraudin, André: Swiss native and White Father born in 1914 and ordained priest in 1939; served as Nyakibanda professor and rector between 1950 and 1956; served as Vicar Apostolic and then Archbishop of Kabgayi between 1956 and 1989; controversial for his linking of ethnicity with social justice and his support of Rwanda's post-colonial Hutu governments.

Preud'homme, André: Belgian resident in Rwanda in late 1950s; known for his sympathy for Catholic missions; replaced by Logiest in December 1959, precipitating further divisions between Belgium and local Rwandan elites.

Rwabugiri: ruled as Rwanda's Mwami between early 1860s and 1895; notable for propagating major expansion of Rwandan kingdom through military conquests; Hutu-Tutsi identities hardened during final years of his rule.

Seumois, Xavier: Belgian White Father who served as rector of Nyakibanda Seminary in late 1940s and early 1950s; failed to manage the nationalist tensions that enveloped Nyakibanda in 1951–1952; his 1952 reassignment led to the appointment of André Perraudin as rector.

Sibomana, André: influential Hutu Catholic priest, journalist and human rights crusader who served as editor of *Kinyamateka* in late 1980s and early 1990s;

exerted strong influence on T. Nsengiyumva; later appointed as administrator of Kabgayi diocese after genocide; died in Rwanda in 1998 after RPF government failed to give him a visa to seek medical care in Europe.

Sibomana, Joseph: Hutu priest who served as superior of Save mission during the November 1959 uprisings; named Bishop of Ruhengeri in October 1961; issued episcopal condemnation of Byumba massacres in April 1962; known for his political moderation; transferred to Kibungo in eastern Rwanda in late 1960s; died in 1999.

Sigismondi, Pierre Cardinal: apostolic delegate to Belgian Congo, Rwanda and Burundi who later served as secretary for Propaganda Fide during late 1950s and early 1960s; skeptical toward White Fathers politics inside Rwanda.

Van Hoof, Alphonse: regional superior for the White Fathers in late 1950s and early 1960s, overseeing missions in Rwanda and Burundi; briefly considered for position of Vicar Apostolic of Kabgayi in 1955; Van Hoof's voluminous correspondence is notable for its detailed descriptions of Rwanda's violence and pro-Parmehutu social analysis.

Volker, Leo: Superior General of the White Fathers in the late 1950s and early 1960s; adapted an increasingly anti-Tutsi and anti-UNAR position as the Rwandan revolution progressed between 1959 and 1962; notable for his staunch opposition to communism.

Notes

ACKNOWLEDGMENTS

1. Cf. J.J. Carney, "Waters of Baptism, Blood of Tribalism?" *African Ecclesial Review* 50, 1–2 (2008): 9–30.

INTRODUCTION

1. Quoted in J.J. Kritzinger, "The Rwandan Tragedy as Public Indictment of Christian Mission," *Missionalia* 24:3 (1996): 345.
2. In the words of Nigel Eltringham, "the genocide occurred because of a perception of racial difference" (Nigel Eltringham, *Accounting for Horror: Post-Genocide Debates in Rwanda* (London: Pluto Press, 2004), 33). Eltringham in turn blames colonial anthropology for teaching Rwandans to see the Hutu-Tutsi distinction as a "hard, constructed, mono-dimensional racial distinction" (33).
3. Cf. Timothy Longman, *Christianity and Genocide in Rwanda* (Cambridge: Cambridge University Press, 2010); Mahmood Mamdani, *When Victims Become Killers: Colonialism, Nativism and the Genocide in Rwanda* (Princeton: Princeton University Press, 2001). Although his argument is more nuanced, Bernard Lugan echoes much of this narrative in *Rwanda: Le Génocide, l'Èglise, et la Démocratie* (Paris: Editions du Rocher, 2004), 31–51.
4. Allison Des Forges, *Defeat is the only bad news: Rwanda under Musinga*. Diss. Yale University, 1972, 99. While my notes will reference Des Forges's original dissertation, this work was recently republished by University of Wisconsin Press (Allison Des Forges, *Defeat is the Only Bad News: Rwanda under Musinga*, ed. David S. Newbury (Madison: University of Wisconsin Press, 2011)).
5. Catherine Newbury, "Ethnicity and the Politics of History in Rwanda," *Africa Today* 45:1 (1998): 9, 14–15.
6. Ian Linden with Jane Linden, *Church and Revolution in Rwanda* (Manchester: University of Manchester Press, 1977), 220.

7. Emmanuel Katongole, *A Future for Africa: Critical Essays in Christian Social Imagination* (Scranton: University of Scranton Press, 2005), xiii–xvi.

8. Linden, *Church and Revolution*, 245.

CHAPTER 1

1. The following narrative draws on Justin Kalibwami, *Le Catholicisme et la société Rwandaise 1900–1962* (Paris: Présence Africaine, 1991), 47–60; Filip Reyntjens, *Pouvoir et droit au Rwanda: droit public et évolution politique, 1916–1973* (Tervuren, Belgium: Musée royal de l'Afrique centrale, 1985), 26–30; Mahmood Mamdani, *When Victims Become Killers*, 41–75; Fortunatus Rudakemwa, *L'évangélisation du Rwanda 1900–1959* (Paris: L'Harmattan, 2005), 23–30; John Iliffe, *Africans: The History of a Continent* (Cambridge: Cambridge University Press, 1994), 106–109; Jan Vansina, *Antecedents to Modern Rwanda: The Nyaginya Kingdom* (Madison: University of Wisconsin Press, 2003), 198; Alison Des Forges, *Defeat is the only bad news: Rwanda under Musinga 1896–1931*, Diss. Yale University, 1972, 1–4.

2. This narrative will largely focus on Hutu and Tutsi, but Rwanda also contains a third ethnic or social group, the pygmy Twa. Twa have lived in Rwanda for several thousand years, residing in the northwestern mountains, western forests, and in the environs of the royal court. They have remained the most endogamous ethnic community in Rwanda, numbering around 1% of Rwanda's total population. There are exceptions to the broad historiographical tendency to ignore the Twa community. For example, Josias Semujanga views the transition from "Munyarwanda tripolarity" to "Hutu-Tutsi bipolarity" as the key turn in the formation of genocidal discourse, as Rwanda's traditional tri-linear system became a "dualistic vision contrasting friend and foe" (Josias Semujanga, *Origins of Rwandan Genocide* (Amherst, NY: Humanity, 2003), 77–81).

3. Cf. Louis de Lacger and Pierre Nothomb, *Ruanda* (Kabgayi: 1961), 56; Léon Classe, "Le Ruanda et ses habitants," *Congo: Revue générale de la Colonie belge I*, no. 5 (1922): 680–81; J.J. Maquet, *The Premises of Inequality in Rwanda* (London: Oxford University Press, 1961), 170.

4. Writing in the late 1930s, De Lacger compared the initial Tutsi conquest to the Germanic invasions of the late Roman world—a political conquest leading to mutual cultural and linguistic mixing (De Lacger, *Ruanda*, 67–68). While his views would change later, Marcel d'Hertefelt wrote in 1960 of the "Tutsi conquest" of central, eastern, and western Rwanda leading to Tutsi monopolization of economic wealth, governmental administration, and political mythology. See M. d'Hertefelt, "Myth and Political Acculturation in Rwanda," in Rhodes Livingstone Institute and Allie A. Dubb, *Myth in Modern Africa; The Fourteenth Conference Proceedings* (1960), 115–19.

5. The following narrative is adapted from Mamdani, *When Victims Become Killers*, 79–80.

6. Bernard Muzungu, "Le problème des races au Rwanda," *Cahiers Lumière et Sociéte* [42] (2009): 61, 67.

7. Jean-Pierre Chrétien, *The Great Lakes of Africa: 2000 Years of History*. Trans. Scott Straus (New York: Zone Books, 2003), 115.

8. On the Hamitic thesis, see Edith R. Sanders, "The Hamitic Hypothesis: its origin and functions in time perspective," *Journal of African History* (1969): 521–32; Paul Rutayisire, "Le Tutsi étranger dans le pays de ses aïeux," *Les Cahiers: Evangile et Société: Les Idéologies* 4 (1996): 42–55. Influential colonial sources include C.G. Seligman, *Races of Africa* (London/New York: Oxford, 1966); John Hanning Speke, *Journal of the Discovery of the Source of the Nile* (Eugene, OR: Resource, 1868, 2007); & Jan Czekanowski, *Investigations in the Area between the Nile and the Congo*. Trans. Frieda Scütze (New Haven, CT: Human Relations Area Files, 1917, 1960).

9. This language is taken from Mamdani, *When Victims Become Killers*, 82. For Mamdani, the Hamitic thesis connected race with the more important issue of indigeneity; the "exotic" origins of the Tutsi would prove most damaging in the post-colonial period. See also Rutayisire, "Le Tutsi étranger dans le pays de ses aïeux," 42–49.

10. De Lacger, *Ruanda*, 56. As early as the First Vatican Council in 1869–1870, Catholic leaders appealed to missionaries going to Central Africa to "alleviate the ancient malediction weighing on the shoulders of the misfortunate Hamites inhabiting the hopeless Nigricy" (quoted in Tharcisse Gatwa, *The Churches and Ethnic Ideology in the Rwandan Crises, 1900–1994* (Milton Keynes: Paternoster, 2005, 65–66)).

11. Léon Classe, "Le Ruanda et ses habitants," 680.

12. Marcel d'Hertefelt, *Les anciens royaumes de la zone interlacustre méridionale Rwanda, Burundi, Buha* (Tervuren, Belgium: Musée royal de l'Afrique centrale, 1962), 18.

13. Stefaan Minnaert, "Les Pères Blancs et la société rwandaise durant l'époque coloniale allemande (1900–1916). Une rencontre entre cultures et religions," 10. I am working from a manuscript version of this article, but it can also be consulted under the same title in *Les Religions au Rwanda, défis, convergences, et competitions, Actes du Colloque International du 18–19 septembre 2008 Butare/ Huye*, eds. Paul Rutayisire, J.P. Schreibner, and Deogratias Byanafashe (Butare, Rwanda: Université Nationale du Rwanda, 2009), 53–101.

14. In the early 1990s, Hutu Power advocates like Col. Leon Mugesera and Ferdinand Nahimana argued that the Tutsi were rapacious foreigners who should be sent back to Ethiopia via the Akagera River. A noted historian, Nahimana helped organize the infamous *Radiotélévision libre des Mille collines* (RTLM) that helped to sustain genocidal rhetoric during April, May and June 1994. On the radicalization of ethnic discourse in the early 1990s, see Longman, *Christianity and Genocide*, 163–86 and Marie-Beatrice Umutesi, *Surviving the Slaughter: The*

Ordeal of a Rwandan Refugee in Zaire. (Madison: University of Wisconsin Press, 2004), 17–44.

15. Cf. J. J. Maquet, *The Premise of Inequality*; Helen Codere, *Biography of an African Society, Rwanda 1900-1960* (Tervuren: Musée Royal de l'Afrique Centrale, 1973); René Lemarchand, *Rwanda and Burundi* (New York: Praeger, 1970); Luc de Heusch, *Le Rwanda et la civilisation interlacustre* (Brussels: Université Libre de Bruxelles, 1966). For a later critique of utilizing "caste" language outside of South Asia, see David M. Todd, "Caste in Africa?" *Africa* 47.4 (1977): 398–412.

16. This section draws on Marcel d'Hertefelt, *Les clans du Rwanda ancien: Eléments ethnosociologie et d'ethnohistoire* (Tervuren: Musée royal de l'Afrique centrale, 1971); Linden, *Church and Revolution in Rwanda;* Claudine Vidal, "Colonisation et décolonisation du Rwanda: La question tutsi-hutu," *Revue française d'études politiques africaines* 91 (1973): 32–47.

17. There is an enormous literature on the roots of ethnic discourse. Relevant secondary works include Aidan Southall, "The Illusion of Tribe," *Journal of Asian and African Studies* 5.1/2 (1970): 28–50; Leo Kuper, *The Pity of It All: Polarisation of Racial and Ethnic Relations* (Minneapolis: University of Minnesota Press, 1977); Donald L. Horowitz, *Ethnic Groups in Conflict* (Berkeley: University of California Press, 1985); M. Crawford Young, "Nationalism, Class, and Ethnicity in Africa: A Retrospective," *Cahiers d'Études Africaines* 26.3 (1986): 421–95; Leroy Vail, ed., *The Creation of Tribalism in Southern Africa* (Berkeley: Univ. of California, 1989); Thomas H. Eriksen, "Ethnicity, race and nation," in *The Ethnicity Reader: Nationalism, Multiculturalism, and Migration*, eds. Montserrat Guibernau and John Rex (Cambridge: Polity, 1997), 33–42; Jean-Pierre Chrétien and Gerard Prunier, eds., *Les Ethnies ont une histoire* (Paris: Karthala, 2003); Nigel Eltringham, *Accounting for Horror: Post-Genocide Debates in Rwanda* (London: Pluto Press, 2004), 6–33.

18. In his widely read journalistic account of the Rwandan genocide, Philip Gourevitch describes Hutu and Tutsi in largely socioeconomic terms; cf. Philip Gourevitch, *We Wish to Inform You that Tomorrow We Will Be Killed with Our Families: Stories from Rwanda* (New York: Farrar, Straus, and Giroux, 1998). On the need to distinguish Hutu-Tutsi language from social class language, see Kalibwami, *Le Catholicisme*, 58–59; Minnaert, "Les Pères Blancs et la société rwandaise," 10.

19. Johan Pottier, *Re-Imagining Rwanda: Conflict, Survival and Disinformation in the Late Twentieth Century* (Cambridge: Cambridge University Press, 2002), 116. In an often contentious dialogue with Jean-Pierre Chrétien, René Lemarchand has voiced a similar perspective over the past two decades, arguing that "European prejudice and misperception" alone cannot explain the recurrent massacres of Tutsi and Hutu in either Rwanda or Burundi (cf. R. Lemarchand, *Burundi: Ethnocide as Discourse and Practice* (Washington, DC: Woodrow Wilson, 1994), xv). For similar perspectives, see Kalibwami, *Le Catholicisme*; Rudakemwa, *L'évangélisation*.

20. Bernard Lugan, *Rwanda: Le Génocide, l'Église, et la Démocratie* (Paris: Editions du Rocher, 2004), 23. Lugan cites genetic evidence to support a "morphological" distinction between Hutu and Tutsi even as he argues that Hutu and Tutsi share a common cultural and national background. "We are in the presence of two peoples, of distinct origins, living on the same territory and constituting one nation" (217). See also Pierre Erny, "'Races' et 'ethnie' au Rwanda selon l'historien Bernard Lugan," *Dialogue* 235 (2004): 3–14.

21. Cf. Joseph Gahama and Augustin Mvuyekure, "Jeu ethnique, idéologie missionnaire et politique coloniale: Le cas du Burundi," in Chrétien and Prunier, *Les Ethnies ont une histoire*, 303–13. For Mvuyekure, the great error of missionary discourse was that Hutu and Tutsi "socio-professional categories...were fixed, ossified in 'races,' in 'ethnicities.'" (Augustin Mvuyekure, "Idéologie missionnaire et classification ethnique en Afrique centrale," in *Les Ethnies ont une histoire*, 321).

22. A longtime scholar at the University of Burundi, Chrétien's writings on the Great Lakes region are voluminous. His overarching views are found in English translation in *The Great Lakes of Africa* (2003). For his specific approach to the Hutu-Tutsi question in Rwanda, see J.P. Chrétien, "Hutu et Tutsi au Rwanda et au Burundi," in *Au coeur de l'ethnie: Ethnie, tribalisme et État en Afrique*, eds. Jean-Loup Amselle and Elikia M'Bokolo (Paris: La Découverte, 1999), 129–66. Similar perspectives can be found in Mamdani, *When Victims Become Killers;* Gourevitch, *We Wish to Inform You*; Emmanuel Katongole, *A Future for Africa* (Scranton, PA: University of Scranton Press, 2005), 95–117.

23. Cf. Bernard Muzungu, "Le problème des races au Rwanda," 51; See also Jean-Loup Amselle and Elikia M'Bokolo's influential *Au coeur de l'ethnie*. For Amselle and M'Bokolo, terms like Hutu and Tutsi are politicized labels that must be understood in specific historical contexts (Amselle and M'Bokolo, *Au coeur de l'ethnie*, ii). They reject "ethnic" language as a colonial construct to classify and homogenize African peoples and see pre-colonial identity as much more fluid and multivalent (cf. J.L. Amselle, "Ethnies et espaces: pour une anthropologie topologique," in Amselle and M'Bokolo, *Au cœur de l'ethnie*, 11–48).

24. For an overview of eighteenth and nineteenth-century Rwandan history, see Vansina's *Antecedents to Modern Rwanda*. Vansina argues that the meaning of Hutu and Tutsi shifted over time, but he also thinks that Hutu-Tutsi tensions predated European arrival. For similar perspectives, see Des Forges, *Defeat is the only bad news*, 8–16; Mamdani, *When Victims Become Killers*, 69–72; Catherine Newbury, *The Cohesion of Oppression: Clientship and Ethnicity in Rwanda 1860–1960* (New York: Columbia University Press, 1988), 207–9; Reyntjens, *Pouvoir et Droit*, 23–30.

25. Centre Lavigerie, Kigali (C.M.L.), Joseph Ntamahungiro, "Eglise Catholique du Rwanda: De la Spiritualité au Prophétisme" (2000): 5. Vansina notes that Hutu was originally a "demeaning term that alluded to rural boorishness or loutish

behavior" and was applied to servants and foreigners but not initially to farmers (Vansina, *Antecedents to Modern Rwanda*, 134). Even Chrétien concurs on
this point. "The term Hutu meant, in the clientage relationship, the subordinate position of the recipient: even if the recipient was Tutsi, the donor spoke
of him as 'my Hutu.' In Rwanda, the term 'Tutsi' little by little was perceived as
an identity closely related to power" (Chrétien, *Great Lakes of Africa*, 190).

26. *Ubuhake* was a patron-client relationship in which the client (*garagu*) offered
his services in exchange for the patron's (*shebuja*) protection and usage of land
and cattle. The client retained full ownership rights over milk, new male calves,
and the meat and skin of deceased cows. The patron also provided for the client's family after death. Client service included accompanying the patron on
trips, working fields, and keeping nightwatch. The patron could also choose
to extend the *ubuhake* relationship to a deceased client's heirs. The clientage
system existed among Tutsi, although it was rare for a Tutsi *garagu* to enter into
relationship with a Hutu *shebuja*. First instituted under Mwami Rwabugiri,
uburetwa required the Hutu client to devote two of every five days to working
his Tutsi patron's land. During the 1920s, the Belgians reduced this rate to
two days per week and made further exceptions for government and mission
workers; the work requirements became more onerous however. Significantly,
only Hutu were required to perform *uburetwa* service. On the roots and evolution of *ubuhake* and *uburetwa*, see Vansina, *Antecedents to Modern Rwanda*, 135–
36; Reyntjens, *Pouvoir et Droit*, 134–42, 206–8; Rutayisire, *La Christianisation
du Rwanda*, 140–47; Linden, *Church and revolution*, 228; Maquet, *Premise of
Inequality*, 129–31.

27. Vansina, *Antecedents to Modern Rwanda*, 137–38. According to Vansina, Hutu
uprisings in eastern and northwestern Rwanda were directed against the
Nyiginya kingdom and its notables but also took on an increasing anti-Tutsi
caste. "The 1897 uprising is particularly significant because it proves without
any ambiguity not only that the population at this time was conscious of a great
divide between Tutsi and Hutu, but also that the antagonism between these two
social categories had already broken into the open. One can therefore summar-
ily reject the views of those who attribute the distinction between Tutsi and Hutu
as well as the engendering of their mutual hostility to each other to the first
Europeans" (138). Paul Rutayisire challenges this thesis, arguing that Vansina
is inappropriately extrapolating a regional conflict to the entire nation (Paul
Rutayisire, "Review of *J.J. Carney, From Democratization to Ethnic Revolution;
Catholic Politics in Rwanda, 1950–1962*" (Butare, Rwanda: [n.p.], 2012), 2).

28. Cf. Linden, *Church and Revolution in Rwanda*, 16–20; Vansina, *Antecedents to
Modern Rwanda*, 134–39. Danielle de Lame agrees that in the 19th century the
term "Hutu" conveyed a general sense of "submissiveness" but argues that
this "had not yet crystallized into a collective identity" (Danielle de Lame,
A Hill among a Thousand: Transformations and Ruptures in Rural Rwanda

(Madison: University of Wisconsin Press, 2005), 48). Even a strident critic of colonial anthropology like Bernardin Muzungu implies the hierarchical and political dimensions of precolonial Hutu-Tutsi labels. While emphasizing the fluidity of *kwihutura* (changing social status), Muzungu admits that "this set-back [becoming Hutu] could be the result of simple misfortune, dispossession or even confiscation of cows by one's patron (*kunyagwa*) or by foreign aggressors in war, or even as a result of famine or cattle epidemics like rinderpest" (Bernardin Muzungu, "Le problème des races au Rwanda," 54).

29. Gatwa, *The Churches and Ethnic Ideology*, 5.
30. Reyntjens, *Pouvoir et droit*, 22.
31. See here David Newbury, *The Land Beyond the Mists: Essays on Identity and Authority in Precolonial Congo and Rwanda* (Athens, OH: Ohio University Press, 2009), 326–29. Building on the research of Jean-François Saucier, Newbury argues that only 10–15 percent of Rwandans were involved in *ubuhake* relationships in the late 19th century. For Newbury, *ubuhake* was designed to build alliances between elite Tutsi rather than as a means of connecting Tutsi nobles with Hutu peasants. *Ubuhake* was not universal, primordial, or exclusively hierarchical, and it was not a "pervasive cultural institution in precolonial Rwanda" (329).
32. As Chrétien notes, clans are Rwanda's oldest social structures, "combining kinship, exogamy, shared symbols, and rules of solidarity" (Chrétien, *Great Lakes*, 88; see also Gahama and Mvuyekure, "Jeu ethnique," 308–9). This does not mean that Rwanda's eighteen clans were not subject to similar ideological influences. See here David Newbury, "The Clans of Rwanda: An Historical Hypothesis," *Africa* 50.4 (1980): 389–403 which shows how royal political ideology shaped pre-colonial clan membership.
33. Catherine Newbury, "Ethnicity and the Politics of History in Rwanda," *Africa Today* 45:1 (1998): 11.
34. Nor does the current Rwandan government's decision to ban Hutu-Tutsi terms in public discourse necessarily resolve the problem. As René Lemarchand has argued in the Burundian context, "By abolishing ethnic otherness as a socially relevant term of reference, Tutsi regimes [in Burundi] removed the critical issue of ethnic hegemony and discrimination from the realm of legitimate debate" (Lemarchand, *Burundi: Ethnocide as Discourse and Practice*, 32).
35. Mamdani, *When Victims Become Killers*, 52.
36. Newbury, *Land Beyond the Mists*, 298, 300. For a similar argument which emphasizes ethnicity as a "contextually configured" identity rather than as either "primordial" or "invented," see David Newbury and Catherine Newbury, "A Catholic Mass in Kigali: Contested Views of the Genocide and Ethnicity in Rwanda," *Canadian Journal of African Studies* 33.2–3 (1999): 292–94.
37. Cf. Jean-François Bayart, *The Illusion of Cultural Identity* (Chicago: University of Chicago Press, 2005), 92. As Chrétien notes, the point is not "to deny how old this cleavage is…but to understand why this cleavage has become so

obsessive to the point of eclipsing every other problem" (Chrétien, *Great Lakes of Africa*, 281–82). See also Claudine Vidal, "Situations ethniques au Rwanda," in Amselle and M'Bokolo, *Au coeur de l'ethnie*, 184.

CHAPTER 2

1. The Catholic historian Adrian Hastings described Lavigerie as "the most outstanding Catholic missionary strategist of the 19th century" (Adrian Hastings, *The Church in Africa 1450–1950* (Oxford: Clarendon, 1994), 254). The first three African bishops and first two African cardinals were all trained in White Father seminaries. By the 1960s, the White Fathers had evangelized one-sixth of African territory and helped form one-quarter of Catholic Christians on the continent (John Baur, *2000 Years of Christianity in Africa: An African History 62-1992* (Nairobi: Paulines Publications, 1994), 187).

2. Paul Rutayisire, *La christianisation du Rwanda (1900–1945): Méthode missionnaire et politique selon Mgr Léon Classe* (Fribourg: Éditions Universitaires Fribourg Suisse, 1987), 53. The metaphor is further developed in Alison des Forges, "Kings without Crowns: the White Fathers in Rwanda," in *Eastern African History*, eds. Daniel McCall, Norman Bennett, and Jeffrey Butler (New York: Praeger, 1969), 176–207.

3. On Lavigerie's life, see François Renault, *Cardinal Lavigerie: Churchman, Prophet, Missionary*, trans. John O'Donohue (London/Atlantic Highlands, NJ: Athlone Press, 1994). On nineteenth-century French church history, see Adrien Dansette and John Dingle, *Religious History of Modern France* (New York: Herder and Herder, 1961); Ralph Gibson, *A Social History of French Catholicism 1789–1914* (New York/London: Routledge, 1989); Mary Heimann, "Catholic revivalism in worship and devotion," in *The Cambridge History of Christianity VIII—World Christianities c. 1815–914*, eds. Sheridan Gilley and Brian Stanley (Cambridge: Cambridge University Press, 2006), 70–83.

4. Stefaan Minnaert, *Premier Voyage de Mgr Hirth au Rwanda, Novembre 1899—Février 1900: Contribution à l'étude de la fondation de l'église catholique au Rwanda* (Kigali: Les Editions Rwandaises, 2006), 205. The early modern period of mission history can be dated from Portugal and Spain's late fifteenth-century explorations to the suppression of the Jesuits in 1773.

5. On African mission history, see Ogbu Kalu, *African Christianity: An African Story* (Trenton, NJ: Africa World Press, 2007); Adrian Hastings, *The Church in Africa 1450–1950*; Elizabeth Isichei, *A History of Christianity in Africa: From Antiquity to the Present* (Grand Rapids, MI: Eerdmans, 1995); Bengt Sundkler and Christopher Steed, *The History of the Church in Africa* (Cambridge: Cambridge University Press, 2000); Baur, *2000 Years of Christianity in Africa*. Next to the White Fathers, the Spiritans were likely the most important missionary congregation in colonial Africa, especially on the East and West African coasts. On the

Spiritans, see Henry J. Koren, *To the Ends of the Earth: A General History of the Congregation of the Holy Ghost* (Pittsburgh: Duquesne University Press, 1983); Paul V. Kollman, *The Evangelization of Slaves and Catholic Origins in East Africa* (Maryknoll, NY: Orbis, 2005).

6. Renault, *Cardinal Lavigerie*, 67–70.

7. For an early account of Lavigerie's work in North Africa, see Marc Fournel, *La Tunisie. Le Christianisme et l'Islam dans l'Afrique septentrionale* (Paris: Challamel, 1886), 161–75.

8. Quoted in Renault, *Cardinal Lavigerie*, 153.

9. Ibid., 427.

10. General Archives of the Missionaries of Africa, Rome (hereafter A.G.M.Afr.), *Lettres de Mgr Lavigerie à la Congrégation de la Propagation de la Foi*, n°10, 1 December 1869. I am grateful to Stefaan Minnaert for sharing this letter with me.

11. Charles Lavigerie and Xavier de Montclos, *Le Cardinal Lavigerie: La Mission Universelle de L'Église* (Paris: Cerf, 1991), 94. See also Renault, *Cardinal Lavigerie*, 107–8.

12. See here A.G.M.Afr., *Lettres de Mgr Lavigerie à la Congrégation de la Propagation de la Foi*, n°10, 1 December 1869. Minnaert sees Lavigerie's "French spirit" as bordering on "chauvinistic patriotism." Even after the initial internationalization of the Missionaries of Africa in the 1880s and 1890s, the congregation remained 60% French in 1900 (S. Minnaert, *Premier Voyage de Mgr Hirth*, 100).

13. See the first-person testimonials about Lavigerie in "À la mémoire du Cardinal Lavigerie a Carthage et a Bayonne," *Bulletin de la Société antiesclavagiste de France* (1895): 34–42.

14. Lavigerie and Montclos, *Le Cardinal Lavigerie*, 94.

15. Ibid., 104.

16. Lavigerie quickly realized the importance of the mission's medical component, instructing his first missionaries in 1868 to learn enough about medicine to be able to treat their Arab patients (cf. A.G.M.Afr., *Lettres de Mgr Lavigerie à la Congrégation de la Propagation de la Foi*, n°10, 1 December 1869).

17. Lavigerie and Montclos, *Le Cardinal Lavigerie*, 103. The legacy of the seventeenth-century Jansenist controversy remained with the nineteenth-century French missions. Lavigerie constantly warned his zealous missionaries against the "Jansenist" temptations of rigorism and perfectionism. For an accessible introduction to Jansenism, see William Doyle, *Jansenism: Catholic Resistance to Authority from the Reformation to the French Revolution* (New York: St. Martin's Press, 2000). The most thorough study can be found in Jacques Gres-Gayer's *Jansénism en Sorbonne: 1643–1656* (Paris: Klincksieck, 1996) and *D'un jansénisme à l'autre: chroniques de Sorbonne (1696–1713)* (Paris: Nolin, 2007).

18. Lavigerie, "Premières instructions aux Pères Blancs de l'Afrique équatoriale (1878)," in Lavigerie and Hamman, *Écrits d'Afrique*, 154.

19. "Polygamy is not contrary to the natural law, since Moses permitted it, so one should not force the prince to renounce his wives before baptism" (Charles Lavigerie, "Lettre au R.P. Livinhac et aux missionnaires du Nyanza (2)," 1 April 1880, in Charles Lavigerie and A.G. Hamman, *Écrits d'Afrique: Lettres chrétiennes 3*, (Paris: B. Grasset, 1966), 196).

20. This reflected Mutesa's style of politics, a style quite similar to that of Rwanda's Mwami Musinga in the early 1900s. As John Rowe writes, "Mutesa ruled by means of a balancing of interest groups, rather than awarding any one exclusive power and privilege" (John Rowe, "Mutesa and the Missionaries: Church and State in Pre-colonial Buganda," in *Christian Missionaries and the State in the Third World*, eds. Holger B. Hansen and Michael Twaddle (Athens, OH: James Currey/Ohio University Press, 2002), 63).

21. On the Buganda missions, see Rowe, "Mutesa and the Missionaries"; Holger B. Hansen, *Mission, Church and State in a Colonial Setting: Uganda 1890–1925* (London: Heinemann, 1984), 6–17; Hastings, *Church in Africa*, 375–381, 391–395; J.F. Faupel, *African Holocaust: The Story of the Uganda Martyrs* (New York: P.J. Kennedy, 1962); M. Louise Pirouet, *Black Evangelists: The Spread of Christianity in Uganda 1891–1914* (London: Rex Collings, 1978).

22. Hastings, *Church in Africa*, 419.

23. At the time of Lavigerie's 1892 death, there were 234 Missionaries of Africa. By 1900 there were over 470, and the congregation would nearly double to include 900 missionaries in 1914 (cf. Minnaert, *Premier Voyage de Mgr Hirth*, 104; Aylward Shorter, *Cross and Flag in Africa: The "White Fathers" during the Colonial Scramble, 1892–1914* (Maryknoll, NY: Orbis Books, 2006), 235).

24. Philip Jenkins, *The Next Christendom: The Coming of Global Christianity*. 2nd Ed. (New York: Oxford University Press, 2007), 46. Jenkins notes that the number of African Catholics doubled between 1914 and 1938. In 2000 the African Catholic population stood at 140 million, or roughly 40 percent of the continent's 360 million Christians.

25. On this transitional period in Rwandan history, see Alison L. Des Forges, *Defeat is the only bad news: Rwanda under Musinga, 1896–1931*. Diss. Yale University (1972), 12–26; Justin Kalibwami, *Le Catholicisme et la société rwandaise, 1900–62* (Paris: Présence africaine, 1991), 140–49; David Newbury, *The Land Beyond the Mists: Essays on Identity and Authority in Precolonial Congo and Rwanda* (Athens, OH: Ohio University Press, 2009), 334–35.

26. On the Congress of Berlin and its impact in Africa, see John Iliffe, *Africans: The History of a Continent* (Cambridge: Cambridge University Press, 1994), 189–90. On how Berlin shaped Christian missions, see Hastings, *Church in Africa*, 397–420.

27. Filip Reyntjens, *Pouvoir et droit au Rwanda: Droit public et évolution politique, 1916–1973* (Tervuren: Musée Royale de L'Afrique Centrale, 1985), 95–100.

28. Minnaert notes that the White Fathers' direct overtures to Musinga's court had been rebuffed as late as December 1898. For more on this initial missionary

outreach, see Stefaan Minnaert, "Un regard neuf sur la première fondation des Missionnaires d'Afrique au Rwanda en février 1900," *Histoire et Missions Chrétiennes* 8 (December 2008): 44–53; Des Forges, *Defeat is the only bad news*, 38–40; Kalibwami, *Le Catholicisme*, 151–53.

29. Marcel D'Hertefelt, "Myth and Political Acculturation in Rwanda," in Rhodes Livingstone Institute and Allie A. Dubb, *Myth in Modern Africa; The Fourteenth Conference Proceedings* (1960), 119. For more on this period, see Bernard Lugan, "L'Eglise Catholique au Rwanda 1900-1976," *Etudes Rwandaises* XI (March 1978): 69–70; Claudine Vidal, "Colonisation et décolonisation du Rwanda: La question tutsi-hutu," *Revue française d'études politiques africaines* 91 (1973): 32–33.

30. In the Roman Catholic hierarchy, a "Vicar Apostolic" was considered to be a bishop and member of the episcopate, but he oversaw mission territories that had not yet been classified as local dioceses. Once a mission territory was classified as a diocese, it would be assigned its own local bishop or archbishop (often the same person who was already serving as Vicar Apostolic). This transition happened in Rwanda in 1959.

31. The original motivation for Hirth's journey into Rwanda was a rumor that the Anglicans were about to enter the country under British patronage (cf. Minnaert, *Premier Voyage de Mgr Hirth*, 303).

32. Ibid, 314.

33. Ibid, 393. This in turn gave rise to what the Rwandan historian Paul Rutayisire has called the "stereotype of the completely devout Hutu" (Paul Rutayisire, "Rapports entre l'église Catholique et l'état Rwandais pendant la période colonial," *Cahiers Lumière et Société: Histoire III*, no. 7 (1997): 19).

34. Quoted in Minnaert, *Premiere Voyage de Mgr Hirth*, 291.

35. Gamaliel Mbonimana, "Ethnies et Église catholique: Le remodelage de la société par l'école missionaire (1900–1931)," *Cahiers lumière et société* 1 (1995): 55. Mbonimana criticizes Linden among others for speaking of a "Hutu Church" in the early years of the 20th century, preferring to call this a "poor church."

36. Timothy Longman focuses almost exclusively on the egalitarian dimensions of Brard's ministry (cf. Timothy Longman, *Christianity and Genocide in Rwanda* (Cambridge: Cambridge University Press, 2010), 46–48). For a more critical view that emphasizes Brard's authoritarianism, see Rutayisire, *La christianisation du Rwanda*, 29.

37. Stefaan Minnaert, "Les Peres Blancs et la société rwandaise durant l'époque coloniale allemande (1900–1916). Une rencontre entre cultures et religions," 5, 12. I am working from a manuscript version of this article, but it can also be located under the same title in *Les Religions au Rwanda, défis, convergences, et competitions, Actes du Colloque International du 18–19 septembre 2008 Butare/Huye*, eds. Paul Rutayisire, J.P. Schreibner, and Deo Byanafashe (Butare, Rwanda: Université Nationale du Rwanda, 2009), 53–101. Minnaert's extensive archival research on this era has uncovered the aggressive and often

violent actions of the missionaries, offering a corrective to Ian Linden's ear-
lier account that portrayed the White Fathers in a more defensive posture.
See here Ian Linden (with Jane Linden), *Church and Revolution in Rwanda*
(Manchester: Manchester University Press, 1977), 54.

38. The following narrative draws on Des Forges, *Defeat is the Only Bad News*,
63–78; Linden, *Church and Revolution*, 32–67; Rutayisire, *La Christianisation du
Rwanda*, 63–65; Minnaert, "Les Peres Blancs et la société rwandaise," 13–14.

39. Des Forges, *Defeat is the only bad news*, 99.

40. De Lacger notes that there were only 1,108 baptized Christians in 1905 (cf. Louis
de Lacger (with Pierre Nothomb), *Ruanda* (Kabgayi: 1961), 442).

41. The following section on Rwandan Catholic history before World War I draws
on Jean-Pierre Chrétien, *The Great Lakes of Africa: 2000 Years of History*, trans.
Scot Straus (New York: Zone, 2003), 254; Linden, *Church and Revolution*,
73–113; Des Forges, *Defeat is the only bad news*, 118–126, 177–197; Kalibwami,
Le Catholicisme, 167–69; Minnaert, "Les Peres Blancs et la société rwandaise,"
12–19; Rutayisire, *La Christianisation du Rwanda*, 23.

42. Centre Missionnaire Lavigerie, Kigali, Rwanda (C.M.L.), Léon Classe, "Batutsi
et Bahutu," [c. 1905–1906], 184. Rutayisire, *La christianisation du Rwanda*,
30–31, 92.

43. C.M.L., Léon Clase, "Batutsi et Bahutu," 185–86. See also Rutayisire, *La christianisation du Rwanda*, 10–11, 41, 49.

44. Kandt quoted in De Lacger, *Ruanda*, 426.

45. Minnaert, "Les Pères Blancs et la société rwandaise," 12. Shorter notes that
Loupias was the only White Father to suffer a violent death in Africa during
the entire 1892–1914 period (Shorter, *Cross and Flag*, 115). As Minnaert argues,
this may have stemmed from the fact that Loupias had been involved in violent
pacification campaigns going back to the 1903-04 period.

46. René Lemarchand, *Rwanda and Burundi* (New York: Praeger, 1970), 47;
Chrétien, *Great Lakes of Africa*, 213; Shorter, *Cross and Flag*, 236.

47. Shorter, *Cross and Flag*, 53.

48. The Benebikira were partially inspired by the Bannabikira congregation in
Uganda, an order founded in 1910 by the White Sister Mother Mechtilde.
Many of the Benebikira sisters have been praised for their witness during
the 1994 genocide. See here Kathleen L. Sullivan, "Cultivating Unity," *The
National Catholic Reporter*, October 28, 2010, http://ncronline.org/news/
cultivating-unity. I am grateful to Sr. Ann Fox for bringing my attention to this.

49. C.M.L., Classe to Livinhac, 28 April 1911. I am indebted to Paul Rutayisire
for pointing out this parallel (P. Rutayisire, "Review of J. J. Carney, *From
Democratization to Ethnic Revolution: Catholic Politics in Rwanda, 1950–1962*"
(Butare, Rwanda, [n.p.], 2012): 3).

50. This section draws on Chrétien, *Great Lakes of Africa*, 236–37, 261; Linden,
Church and Revolution, 123–139; Rutayisire, *La Christianisation du Rwanda*, 98,

120–131; Des Forges, *Defeat is the Only Bad News*, 199–204, 220, 265; Fortunatus Rudakemwa, *L'évangélisation du Rwanda 1900-1959* (Paris: L'Harmattan, 2005), 159, 180–86; Kalibwami, *Le Catholicisme*, 166; Reyntjens, *Pouvoir et droit*, 81–85.

51. To understand better why stories from Belgian Congo raised such fears, see Adam Hochschild's *King Leopold's Ghost* (New York: Mariner, 1998). On Belgian colonial influence and church-state relations in Congo, see Georges Nzongola-Ntalaja, *The Congo from Leopold to Kabila: A People's History* (London: Zed Books, 2002) and Marvin D. Markovitz, *Cross and Sword: The Political Role of Christian Missions in the Belgian Congo 1908–1960* (Stanford: Hoover, 1973).

52. The "indirect" nature of German rule should not be exaggerated. As Reyntjens notes, the Germans pacified the country, opened it to international commerce, introduced Christian missions, abolished slavery, and started a new currency (Reyntjens, *Pouvoir et droit*, 38).

53. Reyntjens, *Pouvoir et droit*, 65–66, 75.

54. De Lacger, *Ruanda*, 463.

55. On church-state relations in early twentieth-century Belgium, see Martin Conway, "Belgium," in *Political Catholicism in Europe, 1918–1965*, eds. Tom Buchanan and Martin Conway (Oxford: Clarendon, 1996): 187–218; Emmanuel Gerard, "Religion, Class and Language: The Catholic Party in Belgium," in *Political Catholicism in Europe 1918–45*, eds. Wolfram Kaiser and Helmut Wohnout (New York: Routledge, 2004): 94–115; Roger Aubert, *150 ans de Vie des Eglises* (Brussels: Legraine, 1982).

56. Reyntjens, *Pouvoir et droit*, 171. See also Des Forges, *Defeat is the only bad news*, 308–309.

57. On the Scramble for Africa and the effects of World War I, see Hastings, *Church in Africa*, 400–13, 541–43; Iliffe, *Africans*, 189–211.

58. Reyntjens, *Pouvoir et droit*, 43.

59. Kalibwami, *Le Catholicisme*, 182–94.

60. This section draws on the more detailed presentation in Rutayisire, *La Christianisation du Rwanda*, 235–90.

61. Growing out of early 20th-century Belgian Catholic efforts to break the link between industrialization and secularization, Catholic Action aimed to "evangelize within the heartlands of Catholicism, to regain for the Catholic Church those sections of modern industrial societies which had fallen victim to secularization along the way" (Gerd-Rainer Horn, *Western European Liberation Theology: The First Wave (1924–1959)* (New York: Oxford University Press, 2008), 20). Turning away from the late 19th and early 20th-century emphasis on forming explicitly Catholic political parties, Catholic Action looked to re-Christianize modern society through forming non-partisan associations of committed Catholic laity. Embraced by Pope Pius XI after 1922, the movement spread across Europe and areas of European influence, gaining particular

traction in Latin America. Horn's *Western European Liberation Theology* offers a thorough recent study of the movement. For a more critical analysis, see William T. Cavanaugh, *Torture and Eucharist: Theology, Politics and the Body of Christ* (Oxford: Blackwell, 1998), 124–150.

62. C.M.L., Classe to Livinhac, 28 April 1911.

63. Classe quoted in Rutayisire, *Le Christianisation du Rwanda*, 112; Kalibwami, *Le Catholicisme*, 194.

64. C.M.L., Classe to Livinhac, 28 April 1911. Classe was not alone in this analysis. As Minnaert notes, most early White Fathers classified the popular masses as "Hutu" and political and economic elites as "Tutsi," even though locals would have placed Hutu and Tutsi in both groups (cf. Minnaert, "Les Pères Blancs et la Société Rwandaise," 10). As it is, a very small minority (perhaps 5 percent) of Tutsi exercised political leadership at the time of the European arrival (Nigel Eltringham, *Accounting for Horror: Post-Genocide Debates in Rwanda* (London: Pluto Press, 2004), 15).

65. Léon Classe, "Le Ruanda et ses habitants," *Congo: Revue générale de la Colonie belge* I, no. 5 (1922): 681. See also Chrétien, *Great Lakes of Africa*, 286. By associating Tutsi exclusively with the nobility, Classe estimated in 1916 that Rwandan Tutsi comprised no more than 20,000 people. By 1922 he had raised this figure to 80,000, but his language still underplayed the far larger numbers of poor Tutsi.

66. C.M.L., Léon Classe, "Batutsi et Bahutu," 184.

67. Rudakemwa, *L'évangélisation du Rwanda*, 202; Gamaliel Mbonimana, "Christianisation indirecte et cristallisation des clivages ethniques au Rwanda (1925-31)," *Enquêtes et documents d'histoire africaine III* (Louvain: Centre d'histoire de l'Afrique, 1978): 153.

68. Classe quoted in Reyntjens, *Pouvoir et droit*, 105 and Lemarchand, *Rwanda and Burundi*, 73.

69. Classe, "Circulaire N°14, Écoles et Apostolat prés des Batutsi, 15 May 1928," in Léon Classe, *Instructions Pastorales 1922–1939* (Kabgayi: 1940), 40–43.

70. Classe, "Circulaire N°11, Les écoles, 16 July 1927," in Classe, *Instructions Pastorales*, 31.

71. Classe, "Circulaire N°14, Écoles et Apostolat," in Classe, *Instructions Pastorales*, 40. See also Mbonimana, "Christianisation indirecte," 139–45 and Linden, *Church and Revolution*, 163–64, 198.

72. Classe, "Le Ruanda et ses habitants," 681. See also Rudakemwa, *L'évangélisation du Rwanda*, 277; Mbonimana, "Ethnies et Église catholique," 63; Des Forges, *Defeat is the only bad news*, 266–67.

73. Classe, "Le Ruanda et ses habitants," 680.

74. Léon Classe, "Un pays et trois Races," in *Grands Lacs* nos. 5–6 (1935): 138.

75. Ibid.

76. Ibid, 139.

77. De Lacger, *Ruanda*, 37.

78. This quotation is taken from a 17 March 1913 Classe letter to his fellow White Fathers, as quoted in Minnaert, "Les Pères Blancs et la Société Rwandaise," 6, 17–18.

79. Léon Classe, "Pour moderniser le Ruanda. Le problème des Batutsi," *L'Essor colonial et maritime* IX (1930): no. 489: 1–2; no. 490: 7; no. 491: 11. See also Mbonimana, "Ethnies et Église catholique," 64; Reyntjens, *Pouvoir et droit*, 105.

80. Classe quoted in Linden, *Church and Revolution*, 162.

81. In this analysis I follow Paul Rutayisire over Mahmood Mamdani. For these alternative views, see Rutayisire, *La Christianisation du Rwanda*, 175–78; Mahmood Mamdani, *When Victims Become Killers: Colonialism, Nativism, and the Genocide in Rwanda* (Princeton: Princeton University Press), 92–93.

82. Reyntjens, *Pouvoir et droit*, 176. The following sections draw on Danielle de Lame, *A Hill Among a Thousand: Transformations and Ruptures in Rural Rwanda* (Madison: University of Wisconsin Press, 2005), 46; Reyntjens, *Pouvoir et droit*, 109–13, 123–29; Rutayisire, *La Christianisation du Rwanda*, 150–68, 182–91; Mbonimana, "Christianisation indirecte," 128–29, 156–57; Kalibwami, *Le Catholicisme*, 164, 197, 208–17; Lemarchand, *Rwanda and Burundi*, 70–71; Des Forges, *Defeat is the only bad news*, 294–301, 318–35; Des Forges, "Kings without Crowns," 350; Mamdani, *When Victims Become Killers*, 99; Linden, *Church and Revolution*, 166–68; Octave Ugirashebuja, "L'ideologie du Tutsi oppresseur," *Les Cahiers: Evangile et Société: Les Idéologies*, no. 4 (1996): 57–61; Eltringham, *Accounting for Horror*, 19; Rudakemwa, *L'évangélisation du Rwanda*, 220. Similar reforms were undertaken at this time in neighboring Burundi (cf. Augustin Mvuyekure, "Idéologie missionnaire et classification ethnique en Afrique centrale," in *Les Ethnies ont une histoire*, 319–20).

83. The Nyanza school was replaced in the 1930s by the *Group Scolaire d'Astrida* in southern Rwanda. The Brothers of Charity, a Catholic religious community based in Belgium, was entrusted with leadership of the new school.

84. Mamdani, *When Victims Become Killers*, 99. Rwandans were required to carry ethnic identity cards for the next 60 years. These cards served an instrumental role in facilitating the massacres of Tutsi during the 1994 genocide. Rwanda's post-genocide government eliminated ethnic identity cards and banned individual Rwandans from publicly describing themselves as Hutu and Tutsi.

85. Clovis, king of the Franks, converted to Christianity in the 590s. In Catholic tradition, he was credited with establishing France as the "first daughter of the Church." A Rwandan historian would later compare the 1943 baptism of Musinga's son Mutara Rudahigwa to "St. Remi's baptism of Clovis in ancient France" (C.M.L., Alphonse Ntezimana, "Brin d'histoire á l'occasion du Sacre du premier évêque du Ruanda," 1952).

86. This is one of the central themes of Des Forges's *Defeat is the only bad news*. Des Forges recognizes the integral connection between religion and politics

in Rwandan thought; the Mwami himself had a central ritual role in these traditions, making him especially loathe to convert to Christianity. See also Des Forges, "Kings without crowns," 180–81.

87. Linden, *Church and Revolution*, 172.

88. This section draws on Des Forges, *Defeat is the only bad news*, 316; Des Forges, *Kings without Crowns*, 195–98; Rudakemwa, *L'évangélisation du Rwanda*, 204, 235, 242; De Lacger, *Ruanda*, 632; Kalibwami, *Le Catholicisme*, 227–265; Linden, *Church and Revolution*, 190; Reyntjens, *Pouvoir et droit*, 126; Rutayisire, *La Christianisation du Rwanda*, 175–78, 329–40; De Lame, *Hill among a Thousand*, 51–53.

89. Burundi experienced an even greater wave of mass conversions at this time. A church that had counted a mere 7,000 Christians in 1916 numbered 176,000 in 1935 and 365,000 in 1940. Two-thirds of Burundian chiefs and one-half of the nation's sub-chiefs had converted to Catholicism by 1933 (Chrétien, *Great Lakes of Africa*, 269).

90. These numbers grew even more by 1947 when 48 of 51 Rwanda's chiefs and 555 of 635 of its sub-chiefs identified as Roman Catholic (Kalibwami, *Le Catholicisme*, 266).

91. Known as the *Balokole*, these evangelical Anglicans were notable for crossing ethnic lines, rejecting traditional religion, turning away from politics, and focusing on the individual experience of salvation. They looked to convert lukewarm Christians, Catholic and Protestant alike, to a more rigorous form of Christianity. The most exhaustive recent study is Kevin Ward and Emma Wild-Wood, eds., *The East African Revival: Histories and Legacies* (Burlington, VT: Ashgate, 2012); on the Rwandan dimensions of this revival, see in particular Kevin Ward, "Revival, mission and church in Kigezi, Rwanda and Burundi," 11–31. See also Tharcisse Gatwa, *The Churches and Ethnic Ideology in the Rwandan Crises, 1900–1994* (Milton Keynes: Paternoster, 2005), 95–96; Linden, *Church and Revolution*, 204–205.

92. This term was famously used in the 1935 issue of the White Fathers periodical *Grands Lacs* to describe the mass conversions in Rwanda: "Où l'Esprit saint souffle en tornade" (cf. Kalibwami, *Le Catholicisme*, 261).

93. John Iliffe sees the youthful nature of Christian conversion as a continental theme in the 1930s and 1940s, comparing this "generational revolt" in Africa to that engendered by communism in 20th-century Asia (Iliffe, *Africans*, 224–25).

94. Classe, "Le Ruanda et ses habitants," 693.

95. De Lacger, *Ruanda*, 548. Elsewhere De Lacger writes that the reign of Mutara Rudahigwa marked "the decisive and ultimately official acceptance of European and Christian civilization" (504).

96. Kalibwami, *Le Catholicisme*, 240.

97. Between 1946 and 1954, 389 Tutsi and 16 Hutu enrolled in the school (cf. "Reportages: Le Groupe Scolaire d'Astrida 1952," *L'Ami* 87 (March 1952): 45.

See also Mbonimana, "Christianisation indirecte," 149; Linden, *Church and Revolution*, 196).

98. Léon Classe, "Roi et Chefs," in *Grands Lacs* nos. 5–6 (1935): 155, 158.

99. Léon Classe, "Circulaire N°106, Conduite a l'égard des chefs, 5 May 1938," in Classe, *Instructions Pastorales*, 341.

100. The Kinyarwanda term was "*Irivuze umwami*," "the word pronounced by the king" or "what the king has said you must follow" (Gatwa, *Churches and Ethnic Ideology*, 91; Rutayisire, *La Christianisation du Rwanda*, 322; Kalibwami, *Le Catholicisme*, 220–21).

101. This description was included in the White Fathers' special Rwanda issue of *Grands Lacs* nos. 5–6 (1935). See also Rutayisire, *La Christianisation du Rwanda*, 325.

102. Classe, "Circulaire N°14, Écoles et Apostolat près des Batutsi, 15 May 1928," in Classe, Instructions Pastorales, 41–42.

103. Rutayisire, *La Christianisation du Rwanda*, 355; Linden, *Church and Revolution*, 189.

104. If Rwandan elites converted in the 1930s, the true *tornade* of the Rwandan people happened during the 1960s. Between 1960 and 1970, the Catholic population doubled from 900,000 to 1.8 million (cf. Rutayisire, *La Christianisation du Rwanda*, 342–48; Lugan, *L'Eglise Catholique au Rwanda*, 72).

105. Gérard Prunier, *The Rwanda Crisis: History of a Genocide* (New York: Columbia University Press, 1995), 34. See also Jean-Pierre Chrétien, "Hutu et Tutsi au Rwanda et au Burundi," in Jean-Loup Amselle and Elikia M'Bokolo, eds., *Au Cœur de l'ethnie: Ethnie, tribalisme, et état en Afrique* (Paris: La Découverte, 1999), 146–47.

106. Bernard Lugan, *Rwanda: Le Génocide, l'Èglise, et la Démocratie* (Paris: Editions du Rocher, 2004), 50.

107. This section draws on Kalibwami, *Le Catholicisme*, 279–86; Rudakemwa, *L'évangélisation du Rwanda*, 224, 254–56; Linden, *Church and Revolution*, 198, 223; De Lacger, 679–80.

108. Aloys Bigirumwami, "Le clergé indigène du Ruanda," *L'Ami* 67–68 (July-August 1950): 125, 131. This represented a stark contrast with Belgian Congo, Rwanda's giant eastern neighbor. While in 1950 only 10% of Congo's priests were African, 36% of Rwanda's clergy were indigenous. Rwandans comprised a similarly large percentage of vowed religious sisters and brothers (*L'Ami* 79 (July 1951): 128–29).

109. Cf. "22 millions de catholiques en Afrique," *Grands Lacs* no. 186 (August-September 1956): 14.

110. Adrian Hastings, *A History of African Christianity 1950–1975* (Cambridge: Cambridge University Press, 1979), 62.

111. Mutara actually had a daughter with his first wife; this daughter died in 1937. Ironically, Mutara never conceived a child with Rosalie (Paul Rutayisire, "Rudahigwa et les missionnaires," *Dialogue* 188 (2009): 24).

112. Quoted in C.M.L., Alphonse Ntezimana, "Brin d'histoire à l'occasion du Sacre du premier évêque du Ruanda," 1 June 1952.

113. These figures included Marshall Pétillon, the vice governor-general for the Belgian colonies; General Sandrart, the colonial resident in Rwanda; Mwami Mutara; and Burundi's Mwami Mwambutsa. (Cf. A.G.M.Afr.N°540758-62, "Le Jubile du Ruanda Catholique 1900–1950.")

114. See Linden, *Church and revolution*, 258; Catherine Newbury, *The Cohesion of Oppression: Clientship and Ethnicity in Rwanda, 1860–1960* (New York: Columbia University Press, 1988), 191.

115. A.G.M.Afr. N° 540758, [Anon.], "Le Jubile du Ruanda Catholique 1900-1950." For similar sentiments, see the July-August 1950 issue of *L'Ami*, especially "Jubilé de Ruanda 1950," *L'Ami* VI, no. 67–68: 121–49, as well as the entire issue of *Grands Lacs* 1, no. 135 (1950).

116. This famine caused the colonial vice-governor to allege that Mutara and other court nobles were more concerned with Mutara's baptism than the welfare of Rwanda's Hutu peasants. The famine would also delegitimize the Belgian colonial project for many Rwandans. Cf. Paul Rutayisire, "Rudahigwa et les missionnaires," *Dialogue* 188 (April-July 2009): 27–29.

117. A.G.M.Afr.N°206706, *Au Cœur du Ruanda Chrétien (1900–1946)*, 3 August 1946, 13. This document is housed as a loose file in the library annex of the General Archives of the Missionaries of Africa, Rome.

118. Ibid, 3–5.

119. On Déprimoz's life, see [Anon.], *Son Excellence Mgr. Laurent Déprimoz, Evêque de Mateur, Vicaire Apostolique de Kabgayi, 1884–1962* (Kabgayi: 1962). This small biography was released at the time of Déprimoz's death but not published outside of Rwanda; I consulted a rare copy in the Roman archives of the Missionaries of Africa. For additional commentary on Déprimoz, see De Lacger, *Ruanda*, 662; André Perraudin, *"Par-dessus tout la charité": un évêque au Rwanda: les six premières années de mon épiscopat (1956–1962)* (Saint Maurice: Editions Saint-Augustin, 2003), 27–28. The most exhaustive recent study is Joseph Ngomanzungu, *L'épiscopat de Mgr Laurent Déprimoz 1943–1955: une période de consolidation de la foi et de rwandisation de l'Église dans une société en transformation*. Thèse de doctorat, Pontifical Gregorian University, 2010.

120. *Son Excellence Mgr. Laurent Déprimoz*, 41.

121. Linden, *Church and Revolution*, 220. Easter duty practices grew out of the Lateran IV council reforms of 1215 that required lay Catholics to confess their sins and receive Eucharist at least once a year, typically during the penitential season of Lent. Prior to Vatican II, Catholic parishes viewed this statistic as a quantifiable measurement of how many local Catholics practiced their faith.

122. *Son Excellence*, 43–47.

123. The greatest Banyarwanda intellectual of his era, Kagame published a remarkable volume of books, articles and monographs on Rwandan history, culture,

philosophy, and language; there is an entire library in Butare dedicated to his published and unpublished works. His most important early work on pre-colonial Rwandan history is *Le code des institutions politiques du Rwanda pre-colonial* (Brussels: Institut royal colonial belge, 1952). See also his multi-volume later history *Un abrégé de l'histoire du Rwanda* (Butare: Editions universitaires du Rwanda, 1972–1975).

124. C.M.L., Endriatis to Priests/Religious, 12 January 1951.

CHAPTER 3

1. The best thematic overview of the intersection of political and religious change in 1950s Africa remains Adrian Hastings, *A History of African Christianity 1950–1975* (Cambridge: Cambridge University Press, 1979), 5–120.

2. Ibid., 86–90. As late as 1956 one prominent Belgian official proposed a "thirty-year plan for the political emancipation of Belgian Africa" (A.A.J. Van Bilsen, "Un plan de 30 ans pour l'émancipation politique de l'Afrique Belge," *Temps Nouveaux d'Afrique*, 13 May 1956, 3). See also Marvin D. Markowitz, *Cross and Sword: The Political Role of Christian Missions in the Belgian Congo, 1908–1960* (Stanford, CA: Hoover, 1973), 156.

3. Filip Reyntjens, *Pouvoir et droit au Ruanda: Droit public et évolution politique, 1916–1973* (Tervuren, Belgium: Musée Royal de L'Afrique Centrale, 1985), 212–13.

4. Louis de Lacger (with Dominic Nothomb), *Ruanda* (Kabgayi: 1961), 682–83.

5. "Page du Ruanda-Urundi: Nouvelle organisation politique au Ruanda-Urundi," *L'Ami* 105 (1953): 187–91. See also Reyntjens, *Pouvoir et droit*, 185–96; Mahmood Mamdani, *When Victims Become Killers: Colonialism, Nativism, and the Genocide in Rwanda* (Princeton: Princeton University Press, 2001), 115.

6. In Mamdani's words, "in the absence of corresponding reform redistributing grazing land monopolized by Tutsi patrons, it left Hutu owners of cattle dependent on former patrons for access to pasturage" (Mamdani, *When Victims Become Killers*, 115).

7. Mwami Mutara, "Problèmes Africains: Project de Suppression du Régime feudal (Ubuhake)," *L'Ami* 90 (1952): 105–109. For more on *ubuhake* and its development in the late colonial period, see Reyntjens, *Pouvoir et droit*, 199–207; Ian Linden (with Jane Linden), *Church and Revolution in Rwanda* (Manchester, U.K.: Manchester University Press, 1977), 225–26; Jean-Pierre Chrétien, *The Great Lakes of Africa: Two Thousand Years of History*. Trans. Scott Strauss (New York: Zone, 2003), 299, 407; Mamdani, *When Victims Become Killers*, 111.

8. General Archives of the Missionaries of Africa, Rome (hereafter A.G.M.Afr.), N°721001, *Rapport du Groupe de Travail concernant le problème politique du Ruanda-Urundi, 1958–59*, September 1959, 35.

9. Cf. A.G.M.Afr.N°543010, Gilles to Durrieu, 19 August 1950; Br. Secundien, "Groupe Scolaire d'Astrida," *Grands Lacs* 156 (1952): 37–41.

10. For examples of this lionization of Bwanakweri, see "Un abbé ruandais: nous parle," *La Presse Africaine*, 21 July 1956; "Des notables ruandais nous parlent," *La Presse Africaine*, 4 August 1956; "Un abbé ruandais nous parle," *La Presse Africaine*, 23 August 1956.

11. Reyntjens, *Pouvoir et Droit*, 225. For a retrospective colonial account that paints Bwanakweri in very flattering terms, see Victor-Clement Nijs, *Souvenirs d'un administrateur territorial: Congo-Rwanda 1950–1962* (Brussels: Editions Racine, 2007), 317.

12. "Les amitiés Belgo-Rwandaises," *L'Ami* 78 (1951): 105–6.

13. "Un Parti Politique in Partibus au Ruanda-Urundi," *Presse Africaine*, 17 September 1955.

14. "Formation politique—la meilleure forme de Gouvernement," *L'Ami* 113 (1954): 178–82; Gregoire Kayibanda, "Les Évolués de campagne," *L'Ami* 110 (1954): 56–63; Gregoire Kayibanda, "Editorial: Un peu d'optimisme," *L'Ami* 118 (1954): 353.

15. Pope Pius XII, *Evangelii Praecones ("On the Promotion of Catholic Mission")*, 2 June 1951, pars. 17, 27, 49, (http://www.vatican.va/holy_father/pius_xii/encyclicals/documents/hf_p-xii_enc_02061951_evangelii-praecones_en.html); Pope Pius XII, *Fidei Donum, "On the present conditions of the Catholic missions, especially in Africa,"* 21 April 1957 (http://www.vatican.va/holy_father/pius_xii/encyclicals/documents/hf_p-xii_enc_21041957_fidei-donum_en.html).

16. Cf. "Savez-vous ce qu'est le communisme?" *L'Ami* 61–63 (1950): 3–4, 6, 25–26, 43–44; "Des Noirs Communistes formés comme Prêtres Catholiques," *L'Ami* 109 (Jan 1954): 27. Launched in 1950 as a weekly newspaper for Catholic intellectual elites in Belgian Africa, *L'Ami's* international pages reflected a deep concern with the fates of Indochina, China, Hungary, Yugoslavia and other nations facing communist governments or insurrections (*L'Ami* 71 (1950): 206; *L'Ami* 93 (1952): 179–80; *L'Ami* 98 (1953): 22–23); *L'Ami* 104 (1953): 164–65; *L'Ami* 113 (1954): 176; *L'Ami* 116 (1954): 304–305). Its successor *Temps Nouveaux d'Afrique* also carried forward the anti-communist theme (cf. "Le communism et l'Afrique noire?" *Temps Nouveaux d'Afrique*, 22 January 1956, 1, 8).

17. A.G.M.Afr.N°543033, Cattin to Durrieu, 3 October 1952; "Actualité sociale: Chasser les communistes n'est rien, il faut établir la justice sociale," *L'Ami* 118 (1954): 383. The 1954 electoral successes of the socialists in Guatemala loomed in the background of this latter article.

18. Centre Missionnaire Lavigerie, Kigali (C.M.L.), André Perraudin to Henry Sillion, 16 February 1955.

19. In sketching what many observers saw as a "third way" between socialist communism and liberal capitalism, Pope Leo XIII's 1891 encyclical *Rerum Novarum* initiated the modern movement of Catholic social teaching. On *Rerum Novarum* and its legacy, see David J. O'Brien and Thomas Shannon, Eds., *Catholic Social Thought: The Documentary Heritage* (Maryknoll, NY: Orbis Books, 1992), 12–41.

20. Gregoire Kayibanda, "Editorial—L'union fait la force," *L'Ami* 107 (1953): 233–34. Burundi also developed cooperatives and mutualities during this time (cf. "Le première congrès mutualiste chrétien du Burundi," *Temps Nouveaux d'Afrique*, 9 September 1956, 3). For background on the European roots of cooperatives, see Gerd-Rainer Horn, *Western European Liberation Theology: The First Wave (1924–1959)* (New York: Oxford University Press, 2008), 5–25.

21. "Questions Sociales—L'Avenir de nos Coopératives," *L'Ami* 116 (1954): 291; "Les Coopératives," *Temps Nouveaux d'Afrique*, 7 August 1955. On the necessity of steering Catholic social teaching on a middle course between communism and liberal capitalism, see "Les abus inhumains du capitalisme liberal," *Temps Nouveaux d'Afrique*, 10 June 1956, 2.

22. "Pour le progrès des Missions," *Theologie et Pastorale au Rwanda* 24 (1952): 524–37.

23. See here Emiel Lamberts, "The Zenith of Christian Democracy," 69–73; Martin Conway, "Belgium," in *Political Catholicism in Europe, 1918–1965*, eds. Tom Buchanan and Martin Conway (Oxford: Clarendon, 1996), 212–13; "La question scolaire en Belgique," *Temps Nouveaux d'Afrique*, 13 March 1955. Mwami Mwambutsa and the Burundian nobility generally took a more pro-missionary line in these debates than Rwanda's local leaders. This helps explain why the White Fathers remained much closer to the Burundian monarchy in later years. Cf. "Le conseil supérieur de l'Urundi, présidé par Le Mwami Mwambutsa, se prononce á l'unanimité contre le création d'écoles officielles laïques dans l'Urundi," *Temps Nouveaux d'Afrique*, 30 January 1955.

24. A.G.M.Afr.N°540034, Cattin to Durrieu, 3 October 1952.

25. Cf. Paul Rutayisire, "Rudahigwa et les missionnaires," *Dialogue* 188 (2009): 39–43.

26. Cf. "La Franc-maçonnerie lutte contre l'Eglise," *Temps Nouveaux d'Afrique*, 23 October 1955.

27. For background, see Fortunatus Rudakemwa, *L'évangélisation du Rwanda 1900-1959* (Paris: L'Harmattan, 2005), 272–275; Linden, *Church and Revolution*, 236.

28. The emphases are found in the original French. "DANS UN PAYS CATHOLIQUE comme l'est le Ruanda, LE SEUL ENSEIGNEMENT OFFICIEL DEVRAIT ETRE L'ENSEIGNEMENT CATHOLIQUE...Nous devons tous revendiquer les droits les plus sacrés de l'Église, ceux de l'éducation des enfants." (A.G.M.Afr.N°540785, *Lettre des Vicaires Apostoliques de Kabgayi et de Nyundo sur le danger qui menace l'enseignement au Ruanda*, 25 October 1954).

29. Laurent Déprimoz, "Mandement en Charité, 1 février 1955," *Trait d'Union* 33 (1955).

30. "Leçons de Morale Sociale: La Patrie," *L'Ami* 88 (1952): 63.

31. Cf. A.G.M.Afr.N°526358, Perraudin to Volker, 19 November 1954; "La question de l'enseignement au Ruanda-Urundi—Les anciens élèves du groupe scolaire

d'Astrida," *L'Ami* 116 (1954): 301–302; "Ecole laïque au Ruanda," *Revue du clergé africain* X, no. 6 (1955): 602; Reyntjens, *Pouvoir et droit au Rwanda*, 225–28; Linden, *Church and Revolution*, 236.

32. Cf. Cardinal Joseph Ernst van Roey, "L'Eglise et Enseignement Moyen," *L'Ami* 90 (1952): 104; Laurent Déprimoz, "Le Jubilé du Ruanda Catholique 1900–1950," *L'Ami* 67–68 (1950): 165.

33. The *biru* were the official keepers of Rwanda's royal customs and played an especially important role in consecrating the Mwami's successor, as we will see in chapter four. The quotation is taken from Alexis Kagame, "Leçons de Morale Sociale: La Justice Distributive," *L'Ami* 84 (1951): 223. For similar sentiments, see Tharcisse Gatwa, "Editorial—Un appel: que penser des questions familiales," *L'Ami* 116 (1954): 284. For Kagame's emphasis on missionary contributions to the development of the written Kinyarwanda language, see Alexis Kagame, "Le Christianisme dans le poésie du Ruanda," *L'Ami* 67–68 (1950): 137–140.

34. Gregoire Kayibanda, "Editorial—Il nous fait aussi des penseurs," *L'Ami* 105 (1953): 169; Gregoire Kayibanda, "La recontre Europe-Afrique," *L'Ami* 109 (1954): 7.

35. Belgium's Socialists took power in 1954, placing the pro-church *Christelijke Volkspartij/Parti social chrétien* (PSC/CVP) in opposition until 1958. In addition to their suspicions of the Catholic Church, the Socialists took a more negative view of Belgian colonial endeavors. Cf. Emile Lamberts, "The Zenith of Christian Democracy: The Christelijke Volkspartij/Parti Social Chrétien in Belgium," in *Christian Democracy in Europe since 1945*, eds. Michael Gehler and Wolfram Kaiser (New York: Routledge, 2004), 67–84.

36. A.G.M.Afr.N°541449, Klep to Durrieu, 8 August 1955.

37. C.M.L., Perraudin to Henry Sillion, 16 February 1955.

38. Gregoire Kayibanda, "Editorial—Un nouveau problème," *L'Ami* 113 (1954): 173–74; Gr. Kayibanda, "En Marche du Progrès: La condition essentielle," *L'Ami* 117 (1954): 344. See also Ignace Nzamwita, "Le Droit d'Intervention de l'Eglise en matière Sociale," *L'Ami* 107 (1953): 236–237.

39. Cf. A.G.M.Afr.N°542130, *Rapport du Vicariat du Ruanda 1950–51*; A.G.M.Afr. N°543036, Volker to Cattin, 22 October 1952; A.G.M.Afr.N°526777, Dejemeppe to Déprimoz, 14 February 1954.

40. [Anon.], "Pour le progrès des Missions," *Theologie et Pastorale au Ruanda 24* (1952): 524–537.

41. A.G.M.Afr.N°540335, Cattin to Durrieu, 3 October 1952; A.G.M.Afr.N°526778, Dejemeppe to Déprimoz, 14 February 1954. See also "Realisations Sociales: La mutualité de Byumba," *L'Ami* 86 (1952): 23–24.

42. Mutara's February 1954 speech is quoted in A.G.M.Afr.N°526777, Dejemeppe to Déprimoz, 14 February 1954.

43. Kayibanda, "En Marche du Progrès," 343, 347.

44. Aloys Munyangaju, "Aux Urnes," *L'Ami* 112 (1954): 155–56.

45. Cf. "Formation politique, L'organisation du pouvoir dans les pays d'Europe et d'Amérique—Les régimes démocratiques," *L'Ami* 112 (1954): 133–37.

46. Paul Rutayisire, "Les signes précurseurs de la crise de la Toussaint rwandaise," *Dialogue 189* (2009): 8–12.

47. Cf. "Le manifeste de la J.O.C. internationale, Bruxelles, 10 Sept. 1950," *L'Ami* 73 (1951): 7; "Contrat et Travail," *L'Ami* (1950): 63–66; 105–108; "Leçons de Morale Sociale," *L'Ami* 76–79 (1951): 63–64, 83–84, 103–104, 123–24; "Le Ruanda-Urundi en 1952," *L'Ami* 112 (1954): 157–61.

48. On the *évolués*, see A.G.M.Afr.N°543009-13, Gilles to Durrieu, 19 August 1950; A.G.M.Afr.N°543027, Derson, "Question des Évolués," 23 March 1951; A.G.M.Afr. N° 731603-05, Innocent Gasabwoya, "Etude sur les relations du Clergé avec les Évolués," 9 February 1955. For an insightful commentary on *évolués* in the late colonial Congolese context, see Georges Nzongola-Ntalaja, *The Congo from Leopold to Kabila: A People's History* (London: Zed Books, 2002), 62–82.

49. Louis Gasore, "L'Evolue face aux problèmes économico-sociaux," *Théologie et Pastorale au Ruanda 1* (1956): 54.

50. Statistical information comes from "Rapport du Vicariat du Rwanda," *Theologie et Pastorale au Ruanda* 18 (1950): 412–15; C.M.L., "Souvenirs du Sacre de Son Excellence Mgr. Aloys Bigirumwami, Vicaire Apostolique du Nyundo," 1 June 1952, 29; A.G.M.Afr.N°542127, *Rapport Annuel du Vicariat du Ruanda*, 1 July 1950 to 30 June 1951; C.M.L., Alphonse Ntezimana, "Brin d'histoire à l'occasion du Sacre du premier évêque du Ruanda," 1952; Dominic Nothomb, *Petite Histoire de L'Eglise Catholique au Rwanda* (Kabgayi: 1962), 121; A.G.M.Afr. N°542212, *Rapport Annuel du Vicariat du Kabgayi*, 1 July 1955 to 30 June 1956.

51. This also stood in contrast to neighboring Burundi where 60% of the population had entered the Catholic catechumenate or received Catholic baptism by 1955 (cf. Jan Adriaenssens, *Rapport sur la situation religieuse, sociale, et économique du Ruanda-Urundi* (Geneva: Institut International Catholique de Recherches Socio-Ecclésiales, 1956), 22).

52. R.P. Endriatis, "L'Eglise actuelle du Ruanda," *L'Ami* 67–68 (1950): 141; Adriaenssens, *Rapport sur la situation religieuse*, 16.

53. A.G.M.Afr.N°542164, *Rapport Annuel du Vicariat Apostolique du Kabgayi, 1 juillet 1953 au 30 juin 1954*.

54. This section draws on R.P. Endriatis, "L'Eglise actuelle du Ruanda," *L'Ami* 67–68 (1950); A.G.M.Afr.N°542146, *Rapport du Vicariat Apostolique du Kabgayi 1 juillet 1952 au 30 Juin 1953*; Laurent Déprimoz, "Mandement de Carême," in *Trait d'Union* 33 (February 1955); A.G.M.Afr.N°543009-13, Gilles to Durrieu, 19 August 1950; A.G.M.Afr.N° 526781-83, Bushayija to Durrieu, 26 July 1955; C.M.L., Perraudin to Ducrey, 8 September 1955.

55. The Belgian Protestant Missionary Society in Rwanda ultimately became the Presbyterian Church of Rwanda. On the history of this church, see Michel Twagirayesu and Jan van Beutselaar, *Ce Don Que Nous Avons Reçu,*

L'Histoire de l'Eglise Presbyterienne au Rwanda 1907–1982 (Brussels: De Jonge, 1982). For a more recent commentary on Presbyterian churches and the 1994 genocide, see Timothy Longman, *Christianity and Genocide in Rwanda* (Cambridge: Cambridge University Press, 2010), 199–300.

56. Quoted in Paul Rutayisire, "L'Eglise catholique et le décolonisation du Rwanda ou les illusions d'une victoire," in *Rwanda: L'Eglise catholique à l'épreuve du génocide*, Eds. F. Rutembesa, J.P. Karegeye, P. Rutayisire (Greenfield Park, Canada: Les Editions Africana, 2004), 42.

57. For a helpful summary of Catholic Action's early impact in Europe, see Horn, *Western European Liberation Theology*, 38–53.

58. Cf. Nothomb, *Petite Histoire*, 135; A.G.M.Afr.N°543012-13, Gilles to Durrieu, 19 August 1950; A.G.M.Afr.N°543024, Volker to Dejemeppe, 8 January 1951; "Action Catholique des Évolués," *Trait d'Union* 28 (1954).

59. A.G.M.Afr.N°543012, Gilles to Durrieu, 19 August 1950; A.G.M.Afr.N°543027, Derson, "Question des Évolués," 23 March 1951; "Pour former une élite: Notre enquête sur les Cercles d'Évoluants," *L'Ami* 81 (1951): 163–65. A.G.M.Afr. N°543192-94, *Rapport Annuel du Vicariate du Kabgayi 1954–55*, 30 June 1955.

60. A.G.M.Afr.N°526774, Dejemeppe to Déprimoz, 14 February 1954.

61. The phrase is taken from "Communications Officielles—Dimanche de la Presse," *Trait d'Union* 30 (1954).

62. The White Fathers' request that Kagame avoid political issues in his doctoral writing led to one of the most influential works of early African theology, Kagame's "Bantu-Rwandan Philosophy of Being"; cf. Alexis Kagame, *La philosophie bantou-rwandaise de l'être* (Brussels: Académie Royale des Sciences Coloniales, 1956). For examples of White Father suspicions of Kagame's political interests, see A.G.M.Afr.N°543089, Van Volsem to Durrieu, 26 July 1952 and A.G.M.Afr.N°543125-26, Wouters to Van Volsem, 3 July and 29 July 1952.

63. A.G.M.Afr.N°542214, *Rapport Annuel du Vicariat du Kabgayi, 1955–56*, 30 June 1956; Linden, *Church and Revolution*, 235.

64. "L'Ami à ses amis," *L'Ami* 102 (1953): 101; Gregoire Kayibanda, "Editorial—Entre autres choses," *L'Ami* 108 (1953): 261–62.

65. A.G.M.Afr.N°526538, *Rapport Annuel du Vicariate du Kabgayi 1953–54*, 7 July 1954.

66. Gregoire Kayibanda, "Editorial, Critique destructrice ou Action?" *L'Ami* 104 (1953): 155–56. See also Clays Bouuaert, "La page du Ruanda-Urundi—Discours de Monseiur Claeys Bouuaert au conseil du Vice-Gouvernement Genéral," *L'Ami* 102 (1953): 107–10; "Conseil de Gouvernement 1953—Discours de Mr. Pétillon," *L'Ami* 104 (1953): 149–151.

67. Gregoire Kayibanda, "Ce sera un peu dur....," *L'Ami* 112 (1954): 129–31.

68. Gregoire Kayibanda, "En Marche du Progrès: La condition essentielle," *L'Ami* 117 (1954): 339–47. See also Reyntjens, *Pouvoir et Droit*, 67–68.

69. Paul Rutayisire, "Les signes précurseurs de la crise de la Toussaint rwandaise," *Dialogue 189* (2009): 16–17.

70. Cf. Laurent Nkongori, "Etudes: la parenté au Ruanda," *L'Ami 82* (1951): 183–186; Marcel Pouwels, "Le Munya-ruanda," *Grands Lacs 164* (1953): 49–55; Marcel Pouwels, "Le Munya-Ruanda," *Grands Lacs 165* (1953): 23.

71. Cf. "Blancs et Noirs, Noirs et Noirs, Blancs et Blancs," *Temps Nouveaux d'Afrique*, 24 April 1955; "Le problème de races," *Temps Nouveaux d'Afrique*, 7 August 1955; "Il n'y a pas de race supérieure," *Temps Nouveaux d'Afrique*, 23 October 1955. In commentaries on South African apartheid, White Fathers offered strident critiques of South Africa's Dutch Reformed Church for allowing segregation in its churches and for retreating from its social responsibility in the public realm. Rather than embrace liberal structural reform or radical civil disobedience, however, the White Fathers emphasized the duty of altruistic whites to help black South Africans raise their economic and cultural aptitude. Nor were the White Fathers free from racial prejudice. "Europeans [in South Africa] are much superior to the others by the level of their culture and their education, by their intellectual and technical capacities, and also by their wealth. They form in fact a sort of especially privileged aristocracy"; (cf "Problèmes sociaux et raciaux en Afrique du Sud," *Grands Lacs 158* (1952): 26). See also "Les Protestants et la question raciale en Afrique du Sud," *L'Ami 112* (1954): 168).

72. A.G.M.Afr.N°526651-52, [Anon.], "Pro Memoria sur quelques difficultés particulières au Ruanda," 30 October 1952.

73. "Tribune Libre—L'évolué, sa place, ses responsabilités," *L'Ami 117* (1954): 333.

74. Gregoire Kayibanda, "Editorial—Un peu d'optimisme," *L'Ami 118* (1954): 352; Louis Gasore, "L'Évolué face aux problèmes économico-sociaux," *Théologie et Pastorale au Ruanda 1* (1956): 7.

75. A.G.M.Afr.N° 731603-05, Innocent Gasabwoya, "Etude sur les relations du Clergé avec les Évolués," 9 February 1955.

76. René Lemarchand, *Rwanda and Burundi* (New York: Praeger, 1970), 107.

77. C.M.L., Christian Gesché, "Le Vicariat Apostolique de Nyundo," 1952, 27–36.

78. This section on the establishment of Nyundo draws on A.G.M.Afr.N°542077-78, Durrieu to Wouters, 10 April 1949; A.G.M.Afr.N°542079, Déprimoz to Durrieu, 11 April 1949; A.G.M.Afr.N°540744, Hove to Mosmans, "Climat du Ruanda Indigène en 1952," [n.d.]; C.M.L., Christian Gesché, "Le Vicariat Apostolique de Nyundo," 1952, 27–36.

79. Rome's advocacy of indigenization can be traced back to the founding of Propaganda Fide in 1622 (cf. Adrian Hastings, *The Church in Africa 1450-1950* (Oxford: Clarendon, 1994), 88–89). Establishing an indigenous hierarchy in the Catholic missions became one of the central goals of Catholic ecclesiology after Pope Benedict XV's 1919 apostolic letter *Maximum Illud*, considered to be the "charter document" of papal missiology in the twentieth century.

80. De Lacger and Nothomb, *Ruanda*, 688; Nothomb, *Petite Histoire*, 130; Kalibwami, *Le Catholicisme*, 291–97.

81. A.G.M.Afr.N°540743, Hove to Mosmans, "Climat du Ruanda Indigène en 1952," [n.d.].

82. Nothomb, *Petite Histoire*, 146.

83. This biographical section draws on *Hommage à Mgr. Aloys Bigirumwami: Premier Evêque rwandais* (Kigali: Editions du Secrétariat général de la C.E.P.R., 2009), 5–13; Alexis Kagame, "Le Page du Ruanda," *L'Ami 82* (1951): 73; Linden, *Church and Revolution*, 244; Aloys Bigirumwami, "Le clergé indigène du Rwanda," *L'Ami 67–68* (1950): 130–31.

84. This description of Bigirumwami's consecration stems from A.G.M.Afr. N°542140, *Rapport du Vicariat du Ruanda du July 1951 au Juin 1952*; "Sacre de Son Excellence Monseigneur Bigirumwami 1 Juin 1952," *L'Ami 91* (1952): 128–33; *Hommage á Mgr. Aloys Bigirumwami*, 14–20; C.M.L., "Souvenirs du Sacre de Son Excellence Mgr. Aloys Bigirumwami, Vicaire Apostolique de Nyundo," 1 June 1952.

85. "Sacre de Son Excellence Monseigneur Bigirumwami 1 Juin 1952," *L'Ami 91* (1952): 133. This echoed his comments at the 1950 Save jubilee that "our [indigenous priests'] apostolic ministry is not only traced to the White Fathers but is absolutely the same" (Aloys Bigirumwami, "Le clergé indigène du Ruanda," *L'Ami 67–68* (1950): 131).

86. A.G.M.Afr.N°543191-92, Durrieu to Bigirumwami, 5 May 1952. See also A.G.M.Afr.N°543193-94, Volker to Bigirumwami, 9 May 1952.

87. A.G.M.Afr.N°526570, "Visite de Mgr. le Supérieur Général au Grand Séminaire Saint Charles à Nyakibanda, 5-11 April 1949"; A.G.M.Afr. 542130, "Rapport du Vicariat du Ruanda du Juillet 1950 au 30 Juin 1951."

88. A.G.M.Afr.N°526651, [Anon.], "Pro Memoria sur quelques difficultés particulières au Ruanda," 30 October 1952; A.G.M.Afr.N°540747, Hove to Mosmans, "Climat du Ruanda Indigène en 1952," [n.d.].

89. A.G.M.Afr.N°543229, Bigirumwami to Hellemans, 11 April 1954; A.G.M.Afr. N°543228, Bigirumwami to Durrieu, 15 April 1954; A.G.M.Afr.N°543226-27, Bigirumwami to Van Volsem, 28 January 1954.

90. A.G.M.Afr.N°540747, Hove to Mosmans, "Climat du Ruanda Indigène en 1952," [n.d.].

91. A.G.M.Afr.N°526774, Dejemeppe to Déprimoz, 14 February 1954. The two priests who served on the CSP in the mid-1950s were Stanislas Bushayija and Boniface Musoni. The former was seen as an ideological opponent of the Mwami, which may explain Mutara's desire to enlist Bigirumwami. (Cf. C.M.L., Joseph Ntamahungiro, "Eglise Catholique du Rwanda: De la Spiritualité au Prophétisme" (2000): 3).

92. A.G.M.Afr.N°543198-99, Bigirumwami to Durrieu, 1 September 1952; A.G.M.Afr.N°543200, Bigirumwami to Durrieu, 24 January 1953.

93. C.M.L., André Perraudin, "Les Grands Séminaires du Centre Africain," 3 December 1950. The Nyakibanda figures even surpassed Uganda's famous Katigondo seminary that had formed 137 priests and enrolled 86 seminarians by 1950. Across the African continent, Rwanda had the third-highest number of priestly ordinations (32) between 1910 and 1940 and the fourth highest number (112) for the 1940 to 1957 period (cf. *Civitas Mariae* 15 (1959): 7–8).

94. C.M.L., André Perraudin to Francis Perraudin, 3 April 1954.

95. A.G.M.Afr.N°731595, *Nyakibanda Rapport Annuel 1954–55*, 9 August 1955.

96. A.G.M.Afr.N° 52670-71, "Visite de Mgr. le Supérieur Général au Grand Séminaire Saint Charles à Nyakibanda, 5-11 April 1949."

97. A.G.M.Afr.N° 526594-97, Van Volsem to Durrieu, *Rapport de Visite du Grand Seminaire Regional de Nyakibanda, 26 Mars au 3 Avril 1952.*

98. This analysis of the 1952 Nyakibanda crisis draws on A.G.M.Afr.N° 526594-97, Van Volsem to Durrieu, *Rapport de Visite du Grand Seminaire Regional de Nyakibanda, 26 Mars au 3 Avril 1952*; A.G.M.Afr.N° 526023-24, *Rapport de la réunion des ordinaires, 7 April 1952*; A.G.M.Afr.N° 526583, Hellemans to Van Volsem, 22 April 1952; A.G.M.Afr.N°526649, Durrieu to Déprimoz, 21 May 1952; A.G.M.Afr.N°526213, *Rapport Annuel 1953, Grand Séminaire de Nyakibanda*, 7 July 1953.

99. This biographical section is drawn from André Perraudin, *Un Évêque au Rwanda: Les six premières années de mon épiscopat (1956-1962)* (Paris: Éditions Saint-Augustin, 2003), 12–16; "Un nouvel évêque au Ruanda," *Revue du Clergé Africain* XI, no. 3 (1956): 276–77; Rudakemwa, *L'évangélisation du Rwanda*, 328–29. Perraudin's nominating documents as rector of Nyakibanda also describe his background (A.G.M.Afr.N°526660, Van Volsem to Fumasoni-Biondi, 22 September 1952).

100. C.M.L., Angeline and Louis Perraudin to Rev. Père Superieur de l'Institut Lavigerie, 11 December 1925; Louis Perraudin to André Perraudin, 17 May 1936. From the archival records in Kigali, it appears that Louis Perraudin continued a close correspondence with André Perraudin throughout the 1920s and 1930s.

101. Perraudin's correspondence with Bruchez in the early 1950s reflected the esteem in which Perraudin held his cousin. This respect only grew after Bruchez was martyred in Kabyilie, Algeria in October 1956 during the Franco-Algerian war (cf. C.M.L., *Lettres de Père Hubert Bruchez*, 11 January 1956, 22 October 1956).

102. In their personal correspondence, Perraudin's brother Jean wrote in 1938 of the "menace of Hitler" and celebrated a recent Swiss victory over the German soccer team (C.M.L., Jean Perraudin to André Perraudin, 19 June 1938). For more on the effect of the Fribourg years on Perraudin's political theology, see Linden, *Church and Revolution*, 223.

103. A.G.M.Afr.N°545023, Bernard Hellemans, "Visite de Règle du 10-21 March 1950 (Kibumbo)."

104. C.M.L., André Perraudin, "Premier voyage à Burundi," 15 December 1947.

105. C.M.L., André Perraudin, "Les fêtes de l'action de grâces du Burundi, 1898–1948," 23 August 1948; André Perraudin, "Sous les étoiles," 7 January 1950.

106. C.M.L., André Perraudin, "Visite d'une succursale au Burundi," Munyange, 1948.

107. Perraudin later regretted that he was not able to spend more time in the mission stations. "I regret often this life which is so true and so near the people. At the Seminary one often has the impression that it is like Europe" (C.M.L., André Perraudin to Francis Perraudin, 3 April 1954). For similar sentiments, see C.M.L., Perraudin to Wyckaert, 14 June 1955.

108. C.M.L., André Perraudin, "Le Jubilé du Rwanda, 1900–1950," 15 August 1950. For Perraudin's retrospective comments on this event, see Perraudin, *Un Évêque au Rwanda*, 16.

109. C.M.L., André Perraudin, "Les Grand Séminaires du Centre Africain," 3 December 1950.

110. This section draws on A.G.M.Afr.N°526658-62, *Nyakibanda Rapport Annuel 1952*, 5 March 1953; A.G.M.Afr.N° 526661, *Rapport Annuel 1952*, 5 March 1953; A.G.M.Afr.N°526516, *Rapport de la Réunion Annuelle des Ordinaires*, 29 March 1954; A.G.M.Afr.N° 526537, *Nyakibanda Rapport Annuel 1953-54*, 7 July 1954; C.M.L., André Perraudin, "Je rends grace à Dieu," 25 August 1989.

111. A.G.M.Afr.N°526006-015, André Perraudin, "Un curriculum nouveau pour le séminaire régionale de Nyakibanda, 1952," [n.d.].

112. C.M.L., Leo Volker to André Perraudin, 12 July 1951.

113. A.G.M.Afr.N°526660, Van Volsem to Fumasoni-Biondi, 22 September 1952.

114. A.G.M.Afr.N°526239, Perraudin to Seumois, 22 September 1952.

115. A.G.M.Afr.N°526658, *Nyakibanda Rapport Annuel 1952*, 5 March 1953.

116. A.G.M.Afr.N°526241, Perraudin to Volker, 16 October 1952.

117. This section draws on A.G.M.Afr.N°526249, Perraudin to Volker, 20 November 1952; A.G.M.Afr.N°526252-53, Perraudin to Durrieu, 22 December 1952; A.G.M.Afr.N°526370, Perraudin to Durrieu, 24 December 1954; A.G.M.Afr. N°526288, Perraudin to Durrieu, 29 September 1953.

118. A.G.M.Afr.N°526254, Perraudin to Volker, 20 January 1953. Perraudin wrote in February 1953 of expressing himself too "crudely" on this issue (A.G.M.Afr. N°526259, Perraudin to Volker, 20 February 1953).

119. A.G.M.Afr.N°526261, Perraudin to Volker, 7 March 1953; A.G.M.Afr.N°526266, Perraudin to Bigirumwami, 29 March 1953; A.G.M.Afr.N°526272, Perraudin to Volker, 3 June 1953.

120. A.G.M.Afr.N°526330, Perraudin to Volker, 4 July 1954; A.G.M.Afr.N°526361, Perraudin to Volker, 23 December 1954.

121. This section draws upon A.G.M.Afr.N°526281, Perraudin to Durrieu, 27 August 1953; A.G.M.Afr.N°526288, Perraudin to Durrieu, 29 September 1953; A.G.M.Afr.N°526330, Perraudin to Volker, 4 July 1954; A.G.M.Afr.N°526338,

Perraudin to Seumois, 7 July 1954; A.G.M.Afr.N°526370, Perraudin to Durrieu, 24 December 1954; A.G.M.Afr.N°731600, *Nyakibanda Rapport Annuel 1954–55*, 9 August 1955.

122. A.G.M.Afr.N°526268, André Perraudin, "Rapport du Conseil du Séminaire sur les Vacances des Séminaristes," 9 April 1953. In a separate circular, Perraudin instructed local priests to keep their distance from the seminarians (A.G.M.Afr. N°526116, André Perraudin, "Circulaire au Prêtres," 8 July 1953).

123. This section draws upon A.G.M.Afr.N°526662, *Nyakibanda Rapport Annuel 1952*, 5 March 1953; A.G.M.Afr.N°526537, *Nyakibanda Rapport Annuel 1953*, 7 July 1953; A.G.M.Afr.N°731599, *Nyakibanda Rapport Annuel 1954-55*, 9 August 1955; A.G.M.Afr.N°731591-94, Perraudin to [Anon.], 15 December 1953.

124. Perraudin, *Un Évêque au Rwanda*, 18. For Leclercq's views on Christian civilization, church-state relations and social ethics, see Jacques Leclercq, *La Vie du Christ dans son Église* (Paris: Cerf, 1947), 217–47, 254–301 and Jacques Leclercq, *Vivre chrétiennement notre temps* (Tournai, Belgium: Casterman, 1957), 11–21, 38–83.

125. Stressing the Christian obligations to address structural sin, work for social justice, and embrace a "preferential option for the poor," liberation theology rose to prominence in Latin America during the 1960s and 1970s. South African "black theology" contained similar resonances during the same period. David Tombs' *Latin American Liberation Theology* (Boston: Brill, 2002) offers the best history of the movement. On the roots of black theology in South Africa, see Daniel Magaziner's *The Law and the Prophets: Black Consciousness in South Africa, 1968–1977* (Athens, OH: Ohio University Press, 2010).

126. C.M.L., André Perraudin, "Premier voyage à Burundi," 15 December 1947. A year later he praised the "frank collaboration" between the Belgian Resident, the Burundian Mwami, and Burundi's Vicar Apostolic. Perraudin was particularly appreciative of the Resident's gift of 300 million Belgian francs and the Mwami's gift of 50 million Rwandan francs to the Catholic missions (C.M.L., André Perraudin, "Les fêtes de l'action de grâces du Burundi, 1898–1948," 23 Aug. 1948).

127. Jean-Paul Harroy, *Rwanda: Souvenirs d'un Compagnon de la marche du Rwanda vers la démocratie et l'indépendance* (Brussels: Hayez, 1984), 228.

128. This section draws on A.G.M.Afr.N°526559, *Rapport Annuel 1952*, 5 March 1953; A.G.M.Afr.N°526272, Perraudin to Volker, 3 June 1953; A.G.M.Afr.N°526343, Volker to Perraudin, 4 September 1954.

129. Perraudin, *Un Évêque au Rwanda*, 19, 134. Perraudin struck a more antagonistic note in a 1995 interview with the Hutu priest and church historian Fortunatus Rudakemwa. "Hutu [seminarians] were considered as second class men by the others who said they were made to command with the mentality of the *Ubermensch* which you have known well in Germany" (quoted in Rudakemwa, *L'évangélisation du Rwanda*, 331–32).

130. This section draws on A.G.M.Afr.N°526539, *Rapport Annuel 1953–54*, 7 July 1954; A.G.M.Afr.N°526374-75, Langevin to Côte, 12 January 1955; A.G.M.Afr.N°526395, Boutry to Volker, 31 July 1955; A.G.M.Afr.N°526542, *Rapport de la réunion annuelle des Ordinaires*, 10 November 1955; A.G.M.Afr. N°526401, Perraudin to Volker, 4 October 1955; A.G.M.Afr.N°526322-23, De Canniere to Volker, 23 February 1954; A.G.M.Afr.N°526363, De Canniere to Volker, 15 December 1954; A.G.M.Afr.N°526380-81, Cogniaux to Volker, 13 March 1955; A.G.M.Afr.N°526380-81, Cogniaux to Volker, 13 March 1955; A.G.M.Afr.N°526609, Hellemans, Nyakibanda *Carte de Visite*, 19-30 March 1954; A.G.M.Afr.N°526401, Perraudin to Volker, 4 October 1955; A.G.M.Afr. N°526398, Perraudin to Durrieu, 12 August 1955.

131. Nothomb mentions a hemorrhage in November 1950 that sent Déprimoz back to Europe for months. Déprimoz also fell seriously ill near the end of 1951 (Nothomb, *Petite Histoire*, 120, 125).

132. A.G.M.Afr.N°542071, Déprimoz to Durrieu, 9 March 1955. The Catholic Church did not announce Déprimoz's resignation publicly until June 1955 (A.D.K., Déprimoz to Clergy & Religious, 3 June 1955).

133. This section draws upon A.G.M.Afr.N°543024, Volker to Dejemeppe, 8 January 1951; A.G.M.Afr.N°526782, Bushayija to Durrieu, 26 July 1955; Nothomb, *Petite Histoire*, 145; A.G.M.Afr.N°541408, Hartmann to Volker, 8 June 1955; A.G.M.Afr. N°541426-27, Van Heeswijk to Durrieu, 25 July 1955; A.G.M.Afr.N°541468-71, Aelvot to Durrieu, 13 October 1955.

134. A.G.M.Afr.N°540034, Cattin to Durrieu, 3 October 1952. Until he was sent to Rome in September 1952, Alexis Kagame had served as Déprimoz's personal secretary (Nothomb, *Petite Histoire*, 122).

135. A.G.M.Afr.N°526774, Dejemeppe to Déprimoz, 14 February 1954.

136. Stanislas Bushayija protested the "intense campaign against Fr. Dejemeppe" which he traced to the Mwami and his entourage (A.G.M.Afr.N°526782, Bushayija to Durrieu, 26 July 1955).

137. Most of this commentary comes from A.G.M.Afr.N°542056-57, Durrieu to Propaganda Fide, 13 May 1955.

138. Hartmann himself endorsed Perraudin, lauding Perraudin's piety, tact, Swiss identity, and the respect he had earned from missionaries and indigenous clergy (A.G.M.Afr.N°541408, Hartmann to Volker, 8 June 1955).

139. This section also draws on the nominating documents for Perraudin (cf. A.G.M.Afr.N°542042, Durrieu to Propaganda Fide, 13 May 1955 and A.G.M.Afr. N°542061, Durrieu to Propaganda Fide, 17 May 1955).

140. Rudakemwa, *L'évangélisation du Rwanda*, 328. Appointing Swedish, Danish, and Swiss missionaries to church leadership was not uncommon in late colonial Africa. They stood outside the national mission model and could theoretically offer the church more political credibility as decolonization accelerated (Hastings, *History of African Christianity*, 43).

141. Grauls quoted in A.G.M.Afr.N°542042, Durrieu to Propaganda Fide, 13 May 1955.

142. A.G.M.Afr.N°542040, [anon.], [n.d.].

143. This section draws on A.G.M.Afr.N°541449, Klep to Durrieu, 8 August 1955; A.G.M.Afr.N°541473-74, Levie to Durrieu, 18 October 1955; A.G.M.Afr. N°541494, Contini to Volker 15 November 1955; A.G.M.Afr.N°542065, Durrieu to Fumasoni-Biondi, 13 October 1955.

144. Cf. "Musenyeri André Perraudin, Umushumba wa vikariyati ya Kabgayi," *Kinyamateka* 25, 279 (1956): 1.

145. A.G.M.Afr.N°541550-51, Gasqui to Durrieu, 23 April 1956. For other positive comments, see A.G.M.Afr.N°526411, Kaisin to Durrieu, 23 December 1955; A.G.M.Afr.N°541513-14, Clemens to Durrieu, 3 January 1956; A.G.M.Afr. N°541519, Volker to Schaetzen, 23 January 1956; A.G.M.Afr.N°541417, Volker to De Canniere, 11 January 1956; A.G.M.Afr.N°526544, Permentier to Durrieu, 6 March 1956; A.G.M.Afr.N°541542, Levie to Durrieu, 5 April 1956.

146. A.G.M.Afr.N°541526, Beghin to Durrieu, 8 January 1956.

CHAPTER 4

1. According to Perraudin's retrospective account, Bigirumwami initially resisted Perraudin's requests. Perraudin does not speculate on Bigirumwami's possible reasons (Centre Missionnaire Lavigerie (C.M.L.), Kigali, André Perraudin "Je rends grâce à Dieu," (25 August 1989): 1). See also General Archives of the Missionaries of Africa (A.G.M.Afr.), N°542203, *Rapport Annuel du Vicariat du Kabgayi, 1 juillet 1955 au 30 juin 1956*.

2. Archives of the Diocese of Kabgayi (A.D.K.), André Perraudin, "Sacré," 25 March 1956. See also "Le Sacré de Monseigneur Perraudin," *Temps Nouveaux d'Afrique* (1 April 1956): 4–5; "Byose bigengwe n'urukundo, Myr Andreya Perraudin umushumba wa Vikariyati ya Kabgayi, y ahawe Ubwepiskopi," *Kinyamateka* 25, 282 (1956): 1, 4–5.

3. A.G.M.Afr.N°526546, Volker to Permentier, 16 March 1956.

4. A.D.K. André Perraudin, "Super omnia caritas," 6 January 1956; A.D.K., André Perraudin, "Aux fidèles du Vicariat apostolique de Kabgayi," 16 February 1956. In his autobiography Perraudin claimed to address social justice questions in these early letters, but I saw no such references in the letters themselves (cf. André Perraudin, *Un évêque au Rwanda: les six premières années de mon épiscopat (1956–1962)*. (Saint Maurice: Editions Saint-Augustin, 2003), 53–54).

5. A.D.K., André Perraudin, "Sacré," 25 March 1956.

6. A.G.M.Afr.N°542203, *Rapport Annuel du Vicariat du Kabgayi, 1 juillet 1955 au 30 juin 1956*.

7. A.G.M.Afr.N°526303, Perraudin to Van Volsem, 13 April 1956. See also *Trait d'Union* 48 (1956).

8. The colonial governor, Jean-Paul Harroy, later noted that he enjoyed very good relations with Mwami Mutara until the close of 1957 (cf. Jean-Paul Harroy, *Rwanda: Souvenirs d'un Compagnon de la marche du Rwanda vers la démocratie et l'indépendance* (Brussels: Hayez, 1984), 208).

9. A.G.M.Afr.N°526306, Perraudin to Durrieu, 15 May 1956; A.G.M.Afr.N°540316, Volker to Perraudin, 14 June 1956.

10. Details on the 1956 elections come from Filip Reyntjens, *Pouvoir et droit*, 185–96, 233; Fortunatus Rudakemwa, *L'évangélisation du Rwanda 1900–1959* (Paris: L'Harmattan, 2005), 268; Perraudin, *Un Évêque au Rwanda*, 126; Linden, *Church and Revolution*, 227; Lemarchand, *Rwanda and Burundi*, 81–88; Kalibwami, *Le Catholicisme*, 360–363; Harroy, *Rwanda: Souvenirs d'un Compagnon*, 226–227.

11. André Perraudin, "En vue des élections du 30 septembre," 9 September 1956, in Vénuste Linguyeneza, *Vérité, justice, charité: lettres pastorales et autres déclarations des évêques catholiques du Rwanda, 1956–1962* (Waterloo, Belgium, 2001), 35–36.

12. Paul Rutayisire, "L'Eglise catholique et le décolonisation du Rwanda ou les illusions d'une victoire," in *Rwanda: L'Eglise catholique à l'épreuve du génocide*, eds. F. Rutembesa, J.P. Karegeye, P. Rutayisire (Greenfield Park, Canada: Les Editions Africana, 2004), 47. These clans had typically dominated the Rwandan nobility. Mutara himself came from the Abanyiginya clan; many of his rivals like Bwanakweri came from the Abega clan.

13. Harroy, *Rwanda: Souvenirs d'un compagnon*, 249; Rutayisire, "L'Eglise catholique et le décolonisation du Rwanda," 50.

14. "Un Abbé Ruandais: nous parle," *La Presse Africaine*, 21 July 1956.

15. "Que valent les affirmations de la 'Presse Africaine'?" *Courrier d'Afrique*, 7 August 1956.

16. Cf. "Des notables Ruandaises nous parlent," *La Presse Africain*, 4 August 1956; "Que se passe-t-il au Ruanda-Urundi?" *Le Courrier d'Afrique*, 1 August 1956 and "Que valent les affirmations de la 'Presse Africaine'?," *Le Courrier d'Afrique*, 7 August 1956; "Procédés discutables," *Temps Nouveaux d'Afrique*, 12 August 1956; "Déclaration du Mwami Mutara au pays," *Temps Nouveaux d'Afrique*, 2 September 1956.

17. [Anon.], "Impressions sur le Ruanda d'un autochtone," *Dépêche du Rwanda-Urundi*, 24 August 1956.

18. Harroy, *Rwanda: Souvenirs d'un Compagnon*, 230.

19. "Déclaration du Mwami Mutara au pays," *Temps Nouveaux d'Afrique*, 2 September 1956. This article was reprinted in the 1 October 1956 issue of *Le Courrier d'Afrique*. Perraudin also quotes this text at length in *Un Évêque au Rwanda*, 114–116.

20. "Les chefs du Rwanda expriment leur loyalisme envers le Mwami," in Fidele Nkundabagenzi, Ed., *Rwanda Politique 1958-1960* (Brussels: Centre de Recherche

et d'Information Socio-Politique (CRISP), 1962), 34. See also "Déclaration des chefs du Ruanda," *Temps Nouveaux d'Afrique*, 7 October 1956, 4.

21. A.G.M.Afr.N°526312-314, Mosmans to Perraudin, 25 May 1956.

22. A.G.M.Afr.N°526307, Perraudin to Durrieu, 15 May 1956; A.G.M.Afr.N°540323, Perraudin to Van Volsem, 23 July 1956.

23. A.G.M.Afr.N°526307, Perraudin to Durrieu, 15 May 1956.

24. Cf. A.G.M.Afr.N°526552, "Nyakibanda rapport annuel pour l'exercice 1955–56," 31 August 1956. Brief Perraudin-Mutara correspondence can be reviewed in a dossier marked "Rwanda 1955-58" in the Diocese of Kabgayi archives (A.D.K., Mutara to Perraudin, 21 May 1956; Mutara to Perraudin, 21 December 1956; Perraudin to Mutara, 28 December 1956).

25. Cf. Jan Adriaenssens, *Rapport sur la situation religieuse, sociale, et économique du Ruanda-Urundi* (Geneva: Institut International Catholique de Recherches Socio-Ecclesiales, 13 July 1956), 10; A.G.M.Afr.N°541588-89, Watteuw to Durrieu, 4 August 1956; A.G.M.Afr.N°541626, Righi to Durrieu, 28 December 1956.

26. Kalibwami, *Le Catholicisme*, 371; C.M.L., Joseph Ntamahungiro, "Église Catholique du Rwanda: De la Spiritualité au Prophétisme," (2000), 4.

27. On the personnel shifts, see A.G.M.Afr.N°541547, Cattin to Durrieu, 20 April 1956; A.G.M.Afr.N°541627, Righi to Durrieu, 28 December 1956; A.G.M.Afr.N°526735-37, [untitled], 9 April 1956; A.D.K., André Perraudin, circular letter to Kabgayi priests & religious, 9 April 1956. The Kabgayi annual report described these appointments as "the most sensational event" since Perraudin's consecration (A.G.M.Afr.N°542206-07, *Rapport Annuel du Vicariat du Kabgayi, 1 juillet 1955 au 30 juin 1956*). Playing on words, Perraudin himself later described this as "*le massacre après le sacré*" (C.M.L., André Perraudin, "Je rends grâce à Dieu" (25 August 1989): 2).

28. This section draws on "Un Jubilé Historique 1906–1956," *Temps Nouveaux d'Afrique*, 16 December 1956, 9; "1906—Kabgayi—1956," *Kinyamateka* (December 1956): 6–7; "Message de Son Exc. Mgr Perraudin," *Grands Lacs* 186 (August-September 1956): 11; Perraudin, *Un Évêque au Rwanda*, 65–67; A.G.M.Afr.N°542210-12, *Rapport Annuel du Vicariat du Kabgayi, 1 juillet 1955 au 30 juin 1956*, 10–12; Adriaenssens, *Rapport sur la situation religieuse*, 9.

29. This report claimed that 80% of Catholic school graduates in education and artisanry had not found employment (A.G.M.Afr.N°738370, *Rapport annuel du Vicariat du Kabgayi*, 1956–57).

30. A.D.K., U.N. Trusteeship Council, T/Ac.36/L.60, "Study of Population, Land Utilization, and Land System in Ruanda-Urundi," 26 March 1957, 3.

31. A.D.K., Fidele Nkundabagenzi to André Perraudin, 25 December 1956. Nkundabagenzi is also notable for his 1962 collection of political primary source documents (cf. Nkundabagenzi, *Rwanda Politique 1958-1960*).

32. Cf. A.G.M.Afr.N°526293, Mosmans to Dejemeppe, 21 February 1956; A.G.M.Afr.N°740003, Mosmans to Van Overschelde, 18 November 1956;

A.G.M.Afr.N°740004, Van Overschelde to Mosmans, 21 November 1956; A.G.M.Afr.N°526308, Volker to Perraudin, 1 June 1956; Adriaenssens, *Rapport sur la situation religieuse*, 10–14; Louis Gasore, "L'Evolue face aux problèmes économico-sociaux," *Théologie et Pastorale au Ruanda 1* (1956): 1–59.

33. Joseph Ngomanzungu, "L'attitude de l'église catholique au Rwanda face aux problèmes sociopolitiques des années 1956-1962: Une pastorale de prévention, de médiation, et d'accompagnement," Mémoire de License, Pontifical Gregorian University, Rome (2000): 4. This manuscript can be consulted in the Nyakibanda Seminary library, Rwanda.

34. Perraudin, *Un Évêque au Rwanda*, 100.

35. Cf. "Déclaration de l'Épiscopat du Congo Belge et Ruanda-Urundi, 1956," *Temps Nouveaux d'Afrique*, 8 July 1956, 2–3. For background on this statement, see Rudakemwa, *L'évangélisation*, 301; Donat Murego, *La Révolution Rwandaise, 1959-1962* (Louvain: Institut des Sciences Politiques et Sociales, 1975), 731–32; Louis de Lacger (with Pierre Nothomb), *Ruanda* (Kabgayi, Rwanda: [n.p.], 1961), 714.

35. This will not be the last time that Rwandan church leaders engage political issues while citing a "distinction of planes" between the spiritual and the political. For a fascinating parallel with post-Vatican II Chile, see William T. Cavanaugh's *Torture and Eucharist: Theology, Politics and the Body of Christ* (Oxford: Blackwell, 1998).

37. For similar sentiments, see "Colonialisme," *Temps Nouveaux d'Afrique*, 20 April 1958, 1.

38. This section draws on "Lettre de Monseigneur le Vicaire Apostolique de Kabgayi," *Trait d'Union* 47 (1956); A.G.M.Afr.N°541552-54, Pien to Durrieu, 28 April 1956; A.G.M.Afr.N°738366, *Rapport Annuel du Vicariat Apostolique du Kabgayi*, 1956-1957; Lemarchand, *Rwanda and Burundi*, 147–48; Linden, *Church and Revolution*, 239; Mamdani, *When Victims Become Killers*, 118.

39. Linden, *Church and Revolution*, 251.

40. On the communist risk, see "Danger Communiste en Afrique," *Temps Nouveaux d'Afrique*, 13 January 1957, 1; "La Franc-maçonnerie," *Temps Nouveaux d'Afrique*, 3 February 1957, 8; "L'Afrique sera-t-elle communiste?" *Temps Nouveaux d'Afrique*, 31 March 1957, 1; "L'Afrique deviendra-t-elle communiste?" *Temps Nouveaux d'Afrique*, 7 April 1957, 3; "L'avenir de l'Afrique est sombre: Ce que l'on sait du Communisme en Afrique," *Temps Nouveaux d'Afrique*, 21 July 1957, 3; "Présence du Communisme en Afrique," *Temps Nouveaux d'Afrique*, 25 August 1957, 3. See also the Belgian missionary reflections contained in the 1957 "Semaine de Missiologie" in Louvain, particularly T. Theuws, "Le danger communiste et la mission au Congo," *Communisme et Missions, XXVII Semaine de Missiologie* (Louvain: 1957): 131–32. On the continuing problem of race relations, see "Un dialogue entre Blancs et Noirs est-il encore possible?" *Temps Nouveaux d'Afrique*, 20 October 1957, 1; "L'Afrique noire perdra-t-elle son âme?" *Temps Nouveaux d'Afrique*, 3 November 1957, 1.

41. Information here is drawn from A.D.K., U.N. Visiting Mission to Trust Territories in East Africa, *1957 Report on Ruanda-Urundi*, 6 December 1957, 7–8; Reyntjens, *Pouvoir et droit*, 214–17.

42. The Superior Council's *Mise au point* is transcribed in its entirety in Murego, *La Révolution Rwandaise*, 754–57.

43. Cf. Jean-Pierre Chrétien, *The Great Lakes of Africa: Two Thousand Years of History*. Trans. Scot Strauss (New York: Zone, 2003), 301; Linden, *Church and Revolution*, 249; Mamdani, *When Victims Become Killers*, 125; Jean Nizurengo Rugagi, "Décolonisation et démocratisation du Rwanda," *Cahiers Lumière et Société* 7 (1997): 48–49.

44. C.M.L., André Perraudin, "Je rends grâce à Dieu," 25 August 1989, 2. Perraudin here rejected the idea that he served as a political counselor for Kayibanda. "Kayibanda was very independent in his political action…He had great respect for the Church; but I have never influenced him politically" (2). See also Perraudin, *Un Évêque au Rwanda*, 138.

45. Kalibwami, *Le Catholicisme*, 386. See also Rudakemwa, *L'évangélisation du Rwanda*, 306.

46. Perraudin's personal secretary was Calliope Mulindahabi, not Gregoire Kayibanda. Perraudin notes that his personal secretary in 1957 was Mulindahabi rather than Kayibanda; Kalibwami and Rudakemwa confirm this (cf. Perraudin, *Un Évêque au Rwanda*, 141; Kalibwami, *Le Catholicisme*, 374; Rudakemwa, *L'évangélisation*, 307–308).The mistaken (and often polemical) claim that Kayibanda was Perraudin's personal secretary has been repeated widely, especially in recent Anglophone literature on Rwanda (cf. Lemarchand, *Rwanda and Burundi*, 143; Mamdani, *When Victims Become Killers*, 118; Gérard Prunier, *The Rwanda Crisis: History of a Genocide* (New York: Columbia University Press, 1995), 45).

47. Murego notes that the *Groupe Scolaire d'Astrida* was only opened to Hutu students in 1955. Prior to this date, the Catholic seminary provided the only viable means for secondary education for Hutu (Murego, *La Révolution Rwandaise*, 679).

48. I have not located a reliable English translation, but the Bahutu Manifesto can be consulted in French in "Le Manifeste des Bahutu, 24 March 1957," in Nkundabagenzi, *Rwanda Politique*, 20–29. Surprisingly, *Temps Nouveaux* did not publish the document until four months after its initial release ("Le manifeste des Bahutu," *Temps Nouveaux d'Afrique*, 14 July 1957, 1; repeated in *Temps Nouveaux d'Afrique*, 4 May 1958, 5). For secondary commentary, see Kalibwami, *Le Catholicisme*, 375–84; Lemarchand, *Rwanda and Burundi*, 149–51; Mamdani, *When Victims Become Killers*, 116–17.

49. "Le Manifeste des Bahutu" in Nkundabagenzi, *Rwanda Politique*, 24.

50. Ibid., 28.

51. Ibid., 29.

52. Harroy quoted in A.D.K., U.N. Visiting Mission to Trust Territories in East Africa, *1957 Report on Ruanda-Urundi*, 6 December 1957, 16. Harroy did not even mention the Hutu-Tutsi question in his long discourse to the Superior Council in August 1957 (cf. "Discours de M. le Vice-Gouverneur Général Harroy au Conseil Général du Ruanda-Urundi," *Temps Nouveaux d'Afrique*, 4 August 1957, 1–8). This silence undermines his later claims that he informed the U.N. Visiting Commission that the Hutu-Tutsi question was the "chief problem of the country" (Harroy, *Rwanda: Souvenirs d'un compagnon de la marche*, 232).

53. Quoted in Murego, *La Révolution Rwandaise*, 863–64 and Perraudin, *Un Évêque au Rwanda*, 134. See also Reyntjens, *Pouvoir et droit*, 218–20.

54. Background information here is drawn from Reyntjens, *Pouvoir et droit*, 218–20; Perraudin, *Un Évêque au Rwanda*, 125–26, 153; Murego, *La Révolution Rwandaise*, 709–10.

55. A.D.K., U.N. Trusteeship Council, T/Ac.36/L.60, "Study of Population, Land Utilization, and Land System in Ruanda-Urundi," 26 March 1957, 4–5.

56. A.D.K., U.N. Visiting Mission, *1957 Report on Ruanda-Urundi*, 6 December 1957, 14–15.

57. Leroy quoted in Murego, *Révolution Rwandaise*, 863–64.

58. All of these quotations are taken from A.D.K., U.N. Visiting Mission to Trust Territories in East Africa, *1957 Report on Ruanda-Urundi*, 9–10.

59. Cf. "Vers une doctrine sociale coloniale," *Temps Nouveaux d'Afrique*, 15 July 1956.

60. This section draws upon A.G.M.Afr.N°541630, Werleye to Durrieu, 5 January 1957; A.G.M.Afr.N°541645-48, Hartmann to Durrieu, 21 April 1957; A.G.M.Afr.N°541644, Durrieu to Derson, 8 June 1957; A.G.M.Afr.N°731083, Volker to Boutry, 14 December 1957. The Perraudin-Noti correspondence can be found in A.G.M.Afr.N°739483-487, 25 September 1957, 30 September 1957, 3 October 1957.

61. A.G.M.Afr.N°542046, Perraudin to [Anon], 15 February 1957.

62. A.G.M.Afr.N°541644, Durrieu to Derson, 8 June 1957.

63. Cf. "Lettre pastorale des Vicaires Apostoliques du Ruanda-Urundi—La Justice," *Temps Nouveaux d'Afrique*, 31 March 1957, 2. For commentary, see Kalibwami, *Le Catholicisme*, 421–22.

64. To highlight just one example, Burundi's Mwami Mwambutsa adopted a far more pro-Belgian line than Mwami Mutara between 1957 and 1959. While Mutara's allies on the Superior Council were calling for Rwandan independence as early as 1957, Mwambutsa requested as late as 1959 that Belgium *not* set a deadline for relinquishing its territorial trusteeship. For an example of Mwambutsa's pro-Belgian rhetoric, see "Discours du Mwami du Burundi au Groupe de Travail—23 April 1959," *Temps Nouveaux d'Afrique*, 10 May 1959, 3.

65. Adriaenssens, *Rapport sur la situation religieuse*, 14.

66. Linden, *Church and Revolution*, 251. On the connections between the Belgian political left and late colonial Hutu nationalism, see Léon Saur, *Influences*

parallèles: L'Internationale démocratie-chrétienne au Rwanda (Brussels: Editions Luc Pire, 1998).

67. Cf. Reyntjens, *Pouvoir et droit*, 231; Linden, *Church and Revolution*, 234.

68. It is always dangerous for the historian to extrapolate from absence. However, in light of the growing ethnic disputes amongst intellectuals, political elites, and Catholic seminarians, one should note the dearth of references to ethnic tensions in the mission stations (cf. A.G.M.Afr.N°739340, Longueval (Astrida) to Volker, 22 July 1957; A.G.M.Afr.N°739343, Duchamps (Mushishoro) to Volker, 8 August 1957; A.G.M.Afr.N°739348, Marien (Kansi) to Volker, 22 September 1957; A.G.M.Afr.N°739355, Franzen (Nyamata) to Volker, 26 September 1957; A.G.M.Afr.N°739362, Tasse (Rwesero) to Volker, 21 November 1957; A.G.M.Afr. N°739375, Landtmeters (Zaza) to Volker, 4 December 1957).

69. Cf. "Les vingt-cinq ans de règne du Mwami du Ruanda," *Temps Nouveaux d'Afrique*, 7 July 1957, 8–9. For background, see Perraudin, *Un Évêque au Rwanda*, 143–44; Rudakemwa, *L'évangelisation*, 313; Linden, *Church and Revolution*, 255.

70. A.G.M.Afr.N°731006, Boutry to Volker, 19 July 1957.

71. A.G.M.Afr.N°731287-88, *Rapport annuel du Nyakibanda*, 1956–1957.

72. Cf. "Yubile y'Ingoma 1931-ya Mutara III-1957," *Kinyamateka* 25, 13 July 1957, 1. For background, see Paul Rutayisire, "Les signes précurseurs de la crise de la Toussaint rwandaise," *Dialogue 189* (November 2009): 18.

73. A.G.M.Afr.N°741610-13, "Rapport de la visite du Grand Séminaire de Nyakibanda du 31 Octobre au 13 Novembre 1956," 14 November 1956.

74. A.G.M.Afr.N°731083, Volker to Boutry, 14 December 1957; A.G.M.Afr. N°731081-82, Boutry to Mondor, 4 December 1957; A.G.M.Afr.N°727057-62, Van Hoof to Cauwe, 5 December 1957.

75. In late 1957 Cogniaux named the arrogance, pride and "profoundly pagan mentality" of the Tutsi seminarians as the root causes of Nyakibanda's problems (A.G.M.Afr.N°7310768, Cogniaux to Mondor, 16 December 1957).

76. A.G.M.Afr.N°541627, Righi to Durrieu, 28 December 1956. For Righi this explained why Perraudin had promoted undeserving indigenous priests to lead local mission stations.

77. A.G.M.Afr.N°739367-68, Hartmann to Volker, 24 December 1957.

78. A.G.M.Afr.N°542049, Perraudin to [Anon.], 15 February 1957; A.G.M.Afr. N°739003, Volker to Perraudin, 3 December 1957.

79. A.G.M.Afr.N°738366, *Rapport Annuel du Vicariat Apostolique du Kabgayi*, 1956-57.

80. A.D.K., André Perraudin, "Allocution aux Anciens du Groupe Scolaire d'Astrida à l'occasion du 150me anniversaire de la Fondation de la Congrégation des Frères de la Charité," 8 November 1957.

81. A.G.M.Afr.N°739345, Levie to Volker, 23 August 1957. Cogniaux credited Perraudin's and Bigirumwami's retreat days for ameliorating intra-clerical tensions at the seminary (A.G.M.Afr.N°731076, Cogniaux to Mondor, 16 December

1957). On Perraudin's commitment to building pastoral capacity, see "Bréve rencontre avec S. Exc. Mgr. Perraudin vicaire apostolique de Nyundo et M. Abbé Cuvellier l'envoyé du diocèse de Namur à Nyanza," *Temps Nouveaux d'Afrique,* 12 May 1957, 2.

82. A.D.K., U.N. Visiting Mission to Trust Territories in East Africa, *1957 Report on Ruanda-Urundi,* 21.

83. "To be sure, nobody in Rwanda in the late 1950s had offered an alternative to a tribal construction of politics" (Philip Gourevitch, *We wish to inform you that tomorrow we will be killed with our children: Stories from Rwanda* (New York: Picador, 1998), 61).

84. Cf. "Les Bahutu au Conseil Supérieur du Ruanda," *Temps Nouveaux d'Afrique,* 23 March 1958, 3. For background see Ernest Mutwarasibo, "Crispation ethnique à la fin du règne de Mutara III Rudahigwa," *Dialogue 188* (2009): 157–180.

85. In Perraudin's words, after these meetings "the rupture was consummated between Hutu and Tutsi [and] a new phase was opened in the conflict which opposed them" (Perraudin, *Un Évêque au Rwanda,* 169).

86. For secondary commentary on the Hutu-Tutsi Study Commission and the reactions of the Mwami and the CSP, see Linden, *Church and Revolution,* 252–255; Perraudin, *Un Évêque au Rwanda,* 153–67; Murego, *La Révolution Rwandaise,* 871; Kalibwami, *Le Catholicisme,* 450–55.

87. Linden, *Church and Revolution,* 252.

88. The quotations are taken from the transcript of the first debate of the CSP commission on the Hutu-Tutsi question (cf. A.D.K., "Comité de l'étude de l'aspect social Muhutu-Mututsi (CSP), 31 March–3 April 1958"). For similar sentiments, see "Interview de M. Joseph Gitera," *Temps Nouveaux d'Afrique,* 27 April 1958, 3.

89. Perraudin, *Un Évêque au Rwanda,* 127–28.

90. A.D.K., "Deuxième Séance de l'étude de l'aspect social muhutu-mututsi, 10-12 April 1958," 5–9.

91. A.D.K., "Comité de l'étude de l'aspect social Muhutu-Mututsi (CSP), 31 March–3 April 1957," 6.

92. A.D.K., "Deuxième Séance de l'étude de l'aspect social muhutu-mututsi, 10-12 April 1958," 7.

93. A.D.K., "Comité de l'étude de l'aspect social Muhutu-Mututsi (CSP), 31 March–3 April 1957," 5.

94. "Egalité raciale au Ruanda," *Revue du clergé africain* X, no. 6 (1955): 602.

95. "Lettre de M.A. Maus au Vice-gouverneur Général," in Nkundabagenzi, *Rwanda Politique,* 13. After colonial administrators ignored his April 1956 letter, Maus left the Belgian administration and later became a pro-Hutu polemicist during the Rwandan revolution.

96. A.D.K., "Deuxième Séance de l'étude de l'aspect social muhutu-mututsi, 10-12 April 1958," 15–16; A.D.K., "Le Comité d'étude du problème social muhutu-mututsi reprend session," 9–11 April 1958, 5–6.

97. A.D.K., "Comité de l'étude de l'aspect social Muhutu-Mututsi (CSP), 31 March–3 April 1957," 3.

98. Ibid.

99. A.D.K., "Le Comité d'étude du problème social muhutu-mututsi reprend session," 9–11 April 1958, 6, 11. A.D.K., "Deuxième Séance de l'étude de l'aspect social muhutu-mututsi, 10–12 April 1958," 13.

100. A.D.K., "Deuxième Séance de l'étude de l'aspect social muhutu-mututsi, 10–12 April 1958," 16.

101. In a contemporaneous article on the CSP debates, the White Fathers' journal *Temps Nouveaux d'Afrique* referred to Hutu and Tutsi as "social groups." Cf. "Pendant quinze jours: Les Bahutu à Nyanza…," *Temps Nouveaux d'Afrique,* 20 April 1958, 1.

102. All of these quotations can be found in A.D.K., "Deuxième Séance de l'étude de l'aspect social muhutu-mututsi, 10-12 April 1958," 13. In a later conversation, Gitera rejected the idea that a "poor Tutsi" could represent the Hutu masses, claiming that this "would not alleviate our fears" (A.D.K., "Le Comité d'étude du problème social muhutu-mututsi reprend session," 9–11 April 1958, 9).

103. Writing seven months later, even the Hutu propagandist Gaspard Cyimana admitted a high degree of ethnic intermixing in central Rwanda. For Cyimana, observers could only make clear racial distinctions between Hutu, Tutsi, and Twa in other regions of the country (G. Cyimana, "Problèmes sociaux et ethniques au Ruanda," *Temps Nouveaux d'Afrique,* 2 November 1958, 3).

104. While Hutu made up a large majority of younger primary school populations, Tutsi comprised a majority in later primary and secondary years. For statistics on 21 Catholic schools in central Rwanda, see A.D.K., "Enquête Bahutu-Batutsi 1956-57, Secteur Nord, Kigali."

105. A.D.K., "Troisième Session du Comité de l'étude la question sociale Muhutu-mututsi," 7–9.

106. A.D.K., Innocent Gasabwoya to School Directors, 30 April 1958; A.D.K., "Troisième Session du Comité de l'étude la question sociale Muhutu-mututsi," 8.

107. "Premier écrit de Nyanza" and "Deuxième écrit de Nyanza," 17–18 May 1958, in Nkundabagenzi, *Rwanda Politique,* 35–37.

108. "Le dernier Conseil Supérieur du Rwanda: Lamentables débats," *Temps Nouveaux d'Afrique,* 6 July 1958, 5. As Ian Linden notes, the document's signatories reflected an older generation of Tutsi chiefs rather than the younger generation of Tutsi *évolués* more enamored with anti-colonial nationalism (Linden, *Church and Revolution,* 253–55).

109. Quoted in "Le dernier Conseil Supérieur du Ruanda: Lamentables débats," *Temps Nouveaux d'Afrique,* 6 July 1958, 5.

110. "Position du Conseil Supérieur et du Mwami," in Nkundabagenzi, *Rwanda Politique,* 37. The Hutu delegation to the CSP immediately protested that "we want the term Muhutu strongly and frequently utilized in view of its

REHABILITATION, a term whose original sense has been associated with slavery (*servage*)." ("Le dernier Conseil Supérieur du Ruanda: Lamentables débats," *Temps Nouveaux d'Afrique*, 6 July 1958, 5.)

111.   Even before the Mwami's statement, the U.N. *tutelle* had approved the statutes of Gregoire Kayibanda's new *Mouvement Social Muhutu*, lending public legitimacy to the MSM's demands for democratization and the promotion of what the MSM termed the "Bahutu race-class."

112.   The text is included in Murego, *La Révolution Rwandaise*, 882.

113.   A.G.M.Afr.N°739394, Gilles to Volker, 3 March 1958.

114.   A.G.M.Afr.N°739414, Reners to Van Volsem, 10 October 1958. The continued importance of winning over the *évolués* is echoed by the director of Catholic Action (cf. A.G.M.Afr.N°739420-24, De Renesse to Volker, 6 November 1958).

115.   A.G.M.Afr.N°731049, Boutry to Volker, 27 March 1958.

116.   Cf. A.G.M.Afr.N°739372, Van Oosterhout to Volker, 7 January 1958; A.G.M.Afr. N°739381, Van der Meersch to Volker, 25 January 1958; A.G.M.Afr.N°739383, Nothomb to Volker, 4 March 1958; A.G.M.Afr.N°739389, Van Oosterhout to Volker, 6 April 1958; A.G.M.Afr.N°739389, Martin to Volker, 7 April 1958; A.G.M.Afr.N°739386, Gasser to Volker, 21 April 1958; A.G.M.Afr.N°739397, Noti to Volker, 22 May 1958; A.G.M.Afr.N°739413, Quanonne to Volker, 20 June 1958; A.G.M.Afr.N°739399, Brutsaert to Volker, 4 July 1958; A.G.M.Afr. N°739140, Werly to Volker, 24 September 1958; A.G.M.Afr.N°739417, Bourgois to Volker, 20 October 1958.

117.   Perraudin, *Un Évêque au Rwanda*, 151; A.G.M.Afr.N°738023, Perraudin to Cauwe, 18 January 1958; A.G.M.Afr.N°738039, Perraudin to Cauwe, 27 January 1958; A.G.M.Afr.N°738033-34, Perraudin to Cauwe, 21 March 1958.

118.   A.G.M.Afr.N°731050, Volker to Boutry, 21 April 1958. The views of the Holy See and the Apostolic Delegate would offer a more complete picture of Catholic hierarchical reactions at this time. Vatican archival sources are released after a 75-year waiting period.

119.   Lemarchand, *Rwanda and Burundi*, 107.

120.   Louis Gasore, "Quelques problèmes de l'élite africaine," *Vivante Afrique 198* (1958): 29–32.

121.   Cf. "Colonialisme," *Temps Nouveaux d'Afrique*, 20 April 1958, 1; "Le Colonialisme est-il légitime?" and "Interview de M. Joseph Gitera," *Temps Nouveaux d'Afrique*, 27 April 1958, 1; "Le Conseil-General du Ruanda-Urundi—Un conseil représentatif de quoi?" *Temps Nouveaux d'Afrique*, 15 June 1958, 1; "L'avenir de l'Afrique n'est pas dans le colonialisme," *Temps Nouveaux d'Afrique*, 22 June 1958, 1; "Le temps de la décolonisation est arrivé," *Temps Nouveaux d'Afrique*, 6 July 1958, 1.

122.   Aloys Bigirumwami, "L'Eglise a raison d'exiger plus de justice," 15 April 1958, in Linguyeneza, *Vérité, Justice, Charité*, 50–56. For background, see Linden, *Church and Revolution*, 256.

123. Bigirumwami, "L'Eglise a raison d'exiger plus de justice," 15 April 1958. Bigirumwami's gradualist, pan-ethnic vision of social justice is reflected in a December 1958 commentary from his diocesan newspaper, *Civitas Mariae*. Here Bigirumwami wrote that the church "looked not only to apostolic and purely spiritual action, but also in the temporal plan, especially in a campaign for the construction of houses in durable materials, searching to help all those who make efforts to improve their homes, work as artisans, and join cooperatives" (Aloys Bigirumwami, *Civitas Mariae* 11, December 1958, 3).

124. The article appeared in the 5 September 1958 edition of *Témoignage Chrétien* and can be consulted in Nkundabagenzi, *Rwanda politique*, 38–42. For analysis, see Kalibwami, *Le Catholicisme*, 422–33; Linden, *Church and Revolution*, 256.

125. Cf. Bigirumwami in Nkundabagenzi, *Rwanda politique*, 42.

126. A.D.K., Bigirumwami to [Anon.], 16 March 1959.

127. A.D.K., Dominique Nothomb, "Note sur la pensée chrétienne, face au conflit Batutsi-Bahutu, tel qu'il se pose au Rwanda."

128. Writing several years later, Dominique Nothomb's brother Pierre Nothomb saw the emergence of "racial language" as one of the major changes in Rwandan political discourse in 1958. Cf. De Lacger and Nothomb, *Ruanda*, 715.

129. Nothomb, "Note sur la pensée chrétienne," 3.

130. A.G.M. Afr.N°720645-66, Guy Mosmans, "L'avenir politique du Ruanda-Urundi," 21 September 1958.

131. Ibid. Emphases are found in the text.

132. Ibid.

133. The risk of nationalism for Christian mission was also a prominent theme in the annual "Semaine de Missiologie" hosted in Belgium in 1958. See in particular R.P. de Soras, "Les tentations du nationalisme," 9–33; M.M. Lihau, "Les aspirations nationales au Congo belge," 157–164; M. Espéret, "Le laïc chrétien devant le nationalisme," 195–214; R.P. Masson, "Le missionaire et le nationalisme," 215–26. All of these articles can be located in *Aspirations Nationales et Missions, 1958. XXVIII Semaine de Missologie* (Louvain: Desclee de Brouwer, 1958). Of course, missionaries tended to be more critical of African nationalism than its European colonial variants.

134. A.G.M.Afr.N°740379, Alphonse van Hoof, *Rapport on le vicariat du Nyundo*, 3 January 1958; A.G.M.Afr.N°739402-07, Rommelaere to Volker, 17 August 1958; A.D.K., Vargas to Perraudin, 25 June 1958.

135. A.G.M.Afr.N°740329-41, *Rapport du Vicariat Apostolique de Nyundo, 1957-58*, 1 July 1958.

136. This paragraph draws on "Sacre de Son Excellence Monseigneur Bigirumwami 1 Juin 1952," *L'Ami* 91 (1952): 133; A.G.M.Afr.N°740209, Bigirumwami to Boutry, 21 July 1958; A.G.M.Afr.N°731130-33, Boutry to Bigirumwami, 8 August 1958; A.G.M.Afr.N°740204, Bigirumwami to Boutry, 20 August 1958.

137. This section draws on A.G.M.Afr.N°731304, *Rapport annuel du Nyakibanda, 1957-58*, December 1958; A.G.M.Afr.N°731066-68, Feys to Cauwe, 7 March 1958; A.G.M.Afr.N°731046, Boutry to Mondor, 8 February 1958; A.G.M.Afr. N°727046-48, Van Hoof to Cauwe, 3 February 1958; A.G.M.Afr.N°738025, Cauwe to Perraudin, 15 February 1958; A.G.M.Afr.N°738027, Cauwe to Perraudin, 4 March 1958; A.G.M.Afr.N°738033-34, Perraudin to Cauwe, 21 March 1958; A.G.M.Afr.N°731060, Mondor to Boutry, 25 June 1958; A.G.M.Afr. N°731063, Slenders to Volker, 17 August 1958.

138. For summaries of the clerical study days, see *Trait d'Union* 62 (1958): 122–23; Rudakemwa, *L'évangélisation du Rwanda*, 326-27.

139. Unfortunately I have not located any records of these deliberations in either the White Fathers archives in Rome or Rwandan diocesan archives. I assume the committee's conclusions informed Perraudin's Lent 1959 pastoral "Super Omnia Caritas."

140. A.D.K., André Perraudin, Circulaire N°17, 9 October 1958.

141. The original Aprosoma manifesto against the Kalinga drums can be consulted in the Diocese of Kabgayi archives (A.D.K., Joseph Gitera, "Ijwi Lya Rubanda Rugufi," October 1958). Perraudin also critiqued Gitera for issuing a political manifesto under the umbrella of the Catholic youth organization *Jeunesse Chrétienne Ruandaise* without obtaining Perraudin's authorization (A.D.K., Perraudin to Gitera, 21 October 1958).

142. The January 1959 dedication of the Benedictine monastery at Gihindamuyaga drew a large crowd and included one of the last joint public appearances of Perraudin and Mwami Mutara (cf. "Bénédiction de la chapelle et inauguration monastique á Gihindamuyaga," *Trait d'Union* 67 (1959), 73–77).

143. A.G.M.Afr.N°738058-060, Perraudin to Cauwe, 27 January 1959; A.G.M.Afr. N°720625, Guy Mosmans, "Note sur l'évolution politique du Ruanda-Urundi," 17 January 1959.

144. A.D.K., André Perraudin, "Super omnia caritas," 11 February 1959. This letter can also be consulted as "Par dessus tout, la charité," *Temps Nouveaux d'Afrique*, 1 March 1959, 8.

145. Perraudin, *Un Évêque au Rwanda*, 187, 194. Perraudin's redactions of the original text reflected his self-confidence—there are very few differences between his original draft and the final version. Early redactions of *Super omnia caritas* can be consulted in the Diocese of Kabgayi archives (A.D.K., André Perraudin, "Lettre pastorale pour l'année 1959," [undated].)

146. Perraudin, "Super omnia caritas," 5.

147. Ibid., 9–13, 23.

148. Ibid., 33.

149. Ibid., 33–37.

150. A.D.K., "Circulaire no. 20, 11 Février 1959."

151. Ibid.

152. Nor would his analysis shift during the polemics of 1959–1960. Writing to Rome in May 1960, Perraudin still described Rwanda according to classic missionary typologies. "The inhabitants all have the same language but they are of different races: we have distinguished the Batutsi, until now the leadership class (around 14% of the population), the Bahutu, cultivators, who form the mass (85% of the population), and some Batwa, pygmies." (A.G.M.Afr.N°739011, André Perraudin, "Renseignement concerne Archidiocèse de Kabgayi," 19 May 1960)

153. Cf. Mamdani, *When Victims Become Killers*, 117–18.

154. C.M.L., André Perraudin, "Je rends grâce à Dieu," 25 August 1989, 2; C.M.L., Bernard Muzungu, "Le rôle des responsables des religions reconnues au Rwanda, pendant le génocide," [n.d.].

155. A.D.K., Harroy to Perraudin, 9 March 1959. Perraudin had sent Harroy and Mutara personal copies of *Super omnia caritas* in February 1959.

156. Perraudin, *Un Évêque au Rwanda*, 192; C.M.L., André Perraudin, "Je rends grace à Dieu," 25 August 1989, 2. Perraudin admitted in this 1989 presentation that "God alone knows what he [the Mwami] wanted to say by this." It should be noted that Mutara developed especially close relations with Dr. Joe Church and the Church Missionary Society at Gahini. Rumors circulated in early 1959 that the Mwami was considering converting to Anglicanism, in part so he could remarry and conceive an heir (Linden, *Church and Revolution*, 259–61; Rudakemwa, *L'évangélisation*, 330–33).

157. The letter was published in full in a 5 March 1959 issue of *Le Courrier d'Afrique*. The Belgian-based *Le Croix* requested a copy of the letter, as did the missiology faculty at the Catholic University of Nijmegen in Holland. See here Perraudin's media file on "Super Omnia Caritas" in the Diocese of Kabgayi archives.

158. Aloys Bigirumwami, "L'évêque de Nyundo parle de l'Aprosoma (10 mars 1959)," in Linguyeneza, *Vérité, Justice, Charité*, 81–91. Rutayisire argues that *Kinyamateka* maintained a broad editorial policy on the Hutu-Tutsi question between 1955 and 1959, serving as a "tribune of expression" for the competing voices in Rwandan politics (P. Rutayisire, "Les signes précurseurs de la crise de la Toussaint rwandaise," *Dialogue 189* (2009): 29–38).

159. A.D.K., Bigirumwami to [Anon.], 16 March 1959. Bigirumwami addresses this letter to "my dear *abbé*" but does not specify his name. Considering the tone of the letter and its housing in the official archives of the Diocese of Kabgayi, I think it plausible to identify the recipient as Innocent Gasabwoya, the Tutsi vicar general of Kabgayi and overall director of *Kinyamateka* at the time.

160. Ibid.

161. *Civitas Mariae* 15 (April 1959): 6–7.

162. M.G. Cyimana, "Plaidoyer pour le menu peuple au Rwanda-Burundi," in F. Nkundabagenzi, *Rwanda Politique*, 55–75. In this article Cyimana praises Belgian colonists for eliminating the worst abuses of Rwanda's pre-colonial

society. He also argues that the pre-colonial ennoblement of Hutu elites undermined Hutu dignity by reclassifying them as Tutsi (63–64).

163. Quoted in Bigirumwami, "L'évêque de Nyundo parle de l'Aprosoma," 10
      March 1959.

164. A.G.M.Afr.N°722156, A. Munyangaju, "L'actualité politique au Ruanda,"
      January 1959, 13, 28.

165. Ibid., 32, 35–36. Munyangaju continued to frame his argument in democratic
      rather than ethnic terms through the spring of 1959 (cf. Aloys Munyangaju,
      "Le Ruanda-Urundi sera-t-il autonome en 1960?" *Temps Nouveaux d'Afrique*, 10
      May 1959, 1).

166. G. Kayibanda, "Ce que visent les Bahutu est une démocratie sans esclavage,"
      Kinyamateka, 15 April 1959. A French translation of this article—along with
      many other key sources from the late 1950s period—was included on the
      Belgium-based website of the *Centre d'Information et d'Étude sur le Rwanda*
      (cf. http://www.cier-be.info). Unfortunately, this website was taken down in
      2011. As will be discussed below, Kayibanda continued to serve as an editor at
      Kinyamateka until Perraudin removed him from the position in October 1959.

167. Kayibanda, "Nos devises sont presque les mêmes (Tunyuranyije kuri bike),"
      Kinyamateka, 15 May 1959.

168. Kayibanda, "Renoncez à la désinformation (Impuha nimuzange)," *Kinyamateka*,
      15 June 1959.

169. "Rapport soumis au Groupe de Travail par le Conseil Supérieur du Pays, April
      1959," in F. Nkundabagenzi, *Rwanda Politique*, 76–84.

170. Ibid., 82–83.

171. "Mr le Vice-gouverneur Général Harroy traite du problème hutu-tutsi," *Temps
      Nouveaux d'Afrique*, 7 December 1958, 3. All of the subsequent quotations are
      taken from this address.

172. Harroy later claimed that he issued this statement as a response to Mwami
      Mutara's denial of the existence of a Hutu-Tutsi problem at the June 1958 CSP
      session (Harroy: *Rwanda: Souvenirs d'un compagnon*, 251).

173. See also Harroy, *Rwanda: Souvenirs d'un Compagnon*, 209–13.

174. A.G.M.Afr.N°721001, *Rapport du Groupe du Travail concernant le problème poli-
      tique du Ruanda-Urundi, 1958–59*, September 1959. For secondary commentary,
      see Murego, *La Révolution Rwandaise*, 892–93. Writing shortly after Belgium's
      announcement, Guy Mosmans argued that the Belgians were sending a work-
      ing group to Rwanda-Burundi "to avoid the reproach of having imposed some
      choice without having taken the advice of interested parties…[the working
      group] will be very useful for giving the government a solid basis for imposing
      reforms" (A.G.M.Afr.N°720625, Guy Mosmans, "Note sur l'évolution politique
      du Ruanda-Urundi," 17 January 1959).

175. J.J. Maquet, *The Premises of Inequality in Rwanda* (London: Oxford University
      Press, 1961).

176. A.G.M.Afr.N°721001, *Rapport du Groupe du Travail*, 4. Leon Saur notes that August de Schryver, the head of the Working Group, was a former leader of the Belgian PSC-CVP (Parti Social Chrétien-Christelijke Volkspartij), a center-left party rooted in the Catholic Church and known for its commitment to decolonization and social justice. The PSC-CVP won a majority in the June 1958 Belgian elections and subsequently led Belgium to disengage from its colonies and support Hutu counter-elites in Rwanda (Saur, *Influences parallèles*, 29).

177. A.G.M.Afr.N°721001, *Rapport du Groupe du Travail*, 29.

178. A.G.M.Afr.N°721001, *Rapport du Groupe du Travail*, 100–109. One should note that the Belgian Working Group applied this language of "non-autochthonous" only to resident Congolese, not to local Tutsi. There are ample references to the Tutsi as a racial group in both Catholic and colonial literature in the 1950s, but I have not located a reference to the Tutsi as a *non-indigenous* race until the 1960s. Mahmood Mamdani thus overstates his case when he alleges that the colonial racialization of the Tutsi transformed them into a non-autochthonous race. "The third phase (in changing Hutu-Tutsi identities) came with the colonial period, when both Hutu and Tutsi were racialized, Tutsi as a nonindigenous identity of (subordinate) power and Hutu as an indigenous identity of (nativized) subjects. To the late nineteenth century dynamic whereby Tutsi symbolized power and Hutu subject, a new and truly volatile dimension was added. This was the dimension of indigeneity; for the first time in the centuries-long history of the Rwandan state, Tutsi became identified with an alien race and Hutu with the indigenous majority" (Mamdani, *When Victims Become Killers*, 102). For another version of this indigeneity thesis, see Paul Rutayisire, "Le Tutsi étranger dans le pays de ses aïeux," *Les Cahiers: Evangile et Société: Les Idéologies*, no. 4 (1996): 42–55.

179. *Rapport du Groupe du Travail*, 7, 33–35.

180. A.G.M.Afr. N°722156, Aloys Munyangaju, "L'actualité politique au Ruanda," January 1959, 19, 23.

181. Harroy echoed this thirty years later, claiming that only 12,000 of Rwanda's 300,000 Tutsi were directly implicated in Rwanda's hierarchical political system (Harroy, *Rwanda: Souvenirs d'un compagnon*, 234). Rutayisire estimates an even lower figure of 1,000 (Paul Rutayisire, "Les mythes fondateurs de 'la Revolution' Rwandaise de 1959"; *Cahiers Lumière Et Société: Dialogue. IV: 40th anniversaire des événements de 1959*, no. 16 (1999): 49).

182. The most prevalent ethno-political division in Burundi separated Baganwa elites associated with the royal court from rising Tutsi and Hutu elites outside of the court. A specifically Hutu-Tutsi dynamic did not emerge until the 1960s. On Burundi and the Great Lakes context, see René Lemarchand, *Rwanda and Burundi* (New York: Praeger, 1970); Chretien, *The Great Lakes of Africa*; Patricia Daley, *Gender and Genocide in Burundi* (Bloomington, IN: Indiana University Press, 2008); Liisa Malkki, *Purity and Exile: Violence, Memory and National*

Cosmology among Hutu Refugees in Tanzania (Chicago: University of Chicago Press, 1995).

183. A.G.M.Afr.N°721001, *Rapport du Groupe du Travail*, 37–38. Elsewhere social tension is attributed to two other modernizing currents—the rise of individualism and the undermining of traditional social structures (25–27).

184. A.D.K., "Summary of the Discussion of Ruanda-Urundi at the Twenty-First Session of the Trusteeship Council January-March 1958," 12 May 1959, 1, 8.

185. Ibid., 1, 3.

186. Ibid., 6–8.

187. This section draws on A.G.M.Afr.N°739278, Alphonse van Hoof, "Rapport de la visite de Save," 6 May 1959; A.G.M.Afr.N°739444, C.A. de Vincke to Volker, 15 June 1959; A.D.K., Père Watteuw, "Que se passé-t-il au Kinyaga?" 22 April 1959.

188. A.D.K., Père Watteuw, "Que se passé-t-il au Kinyaga?" 22 April 1959.

189. Cf. A.G.M.Afr.N°739428, Frauzen (Simbi) to Volker, 11 January 1959; A.G.M.Afr.N°739435, Arcelay (Byumba) to Volker, 2 February 1959; A.G.M.Afr.N°740422, Hechedel (Ruhengeri) to Volker, 22 February 1959; A.G.M.Afr.N°739440, Gasser (Mibirizi) to Volker, 8 April 1959; A.G.M.Afr. N°739437, Martin (Kabgayi) to Volker, 3 May 1959; A.G.M.Afr.N°739445, Franzen (Nyamata) to Volker, 22 July 1959. In addition, Alphonse van Hoof's semi-annual reports from April-May 1959 omit references to ethnic tensions in the mission stations. Cf. A.G.M.Afr.N°739260, "Rapport de la visite de Kabgayi," 3 April 1959; A.G.M.Afr.N°739270, "Carte de visite de Mushishiro," 8 April 1959; A.G.M.Afr.N°739266, "Carte de visite de Kanyanza," 13 April 1959; A.G.M.Afr.N°739272, "Carte de visite de Nyanza," 19 April 1959; A.G.M.Afr.N°739274, "Carte de visite de Kaduha," 24 April 1959; A.G.M.Afr. N°739276, "Carte de visite de Kiruhura," 29 April 1959; A.G.M.Afr.N°739268; "Carte de visite de Simbi," 10 May 1959; A.G.M.Afr.N°739284-85, "Carte de visite de Nyumba," 19–25 May 1959; A.G.M.Afr.N°739286-87, "Carte de visite de Kansi," 28 May 1959; A.G.M.Afr.N°739264, "Carte de visite de Cyanika," 8 June 1959.

190. A.G.M.Afr.N°731335-39, *White Father Regional Superior for Seminaries, Report on the Major Seminary of Nyakibanda*, 14-30 April 1959.

191. "Pour les Bahutu j'ai le tord d'être mututsi, pour les Batutsi le tord de ne pas vouloir me mêler de leur particularisme, et pour tous celui d'être murundi." (A.G.M.Afr.N°731108, Makarakiza to Mondor, 8 June 1959).

192. A.G.M.Afr.N°738063, Volker to Perraudin, 21 May 1959.

193. A.G.M.Afr.N°740197, Volker to Bigirumwami, 2 May 1959; A.G.M.Afr. N°738604, Cauwe to Perraudin, 27 May 1959; A.G.M.Afr.N°731009-103, Baers to Volker, 8 February 1959. Candidates for seminary rector included Manyurane, Gasore, the Tutsi priest Jean-Baptiste Gahamanyi, and two other Tutsi priests—Kabgayi's schools inspector, Aldephonse Kamiya, and the vicar general of Kabgayi, Innocent Gasabwoya.

194. A.G.M.Afr.N°739272, Alphonse van Hoof, "Rapport de la visite de Nyanza," 14-20 April 1959.

195. "Les événements de Léopoldville," *Temps Nouveaux d'Afrique*, 11 January 1959, 1.

196. A. Bruniera, "L'Église au Congo et au Ruanda-Urundi," *Vivante Afrique 198* (1958): 1–2; "Il n'y a pas de coïncidences! L'agitation en AFRIQUE est (avant tout) COMMUNISTE," *Temps Nouveaux d'Afrique*, 22 March 1959, 2. For background, see Marvin Markowitz, *Cross and Sword: The Political Role of Christian Missions in the Belgian Congo 1908–1960* (Stanford, CA: Stanford University Press, 1973), 167.

197. Reyntjens, *Pouvoir et droit*, 240–41. On the possible causes of Mutara's death, see A. Bushayija, "Le décès de Mutara III Rudahigwa et les différentes interprétations," *Dialogue 188* (2009): 227–32.

198. Cf. "La Pays demande le lumière," *Kinyamateka*, 1 August 1959, 11; "Charles Mutara III Rudahigwa est décédé," *Temps Nouveaux d'Afrique*, 2 August 1959, 1. Whatever their frustrations with Mutara, Reyntjens doubts the Belgians would have risked the political vacuum that would follow an assassination, although he admits that the whole truth may never be known (Reyntjens, *Pouvoir et droit*, 241).

199. Harroy cites as evidence the Queen Mother's refusal of an autopsy, the Mwami's alleged farewells to close friends in the weeks leading up to his death, the predictions of his death that circulated in July 1959, the scandal of Mutara's alcoholism, and Mutara's March 1959 decision to begin preparing Jean-Baptiste Ndahindurwa as his successor after years of ignoring the succession question (Harroy, *Rwanda: Souvenirs d'un compagnon*, 269–70). As colonial governor, Harroy had ample incentive to deflect attention from himself and other Belgian officials.

200. "Curriculum vitae de Charles, Léon, Pierre, Mutara III, Mutara, Mwami du Ruanda," *Temps Nouveaux d'Afrique*, 2 August 1959.

201. A.G.M.Afr.N°738075, Cauwe to Perraudin, 1 August 1959.

202. A.G.M.Afr.N°727161, Van Hoof to Volker, 8 August 1959. For Perraudin's own recollections, see C.M.L., André Perraudin, "Je rends grace à Dieu," 25 August 1989, 2.

203. A.D.K., André Perraudin, "Oraison Funèbre 28 juillet 1959."

204. A.D.K., Kagame to Perraudin, 27 July 1959; Kagame to Perraudin, 30 July 1959. Interestingly, Kagame notified Perraudin of the *biru's* intentions but did not tell Belgian colonial officials. A contemporary Perraudin defender, Venuste Linguyeneza, interpreted Kagame's actions as an effort to enlist Perraudin in a Classe-like coup to install a new Catholic king. Perraudin refused, thereby demonstrating his apolitical inclinations (V. Linguyeneza, "Mgr. André Perraudin: L'homme de la justice," *Dialogue 234* (2004): 101).

205. This polemical label was supplied by M.A. Maus in a 1 August 1959 article in *Eurafrica*. Maus was the pro-Hutu Belgian colonial official who had resigned over the Hutu-Tutsi question in April 1956. The language of *coup d'état* implied

that Belgium or the Hutu people were the proper repositories of political power in Rwanda. I would agree with Filip Reyntjens that the events of 28 July 1959 did not fundamentally violate the traditional mode of succession. In many ways the 1959 succession was more legitimate than the coups of 1897 and 1931. (Cf. M. Maus, "Le coup d'Etat de Nyanza, *Eurafrica* VIII (August 1959)," in Nkundabagenzi, *Rwanda Politique*, 87–92; Reyntjens, *Pouvoir et droit*, 246–48).

206. "Kigeli V, Mwami du Rwanda," *Le Courrier d'Afrique*, 30 July 1959.

207. A.G.M.Afr.Nº727162, Van Hoof to Volker, 8 August 1959. This was no small matter, as the Queen Mother traditionally retained strong influence in Rwandan politics. Mutara's 1950s turn against the missionary church was blamed in part on the supposed anti-clerical opinions of his mother.

208. A. Munyangaju, "Supplément: L'avènement du premier mwami constitution-nel du Ruanda," in *L'Actualité Politique au Ruanda*, 50–51. For background, see Reyntjens, *Pouvoir et droit*, 242–43.

209. A.D.K., Perraudin, "Accueil du nouveau roi Kigeli V à Kabgayi, 31 July 1959"; *Civitas Mariae* 19, August 1959, 5.

210. "Charte de fondation du Parti UNAR," in Nkundabagenzi, *Rwanda Politique*, 92–94.

211. Linden, *Church and Revolution*, 263.

212. A.D.K., "Première réunion du Parti de l'Union nationale Ruandaise, Kigali, 13 septembre 1959," 1. For background, see Linden, *Church and Revolution*, 264.

213. "Première réunion du Parti de l'Union nationale Ruandaise, Kigali," 5. See also "Manifeste du Parti Politique 'Abashyirahamwe B'Urwanda (UNAR),' 13 September 1959," in F. Nkundabagenzi, *Rwanda Politique*, 98.

214. A.D.K., "Première réunion du Parti de l'Union nationale Ruandaise, Kigali, 13 septembre 1959," 2.

215. Ibid. "Partons tous avec la même volonté de lutter pour l'unité du pays, pour son autonomie d'abord et pour son indépendance ensuite, contre ceux qui cherchent à nous diviser que vous connaissez tous, combattons le mono-pole des blancs et celui des missions dans les écoles, luttons contre les autres Banyarwanda qui ne sont pas de ce parti, parce qu'ils sont contre l'unité, contre le Rwanda, contre le Mwami, contre les coutumes du pays."

216. Cf. *Rudipresse (Bulletin Hebdomadaire d'Information)* 132, 26 September 1959.

217. A.D.K., "Meetings d'APROSOMA, Parti social hutu en date du 27.9.59 à Astrida," 7. See also A.D.K., Aprosoma, "Fête la liberation des Bahutu à l'égard de l'esclavagisme séculaire des Batutsi," 27 September 1959.

218. Ibid., 7–8.

219. Quoted in Murego, *La Révolution Rwandaise*, 885. This is clearly an example of the emerging "corporate view of ethnicity" that Catherine Newbury traces to the late colonial period. In Newbury's words, "one principal strategy for mobi-lizing a political following was to consolidate the mental image of a corporate

view of ethnicity" (Catherine Newbury, "Ethnicity and the Politics of History in Rwanda," *Africa Today* 45:1 (1998): 14).

220. Reyntjens, *Pouvoir et droit*, 253; Linden, *Church and Revolution*, 258. See also "Le mouvement social muhutu," *Temps Nouveaux d'Afrique*, 9 November 1958, 3–4.

221. Quoted in Murego, *La Révolution Rwandaise*, 904.

222. "Manifeste-Programme du Parmehutu, 18 October 1959," in F. Nkundabagenzi, *Rwanda Politique*, 114.

223. Ibid., 119–21.

224. "Manifeste du RADER, 1 October 1959," in F. Nkundabagenzi, *Rwanda Politique*, 129. The manifesto was printed as "Manifeste du Rassemblement Démocratique Ruandais," *Temps Nouveaux d'Afrique*, 11 October 1959, 2.

225. "Manifeste du RADER, 1 October 1959," in F. Nkundabagenzi, *Rwanda Politique*, 127–28.

226. Reyntjens, *Pouvoir et droit*, 252.

227. Ordinaires of Congo and Rwanda-Urundi, "Le Chrétien et la politique," 15 August 1959, in Linguyeneza, *Vérité, Justice, Charité*, 104–120; Vicaires Apostoliques du Rwanda-Urundi, "Consignes et Directives," 25 August 1959, in Linguyeneza, *Vérité, Justice, Charité*, 121–134. This letter was also reprinted as "Lettre pastorale des leurs excellences les vicaires et préfets apostoliques du Congo belge et du Ruanda-Urundi," *Temps Nouveaux d'Afrique*, 30 August 1959, 9. For background, see Lemarchand, *Rwanda and Burundi*, 161.

228. Vicaires Apostolique du Rwanda-Urundi, "Consignes et Directives," 25 August 1959. A *Temps Nouveaux* article that appeared around this time also castigated those who would abstain from voting. "At the same time those who do not vote allow the election of bad candidates…Therefore those who do not vote contribute as well to an evil made by these [bad] candidates." ("La politique et les chrétiens en Afrique Noire," *Temps Nouveaux d'Afrique*, 16 August 1959, 3).

229. Ordinaires of Congo and Rwanda-Urundi, "Le Chrétien et la politique," 15 August 1959. Paul's language in Romans 13:1–7 is typically invoked to justify Christian obedience to established state powers. "Let every person be subordinate to the higher authorities, for there is no authority except from God, and those that exist have been established by God. Therefore, whoever resists authority opposes what God has appointed, and those who oppose it will bring judgment upon themselves" (Romans 13:1-2, NAB).

230. Vicaires Apostolique of Rwanda-Urundi, "Consignes et Directives," 25 August 1959.

231. Ibid.

232. *Trait d'Union* 71 (1959): 7–20 offers a detailed overview of the Synod of Nyakibanda. See also A.D.K., "Le Synode à Nyakibanda," 29 August 1959.

233. A.D.K., André Perraudin, "Circulaire N°21," 26 June 1959. See also Perraudin, *Un Évêque au Rwanda*, 206.

234. *Trait d'Union* 71 (1959): 19.

235. Perraudin and Bigirumwami, "Le Synode à Nyakibanda," 29 August 1959.

236. *Trait d'Union* 70 (1959): 122. For further commentary on the Perraudin-Bigirumwami analytical dispute, see A.G.M.Afr.N°727089-90, Van Hoof to Cauwe, 6 September 1959.

237. A.D.K., Bigirumwami to [Anon.], 16 March 1959. As noted above, I believe that this letter was addressed to Innocent Gasabwoya, vicar general of Kabgayi and overall director of *Kinyamateka* at the time.

238. A.G.M.Afr.N°740223-26, Bigirumwami to Grauls, Martin, Perraudin, Ntuyahaga, and Volker, 8 August 1959.

239. Bigirumwami overlooked here the glowing press that *Temps Nouveaux* continued to offer to the Burundian monarchy, especially the crown prince Louis Rwagasore who was known for his anti-colonial nationalism and his pro-Catholic sentiments. See here Matthieu Akobaseka, "Louis Rwagasore," *Temps Nouveaux d'Afrique*, 13 September 1959, 3; "Le mariage du prince Rwagasore et de Marie Rose Ntamikevyo," *Temps Nouveaux d'Afrique*, 20 September 1959, 9; "Allocutions du Mwami et du Prince Rwagasore," *Temps Nouveaux d'Afrique*, 18 October 1959, 1.

240. This appears to be an exaggerated claim in light of the fact that Alexis Kagame, court historian and royal confidant, served as the editor of *Kinyamateka* until 1953.

241. A.G.M.Afr.N°740226, Bigirumwami to Grauls, Martin, Perraudin, Ntuyahaga, and Volker, 8 August 1959.

242. A.G.M.Afr.N°740227, Bigirumwami to Volker, 10 August 1959. For similar critiques of the missionary press, see A.G.M.Afr.N°739497-98, De Schrevel to Volker, 5 August 1959; A.G.M.Afr.N°740220-22, Anonymous to Bigirumwami, 15 August 1959.

243. A.G.M.Afr.N°727099, Volker to Van Hoof, 24 August 1959. See also A.G.M.Afr. N°740203, Cauwe to Bigirumwami, 3 September 1959. *Temps Nouveaux* would have also benefitted from broadening their interlocutors. Likely reflecting the prominent presence of *TN* correspondent and Aprosoma leader Aloys Munyangaju, their interviews typically engaged prominent Hutu spokesmen rather than their Tutsi critics (cf. "Interview de M. Joseph Gitera, Président de la Délégation Bahutu à Nyanza," *Temps Nouveaux d'Afrique*, 27 April 1958, 1; "Le délégation des Bahutu à l'Ibwami, Nyanza-Ruanda," *Temps Nouveaux d'Afrique*, 8 June 1958, 7; "Kalinga drapeau du Ruanda?" *Temps Nouveaux d'Afrique*, 12 April 1959, 3; G. Cyimana, "Plaidoyer pour le menu peuple au Ruanda-Urundi," *Temps Nouveaux d'Afrique*, 7 June 1959, 6; A. Munyangaju, "Le pays demande la lumière," *Temps Nouveaux d'Afrique*, 16 August 1959, 1, 10). For a rare exception to this generally pro-Hutu line, see "S'accrocher au passé ou construire l'avenir: Une voix tutsi, Une voix Hutu," *Temps Nouveaux d'Afrique*, 27 July 1958, 3.

244. A.G.M.Afr.N°727089-90, Van Hoof to Cauwe, 6 September 1959.

245. *Trait d'Union* 70 (1959): 115; A.G.M.Afr.N°727138, Van Hoof to Cauwe, 20 January 1960. Van Hoof notes that Ntezimana was a Hutu priest. This account contradicts Ian Linden's claim that Perraudin appointed "Ntezimana, a more hard-core Tutsi priest," to the editorial staff in late 1959 (Cf. Linden, *Church and Revolution*, 270).

246. Bigirumwami and Perraudin, "Mise en garde des Vicaires Apostoliques contre l'UNAR 24 September 1959," in Linguyeneza, *Vérité, Justice, Charité*, 141–144.

247. Aloys Bigirumwami, "Lettre circulaire," 26 September 1959, in Linguyeneza, *Vérité, Justice, Charité*, 144–149.

248. Ibid. In a recent memoir, Victor Clement-Nijs, a Belgian territorial administrator in northwestern Rwanda, recounts a conversation with Bigirumwami in August 1959 in which the latter expressed fears that the young Mwami could be manipulated by extremist elements around the court. This reinforced Nijs' impression that Bigirumwami offered a measure of "objectivity" on political matters (Victor-Clement Nijs, *Souvenirs d'un administrateur territorial: Congo-Rwanda 1950-1962* (Brussels: Editions Racine, 2007), 349).

249. A. Bigirumwami, "Lettre circulaire," 26 September 1959, in Linguyeneza, *Vérité, Justice, Charité*, 144–149.

250. Perraudin and Bigirumwami, "Mise en garde des Vicaires Apostoliques contre le Parti Social Hutu 11 octobre 1959," in Linguyeneza, *Vérité, Justice, Charité*, 149–53.

251. Cf. Linden, *Church and Revolution*, 251; Rudakemwa, *L'évangélisation du Rwanda*, 341; Perraudin, *Un Évêque au Rwanda*, 173–75; Murego, *La Révolution Rwandaise*, 932.

252. Perraudin and Bigirumwami, "Mise en garde des Vicaires Apostoliques contre le Parti Social Hutu 11 octobre 1959," in Linguyeneza, *Vérité, Justice, Charité*, 151. As early as spring 1958, Joseph Gitera draped his Hutu emancipation movement in the flag of Christian civilization. "Their [Hutu] inferiority complex and their desire for emancipation from the social, economic and industrial point of view, cannot find satisfaction other than in a Western, human and Christian civilization" ("Interview de M. Joseph Gitera," *Temps Nouveaux d'Afrique*, 27 April 1958, 3).

253. Cf. "Les Craintes de la population des Bahutu," *La Libre Belgique*, 27 October 1959; A.D.K., "Lettre Perraudin à *La Libre Belgique*," 31 octobre 1959.

254. Kalibwami, *Le Catholicisme*, 479.

255. UNAR leaders consistently denied the reported xenophobic and anti-Catholic statements from their September 13 meeting. In a November 7, 1959 "statement of views," they professed their respect for the Catholic hierarchy, thanked the missions for their development work with the Rwandan people, and credited Belgium for ushering Rwanda into the modern world. Calling the Belgians "honored and privileged friends of Rwanda," UNAR reiterated that it "wanted to be the party of

fraternal unity." (cf. A.D.K., "Une Mise au Point de l'UNAR," 7 November 1959; "L'UNAR fait une mise au point," *Temps Nouveaux d'Afrique*, 15 November 1959).

256. Cf. A.G.M.Afr.N°720623, "Les 10 commandements des ABATABAZI," October 1959; "Une mise au point de l'UNAR," in Nkundabagenzi, *Rwanda Politique*, 108–11; Murego, *La Révolution Rwandaise*, 903; Linden, *Church and Revolution*, 267.

257. Cf. "Une explosion de xénophobie au Ruanda," *La Libre Belgique*, 16 October 1959.

258. Kigeli's stern letter to Governor Harroy can be found in "Lettre du 14 Octobre 1959 à M. le Ministre du Congo belge et du Rwanda-Burundi," in Nkundabagenzi, *Rwanda Politique*, 103–105. See also Reyntjens, *Pouvoir et droit*, 260; Linden, *Church and Revolution*, 267; Murego, *Révolution Rwandaise*, 911–14.

259. In the words of one recent RPF official, "The first genocidal massacres were in 1959, propagated by the Belgians in close collaboration with the Catholic Church" (quoted in Nigel Eltringham, *Accounting for Horror: Post-Genocide Debates in Rwanda* (London: Pluto Press, 2004): 36). See also Deogratias Byanafashe, "Mgr. A. Perraudin et les changements politiques au Rwanda entre 1952 et 1962." *Etudes rwandaises: série lettres et sciences humaines 1* (July 2000): 120–37. This is not to say that Perraudin lacks any contemporary support, especially in the predominantly Hutu exile community in Europe. In Eltringham's words, many Hutu exiles continue to see Perraudin as a champion of "social rights, justice, and equality" who "preached the equality of races and a respect for social justice" (Eltringham, *Accounting for Horror*, 170). However, when I attended a Rome commemoration of the genocide in May 2009, I was struck by the depth of anti-Perraudin sentiment among the Rwandan expatriate community.

260. Mamdani, *When Victims Become Killers*, 232.

261. Eltringham, *Accounting for Horror*, 171.

262. As noted above, the Tutsi priest Innocent Gasabwoya served as general editor of *Kinyamateka* between 1956 and 1959. The Tutsi priest Justin Kalibwami took over from Gasabwoya in 1959 (Kalibwami, *Le Catholicisme*, 443).

263. In saying this I do not mean to imply that all post-Vatican II Latin American liberation theology supported violent revolution. On the complexity and depth of this movement, see Alfred Hennelly, Ed., *Liberation Theology: A Documentary History* (Maryknoll: Orbis, 1990) and David Tombs, *Latin American Liberation Theology* (Boston: Brill, 2002).

264. The pejorative term "Constantinianism" references the Roman Emperor Constantine's 312 AD conversion to Christianity and the subsequent legalization and then establishment of Christianity across the Roman Empire. The early church of martyrs was replaced by caesaro-papism in the Greek East and medieval Christendom in the Latin West. The "Constantinian" tradition of political theology assumes a close relationship between church and state to support the spread of Christianity and the growth of Christian civilization.

265. A.G.M.Afr.N°720666, G. Mosmans, "L'avenir politique du Ruanda-Urundi," 21 September 1958.

266. See here Josias Semujanga, *Origins of Rwandan Genocide* (Amherst: NY: Humanity, 2003), 78–81. Although more nuanced than Semujanga, Paul Rutayisire also generally shares this vision of Perraudin.

267. In Anglophone literature, Mamdani and Gourevitch are representative of the post-genocide tendency to search the 1950s for the pernicious roots of Hutu power. In contrast, Linden writes that "Tutsi intransigence and (their) egregious sense of historical superiority attracted waverers and forced on the Hutu a militant ethnic consciousness" (Linden, *Church and Revolution*, 227). Newbury concurs, writing that "for Rwanda it would be more accurate to argue that Tutsi chiefs, through their use and abuse of power, created Hutu consciousness. It is in this sense that the analysis concerns the 'cohesion of oppression'" (Catherine Newbury, *The Cohesion of Oppression: Clientship and Ethnicity in Rwanda 1860–1960* (New York: Columbia, 1988), 209).

268. This in fact happened later in neighboring Burundi. Here Catholic authorities stood in pusillanimous silence as the Tutsi-dominated military massacred 200,000 Hutu in 1972 (cf. Adrian Hastings, *A History of African Christianity 1950–1975* (Cambridge: Cambridge University Press, 1979), 200–202). The most thorough recent study of the 1972 genocide is Jean-Pierre Chrétien's *Burundi 1972: Au bord des génocides* (Paris: Karthala, 2007). See also Patricia Daley, *Gender and Genocide*, 68–72.

269. Paul Rutayisire, "Les mythes fondateurs de 'la Révolution Rwandaise' de 1959"; *Cahiers Lumière et Société 16* (1999): 54.

270. Perraudin, *Un Évêque au Rwanda*, 194–95.

271. "Le féodalité n'est pas éternelle," *Temps Nouveaux d'Afrique*, 12 October 1958, 3. On economic developments in the 1950s, see Jean-Pierre Chrétien, *Great Lakes of Africa*, 299.

272. A.G.M.Afr., Jan Adriaenssens, *La situation politique et sociale du Ruanda*, 30 May 1960, 2.

273. Cf. "Graves Incidents au Ruanda," *Courrier d'Afrique*, 9 November 1959. The revolutionary violence of November 1959 is described here as originating in the sudden rise of political consciousness among the Hutu "after centuries of servitude under the Tutsi." Similarly, the Belgian U.N. representative Clays-Bouuaert attributed the violence to ethno-social tensions between Hutu and Tutsi, tensions that originated in "raised Hutu consciousness" which could be traced to the spread of Christianity with its "diffusal of the principles of fundamental equality between all men" ("La situation reste grave au Ruanda," *Courrier d'Afrique*, 10-11 November 1959). Even as many Hutu initially supported parties like UNAR, Hutu leaders argued that they would ultimately win elections if they successfully "crystallized the Hutu conscience" ("Les Leaders

Bahutu de R-U précisent leurs craintes de voir se renforcer la féodalité et la discrimination raciale," *Temps Nouveaux d'Afrique*, 8 November 1959).

274. A.G.M.Afr.N°738265, André Perraudin, "Note rectificative á propos d'un document de Monseigneur Gasore," 18 May 1962.

275. "Le Conseil Général du Ruanda-Urundi: Un Conseil Représentatif de Quoi?" *Temps Nouveaux d'Afrique*, 15 June 1958, 1; "Le dernier Conseil Supérieur du Rwanda: Lamentables débats," *Temps Nouveaux d'Afrique*, 6 July 1958, 5.

276. See here Cavanaugh, *Torture and Eucharist*, 205–81. Cavanaugh combines a close historical reading of Chilean Catholicism under Pinochet with a Eucharistic ecclesiological vision, emphasizing how Catholic practices helped to "build a visible social body capable of resisting the state's strategy of disappearance" (251).

277. Linden, *Church and Revolution*, 278.

278. On the civil rights movement as a nonviolent, grassroots Christian alternative to state politics, see Charles Marsh, *The Beloved Community: How Faith Shapes Social Justice from the Civil Rights Era to Today* (New York: Basic, 2004). On Tutu's vision, see Desmond Tutu, *No Future without Forgiveness* (New York: Doubleday, 1999).

279. Cavanaugh's *Torture and Eucharist* demonstrates a similar dynamic in a post-Vatican II Chilean church whose rush to relevancy sacrificed its ability to offer a viable communal alternative to Pinochet's regime.

280. A.D.K., Bigirumwami to [Anon.], 16 March 1959. Emphases are from the original text.

CHAPTER 5

1. Scott Straus, *The Order of Genocide: Race, Power, and War in Rwanda* (Cornell: Cornell University Press, 2006), 25. For a similar narrative, see Linda Melvern's account of a Rwandan military meeting on 4 December 1991. "The principal enemy is the Tutsi inside or outside the country, extremist and nostalgic for power and who have never recognized and will never recognize the realities of the social revolution of 1959 and who want to take back their power by any means, including weapons. The accomplice of the enemy is anyone who supports the enemy" (Linda Melvern, "Past is Prologue: Planning the Rwandan Genocide," in *After Genocide: Transitional Justice, Post-Conflict Reconstruction and Reconciliation in Rwanda and Beyond*, eds. Phil Clark and Zachary Kaufman (New York: Columbia University Press, 2009), 27). As Straus notes, such rhetoric continued after the outbreak of the genocide. A 12 April 1994 government radio broadcast called on "all Rwandans [to] unite against the enemy, the only enemy...the enemy who wants to reinstate the former feudal monarchy" (Straus, *Order of Genocide*, 50).

2. Cf. Phillip Gourevitch, *We Wish to Inform You that Tomorrow We Will Be Killed with Our Families: Stories from Rwanda* (New York: Picador, 1998); Mahmood

Mamdani, *When Victims Become Killers: Colonialism, Nativism and the Genocide in Rwanda* (Princeton: Princeton University Press, 2001).

3. Cf. René Lemarchand, *Rwanda and Burundi* (New York: Anchor, 1970); Filip Reyntjens, *Pouvoir et droit au Rwanda: Droit publique et évolution politique, 1916-1973* (Tervuren, Belgium: Musée royale de l'Afrique centrale, 1985); Donat Murego, *La Révolution Rwandaise 1959-1962* (Louvain: Institut des Sciences Politiques et Sociales, 1975).

4. Ian Linden (with Jane Linden), *Church and Revolution in Rwanda* (Manchester, U.K.: University of Manchester Press, 1977); Justin Kalibwami, *Le Catholicisme et le société Rwandaise 1900-1962* (Paris: Présence africaine, 1991); Tharcisse Gatwa, *The Churches and Ethnic Ideology in the Rwandan Crises, 1900-1994* (Milton Keynes: Paternoster, 2005); Timothy Longman, *Christianity and Genocide in Rwanda* (Cambridge: Cambridge University Press, 2010).

5. I am grateful to the Missionaries of Africa in Rome for granting me access to newly-released archival material for the 1959-1962 period. I also thank the Diocese of Kabgayi for sharing a wide range of newspapers and correspondence from this critical period.

6. As with most areas of Rwandan history, intense debate surrounds the terminology one should use to describe the events of November 1959. In Kinyarwanda, the events have been labeled as the "muyaga"—a "strong but variable wind with unpredictable consequences" (Gérard Prunier, *Africa's World War* (New York: Oxford University Press, 2009), 458). Prior to the 1994 genocide, Hutu historians and most Western commentators described the events of 1959–1962 as the "Hutu social revolution" (Donat Murego's *La Révolution Rwandaise* (1975) is representative here). After the genocide, historians—and particularly Rwandan commentators—largely rejected the label of "revolution," arguing that such terminology implied a "homogeneity and political consciousness" that did not in fact exist (cf. Paul Rutayisire, "Les mythes fondateurs de 'la Revolution' Rwandaise de 1959" *Cahiers Lumière Et Société 16* (December 1999): 45; Déogratias Byanafashe, *Les Défis de l'Historiographie rwandaise: Le Rwanda précolonial* (Butare: Editions de l'Université Nationale du Rwanda: 2004), 9–10). I will describe the November 1959 events in terms of "uprising," "*jacquerie*," and "government-ordered assassinations," but I will also utilize revolutionary language. Here I follow Filip Reyntjens in seeing the November events as precipitating a "transformation of the political order" which replaced a Tutsi-dominated monarchy with a Hutu-dominated republic in less than three years (Reyntjens, *Pouvoir et droit*, 233–34). For all of the discontinuity, however, Belgian colonial influence remained an important factor of continuity throughout this period.

7. In 1994 many Tutsi took refuge in churches thinking that they would again serve as places of asylum as they had in 1959. Churches in fact became some of the

worst killing grounds during the genocide (cf. African Rights, *Rwanda: Death, Despair, Defiance* (London: African Rights, 1994), 485–88).

8. Timothy Longman's 2010 *Christianity and Genocide in Rwanda* is a case in point. While offering the most thorough English-language study of the intersection of Christianity, politics, and ethnicity since Ian Linden's *Church and Revolution in Rwanda*, Longman attributes the paradigm of 20th-century Catholic politics to Classe's efforts to ally the church with political elites. He does not mention Bigirumwami and gives short shrift to Perraudin, failing to even mention Perraudin's 1959 *Super Omnia Caritas*. This may stem in part from Longman's desire to oppose "a conservative, hierarchical, bigoted version of Christianity" with his preferred ecclesial politics of grassroots democracy (304). Considering his pro-democracy and pro-social justice worldview, Perraudin problematizes such a binary narrative.

9. Perraudin is still viewed this way among many former exiles, as multiple conversations in Rwanda revealed in 2010. If Perraudin's reputation has declined since 1994, Bigirumwami has received an ecclesial rehabilitation. For example, Rwandan Catholic leaders used the fiftieth anniversary of the institution of the local hierarchy to issue a special tribute to Bigirumwami (*Hommage à Mgr. Bigirumwami: Premier Evêque Rwandais* (Kigali: Editions du Secrétariat général de la C.E.P.R., 2009)).

10. The most comprehensive and balanced international account of the November violence comes from the U.N. Visiting Mission's June 1960 report, although the Belgian Commission of Inquiry report from January 1960 should also be consulted (cf. General Archives of the Missionaries of Africa, Rome (A.G.M.Afr.), N°720669, "Report of the United Nations Visiting Mission to Trust Territories in East Africa, 1960, on Ruanda-Urundi (T/1538)," 14 April to 30 June 1960; "Rapport de la commission d'enquête au Ruanda, 7-17 January 1960," 26 February 1960). The heart of this latter Belgian document is transcribed in Fidele Nkundabagenzi, *Rwanda Politique 1958-1960* (Brussels: Centre de Recherche et d'Information Sociopolitique (CRISP), 1962, 148–56). On the Catholic side, Alphonse van Hoof's November 1959 article in the White Fathers journal *Petit Echo* offers a thorough overview of the November violence and the official Catholic response (A.G.M.Afr. N°727114-16). For the self-serving but important perspectives of two influential colonial leaders, see Jean-Paul Harroy, *Rwanda: Souvenirs d'un Compagnon de la marche du Rwanda vers la démocratie et l'indépendance* (Brussels: Hayez, 1984), 301–12; Guy Logiest, *Mission au Rwanda: Un blanc dans le bagarre Tutsi-Hutu* (Brussels: Didier Hatier, 1988), 43–50.

11. A.G.M.Afr.N°727106, Van Hoof to Volker, 13 November 1959.

12. This "Déclaration des Ruandais authentiques" document is discussed in "Climat de terreur au Ruanda: ou les féodaux menacent de mort les progressistes," *La Cité*, 7-8 November 1959. This article can be consulted in the archives of the Diocese of Kabgayi, Rwanda.

13. U.N. Visiting Mission, *1960 Report on Rwanda-Urundi*, 39.

14. Cf. RADER, "La voie de la paix au Ruanda, 15 November 1959," in F. Nkundabagenzi, *Rwanda Politique*, 134; Nkundabagenzi, "La guerre civile de Novembre 1959," in *Rwanda Politique*, 141–42. Kalibwami notes that Mwami Mutara had respected Mbonyumutwa for his administrative abilities but feared that the Hutu sub-chief had acquired the "ideas of Gitera"—a seeming reference to the latter's increasingly strident emphasis on Hutu nationalism (Kalibwami, *Le Catholicisme*, 480).

15. A.G.M.Afr.N°727119, Van Hoof to Volker, 21 November 1959; Kalibwami, *Le Catholicisme*, 480.

16. Linden notes that Ndiza had been the center of the monarchy's political repression after Ndungutse's 1912 uprising; local Hutu resentment of the imposed Tutsi chiefs ran deep (Linden, *Church and revolution*, 267).

17. "A propos des troubles," *Civitas Mariae* 21, November 1959.

18. Nkundabagenzi, *Rwanda Politique*, 142; A.G.M.Afr.N°727115, Alphonse Van Hoof, *Petit Echo*, November 1959. As Nkundabagenzi notes, the Belgian Force Publique in Rwanda grew from 4 divisions and 300 soldiers on November 1 to 24 divisions and 1,800 soldiers on November 11.

19. A.G.M.Afr.N°722008, U.N. Trusteeship Council, "Petition from the 'Union Nationale Rwandaise' concerning Rwanda-Urundi," 11 November 1959.

20. U.N. Visiting Mission, *1960 Report on Rwanda-Urundi*, 30.

21. Cf. "Discours de M. De Schrijver," 12 November 1959, in Nkundabagenzi, *Rwanda Politique*, 146–47; "Rapport de la commission d'enquête au Ruanda," in *Rwanda Politique*, 152–55; *1960 U.N. Visiting Mission Report*, 30–31; Kalibwami, *Le Catholicisme*, 481.

22. Mwami Kigeli V, "Déclaration du Mwami Kigeli V à tous les Banyarwanda," in Nkundabagenzi, *Rwanda Politique*, 105. See also "Graves Incidents au Ruanda," *Courrier d'Afrique*, 9 November 1959.

23. Cf. Henri Bazot, "Ma vie de Missionnaire au Liban, au Rwanda, au Burundi, au Zaïre, en France," (2006), 13. This manuscript can be consulted in the General Archives of the Missionaries of Africa in Rome.

24. Even UNAR did not write of thousands of deaths in their early statements to the U.N. In fact, their early protests were marked by a surprising absence of speculation on the number of deaths in the November uprisings (Cf. A.G.M.Afr.N°722005-013, Kigali, 11 November 1959, UN Trusteeship Council, Petition from the "Union Nationale Rwandaise" concerning Ruanda-Urundi (T/PET 3/100, 8 December 1959); A.G.M.Afr. N°720672-75, UNAR in Exile to Harroy, 14 November 1959; A.G.M.Afr.N°722015-17, UN Trusteeship Council, T/PET.3/102, 15 January 1960; "Petition from Messrs. KS Ntauruhunga and BK Kavutse, on behalf of all Banyaruanda in Kigezi, Uganda, concerning Ruanda-Urundi," 24 November 1959; A.G.M.Afr.N°722040-51, UN Trusteeship Council T/PET.3/111, 11 January 1960).

25. A.G.M.Afr.N°720310, Jan Adriaenssens, *La situation politique et sociale du Ruanda,* 30 May 1960, 9; U.N. Visiting Mission, *1960 Report on Rwanda-Urundi,* 31–32; "Rapport de la commission d'enquête au Ruanda," 151–52. For a first-person account of how a joint Tutsi-Hutu force fought off Bakiga Hutu arsonists, see Victor-Clement Nijs, *Souvenirs d'un administrateur territorial: Congo-Rwanda 1950-1962* (Brussels: Editions Racine, 2007), 359.

26. Harroy, *Rwanda: Souvenirs d'un compagnon,* 322–24.

27. A.G.M.Afr.N°741102, Letter from B. Manyurane to his Parents, 8 December 1959.

28. Quoted in A.G.M.Afr.N°722023-24, United Nations T/L 955, "Conditions in the Trust-Territory of Ruanda-Urundi," 19 January 1960.

29. Cf. "Rapport de la commission d'enquête au Ruanda, January 7-17 1960," in *Rwanda Politique,* 150; A.G.M.Afr.N°727107, Van Hoof to Volker, 13 November 1959; *1960 U.N. Visiting Mission Report,* 28.

30. For more on Logiest's controversial actions in late 1959, see Archives of the Diocese of Kabgayi (A.D.K.), Guy Logiest, "Communication N°3 du Résident Militaire du Ruanda," 10 December 1959. See also U.N. Visiting Mission, *1960 Report on Rwanda-Urundi,* 32–33; "Le bilan des événements," in Nkundabagenzi, *Rwanda Politique,* 157; A.D.K., Rudipresse N°148, 19 December 1959; A.G.M.Afr. N°721012, CRISP no. 51, 5 February 1960; Reyntjens, *Pouvoir et droit,* 268–70; "Mr le Vice-gouverneur Général Harroy traite du problème hutu-tutsi," *Temps Nouveaux d'Afrique,* 7 December 1958, 3.

31. A.D.K., Guy Logiest, "Communication N°3 du Résident Militaire du Ruanda," 10 December 1959. See also *U.N. Visiting Mission Report,* 32–33; Logiest, *Mission au Rwanda,* 59–60.

32. Logiest, *Mission au Rwanda,* 60.

33. U.N. Visiting Mission, *1960 Report on Rwanda-Urundi,* 31; Reyntjens, *Pouvoir et droit,* 262–63.

34. A.G.M.Afr.N°739452, De Renesse to Volker, 10 November 1959. As a leader of both Catholic Action and the Kabgayi mission, De Renesse had critiqued Tutsi authorities in Rwanda and shared Perraudin's pro-Hutu social justice vision. As an ideological ally of Kayibanda, De Renesse's comments have even more legitimacy.

35. Ibid.

36. A.D.K., Belgian Parliament, "Déclaration du gouvernement sur la Politique de la Belgique au Ruanda-Urundi," 10 November 1959.

37. For historian Justin Kalibwami, this move initiated both centrifugal and centripetal political tendencies. *De facto* political power was redistributed more broadly from the *chefferie* to the commune level. At the same time, the number of communes was fewer than half the previous number of *sous-chefferies,* leading to more centralization of power at the local level (Kalibwami, *Le Catholicisme,* 486).

38. A.D.K., "Communiqué spécial de Rudipresse," Administration Supérieure du Ruanda, 5 December 1959.

39. The superior of Kigali, Fr. Bourgois, wrote of his fears that the "liberal" Harroy would gain more influence in Rwanda with Preud'homme removed from the scene, encouraging the "very anticlerical tendencies coming from Usumbura [Bujumbura] to the detriment of the country" (A.D.K., Bourgois to Mosmans, 8 December 1959). Although they would become closer during the revolutionary years, Perraudin initially dismissed Harroy as a "liberal free-mason" and predicted that the Catholic people would reject Harroy's plan to transform Catholicism into a "religion of the sacristy" (Centre Missionnaire Lavigerie, Kigali (C.M.L.), Perraudin to Sillion, 16 February 1955).

40. Some had accused Preud'homme of actually starting Rader in his Kigali office. If so, he would have appreciated Rader's official protest of his early removal. (cf. "Ruanda," *Temps Nouveaux d'Afrique*, 13 December 1959).

41. Reyntjens, *Pouvoir et droit*, 271–72.

42. A.G.M.Afr.N°722052-067, UN Trusteeship Council, "Conditions in the Trust Territory of Ruanda-Urundi—Interim decree of 25 December 1959 on the political organization of Ruanda-Urundi," 25 December 1959. See also Reyntjens, *Pouvoir et droit*, 275.

43. "Institution de la hiérarchie au Congo-Belge et au R-U," *Trait d'Union* 4 (1960): 90–99.

44. A.D.K., "Message de leurs excellences Monseigneurs Bigirumwami and Perraudin aux chrétiens du Ruanda," 6 November 1959.

45. A.G.M.Afr.N°738097, Perraudin to Cauwe, 8 November 1959. Ian Linden notes that this was "hardly the letter of a man pushing ruthlessly for a Catholic Hutu republic" (Linden, *Church and revolution*, 269).

46. A.D.K., Perraudin to Logiest, 12 November 1959.

47. A.D.K. André Perraudin, "L'heure de la charité (Circ. N°23)," 21 November 1959.

48. A.D.K., "Note pour Mgr. Perraudin novembre 1959." For more commentary on Perraudin's reactions, see A.G.M.Afr.N°727122, Van Hoof to Volker, 21 November 1959 and A.G.M.Afr.N°727120, Van Hoof to Volker, 5 December1959.

49. Cf. A.G.M.Afr.N°720623, "Comité de libération nationale (INGANGURARUGU), 'Les 10 commandements des ABATABAZI," October 1959; A.G.M.Afr.N°738140, "Extrait de La Cité," 7-8 November 1959; A.G.M.Afr. N°720672-75, UNAR in Exile to Harroy, 14 November 1959; A.G.M.Afr. N°722015-17, "Petition from Messrs. K.S. Ntauruhunga and B.K. Kavutse on behalf of all Banyaruanda in Kigezi, Uganda, concerning Ruanda-Urundi," 24 November 1959; A.G.M.Afr.N°727122, Van Hoof to Volker, 21 November 1959. A.G.M.Afr.N°722028-39, "Petition from the Banyarwanda and Barundi Abadhemuka of Kampala concerning Ruanda-Urundi," 14 December 1959.

50. This incident led to the arrest of a Tutsi priest seen as a liaison to local UNAR leaders ("La guerre civil au Ruanda: Nécessité d'une forte authorité," *La Libre Belgique*, November 1959; A.D.K., Logiest to Perraudin, 24 November 1959).

51. "Les leaders Bahutu de R-U précisent leurs craintes de voir se renforcer la féodalité et la discrimination raciale," *Temps Nouveaux d'Afrique*, 8 November 1959.

52. U.N. Visiting Mission, *1960 Report on Rwanda-Urundi*, 25.

53. Adriaenssens, *La situation politique*, 23. In a personal letter, Adriaenssens praised Perraudin for intervening in the Hutu-Tutsi conflict, claiming that "abstention would not have been neutrality but more complicity in injustice" (A.D.K., Adriaenssens to Perraudin, 17 November 1959).

54. Logiest, "Mission au Rwanda," 50, 219.

55. A.D.K., André Perraudin, "L'heure de la charité (Circ n°23)," 21 November 1959.

56. A.G.M.Afr.N°727122, Van Hoof to Volker, 21 November 1959. Perraudin himself repeated these sentiments in 1962, claiming that UNAR persecution incited the Hutu masses to revolt against the feudal regime that "had decided to decapitate the parties who demanded a democratic regime" (A.G.M.Afr.N°738265, André Perraudin, "Note rectificative a propos d'un document de Monseigneur Gasore," 18 May 1962).

57. A.G.M.Afr.N°738098, Perraudin to Volker, 8 January 1960. Perhaps to make up for this overly sanguine analysis, Perraudin in his autobiography admitted that the principal leaders of the revolution were Christian and that many were former seminarians. Even here, though, Perraudin stopped short of any kind of apology. "It is undeniable that the Christians and the catechumens took part in the revolutionary actions...But is it not the case in all popular revolutions?" (Perraudin, *Un Évêque au Rwanda*, 252).

58. A.G.M.Afr.N°738097, Perraudin to Cauwe, 8 November 1959.

59. *Civitas Mariae* 22 (1959): 4–5.

60. A.D.K., Aloys Bigirumwami, "Vivre chrétiennement les événements," 15 November 1959.

61. Ibid.

62. Cf. "Les Leaders Bahutu de R.-U. précisent leurs craintes de voir se renforcer la féodalité et de la discrimination raciale," *Temps Nouveaux d'Afrique*, 8 November 1959, 1.

63. "A propos des troubles," *Civitas Mariae* 21 (1959).

64. A.D.K., Nyrinkindi to Perraudin, 8 November 1959.

65. A.D.K., Pierre Cattin, "Relevé du diaire de la Mission de Janja," November-December 1959, 2.

66. A.D.K., Joseph Sibomana to André Perraudin, 16 November 1959. It should also be noted here that the Save superior Joseph Sibomana is not the same Joseph Sibomana who served in Parmehutu leadership and suffered a UNAR attack in early November 1959. Linden conflates the two individuals, making it appear that the future Catholic bishop Joseph Sibomana was also a Parmehutu

political leader (Cf. Linden, *Church and Revolution*, 267). For a listing of the *Mouvement Social Muhutu* leadership in late 1958, see "Le mouvement social muhutu," *Temps Nouveaux d'Afrique*, 9 November 1958, 3–4.

67. A.G.M.Afr.N°741127, Alphonse Van Hoof, Visite de Runaba, 5–15 November 1959.

68. Van Hoof claims that Ruhengeri's colonial administrator put the mission under surveillance and lobbied Perraudin to replace Cattin as superior (A.G.M.Afr. N°727122, Van Hoof to Volker, 21 November 1959). For Cattin's fascinating account of the November 1959 events, see A.G.M.Afr.N°741132, "Carte de visite de Janja," 30 November 1959; A.D.K., Cattin to Perraudin, 10 December 1959; A.G.M.Afr.N°739454, Cattin to Volker, 15 December 1959.

69. A.D.K., "Evènements de Novembre 1959 à Runaba," November 1959; P. Cattin, "Relevé du diaire de la Mission de Janja," November-December 1959, 3.

70. A.G.M.Afr.N°727122, Van Hoof to Volker, 21 November 1959.

71. A.G.M.Afr.N°727115, Van Hoof, *Petit Echo*, November 1959; A.G.M.Afr. N°727108-09, Van Hoof to Volker, 13 November 1959; A.D.K., A. Kazubwenge to Perraudin, 16 November 1959.

72. A.D.K., J. Sibomana to A. Perraudin, 16 November 1959.

73. Two Tutsi clergy fled abroad, and two others were placed under surveillance. One Tutsi priest had been seen marching with Tutsi arsonists looking to burn down Kabgayi cathedral in early November (A.G.M.Afr.N°727119-20, Van Hoof to Volker, 5 December 1959; A.G.M.Afr.N°738098, Perraudin to Volker, 8 January 1960; A.G.M.Afr.N°740020-31, T. Bazarusanga to Volker, 23 January 1960). Van Hoof notes that Hutu priests at Kanyanza did not take in Tutsi refugees but sent them to the homes of the nearby Josephite brothers. He neglects to mention that one of these refugees was Athanase Gashagaza, the Tutsi chief whose political conflict with Dominique Mbonyumutwa had precipitated the violence in the first days of November (Kalibwami, *Le Catholicisme*, 480).

74. Cf. A.G.M.Afr.N°727118, Van Hoof to Volker, 5 December 1959; A.D.K., Mgr. Cattin, "Relevé du diaire de la Mission de Janja, 5 November–5 December," 4–10.

75. A.D.K. Guy Logiest, "Communication N°3 du Resident Militaire du Ruanda," 10 December 1959; A.D.K., Rudipresse n°148, 19 December 1959; A.G.M.Afr. N°727126, Van Hoof to Volker, 19 January 1960.

76. A.G.M.Afr.N°740211, Bigirumwami to Volker, 28 November 1959. Subsequent quotations are taken from this letter.

77. A.D.K., "Prêtres ruandais dont les familles sont sinistrées." [undated].

78. A.G.M.Afr.N°739458-59, Gilles to Volker, 14 December 1959.

79. A.G.M.Afr.N°727114, Alphonse Van Hoof, *Petit Echo*, November 1959.

80. A.G.M.Afr.N°727117, Van Hoof to Volker, 5 December 1959.

81. A.G.M.Afr.N°741102, Manyurane to Parents, 8 December 1959.

82. Nor did Perraudin's perspective change 40 years later. Writing in his autobiography, Perraudin claimed that "I am personally convinced that the Hutu Revolution was a response of an exasperated mass to the systematic

provocation organized by the Tutsi power of this epoch" (Perraudin, *Un Évêque au Rwanda*, 237).

83. A.G.M.Afr.N°739455, Cattin to Volker, 15 December 1959.

84. Unlike Cattin, Adriaenssens doubted that UNAR had any ideological commitment to communism. He interpreted UNAR's rumored outreach to China and the USSR as merely tactical. "The Unarists do not desire to introduce communism in their country. Their real goal is to conserve the monopoly of power and its advantages" (*La situation politique*, 18–19).

85. A.G.M.Afr.N°727119, Van Hoof to Volker, 5 December 1959.

86. A.G.M.Afr.N°727155, Van Hoof to Volker, 27 December 1959. Adriaenssens went further, stating that Nyundo's Tutsi clergy actually founded *Rwanda Nziza* in mid-1959 as a mouthpiece for Rwandan nationalism (Adriaenssens, *La situation politique*, 24).

87. Catholic reactions stood in stark contrast to the official Anglican position at the time. For example, a February 1960 gathering of Anglican church leaders rejected the thesis that Rwanda's conflict should be described as a "conflict between Bahutu and Batutsi," arguing instead that "the Banyarwanda are fundamentally one people, with one language, one culture and one king, in spite of differences of origin." Echoing UNAR, the Anglicans went so far as to propose eliminating the terms "Hutu" and "Tutsi" from public discourse (Cf. A.D.K., "Church Puts Forward Proposals to Heal Ruanda Dissension," *Uganda-Argus*, 27 February 1960).

88. The following political history draws from Nkundabagenzi, *Rwanda Politique*, 181–383; U.N. Visiting Mission, *1960 Report on Rwanda-Urundi*, 1–5, 39–42; Lemarchand, *Rwanda and Burundi*, 171–94; Reyntjens, *Pouvoir et droit*, 276–88; and Kalibwami, *Le Catholicisme*, 487–94.

89. J. Adriaenssens, *La situation politique*, 6.

90. U.N. Visiting Mission, *1960 Report on Rwanda-Urundi*, 25.

91. Rader, "Situation politique actuelle du Ruanda," *Le Dépêche du Ruanda-Urundi*, 8 January 1960.

92. Cf. "Appel des partis politiques á la tolérance," 14 March 1960, in Nkundabagenzi, *Rwanda Politique*, 198–99. The U.N. Visiting Commission noted that this was the only post-November document signed by all four political parties, the Belgian government, and the Mwami (U.N. Visiting Mission, *1960 Report on Rwanda-Urundi*, 4). Kayibanda also issued a personal appeal to his supporters to maintain order in the hills, arguing that the fight against the "secular feudalism of the Tutsi" must be waged in a "peaceful spirit" (A.D.K., Gregoire Kayibanda, "Lettre au Parmehutu," 15 March 1960).

93. A.G.M.Afr.N°727173, Van Hoof to Volker, 25 March 1960; "Echo á une letter des eveques de l'Urundi et nouvelles," *Civitas Mariae* 26, April 1960.

94. A.D.K., Guy Logiest, "Communique n°10," 21 March 1960.

95. Van Hoof provides the most comprehensive recounting of these incidents (A.G.M.Afr.N°727177-78, Van Hoof to Volker, 14 April 1960). For Bigirumwami's

own commentary, see A.D.K., Aloys Bigirumwami, "Quel avenir?" 25 March 1960 and "Les événements lors du passage de l'ONU," *Civitas Mariae* 25, March 1960.

96. A.G.M.Afr.N°727176, Alphonse Van Hoof to [Anon.], May 1960; A.D.K., *Rudipresse* n°166, 23 April 1960.

97. Cf. Nkundabagenzi, *Rwanda Politique*, 199–202.

98. A.D.K., Bwanakweri to De Schrijver, 8 June 1960; A.D.K., Ndazaro to Perraudin, 3 May 1960.

99. "Déclaration du Parmehutu (M.D.R.)," in Nkundabagenzi, *Rwanda Politique*, 245.

100. "Appel pathetique du Ruanda," in Nkundabagenzi, *Rwanda politique*, 247–52.

101. Mamdani, *When Victims Become Killers*, 9–39.

102. In the words of Lemarchand, the communal council elections of June 1960 enabled Parmehutu to achieve "virtually unlimited control over local affairs, and thus to make full use of their prerogatives to hasten the tempo of revolutionary change" (Lemarchand, *Rwanda and Burundi*, 183).

103. Nkundabagenzi, *Rwanda Politique*, 269.

104. Cf. A.G.M.Afr.N°727169, Van Hoof to Volker, 15 July 1960. *Temps Nouveaux's* July 1960 issues chronicle Congo's rapid descent from celebratory independence ceremonies to political conflict and territorial division. See here "Le Congo est indépendant," *Temps Nouveaux d'Afrique*, 3 July 1960; "Proclamation de l'Indépendance," *Temps Nouveaux d'Afrique*, 10 July 1960; "La situation au Congo," *Temps Nouveaux d'Afrique*, 17 July 1960; "Situation tragique au Congo," *Temps Nouveaux d'Afrique*, 24 July 1960. On Congo's political developments during this period, see Georges Nzongola-Ntalaja, *The Congo from Leopold to Kabila: A People's History* (London: Zed Books, 2002), 62–89.

105. A.D.K., Gregoire Kayibanda, "Communique n°2 sur la Paix," 1 November 1960.

106. Nkundabagenzi, *Rwanda Politique*, 323–24.

107. D. Murego, *La Révolution Rwandaise*, 957–58; Bernard Lugan, *Rwanda: Le Génocide, l'Èglise, et la Démocratie* (Paris: Editions du Rocher, 2004), 84.

108. "Institutions nouvelles au Rwanda et au Burundi," *Temps Nouveaux d'Afrique*, 29 January 1961.

109. A.G.M.Afr.N°738099, Volker to Perraudin, 30 January 1960; A.G.M.Afr. N°739456, Volker to Cattin, 12 January 1960.

110. A.G.M.Afr.N°727171, Van Hoof to Volker, 24 July 1960.

111. A.D.K., André Perraudin, "Circulaire réservée aux prêtres: la charité," 6 July 1960; A.D.K., Perraudin to Agagianian, 9 August 1960.

112. A.D.K., Joseph Tenret to Perraudin, 1 February 1960; A.D.K., Perraudin to Tenret, 19 February 1960. This priest, Abbé Godefroid Sumbili, may not have given up his political pursuits; he died in a mysterious car accident in November 1961 (A.D.K., Perraudin, Circ. n°30, 28 November 1961).

113. A.D.K., Aloys Bigirumwami, "Echo á un pressant appel de Rome," 10 June 1960. See also A.D.K., Aloys Bigirumwami, "Voir, juger, agir," 22 January 1960; C.M.L., Leo Volker, "Fidélité à notre vocation," 7 September 1960; A.G.M.Afr. N°740386, Van Hoof, "Carte de visite de Kibungo," 3 April 1960.

114. A.D.K., André Perraudin, "Circulaire réservée aux prêtres: la charité," 6 July 1960.

115. A.D.K., Perraudin to Kigeli V Ndahindurwa, 1 January 1960; A.D.K., Kigeli V Ndahindurwa to Perraudin, 1 May 1960; *Civitas Mariae* 24 (1960): 2.

116. A.D.K., Ndazaro to Perraudin, 3 May 1960; A.D.K., Perraudin to Ndazaro, 9 May 1960; A.D.K., "Carte de Membre du Parti Aprosoma," July 1960. This latter card was personally addressed to Perraudin and signed by Joseph Gitera.

117. A.G.M.Afr.N°741124, Van Hoof, "Carte de visite de Ruhengeri," 21 March 1960; A.G.M.Afr.N°740386, Van Hoof, Carte de visite de Kibingo, 3 April 1960; A.G.M.Afr.N°727171, Van Hoof to Volker, 24 July 1960.

118. A.G.M.Afr.N°740240, Bigirumwami to Volker, 30 August 1960.

119. Aloys Bigirumwami, "Etre prudents et nous taire, ou parler á temps et á contre-temps?" 27 January 1959.

120. A.G.M.Afr.N°740212, Volker to Bigirumwami, 19 December 1959.

121. A.G.M.Afr.N°727127, Van Hoof to Volker, 19 January 1960; A.G.M.Afr. N°727140, Van Hoof to Cauwe, 2 February 1960; A.D.K., André Perraudin, Circ. N°24, 21 September 1960.

122. A.D.K., Aloys Bigirumwami, "La pire des calamités: persévéré dans le mal," 25 January 1960.

123. A.D.K., Aloys Bigirumwami, "Echo à un pressant appel de Rome," 10 June 1960.

124. The White Father Jean Massion even claimed that Perraudin approved such parties, although I have not found any explicit directives to this regard. "This [Bigirumwami's position] is in opposition to the directives of Mgr. Perraudin who has approved parties with a racial base, so long as they are not founded on racism" (A.G.M.Afr.N°720305, Jean Massion, "Note sur la situation de l'église au Ruanda," May 1960).

125. A.G.M.Afr.N°727183, Van Hoof to Cauwe, 13 December 1960.

126. A.D.K., Catholic Bishops of Rwanda and Burundi, "*Verité, Justice, Charité,*" October 1960. This document can also be consulted in Venuste Linguyeneza's book of the same name. All subsequent quotations in this section are taken from this document.

127. The analytical differences with White Fathers in Burundi should be noted. For example, the White Fathers in Burundi offered a glowing tribute to the Burundian prince Louis Rwagasore after his assassination in October 1961, describing him as the "true liberator of their country" and praising him for surrounding himself with a "ministerial team of remarkable Catholics" (A.G.M.Afr.N°720670-71, J. Keuppens, "L'Urundi en Deuil," 19 October 1961; see also "Tragique assassinat du Premier Ministre du Burundi" and "Allocution

de S. Exc. Mgr Grauls Archevêque de Kitega," *Temps Nouveaux d'Afrique*, 22 October 1961). This was despite the fact that Rwagasore led UPRONA (*Union du Progrès National*), a party that shared UNAR's nationalist and anti-colonial agenda. Unlike UNAR, UPRONA's party motto placed the party and nation under God, and its manifestoes strongly supported a central role for the Catholic Church in post-colonial Burundian society.

128. On the connections between modern Catholicism, anti-communism, authoritarianism, and 20th-century Marian apparitions, see Léon Saur, *Le sabre, la machete et le goupillon: Des apparitions de Fatima au genocide rwandais.* (Paris: Editions mols, 2004).

129. The influence of Bigirumwami and the Burundian bishops may explain why Perraudin never mentions this document in his 2003 autobiography, *Un Évêque au Rwanda*. In addition, while Perraudin retained draft versions of nearly every other pastoral letter issued during his episcopate, I found scant references to this document in his personal dossiers at the Diocese of Kabgayi archives in Rwanda. Perraudin did instruct his priests to read "Vérité, Justice, Charité" in all parishes and Catholic institutions "on reception, without commentary" (A.D.K., André Perraudin, Circ. N°24, 21 September 1960).

130. Kayibanda voiced this proposal almost as soon as the violence had subsided (cf. "La situation reste sérieuse au Ruanda," *Courrier d'Afrique*, 14-15 November 1959; "Ruanda: Calme apparent dans tout le pays," *Temps Nouveaux d'Afrique*, 22 November 1959).

131. A good summary of these allegations can be reviewed in A.G.M.Afr. N°720667-68, "Griefs formulées contre les Missions Catholiques, auprès de l'ONU, á l'occasion des récents événements du Ruanda," 1960. Most of these accusations were included in official UNAR protest letters sent to the United Nations in late 1959.

132. A.G.M.Afr.N°738107, Volker to Perraudin, 26 March 1960. Behind the scenes Volker lobbied for the appointment of a new Hutu bishop in Kigali to offset Perraudin's tarnished reputation (cf. A.G.M.Afr.N°739036, Volker to Sigismondi, 3 January 1960).

133. "Démenti aux représentants de l'ONU," 1 March 1960, in *Théologie et Pastorale au Rwanda* VI, 2 (1960): 31–54. This document is also transcribed in Perraudin, *Un Évêque au Rwanda*, 340–50.

134. André Perraudin, "Démenti aux représentants de l'ONU," *Théologie et Pastorale au Rwanda VI*, 2 (1960): 53.

135. A.G.M.Afr.N°731570, Manyurane to U.N. Visiting Commission, 10 March 1960.

136. A.G.M.Afr.N°738148, Gahamanyi to President of U.N. Trusteeship Council, 22 April 1960. Perraudin clearly prized this defense, including it as an annex in his autobiography (cf. Perraudin, *Un Évêque au Rwanda*, 351–54). Although some have speculated that Gahamanyi gave this testimony in exchange for a

promised episcopal appointment, it appears that Perraudin did not initially recommend him to the Vatican in October 1960. As discussed below, Perraudin's two initial episcopal nominees were both Hutu (cf. A.G.M.Afr.N°738375, Perraudin to Sigismondi, 24 October 1960).

137. Even in a retrospective account delivered to his fellow White Fathers in 1989, Perraudin still implied that he made Kayibanda and Calliope Mulindahabi (who served as Perraudin's personal secretary in the late 1950s) choose between "their employment or politics." He does not specify when these conversations happened, however (A.D.K., André Perraudin, "Je rends grace à Dieu," 25 August 1989, 2).

138. A.G.M.Afr.N°739034-36, Volker to Sigismondi, 3 January 1960.

139. All of the above quotations are taken from A.G.M.Afr.N°739034, Volker to Sigismondi, 3 January 1960.

140. A.G.M.Afr.N°727173, Van Hoof to Volker, 25 March 1960.

141. A.G.M.Afr.N°727177, Van Hoof to Volker, 14 April 1960.

142. A.G.M.Afr.N°727127, Van Hoof to Volker, 19 January 1960.

143. A.G.M.Afr.N°720303, Abbé Massion, "Note sur la situation de l'église au Ruanda," May 1960. "Laicism" referred to a government policy of disestablishing Catholic schools. Perhaps reflecting fears that its anticlerical rhetoric risked popular support, a UNAR party congress in Uganda voted in April 1960 to continue a government partnership with Catholic schools (A.D.K., Joseph Rutsindintwarane to André Makarakiza (Bishop of Ngozi), 15 May 1960; A.D.K., UNAR, "Discours d'introduction au Congres," 17–18 April 1960).

144. A.G.M.Afr.N°738389, *Rapport Annuel 1959–1960*, Archdiocese of Kabgayi, 30 June 1960. While this Kabgayi annual report appears to reverse the order of events (implying that the Tutsi counter-revolution preceded the revolution), the document at least acknowledges other dimensions of the crisis. For example, this report notes that in some areas the struggle was "purely racial, the Hutu driving out the Tutsi."

145. A.G.M.Afr.N°738375, Perraudin to Sigismondi, 24 October 1960.

146. "L'UNAR est-elle un danger?" *Temps Nouveaux d'Afrique*, 3 April 1960.

147. A.G.M.Afr.N°727169, Van Hoof to Volker, 15 July 1960.

148. In the midst of such ethnic cleansing in northern Rwanda, Van Hoof wondered "if the Hutu of all of Rwanda will not in the end chase the Tutsi from their homes" (A.G.M.Afr.N°727173, Van Hoof to Volker, 25 March 1960). However, he never attributed any blame here to the Hutu political parties, even those like Parmehutu that advocated the ethnic zoning of the country.

149. A.G.M.Afr.N°738374, Perraudin to Sigismondi, 24 October 1960.

150. A.G.M.Afr.N°727184, Van Hoof to Cauwe, 28 December 1960.

151. A.D.K., Aloys Bigirumwami, "Quel avenir?" June 1960.

152. Ibid.

153. The Belgian Administration's official mouthpiece, *Rudipresse*, noted that 500 Tutsi homes were burnt during the week of April 15, leading 3,000 to take refuge in the missions of Gisagara and Mugombwa. They traced the causes of the violence not to Hutu agitation, but rather to Tutsi residents' refusal to accept a Belgian DDT program (A.D.K., *Rudipresse* n°166, 23 April 1960).

154. A.G.M.Afr.N°727173, Van Hoof to Volker, 25 March 1960.

155. A.D.K., André Perraudin, "Appel pressant et angoissé," 14 March 1960. See also the accompanying "Prayer for Rwanda" that Perraudin asked to be recited in all parishes (A.D.K., André Perraudin, "Prière pour le Rwanda," 15 March 1960).

156. The Diocese of Kabgayi archives contains the meeting minutes from the first gathering of *Secours catholique ruandais*, Rwanda's new refugee outreach ministry. Later in the 1960s this operation merged with Caritas, the Catholic Church's international relief agency. Kabgayi Diocese also partnered with the U.S. Bishops' aid group Catholic Relief Services (cf. A.D.K., "Secours Catholique Ruandais," 22 April 1960; A.D.K., Père Depienne, "Secours catholique ruandais," 2 May 1960; A.G.M.Afr.N°738390, *Rapport Annuel 1959-60*, Archdiocese of Kabgayi, 30 June 1960).

157. A.G.M.Afr.N°720307, Jean Massion, "Note sur la situation de l'église au Ruanda," May 1960.

158. A.G.M.Afr.N°727177, Van Hoof to Volker, 14 April 1960; A.G.M.Afr.N°727142, Van Hoof to Cauwe, 20 March 1960.

159. A.D.K., Bigirumwami, "La pire des calamités: persévéré dans le mal," 25 January 1960; Bigirumwami, "Etre prudent et nous taire, ou parler à temps et à contretemps?" 27 January 1960.

160. A.D.K., Aloys Bigirumwami, "La pire des calamités: persévéré dans le mal," 25 January 1960.

161. A.D.K., Aloys Bigirumwami, "Quel avenir?" 25 March 1960. See also A.D.K., A. Bigirumwami, "Voir, juger, agir," 22 January 1960.

162. A.D.K., Perraudin, Circ. N°24, 21 September 1960.

163. Ibid.

164. A.D.K., Aloys Bigirumwami, "Echo à un pressant appel de Rome," 10 June 1960.

165. Mamdani, *When Victims Become Killers*, 226.

166. A.G.M.Afr.N°739393, *Rapport Annuel 1959-60*, Archdiocese of Kabgayi, 30 June 1960; A.G.M.Afr.N°731388-89, *Rapport Annuel de Nyakibanda*, 21 September 1960; André Perraudin, "Consigne d'union," *Trait d'Union*, January 1960.

167. A.G.M.Afr.N°739393, *Rapport Annuel 1959-60*, Archdiocese of Kabgayi, 30 June 1960. The subsequent material is also drawn from this annual report (cf. pp. 393–403).

168. Ibid.

169. A.G.M.Afr.N°738102, Cauwe to Perraudin, 9 February 1960; A.G.M.Afr. N°739015-032, "Renseignements concernant Erection d'une nouvelle juridiction ecclésiastique dite Diocèse de Ruhengeri, Diocèse d'Astrida, et Diocèse de Nyundo," 19 May 1960; A.G.M.Afr.N°739007-08, Perraudin to Propaganda Fide, 20 May 1960.

170. A.G.M.Afr.N°738375, Perraudin to Sigismondi, 24 October 1960.

171. A.D.K., Aloys Bigirumwami, "Soyez missionnaires," 24 July 1960.

172. A.D.K., André Perraudin, "Surveillez votre Cœur et votre langue," 8 September 1960.

173. Cardinal Sigismondi and Cardinal Agagianian, secretary and prefect of Propaganda Fide, signed the 10 June 1960 letter, addressing this to both Perraudin and Bigirumwami (cf. A.D.K., Aloys Bigirumwami, "Echo à un pressant appel de Rome," 10 June 1960).

174. A.G.M.Afr.N°740239-41, Bigirumwami to Volker, 30 August 1960.

175. A.G.M.Afr.N°740244, Volker to Bigirumwami, 29 November 1960.

176. A.G.M.Afr.N°727180, Van Hoof to Cauwe, 1 September 1960.

177. Cf. A.G.M.Afr.N°731351-58, *Rapport de la Réunion annuelle des Ordinaires ayant des Séminaristes à Nyakibanda*, 6 November 1959; A.G.M.Afr.N°741103, Manyurane to Parents, 8 December 1959; A.G.M.Afr.N°731139-40, Nothomb to Volker, 23 December 1959.

178. A.G.M.Afr.N°731163, Baers to Volker, 3 April 1960; A.G.M.Afr.N°731485, Baers, "D'état d'Esprit du Séminaire," 12 November 1960.

179. A.G.M.Afr.N°731460, 463, Gabriel Serugendo to Baers, 4 November 1960 (emphases in text).

180. Cf. A.G.M.Afr.N°731466, Denis Nbabagi to Baers, "La formation du clergé indigène au Rwanda," 6 November 1960. For similar sentiments, see A.G.M.Afr.N°731453, Claude Bahistan to Baers, 8 November 1960; A.G.M.Afr. N°731468, Jean Mwambari to Baers, 14 November 1960; A.G.M.Afr.N°731457, Beluhungiseh to Baers, November 1960. In this correspondence, these seminarians express continual frustrations over Tutsi failures to recognize Hutu agency and the tendency for Tutsi commentators to attribute Hutu insurrections to European manipulation.

181. A.G.M.Afr.N°731500, Bernard Manyurane, "L'Esprit Actuel du Grand Séminaire de Nyakibanda," 12 November 1960.

182. Cf. A.G.M.Afr.N°731470, Paul Feys to Baers, "Rapport sur la tension existent au Grand Séminaire de Nyakibanda," November 1960; A.G.M.Afr.N°731460-61, Gabriel Serugendo to Baers, 4 November 1960; A.G.M.Afr.N°731458, Beluhungiseh to Baers, November 1960.

183. Baers's allies at the seminary included Paul Feys, Bernard Manyurane, and Leopold Vermeersch. Perraudin did not take sides in November 1960 but came out in favor of Baers in early 1961. The Burundian André Makarakiza, Tutsi professor Deogratias Mbandiwimfura, and the two new Sulpicians, Frs. Renier

and Müller, were more sympathetic to the Tutsi seminarians and could count on the strong support of Bigirumwami.

184. A.G.M.Afr.N°731381, [Anon.], "Le problème de la formation sacerdotale au Séminaire de Nyakibanda," November 1960.

185. A.G.M.Afr.N°731481, Paul Baers, "D'état d'Esprit du Séminaire," 12 November 1960; A.G.M.Afr.N°731611, Baers to Bigirumwami, 14 November 1960. For similar sentiments, cf. A.G.M.Afr.N°731522, Donat Murego, "La vie du Séminaire Vue et Vécue par les Séminaristes," December 1960.

186. A.G.M.Afr.N°731398, Paul Baers, "L'évolution de l'état d'esprit des Séminaristes depuis la visite du T.R. Père General," 17 April 1961.

187. A.G.M.Afr.N°731478, Paul Baers, "D'état d'Esprit du Séminaire," 12 November 1960.

188. A.G.M.Afr.N°731498-99, Bernard Manyurane, "L'Esprit Actuel du Grand Séminaire de Nyakibanda," 12 November 1960.

189. A.G.M.Afr.N°731502-03, Bigirumwami to Baers, 14 November 1960.

190. A.G.M.Afr.N°731610, Deogratias Mbandiwimfura, "Counseil du Grand Séminaire de Nyakibanda," 9 November 1960.

191. A.G.M.Afr.N°731381, [Anon.], "Le problème de la formation sacerdotale au Séminaire de Nyakibanda," November 1960. Baers admitted that Perraudin's application of Catholic social doctrine to Rwanda's social context had "hardened" many Tutsi priests, undermining the "cordial and sincere attachment to their bishop" essential to the Catholic priesthood (A.G.M.Afr.N°731482, Baers, "D'état d'Esprit du Séminaire," 12 November 1960).

192. A.G.M.Afr.N°731473, L. Vermeersch, "Réflexions au sujet du rapport fait par le R.P. Baers," November 1960.

193. A.G.M.Afr.N°731615-16, A. Bigirumwami, "Réflexions et commentaires de S.E. Mgr. Bigirumwami sur la situation du Grand Séminaire et la solution proposée," November 1960.

194. A.G.M.Afr.N°731483, Baers, "D'état d'Esprit du Séminaire," 12 November 1960.

195. The following political history is drawn from Reyntjens, *Pouvoir et droit*, 289–310; Kalibwami, *Le Catholicisme*, 494–505; Lemarchand, *Rwanda and Burundi*, 188–94; Murego, *La Révolution Rwandaise*, 959–65.

196. Gitarama was Parmehutu's political base in central Rwanda; it also lay a mere three kilometers from Perraudin's see at Kabgayi.

197. Logiest, *Mission au Rwanda*, 189–90.

198. A.G.M.Afr.N°720315, *IMVAHO—Bulletin d'information bi-mensuel* 33 (28 February 1961).

199. Belgium was the only dissenting vote against U.N. Resolution 1605 declaring the Gitarama coup as an illegal transfer of power (Reyntjens, *Pouvoir et droit*, 297).

200. This narrative draws on A.G.M.Afr.N°727216, Van Hoof to Volker, 14 July 1961; A.G.M.Afr.N°727229, Alphonse van Hoof, "Nouvelles bagarres au Ruanda," 28 August 1961; A.G.M.Afr.N°738237, Perraudin to Mondor, 16 August 1961;

A.G.M.Afr.N°738234, Perraudin to Agagianian, 22 August 1961; A.G.M.Afr. N°738233, Perraudin to Volker, 24 August 1961; A.G.M.Afr.N°731184, Matthieu Ntahoruburiye to Volker, 17 October 1961.

201. A.G.M.Afr.N°727244, Van Hoof to Volker, 15 November 1961; A.D.K., Dejemeppe to Moeremans d'Emaus, 22 February 1961; "17,234 réfugiés Rwandais arrivent en Uganda," *Temps Nouveaux d'Afrique*, 26 November 1961. The 1961 violence produced much higher refugee numbers than the disturbances of 1959 and 1960.

202. A.G.M.Afr.N°727263, Van Hoof to Cauwe, 20 February 1962. Kagame had nationalist sympathies and is rightly seen as the godfather of the 1930s-40s school of Rwandan Christian nationalism. However, he also had problems with some of UNAR's tactics. In March 1960 testimony to the U.N. Visiting Commission, Kagame described Rwanda's major parties as "more or less totalitarian" and claimed that "forms of European democracy do not have any basis in our culture" (A. Kagame, "Point de vue d'abbé Kagame, Astrida, 13 March 1960," *Dialogue 183* (2007): 56).

203. A.G.M.Afr.N°727292, Van Hoof to Cauwe, 3 April 1962; A.G.M.Afr.N°738254, Boutry to Volker, 5 April 1962; A.G.M.Afr.N°727276, Van Hoof to Tiquet, 14 May 1962. The final death total remains uncertain; sources cite between 500 and 3,000 dead. The militia targeted men and mostly spared women and children. I would agree with Mamdani that the violence of 1962 was the first truly genocidal event in Rwanda's history, opening "the gateway to a blood-soaked political future for Rwanda" (Mamdani, *When Victims Become Killers*, 130).

204. "Message de Monsieur Kayibanda, Président de la République Rwandaise à l'occasion des fêtes de l'indépendance du Rwanda," *Trait d'Union* 22 (1962): 155–165; Perraudin, "Sermon à la fête de l'indépendance," *Trait d'Union* 22 (1962): 153–155.

205. A.G.M.Afr.N°720076, "Rapport de la Réunion des aumôniers diocésains d'action Catholique," 26-27 January 1961; A. Perraudin, "Partie Officielle: Lettre de Monseigneur l'Archevêque," *Trait d'Union* 9 (1961), 4–5. Perraudin continued his anti-communist theme in subsequent issues of *Trait d'Union* (cf. "Lettre de Monseigneur Perraudin," *Trait d'Union* 14 (1961), 126–128; "Lettre de Monseigneur," *Trait d'Union* 18 (1962), 34–35).

206. A.D.K., André Perraudin, "Message Pascal 1961 à Radio-Rwanda," April 1961.

207. A.D.K., André Perraudin, "A propos de l'aide en personnel à trouver," 5 June 1961.

208. *Trait d'Union* 13 (1961): 111. In 1962 Perraudin justified the *coup d'état de Gitarama* as a necessary political step to prevent the U.N. from delaying democratic elections (A.G.M.Afr.N°738265, André Perraudin, "Note rectificative à propos d'un document de Monseigneur Gasore, Vicaire Général du diocèse de Nyundo," 18 May 1962).

209. A.D.K., André Perraudin, Circ. N°29, 19 November 1961.

210. A.G.M.Afr.N°740290-99, Bigirumwami to Volker, 23 January 1961. Subsequent quotations are taken from this letter.

211. A.D.K., André Perraudin, "Visite M. Mbonymutwa," 14 February 1961.

212. *Trait d'Union* 18 (1962): 42.

213. "Lettre Pastorale des Evêques du Rwanda," *Trait d'Union* 21 (1962): 126–27.

214. A. Perraudin, "Sermon á la fête de l'indépendance," *Trait d'Union* 22 (1962): 153–55.

215. A.G.M.Afr.N°720112, Conférences des Ordinaires du Rwanda-Burundi (COREB), "Conférence Extraordinaire," February 1961.

216. A.G.M.Afr.N°727235, Van Hoof, "Évènements du Ruanda," 6 October 1961; N°727244, Van Hoof to Volker, 15 November 1961; N°727275, Van Hoof to Tiquet, 4 March 1962; N°727301, Van Hoof to Volker, 6 July 1962.

217. A.G.M.Afr.N°741170, [Anon.], "Consécration de Gahamanyi," 6 January 1961; A.G.M.Afr.N°727244, Van Hoof to Volker, 15 November 1961; "Astrida en fête: Le sacre de Mgr. Gahamanyi," *Temps Nouveaux d'Afrique*, 14 January 1962. Kayibanda allegedly told Perraudin and the assembled church that "the day we deviate from this [Pope John XXIII's 1961 social encyclical *Mater et Magistra*], I counsel you to no longer vote for us."

218. A.G.M.Afr.N°740295, Bigirumwami to Volker, 23 January 1961.

219. I refer here to two famous examples from past church-state disputes. Chancellor under King Henry VIII in the early 1530s, Thomas More resigned his position after Henry rejected papal authority and nationalized the church in England. However, More did not publicly critique the king until he (More) was put on trial for charges of treason. Romero, the Archbishop of San Salvador between 1977 and 1980, used his public addresses and Sunday sermons to criticize state-sponsored violence, leading El Salvador's government to arrange his assassination in March 1980.

220. See here A.G.M.Afr.N°740301-03, Bigirumwami to Volker, 18 July 1962; A.G.M.Afr.N°740305, Bigirumwami to Volker, 27 December 1962; *Civitas Mariae* 49–54 (1962).

221. Cf. A.G.M.Afr.N°739071-72, Armand Vandeplas, "Rapport sur le premier entretien avec son excellence Mgr. P. Sigismondi," 5 October 1962. Not surprisingly, this document was marked "strictly confidential for 50 years" in the General Archives of the Missionaries of Africa.

222. The following narrative is drawn from A.G.M.Afr.N°727197, Van Hoof to Volker, 2 May 1961; A.G.M.Afr.N°722214, Van Hoof to Cauwe, 3 July 1961; A.G.M.Afr.N°727223, Van Hoof to Mondor, 30 July 1961. A.G.M.Afr.N°727227, Van Hoof to Mondor, 23 August 1961; A.G.M.Afr.N°727235, Van Hoof, "Événements du Ruanda," 6 October 1961; A.G.M.Afr.N°727274, Van Hoof to Tiquet, 20 December 1961; A.G.M.Afr.N°727295, Van Hoof to Cauwe, 15 May 1962: *Civitas Mariae* 42 (1961).

223. A.D.K., André Perraudin and Aloys Bigirumwami, "Lettre de l'Episcopat du Rwanda sur l'attitude des chrétiens face aux événements actuels," 24 August

1961. They both signed the October 1960 document *Vérité, Justice, Charité*, but this was a regional statement rather than a joint letter from Rwanda's two bishops.

224. *Civitas Mariae* 43 (1961): 1–4.

225. *Trait d 'Union* 13 (1961): 111.

226. A.D.K., Pierre Boutry, "Décisions de S.E. Monseigneur Perraudin concernant certaines mesures de prudence à prendre à Kabgayi, prises en Conseil de l'Archidiocèse," 13 June 1961.

227. A.D.K., Joseph Sibomana, "Condamnation des attentats et des réactions," April 1962.

228. "Message pascal des Ordinaires du Rwanda," *Trait d'Union* 20 (1962): 94–98. This document can also be consulted as "Message des Evêques du Rwanda," *Temps Nouveaux d'Afrique*, 29 April 1962.

229. C.M.L., Leo Volker, "L'esprit surnaturel dans les épreuves," 2 February 1962. Church-state tensions were even higher in Congo than in Rwanda and Burundi during the 1959-62 period. Nearly a year before this incident, followers of the assassinated Congolese prime minister Patrice Lumumba accused the Catholic bishops of complicity in his death (cf. "Déclaration de l'Episcopat du Congo," *Temps Nouveaux d'Afrique*, 19 March 1961).

230. Cf. A.G.M.Afr.N°738258, Perraudin to Volker, 11 April 1962; A.G.M.Afr. N°738267, Perraudin, "Note rectificative á propos d'un document de Monseigneur Gasore," 18 May 1962.

231. A.G.M.Afr.N°738254, Boutry to Volker, 5 April 1962.

232. A.G.M.Afr.N°727274, Van Hoof to Tiquet, 20 December 1961; A.G.M.Afr. N°727292, Van Hoof to Cauwe, 3 April 1962.

233. A.G.M.Afr.N°727229, Van Hoof, "Nouvelles bagarres au Ruanda," 28 August 1961.

234. C.M.L., André Perraudin, "Je rends grâce à Dieu," 25 August 1989: 3.

235. Shortly before the publication of this document, Van Hoof alleged that Gasore transmitted three million francs to UNAR through a Belgian intermediary (A.G.M.Afr.N°727297, Van Hoof to Cauwe, 15 May 1962). In March 1962, the bishops of Rwanda and Burundi banned priests from diverting aid money for political purposes or accepting third party deposits (A.D.K., Les Archevêques et Evêques du Rwanda et du Burundi, "Au clergé du Rwanda et du Burundi," 17 March 1962).

236. A.G.M.Afr.N°738264-67, André Perraudin, "Note rectificative á propos d'un document de Monseigneur Gasore," 18 May 1962.

237. A.D.K., Gasore to Boutry, 11 October 1962.

238. A.G.M.Afr.N°738182, Casier to Boutry, 28 January 1961.

239. A.D.K., André Perraudin, Circ. N°28, 9 May 1961.

240. Manyurane's commitment to the White Fathers is reflected in one of his first (and only) requests after his appointment to the Ruhengeri see. In a

February 1961 letter to the White Fathers in Rome, Manyurane requested the services of ten additional White Fathers to staff three new parishes in his diocese so as to "promote a fraternal and confident collaboration with the Society of the White Fathers" (A.G.M.Afr.N°741028, Manyurane to Volker, 18 February 1961).

241. Oddly, Manyurane's death goes unmentioned in most English-language histories of Rwanda. This narrative is adapted from the following sources: A.G.M.Afr. N°741104, Alphonse Ntezimana to [anon.], 6 March 1961; A.G.M.Afr.N°738281, Perraudin to Volker, 10 March 1961; A.G.M.Afr.N°738291, Perraudin to Volker, 11 March 1961; A.G.M.Afr.N°741006, Bernard Hoste to Volker, 25 March 1961; A.G.M.Afr.N°741025, Hoste to Volker, 12 April 1961; A.G.M.Afr.N°741024, Hoste to Volker, 19 April 1961; A.G.M.Afr.N°741012-014, De Moor to Van der Rick, 25 April 1961; A.G.M.Afr.N°741020, [anon.], 25 April 1961; A.G.M.Afr. N°738201, Volker to Perraudin, 13 May 1961; A.G.M.Afr.N°738201, Volker to Perraudin, 13 May 1961; A.G.M.Afr.N°741008-10, [Anon.], May 1961; A.D.K., André Perraudin, Circ. N°29, 24 May 1961; A.D.K., Circ. N°28, 9 May 1961; *Civitas Mariae* 39 (1961): 2.

242. The Rwandan Dominican scholar Bernardin Muzungu has been the foremost proponent of the thesis that Perraudin and the White Fathers conspired in the poisoning of Manyurane. Not only is Muzungu's argument based largely on hearsay, but his presentation of Manyurane as a pan-ethnic nationalist should be corrected in light of archival evidence which demonstrates that Manyurane supported the Hutu social revolution (cf. Bernardin Muzungu, Ed., "Église Catholique: Pendant le Génocide," *Cahiers Lumière et Société 43* (2010): 62–63; C.M.L., Bernardin Muzungu, "Le rôle des responsables des religions reconnues au Rwanda, pendant le génocide," 6, 9 [n.d.]).

243. A.G.M.Afr.N°738205, Perraudin to Volker, 9 May 1961.

244. A.G.M.Afr.N°738234, Perraudin to Agagianian, 22 August 1961. Perraudin added here that "further delay, considering the social and political orientations which are taking place, not only would settle nothing, but could be very damaging." In a rare departure from his typical diplomatic decorum, Perraudin included no fraternal greetings at the end of this letter.

245. Biographical information is drawn from "Deux nouveaux évêques pour le Rwanda," *Trait d'Union* 15 (1961): 146–49.

246. A.G.M.Afr.N°741167, Gahamanyi to Volker, 23 October 1961; A.G.M.Afr. N°727238, Van Hoof to Volker, 28 October 1961.

247. Both were also controversial White Fathers. Sibomana requested the deposed rector of Nyakibanda, Paul Baers, as his new chancellor. Gahamanyi solicited the help of Fr. Cogniaux, the former Nyakibanda professor who had been dismissed in 1958 (A.G.M.Afr.N°727238, 28 October 1961, Van Hoof to Volker). Sibomana would take a relatively independent line in post-colonial Rwanda; Gahamanyi would remain a much closer ally of Perraudin.

248. Cf. A.G.M.Afr.N°731540-45, "Rapport sur les problèmes à Nyakibanda," 30 January 1961.

249. Ibid.

250. A.G.M.Afr.N°731178, Lanfry to Garitan, 29 April 1961; A.G.M.Afr.N°731298, Paul Baers, "L'évolution de l'état d'esprit des Séminaristes depuis la visite du T.R. Père General," 17 April 1961; A.G.M.Afr.N°731432, "Pourquoi la compagnie de St. Sulpice quitte le séminaire de Nyakibanda," January-February 1961.

251. A.G.M.Afr.N°731429-38, "Pourquoi la compagnie de St. Sulpice quitte le séminaire de Nyakibanda," January-February 1961.

252. Ibid.

253. Ibid. Their rapid gathering may have also stemmed from Manyurane's imminent appointment to the episcopate and the White Fathers' desire to insure that his vote was included in the Seminary Council decisions.

254. A.G.M.Afr.N°731617, Baers to Bigirumwami, 19 February 1961.

255. A.G.M.Afr.N°731618, Bigirumwami to Baers, 28 February 1961.

256. A.G.M.Afr.N°731618, Bigirumwami to Perraudin, 28 February 1961; A.G.M.Afr. N°731622-23, Perraudin to Agagianian, 7 March 1961; A.G.M.Afr.N°731624-25, Perraudin to Bigirumwami, 7 March 1961; A.G.M.Afr.N°731628, Volker to Bigirumwami, 10 March 1961.

257. Van Hoof complained about this perceived Vatican bias in 1961, wondering how long Rome would continue to support the local *abbés* when so many possessed Unarist sympathies (A.G.M.Afr.N°727223, Van Hoof to Mondor, 30 July 1961).

258. Cf. A.G.M.Afr.N°731176, Volker to Perraudin, 22 April 1961; A.G.M.Afr. N°727197, Van Hoof to Volker, 2 May 1961; A.G.M.Afr.N°738203, Perraudin to Volker, 10 May 1961; *Civitas Mariae* 38 (1961): 2–6.

259. The following narrative is drawn from A.G.M.Afr.N°731398-404, Paul Baers, "L'évolution de l'état des Séminaristes depuis la visite du T.R. Père General," 17 April 1961; A.G.M.Afr.N°731175, Perrraudin to Volker, 15 April 1961; A.G.M.Afr. N°740276-77, Bigirumwami to Volker, 15 May 1961.

260. Cf. A.G.M.Afr.N°720670-71, J. Keuppens, "L'Urundi en Deuil," 19 October 1961.

261. A.G.M.Afr.N°727200-01, Van Hoof to Volker, 10 May 1961. For similar sentiments, see also A.G.M.Afr.N°738203, Perraudin to Volker, 10 May 1961.

262. Only 18% of Ruhengeri's population had received Catholic baptism by the end of 1962, versus 36% in Astrida, 29% in Kabgayi and 26% in Nyundo ("Statistiques comparées des Diocèses du Rwanda," *Trait d'Union* 19 (1962): 75–83).

263. The following narrative is drawn from A.G.M.Afr.N°738231-32, Perraudin to Sigismondi, 25 July 1961; A.G.M.Afr.N°731181-83, Feys, Biname & Vermeersch to Volker, 26 July 1961; A.G.M.Afr.N°731184, Matthieu Ndahoruburiye to Volker, 17 October 1961; A.G.M.Afr.N°731194-95, Feys to Volker, 22 December 1961.

264. This section draws on A.G.M.Afr.N°727260, Van Hoof to Volker, 25 February 1962; A.G.M.Afr.N°727244, Van Hoof to Volker, 15 November 1961; A.G.M.Afr.

N°727299, Van Hoof to Cauwe, 20 February 1962; A.G.M.Afr.N°731200-03, Paul Feys, "Conseil du 28 Février 1962," March 1962.

265. A.G.M.Afr.N°731418-21, "Rapport de la réunion annuelle des Ordinaires avant des séminaristes à Nyakibanda, 1961-62," 30 June 1962; A.G.M.Afr. N°738272-73, Perraudin to Agagianian, 8 June 1962; A.G.M.Afr.N°40301, Bigirumwami to Volker, 18 July 1962; A.G.M.Afr.N°731209-10, Feys to Perraudin, 25 November 1962.

266. Jean-Paul Myasibo, "Butare: les Tutsi du Grand Séminaire de Nyakibanda continuent à persécuter les Hutu" *Ijambo* 33, 31 December 1991, in *Les crises politiques au Burundi et au Rwanda (1993-1994): Analyses, faits, et documents*, ed. A. Guichaoua (Paris: Université de Lille, 1995): 648.

267. Venuste Linguyeneza and Smaragde Mbonyintege quoted in C.M.L., Joseph Ntamahungiro, "Eglise Catholique du Rwanda: De la Spiritualité au Prophétisme" (2000): 9. Linguyeneza was a close confidant of Perraudin and has made many of Perraudin's writings available to a broader reading public; Mbonyintege is a former rector of Nyakibanda seminary and current bishop of Kabgayi.

268. Nor was this tendency limited to Rwanda. For a similar narrative of prioritizing institutional self-interest in 20th-century European Catholic politics, see Carolyn M. Warner, *Confessions of an Interest Group: The Catholic Church and Political Parties in Europe* (Princeton, N.J.: Princeton University Press, 2000).

269. A.G.M.Afr.N°727223, Van Hoof to Mondor, 30 July 1961.

270. A.G.M.Afr.N°727181, Van Hoof to Cauwe, 1 September 1960.

271. A.G.M.Afr.N°740296, Bigirumwami to Volker, 23 January 1961.

272. In this sense, I would strongly disagree with Joseph Ngomazungu who argues that "there were no major philosophical differences between Bigirumwami and Perraudin" during the 1956-62 period (Joseph Ngomanzungu, "L'attitude de l'église catholique au Rwanda face aux problèmes sociopolitiques des années 1956-1962: Une pastorale de prévention, de médiation, et d'accompagnement," Mémoire le License, Pontifical Gregorian University, Rome (2000): 105).

273. Gourevitch, *We Wish to Inform You*, 61.

274. A.G.M.Afr.N°738264, André Perraudin, "Note rectificative a propos d'un document de Mgr. Gasore," 18 May 1962.

275. A.G.M.Afr.N°731178, Lanfry to Garitan, 29 April 1961; A.G.M.Afr.N°731431, "Pourquoi la compagnie de St. Sulpice," January-February 1961.

276. A.G.M.Afr.N°731616, Bigirumwami, "Réflexions et commentaires de S.E. Mgr. Bigirumwami sur la situation du Grand Séminaire et la solution proposée," November 1960.

277. In explaining popular participation in the 1994 genocide, Scott Straus argues that "collective ethnic categorization" was a more important factor than long-standing ethnic antagonism. Particularly important was the rhetorical linking of "Tutsi" with the government's political and military opponents (Scott

Straus, *Order of Genocide: Race, Power and War in Rwanda* (Ithaca, NY: Cornell University Press, 2006), 9).

278. Cf. Linda Alcoff and Eduardo Mendietta, Eds., *Thinking from the Underside of History: Enrique's Dussel's Philosophy of Liberation* (London: Roman and Littlefield, 2000).

279. See for example the 2009 Rwandan church document, *Hommage à Mgr. Aloys Bigirumwami: Premier Evêque rwandais* (Editions du Secrétariat General de la C.E.P.R.: Kigali, 2009).

280. A.G.M.Afr.N°740270, Bigirumwami to Volker, 6 December 1960.

CHAPTER 6

1. For all of its politicization, the current Rwandan government's post-1994 "never again" credo and network of national memorial sites have kept the risk of ethnic violence in both local and global consciousness.

2. This chapter is intended as a coda for the primary body of research presented in chapters three through five. The General Archives for the Missionaries of Africa in Rome restricted my archival access after 1962, limiting my ability to engage new material for the 1963 to 1973 period. And while the Diocese of Kabgayi archives included major pastoral statements, homilies and limited correspondence from the 1960s and early 1970s, the Diocese of Nyundo archives were wholly disrupted by the genocide and war of the 1990s. This helps to explain the relative disappearance of Aloys Bigirumwami from this narrative. My hope is that this brief narrative will reveal lines for further research; the history of the Catholic Church under Rwanda's First and Second Republics merits a more detailed study.

3. The following narrative is drawn from René Lemarchand, *Rwanda and Burundi* (New York: Anchor, 1970), 220–24; Filip Reyntjens, *Pouvoir et droit au Rwanda: Droit public et évolution politique, 1916–1973* (Tervuren, Belgium: Musee Royal de l'Afrique Centrale, 1985), 456–71; "En pleine épreuve racial: Le Rwanda," *Informations Catholiques Internationales* 212 (1964): 15–25.

4. Only 26 of Rwanda's 1,138 communal councilors did not belong to the Parmehutu party after the August 1963 parliamentary elections ("En pleine épreuve racial: Le Rwanda," *Informations Catholiques Internationales* 212 (1964): 22).

5. The fact that the UNAR exiles proceeded over the Mwami's opposition demonstrated the exiles' increasing distance from Kigeli during 1963-64 (Reyntjens, *Pouvoir et Droit*, 457–59). Kigeli also opposed the Rwanda Patriotic Front's plans to invade Rwanda in the fall of 1990 (Unattributable interview in Rwanda, June 2010).

6. Bernard Lugan, *Rwanda: Le Génocide, l'Èglise, et la Démocratie* (Paris: Editions du Rocher, 2004), 93.

7. Reyntjens, *Pouvoir et Droit*, 462–463.

8. Henri Bazot, et. al., "Un appel à la Chrétienté Européenne, par un groupe de Missionnaires au Rwanda le 15 janvier 1964," in Henri Bazot, *Ma vie de Missionnaire au Liban, au Rwanda, au Burundi, au Zaïre, en France* (Rome: 2006), 21. I located this copy in the General Archives of the Missionaries of Africa in Rome.

9. "En pleine épreuve racial: Le Rwanda," *Informations Catholiques Internationales* 212 (1964): 22.

10. A.G.M.Afr., Henri Bazot, et. al., "Un appel à la Chrétienté Européenne," 22. As with the 1994 genocide, the statistics themselves became the subject of intense political wrangling. The Rwandan government's subsequent white paper investigation estimated 400 deaths, while some Tutsi exiles alleged 25,000 deaths. Independent Red Cross and United Nations reports placed the range at 5,000–10,000. Reyntjens estimates 10,000 to 14,000 deaths (Reyntjens, *Pouvoir et Droit*, 467). The Rwandan scholar J.D. Bizimana has estimated 20,000 deaths (J.D. Bizimana, *L'église et le génocide au Rwanda: Les Peres Blancs et le Négationnisme* (Paris: L'Harmattan, 2004), 26).

11. Lemarchand, *Rwanda and Burundi*, 224. A.G.M.Afr., Henri Bazot, et. al., "Un appel à la Chrétienté Européenne," 22. For a more recent account that emphasizes 1964 as a precursor of 1994, see Nigel Eltringham, *Accounting for Horror: Post-Genocide Debates in Rwanda* (London: Pluto Press, 2004), 42–44.

12. A.D.K., A. Perraudin, "Message de Noël 1963," 25 December 1963.

13. "Message des Evêques du Rwanda à la occasion de la nouvelle année, 1 janvier 1964" *Trait d'Union* 36 (1964): 12–16. Aloys Bigirumwami issued a separate condemnation of the violence on 29 December 1963, but I have not been able to locate this document. Bigirumwami did sign the joint January 1 statement.

14. *Civitas Mariae* 70 (1964): 2.

15. Eltringham, *Accounting for Horror*, 41.

16. "Message des Evêques du Rwanda à la occasion de la nouvelle année, 1 janvier 1964" *Trait d'Union* 36 (1964): 15–16.

17. Perraudin echoed this language in a corresponding commentary in the January 1964 issue of *Trait d'Union*, expressing his regret that "even innocents have paid for the madness of the assailants." Again, one could be forgiven for thinking that it was the UNAR "assailants" who committed the Gikongoro massacres rather than Hutu self-defense units directed by local Parmehutu government officials ("Lettre de S.E. Monseigneur Perraudin Archevêque de Kabgayi, 1 January 1964," *Trait d'Union* (1964): 6).

18. Ibid., 7. Gregoire Kayibanda echoed these sentiments in his own early 1964 letter to the Rwandan exiles. Here he argued that the fate of Rwanda's internal Tutsi rested in the hands of the Tutsi exiles. If these "fanatics" and "impenitent feudalists" continued to attack Rwanda, they would in essence be killing their own Tutsi relatives (Gr. Kayibanda, "Adresse du Président Kayibanda aux

Rwandais Emigrés ou Réfgiés a l'Etranger," *Rwanda: Carrefour d'Afrique 31* (1964): 2).

19. A.D.K., "Lettre Pastorale des Evêques du Burundi et du Rwanda sur l'Eglise," 18 February 1967, 17.

20. A.D.K., André Perraudin, *Lettre Pastorale, Carême 1964* (15 February 1964): 12. Here at least Perraudin names the sin—if not the sinners.

21. *Trait d 'Union* 38 (1964): 65–66. Nor did Perraudin's analysis fundamentally change over the subsequent 40 years. Writing in his 2003 autobiography, he still blamed UNAR insurgents for intentionally precipitating an ethnic blood-bath and claimed that the 1963-64 massacres occurred outside of government control, making no mention of the involvement of local Parmehutu officials (André Perraudin, *Un Evêque au Rwanda: Les six premières années de mon épisco-pat (1956-1962)* (Paris: Editions Saint-Augustin, 2003), 275–77).

22. A.D.K., Perraudin to José Zunzunegui, 23 February 1964.

23. A.G.M.Afr., Henri Bazot, et. al., "Un appel à la Chrétienté Européenne," 23.

24. Antoine Mugesera, "*Kinyamateka* contre les *inyenzi* et leurs complices," *Dialogue 189* (2009): 43–47.

25. Denis-Gilles Vuillemin, "L'Extermination des Tutsis: Les massacres du Ruanda sont le manifestation d'une haine raciale soigneusement entretenue," *Le Monde,* 4 February 1964, 16. Vuillemin had worked as an advisor for the Rwandan government at Butare's Groupe Scolaire before resigning in protest over the Gikongoro massacres.

26. Cf. "Le massacre des Tutsis," *Informations Catholiques Internationales* 211 (1964): 7–8.

27. Audax Hodari, "La Confession de Monseigneur Perraudin," *Remarques congo-laises et africaines VI,* 11 (1964): 260–64.

28. Lemarchand, *Rwanda and Burundi,* 224.

29. A.G.M.Afr.N°721014, "Brève réponse à quelques grossières calomnies que l'on a lancées contre l'Eglise au Rwanda," 1.

30. *Civitas Mariae* 72 (1964): 2. The Holy See established diplomatic relations with Rwanda less than six months later, demonstrating that the Vatican Radio fracas of February 1964 did not mark a permanent diplomatic break between Vatican City and Kigali ("Echoes et nouvelles," *Revue du Clergé Africain 19,* 4 (1964): 409).

31. S. Thomas, "Au Rwanda: pour le peuple, par le peuple," *Vivante Afrique 230* (1964): 47–48. The Congo-based *Revue du Clergé Africain* offered a similarly sanguine analysis, noting that the Rwandan population reacted violently against those "estimated as accomplices of the enemy" (*Revue du Clergé Africain* 19, 1 (1964): 122–23). A special 1965 issue of the Belgian Catholic journal *Pro Mundi Vita* also reinforced this one-sided analysis ("Le Rwanda: Force et Faiblesse du Centre Chrétien de l'Afrique," *Pro Mundi Vita* VI (1965): 1–35). In 1971 *Vivante Afrique* still described the 1964 events in terms of a "vast terrorist

attack launched from abroad by Tutsi exiles" which precipitated lamentable violence in which "once again Tutsi and Hutu killed each other without pity" ("Au carrefour de deux ères," *Vivante Afrique* 271 (1970): 3). This account implies mutual killings when in fact very few Hutu died during the 1964 events.

32. Dominic Nothomb, "Le Rwanda est-il Chrétien?" *Etudes* CCCXX (1964): 700–705.

33. A.G.M.Afr.N°721014, "Brève réponse à quelques grossières calomnies que l'on a lancées contre l'Eglise au Rwanda," 1964. The authors remain anonymous but claim to be "missionaries in Rwanda." I obtained a copy of this document from the Missionaries of Africa General Archives' annex library (housed under file folder 0345). Copies are also available in the Diocese of Kabgayi archives, the archives of the Missionaries of Africa in Kigali, and the library of Nyakibanda Major Seminary, Rwanda. The Vatican Radio statement and *Témoignage Chrétien* article mentioned above are transcribed and discussed in this document as well.

34. Ibid., 1.

35. I have not located Kayihura's and Kayonda's original document, but much of their text is transcribed verbatim in the missionaries' "Brève réponse" document.

36. Ibid., 14.

37. Ibid., 31.

38. Ibid, 40. Correspondence in the Diocese of Kabgayi archives supports the contention that the Rwandan Catholic Church made a concerted effort to support Tutsi refugees in 1963-64 (cf. A.D.K., Perraudin to Ballen, 2 April 1964; Comité de Caritas de Nyamirambo à Kigali, 15 March 1964; Octave Hakiba to Perraudin, 15 April 1964; Delpienne to Perraudin, 21 June 1964; Arthur Dejemeppe, "Rapport du Secrétaire-Général sur les activités de Caritas-Rwanda durant l'exercise 1963-1964," 1 July 1963 to 30 June 1964). However, this last document devoted more attention to victims of a 1963 flood than those who suffered in the "events of December 1963." In a brief paragraph, Dejemeppe described this violence as "a phase of the revolution...more deadly than the preceding ones but happily also more localized" (Dejemeppe, "Rapport du Secrétaire Général," 7).

39. A.G.M.Afr.N°721014, "Brève réponse...," 30, 33, 42. I make this argument with a degree of caution given my lack of access to the original Kayihura/Kayonda document.

40. Ibid., 43.

41. Ibid., 49. Here the missionaries quote Perraudin's February 21, 1964 protest to *Le Monde*—a protest that was never actually published in the newspaper.

42. Ibid, 53. As this commentary demonstrates, the term "genocide" was already politicized thirty years before the U.N. Security Council labored over how to designate the far greater massacres of April-May 1994. As in the early weeks of the 1994 genocide, the United Nations rejected applying the label of

"genocide" to the Gikongoro massacres in the official Dorsainville report of 5 March 1964 ("Church and Revolution in Rwanda," *Herder Correspondence,* September-October 1964; Reyntjens, *Pouvoir et droit,* 467). On the May 1994 U.N. debates over whether to invoke the term "genocide," see Samantha Power, "Bystanders to Genocide: Why the United States Let the Rwandan Tragedy Happen," *Atlantic Monthly 288.*2 (2001): 84–108.

43. Perraudin, *Un Évêque au Rwanda,* 278–79. In March 1964 Kayibanda also lobbed the "genocide" charge back at UNAR, describing them as "impenitent feudalists" whose attacks on Rwanda provoked "popular furor" (as quoted in Saur, *Le Sabre,* 30).

44. C.M.L., André Perraudin, "Je rends grâce à Dieu" (25 August 1989): 3. A quarter-century after the events, Perraudin claimed that in the days following the Gikongoro massacres, he "had gone many times to the house of President Kayibanda to ask him to stop all this." This implies that Perraudin thought that Kayibanda *could* stop the violence, granting the government a level of agency that Perraudin was reluctant to acknowledge publicly in 1964 (or in his 2003 autobiography for that matter).

45. Correspondence I reviewed in the Diocese of Kabgayi archives focused almost solely on the statistical and etymological dimensions of the 1963-64 violence. In addition to the Perraudin/Zunzunegui letter cited above, the founder of TRAFIPRO, Louis Pien, wrote that the European media statistics should be "cut by a factor of ten," while a European friend of Perraudin lamented that "certain publications have continued to make believe that this was a genocide pure and simple" (A.D.K., Pien to Perraudin, 18 March 1964; A.D.K., Counachamps to Perraudin, 2 March 1964). Notably missing here were any notes of empathy for the Tutsi victims themselves.

46. Dominic Nothomb, "Le Rwanda est-il Chrétien?" *Etudes CCCXX* (1964): 705.

47. "En pleine épreuve racial: Le Rwanda," *Informations Catholiques Internationales* 212 (15 March 1964): 24.

48. Reyntjens's *Pouvoir et Droit* (1985) offers the most thorough secondary account of political history during Rwanda's First Republic. Lemarchand's *Rwanda and Burundi* (1970) remains the best study in English. Post-genocide studies tend to gloss over the First Republic, focusing more on developments in Juvenal Habyarimana's Second Republic (1973–1994). Gerard Prunier's *The Rwanda Genocide: History of a Crisis* (New York: Columbia, 1995) and Mahmood Mamdani's *When Victims Become Killers: Colonialism, Nativism and the Genocide in Rwanda* (Princeton: Princeton University Press, 2001) are good examples of this tendency. Eltringham's *Accounting for Horror* offers an admirable focus on the 1964 events but little else from the 1960s.

49. Reyntjens, *Pouvoir et droit,* 366. Lemarchand notes the similarities between Parmehutu cadres in the 1960s and French Jacobins in the 1790s, namely a reign of terror in the name of justice giving way to a public modeling of ascetic virtue (Lemarchand, *Rwanda and Burundi,* 258–59).

50. Reyntjens, *Pouvoir et Droit*, 470–71, 494–98.

51. Reyntjens, *Pouvoir et Droit*, 395–98, 401–402, 471; Ian Linden, *Christianisme et Pouvoirs au Rwanda (1900–1990)*. Trans. Paulette Géraud (Paris: Karthala, 1999), 369–70; C.M.L., Joseph Ntamahungiro, "Eglise Catholique du Rwanda: De la Spiritualité au Prophétisme" (2000): 4.

52. International Catholic newspapers continued to adopt a sanguine view of Kayibanda. The British Catholic *Herder Correspondence* wrote in 1964 that "Kayibanda's regime was distinguished from the first by the seriousness of its efforts to develop the country and promote education as well as by the personal austerity of the political leaders who have not used their positions to amass spoils" ("Church and Revolution in Rwanda," *Herder Correspondence*, September-October 1964, 292). The Belgian Catholic journal *Pro Mundi Vita* also supported the Rwandan church's pro-revolutionary stance by arguing that "it is unworthy of man to perpetuate a state of unjust affairs for love of peace."

53. A.D.K., "Jubilé au Rwanda," 29 June 1964; "Le Jubile sacerdotal de S.E. Mgr. Perraudin," *Trait d'Union* 42 (1964): 139–51.

54. A.D.K., Adriaenssens to Perraudin, 16 June 1963.

55. Reyntjens, *Pouvoir et droit*, 341–43.

56. A.D.K., "Lettre Pastorale sur L'Education Chrétienne," 15 March 1966.

57. "Rwanda et Burundi: cas unique dans le monde missionnaire," *Vivante Afrique* 254 (1968): 14–15.

58. Walter Aelvot, "Le cercle vicieux de sous-développement," *Vivante Afrique 240* (1965): 48–50. This article notes that only 55% of the population aged 5–14 attended school in 1965.

59. This section draws on "Le Rwanda: Force et Faiblesse du centre Chrétien de l'Afrique," *Pro Mundi Vita* VI (1965): 24–34; "Rwanda et Burundi: cas unique dans le monde missionnaire," *Vivante Afrique* 254 (1968): 13; A.D.K., Perraudin to Michellod, 5 June 1969; A.D.K., Perraudin to Benefectors, 30 July 1971; A. Sosson, "Bientot 100% de Baptisés," *Vivant Univers 271* (1970): 33–42; Linden, *Christianisme et pouvoirs au Rwanda*, 368.

60. The phrase is borrowed from Justin Kalibwami, "Le Rwanda en question," *Remarques Africaines* 291 (1967): 302.

61. On Burundian politics in the post-colonial period, see Patricia Daley, *Gender and Genocide in Burundi: The Searches for Spaces of Peace in the Great Lakes Region* (Bloomington, IN: Indiana University Press, 2007), 61–72.

62. C.M.L., Perraudin to Jean Germanier, 8 October 1966; Perraudin to Joseph Balet, 9 October 1966; Perraudin to Amélie and Henry Sillion, 28 February 1968.

63. Cf. "Union fraternelle du clergé rwandais (U.F.C.R.)," *Cum Paraclito* 25 (1969): 95–99; "Assemblée générale du clergé rwandaise a Nyundo," *Cum Paraclito* 26 (1969): 152–59; Aloys Bigirumwami, "L'Union Fraternelle du Clergé Rwandais," *Cum Paraclito* 27 (1969): 79–81; "L'U.F.C.R.," *Foi et Culture* 7, 34 (1971): 88–95; Linden, *Christianisme et Pouvoirs*, 370–371.

64. Lemarchand, *Rwanda and Burundi*, 260; Reyntjens, *Pouvoir et Droit*, 501–502. In 1972, 120 of the *Groupe Scolaire's* 260 students and 200 of the National University's 500 students were Tutsi.

65. Ian Linden, "The Roman Catholic Church in Social Crisis: The Case of Rwanda," in *Christianity in Independent Africa*, eds. E. Fasholé Luke, R. Gray, A. Hastings, G. Tasie (Bloomington, IN: Indiana University Press, 1978), 249. Linden's pro-Hutu rhetoric emerged several times in this narrative. "The culturally conditioned disdain for *le petit Hutu* meant that Hutu pupils in the minor and major seminaries experienced the humiliating contempt of their superiors, and this acted as a brake on their attainment. They were expected to be inferior to Tutsi pupils, and such predictions tended to be self-fulfilling" (247). In light of this, Linden called on the African church to develop a new "theology of revolution" (244), arguing that inculturation in and of itself could not resolve the church's political quandary. "In other words, what was the church: a custodian of ruling class interests and culture, an embodiment of social inequality, or an agency for the transformation of society, a generator of social justice?" (253). In light of the amount of Rwandan violence committed in the name of revolutionary justice, one wishes here for a fourth option.

66. Linden, *Christianisme et Pouvoirs*, 370–72.

67. On the 1972 genocide in Burundi, see Daley, *Gender and Genocide*; Leo Kuper, *The Pity of It All: Polarization of Racial and Ethnic Relations* (Minneapolis: University of Minnesota, 1977); René Lemarchand, *Burundi: Ethnocide as Discourse and Practice* (Cambridge: Woodrow Wilson Center/University of Cambridge, 1994); Jean-Pierre Chrétien & Jean-François Dupaquier, *Burundi 1972: au bord des génocides* (Paris: Karthala, 2007).

68. Quoted in Adrian Hastings, *A History of African Christianity 1950–1975* (Cambridge: Cambridge University Press, 1979), 201.

69. Linden, "The Roman Catholic Church in Social Crisis," 252.

70. C.M.L., Perraudin to Benefactors, 16 December 1972. Subsequent quotations are taken from this document.

71. Vincent Linguyeneza, "Mgr. André Perraudin: L'homme de la justice," *Dialogue* 234 (2004): 101.

72. Sylvestre Nsanzimana, "Rapport sur les événements qui se sont produits a l'UNR à partir de la nuit du 15 au 16 février 1973," *Dialogue 183* (2007): 65. Kayibanda's influence in the Kabgayi-Gitarama area has led commentators like Filip Reyntjens to conclude that the president himself initiated the expulsions (Reyntjens, *Pouvoir et droit*, 502–503). Such suspicions remain today. Having witnessed the 1973 uprisings, one observer confessed that Kayibanda's "racist" ideology overcame his social justice ideals. "Kayibanda had lost his head." (Unattributable interview in Rwanda, May 2010). For an alternative view that traces the violence to an anti-Kayibanda Hutu faction, see David and Catherine Newbury, "A Catholic Mass in Kigali: Contested Views of the Genocide and Ethnicity in Rwanda," *Canadian Journal of African Studies 33.2/3* (1999): 299.

73. Reyntjens, *Pouvoir et droit*, 502–504; Linden, "The Roman Catholic Church in Social Crisis," 249–251; Linden, *Christianisme et pouvoirs*, 372–75. As Reyntjens notes, Kayibanda saw Kanyarengwe as his greatest potential rival in the military. In addition to infringing on the autonomy of the church, appointing him to take over Nyundo Seminary served Kayibanda's political purposes of isolating a potential leader of a *coup d'état*. Habyarimana would also turn against Kanyarengwe; the latter joined the RPF in exile in Tanzania in 1981 (Lugan, *Rwanda: Le Génocide*, 105).

74. Reyntjens, *Pouvoir et droit*, 505–508.

75. Unattributable interview in Rwanda, May 2010.

76. All quotations are taken from "Lettre Pastorale des Evêques du Rwanda à l' occasion du Carême 1973," 23 February 1973, 1–8.

77. A.D.K., "Réunion du Conseil Presbytéral de l'Archidiocèse de Kabgayi," 7–8 May 1973; Ian Linden, *Church and Revolution in Rwanda* (Manchester: Manchester University Press, 1977), 285. Radio Bujumbura in Burundi also critiqued the Rwandan bishops' statement, as did a group of Hutu priests writing from Rwesero (Saur, *Le Sabre*, 32; Paul Rutayisire, Review of *J. J. Carney, From Democratization to Ethnic Revolution: Catholic Politics in Rwanda, 1950–1962,"* (Butare, Rwanda: [n.p.], 2012), 19).

78. The above quotations are all taken from "Lettre des évêques du Rwanda a leurs prêtres, religieux, religieuses, et aides laïcs, 23 March 1973," *Trait d'Union* 123 (1973): 30–32.

79. A.D.K., Cerri to Perraudin, 4 March 1973. For another critical perspective on the ecclesial response to the events of 1973, see the April 1973 letter from exiled Tutsi priests in Burundi. "La mort des séminaires au Rwanda par les prêtres de Nyundo réfugiés au Burundi," *Dialogue* 183 (2007): 80–89.

80. A.D.K., Cerri to Perraudin, 4 March 1973.

81. Ibid. Perraudin granted Cerri's leave request but described this as a "holiday" in a letter to Cerri's superior. Cerri never returned to Rwanda (cf. A.D.K., Perraudin to Bartoletti (Secretary General of Italian Episcopal Conference), 17 March 1973).

82. A.D.K., Bureau presbytéral de l'Archidiocèse de Kabgayi, "Compte-rendu de la rencontre du mardi 27 mars 1973," 27 March 1973.

83. A.D.K., Perraudin, "Homélie de Pâques," 1973.

84. Ironically, the government succeeded here in accomplishing what many White Fathers had desired back in 1961–1962—sacking Fr. Mathieu Ndahoruburiye, the first indigenous rector of Nyakibanda who had been appointed in the heat of the 1960–1962 crisis. Fr. Mathieu moved from Nyakibanda to St. Joseph's when Bigirumwami opened Nyundo's new major seminary in November 1963. After the government transferred the seminary back over to church control in August 1973, Perraudin and Vincent Nsengiyumva, Nyundo's new bishop, reunited the two seminaries in October 1974 and deposed Ndahoruburiye (Linden, *Christianisme et Pouvoirs*, 377).

85. Guy Theunis, "Le rôle de l'Église catholique dans les événements récents," in *Les crises politiques au Burundi et au Rwanda (1993–1994): Analyses, faits, et documents,* Ed. André Guichaoua (Paris: Université de Lille, 1995), 292.

86. Cf. "Lettre de Monseigneur l'Archevêque, 28 July 1973" *Trait d'Union* (1973): 82–83; A.D.K., A. Perraudin, "Noel 1973—Ouverture de l'année sainte," 25 December 1973. Lugan notes that Habyarimana's father had been one of the first baptized Christians in Rwanda (Lugan, *Rwanda: Le Génocide,* 102).

87. Saur, *Le Sabre,* 32–33, 289–297. For a popular recent presentation of the Kibeho message, see Immaculée Ilibagiza, *Our Lady of Kibeho: Mary Speaks to the World from the Heart of Africa* (Carlsbad, CA: Hay House, 2008).

88. Bernardin Muzungu, *Histoire du Rwanda sous la colonisation* (Kigali: Edition Cahiers Lumière et Société, 2009), 100.

89. See here the special June 1986 issue of *Civitas Mariae,* n°343, "En hommage a son Excellence Monseigneur Aloys Bigirumwami, premier évêque de Nyundo, que Dieu a rappelé à lui le 3 juin 1986."

90. Leon Saur, *Le sabre, la machete et le goupillon: Des apparitions de Fatima au génocide rwandais* (Paris: Editions mols, 2004), 32.

91. Quoted in Bizimana, *L'Église et le genocide au Rwanda,* 22. See also Hugh McCullum, *The Angels Have Left Us: The Rwanda Tragedy and the Churches* (Geneva; WCC Publications, 1995), 79.

92. Antoine Mugesera, "André Perraudin, Un Évêque au Rwanda," *Dialogue 183* (2007): 142.

93. C.M.L., André Perraudin, "Je rends grâce à Dieu" (25 August 1989): 4.

94. Pères Blancs de Suisse, "Vie et œuvre de Mgr Perraudin," *Dialogue 234* (2004): 84–85.

95. The most exhaustive study of the Rwandan genocide is Alison Des Forges, *Leave None to Tell the Story: Genocide in Rwanda* (New York: Human Rights Watch, 1999; this can also be consulted online at http://www.hrw.org/reports/1999/rwanda). Gérard Prunier offers a balanced overview in *The Rwanda Crisis: History of a Genocide* (New York: Columbia University Press, 1995) and an important revision in *Africa's World War: Congo, the Rwandan Genocide, and the Making of a Continental Catastrophe* (New York: Oxford University Press, 2009). Philip Gourevitch's *We wish to inform you that tomorrow we will be killed with our families: Stories from Rwanda* (New York: Picador, 1998) and African Rights' *Rwanda: Death, Despair, and Defiance* (London: African Rights, 1994) offer powerful first-person testimonies but are shaped strongly by RPF ideology. Mamdani's *When Victims Become Killers* offers one of the more probing analytical studies of what made the genocide thinkable. Scott Straus's *The Order of Genocide: Race, Power and War in Rwanda* (Ithaca, NY: Cornell University Press, 2006) provides detailed insight into the motivations of individual killers. The late Catholic priest and human rights advocate André Sibomana provides an important ecclesial perspective in *Hope for*

Rwanda: Conversations with Laure Guilbert and Herve Deguine. Trans. Carina Tertsakian (Sterling, VA: Pluto Press, 1999). For critical perspectives on church involvement in the genocide, see Timothy Longman, *Christianity and Genocide in Rwanda* (Cambridge: Cambridge University Press, 2010); Collette Braeckman, *Terreur africaine: Burundi, Rwanda, Zaire, les racines de la violence* (Paris: Fayard, 1996); Bizimana, *L'Église et le genocide au Rwanda*; Carol Rittner, et. al., *Genocide in Rwanda: Complicity of the Churches?* (St. Paul, MN: Paragon House, 2004); Saskia Hoyweghen, "The Disintegration of the Catholic Church of Rwanda: A Study of the Fragmentation of Political and Religious Authority." *African Affairs 95* (1996): 379–401.

96. In the midst of Uganda's vicious civil war between President Milton Obote and Yoweri Museveni's National Revolutionary Movement (NRM), thousands of Rwandan refugees attempted to cross into Rwanda in the early 1980s. Citing Rwanda's growing population and lack of cultivable land, the Habyarimana government refused to allow these Tutsi refugees to resettle in Rwanda. In the meantime, Tutsi exiles like Fred Rwigyema and Paul Kagame helped Museveni's NRM defeat Obote and take power in Uganda in 1986. While Rwigyema and Kagame initially served in high-level positions in Museveni's government, Ugandans were increasingly resentful of their Rwandan rivals. Ostracized by Museveni in the late 1980s, Rwigyema and Kagame organized an exile army to return to Rwanda. For more on the Ugandan dimensions of the Rwandan refugee crisis, see Lugan, *Rwanda: Le Génocide,* 117–19; David and Catherine Newbury, "A Catholic Mass in Kigali," 302–303; Prunier, *Africa's World War,* 12–14.

97. Particularly notable was the February 1993 RPF offensive that led to the deaths of thousands in northern Rwanda and the internal displacement of nearly one million Hutu residents (Lugan, *Rwanda: Le Génocide,* 135). The Rwandan bishops strongly condemned this attack (cf. A.G.M.Afr., *Communique des Eveques Catholiques du Rwanda,* 13 February 1993). Longman underplays the scale of the violence, describing the February 1993 RPF attacks as "killing a number of civilians" (Longman, *Christianity and Genocide,* 179). For a much more critical first-person account of these events and their aftermath, see Marie Beatrice Umutesi, *Surviving the Slaughter: The Ordeal of a Rwandan Refugee in Zaire* (Madison: University of Wisconsin Press, 2004), 24–34.

98. David and Catherine Newbury note Arusha's calls for the RPF to comprise 40% of the new integrated military. In order to meet this quota, thousands of FAR soldiers would have needed to be demobilized. Fearful of this, Hutu FAR soldiers cooperated in hardliners' plans and implementation of the genocide (David and Catherine Newbury, "A Catholic Mass in Kigali," 308).

99. Bizimana, *L'Église et le genocide au Rwanda,* 33–34; Eltringham, *Accounting for Horror,* 41–42.

100. Fierce controversy lingers over which side actually shot the plane down. The early consensus pointed to a *coup d'état* by Hutu hardliners who felt

that Habyarimana was selling them out in Arusha. More recent arguments (and a French court) have implicated the RPF. For the first perspective, see Lugan, *Rwanda: Le Génocide*, 172. On the second theory, see Straus, *Order of Genocide*, 45.

101. The initial U.N. investigative team estimated 800,000 genocide deaths. Alison Des Forges and her research team calculated a figure closer to 500,000, or approximately 75% of Rwanda's Tutsi population in 1994. Des Forges estimated that the RPF killed around 60,000 people between April 1994 and August 1995. The 1994 "Gersony Report" also implicated the RPF in major massacres, but this report was suppressed by the U.N. under pressure from the new RPF government (cf. Des Forges, *Leave None to Tell the Story*, http://www.hrw.org/reports/1999/rwanda/Geno1-3-04.htm#P95_39230; Prunier, *Africa's World War*, 15–20).

102. Prunier's *Africa's World War* is the most comprehensive account of the Congolese war. See also Filip Reyntjens, *The Great African War: Congo and Regional Geopolitics, 1996–2006* (Cambridge: Cambridge University Press, 2009); Jason K. Stearns, *Dancing in the Glory of Monsters: The Collapse of the Congo and the Great War of Africa* (New York: Public Affairs, 2012).

103. Cf. "Lettre Pastorale du presbyterium de Kabgayi, 'Convertissons-nous pour vivre ensemble dans la paix,' 1 December 1991," in Guichaoua, *Les crises politiques au Burundi et au Rwanda (1993-1994)*, 647–48. For further commentary, see Longman, *Christianity and Genocide*, 153–55; Saur, *Le sabre*, 133–34; McCullum, *Angels Have Left Us*, 79–80.

104. C.M.L., Joseph Ntaho, "Eglise Catholique du Rwanda: De la Spiritualité au Prophétisme," (2000), 4. See also Sibomana, *Hope for Rwanda*, 121–22.

105. The most detailed account of Catholic mediation efforts can be found in Joseph Ngomanzungu, *Efforts de Mediation oecumenique des eglises dans la crise rwandaise: Le comite de contacts (1991-1994)* (Kigali, 2003): 3–76. Longman offers a more critical account, noting that the Catholic bishops' active involvement in political talks declined significantly after the RPF's February 1993 offensive (Longman, *Christianity and Genocide*, 185–86).

106. Theunis, "Le rôle de l'Église catholique dans les événements récents," in Guichaoua, *Les crises politiques au Burundi et au Rwanda (1993–1994)*, 294.

107. A.D.K., Conférence des Evêques Catholiques du Rwanda (CECR), *Recueil des lettres et messages de la Conférence des Evêques Catholiques du Rwanda publies pendant la période de guerre (1990–1994)* (Kigali, Rwanda: Pallotti Press, 1995), 121, 147, 200–201. The refugee issue was first mentioned in the bishops' November 1990 pastoral letter (CECR, "Heureux les artisans de paix, car ils seront appeles fils de Dieu" (Mt 5:9), 7 November 1990, 119–131).

108. A.G.M.Afr., "Message de Mgr. Vincent Nsengiyumva, Archêveque de Kigali, 12 October 1990." I located this as a loose file in the Missionaries of Africa archives in Rome.

109. Straus convincingly demonstrates the importance of the national security and self-defense narratives for Hutu *génocidaires* (see Straus, *Order of Genocide*, 9–12, 97–120).

110. CECR, "Convertissez-vous et croyez a l'evangile," 11 March 1992, in CECR, *Recueil des lettres et messages*, 211.

111. Longman, *Christianity and Genocide*, 163. For example, in their Easter message of March 1991, the Catholic bishops preached love of enemy but did not mention the Tutsi massacre at Ruhengeri the previous month (cf. Message de Carême, 2 March 1991, in CECR, *Recueil des lettres et messages*, 135–49).

112. The most detailed recounting of clerical deaths during the Rwanda genocide and its aftermath can be found in Joseph Ngomanzungu, *La Souffrance de l'église a travers son personnel: Massacres, emprisonnements et expulsions d'ouvriers apostoliques (1990–2002)* (Kigali: Pallotti Press, 2002).

113. The Vatican had announced Muvara's promotion to the episcopate in late 1988. Nsengiyumva opposed the appointment of another Tutsi to the hierarchy. Shadowy allegations emerged that Muvara had fathered a child, and Muvara stepped down days before his scheduled installation as bishop. The woman who first accused Muvara later recanted her story (cf. Bizimana, *L'Église et le genocide au Rwanda*, 23). A respected church historian, Muvara went on to write *Introduction à l'histoire de l'évangélisation du Rwanda* (Kigali: Pallotti Press, 1990). He was killed early in the genocide in April 1994.

114. "Le massacre de religieux au Rwanda," in A Guichaoa, *Les crises politiques au Burundi et au Rwanda (1993–1994)*, 702.

115. While the focus here is on the Catholic Church, Protestant leaders have also faced strong critiques for their muted reaction to the genocide. Cf. André Karamaga, "Les Églises Protestantes et la Crise Rwandaise," in Guichaoua, *Les crises politiques au Burundi et au Rwanda (1993–1994)*, 299–308; Longman, *Christianity and Genocide*, 186–97.

116. McCullum, *Angels Have Left Us*, 63–64.

117. Saur, *Le Sabre*, 23.

118. "Déclaration des responsables des Églises catholique et protestante, Kabgayi, 13 May 1994," in Guichaous, *Les crises politiques au Burundi et au Rwanda (1993–1994)*, 650. Thadée Nsengiyumva was the first bishop to name the "Tutsi" dimension of the genocide in a statement issued on May 18 (Saur, *Le Sabre*, 24). Joseph Ngamazungu claims that Radio Rwanda refused to transmit a Rwandan bishops' statement on the violence on April 9, but I have seen no other reference to this (Ngomanzungu, *Efforts de Mediation*, 87). Ngomanzungu also offers a detailed recounting of the bishops' May 13 statement (87–88).

119. Cf. Carol Rittner, et. al., *Genocide in Rwanda: Complicity of the Churches?* (St. Paul, MN: Paragon Press, 2004), 13; C.M.L., Joseph Ntamahungiro, "Eglise Catholique du Rwanda: De la Spiritualité au Prophétisme"(2000): 10. While

defending the church response, Ntamahungiro notes that church leaders did not issue an official pastoral letter condemning the massacres until March 1995, nearly a year after the beginning of the genocide.

120. Lugan, *Rwanda: Le Génocide,* 178. Guy Theunis, a White Father priest and respected human rights advocate, argues that Vincent Nsengiyumva began distancing himself from the Habyarimana regime in the early months of 1994, noting Nsengiyumva's participation in the 1 January 1994 March for Peace (G. Theunis, "Le rôle de l'Église catholique dans les événements récents," 291).

121. As mentioned above, observers have estimated that the RPF killed between 25,000 and 45,000 Hutu between April and August 1994. While the RPF should be held accountable for these human rights violations, this is not remotely equivalent in scale or intent to a "double genocide" (Prunier, *Africa's World War,* 20).

122. Cf. Ngomanzungu, *Efforts de Mediation,* 90–95.

123. Prunier, *Africa's World War,* 6. According to Bernardin Muzungu, Nikwigize claimed in a 1995 newspaper interview that "the Tutsi are evil by nature…if we did not kill them, they would kill us." Likely in response to such inflammatory statements, Nikwigize was abducted at the end of 1996 near the Congo border; his body has never been located. The RPF is strongly suspected in his presumed death (C.M.L., Bernard Muzungu, "Le role des responsables des religions reconnues au Rwanda, pendant le génocide," [n.d.]. See also Ntamahungiro, "Eglise Catholique du Rwanda: De la Spiritualité au Prophétisme," 12–13).

124. Saur describes the genocide cases against Mgr. Augustin Misago, who allegedly refused aid to Tutsi clergy seeking refuge from the massacres; Fr. Athanase Seromba, a diocesan priest who reportedly burned down a church with 2,000 Tutsi sheltering inside; Fr. Emmanuel Rukondo, a former military chaplain and rector of the College of Christ the King in Nyanza; and Fr. Wenceslas Munyeshyaka, the former rector of Saint-Famille parish in Kigali who allegedly turned over lists of Tutsi to Hutu *génocidaires* (Saur, *Le Sabre,* 241–250). For a more detailed indictment of Misago, see Bizimana, *L'Eglise et le génocide,* 96–129. One of the more infamous cases involving Catholic women religious was the trial of Sr. Gertrude and Sr. Kisito, two Catholic Benedictine sisters from Sovu convent who turned over Tutsi refugees and supplied the petrol that *interahamwe* then used to burn down Sovu's health center (cf. Max Rettig, "The Sovu Trials: The Impact of Genocide Justice on One Community," in Straus and Waldorf, *Remaking Rwanda,* 195). After the genocide these sisters were given refuge at convents in Europe, and the Vatican stood by them even after their convictions on genocide charges (cf. Gill Donovan, "Vatican Criticizes Conviction of Nuns in Genocide Case," *The National Catholic Reporter,* 29 June 2001).

125. Saur, *Le Sabre*, 22. For other examples of collaboration, see Ntamahungiro, "Eglise Catholique du Rwanda: De la Spiritualité au Prophétisme," 11; Longman, *Christianity and Genocide*, 191–97.

126. G. Theunis, "Le rôle de l'Église catholique dans les événements récents," 297. For other accounts of Christian resistance to the genocide, see Sibomana, *Hope for Rwanda*, 54–76, 123–26 and McCullum, *Angels Have Left Us*, 78.

127. Roger de Diesbach, "L'ancien archevêque Suisse du Rwanda crie son angoisse," *Journal de Genève*, 18 April 1994. Further quotations in this paragraph are taken from this article.

128. "Mgr. Perraudin répond," *Journal de Genève*, 23 June 1994. Perraudin reiterated such sentiments in his 2003 memoir. "Without hesitation, one should affirm that the first and principal cause of the Tutsi genocide of April 1994 was the attack on the country by the Tutsi themselves." One should note here Perraudin's tendency to substitute ethnic for political language, associating "Tutsi" with "RPF" (Perraudin, *Un Évêque au Rwanda*, 277).

129. Roger de Diesbach, "L'ancien archevêque Suisse du Rwanda crie son angoisse," *Journal de Genève*, 18 April 1994.

EPILOGUE

1. Over the past decade, the term "theopolitical" has become a buzzword in Christian theological circles. The term intentionally blurs the modern distinctions between theology and politics, recognizing the relatively recent separation of church and state and theology and political science in post-Enlightenment Europe. Constructive theopolitics has focused in recent years on the political implications of Christian practices, particularly the sacrament of the Eucharist. On recent developments in theopolitics and political theology, see William T. Cavanaugh, *Theopolitical Imagination: Christian Practices of Space and Time* (London/New York: T&T Clark: 2003); C.C. Pecknold, *Christianity and Politics: A Brief Guide to the History* (Eugene: Cascade, 2010); Michael Kirwan, *Political Theology: An Introduction* (Minneapolis: Fortess, 2009); Graham Ward, *The Politics of Discipleship: Becoming Postmaterial Citizens* (Grand Rapids, MI: Baker, 2009); Peter Scott and William T. Cavanaugh, eds., *The Blackwell Companion to Political Theology* (Oxford: Blackwell, 2004) and Hent de Vries and Lawrence E. Sullivan, eds., *Political Theologies: Public Religions in a Post-Secular World* (New York: Fordham, 2006).

2. The best account of church-led prison and reconciliation ministries is Anglican Bishop John Rucyahana's *The Bishop of Rwanda* (Nashville, TN: Thomas Crown, 2006). On the communal justice system of *gacaca*, see Timothy Longman, "Justice at the grassroots? Gacaca trials in Rwanda," in *Transitional Justice in the Twenty-First Century: Beyond Truth versus Justice*, eds. Naomi Roht-Arriaza and Javier Mariezcurrena (Cambridge: Cambridge University Press,

2006): 206–228; Don Webster, "The Uneasy Relationship between the ICTR and Gacaca," in *Remaking Rwanda: State Building and Human Rights after Mass Violence*, eds. Scott Straus and Lars Waldorf (Madison: University of Wisconsin Press, 2011): 184–193.

3. If anything, post-genocide statements like the bishops' Christmas 1994 message betrayed an attitude of "we told you so" rather than one of contrition. See here "Message aux Chretiens a l'occasion de Noel et du nouvel An," 21 December 1994, in A.D.K., Conférence des Évêques Catholiques du Rwanda (CECR), *Recueil des lettres et messages de la Conférence des Évêques Catholiques du Rwanda publies pendant la période de guerre (1990–1994)* (Kigali, Rwanda: Pallotti Press, 1995), 281–294.

4. Mbonyintege has called for the drafting of a general confession of sin similar to the German bishops after World War II, noting that this could serve as a first step in Rwanda's "true reconciliation with ourselves." Tried and later acquitted of genocide charges, the Bishop of Gikongoro, Augustin Misago, has been the strongest opponent of the Catholic Church issuing a collective statement of repentance, arguing that Rwanda's sins were individual rather than collective. Misago gained important support for his views from Pope John Paul II in March 1996. In a letter to the Rwandan hierarchy, the late pope posited that individual Christians but not church institutions bore responsibility for the 1994 genocide (cf. C.M.L., Joseph Ntamahungiro, "Eglise Catholique du Rwanda: De la Spiritualité au Prophétisme," 14–15; Timothy Longman, *Christianity and Genocide in Rwanda* (Cambridge: Cambridge University Press, 2010), 5–7).

5. Longman, *Christianity and Genocide*, 304–323.

6. C.M.L., Joseph Ntamahungiro, "Eglise Catholique du Rwanda: De la Spiritualité au Prophétisme" (2000): 9.

7. Mary Grey, *To Rwanda and Back: Liberation Spirituality and Reconciliation* (London: Darton, Longman and Todd, 2007), 176.

8. Second Vatican Council, *Lumen Gentium (Dogmatic Constitution on the Church)*, par. 8 (cf. http://www.vatican.va/archive/hist_councils/ii_vatican_council/documents/vat-ii_const_19641121_lumen-gentium_en.html).

9. Saur, *Le Sabre*, 77.

10. Philip Pullella, "'Sin within the Church' threat to Catholicism: Pope Benedict," *Reuters*, 11 May 2010. http://www.reuters.com/article/2010/05/11/us-pope-abuse-portugal-idUSTRE64A1W220100511.

11. A.G.M.Afr., Guy Theunis, "Le présence des Missionnaires d'Afrique (Pères Blancs) parmi les Rwandais, aujourd'hui," 12 September 1994. A White Father, human rights advocate and former editor of *Dialogue*, the leading Catholic intellectual journal in Rwanda, Theunis was convicted on trumped-up "genocide ideology" charges in 2005 and forced out of the country. He now works in Israel.

12. Cf. Antoine Mugesera, "Review of *Un Évêque auRwanda*, by André Perraudin," *Dialogue 183* (2007): 139.

13. On Sant'Egidio's work in Mozambique, see Helena Cobban, *Amnesty after Atrocity? Healing Nations after Genocide and War Crimes* (Boulder, CO/London: Paradigm: 2007), 158–165.

14. Prunier notes that the Vatican newspaper *L'Osservatore Romano* still invoked "double genocide" language in 1999 (Prunier, *Africa's World War*, 356). Nor is this "temptation to neutrality" limited only to churches. In attempting to be value-neutral and apolitical, humanitarian NGOs were complicit to great political evils during the Congolese wars of the late 1990s and early 2000s (Prunier, *Africa's World War*, 359).

15. CECR, "Message des Évêques Catholiques du Rwanda aux prêtres, religieux et religieuses, 21 November 1991: Au service de l'Eglise dans une societe de multi-partisme," in CECR, *Recueil des lettres et messages*, 181.

16. Nor have such claims dissipated in recent years. In Pope Benedict's November 2011 post-apostolic exhortation *Africae Munus* after the Second African Synod of 2009, the pope repeatedly denies that the church has any explicitly "political" dimension. In doing so, Benedict narrowly limits "politics" to the machinations of the modern nation-state (cf. Pope Benedict XVI, *Africae Munus* (On the Church in Africa in Service to Reconciliation, Justice and Peace), November 2011 (cf. http://www.vatican.va/holy_father/benedict_xvi/apost_exhortations/documents/hf_ben-xvi_exh_20111119_africae-munus_en.html)).

17. Augustine develops these contrasting visions in his magnum opus, *The City of God* (London/New York: Penguin Books, 2003). One should note that Augustine never loses site of the eschatological horizons for both the city of man and the city of God.

18. See here Emmanuel Katongole, *The Sacrifice of Africa: A Political Theology for Africa* (Grand Rapids, MI: Eerdmans, 2011), 135–192. For further commentary on the theopolitical visions underlying these ministries, see my "Roads to Reconciliation: An Emerging Paradigm of African Theology," *Modern Theology* 26:4 (2010): 549–565.

19. One could argue that this is the biggest shortcoming of contemporary national reconciliation efforts in Rwanda—namely, the government will not admit any fault or subject its own military to outside review. For a comprehensive and stringing critique of the contemporary Rwandan politics of reconstruction, reconciliation, and development, see Scott Straus and Lars Waldorf, Eds., *Remaking Rwanda: State Building and Human Rights after Mass Violence* (Madison, WI: University of Wisconsin Press, 2011). For a more sympathetic account, see Phil Clark and Zachary Kaufman, Eds., *After Genocide: Transitional Justice, Post-Conflict Reconstruction and Reconciliation in Rwanda and Beyond* (New York: Columbia University Press, 2009).

20. Cf. Gabriel Santos, *Redeeming the Broken Body: Church and State after Disaster* (Eugene, OR: Cascade, 2009), 236. While based on the recent American context, Santos's conclusions would be applicable to ecclesiology in the Rwandan context, particularly his sense that the church must break the friend-foe dynamic that builds love of "my own" by fostering hatred towards "the other." For Santos, the church is a "transnational body and not simply Americans" which calls "peoples and nations (including the nations of those who carried out the (9/11) attacks) to be brothers and sisters in the household of God" (126).

21. For a helpful comparative study of the "masculine" violence of the colonial state in Burundi, see Patricia Daley, *Gender and Genocide in Burundi* (Bloomington, IN: Indiana University Press, 2007), 41–60.

22. Desmond Tutu, *No Future without Forgiveness* (New York: Doubleday, 1999), 268.

23. Scott Straus interviewed hundreds of *génocidaires* during research in the early 2000s. He found that war-related fear, in-group pressure, and obedience were far more important motivating factors than ethnic animosity. In Straus's words, "perpetrators frame the logic of violence as self-defense in war or as retaliation for the death of the president (Habyarimana)" (Straus, *The Order of Genocide*, 154). On the militarization of the Rwandan state in the early 1990s, see David and Catherine Newbury, "A Catholic Mass in Kigali: Contested Views of the Genocide and Ethnicity in Rwanda," *Canadian Journal of African Studies* 33.2/3 (1999): 296, 304–305.

24. Cf. Ngomanzungu, *Efforts de Mediation*, 81; C.M.L., Joseph Ntamahungiro, "Eglise Catholique du Rwanda: De la Spiritualité au Prophétisme," 20; A.G.M.Afr., [Anon.], 5 Jan. 1993. This latter document was issued by the regional White Fathers house in Kigali and offered a summary of the local church's recent work for peace in late 1992; I located this article in a binder of news articles in the White Fathers' archives in Rome.

25. Linda Melvern, Romeo Dallaire and Samantha Power have all argued that rapid international intervention in the first weeks of the genocide could have stopped most of the killing. As the leader of the UNAMIR force on the ground in Kigali, Dallaire felt especially impotent. See Samantha Power, "Bystanders to Genocide: Why the United States Let the Rwandan Tragedy Happen," *Atlantic Monthly* 288.2 (2001): 84–108 and *A Problem from Hell: America in the Age of Genocide* (New York: Basic Books, 2002); Roméo Dallaire, *Shake Hands with the Devil: The Failure of Humanity in Rwanda* (New York: Carroll & Graf, 2005); Linda Melvern, *A People Betrayed: The Role of the West in Rwanda's Genocide* (New York: Palgrave Macmillan, 2000).

26. The best epidemiological study of mortality during the recent wars in Congo is Benjamin Coghlan, et. al, "Mortality in the Democratic Republic of Congo: A Nationwide Survey" *The Lancet* 367 (2006): 44–51. See also John Kiess, *When War is Our Daily Bread: Congo, Theology and the Ethics of Contemporary*

Conflict. Diss. Duke University, 2011. Kiess explores how the Congolese wars reframe questions of Christian ethics and just war theory.

27. See Cobban, *Amnesty after Atrocity*, 158–65. On medieval penitential practices during war, see Daniel M. Bell, *Just War as Christian Discipleship* (Grand Rapids, MI: Brazos Press, 2009), 44–46 and Bernard J. Verkamp, *The Moral Treatment of Returning Warriors in Early Medieval and Modern Times* (Scranton, PA: University of Scranton Press, 1993).

28. Guy Theunis argues that Catholic seminaries never addressed the ethnic question or Catholic social teaching in sufficient depth. Cf. G. Theunis, "Le rôle de l'Église catholique dans les événements récents," in André Guichaoua, *Les crises politiques au Burundi et au Rwanda (1993–1994): Analyses, faits, et documents* (Paris: Université de Lille, 1995), 292.

29. This title is given to Perraudin by Roger de Diesbach, "L'ancien archevêque Suisse du Rwanda crie son angoisse," *Journal de Genève*, 18 April 1994. On the justifications for violence in the modern world, see Hannah Arendt's classic studies *On Revolution* (New York: Viking, 1963) and *On Violence* (New York: Harcourt, 1970).

30. CECR, "La paix et la reconciliation des Rwandais," 17 February 1993, in CECR, *Recueil des lettres et messages*, 259.

31. Quoted in J.J. Kritzinger, "The Rwandan Tragedy as Public Indictment of Christian Mission," *Missionalia* 24:3 (1996): 345.

32. "Being Muslim is not simply a choice dictated by religion; it is a global identity choice. [Rwandan] Muslims are often socially marginal people, and this reinforces a strong sense of community identification that supersedes ethnic tags, something the majority Christians have not been able to achieve" (Gerard Prunier, *The Rwanda Crisis: History of a Genocide* (New York: Columbia University Press, 1995), 253).

33. Marie Beatrice Umutesi's *Surviving the Slaughter* (Madison: University of Wisconsin Press, 2004) is perhaps the best account of these atrocities.

34. Paul Rutayisire, "Le Tutsi étranger dans le pays de ses aïeux," *Cahiers Évangile et Société 4* (1996): 52.

35. Pope Benedict XVI, *Africae Munus* (2011), par. 152.

36. This proposal is discussed in C.M.L., Joseph Ntamahungiro, "Eglise Catholique du Rwanda: De la Spiritualité au Prophétisme" (2000): 21.

37. "Le massacre de religieux au Rwanda," in A. Guichaoua, *Les crises politiques au Burundi et au Rwanda*, 704.

38. Dietrich Bonhoeffer, *The Cost of Discipleship* (New York: Touchstone, 1995). One thinks here of Bonhoeffer's opening words that "when Christ calls a man, he bids him to come and die" (1).

39. Lemarchand contrasts this with the oft-repeated "duty of memory" which typically implies an enforced, univocal narrative. "Thinking or grappling with the past is what is conspicuously missing from Rwanda's official memory— in other words, a sustained effort to recognize the profound ambivalence of

the notion of guilt" (Lemarchand, "The Politics of Memory in Post-Genocide Rwanda," in Clark and Kaufman, *After Genocide: Transitional Justice,* 69).

40. Roger de Diesbach, "L'ancien archevêque Suisse du Rwanda crie son angoisse," *Journal de Genève,* 18 April 1994. This view that liberation theology and/or genuine democratization would have preserved Rwanda from its postcolonial nightmare is found throughout recent ecclesial and theological commentaries on Rwanda. See in particular Timothy Longman, *Christianity and Genocide in Rwanda,* 303–23; Léon Saur, *Le sabre, la machete et le goupillon: Des apparitions de Fatima au genocide rwandais* (Paris: Editions mols, 2004); Mario Aguilar, *Theology, Liberation and Genocide: A Theology of the Periphery* (London: SCM, 2009); Mary C. Grey, *To Rwanda and Back: Liberation Spirituality and Reconciliation* (London: Darton, Longman and Todd, 2007).

41. This would summarize my critique of Emmanuel Katongole's *Mirror to the Church: Resurrecting Faith after Genocide in Rwanda* (Grand Rapids, MI: Zondervan, 2009). Katongole fails to sufficiently analyze the complexities of Rwandan history, offering a thin reading of the Hutu-Tutsi dynamic that attributes nearly all blame to the Belgians.

42. As Catherine Newbury has argued, "here (in Rwanda) with an intensity that surpasses normal clichés, there is no single history; rather there are competing 'histories" (Catherine Newbury, "Ethnicity and the Politics of History in Rwanda," *Africa Today* 45:1 (1998): 9). Likewise, Nigel Eltringham traces many of Rwanda's social conflicts to elite efforts to impose a single history on a complex past. "While Rwanda has a single past, a single, definitive history is unattainable" (Eltringham, *Accounting for Horror,* 182). See also Sarah Warshauer Freedman, Harvey M. Weinstein, K.L. Murphy, and Timothy Longman, "Teaching History in Post-Genocide Rwanda," in Straus and Waldorf, *Remaking Rwanda,* 297–315.

Bibliography

ARCHIVAL AND PRIMARY SOURCES

I conducted my primary archival work in the General Archives of the Missionaries of Africa in Rome (abbreviated A.G.M.Afr. in footnotes). In Rwanda, I undertook research in the archives of the Diocese of Kabgayi (abbreviated A.D.K.); the *Bibliothèque du Centre Missionaire Lavigerie* (abbreviated C.M.L.), the White Fathers' local archives in Kigali, Rwanda; and the library of Nyakibanda Major Seminary. These archives provided the vast majority of diocesan reports, missionary correspondence, political analyses, United Nations reports, and other key Belgian colonial documents. In addition, I consulted many pastoral letters, newspaper articles, and other primary sources in Vénuste Linguyeneza's online archive, www.cier-be. info. Although this website was taken down in 2011, most pastoral statements can be found in Linguyeneza's *Vérité, justice, charité: lettres pastorales et autres déclarations des évêques catholiques du Rwanda, 1956-1962* (Waterloo, Belgium, 2001). Many of Linguyeneza's other primary sources can be consulted in the Diocese of Kabgayi archives in Rwanda. I am grateful to the Missionaries of Africa and the Diocese of Kabgayi for offering me such extensive access to archival material, especially considering the sensitivity of this history.

Newspaper and media sources include the Bujumbura-based *Temps Nouveaux d'Afrique*, the White Fathers' biweekly newspaper for Rwanda, Burundi, and Eastern Congo between 1954 and 1962; *L'Ami: La revue des elites de l'Est de la Colonie*, an influential White Father monthly for Catholic lay elites in the early 1950s; *Grands Lacs*, the White Fathers' international journal between the 1930s and the mid-1950s; and *Vivant Univers*, the White Fathers' successor to *Grands Lacs* in the late 1950s and 1960s. I also reviewed late 1950s issues of the Catholic Kinyarwanda weekly *Kinyamateka*. Several diocesan journals proved invaluable, such as the academic journals *Théologie et Pastorale au Rwanda* and its successor *Théologie et Pastorale au Rwanda et Burundi*; Kabgayï's diocesan newspaper *Trait d'Union*; and Nyundo's diocesan newspaper *Civitas Mariae*. On the 1963–1964 Gikongoro massacres, I located a range of contemporary articles from the international Catholic press in the University of Notre Dame's Hesburgh library.

Finally, Fidele Nkundabagenzï's *Rwanda Politique 1958–1960* (Brussels: Centre de Recherche et d'Information Sociopolitique (CRISP): 1962) collects over 400 pages of primary sources from the period, focusing mostly on political documents from colonial officials and indigenous political leaders.

SECONDARY SOURCES

Adriaenssens, Jan. *Rapport sur la situation religieuse, sociale, et économique du Ruanda-Urundi*. Geneva: Institut International Catholique de Recherches Socio-Ecclésiales, 1956.

Aguilar, Mario. *Theology, Liberation and Genocide: A Theology of the Periphery*. London: SCM Press, 2009.

African Rights. *Rwanda: Death, Despair, and Defiance*. London: African Rights, 1994.

Alcoff, Linda and Eduardo Mendietta, Eds. *Thinking from the Underside of History: Enrique's Dussel's Philosophy of Liberation*. London: Roman & Littlefield, 2000.

Amselle, Jean-Loup and Elikia M'Bokolo, Eds. *Au Coeur de l'ethnie: Ethnie, tribalisme, et état en Afrique*. 2nd Edition. Paris: La Découverte/Poche, 1999.
- Amselle, Jean-Loup. "Ethnies et espaces: pour une anthropologie topologique," 11–48.
- Chretien, Jean-Pierre. "Hutu et Tutsi au Rwanda et au Burundi," 129–66.
- Vidal, Claudine. "Situations ethniques au Rwanda," 167–84.

Arendt, Hannah. *On Revolution*. New York: Viking Press, 1963.

Arendt, Hannah. *On Violence*. New York: Harcourt, Inc., 1970.

Aubert, Roger. *150 ans de vie des Églises. 1830-1980*. Bruxelles: P. Legrain, 1980.

Augustine of Hippo. *City of God*. Trans. Gill Evans and Henry Bettenson. London/New York: Penguin Classics, 2003.

Barth, Frederick. *Ethnic Groups and Boundaries*. London: Allen and Unwin, 1969.

Baur, John. *2000 Years of Christianity in Africa: An African History 62-1992*. Nairobi: Paulines Publications Africa, 1994.

Bayart, Jean-Francois. *The Illusion of Cultural Identity*. Trans. Steven Rendall, Janet Roitman, Cynthia Schoch, and Jonathan Derrick. Chicago: University of Chicago Press, 2005.

Bazot, Henri. *Ma vie de Missionnaire au Liban, au Rwanda, au Burundi, au Zaïre, en France*. [N.P]: 2006.

Bell, Daniel M. *Just War as Christian Discipleship: Recentering the Tradition in the Church rather than the State*. Grand Rapids, MI: Brazos Press, 2009.

Bizimana, J.D. *L'église et le génocide au Rwanda: Les Peres Blancs et le Négationnisme.* Paris: L'Harmattan, 2004.

Bonhoeffer, Dietrich. *The Cost of Discipleship.* New York: Touchstone, 1995.

Braeckman, Collette. *Terreur africaine: Burundi, Rwanda, Zaire, les racines de la violence.* Paris: Fayard, 1996.

Brass, Paul R. "Ethnicity and Nationality Formation." *Ethnicity* 3 (1976): 225–41.

Bushayija, A. "Le décès de Mutara III Rudahigwa et les différentes interprétations," *Dialogue* 188 (2009): 227–32.

Byanafashe, Déogratias, Ed. *Les Défis de l'Historiographie rwandaise: Le Rwanda précolonial.* Butare: Editions de l'Université Nationale du Rwanda: 2004.

Byanafashe, Deogratias. "Mgr. A. Perraudin et les changements politiques au Rwanda entre 1952 et 1962." *Etudes rwandaises: série lettres et sciences humaines 1* (2000): 120–37.

Carney, J.J. "Roads to Reconciliation: An Emerging Paradigm of African Theology," *Modern Theology* 26, no. 4 (2010): 549–65.

Carney, J.J. "Waters of Baptism, Blood of Tribalism?" *African Ecclesial Review* 50, nos. 1-2 (2008): 9–30.

Cavanaugh, William T. *Theopolitical Imagination: Christian Practices of Space and Time.* London/New York: T&T Clark: 2003.

Cavanaugh, William T. *Torture and Eucharist: Theology, Politics and the Body of Christ.* Oxford: Blackwell, 1998.

Chrétien, Jean-Pierre. "L'Afrique des Grands Lacs existe-t-elle?" *Culture et Société (Revue de Civilisation Burunduise) VIII* (1986): 71–89.

Chrétien, Jean-Pierre. *The Great Lakes of Africa: Two Thousand Years of History.* Trans. Scott Straus. New York: Zone, 2003.

Chrétien, Jean-Pierre and Gérard Prunier, Eds. *Les Ethnies ont une histoire.* Paris: Karthala, 1989.

> • Gahama, Joseph and Augustin Mvuyekure. "Jeu ethnique, idéologie missionnaire et politique coloniale: Le cas du Burundi," 303–13.

Chrétien, Jean-Pierre and Jean-François Dupaquier. *Burundi 1972: Au bord des génocides.* Paris: Karthala, 2007.

Clark, Phil and Zachary Kaufman, Eds. *After Genocide: Transitional Justice, Post-Conflict Reconstruction and Reconciliation in Rwanda and Beyond.* New York: Columbia University Press, 2009.

> • Melvern, Linda. "The Past is Prologue: Planning the 1994 Rwandan Genocide," 21–32.
> • Lemarchand, René. "The Politics of Memory in Post-Genocide Rwanda," 65–76.

Classe, Léon. *Instructions Pastorales 1922-1939.* Kabgayi: 1940.

Classe, Léon. "Le Ruanda et ses habitants; organisation politique, la religion, la famille," *Congo: Revue générale de la colonie belge I*, no. 5 (1922): 677–93.

Cobban, Helena. *Amnesty after Atrocity? Healing Nations after Genocide and War Crimes.* Boulder, CO/London: Paradigm: 2007.

Codere, Helen. *The Biography of an African Society: Rwanda, 1900–1960.* Tervuren: MRAC, 1973.

Conway, Martin. "Belgium." In *Political Catholicism in Europe, 1918–1965*, edited by Tom Buchanan and Martin Conway, 187–218. Oxford: Clarendon, 1996.

Coghlan, Benjamin, et. al, "Mortality in the Democratic Republic of Congo: A Nationwide Survey," *The Lancet* 367 (2006): 44–51.

Czekanowski, Jan. *Investigations in the Area between the Nile and the Congo.* Trans. Frieda Scütze. New Haven, CT: Human Relations Area Files, 1917, 1960.

Daley, Patricia. *Gender and Genocide in Burundi: The Searches for Spaces of Peace in the Great Lakes Region.* Bloomington, IN: Indiana University Press, 2007.

Dallaire, Roméo. *Shake Hands with the Devil: The Failure of Humanity in Rwanda.* New York: Carroll & Graf, 2005.

Dansette, Adrien and John Dingle. *Religious History of Modern France.* New York: Herder and Herder, 1961.

De Lacger, Louis and Pierre Nothomb. *Ruanda.* 2nd Edition. Kabgayi, Rwanda: 1959.

De Lame, Danielle. *A Hill among a Thousand: Transformations and Ruptures in Rural Rwanda.* Madison: University of Wisconsin Press, 2005.

De Vries, Hent and Lawrence E. Sullivan, Eds. *Political Theologies: Public Religions in a Post-Secular World.* New York: Fordham University Press, 2006.

Des Forges, Alison L. *Defeat is the only bad news: Rwanda under Musinga, 1896–1931.* Diss. Yale University, 1972.

Des Forges, Alison. "Kings without crowns: the White Fathers in Rwanda." In *Eastern African History*, edited by Daniel McCall, Norman Bennett, and Jeffrey Butler, 176–207. New York: Praeger, 1969.

Des Forges, Alison. *Leave None to Tell The Story: Genocide in Rwanda.* New York: Human Rights Watch, 1999.

D'Hertefelt, Marcel. *Les anciens royaumes de la zone interlacustre méridionale, Rwanda, Burundi, Buha.* London: International African Institute, 1962.

D'Hertefelt, Marcel. *Les clans du Rwanda ancien: éléments d'ethnosociologie et d'ethnohistoire.* Tervuren: MRAC, 1971.

D'Hertefelt, Marcel. "Myth and political acculturation in Rwanda," in Rhodes-Livingstone Institute, and Allie A. Dubb. Eds., *Myth in Modern Africa; The Fourteenth Conference Proceedings* (1960): 114–35.

Doyle, William. *Jansenism: Catholic Resistance to Authority from the Reformation to the French Revolution.* New York: St. Martin's Press, 2000.

Eltringham, Nigel. *Accounting for Horror: Post-Genocide Debates in Rwanda.* London: Pluto Press, 2004.

Eriksen, Thomas H. "Ethnicity, race and nation," in *The Ethnicity Reader: Nationalism, Multiculturalism, and Migration*, edited by Montserrat Guibernau and John Rex, 33–42. Cambridge: Polity Press, 1997.

Erny, Pierre. "'Races' et 'ethnie' au Rwanda selon l'historien Bernard Lugan," *Dialogue* 235 (2004): 3–14.

Faupel, J.F. *African Holocaust: The Story of the Uganda Martyrs*. New York: P.J. Kennedy, 1962.

Fournel, Marc. *La Tunisie: Le Christianisme et l'Islam dans l'Afrique septentrionale*. Paris: Challamel, 1886.

Gatwa, Tharcisse. *The Churches and Ethnic Ideology in the Rwandan Crises, 1900–1994*. Milton Keynes: Paternoster, 2005.

Gerard, Emmanuel. "Religion, Class and Language: The Catholic Party in Belgium." In *Political Catholicism in Europe 1918–45*, edited by Wolfram Kaiser and Helmut Wohnout, 94–115. New York: Routledge, 2004.

Gibson, Ralph. *A Social History of French Catholicism 1789–1914*. New York: Routledge, 1989.

Guichaoua, André, Ed. *Les crises politiques au Burundi et au Rwanda (1993–1994): Analyses, faits, et documents*. Paris: Université de Lille, 1995.

- Karamaga, André. "Les Églises Protestantes et La Crise Rwandaise," 299–308.
- Theunis, Guy. "Le rôle de l'Église catholique dans les événements récents," 289–299.

Gourevitch, Phillip. *We Wish to Inform You that Tomorrow We Will Be Killed with Our Families: Stories from Rwanda*. New York: Free Press, 1998.

Gres-Gayer, Jacques. *Jansénism en Sorbonne: 1643-1656*. Paris: Klincksieck, 1996.

Gres-Gayer, Jacques. *D'un jansénisme à l'autre: chroniques de Sorbonne (1696–1713)*. Paris: Nolin, 2007.

Hansen, Holger B. *Mission, Church and State in a Colonial Setting: Uganda 1890–1925*. London: Heinemann Press, 1984.

Harroy, Jean-Paul. *Rwanda: Souvenirs d'un Compagnon de la marche du Rwanda vers la démocratie et l'indépendance*. Brussels: Hayez, 1984.

Hastings, Adrian. *The Church in Africa 1450–1950*. Oxford: Clarendon Press, 1994.

Hastings, Adrian. *A History of African Christianity 1950–1975*. Cambridge: Cambridge University Press, 1979.

Hastings, Adrian, ed. *Modern Catholicism: Vatican II and After*. New York: Oxford, 1991.

Heimann, Mary. "Catholic revivalism in worship and devotion." In *The Cambridge History of Christianity VIII—World Christianities c. 1815–1914*, edited by Sheridan Gilley and Brian Stanley, 70–83. Cambridge: Cambridge University Press, 2006.

Hennelly, Alfred, ed. *Liberation Theology: A Documentary History*. Maryknoll: Orbis, 1990.

De Heusch, Luc. *Le Rwanda et la civilisation interlacustre*. Brussels: Université Libre de Bruxelles, 1966.

Hochschild, Adam. *King Leopold's Ghost*. New York: Mariner Books, 1998.

Hommage à Mgr. Bigirumwami: Premier Evêque Rwandais. Kigali: Editions du Secrétariat général de la C.E.P.R., 2009.

Horn, Gerd-Rainer. *Western European Liberation Theology: The First Wave (1924–1959)*. New York: Oxford University Press, 2008.

Horowitz, David L. *Ethnic Groups in Conflict*. Berkeley: University of California Press, 1985.

Hoyweghen, Saskia. "The Disintegration of the Catholic Church of Rwanda: A Study of the Fragmentation of Political and Religious Authority." *African Affairs 95* (1996): 379–401.

Ilibagiza, Immaculée. *Our Lady of Kibeho: Mary Speaks to the World from the Heart of Africa*. Carlsbad, CA: Hay House, 2008.

Iliffe, John. *Africans: The History of a Continent*. Cambridge: Cambridge University Press, 1994.

Isichei, Elizabeth. *A History of Christianity in Africa: From Antiquity to the Present*. Grand Rapids, MI: Eerdmans Press, 1995.

Jadoulle, Jean-Louis. *Chrétiens modernes?: l'engagement des intellectuels catholiques "progressistes" belges de 1945 à 1958 à travers La revue nouvelle, La relève et l'édition belge de Témoignage chrétien*. Louvain-la-Neuve: Academia Bruylant, 2003.

Jenkins, Philip. *The Next Christendom: The Coming of Global Christianity*. 2nd Ed. New York: Oxford University Press, 2007.

Kagame, Alexis. *Un abrégé de l'histoire du Rwanda*. 2 vols. Butare: Editions universitaires du Rwanda, 1972–1975.

Kagame, Alexis. *Le code des institutions politiques du Rwanda precolonial*. Brussels: Institut royal colonial belge, 1952.

Kagame, Alexis. *La philosophie bantou-rwandaise de l'être*. Brussels: Académie Royale des Sciences Coloniales, 1956.

Kagame, Alexis. "Point de vue d'abbé Kagame, Astrida, 13 March 1960," *Dialogue 183* (2007): 52–63.

Kalibwami, Justin. *Le Catholicisme et la société rwandaise, 1900-62*. Paris: Présence africaine, 1991.

Kalu, Ogbu. *African Christianity: An African Story*. Trenton, NJ: Africa World Press, 2007.

Katongole, Emmanuel. *A Future for Africa: Critical Essays in Christian Social Imagination*. Scranton, PA: University of Scranton Press, 2005.

Katongole, Emmanuel. *Mirror to the Church: Resurrecting Faith after Genocide in Rwanda*. Grand Rapids, MI: Zondervan Press, 2009.

Katongole, Emmanuel. *The Sacrifice of Africa: A Political Theology for Africa*. Grand Rapids, MI: Eerdmans Press, 2011.

Kiess, John. *When War is Our Daily Bread: Congo, Theology and the Ethics of Contemporary Conflict*. Diss. Duke University, 2011.

Kirwan, Michael. *Political Theology: An Introduction*. Minneapolis: Fortess Press, 2009.

Kollman, Paul V. *The Evangelization of Slaves and Catholic Origins in East Africa*. Maryknoll, NY: Orbis Books, 2005.

Koren, Henry J. *To the Ends of the Earth: A General History of the Congregation of the Holy Ghost*. Pittsburgh: Duquesne University Press, 1983.

Kritzinger, J.J. "The Rwandan Tragedy as Public Indictment of Christian Mission." *Missionalia 24*, no. 3 (1996): 340–57.

Kuper, Leo. *The Pity of It All: Polarization of Racial and Ethnic Relations.* Minneapolis: University of Minnesota Press, 1977.

Lamberts, Emiel. "The Zenith of Christian Democracy: The Christelijke Volkspartij/ Parti Social Chrétien in Belgium." In *Christian Democracy in Europe Since 1945* (Vol. 2), edited by Michael Gehler and Wolfram Kaiser. New York: Routledge, 2004: 67–84.

Lavigerie, Charles Martial Allemand and A.-G. Hamman. *Écrits d'Afrique. Lettres chrétiennes, 3.* Paris: B. Grasset, 1966.

Lavigerie, Charles Martial Allemand and Xavier de Montclos. *Lavigerie: la mission universelle de l'église.* Paris: Éditions du Cerf, 1991.

Leclercq, Jacques. *La Vie du Christ dans son Église.* Paris: Cerf, 1947.

Leclercq, Jacques. *Vivre chrétiennement notre temps.* Tournai, Belgium: Casterman, 1957.

Lemarchand, René. *Burundi: Ethnocide as Discourse and Practice.* Washington, DC: Woodrow Wilson Press, 1994.

Lemarchand, René. *The Dynamics of Violence in Central Africa.* Philadelphia: University of Pennsylvania Press, 2009.

Lemarchand, René. *Rwanda and Burundi.* New York: Praeger, 1970.

Linden, Ian. "The Roman Catholic Church in Social Crisis: The Case of Rwanda," in *Christianity in Independent Africa*, edited by E. Fasholé Luke, R. Gray, A. Hastings, G. Tasie, 242–53. Bloomington, IN: Indiana University Press, 1978.

Linden, Ian (with Jane Linden). *Church and Revolution in Rwanda.* Manchester, UK: Manchester University Press, 1977.

Linden, Ian (with Jane Linden and Paulette Géraud). *Christianisme et Pouvoirs au Rwanda, 1900-1990.* Paris: Karthala, 1999.

Linguyeneza, Venuste. "Mgr. André Perraudin: L'homme de la justice," *Dialogue 234* (2004): 97–104.

Logiest, Guy. *Mission au Rwanda: Un blanc dans le bagarre Tutsi-Hutu.* Brussels: Didier Hatier, 1988.

Longman, Timothy. *Christianity and Genocide in Rwanda.* Cambridge: Cambridge University Press, 2010.

Longman, Timothy. "Justice at the grassroots? Gacaca trials in Rwanda," in *Transitional Justice in the Twenty-First Century: Beyond Truth versus Justice*, edited by Naomi Roht-Arriaza and Javier Mariezcurrena, 206–28. Cambridge: Cambridge University Press, 2006.

Lugan, Bernard. "L'Eglise catholique au Rwanda, 1900–1976," *Etudes Rwandaises XI* (1978): 69–75.

Lugan, Bernard. *Rwanda: Le Génocide, l'Église, et la Démocratie.* Paris: Editions du Rocher, 2004.

Magaziner, Daniel. *The Law and the Prophets: Black Consciousness in South Africa, 1968–1977.* Athens, OH: Ohio University Press, 2010.

Malkki, Liisa. *Purity and Exile: Violence, Memory and National Cosmology among Hutu Refugees in Tanzania*. Chicago: University of Chicago Press, 1995.

Mamdani, Mahmood. *When Victims Become Killers: Colonialism, Nativism, and the Genocide in Rwanda*. Princeton: Princeton University Press, 2001.

Maquet, J.J. *The Premises of Inequality in Rwanda*. London: Oxford University Press, 1961.

Markowitz, Marvin. *Cross and Sword: The Political Role of Christian Missions in the Belgian Congo 1908-1960*. Stanford: Stanford University Press, 1973.

Marsh, Charles. *The Beloved Community: How Faith Shapes Social Justice from the Civil Rights Era to Today*. New York: Basic Books, 2004.

Mayeur, Jean-Marie. *Catholicisme social et démocratie chrétienne: principes romains, expériences françaises*. Paris: Cerf, 1986.

Mbonimana, Gamaliel. "Christianisation indirecte et cristallisation des clivages Ethniques au Rwanda (1925–1931)," *Enquêtes et documents d'histoire africaine III*, Louvain, Centre d'histoire de l'Afrique (1978): 125–63.

Mbonimana, Gamaliel. "Ethnies et Eglise Catholique: Le remodelage de la société par l'école missionaire, 1900-1931." *Cahier du centre Saint Dominique* 1 (1995): 55–67.

Mbonimana, Gamaliel. *L'instauration d'un royaume chrétien au Rwanda (1900–1931)*. Doctoral Thesis Catholic University of Louvain, 1981.

McCullum, Hugh. *The Angels Have Left Us: The Rwanda Tragedy and the Churches*. Geneva: WCC Publications, 1995.

Melvern, Linda. *A People Betrayed: The Role of the West in Rwanda's Genocide*. New York: Palgrave Macmillan, 2000.

Minnaert, Stefaan. "Les Pères Blancs et la société rwandaise durant l'époque coloniale allemande (1900–1916). Une rencontre entre cultures et religions," in *Les Religions au Rwanda, défis, convergences, et competitions, Actes du Colloque International du 18-19 septembre 2008 Butare/Huye*, edited by Paul Rutayisire, J.P. Schreibner, and Deogratias Byanafashe (Butare: Université Nationale du Rwanda, 2009), 53–101.

Minnaert, Stefaan (Jean-Joseph Hirth). *Premier voyage de Mgr Hirth au Rwanda: de novembre 1899 à février 1900: contribution à l'étude de la fondation de l'Église catholique au Rwanda*. Kigali: Editions Rwandaises, 2006.

Minnaert, Stefaan. "Un regard neuf sur la première fondation des Missionnaires d'Afrique au Rwanda en février 1900," *Histoire et Missions Chrétiennes* 8 (December 2008): 39–66.

Mudimbe, V.Y. *The Idea of Africa*. Bloomington, IN: University of Indiana Press, 1994.

Mudimbe, V.Y. *The Invention of Africa*. Bloomington, IN: University of Indiana Press, 1988.

Mugesera, Antoine. "Kinyamateka contre les inyenzi et leurs complices," *Dialogue* 189 (2009): 39–54.

Mugesera, Antoine. Review of "Un Évêque au Rwanda," by André Perraudin, *Dialogue* 183 (2007): 125–44.

Murego, Donat. *La Révolution Rwandaise, 1959–1962.* Louvain: Institut des Sciences Politiques et Sociales, 1975.

Mutwarasibo, Ernest. "Crispation ethnique à la fin du règne de Mutara III Rudahigwa," *Dialogue* 188 (2009): 157–80.

Muvara, Felicien. *Introduction à l'histoire de l'évangélisation du Rwanda.* Kigali: Pallotti Press, 1990.

Muzungu, Bernardin. "Eglise Catholique: Pendant le Génocide," *Cahiers Lumière et Société* 43 (2010): 1–63.

Muzungu, Bernardin. *Histoire du Rwanda sous la colonisation.* Kigali: Edition Cahiers Lumière et Société, 2009.

Muzungu, Bernardin. "Le problème des races au Rwanda," *Cahiers Lumière et Société* 42 (2009): 51–69.

Newbury, Catherine. *The Cohesion of Oppression: Clientship and Ethnicity in Rwanda, 1860-1960.* New York: Columbia University Press, 1988.

Newbury, Catherine. "Ethnicity and the Politics of History in Rwanda," *Africa Today* 45, no. 1 (1998): 7–24.

Newbury, David. "The Clans of Rwanda: An Historical Hypothesis," *Africa* 50, no. 4 (1980): 389–403.

Newbury, David. *The Land Beyond the Mists: Essays on Identity and Authority in Precolonial Congo and Rwanda.* Athens, OH: Ohio University Press, 2009.

Newbury, David and Catherine Newbury. "A Catholic Mass in Kigali: Contested Views of the Genocide and Ethnicity in Rwanda," *Canadian Journal of African Studies* 33, no. 2/3 (1999): 292–328.

Ngomanzungu, Joseph. *L'attitude de l'église catholique au Rwanda face aux problèmes sociopolitiques des années 1956–1962: Une pastorale de prévention, de médiation, et d'accompagnement.* Mémoire de License, Pontifical Gregorian, 2000.

Ngomanzungu, Joseph. *Efforts de Mediation oecumenique des eglises dans la crise rwandaise: Le comite de contacts (1991–1994).* Kigali: [n.p.], 2003.

Ngomanzungu, Joseph. *L'épiscopat de Mgr Laurent Déprimoz, 1943-1955: une période de consolidation de la foi et de rwandisation de l'Église dans une société en transformation.* Doctoral Thesis Pontifical Gregorian University, 2010.

Ngomanzungu, Joseph. *La Souffrance de l'église a travers son personnel: Massacres, emprisonnements et expulsions d'ouvriers apostoliques (1990–2002).* Kigali: Pallotti Press, 2002.

Nijs, Victor-Clement. *Souvenirs d'un administrateur territorial: Congo-Rwanda 1950–1962.* Brussels: Editions Racine, 2007.

Nothomb, Dominic. *Petite Histoire de L'Eglise Catholique au Rwanda.* Kabgayi: 1962.

Ntamahungiro, Joseph. "Eglise Catholique du Rwanda: De la Spiritualité au Prophétisme." Unpublished manuscript, Centre Missionnaire Lavigerie, Kigali, 2000.

Nzongola-Ntalaja, Georges. *The Congo from Leopold to Kabila: A People's History.* London: Zed Books, 2002.

O'Brien, David J. and Thomas Shannon, eds. *Catholic Social Thought: The Documentary Heritage*. Maryknoll, NY: Orbis Books, 1992.

Pecknold, C.C. *Christianity and Politics: A Brief Guide to the History*. Eugene, OR: Cascade Press, 2010.

Pères Blancs de Suisse. "Vie et œuvre de Mgr Perraudin," *Dialogue* 234 (2004): 77–85.

Perraudin, André. *Un évêque au Rwanda: les six premières années de mon épiscopat (1956–1962)*. Saint Maurice: Editions Saint-Augustin, 2003.

Pirouet, M. Louise. *Black Evangelists: The Spread of Christianity in Uganda 1891–1914*. London: Rex Collings, 1978.

Pottier, Johan. *Re-imagining Rwanda: Conflict, Survival and Disinformation in the Late Twentieth Century*. Cambridge: Cambridge University Press, 2002.

Power, Samantha. "Bystanders to Genocide: Why the United States Let the Rwandan Tragedy Happen." *Atlantic Monthly* 288, no. 2 (2001): 84–108.

Power, Samantha. *A Problem from Hell: America in the Age of Genocide*. New York: Basic Books, 2002.

Prunier, Gérard. *Africa's World War: Congo, the Rwandan Genocide, and the Making of a Continental Catastrophe*. New York: Oxford University Press, 2009.

Prunier, Gérard. *The Rwanda Crisis: History of a Genocide*. New York: Columbia University Press, 1995.

Renault, François. *Cardinal Lavigerie: Churchman, Prophet, Missionary*. Translated John O'Donohue. London: Athlone Press, 1994.

Reyntjens, Filip. *The Great African War: Congo and Regional Geopolitics, 1996–2006*. Cambridge: Cambridge University Press, 2009.

Reyntjens, Filip. *Pouvoir et droit au Rwanda: droit public et évolution politique, 1916–1973*. Tervuren, Belgium: Musée royal de l'Afrique centrale, 1985.

Rittner, Carol, John K. Roth and Wendy Whitworth, eds. *Genocide in Rwanda: Complicity of the Churches?* St. Paul, MN: Paragon Press, 2004.

Rowe, John, "Mutesa and the Missionaries: Church and State in Pre-colonial Buganda." In *Christian Missionaries and the State in the Third World*, edited by Holger B. Hansen and Michael Twaddle, 52–65. Oxford/Athens, OH: James Currey/Ohio University Press, 2002.

Rucyahana, John. *The Bishop of Rwanda*. Nashville, TN: Thomas Crown, 2006.

Rudakemwa, Fortunatus. *L'évangélisation du Rwanda, 1900–59*. Paris: Harmattan, 2005.

Ruffieux, Roland (with Bernard Prongué). *Le Mouvement chrétien-social en Suisse romande 1891–1949*. Fribourg: Éditions Universitaires, 1969.

Rugagi, Jean Nizurengo. "Décolonisation et démocratisation du Rwanda," *Cahiers Lumière et Société* 7 (1997): 43–54.

Rutayisire, Paul. *La christianisation du Rwanda (1900-1945): méthode missionaire et politique selon Mgr. Léon Classe*. Fribourg: Editions universitaires Fribourg Suisse, 1987.

Rutayisire, Paul. "L'Eglise catholique et le décolonisation du Rwanda ou les illusions d'une victoire." In *Rwanda: L'Eglise catholique à l'épreuve du génocide*, edited by F. Rutembesa, J.P. Karegeye, and P. Rutayisire, 42–74. Greenfield Park, Canada: Les Editions Africana, 2004.

Rutayisire, Paul. "Les mythes fondateurs de 'la Révolution' Rwandaise de 1959" *Cahiers Lumière Et Société 16* (1999): 43–59.

Rutayisire, Paul. "Rapports entre l'Eglise catholique et l'Etat rwandaise pendant la période coloniale," *Cahiers Lumière et Société* (1997): 19–41.

Rutayisire, Paul. "Rudahigwa et les missionnaires," *Dialogue 188* (2009): 23–53.

Rutayisire, Paul. "Les signes précurseurs de la crise de la Toussaint rwandaise," *Dialogue 189* (2009): 6–38.

Rutayisire, Paul. "Le Tutsi étranger dans le pays de ses aïeux," *Cahiers Lumière et Société 4* (1996): 42–55.

Sanders, Edith R. "The Hamitic Hypothesis: Its Origin and Functions in Time Perspective," *Journal of African History 10*, no. 4 (1969): 521–32.

Santos, Gabriel. *Redeeming the Broken Body: Church and State after Disaster.* Eugene, OR: Cascade, 2009.

Saur, Léon. *Influences parallèles: L'Internationale démocratie-chrétienne au Rwanda.* Brussels: Editions Luc Pire, 1998.

Scott, Peter and William T. Cavanaugh, eds. *The Blackwell Companion to Political Theology.* Oxford: Blackwell Press, 2004.

Seligman, C.G. *Races of Africa.* 4th Ed. London/New York: Oxford, 1966.

Semujanga, Josias. *Origins of the Rwandan Genocide.* Amherst, NY: Humanity Books, 2003.

Sibomana, André. *Hope for Rwanda: Conversations with Laure Guilbert and Herve Deguine.* Trans. Carina Tertsakian. Sterling, VA: Pluto Press, 1999.

Shorter, Aylward. *Cross and Flag in Africa: The "White Fathers" during the Colonial Scramble, 1892–1914.* Maryknoll, NY: Orbis Books, 2006.

Southall, Aidan. "The Illusion of Tribe," in *Journal of Asian and African Studies 5*, no. 1/2 (1970): 28–50.

Speke, John Hanning. *Journal of the Discovery of the Source of the Nile.* Eugene, OR: Resource, 2007.

Stearns, Jason K. *Dancing in the Glory of Monsters: The Collapse of the Congo and the Great War of Africa.* New York: Public Affairs, 2012.

Stenger, Friedrich. *White Fathers in Colonial Central Africa: A Critical Examination of V.Y. Mudimbe's Theories on Missionary Discourse in Africa.* Munich, 2001.

Straus, Scott. *The Order of Genocide: Race, Power and War in Rwanda.* Ithaca, NY: Cornell University Press, 2006.

Straus, Scott and Lars Waldorf, eds. *Remaking Rwanda: State Building and Human Rights after Mass Violence.* Madison, WI: University of Wisconsin Press, 2011.

- Eltringham, Nigel. "The Past is Elsewhere: The Paradoxes of Proscribing Ethnicity in Post-Genocide Rwanda," 269–82.
- Warshauer-Freedman, Sarah, Harvey M. Weinstein, K.L. Murphy, and Timothy Longman. "Teaching History in Post-Genocide Rwanda," 297–315.

- Webster, Don. "The Uneasy Relationship between the ICTR and Gacaca," 184–93.

Sundkler, Bengt and Christopher Steed. *A History of Christianity in Africa.* Cambridge: Cambridge University Press, 2000.

Todd, David M. "Caste in Africa?" *Africa 47*, no. 4 (1977): 398–412.

Tombs, David. *Latin American Liberation Theology.* Boston: Brill, 2002.

Tutu, Desmond. *No Future without Forgiveness.* New York: Doubleday, 1999.

Twagirayesu, Michel and Jan van Beutselaar. *Ce Don Que Nous Avons Reçu, L'Histoire de l'Eglise Presbyterienne au Rwanda (1907-1982).* Brussels: De Jonge, 1982.

Umutesi, Marie-Beatrice. *Surviving the Slaughter: The Ordeal of a Rwandan Refugee in Zaire.* Trans. Julia Emerson. Madison: University of Wisconsin Press, 2004.

Ugirashebuja, Octave. "L'idéologie du Tutsi oppresseur," *Les Cahiers Lumière et Société 4* (1996): 57–61.

Vail, Leroy, ed. *The Creation of Tribalism in Southern Africa.* 2nd Edition. Berkeley: University of California Press, 1991.

Vansina, Jan. *Antecedents to Modern Rwanda: The Nyiginya Kingdom.* Madison: University of Wisconsin Press, 2003.

Vansina, Jan. "The Politics of History and the Crisis in the Great Lakes." *Africa Today 45*, no. 1 (1998): 37–44.

Verkamp, Bernard J. *The Moral Treatment of Returning Warriors in Early Medieval and Modern Times.* Scranton, PA: University of Scranton Press, 1993.

Vidal, Claudine. "Colonisation et décolonisation du Rwanda: La question tutsi-hutu," *Revue française d'études politiques africaines 91* (1973): 32–47.

Ward, Graham. *The Politics of Discipleship: Becoming Postmaterial Citizens.* Grand Rapids, MI: Baker Press, 2009.

Ward, Kevin and Emma Wild-Wood, eds. *The East African Revival: Histories and Legacies.* Burlington, VT: Ashgate, 2012.

Warner, Carolyn M. *Confessions of an Interest Group: The Catholic Church and Political Parties in Europe.* Princeton, N.J.: Princeton University Press, 2000.

Young, M. Crawford. "Nationalism, Class, and Ethnicity in Africa: A Retrospective," *Cahiers d'Études Africaines 26*, no. 3 (1986): 421–95.

Index

Printed and bound by CPI Group (UK) Ltd, Croydon, CR0 4YY